CHAMBER MUSIC

MUSIC RESEARCH AND
INFORMATION GUIDES
(Vol. 8)

GARLAND REFERENCE LIBRARY
OF THE HUMANITIES
(Vol. 704)

MUSIC RESEARCH AND INFORMATION GUIDES

CHAMBER MUSIC
A Research and Information Guide

John H. Baron

GARLAND PUBLISHING, INC. · NEW YORK & LONDON
1987

Library of Congress Cataloging-in-Publication Data

Baron, John H.
Chamber Music.

(Music Research and Information Guides; vol. 8)
(Garland Reference Library of the Humanities; vol. 704)
Includes indexes.
1. Chamber music–Bibliography. I. Title. II. Series.
III. Series: Garland Reference Library of the Humanities;
vol. 704.

ML128.C4B37   1987   016.7857   87-8751
ISBN 0-8240-8346-6

Printed on acid-free, 250-year-life paper
Manufactured in the United States of America

In Memory of

My Grandfather, Julius Singer, Violinist

and

My Aunt, Romola Singer Rice, Pianist

Chamber Musicians par excellence

and in Honor of

John Ward and Paul Brainard

My Teachers, par excellence

CONTENTS

CHAPTER III ANALYTIC STUDIES

CHAPTER IV PERFORMANCE PRACTICE OF CHAMBER MUSIC

CHAPTER V PERFORMERS OF CHAMBER MUSIC

CHAPTER VI MISCELLANEOUS TOPICS

ABBREVIATIONS

a......scored for the following number of instruments
AMD....see MAD
DA.....Dissertation Abstracts
DAI....Dissertation Abstracts International
DD.....doctoral dissertation
DMA....Doctor of Musical Arts degree
ed.....edited by/edition
EdD....Doctor of Education degree
fl.....flourished
HML....Harvard Music Library
ISBN   International Standard Book Number
LC.....Library of Congress
NYPL...New York Public Library
m......measure
M......Musical score, Library of Congress classification
MAD....Music Arts Degree
ML.....Musical literature, Library of Congress classification
MM.....Master of Music degree
MT.....Music theory, Library of Congress classification
NL.....Newberry Library
op.....opus or opera
PhD....Doctor of Philosophy Degree
RILM...Répertoire International de la Littérature Musicale
SBN....Standard Book Number
trl....translated by/translator/translation
UM.....University Microfilms
UMI....University Microfilms International

ACKNOWLEDGMENTS

Research for this book was made possible through the generosity of Tulane University (Summer Research Grant) and the National Endowment for the Humanities (Travel Grant). Work was carried on in the Maxwell Music Library of Tulane University, in the libraries of Harvard University, Louisiana State University, Hunter College, and Memphis State University, and at the Library of Congress, Boston Public Library, Newberry Library, and the New York Public Library. Many libraries from all over the United States provided books on interlibrary loan through Howard-Tilton Memorial Library of Tulane University. Computer facilities have been provided by Tulane University Music Department, Francis Monachino, chairperson. Special thanks to Liselotte Andersson, Wayne Shirley, Jeannette Thompson, Paul Kovenock, Elliott Kaback, Robert Voss, Richard and Hermine Makman, Bernice Baron, Andrew Acs, Yosif Feigelson, Bailey Berry, Faina Lushtak, Vladimir Hirsu, Joel Sheveloff, Robert Falck, Heinrich Schwab, Alison Hartman, Leonard Bertrand, Lynn Gelpi, Vicky Blanchard,and the many university librarians who reported to me on the status of dissertations and theses. Last but certainly not least this book could not have been written without the sacrifices, tolerance and patience of my wife Doris and children Beth, Jeffrey, and Miriam.

INTRODUCTION

Any consideration of chamber music must start with its performance and with hearing its unique, intimate sounds. But how much more meaningful it is if, with the guidance of a specialist talking or writing on music, we can play it better and catch exciting moments in the music which we would otherwise miss. Much has been written about chamber music, but where do we find what we need or want to know?

This is a reference tool for anyone interested in chamber music. It is not a history or an encyclopedia but a guide to where to find answers to questions about chamber music. It may even suggest some questions the reader hadn't thought of yet. In pointing the way, however, I have repeated here many facts gleaned from studies about chamber music so that some readers will not need to go further and actually find the source cited. The scholar might find the book useful when stepping beyond the confines of his/her specialization, and the layperson and performer (amateur or professional) hopefully can use this to broaden his/her knowledge about this special kind of music.

Many have defined chamber music differently from the way I do (see chapter III). Rather than considering chamber music as music performed in a particular locale or by a certain type of performer or as written in a set form and style, I have chosen to define it by describing that music which is most commonly accepted here and in Europe today as germane (for example, see Denis Arnold, "Chamber Music," in *The New Oxford Companion to Music* [Oxford/New York: Oxford University Press, 1983]). Chamber music is classical European instrumental ensemble music for two to approximately twelve performers with no more than one player to a part. Music for two or more keyboard instruments without additional, non-keyboard instruments, and percussion music by itself are not included. I regard non-European offshoots of the European classical tradition as relevant, but not jazz or ethnic manifestations of ensemble music not in the classical European tradition.

Although there have been a few chamber music bibliographies published through the years, it seems that this is the first comprehensive, annotated bibliography that includes the huge number of studies of the past quarter century. Relatively few reliable studies were written before 1950, though some of these have stood the test of time and remain standard tools. New conceptions of chamber music history, new methods of analysis, new perceptions of what constitutes chamber music, and the explosion in the numbers of musicologists and music theorists have inevitably brought forth an extensive new literature. To find one's way in this array of chamber music studies is an overwhelming task,

especially for the non-specialist. I hope this guide will
provide useful directions.
       A great many facts have only recently come to light,
and some interpretations are relatively new. Some readers
may need to study the following pages carefully in order to
correct long-standing misconceptions or no-longer tenable
biases. For example, despite the convincing proof over 20
years ago that Haydn's so-called Opus 3 quartets are not by
Haydn and probably by Hoffstetter, the authors of several
recent books, in discussing Haydn's quartets, show total
ignorance of the facts. Yet one must be careful not to let
historical data unduly influence taste; if a listener loved
Haydn's Opus 3, he/she should feel no shame at loving Hoffstetter. What has changed is the history of the early Haydn
quartets, not their aesthetic value nor that of the now re-
assigned ones. The bias against brass and some other instruments in chamber music can no longer be defended without
serious omissions of what are clearly masterpieces. A great
many readers and writers associate chamber music with string
quartets, and certainly string quartets are the core of the
repertory. But much intimate, solo-ensemble music for other
combinations fulfils all the requirements of chamber music
as well. For example, the Beethoven *Equali* have legitimate
claims to be called chamber music. This is not to dictate
that everyone must love these pieces as much as an Opus 59
Beethoven string quartet; it is to suggest that string quartet devotees might open their ears a bit to enhance their
enjoyment of chamber music.
       Most of the literature is books, articles in journals
and magazines, dissertations and theses, and essays or chapters in Festschriften, treatises and biographies. A few
prefaces to scholarly editions have been entered as well.
In addition to the core literature, I have sometimes brought
in more obscure citations when they are the only studies in
a particular field. When there is only one study of a particular subject, it is included even if it is not especially
brilliant, but when there are hundreds of possible entries
(for example, under Beethoven, Bartók, Haydn or Mozart), I
have tried to limit myself to the best, most recent, more
interesting ones. In general I have concentrated on more
recent works, mostly in English and German (where the bulk
of the literature is), but older, pioneering studies are of
course not neglected. Access to works in other European
languages has been limited to what appears to be the major
literature.
       I have tried to be as accurate as possible in the cita-
tions; where numerous, sometimes confusing editions have
appeared, I have attempted to sort them out and describe
them. I have followed the spelling exactly as given on
title pages; transliterations from cyrillic script follow
the Library of Congress or RILM citations. I have used
forms of names and biographic data as found in *The New Grove*
{1} and the 1984 Slonimsky-Baker *Dictionary {4}*. I have
been fortunate in having in hand nearly every item (except

dissertations) so that I could verify contents and titles. Since few of the more than 400 dissertations and theses on chamber music or related topics have been available to me, I have relied primarily on *Dissertation Abstracts International* for descriptions of contents. Readers who need to study a particular thesis or dissertation can visit or write to the university where the degree was received or order a microfilm or duplicate copy from University Microfilms International in Ann Arbor (MI) giving the UM or UMI number in my entries.

Any bibliography is out of date by the time it reaches press. The last items entered were on November 1, 1986, yet even some studies published before then have not reached me in time to be included. Hopefully there are not many important omissions or any egregious errors; if there are, perhaps the reader will kindly apprise me of them so that, if further editions of this guide should appear, I can make the necessary improvements.

Chamber Music

GENERAL MUSIC REFERENCE

Most music reference books have entries on the term "chamber music" itself and specific topics within chamber music such as "string quartet" and "duet." Others with biographical information usually cover the chamber music of the major composers in the course of the general discussion. Several dictionaries and encyclopedias stand out, however, for their comprehensiveness or for the depth of their information on chamber music, and only these will be mentioned here.

1. *The New Grove Dictionary of Music and Musicians*, 6th edition, gen. ed. Stanley Sadie. 20 volumes. London: Macmillan, 1980. ML 100.N48.
   One of the most comprehensive musical dictionaries ever written, with contributions from scholars around the world. Important articles on performers of chamber music (see Chapter 5) and on composers (where chamber music is usually listed in the course of a general discussion). Also important articles on: *chamber music, accompanied keyboard music, canzona 3 (the ensemble canzona), consort, fantasia, fantasia suite, nonet, octet, piano trio, piano quartet, piano quintet, ricercare, septet, sextet, sonata, sonata da chiesa, sonata da camera, string quartet, string quintet, string trio, wind quintet, quatuor concertant, divertimento, duet, Hausmusik, continuo, suite, violin 3, violoncello 3, concert rooms and halls, solo sonata*, and *serenade*. While extremely useful, the *New Grove* is neither perfect nor complete and many subjects need be consulted in additional sources.

2. *Die Musik in Geschichte und Gegenwart*, gen. ed. Friedrich Blume. 16 volumes. Kassel: Bärenreiter, 1949-1979. ML 100.M92.
   For German readers the best overall encyclopedia of music. Its best features are its extensive bibliographies of primary materials and of secondary literature, of which English readers can make good use as well. Articles of particular relevance to chamber music are *Kammermusik, Blasmusik, Klaviertrio, Streichquartett, Streichquintett, Streichsextett, Streichtrio*, and *Trio Sonata*. See also the articles on composers, which frequently discuss chamber music.

3. *Dizionario Enciclopedico Universale della Musica e dei Musicisti*, gen. ed. Alberto Basso. *Il Lessico* (Subject), 4 vols. Turin: Unione Tipografico - Editrice

Torinese, 1983. ML 100.D63.1983. I: xv + 742 pages;
II: xi + 765 pages; III: xi + 746 pages; IV: xi + 784
pages.
The newest international dictionary, though not as comprehensive as {1} and {2}. Articles of relevance to
chamber music include *camera (Musica da)*, *sonata*, *quartetto*, *quintetto*, *sestetto*, *trio*, and *duetto*. William
Newman's article on "sonata" is by far the best of
these, with a huge bibliography, while most of the
others are somewhat superficial with modest or mediocre
bibliographies. Some other articles, with indirect
relevance to chamber music, are excellent, such as
Carolyn Gianturco's "Barocco."

Le Biografie (Biography), 2 vols. to date (A-F).
Turin: Unione Tipografico - Editrice Torinese, 1985.
I: xiii + 757; II: xiii + 812.
Much more impressive than the subject volumes, includes
some schematic listing of composer's works which make
chamber music easy to spot (for example Boccherini).

4. Slonimsky, Nicolas, ed. *Baker's Biographical Dictionary
of Musicians*, 7th ed. New York: Schirmer/London:
Collier Macmillan, 1984. ML 105.B16.1984. ISBN 0-
02-870-270-0. xlii + 2577 pages. 1st ed. by
Theodore Baker: New York: G. Schirmer, 1900.
A fine supplement to {1} and {2} for biographical information on chamber performers and composers and more
up-to-date. The basic reference tool for biographies.

5. Randel, Don Michael, ed. *The New Harvard Dictionary of
Music*. Cambridge: Harvard University Press, 1986.
ML 100.R3.1986. ISBN 0-674-61525-5. xxii + 942
pages. 3rd ed. of Willi Apel, *Harvard Dictionary of
Music*, 1st ed. 1958, 2nd ed. Cambridge: Harvard
University, 1969. xviii + 935 pages. ML 100.A64.
1969. SBN 674-37501-7.
The best 1-volume English language dictionary of musical terms, edited by a team of expert musicologists.
The explanations are very brief, as opposed to much
more lengthy ones in some cases in {1} and {2}. The 2
most relevant articles on "chamber music" and "string
quartet," which remain unchanged for the first and
second editions, have been completely rewritten for the
third edition. Comparison of the earlier and present
entries reflects the vast changes in concepts as well
as historical detail of the past several decades. The
third edition de-emphasizes the idea that all good chamber music must follow a 4-movement sonata form. Eugene
K. Wolf's discussion of the string quartet is the best
brief history and definition of the genre in the English language; it greatly expands the pre-1780 and

20th-century history of the string quartet and gives a
much more balanced view of the Romantic quartet.

6. Dahlhaus, Carl, and Hans Heinrich Eggebrecht, ed. *Brock-
    haus Riemann Musiklexikon.* Wiesbaden: F.A. Brock-
    haus/Mainz: B. Schott's Söhne, 1978-1979. ML 100.
    B849. ISBN 3-7653-0303-8. 2 vols. I: 699 pages;
    II: 732 pages. Names and subjects interspersed. Very brief but cogent
    bibliographies and articles. For nearly a century the
    standard German short reference on all facets of music.

CHAMBER MUSIC REFERENCE

The most important overall chamber music reference work is:

7. Cobbett, Walter Willson. *Cyclopedic Survey of Chamber
    Music.* London: Humphrey Milford for Oxford Univer-
    sity Press, 1929. ML 1100.C7. 2 vols. I: xii + 585
    pages; II: vii + 641 pages. *Cobbett's Cyclopedic
    Survey of Chamber Music,* vol. III, ed. Colin Mason.
    London: Oxford University Press, 1963. ML 1100.C7.
    1963 v.3. 211 pages. Reprint vols. I-III: 1964.
    Despite its age, still the most useful reference work
    for chamber music. Most entries by Cobbett himself but
    also major contributions by 139 others of many nation-
    alities (vols. 1-2). Alphabetical entries on compo-
    sers, performers, patrons, instruments, nationalities,
    conservatories, and special topics (tuning, humor, com-
    mercialism, color, atonality, quartet playing and so
    on). Names include the very famous down to the most
    obscure composers and performers; biographies are
    followed in many cases by lists of works and some dis-
    cussion of them. Also of value for its reflections on
    aesthetics and for Cobbett's (1847-1937) interjections
    of personal experiences with Brahms, Dvořák, and many
    others. Hugo Leichtentritt's entry on "German Organ-
    izations" lists a large number of chamber groups, their
    dates, and their membership; Marc Pincherle does the
    same for French groups, and others for some other na-
    tionalities, including A.L. Goldberg on American organ-
    izations. Mason's supplement (vol. 3) includes his
    "European Chamber Music since 1929," "Chamber Music in
    Britain since 1929," and "Stravinsky," I.I. Martinov's
    "Soviet Chamber Music," and Nicolas Slonimsky's "Cham-
    ber Music in America," "Additions and Corrections to
    Dates Given in the Original Edition," as well as up-
    dated bibliographies and an index.

8. Campanha, Odette Ferreira, and Antonio Torchia. *Música
    e Conjunto de Câmara.* São Paulo: Ricordi Brasileira,

1978. ML 1100.C29. iii + 290 pages. In Portuguese.
An excellent general handbook on chamber music, including history of types, instruments, combinations of
instruments, forms, seating arrangements, and so on.
Brazilian chamber music and ensembles of the 19th and
20th centuries given separate treatment. Detailed
analyses of 2 works by Beethoven (Opus 18, no. 3, and a
piano sonata) and another piece by a Brazilian composer.

*Several books contain non-technical discussion of a large
repertory of chamber music; although these are not designed
as cyclopedias or dictionaries, they can serve as reference
sources for information on chamber music. See Melvin Berger's Guide to Chamber Music {163} and Reclams Kammermusikführer {162}.*

9. Coeuroy, André, and Claude Rostand. *Les Chefs-d'Oeuvre
   de la Musique de Chambre,* in *Amour de la Musique:
   Petit Guide de l'Auditeur de Musique.* Paris:
   Éditions le Bon Plaisir, Plon, 1952. MT 140.C633.
   282 pages.
   An amateur listener's non-technical guide to the standard classics of chamber music, arranged by composer.
   79 composers from J.S. Bach and sons to Hugo Wolf; besides famous composers, a few less well known (mostly
   French). Brief discussion of the composer's oeuvre,
   dates and titles or tempos of movements, and general
   characteristics of each movement.

*A catchall with little accuracy but covering a wide terri-
tory of (German) chamber music is:*

10. Lemacher, Heinrich. *Handbuch der Hausmusik.* Graz/Salz-
    burg/Vienna: Anton Pustet, 1948. ML 128.C4L4. xv +
    454 pages. On poor paper.
    A mixture of lists of works, essays, and documents re-
    lating to Hausmusik. Part I contains essays and docu-
    ments on 200 years of Hausmusik, including personali-
    ties, generic lists of chamber music (trio sonatas,
    string quartets, and so on) and precursors back to
    Heinrich Isaac. Contains lists of the works of the
    classic composers (Haydn, Beethoven, Mozart, Schubert,
    Schumann, Brahms and Reger). Part II opens with poems
    about chamber music, including a poetic dialogue be-
    tween 2 violins, a viola and a cello. Then follows a
    long list of chamber music (Hausmusik) generically or-
    ganized, including concertos, piano works, and an occa-
    sional poem. Part III is vocal music. Designed for
    the music lover and amateur performer who is looking
    for available repertory. The statements about the
    music are essentially useless.

PERIODICALS

There is a large number of music periodicals which contain
articles on various facets of chamber music. These can be
seen on the following pages in the listings of various
studies of chamber music and its history. Some of these are
scholarly journals, others are theoretical, still others
popular; some are devoted to a particular instrument or
family of instruments or to a particular era or nationality.
There are newspapers, weeklies, monthlies, quarterlies and
annuals. Only a few periodicals are devoted exclusively to
chamber music and are listed here. Since many chamber music
periodicals seem to have come and gone quickly, the following is merely a sketch list.

11. *American Ensemble.* 1978-1983. 6 vols, 4 numbers each
    vol. except I with only 2. Publication of Chamber
    Music America, New York. Replaced by *Chamber Music
    Magazine* in 1984.
    An extremely important periodical for all professional
    and amateur chamber musicians. Includes feature
    articles on performance, business aspects, new
    findings, activities, opportunities, premiers, and
    advertisements.

12. *Blätter für Haus- und Kirchenmusik.* 1897-1915. 18
    vols., issued monthly. Langensalza (Germany). E.
    Rabich, editor.

13. *Chamber Music,* supplement to *The Music Student.* 1913-
    1916. ML 5.C29. 22 numbers. Great Britain. Percy
    Scholes, editor.

14. *Chamber Music Magazine.* 1984-. Issued quarterly. Pub-
    lication of Chamber Music America, New York. Suc-
    ceeds *American Ensemble.* See description under {11}.

15. *Chamber Music News.* 1955-1962. 7 issues. Publication
    of New Zealand Federation of Chamber Music Societies.

16. *Chamber Music Quarterly.* 1982-. ML 1100.C5. Spring
    1984 issue from Bellingham, Washington 98226. In-
    cludes scholarly essays, information on chamber music
    performances, reviews of music and books on chamber
    music, and advertisements.

17. *Collegium Musicum.* 1932. 1933-1943 renamed *Zeit-
    schrift für Hausmusik.* After World War II retitled
    Hausmusik (2).

18. *The Consort.* 1929-. Annual (except 1 issue 1968-
    1969). Publication of the International Society for

Early Music and Instruments, London, etc. Originally
a publication of the Dolmetsch Foundation.

19. Devotée: the Magazine for Chamber Music Players and
    Listeners. Vol. I, no. 1 (Spring, 1979). Vol. II,
    no. 3 (March/April, 1981) only copy seen. Troy (New
    York). ML 1100.D48.

20. Der Dilettant. 1909-1938. From 1910 entitled Haus-
    musik (1). Munich.

21. The Ensemble News. Spring 1926-Summer 1927.

Hausmusik (1). See Der Dilettant.

Hausmusik (2). Continuation of Zeitschrift für Hausmusik,
1946-1961.

22. Die Kammermusik: Zeitschrift für Pflege der Instrumen-
    talmusik unter besonderer Berücksichtigung des Kam-
    merstyls. 1897-1901. 5 vols. Heilsbronn (vol. V
    Düsseldorf). A. Eccarius-Sieber, editor.

23. La Musique de Chambre. 1923-1925. France.

Zeitschrift für Hausmusik. 1932-1943. See Collegium Musicum and Haumusik (2).

                        BIBLIOGRAPHIES

Bibliographies of chamber pieces are listed here. Bibliographies of studies on historical matters can be found in
chapters 2 and 6 and on analytical matters in chapter 3.
The principal bibliographies of studies of performance practice by Newman {1434}, Garretson {1435}, Rutan {1437}, and
Squire {1436} are in chapter 4.

General bibliographies:

24. Altmann, Wilhelm. Chamber Music Literature: Catalogue
    of Chamber Music Works Published since 1841. Leip-
    zig: C. Merseburger/New York: C. Fischer, 1923. ML
    128.C4A53.1923. viii + 170 pages. German title,
    1st, 2nd and 3rd eds.: Kammermusik-literatur: Ver-
    zeichnis von seit 1841 erschienenen Kammermusik-
    werken. 1st ed. 1910. ML128.C4A5. 2nd ed. 1918.
    3rd enlarged and revised ed. Leipzig: Carl Merse-
    burger, 1923. German title 4th, 5th and 6th eds.:
    Kammermusik-Katalog: ein Verzeichnis von seit 1841
    erchienenen Kammermusikwerken, 1931, 1942, and 1945.

Reprint 1945 ed.: Hofheim am Ts.: Hofmeister, 1967.
Designed not as a thorough bibliography but as a handy
list of available chamber music editions published from
1841 to 1923. No distinction between great composers
and insignificant ones; composers before 1841 well
represented in later editions. Systematically presented: I: Chamber Music for Strings and Winds, II:
Chamber Music for Pianoforte, III: Chamber Music for
Harp and Other Instruments, and IV: Chamber Music with
Voice. For updating see {31}.

25. _____. "Zu Unrecht vergessene Kammermusik-
    werke," in *Neue Musik Zeitschrift* (1950), 89-91.
    Lists 25 composers -- some famous, some obscure -- and
    their unjustly neglected chamber works. Includes music
    by Cherubini, Glazunov, Glière, Goldmark, d'Indy,
    Raff, Anton Rubinstein, Saint-Saëns, Schumann, Spohr,
    and Weingartner, among others.

26. Stein, Franz A. *Verzeichnis der Kammermusik von 1650
    bis zur Gegenwart*, in *Dalp-Taschenbücher*, Band 360.
    Bern/Munich: Francke, 1962. ML 128.C4S7x. 107 pages.
    A practical list arranged by composer, then genre. In-
    cludes string, wind, and some solo keyboard music.
    Gives title of collection, date of composition or first
    edition, titles of individual pieces with key, opus
    number, movements, and scoring. Most composers are
    well-known; a small number of 20th-century composers
    are less well-known, but even here most of them are the
    expected ones: Hindemith, Stravinsky, Ravel, Roy Har-
    ris, Samuel Barber, and so forth.

27. Hillman, Adolf. *Kammarmusiken och dess mästare intill
    1800-talets början: jämte Förteckning över Kammar-
    musikkomponister intill Nuvarande Tid*. Stockholm:
    Wahlström & Widstrand, [1918]. ML 1100.H45. 129
    pages.
    The first half of the book is an intelligent, though
    undocumented and dated history of chamber music in-
    fluenced by Nohl {461} and Kilburn {165}. The second
    half is a list of composers of European and Ameri-
    can chamber music from 1600 to 1918, including many
    obscure names but not weighted toward Scandinavia.

28. National Music Camp. *The Interlochen List of Recom-
    mended Materials for Instrumental Ensembles*. 1st ed.
    1946. 3rd ed. Interlochen (Michigan): no publisher,
    1953. ML 132.C4I6 (ML 132.A2N37.1953). 61 pages.
    Divided into 4 categories: strings, woodwinds, brass,
    and mixed string + winds including saxophone and piano.
    Each subdivided by number of players and scoring. Data
    on composer, short title, scoring, publisher, and dif-
    ficulty. Impressive for its length, organization,
    quality of entries and varieties of scorings. Con-

ceived as an updating not only of the 2 previous editions but also of the National School Band Association
list.

29. National School Band, Orchestra and Vocal Association.
    *Instrumental Ensembles: Woodwind, Brass, String and
    Mixed: Graded Lists of Recommended Materials.* Chica-
    go: no publisher, 1948. ML 132.C4N3. 39 pages.
    A large and significant list of chamber works for stu-
    dents, professionals, and devotees. Organized by
    scoring under 4 main headings: woodwind, brass, mixed
    string-wind, and string.

30. Waln, George E., Chairman. *Materials for Miscellaneous
    Instrumental Ensembles: Prepared by the Committee on
    Literature and Interpretation of Music for Instru-
    mental Ensembles.* Washington, D.C.: Music Educators
    National Conference, 1960. ML 128.C4M9. 89 pages.
    Lists of chamber works organized by strings, woodwinds,
    brass and percussion, then by size of ensembles, then
    by composer. Information on title, publisher, diffi-
    culty, scoring, and some elementary observations on
    suitability for students. Brass category includes
    voice and short discography. Some arrangements.
    Famous as well as minor composers.

31. Richter, Johannes Friedrich. *Kammermusik-Katalog: Ver-
    zeichnis der von 1944 bis 1958 veröffentlichten Werke
    für Kammermusik und für Klavier vier- und sechshändig
    sowie für zwei und mehr Klavier.* Leipzig: Friedrich
    Hofmeister, 1960. ML 128.C4R55. 318 pages.
    A huge, detailed catalogue of chamber music published
    from 1944 to 1958, arranged generically from a10 down
    to a1 for winds and strings mixed or alone; from sex-
    tets to duets for piano with winds and/or string; for
    plucked strings in various combinations to solos; for
    accordion with other instruments or alone; and vocal
    chamber music and piano chamber music without winds and
    strings, including piano solos and arrangements. In-
    formation includes brief title, scoring, publishing
    data, and original dates. Conceived as a continuation
    of Altmann's chamber music catalogue {24}.

32. American Music Center. *Chamber Music by Contemporary
    Composers.* [New York: American Music Center, 1954.]
    ML 128.C4A6. 16 pages.
    List of chamber music by composers of the first half of
    the 20th century of different nationalities. The music
    was selected on the basis of its quality and its ser-
    viceability to performers, teachers, students, and mu-
    sic organizations. Organized by instrument class,
    then by genre. Information on composer, title, publi-
    sher, cost in 1954, and sometimes duration. A list of
    12 publishers at the beginning with addresses. A use-

ful list but by no means exhaustive, replaced by the
numerous specialized bibliographies of later times. A
similar list by Ray Green is published in *American Music Teacher*, ii (March-April, 1953), 6-7 and 18-21.

33. Mazzeo, Rosario. *A Brief Survey of Chamber Music for
    Small Groups*. Boston: The Cundy-Bettoney Co., 1937.
    2nd ed. 1938. ML 128.C4M3. 16 pages.
    Highly selective list of chamber music involving
    winds, compiled by a clarinetist of the Boston Symphony
    Orchestra. Includes strings and piano but always at
    least one wind. Information on composer, title, scor-
    ing, arranger and arrangement, character, and diffi-
    culty. A few works with voice at the end.

34. Schaffner, Anne. *Expandable Chamber Music at Various
    Levels: a Source Book for Performers and Teachers*.
    Austin (Texas): privately printed by author, 1982.
    ML 128.C4S32.1982. 45 unpaginated pages.
    Short list of chamber music including ensembles of un-
    like (standard) instruments where the number of perfor-
    mers can be changed *ad libitum* "without loss of solo
    and ensemble feeling." Gives composer, title, source
    (manuscript or publisher), and range of performers.
    Mostly contemporary American or arrangements of Bach,
    Vivaldi, and others.

35. Schumann, Otto. *Schumanns Kammermusikbuch*. Wilhelms-
    haven: Hermann Hübener, 1951. MT 140.S32. 538
    pages. 2nd ed. *Handbuch der Kammermusik*, 1956.
    Reprint 1970. MT 140.S32.1970. 557 pages.
    A handbook for laypersons consisting of a list of 71
    composers of chamber music arranged chronologically
    from Rosenmüller to Messiaen, with biographical infor-
    mation and brief, non-technical commentary on overall
    chamber style and on specific pieces. Adds a much
    longer list at end. Very strong on now somewhat ob-
    scure as well as famous composers, mostly German, of
    the late 19th-century to c.1950.

36. Cosme [Come?], Luiz. *Música de Câmera*. Rio de
    Janeiro: Ministério da Educaçao e Cultura, Serviço de
    Documentaçáo, 1961. ML 1100.C77. 143 pages. In
    Portuguese.
    An outgrowth of weekly radio programs, commentary on 40
    composers of chamber music from J.S. Bach to William
    Walton. Includes lists of each of their major chamber
    music and selected discography. For the layperson.

37. Baldwin, Lillian. *A Repertory of Chamber Music*.
    Cleveland: Lillian Baldwin typewritten copy, 1944.
    MT 140.B3. 77 pages.
    List of 19 pieces of chamber music by 15 composers with
    naive analyses of each. Standard repertory except for

Charles Huguenin's *Second Trio for Oboe + Clarinet +
Bassoon*, Opus 31.

38. Helm, Everett. "New Chamber Music," in *Musical Ameri-
    ca*, lxxxii (April, 1962), 58.
    A brief description of difficulty, style, texture and
    form of a few new works by Lou Harrison, Ned Rorem,
    Chou Wen-Chung, Paul Pisk, David Diamond, Earle Brown,
    and François Devienne, as well as works by older com-
    posers such as Danzi and Haydn.

*For most bibliographies of chamber music pertaining to a
specific nationality, see the last section in Chapter 2. An
additional list is in {148}. Some libraries and specific
collections of importance to chamber music have been inven-
toried, among which are the following:*

39. Clinton, Ronald Dale. "The Edwin Bachmann Collection
    at the University of Texas at Austin: Perspectives on
    the Solo and Chamber Music with Keyboard." DMA
    dissertation. University of Texas, 1984. UMI DA83-
    19553. DAI xliv.4A, p. 903. 81 pages.
    A discussion of the collection, of music printing used
    in the editions in the collection, and of the early
    Beethoven editions in the collection which apparently
    are the principle items in it. Discusses at length the
    early Breitkopf and Härtel edition of Op. 12, no. 1
    (solo piano sonata) and compares it to later editions.
    An appendix has a list of the complete collection,
    including chamber music.

40. Eddy, Marmee Alexandra. "The Rost Codex and its
    Music." PhD dissertation. Stanford University,
    1984. UMI 84-20518. DAI xlv.6A, p. 1567. 304
    pages.
    The Rost Codex (in the Paris Bibliothèque National,
    Mus. Rès. Vm⁷673) is a 17th-century collection of in-
    strumental chamber music in 3 part books (violin, vio-
    lin, organ). Contains c.150 pieces, composed from be-
    fore 1649 to c.1675 and compiled in Baden-Baden and
    Strasbourg by François Rost c.1660-c.1680. Mostly trio
    sonatas (2 violins + continuo) by German and Italian
    composers like Schmelzer and Cazzati. An important
    historical document for the trio sonata. Considers
    concordances, styles, and the biography of Rost.

41. *A Catalogue of the String Music Library of Gustave
    Schirmer, Kneisel Hall, Blue Hill, Maine.* No publ.
    information. ML 138.S34. i + 12 pages.
    A simple list of chamber music, by genre and scoring,
    in the private possession of one of the leading chamber
    music patrons of the late 19th century, Gustave Schir-

mer (1864-1907). Mostly string quartets, trios and a
few duets.

42. Detroit Public Library, Music and Drama Department.
    Music for Orchestra and Chamber Music. Detroit:
    Detroit Public Library, 1929. NL v.2.225. 58 pages.
    List of a sizeable collection of chamber scores and
    parts in the Detroit Public Library, partially acquired
    from the estates of the violinist Maud Powell in 1923
    and the conductor-violinist Theodore Spiering in 1925.
    Organized by number of players (trios to nonets) and
    scoring; gives only composer, title, and publisher.

*For an inventory of wind ensemble music in the Oettingen-
Wallerstein Hofkapelle library, see Jon Piersol's
dissertation {290}.*

43. Composers Guild of Great Britain. *Chamber Music by Liv-
    ing British Composers.* London: British Music Infor-
    mation Centre, 1969. ML 120.G7B74. ii + 42 pages.
    A list of published and unpublished chamber works for 3
    or more instruments by more than 250 British composers
    living in 1969, housed in the British Music Information
    Centre, 10 Stratford Place, London W.1. Gives compo-
    ser's birthdate, title and date of composition, scor-
    ing, duration, publisher if any, and how the material
    may be used (for rent or sale).

44. British Broadcasting Corporation. *BBC Music Library:
    Chamber Music Catalogue: Chamber Music, Violin and
    Keyboard, Cello and Keyboard,* ... London: J.
    Smethurst and Novello, 1965. ML 128.C4B7.1965. xix
    + 612 pages.
    A catalogue of the BBC's extensive chamber music hold-
    ings of scores and parts. Within broad sections an
    alphabetical list by composer (or title if anonymous)
    followed by title, scoring, publisher, date of publica-
    tion, and BBC shelf numbers.

45. [Chester, J. and W.] *A Complete Handbook and Guide to
    Chamber Music.* London: J. and W. Chester, [1923].
    ML 128.C54C45. 36 pages. Suppl. 1 (Sept. 1923), 2
    pages. Suppl. 2 (Sept. 1924), 2 pages. Suppl. 3
    (Sept. 1925), 2 pages. Suppl. 4 (Sept. 1926), 1
    page.
    A systematic list of chamber music from nonets to duets
    without piano and piano octets to piano duets with vio-
    lin or cello. Also short list of wind chamber music.
    17th to 20th century, great and obscure composers, all
    European nationalities. A catalogue of the J. and W.
    Chester lending library which opened in 1915 with the
    aim of obtaining every piece of chamber music in print,

whether worthy or not (the library recognized that
taste changes). Over 2000 items.

46. Famera, Karen McNerney, ed. *Catalog of the American
    Music Center Library*, vol. 2: *Chamber Music*. New
    York: American Music Center, 1978. ML 120.U54A7.
    ISBN 0-916052-04-4. xv + 164 pages.
    Important catalogue of the New York-based library con-
    taining 20th-century chamber music by American compo-
    sers. In 3 parts: instrumental, with voices, and mis-
    cellaneous (including multi-media). Systematically ar-
    ranged. Information on composer, title, scoring, pub-
    lisher, number of pages, and duration. 2735 titles.
    While not including all chamber music of the composers
    listed, it contains many works not listed elsewhere,
    especially by lesser-known American composers.

47. Australia Music Centre. *Catalogue of Instrumental and
    Chamber Music*. Sydney: Australia Music Centre, 1976.
    ML 120.A86A93. ISBN 0-909168-01-6. vi + 147 pages.
    A catalogue of music by Australian composers in the
    Music Centre's library in Sydney. In 2 parts, the
    second -- chamber music -- comprises nearly all the
    catalogue. Works listed by composer (birth dates
    given), then title, date of composition, duration,
    publisher, and scoring.

48. New South Wales State Conservatorium of Music Library.
    Catalogue of Chamber Music 1960. Sydney: NSWSCM,
    1960. ML 136.S97N5. 79 pages.
    List of works from solos to octets for strings with or
    without piano, songs with strings, and wind ensembles.
    Gives shelf number, composer, title, scoring and
    publisher.

49. Mallows, Katherine. *Chamber Music by South African
    Composers in South African Libraries*. Cape Town:
    University of Cape Town, 1979. ML 120.S58M3. ISBN
    0-7992-0304-1. viii + 88 pages. Publication of
    Librarianship Diploma thesis. University of Cape
    Town, 1977.
    List of manuscripts and prints of South African chamber
    music. Gives scoring, composer with dates, title, lo-
    cation of score, size of score or parts, movements, and
    some other data.

50. Russell, John F. *List of Chamber Music in the Henry
    Watson Music Library*. Manchester: Henry Watson Music
    Library, 1913. ML 136.M2H32 no.2. vi + 143 pages.
    A catalogue in 2 parts: by scoring and alphabetical by
    composer. Mostly strings and piano, a few wind pieces.
    Gives title and in a few cases publisher. This is a
    public library in Manchester, England.

51. Holecek, Jaroslav, ed. *J.A. Seydl Decani Beronensis Operum Artis Musicae Collectio: Catalogus*, in *Catalogus Artis Musicae in Bohemia et Moravia Cultae*, No. 2. Prague: Supraphon, 1976. 201 pages. In German, Czech, and English.
     A thematic catalogue of 585 chamber pieces (mostly violin music) once owned by J.A. Seydl (1775-1837) and now in the Bezirksarchiv Beroun (Bohemia).

52. Stevens, Denis. "Seventeenth-Century Italian Instrumental Music in the Bodleian Library," in *Acta Musicologica*, xxvi (1954), 67-74.
     A list of works in the Bodleian Library, alphabetical by composer, with date, opus number, publishing data, number of volumes, and shelf number. A large number of sonatas and divertimenti.

53. Lippmann, Friedrich, and Ludwig Finscher. "Die Streichquartett-Manuskripte der Bibliothek Doria-Pamphilj in Rom," in *Studien zur italienisch-deutschen Musikgeschichte*, vi, in *Analecta Musicologica*, vii (1969), 120-144.
     A scholarly inventory of string quartet manuscripts from the last third of the 18th century, with themes of all the movements and concordances. Composers include Federico Abel, Michele Barbici, Boccherini, Giuseppe Demachi, Anton Kammel, Josef Mysliveček, Pugnani, and Antonio Vanhs (= Jan Krtitel Vanhal).

The following bibliographies are designed to assist those wishing to build a library:

54. Forsyth, Ella Marie. *Building a Chamber Music Collection: a Descriptive Guide to Published Scores*. Metuchen (New Jersey)/London: The Scarecrow Press, 1979. ML 128.C4F7. ISBN 0-8108-1215-0. xix + 191 pages.
     An annotated, selective bibliography of basic chamber music, systematically arranged. Includes primarily the most popular music, and only in wind music ensembles do many lesser-known names appear. Information on publishers of currently available scores and parts, references to analyses in Cobbett {7}, Tovey {157} and a few other books, and a few assessments of difficulty of performance and moods in the music. Designed for the the librarian who wishes to build a music library.

55. Forbes, Watson. *Catalogue of Chamber Music*. London: National Federation of Music Societies, 1965. ML 128.C4F67. 68 pages.
     Selected lists of chamber music a3 to a9 or a10. Section I gives the basic classics and contemporary works popular in England. Lists composers with dates, titles, duration, tempos of movements, scoring, and publisher.

Section II contains easy works for the beginner
(marked with "a") and more challenging works for advanced players (marked with "b"). Designed to help music clubs build programs and performers find repertory.

*Several bibliographies are designed especially for the ama-
teur "Hausmusikant": see also Lemacher and Schmidt's* Almanach der Hausmusik *{465} and Bruno Aulich's* Alte Musik für
Hausmusikanten *{1430}.*

*Bibliographies of specific types of chamber music vary in
scope.*

56. Vidal, Antoine. *Les Instruments á Archet: les Feseurs,
    les Joueurs d'Instruments, leur Histoire sur le Con-
    tinent Européen: suivi d'un Catalogue Général de la
    Musique de Chambre.* 3 vols. Paris: 1876-1878.
    Reprint London: The Holland Press, 1961. ML 755.
    V53L4. 3 vols. I: xvi + 357 pages; II: vi + 383
    pages; III: vii + 160 pages.
    Particularly valuable for its bibliography of chamber
    music in vol. III. Though dated and incomplete, it
    nonetheless is so large as to contain many names not
    encountered in any other chamber music list. Vol. I:
    history of bowed string instruments, their makers, and
    some of the players. Vol. II: history of the players
    concluded, history of cellists, and a list of cellists
    from "the beginning" to B. Romberg with brief bio-
    graphical information. Vol. III: history of musical
    printing, biographies of composers of chamber music,
    catalogue of chamber music for bowed strings a2 to a10,
    and a list of violinist-composers in Italy in the 16th
    and 17th centuries. The biographies are also dated
    but, in some cases, are the best that are available.
    Originally designed for both layperson and scholar, it
    would serve as secondary reading for the same clien-
    telle today.

57. Wilkins, Wayne. *Index of Violin Music (Winds) Including
    Index of Baroque Trio Sonatas.* Magnolia (Arkansas):
    The Music Register, 1973. ML 128.V4W5. ii + 38 + 14
    pages. Supplements 1976-1977 (ii + 15 pages) and
    1978 (ii + 25 pages).
    Systematic list of works for violin with woodwinds, a2
    to more than 10 instruments. Information is limited to
    composer, title, scoring and publisher.

58. Farish, Margaret K. *String Music in Print.* 2nd ed.
    New York/London: R.R. Bowker Company, 1973. ML 128.
    S7F4.1973. ISBN 0-8352-0596-7. 1984 suppl. in
    Music-in-Print Series (Philadelphia: Musicdata, Inc.,
    1984), ML 128.S7F4.suppl., ISBN 0-88478-016-3, xiii +
    262 pages. 1st ed. 1965; suppl. 1968.

Almost entirely chamber music. The most comprehensive and significant current bibliography of string chamber music. Listed by scoring, then alphabetically by composer (1984 suppl. adds dates). Gives only title and publisher. Index and list of publishers.

59. West, Charles Wayne. "Music for Woodwinds and Strings, Five to Thirteen Players, Composed between *ca.*1900 and *ca.*1973: a Catalogue of Compositions and Analyses of Selected Works by Composers Active in the United States after 1945." DMA dissertation. University of Iowa, 1975. UMI 76-2204. DAI xxxvi.8A, p. 4844. xvi + 257 pages.
   Includes a catalogue of works, published and in manuscript, for large woodwind + string ensembles, and an historical study of the development of these ensembles in the 19th century. Ten 20th-century works are analyzed in detail.

60. Voxman, Himie, and Lyle Merriman. *Woodwind Ensemble Music Guide.* Evanston: The Instrumentalist Co., 1973. ML 128.W5V7. viii + 280 pages.
   An extensive list of woodwinds in ensemble with other woodwinds, brass, string, percussion and tape. Organized by number of players (2 to 13), scoring, and alphabetically by composers. Information on title and publisher. List of 262 publishers at end.

String quartets:

61. Altmann, Wilhelm. *Handbuch für Streichquartettspieler: ein Führer durch die Literatur des Streichquartetts.* 1st ed. Berlin: M. Hesse, 1928-1929. 3 vols. 2nd ed. Wilhelmshaven: Heinrichshofen's Verlag, 1972-1974. 4 vols. MT 140.A582. ISBN 3-7959-0112x. I:340 pages; II: 354 pages; III: 373 pages, IV: 234 pages.
   Vols. I and II discuss all major and many minor composers of string quartets, chronologically. An intelligent, useful guide. Gives composer's dates and dates of known quartets, and discusses each quartet briefly. Vol. III covers the same for trios, quintets, sextets, septets, and octets for strings only. Vol. IV covers works for strings + winds. Especially strong on obscure composers c.1880-1920's.

62. _____. *Kleiner Führer durch die Streichquartette für Haus und Schule,* in *Hesses Handbücher der Musik,* Band 102. Berlin-Halensee/Wunsiedel: Deutsche Musikliteratur-Verlag, 1950. MT 140.A5823. 166 pages.
   A simple review of "easy" string quartets by the mas-

ters as well as many minor composers. The appendix
lists "easy" string trios.

63. Chapman, Roger E.   "The American String Quartet: 1924 -
    1949."   MA thesis.   University of California at Los
    Angeles, 1950.   102 pages.
    Lists more than 400 quartets, both printed and in manu-
    script.   "American" is defined as any composer native
    and foreign born who writes a quartet in the United
    States.   Also includes a discussion of style, form and
    techniques in representative samples.

Sonatas:

*For the most extensive list of 17th-century Italian violin
composers and their sonatas, see Willi Apel's* Die italienische Violinmusik *and related article {222}.   For a list of
17th- and 18th-century violin sonatas in editions published
in Europe 1850-1899, see Volker Freywald's monograph {246}.
For lists of a large number of French violin sonatas from
Lully to Viotti, see La Laurencie's book {236}.*

64. Loft, Abram.   *Violin and Keyboard: the Duo Repertoire.*
    New York: Grossman Publishers, 1973.   ML 1165.L635V6.
    ISBN 0-670-74700-9.2 vols: I: xiv + 360 pages, 312
    musical examples (from the seventeenth century to
    Mozart); II: xii + 417 pages, 408 musical examples
    (from Beethoven to the Present).
    Primarily an annotated bibliography designed for the
    performer who is looking for repertory and some expla-
    nation of that repertory.   Containing little biographi-
    cal information, the thrust is on the technical violin
    + keyboard achievements or problems of each piece and
    some concern with variant sources, ornamentation, and
    performance suggestions.   Repertoire before 1950 is
    extensive, of 1950-1973 highly selective.

*For an index of Baroque trio sonatas, see {108}.   For a list
of cello sonatas, see Gertrude Shaw's* "The Violoncello
Sonata Literature in France during the Eighteenth Century"
{241}.

65. Fisher, Huot.   "A Critical Evaluation of Selected Clari-
    net Solo Literature Published from January 1, 1950 to
    January 1, 1967."   AMD dissertation.   University of
    Arizona, 1970.   UMI 70-13730.   DAI xxxi.3A, p. 1308.
    146 pages.
    Among the 514 pieces examined are 104 sonatas, sonati-
    nas, or suites for clarinet + piano; 13 are annotated
    in some detail (brief stylistic and formal analyses,
    some performance factors, and critical comments on
    editions).   Also annotates 10 of the 286 other pieces
    for clarinet + piano.

66. Bartlett, Loren Wayne. "A Survey and Checklist of
    Representative Eighteenth-Century Concertos and
    Sonatas for Bassoon." PhD (performance) disserta-
    tion. University of Iowa, 1961. UM 61-5544. DA
    xxii.12, p. 2815. 247 pages.
    An annotated list of over 120 works (sonatas and con-
    certos), with thematic index, information on biography
    of the composers, location of works, and brief formal
    and stylistic analyses. Opens with a history of the
    bassoon to c.1800, and emphasizes the 1645 bassoon
    sonatas of Giovanni Antonio Bertoli.

67. Houser, Roy. *Catalogue of Chamber Music for Woodwind
    Instruments.* 1st ed. Bloomington (Indiana): Indiana
    University School of Music, 1962. Reprint New York:
    Da Capo, 1973. ML 128.W5H7.1973. ISBN 0-306-70257-
    6. xx + 159 pages.
    An extensive, practical catalogue of college woodwind
    ensembles from trios with or without piano up to more
    than 10 instruments. Includes instructions for student
    performers on how to play chamber music. Gives publi-
    shers.

Woodwind ensembles:

68. Helm, Sanford M. *Catalogue of Chamber Music for Wind
    Instruments.* Ann Arbor: National Association of
    College Wind and Percussion Instrument Instructors,
    1952. Rev. ed. New York: Da Capo, 1969. ML 128-
    C4H4.1969. ISBN 0-306-71490-6. ix + 85 pages.
    Systematic listing from a3 to larger than a12, subdi-
    vided by number of winds in the ensemble and then by
    specific scoring. Gives only author, title (often ab-
    breviated), scoring, editor, publisher, and some dates.

69. Simon, Eric. "Woodwind Ensemble Literature," in *Wood-
    wind World*, iii (Sept. 15, 1959), 13.
    In essay form a list of original woodwind ensemble
    pieces with brief commentary. Starts with Beethoven's
    3 Duos for clarinet + bassoon and Poulenc's Duos for
    clarinets and clarinet + bassoon, and continues with
    relatively little known works by Rossini, Bridge,
    Ibert, Hindemith, d'Indy, Mozart, Milhaud, Strauss,
    Ludwig Thuille, Berg, Riegger, and Stravinsky.

70. Weerts, Richard K., ed. *Original Manuscript Music for
    Wind and Percussion Instruments.* Washington, D.C.:
    Music Educators National Conference, 1973. ML 132.
    C4W4. 42 pages. Originally published in National
    Association of College Wind and Percussion Instruc-
    tor's *Bulletin*, then updated and published in 1964.
    ML 128.C4N4.1964a. 52 pages.
    List of works in manuscript owned by composers (a few
    distributed by publishers), arranged by genre (solos,

brass, percussion, woodwind ensembles, mixed, with or
without voices, and others). Information on title,
composer, grade, duration, scoring, date of composition, recording, and address of composer. The composers are exclusively minor figures in the overall field
of chamber music but who have contributed to these
special genres.

*For a list of 861 pieces of mixed-wind chamber music by more
than 300 composers, see Ralph Wahl's dissertation {292}.
For a list of representative compositions for woodwind ensemble c.1695-1815, see Harry Hedlund's dissertation {257}.
For a catalogue of ensemble music for woodwinds alone or
with brass from c.1700 to c.1825, see Saul Kurtz's dissertation {288}.*

71. Horne, Aaron. "Solo and Chamber Music for Woodwinds by
      Black Composers Composed from 1893 to 1976." DMA
      dissertation. University of Iowa, 1976. UM 77-
      13152. DAI xxxvii.12A, p. 7394. 121 pages.
   A history of significant Black composers and their
   woodwind music, biographies of selected 20th-century
   Black composers of woodwind music, analyses of selected
   works, and "a catalogue of original works for solo
   woodwind and for chamber ensembles that include one or
   more woodwind instruments" written 1893-1976. In addition to traditional European woodwinds, Horne also includes the African flute *atenteben*.

72. O'Loughlin, Niall. "Classical Wind Chamber," in *Musical
      Times*, cxxv (1984), 34.
   A brief review of various new publications for differ-
   ent scorings involving woodwinds, by Antonio Polzelli
   (1783-1855), Alexander Pössinger (1766-1827), François
   Joseph Garnier (1755-1825), Gassmann, Jacques-Jules
   Bouffil (1783-18??), Johann Rösler (= Jan Josef Röss-
   ler, 1771-1813), Joseph Fiala (1749-1816), and
   Wagenseil.

*See Walter Jones dissertation on the unaccompanied flute
duets in 18th-century France {266}. For the clarinet duet
c.1715 to c.1828, see David Randall's dissertation {270}.*

73. Weiner, Lowell Barry. "The Unaccompanied Clarinet Duet
      Repertoire from 1825 to the Present: an Annotated
      Catalogue." PhD dissertation. New York University,
      1980. UMI 80-17535. DAI xli.2A, p. 458. 236 pages.
   Organized by difficulty into 4 categories, then by composer, with brief information on title, duration, composition date, publisher, movement titles and tempos,
   type of clarinet required, musical elements, and reviews. Includes unpublished works as well. Considers
   the history of the clarinet duet.

74. Gillespie, James E., Jr. *The Reed Trio: an Annotated Bibliography of Original Published Works*, in Detroit Studies in Music Bibliography, no. 20. Detroit: Information Coordinators, 1971. ML 128.W5G54. 84 pages.
An excellent list of published works for oboe + clarinet + bassoon from 1897 to 1968. Gives composer with dates and nationality, trio title, duration, publisher, difficulty, list of movements, and extensive annotations on stylistic influences, scoring, idiosyncracies, and technical matters for each of the 3 instruments. Opens with a history of the reed trio and some major performing groups.

75. Oberlag, Herbert Henry. "An Annotated Bibliography of Original, Published Quartets for Flute, Oboe, Clarinet, and Bassoon." DMA dissertation. Indiana University, 1974. RILM 74-68. viii + 98 pages.
A well-annotated list including, among much else, difficulty, publisher, movements, and dating.

76. Hosek, Miroslav. *Das Bläserquintett: the Woodwind Quintet*. Grünwald: Bernhard Brüchle Edition, 1979. ML 128.W5H67. 234 pages. In German and English.
Primarily a bibliography of pieces for woodwind quintet, alphabetically by composer, with dates, title, sometimes duration, arranger if relevant, and publisher. Also includes lists of works for woodwind quintet with other instruments and a list of woodwind ensembles with date of their organization, original membership, current membership, and mailing address. Opens with a brief history of the woodwind quintet.

77. Peters, Harry B. *The Literature of the Woodwind Quintet*. Metuchen (New Jersey): Scarecrow Press, 1971. ML 128.C4P5. ISBN 0-8108-0368-2. 174 pages.
An attempt at an all-inclusive list of pieces for woodwind quintet including arrangements and pieces for such a quintet with other instruments. Gives composer's dates, arranger, title, publisher, source for data on the piece, and in some cases annotations on difficulty, length, movements, general characteristics, and suitability for concert performance. A basic resource tool for this genre.

For a huge bibliography of woodwind quintets (over 800), see Ronald Wise's dissertation {264}.

78. Price, Jeffrey Keith. "A Study of Selected Twentieth-Century Compositions for Heterogeneous Brass Ensemble and Organ by United States Composers." DMA dissertation. University of Missouri-Kansas City, 1976. UMI 76-25150. DAI xxxvii.5A, p. 2484. 308 pages.
A brief history of brass + organ compositions in

general, then analyses in outline of 31 pieces as
defined in the title. Two or more different brass
parts to be included here, and a few with percussion.
Includes data on range, number and character of movements, musical style, and technical requirements of
each piece.

79. Walker, B.H. "I Teach Solo Brass," in *The School
    Musician*, xxi (January 1950), 34-37, and (February
    1950), 40-41.
    An informal, selective list of brass music at the high
    school level for brass sextets, quintets and quartets,
    trumpet, trombone and French horn quartets, cornet
    trios, and trombone duets. Gives title, composer,
    publisher, difficulty, and a very brief description.

80. Richards, John K. "The Brass Sextet: a Study of its
    Instruments, History, Literature and Position in
    Instrumental Music Education." MM thesis, University
    of Southern California, 1947. USC catalogue no. MU
    148 R516. 175 pages.
    Discusses the instruments that make up the brass sextet
    and gives a graded list of the available literature for
    the standard sextet and a small, representative list of
    literature for the non-standard sextet. Dates the
    beginning of literature for the standard brass sextet
    as 1929 by J. Irving Tallmadge, and notes that it is
    unique to America.

*For a large survey of the literature of ensemble music for
lip-reed instruments (brass and some others such as zink and
cornett), see Willard Starkey's dissertation {291}.*

81. Shoemaker, John Rogers. "A Selected and Annotated List-
    ing of Twentieth-Century Ensembles Published for
    Three or More Heterogeneous Brass Instruments." EdD
    dissertation. Washington University, 1968. UM 69-
    9009. DA xxix.12A, p. 4519. RILM 69-3261. v + 292
    pages.
    The results of a survey in which 40 teachers of brass
    ensemble music were asked to add to or delete works
    from a list of such pieces compiled by Mary Rasmussen
    and Robert Tyker. 35 teachers responded and a list of
    58 scores decided upon. Each score is then described:
    scoring, movements, and other characteristics.

82. Decker, Richard George. *A Bibliography of Music for
    Three Heterogeneous Brass Instruments Alone and in
    Chamber Ensembles.* Oneonta (New York): Swift-Dorr
    Publications, 1976. ML 128.W5D4. v + 82 pages.
    A list of brass trios (mostly for trumpet + horn +
    trombone) alone, with piano or organ, or in ensembles
    with up to 6 additional players including strings.

Includes arrangements and at the end vocal music and
band/orchestral music.

*For a comprehensive list of original, published brass
ensemble works 1900-1966, see Arthur Swift's dissertation
{275}. For a list of 293 brass quintets by American composers 1938-1980, see Michael Tunnell's dissertation {285}.
For a list of contemporary brass ensemble music from Poland,
see Juliusz Pietrachowicz's article {410}. For a list of
trombone quartets since the 16th century, see Wallace
Tucker's article {280}.*

83. Hummel, Donald Austin. "A Selected and Annotated
    Bibliography of Original Works for Trombone Trio."
    DMA dissertation. University of Missouri-Kansas
    City, 1976. UMI 76-25147. DAI xxxvii.5A, pp. 2481-
    2481. 149 pages.
    Lists 53 original trios by 46 composers in 14 coun-
    tries. At the most 5 date before 1900, none before
    1800; 38 are published and 35 were available in 1976.
    Cites composers (with dates and nationality), title,
    date of composition, format (score and/or parts), dura-
    tion, publisher, and movement titles or tempos. Gives
    background information, editorial procedures, and per-
    formance suggestions. Reviews and composers's
    comments.

*Duets, trios, quintets, and other combinations not exclu-
sively winds:*

84. Iotti, Oscar R. *Violin and Violoncello in Duo without
    Accompaniment,* in *Detroit Studies in Music Biblio-
    graphy,* no. 25. Detroit: Information Coordinators,
    1972. ML 128.V4I6. SBN 911772-48=0. 78 pages.
    An updated version of Alexander Feinland, *The Combina-
    tion of Violin and Violoncello without Accompaniment*
    (Calvert County [Maryland]: Calvert Independent, 1947).
    Alphabetical list by composers of such duos, with
    title, original date, and current publisher.

85. Mellado, Daniel. "A Study of 20th-Century Duets for
    Violin and Violoncello." PhD dissertation. Michigan
    State University, 1979. UMI 79-21173. DAI xl.3A, p.
    1144. 121 pages.
    Analyses of duets by Glière, Ravel, Kodaly, Villa-
    Lobos, Toch, Martinú, Honegger, and Rochberg. A brief
    history of the medium, discography, and categorical
    listing of duets.

86. Altmann, Wilhelm. *Handbuch für Klaviertriospieler:
    Wegweiser durch die Trios für Klavier, Violine und
    Violoncell: mit fast 400 Notenbeispielen.* Wolfen-
    büttel: Verlag für musikalische Kultur und Wissen-
    schaft, 1934. MT 140.A58. 237 pages, supplement of

389 musical examples.
Designed for performers, not scholars. From Rameau to
Sigfrid Walther Müller (b.1905, his 1926 trio). Chronological by composer, with composer's dates, title,
names or tempos and meters of movements and some subjective opinions about the whole and individual movements (including both praise and condemnation). As in
Altmann's other books, this one is especially strong on
late 19th-century to early 20th-century.

87. Ping-Robbins, Nancy R. *The Piano Trio in the Twentieth
Century: a Partially Annotated Bibliography with
Introduction and Appended Lists of Commissioned Works
and Performing Trios*. Raleigh (North Carolina):
Regan Press, 1984. ML 128.C4P55.1984. 153 pages.
Considers the basic incompatibility of the piano with
the cello and violin. Lists piano trios alphabetically
by composer. No bibliography, no indication where the
author found her information. A great many trios are
by composers not generally known, so that when no
biographical or bibliographical information is given,
the work's significance is a mystery. Includes a much
shorter list of trios dedicated to a specific performing group or other commission; the value of this list
is not clear. Finally, a list of trio ensembles is the
biggest anywhere; alphabetical by the group's name, it
has very little information about the group.

For a list of 30 piano trios by native-born American
composers 1920-1970, see Arno Drucker's dissertation {303}.
For a thematic catalogue of Haydn's baryton trios, see Béla
Csuka's essay "Haydn és a Baryton" {980}.

88. Altmann, Wilhelm. *Handbuch für Klavierquartettspieler:
Wegweiser durch die Klavierquartette*. Wolfenbüttel:
Verlag für musikalische Kultur und Wissenschaft,
1937. ML 128.C4A47. 147 pages, supplement of 237
musical examples.
Designed for the amateur and professional player and
music lover and not for the scholar. Not as all-inclusive as the *Kammermusikliteratur* {24}. Organized by
composer according to birth year. The Klavierquartett
is usually for piano + violin + viola + cello, but also
recognizes Baroque sonatas for 2 treble instruments +
continuo and later wind ensembles with piano.

89. _____. *Handbuch für Klavierquintettspieler:
Wegweiser durch die Klavierquintett*. Wolfenbüttel:
Verlag für musikalische Kultur und Wissenschaft,
1936. ML 128.C4A48. 178 pages, supplement of 343
musical examples.
Designed for players, whether amateur or professional,
a discussion of each of the major works from Mozart to
Miklos Rózsa, organized chronologically. Discusses

composer's dates; key, meter and tempo of each movement; and general characteristics of each. Compares
one composer to another and points out unusual harmonies and techniques. Especially strong on composers
of the late 19th century to early 20th century, including many forgotten names. Includes many nationalities.

*For lists of string quintets, see Tilman Sieber's book
{245}.*

90. Haas, Karl. "Fifty Years of Unusual Music, 1898-1948,"
in *Chesterian*, xxiii (1948), 11-16.
Describes unusually scored chamber music in the given
time span. Includes many interesting and rarely heard
works by famous composers (usually): Stravinsky, Glazunov, Prokofiev, Krenek, Hindemith, Arnold Cooke, Franz
Reizenstein, Schoenberg, Antony Hopkins, Lennox Berkeley, Honegger, Richard Strauss, Francesco Malipiero,
Milhaud, and so on. Begins with Janaček's *Capriccio*
for piano (left hand) + piccolo + flute + 2 trumpets +
3 trombones + tenor tuba, and ends with Bhuslav
Martinú's *Le Revue de Cuisine* (ballet) for clarinet +
bassoon + trumpet + violin + cello + piano.

*The following bibliographies feature a single instrument in
consort with others in chamber pieces:*

91. Wilkins, Wayne. *The Index of Violin Music.* Magnolia
(Arkansas): The Music Register, [1973]. ML 128.V4W5.
iii + 246 pages.
Systematic list of violin compositions; most categories
are chamber music. Information is limited to composer,
title, scoring, and publisher.

*For a representative list of violin music from solos and
duets to octets, see chapter 25 of Alberto Bachmann's* An
Encyclopedia of the Violin *{1519}.*

92. Baudet-Maget, A. *Guide du Violoniste: Oeuvres Choisies
pour Violon ainsi que pour Alto et Musique de Chambre
Classées d'après leur Degré de Difficulté.* Lausanne/
Paris: Foetisch Frères, [1920]. ML 128.V4B2. xvi +
296 pages.
Brief introduction explaining the purpose of the guide
in French, German, Italian, and English. Claims this
to be the first extensive list of works for the violin
and viola in French. Works are listed by genre, then
by composer with title and publisher, and by difficulty. Still valuable for the extent of its listings from
c.1650 to c.1920. Includes transcriptions and arrangements.

93. Wilkins, Wayne. *The Index of Viola Music.* Magnolia
    (Arkansas): The Music Register, 1976. ML 128.V36W5.
    i + 94 pages. *Supplement to The Index of Viola Music,*
    1976-1977 (i + 9 pages) and 1978 (i + 14 pages).
    Systematic list of works for viola, nearly all chamber
    music categories. Information is limited to composer,
    title, scoring, and publisher.

94. Williams, Michael D. *Music for Viola,* in *Detroit
    Studies in Music Bibliography,* no. 42. Detroit:
    Information Coordinators, 1979. ISBN 0-911772-95-2.
    362 pages.
    A basic list of chamber music with significant viola
    part. Gives composer, title, publisher, and scoring.

95. Altmann, Wilhelm, and Wadim Borisovskij. *Literaturver-
    zeichnis für Bratsche und Viola d'Amore: eine Voll-
    ständigkeit anstrebende, auch ungedruckte Werke be-
    rücksichtigende Bibliographie.* Wolfenbüttel: Verlag
    für musikalische Kultur und Wissenschaft, 1937. ML
    128.V36A48. 148 pages.
    A list, by scoring, of a large variety of works for
    viola and other instruments as well as viola duets and
    trios, but often not many works under each category.
    Includes many arrangements, works of lesser dimension,
    and excerpts. Surprisingly popular combinations were
    viola + flute + guitar, viola + flute + piano, and
    viola + violin + guitar. The viola d'amore list is
    vastly shorter. Gives publisher's data and general
    comments about the pieces, but the original dates of
    composition are not included.

96. Zeyringer, Franz. *Literatur für Viola: Verzeichnis.*
    2nd ed. Hartberg (Austria): Julius Schönwetter jr.,
    1976. ML 128.V36Z5.1976. 1st ed. 1963, suppl. 1965.
    418 pages. Forward and introduction in both German
    and English.
    Exhaustive list of works for viola a1, a2 with various
    instruments, and a3 with various instruments. Also
    viola + voice, viola + orchestra, and studies. Clearly
    indicates whether the work is originally for viola,
    borrowed, or arranged. By scoring, then by composer
    with title, publisher (manuscripts included as well),
    and occasionally other information.

*For a list of over 50 works for viola, mostly chamber music,
written in England 1890-1937, see Thomas Tatton's dissertation {320}.*

97. Weigl, Bruno. *Handbuch der Violoncell-Literatur.* 1st
    ed. 1911. 3rd enl. ed. Vienna/Leipzig: Universal-
    Edition, 1929. ML 128.V5W3. 357 pages.
    A large list of cello works by genre, then by composer.
    Separate listings for arrangements. Includes concertos

and other orchestrally accompanied works as well as
chamber music. Gives opus number and/or abbreviated
title, price in marks or francs, publisher, date or
city, and in some cases brief subjective descriptions.
A 6-page introduction chronicles cellists from the late
16th century to the end of the 19th.

98. Groschwitz, Gustav. *Violoncello-Musik und Kammermusik-
    werke: vollständiges Verzeichnis mit ausführlichen
    Angaben über Inhalt der Werke, Tempi, Tonarten,
    Schwierigkeitsgrade, Besetzungen, Bearbeiten und
    Preis.* Leipzig: D. Rahter/N. Simrock/Anton J.Benja-
    min, [1931]. NYPL *MC(Rahter). viii + 218 pages.
    After a large list of exercises, solos, teaching
    pieces, and concert pieces for the cello, a more modest
    but nonetheless sizeable list of pieces a3 to a9 and
    for chamber orchestra with a cello part. Also lists
    chamber music arrangements.

99. Grodner, Murray. *Comprehensive Catalog of Available
    Literature for the Double Bass.* 3rd ed. Bloomington
    (Indiana): Lemur Musical Research, 1974. ML 128.
    D6G7.1974. xxx + 163 pages.
    After sections on etudes, orchestral studies and solo
    literature, half the catalogue lists chamber works with
    bass, from 2 basses to more than 4 basses, from duets
    to ensembles with 14 other instruments. Gives compo-
    ser, arranger (most chamber works are original), title,
    exact scoring, source, price, comments (by code ex-
    plained in the introduction), and in the smaller
    combinations the difficulty.

100. Posell, Jacques. "The String Bass in Chamber Music,"
     in *The Instrumentalist*, xvii (Nov. 1962), 69-71.
     An informative essay on the problems of the string bass
     in chamber music and an historical overview from
     Mozart, Beethoven and Schubert to Stravinsky and
     Schuller. Then a simple list of 51 chamber works
     including string bass. Posell is a bassist.

101. Dodd, Gordon. *Thematic Index of Music for Viols*, 2nd
     installment. London?: The Viola da Gamba Society of
     Great Britain, 1982. ML 128.V35D6.1980. 174 pages
     unbound.
     An attempt to index all British solo and ensemble viol
     music, mostly of the 16th and 17th centuries. Part 2
     of what is proposed as a 3-part index. Extensive
     bibliography, well-documented, with concordances. Part
     2 also includes corrections of part 1.

102. De Smet, Robin. *Published Music for Viola da Gamba and
     Other Viols*, in *Detroit Studies in Music Biblio-
     graphy*, no. 18. Detroit: Information Coordinators,
     1971. ML 128.S7D48. 105 pages.

Includes a large number of works for viol ensmble and
for viol with other instruments. Listed by scoring,
then by composer. Gives composer's dates, titles of
collections, titles of pieces, exact scoring, editor,
and modern publisher. Brief bibliography and list of
publishers with addresses.

103. Mellott, George Kenneth. "A Survey of Contemporary
     Flute Solo Literature with Analyses of Representative
     Compositions." PhD dissertation. University of
     Iowa, 1964. UMI 64-7932. DA xxv.2, pp. 1249-1250.
     393 pages.
     Surveys solo flute literature from c.1930 to 1964 and
     categorizes it according to medium and then nationality
     of the composer. "The appendices contain classified
     lists of works for flute arranged alphabetically by
     composers." Includes also detailed analyses of 12 solo
     flute works including chamber music by Hindemith,
     Prokofiev, Dutilleux, Boulez, and Poulenc.

104. Pellerite, James J. *A Handbook of Literature for the
     Flute: Compilation of Graded Method Materials, Solos,
     and Ensemble Music for Flutes.* Bloomington (Indi-
     ana): Frangipani Press, 1963. 2nd ed. 1965. 3rd ed.
     1978. ISBN 0-931200-69-5. xxii + 408 pages.
     An extensive list of flute chamber music. Gives compo-
     sers and dates, titles, difficulty, and brief annota-
     tion as to flute technique, basic structure, and dis-
     tinctive features. Aimed primarily at teachers and
     students of flute.

105. Vester, Frans. *Flute Music of the 18th Century: an An-
     notated Bibliography.* Monteux: Musica Rara, 1985.
     ISBN 2-9500646-0-4. 573 pages.
     Contains a vast repertory for flute, including chamber
     music (sonatas and larger groups). Listed generically
     by scoring, then by composer; gives title, scoring,
     publisher, and library location.

106. Otten, Marÿke. "De Blokfluit in de Kamermuziek," in
     Mens en Melodie, ix (1954), 384-386.
     Reviews trio sonatas and other works by famous compo-
     sers that use the recorder; the term "flute" by itself
     nearly always meant recorder before 1750, flute after
     1750. Omits sonatas for 1 recorder + continuo. Be-
     sides 18th-century composers, includes 20th-century
     figures such as Normann Dello Joio, Mathias Seiber,
     Karl Marx, Hanz Kammeyer, Walter Leigh, Stanley Bate,
     P. Glanville Hicks, and Herbert Baumann.

107. Haynes, Bruce. *Catalogue of Chamber Music for the Oboe
     1654-c.1825.* 4th ed. The Hague: Royal Conservatory,
     1980. ML 128.02H396.1980. vi + 80 pages.
     A list of chamber works including the oboe, arranged

generically from solos without bass, ensembles without
bass, solos with bass, up to mixed strings and winds,
wind combinations a6-10, on to combinations of oboe +
voice. Each category includes alphabetical list of
composers, with title, date, publisher, and library
location. Large number of entries.

108. Wilkins, Wayne. *The Index of Oboe Music including the
     Index of Baroque Trio Sonatas.* Magnolia (Arkansas):
     The Music Register, 1976. ML 128.O2W5. iii + 96 +
     11 pages.
     An index of oboe chamber music including woodwind quin-
     tets and many other types. Useful table of contents
     for finding the type of scoring, and list of publishers
     with addresses. The last 11 pages are an alphabetical
     list by composers of trio sonatas, with editor (or
     arranger), title, and publisher.

109. Gifford, Virginia Snodgrass. *Music for Oboe, Oboe
     D'amore, and English Horn: a Bibliography of
     Materials at the Library of Congress,* in *The Music
     Reference Collection,* No. 1. Westport (Connecti-
     cut)/London: Greenwood Press, 1983. ML 128.O2G5.
     ISBN 0-313-23762-X. xlii + 431 pages.
     Most of the introduction is a list of the possible uses
     and combinations of these 3 instruments with themselves
     and with other instruments, from solo up to orchestral
     -- 5617 entries (many not chamber music). A basic list
     of wind chamber music, especially for the 3 instruments
     but useful for all wind, brass and string chamber musi-
     cians as well. Information includes title, composer
     with dates, publisher, and Library of Congress call
     number. No annotations.

110. Opperman, Kalmen. *Repertory of the Clarinet.* New
     York: Ricordi, 1960. ML 128.C58O66. 140 pages.
     A systematic list of works for clarinet, mostly chamber
     music a2 to 15 with at least 1 clarinet.

111. Hiscock, Sherrick Sumner, II. "An Annotated Biblio-
     graphy of Selected Published and Mixed Trios for One
     Clarinetist and Two Other Musicians." DMA disserta-
     tion. University of Miami, 1978. UMI 78-18727. DAI
     xxxix.4A, p. 1917. 204 pages.
     An annotated list of over 400 trios in 11 different in-
     strumental combinations; besides clarinet there are
     other winds, strings, brass, percussion and voice.
     Considers style, performance practice, and difficulty.

112. Sacchini, Louis Vincent. "The Concerted Music for the
     Clarinet in the 19th Century." PhD dissertation.
     University of Iowa, 1980. UMI 80-22063. DAI xli.4A,
     p. 1276. 401 pages.
     Mostly involves concertos, but also "concertpieces

which require an ensemble accompaniment." Divides the
pieces into those by famous composers and clarinetists
and those by lesser known ones. Within these 2 divisions, lists composers alphabetically with biographical
information and discussion of works. A thematic index
gives location, date of publication, and accompaniment
of works discussed in the text.

*See also Orval Oleson's dissertation "Italian Solo and Cham-
ber Music for the Clarinet 1900-1973" {399}.*

113. Sundet, Jerold A. "A Study of Manuscript, Out-of-
     Print, and Currently Published Compositions for Sin-
     gle Oboe or Single Clarinet with Small String Group
     (c.1750-1820)." EdD dissertation. Colorado State
     College, 1964. UMI 65-4780. DA xxvi.2, p. 1083.
     333 pages.
     Aims to increase the school and college wind and string
     ensemble repertory. 24 titles no longer in print were
     chosen to be investigated from submissions of holdings
     by 63 international libraries, and works by 14 compo-
     sers now in print (1964) were chosen from lists submit-
     ted by publishers. List of 43 such works based on con-
     siderable research. Composers include Giardini, Van-
     hal, Gassmann, Canabich, Brunetti, Wiegl, and others.
     Partially published as "Some Out-of-Print and Unpubli-
     shed Compositions for Oboe with Small String Group ca.
     1750-1820," in *Woodwind World,* xi (1972), no. 5, 7-9.

114. Valenziano, Nicholas, J. "Twenty-one Avant-Garde Com-
     positions for Clarinet Published between 1960 and
     1972: Notational Practices and Performance Techni-
     ques." DMA dissertation. University of Missouri at
     Kansas City, 1973. UM 74-14875. DAI xxxv.1A, p.
     505. 262 pages.
     An annotated listing of 21 pieces selected on the re-
     commendation of performers, publishers, composers, and
     university teachers of clarinet. The pieces fall into
     6 categories: 1) clarinet alone, 2) clarient + piano,
     3) clarinet + percussion, 4) clarinet + tape, 5) clari-
     net + ensemble (only 4 players), and 6) clarinet in un-
     specified ensembles. Deals with the notational pro-
     blems in these pieces and indexes notational symbols.

115. Fletcher, Richard Wesley. "Music for Bassoon and Small
     String Ensemble, circa 1700-1825." DMA dissertation.
     University of Iowa, 1974. UM 74-21958. DAI xxxv.4A,
     p. 2318. xvii + 230 pages.
     A catalogue of 98 compositions written 1700-1825 for 1
     bassoon with 2 or more string instruments and, if in-
     cluded, continuo or keyboard, with "source information"
     (publication data, library location, and citation in
     Eitner's *Quellen-Lexikon,* Fétis's *Biographie Univer-
     selle,* Melville-Mason's bibliography in Lyndesay Lang-

will's *The Bassoon and Contrabassoon*, and various
other catalogues) and brief biographies of the composers. Analyzes form and structure in 5 such pieces,
and prepares performing editions of 2 quartets for
bassoon and strings by Jean Baptiste Bréval and Georg
Abraham Schneider. Includes a thematic index.

116. Wilkins, Wayne. *The Index of Bassoon Music Including
     the Index of Baroque Trio Sonatas*. Magnolia
     (Arkansas): The Music Register, 1976. ML 128.B25W5.
     76 pages + 11 pages.
     List of bassoon chamber pieces arranged by genre.
     Information includes only composer, title, scoring and
     publisher. Trio sonatas on supplementary 11 pages.
     Supplemental addenda appeared in 1976-77 (8 pages) and
     1978 (9 pages).

117. _____. *The Index of Saxophone Music*. Magno-
     lia (Arkansas): The Music Register, 1979. ML 128.
     S247W5. ii + 59 pages.
     Extensive catalogue of music for saxophone available in
     print, from solos to large combinations with only saxo-
     phones or in combination with other instruments.
     Listed by number of instruments and scoring. Gives
     composer, title, and publisher. Many arrangements, but
     also considerable amount of original saxophone music.

118. Brüchle, Bernhard. *Horn Bibliographie*. Wilhelmshaven:
     Heinrichshofen's Verlag, 1970. ML 128.H67B8. ISBN
     3-7959-0025-5. 272 pages + 14 pages of illustra-
     tions.
     Catalogue of horn music from solos to 10 or more in-
     struments including horn concertos. By scoring, then
     by composer. Includes title and publisher. Brief
     bibliography of studies on horn music.

119. Wilkins, Wayne. *The Index of French Horn Music*.
     Magnolia (Arkansas): The Music Register, 1978. ML
     128.H67W5. ii + 120 pages.
     Comprehensive catalogue of horn music available in
     print from solo to 15-piece and larger ensembles (other
     brass or other kinds of instruments). Gives author,
     title and publisher. List of publisher and addresses.

120. Pinkow, David James. "A Selected and Annotated Biblio-
     graphy of Music for Horn and Piano with Analysis of
     Representative Works." DMA dissertation. University
     of Maryland, 1983. UMI 84-29928. DAI xlv.10A, p.
     3023.
     A graded list of 82 works originally written for horn +
     piano. Includes duration, range, and style.

*For a list of available chamber music with trumpet for
students, teachers, and performers, see Mario Oneglia's
dissertation {294}.*

121. Cansler, Philip Trent. *Twentieth-Century Music for
     Trumpet and Organ: an Annotated Bibliography*, in
     Brass Research Series, no. 11. Nashville: The Brass
     Press, 1984. ML 128.T78C32.1984. ISBN 0-914282-30-
     1. 46 pages. Revision of "An Analytical Listing of
     Published Music of the Twentieth Century for Trumpet
     and Organ." DMA dissertation. University of Oregon,
     1984.
     A list by composer of 87 such compositions from numer-
     ous countries. Sizeable discussions of each piece, in-
     cluding biography of the composer, reason for the writ-
     ing of the piece, and demands made on both the trumpe-
     ter and organist. Lists publishers with addresses and
     the pieces by difficulty.

122. Arling, Harry J. *Trombone Chamber Music: an Annotated
     Bibliography*, in *Brass Research Series*, no. 8.
     Nashville: The Brass Press, 1978. ML 128.T76A7.
     ISBN 0-914282-23-9. viii + 48 pages.
     Alphabetical list by composer of chamber music with
     trombone (almost entirely 1 trombone). Annotations
     include title, publishing information, trombone tessi-
     tura, duration, difficulty, instrumentation, special
     effects and techniques, clefs, and style.

123. Roberts, James E. "A Preliminary List of Seventeenth-
     Century Chamber Music Employing the Trombone," in
     Journal of the International Trombone Association,
     viii (1980), 19-22.
     A list of apparently original chamber music including
     trombone or optional trombone, divided into works by
     Italian and non-Italian composers. Includes no intro-
     ductory commentary but does give sources. Gives titles
     of collections but not titles of pieces within collec-
     tions. A basic reference on chamber works for trombone
     players.

124. Gifford, Robert Marvin, Jr. "A Survey of the Use of
     the Trombone in Chamber Music with Mixed Instrumenta-
     tion Composed since 1956." DMA dissertation. Uni-
     versity of Iowa, 1978. UMI 79-05662. DAI xxxix.9A,
     p. 5198. vii + 137 pages (DAI = 266 pages).
     Discusses trends and techniques in the pieces in the
     list. Excludes brass ensemble music; it is con-
     ceived as a continuation of Robert E. Gray's work on
     the same subject. Includes other winds, voice,
     strings, percussion, electronic and multimedia re-
     sources. List compiled from publishers's catalogues,
     composers's and performers's suggestions, and in
     library resource lists. Over 1000 works included.

125. Everett, Thomas G. *Annotated Guide to Bass Trombone
     Literature.* 2nd rev. and enl. ed. Nashville: The
     Brass Press, 1978. ML 128.T76E9.1978. ISBN 0-
     914282-03-4. v + 78 pages.
     Systematized list of bass trombone works including both
     chamber as well as non-chamber music categories. Anno-
     tations include publisher, date, duration, tessitura,
     scoring and general stylistic features.

126. Louder, Earle L. and David R. Corbin, Jr. *Euphonium
     Music Guide.* Evanston: the Instrumentalist Company,
     1978. ML 128.B24L7. vi + 46 pages.
     Includes a list of chamber music where the euphonium
     can be substituted for trombone, French tuba, F tuba,
     bassoon, and cello. Much of the repertory is arrange-
     ments, and the authors also suggest orchestra (band)
     performance of some of the pieces.

127. Hinson, Maurice. *The Piano in Chamber Ensemble: an
     Annotated Guide.* Bloomington: Indiana University
     Press, 1978. ML 128.C4H5. xxxiii + 570 pages.
     Systematic list, by composer, of music for 1 piano and
     other instruments (occasionally 2 pianos + other in-
     struments) a2 to a8; the other instruments include the
     standard strings, woodwinds and brass, plus saxophone,
     percussion, tape, harp, and others. Annotations
     include title, date of composition, available edition,
     exact scoring, description of basic style in each
     movement, and special performance requirements.

128. Bedford, Frances, and Robert Conant. *Twentieth-Century
     Harpsichord Music: a Classified Catalog,* in *Music
     Indexes and Bibliographies.* Hackensack (New Jersey):
     Joseph Boonin, 1974. ML 128.H35B4. ISBN 0-913574-
     08-2. xxi + 95 pages.
     Extensive listing by genre and scoring, including
     mostly chamber music but also solo harpsichord, vocal,
     and orchestral music. Gives composer and dates, title,
     year of composition, duration, and source.

129. Purswell, Joan. "20th-Century Chamber Music for Harp-
     sichord," in *Clavier,* xix (1980), no. 4, 36-39, and
     no. 5, 36-38.
     Notes the popularity of the harpsichord in neo-classic,
     neo-baroque chamber compositions 1960-1980 and its con-
     trapuntal style. Also, in distinction to these, notes
     some Italian and French pieces which use the harpsi-
     chord as a color instrument in a freer, often aleatoric
     style. Lists the compositions by composer, with title,
     scoring, publisher and date. Composers, from various
     countries, are mostly well-known contemporaries.

130. Spelman, Leslie P. *Organ Plus: a Catalogue of Ensemble
     Music for Organ and Instruments.* 3rd ed. New York:

34   *Bibliographies*

The American Guild of Organists, 1981. ML 128.O6S7.
1981. 46 pages. 1st ed. 1975, 2nd ed. 1977.
Well-organized list of chamber music with organ and
also some chamber orchestra works. Composers from 17th
to 20th centuries, music currently in print or readily
available. Gives composer, title, number of pages,
difficulty, and publishing data.

131. Crago, Bartholomew. "A Descriptive List of Infrequently
Played Chamber Music and Some Suggestions for Transcription," in *The Soundboard*, vii (1980), 171-172.
Provides modern-day guitar students with ensemble
music. Lists a few works, which in some cases need
transcription for guitar (from lute), by Silvius
Leopold Weiss (1686-1750), Ernst Gottfried Baron (1690-
1760), Ferdinando Carulli (1770-1841), Mauro Giuliani
(1781-1829), Diabelli, Paganini, Wenzel Thomas Matiegka
(1773-1830), Rudolphe Kreutzer (1766-1831), Sor, Diony-
sio Aguado (1784-1849), Henze, Eugène Bozza (b.1905),
Louise Moyse, Hans Martin Linde (b.1930), among others.
Aimed at the unsophisticated guitar student.

132. Canadian Music Centre. *List of Canadian Music for
Guitar*. Toronto/Calgary/Vancouver/Montreal: Canadian
Music Centre, 1980. ML 120.C2C3617. ii + 18 pages.
Besides solo guitar pieces includes numerous guitar
duets, duets for guitar + 1 other instrument, and
chamber ensembles with guitar. Gives scoring,
composer, title, date of composition, duration,
publisher (or manuscript), and recording.

133. MacAuslan, Janna. *A Catalog of Compositions for Guitar
by Women Composers*. Portland (Oregon): Dear Horse
Publications, 1984. ML 128.G8M3.1984. ISBN 0-
9614170-0-5. iv + 47 pages + 1 page insert of last
minute corrections and additions.
Includes guitar ensembles and guitar with 1 or more
other instruments, along with non-chamber pieces for
guitar. Gives title, scoring, date, and publisher.

134. Witoszynskyj, Leo. "Die Gitarre in der Kammermusik und
der Beitrag Wiens," in *Österreichische Musikzeitschrift*, xxxi (December 1976), 640-644.
Not seen.

135. Gilmore, George. *Guitar Music Index: a Cross-Indexed
and Graded Listing of Music in Print for Classical
Guitar and Lute*. 2 vols. Honolulu: Galliard Press,
1976-1981. ML 128.G8G5. I: ii + 108 pages. II: v +
113 pages.
A list by title, composer and scoring in each volume --
2 separate, non-duplicating indices. Includes guitar
or lute + guitar or lute ensembles and those for guitar
or lute + 1 other instrument (standard and unusual).

Gives title, publisher, period of composer, a few
dates, and difficulty.

136. "Chamber Music for Harp in Instrumental Ensemble," in
     Harp News, i, no. 10 (Fall 1954), 10-16.
     A modest bibliography, by instrumentation, of chamber
     music for harp and others, including some arrangements.
     Gives composer, title, and publisher.

*For a bibliography of bibliographies, see {1589}. A number
of studies and some bibliographies include discography. The
following are exclusively discographies:*

137. Schonberg, Harold C. *Chamber and Solo Instrument
     Music*, in *Guide to Long-Playing Records*, vol. III.
     New York: Knopf, c.1955. Reprint Westport (Connecti-
     cut): Greenwood Press, 1978. ML 156.4.C453.1978.
     ISBN 0-31-3202-966. xi + 280 + vi pages.
     A richly annotated discography with historical informa-
     tion and evaluation of the performance. Designed to
     help the record buyer choose the appropriate record.
     Approximately evenly divided between solo keyboard
     music and chamber music.

138. Bahr, Edward Richard. "A Discography of Classical
     Trombone/Euphonium Solo and Ensemble Music on Long-
     Playing Records Distributed in the United States."
     DMA dissertation. University of Oklahoma, 1980. DAI
     xli.6A, p. 451. 324 pages.
     A list of recordings and a cross-reference list of com-
     positions. Included are album title, performers or
     ensemble, other soloists or ensembles, accompanists,
     conductors, record size, number of sides, label and
     number, mono, stereo or quadraphonic. An introduction
     explains the methodology of the discography.

139. Vokurka, Klaus Alexander. "Tschechische Kammermusik
     auf Schallplatten," in *Phono: Internationale Schall-
     platten-Zeitschrift*, xii (1966), 124-6.
     Lists 19 recordings of Czech chamber music from the
     18th to 20th centuries and discusses the works as much
     as the performers.

CHAPTER II. HISTORY OF CHAMBER MUSIC

GENERAL STUDIES

There are no comprehensive, up-to-date histories of the
whole area of chamber music, but there are older books, some
limited ones, and some shorter essays that attempt to view
chamber music as a whole.

140. Mersmann, Hans. *Die Kammermusik*, in Hermann Kretzschmar, *Führer durch den Konzertsaal.* 4 vols. Leipzig:
Breitkopf & Härtel, 1930-1933. I: Die Kammermusik
des xvii. und xviii. Jahrhunderts bis zu Haydn und
Mozart. II: Beethoven. III: Deutsche Romantik. IV:
Europäische Kammermusik des xix. und xx. Jahrhunderts. MT 90.K92. I: xv + 326 pages; II: vi + 187
pages; III: v + 157 pages; IV: viii + 202 pages.
One of the most comprehensive studies of chamber music
in any language. Historical study of style, progres-
sing systematically from period to period, country to
country, composer to composer, genre to genre. Large
chapters on the major composers (whole book on Beethoven), significant statements on the many minor ones.
Includes solo violin sonatas (such as by Bach, Reger).
20th-century chamber music to 1930 is reasonably
complete, but only one paragraph devoted to American
chamber music. Concentrates on form, thematic development, and general "emotional" content.

141. Ulrich, Homer. *Chamber Music.* 1st ed. 1948. 2nd ed.
New York/London: Columbia University Press, 1966. ML
1100.U4. xviii + 401 pages, 62 musical examples.
Standard general history of chamber music, which is
defined as "instrumental ensemble music written in the
largest forms available to the composer, for groups of
two to eight players, having one player to a part, and
in which piano or string instruments supply the principal interest." Most attention is given to biography
and generalizations, with few specific pieces analyzed
in detail. If this book must be used, do so with extreme caution. It contains numerous factual errors and
suffers from the author's rather extreme prejudices:
the 20th-century is basically ignored, and the poor
treatment of wind music and of slightly out-of-the-
mainstream ensembles is symptomatic.

142. Ewen, David. *Solo Instrumental and Chamber Music: its
Story Told through the Lives and Works of its Fore-
most Composers*, in *Mainstreams of Music*, Vol. 3. New

York: Franklin Watts, 1974. ML 460.E9. ISBN 0-531-
02685-X. viii + 278 pages.
A general history of instrumental music designed for
the layperson who has no background. A simplistic
approach that should make easy reading for its intended
audience and infuriate the scholar ("Before Corelli,
violinists were amateurs, hack musicians, or plain
mediocrities," "By the time he completed the six works
in Op. 20 [1772], Haydn had written about twenty-four
string quartets," and similar nonsense). No discussion
of the woodwind quintet phenomenon or any brass chamber
music. Anecdotal, but also contains a great many
facts. By going from composer to composer, there is
considerable discontinuity. Nonetheless, this sur-
passes Ulrich {141} as the best available 1-volume
history of chamber music in English.

143. Gleason, Harold, and Warren Becker. *Chamber Music from*
     Haydn to Bartok, in *Music Literature Outlines*, No. 5.
     2nd ed. Bloomington (Indiana): Frangipani Press,
     1980. ML 1100.G54.1980. ISBN 0-89917-267-9. iii +
     112 pages. 1st ed. Harold Gleason, *Chamber Music*
     from Haydn to Ravel, in *Music Literature Series*, No.
     4. Rochester: Eastman School of Music mimeograph,
     1954. iv + 136 pages.
     A dangerously misinformed presentation which should be
     avoided by all constituencies. Presents in outline the
     history of chamber music before Haydn and then the
     principle chamber works (mostly string quartets) of 14
     major composers. Omits all wind music and all 2-in-
     strument music. The composer's life is outlined, then
     his works summarized, and finally selected works are
     analyzed in outline. At the end of each chapter is a
     bibliography that includes few works past 1970, and the
     authors seem not to have read anything after 1960.

144. Indy, Vincent d'. *Cours de Composition Musicale*, II.1,
     ed. Auguste Sérieyx, *D'après les Notes Prises aux*
     Classes de Composition de la Schola Cantorum en 1899-
     1900. Paris: A. Durand et Fils, n.d. 500 pages.
     II.2, ...*en 1901-1902*. Paris: A. Durand, 1933. 340
     pages. BPL 4052.74.V.2.
     Lectures covering a wide range of topics, including
     sonatas, accompanied chamber music, string quartets,
     and many non-chamber music genres. In each case de-
     fines the type of music, gives its principal and other
     features, then presents a history, and concludes with
     modern (late-19th-century) practices. Dated but his-
     torically important presentation by one of the leading
     French musical personalities of the time.

145. Ackere, Jules. *De intieme Vormen der Muziek: De Kamer-*
     muziek en het Lied. Antwerp/Brussels/Gent/Leuven:

Standaard-Boekhandel, n.d. ML 1100.A3 or ML 1104.
A25. 238 pages with 8 separate pages of music.
Discussion of only a few select composers of chamber
music, including art song, beginning with Corelli and
concluding with Ravel. Aimed at a popular audience
that wants to know the atmosphere of the hit classics.
Regards the sonority of chamber music to have been
realized by 1650 but the emotions of chamber music are
realized only in the 19th century. Corelli and the
Italians transform the suite by intensifying its spirit
and making the performer more conscious of pleasing
himself rather than an audience -- the purity of style
and elasticity of form of the Italian solo violin
sonata. Falsely credits Tartini with the first triple
stops. Before and after Beethoven, analyzes a few
works which generalize about whole genres and
outputs. Lots of praise for Haydn but not much substance to the discussions. Discusses each of the
Beethoven quartets, the violin + piano sonatas, and
some early chamber music. Without documentation the
historical discussion is weak, and the analyses are
entirely subjective.

146. Brunn, Kai Aage. *Kammermusik*. Copenhagen: Thaning &
     Appel, 1960-1968. ML 1104.B8. 3 vols. I: Fra Haydn
     til den Unge Beethoven, 176 pages; II: Fra Beethoven
     til Schubert, 228 pages; III: Den Romantiske Epoke,
     223 pages. In Danish.
     A history of the traditionally-conceived core period of
     chamber music, mostly string, with discussion of na-
     tional schools (German, Bohemian, Russian, Scandi-
     navian, Italian and French), the major composers, and
     the principal works (detailed stylistic and thematic
     analyses).

See also Adolf Hillman's Kammarmusiken {27}.

147. Headington, Christopher. *The Listeners Guide to Cham-
     ber Music*. Poole, Dorset: Blandford Press, 1982. ML
     1100.H3.1982. v + 138 pages. 22 portraits.
     A very brief history of chamber music for the layper-
     son, from the 17th century to the present. Emphasis on
     the principal masterworks of the most famous composers,
     with the purpose of recommending specific recordings to
     the beginning collector.

148. Hemel, Victor van. *De Kamermuziek: Geschiedenis, Kom-
     ponisten, befaamde Ensembles, Kamermuziekkompozites
     e.a.* 3rd ed. Antwerp: Cupido-Uitgaven, [1959?]. ML
     1100.H35.1959. 108 pages. 2nd ed. Antwerp: 1960.
     In Dutch.
     A superficial history of chamber music from the end of
     the 16th century to Bartók that covers a lot of terri-
     tory. Gives a list of 20th-century composers of cham-

ber music by nationality (a few 19th-century excep-
tions). Also lists famous chamber ensembles. Gives a
bibliography of chamber music by genre and difficulty,
and a discography.

*Shorter books, mostly for laypersons, tend to do a better
job within their imposed limitations.*

149. Fiske, Roger. *Chamber Music.* London: BBC, 1969. ML
     1120.F58. SBN 563-08465-0. 80 pages, 51 examples, 4
     photos, 13 drawings and paintings, 1 facs.
     Designed for the reader who has little or no previous
     knowledge of chamber music but who is acquainted with
     other forms of classical music. Written to accompany 7
     broadcasts on BBC Radio 3. Emphasis on England in the
     discussion of chamber music before 1750, better
     balanced afterwards. Beware of many false statements,
     but in a superficial way this is a readable, informa-
     tive introduction to chamber music.

150. King, Alexander Hyatt. *Chamber Music,* in *The World of
     Music,* ed. George Franckenstein and Otto Erich
     Deutsch. New York: Chanticleer Press/London: M. Par-
     rish, 1948. ML 1100.K5. 72 pages, 40 illustrations.
     A brief, comprehensive history of chamber music which,
     despite numerous historical inaccuracies, is valuable
     for attention to English and American examples and for
     its beautiful illustrations.

151. Höcker, Karla. *Grosse Kammermusik.* Berlin: Rembrandt,
     1962. ML 1100.H55. 64 pages, 34 photos of chamber
     players.
     A brief, very general introduction to chamber music
     concepts and history for the layperson with special
     comments on sonatas, piano chamber music, string
     quartets, and other ensembles (including winds). Less
     emphasis on repertory than on the new performers.

152. Unverricht, Hubert. *Die Kammermusik.* Köln: Arno Volk,
     1972. M 2.M945.Heft 46. 160 pages.
     An edition of 12 complete movements of chamber pieces,
     given in score, from Roman Hoffstetter's String Quartet
     c.1765 to Bo Nilsson's "Zwanzig Gruppen" 1958. The
     introduction and large, comprehensive bibliography are
     valuable for students and scholars. An excellent sum-
     mary of current thought (1972) on the development of
     chamber music 1750-1800, and a fine summary of its
     continued development to the mid-20th century.

153. Gaidamovich, Tat'iana Alekseevna. *Instrumental'nye
     Ansamble.* Moscow: Gos. Myuzikalnoi, 1963. ML 1100
     G3.1963. 54 pages. In Russian.
     A brief introduction to the concept of ensemble music,
     which is chamber music. An essay on sonata, quartet,

trio, and larger ensembles. Gives a brief history of
ensemble playing, with sonata the first type historically. Gives most famous examples. For the layperson.

154. Stupel', Aleksandr Moiseevich. *Beseda o Kamernoi
     Muzyke*. Leningrad: Gos. Muzikalnoi, 1963. ML 1100
     S85. 67 pages. In Russian.
     A well-written "conversation about chamber music" de-
     signed for the layperson. A history of different as-
     pects of chamber music in different countries. Chamber
     music, which is always Hausmusik, includes here vocal,
     solo keyboard, and chamber orchestra music. When Haus-
     musik is brought into the concert hall, it becomes
     democratized. Special attention to the piano trio,
     string quartet, and piano quintet.

155. Hutschenruÿter, Wouter. *De Geschiedenis der Kamer-
     muziek: een Beknopt Overzicht*, in *Musica-Bibliotheek*,
     No. 11. Hilversum: J.J. Lispet, [1935]. ML 1100.
     H8G4. 83 pages.
     A brief, shallow, dated history of chamber music from
     the 17th to the late 19th centuries for the layperson.
     No musical analysis but general concepts of genres and
     styles. Considers string quartets, sonatas for piano +
     1 other instrument, piano trio, string trio, piano
     quartets and quintets, and chamber music for more than
     4 strings.

*Essays on chamber music in several encyclopedias offer ade-
quate overviews, but they, too, are limited. Collectively,
however, they present some of the major issues and problems
in writing a comprehensive history.*

156. Geiringer, Karl. "The Rise of Chamber Music," in *New
     Oxford History of Music*, vol. vii (1973), *The Age of
     Enlightenment 1745-1790*, pages 515-573. ML 160.N44.
     A good survey, for the student and performer, of the
     basic types of chamber music in the transitional period
     from Baroque to Classical, with many compositions
     mentioned. For the scholar, however, this represents a
     marvelous summary of conceptions of chamber music
     history that have become outdated by the research of
     the past 20 years.

157. Tovey, Donald Francis. Ed. Hubert J. Foss. *Chamber
     Music*, in *Musical Analysis, Supplementary Volume*.
     London: Oxford University Press, 1944. 6th reprint
     1967. MT 140.T69. vi + 218 pages, 377 musical
     examples.
     A collection of 20 essays assembled posthumously in the
     form of musical analyses of 19 masterworks by Bach,
     Haydn, Mozart, Beethoven, Schubert, Schumann, Chopin,
     and Brahms, of which 10 are solo keyboard pieces (or
     collections), 1 is a song, 1 is a fragment of a violin

concerto, 6 are true chamber pieces, and 1 (*Die Kunst
der Fuge*) can be regarded as chamber music. An introductory essay (originally in Cobbett, *Cyclopedic Survey*) on what constitutes chamber music is rife with
prejudices of a sophisticated snob of 1928; while there
is much worthy in pre-1760 chamber music, the real
stuff begins with Haydn and Mozart who appreciate the
individuality of members of a chamber ensemble and who
first recognize the need for at least one large,
sonata-form movement in any substantial chamber music
piece (Nohl's contention). Tovey does not include
vocal music or solo keyboard music in this essay on
chamber music, so that Foss's collection does some
violence to Tovey's understanding of the term. The
essay includes an exposé on "correct" realization of
the continuo. Other essays include detailed analyses
of Mozart's Quintet for Piano and Winds K.452, Beethoven's Kreutzer Sonata, Schumann's Quintet, and Brahms's
Piano Quartets Op. 25, 26, and 60.

158. Wirth, Helmut. "Kammermusik," in *Die Musik in Geschichte und Gegenwart* {2}, vii (1958), cols. 477-499.
Useful summary but necessarily limited by space. Also
somewhat biased against non-Germanic chamber music and
heavily weighted toward the string quartet. Not good
on 20th-century works and later research.

159. Tilmouth, Michael. "Chamber Music," in *The New Grove
Dictionary* {1}, iv, 113-118.
Defines chamber music as "music for small ensembles of
solo instruments, written for performance under domestic circumstances in a drawing-room or small hall before an audience of limited size or indeed without the
necessity of any listeners." Careful description emphasizes intimate character and recognizes that in certain periods chamber music is something else. Considers function and locale of chamber music from the Middle Ages to the 20th century. Brief, good overview,
with ample bibliography.

*The following books, while not offering a comprehensive
history, do offer a number of important topics in the
history of chamber music.*

160. Robertson, Alec, ed. *Chamber Music.* 1st ed. Harmonds-
worth: Penguin Books, 1957; reprints 1960, 1963,
1967, 1970 (also printed in Baltimore). MT 140.R6.
1970. 427 pages.
A collection of essays by numerous authors on chamber
music from 1700 to c.1950, in 3 parts. I: chamber
works of specific composers (Haydn, Boccherini, Mozart,
Beethoven, Schubert, Mendelssohn, Schumann, Brahms,
Smetana, Dvořák, Bloch, and Bartók). II: duet sonatas

without winds and chamber music with winds after 1700.
III: several national schools of chamber music (England, U.S.A., France, Germany, and Russia). Designed
for the layperson or student who understands basic definitions. Reliable, informative, well written and
edited, but by being selective and somewhat out of
date, it cannot serve as a basic text. Many individual
essays are cited below.

161. Fleischhauer, Günter, and Walther Siegmund-Schultze
and Eitelfriedrich Thom. *Zur Entwicklung der instrumentalen Kammermusik in der 1. Hälfte des 18. Jahrhunderts,* in *Studien zur Aufführungspraxis und Interpretation von Instrumentalmusik des 18. Jahrhunderts:
Konferenzbericht der xi. wissenschaftlichen Arbeitstagung Blankenburg/Harz, 17. Juni bis 19. June 1983,*
Vol. 22. (No further publishing information.) ML
1102.Z97.1984. 92 pages.
A collection of 10 essays on various aspects of 18th-
century chamber music. 1) Walther Siegmund-Schultze,
"Die Individualisierung der instrumentalen Kammermusik
im 18. Jahrhundert" (pp. 11-16), suggests that the
intimate, often minor works ultimately are more important than major ones because there the composer experimented or expressed himself strongest. 2) Wolfgang
Ruf, "Die Kammermusik in der Musiklehre des 18. Jahrhunderts (pp. 17-22), notes the change from the aristocratic concept of music as handiwork to the middle-
class idea of work of genius, as evinced in Mattheson's
writings and resulting in the string quartet as perfect
synthesis. 3) Jürgen Eppelsheim, "Funktionen des Tasteninstruments in J.S. Bachs Sonaten mit obligatem
Cembalo" (pp. 23-33), analyzes in detail the relationship of top instrument to the cembalo in Bach's 6
violin, 6 flute and 3 viola da gamba sonatas. 4) Gert
Oost, "Die Bedeutung der niederländischen Hausorgel in
der Kammermusik der ersten Hälfte des 18. Jahrhunderts"
(pp. 34-46), chronicles the wide-spread use of small
house organs as continuo, especially by amateurs, in
the 17th and 18th centuries in numerous countries.
Gives detailed photos and shows how organs were hidden
in furniture. 5) Bernd Baselt, "Zu einigen Fragen der
Authentizität in G.F. Händels Kammermusik für ein Soloinstrument und Basso Continuo" (pp. 47-49), considers
the authenticity of the 15 so-called Opus 1 solo sonatas (first gathered together not by Handel but by Chrysander in 1879). Early editions show discrepancies as
to what is really Handel's (the 4 in A, E, g, and F).
None have Handel's trait of parodying his own works, as
found in other authentic sonatas in Handel's own hand.
Explains the 16 sonatas in Chrysander's edition. 6)
Franciszek Wesolowski, "'Pièces de Clavecin en Concerts' von J.Ph. Rameau als Beispiel der französischen
Kammermusik für Klavier mit Begleitung anderer Instru-

mente" (pp. 50-52), shows that despite Rameau's claims
to the contrary, these works cannot be played solo
without serious harm to them.   7) Zdenka Pilková, "Die
Violinsonaten der böhmischen Komponisten in den Jahren
1730-1770" (pp. 53-61), finds 2 types: virtuoso baroque
violin part with basso continuo written by violinists,
and obligato keyboard sonatas with violin accompaniment, especially written for dilettantes.   In Bohemia,
only the second type is considered (music by Benda,
Václav Vodička, J.V. Stomič, Anton Kammel, and Josef
Mysliveček).   8) Rudolf Zelenka, "Verzierungsmöglichkeiten in der Violinsonate A-Dur von František Benda:
ein Beitrag zur Entwicklung der Kammermusik in der 1.
Hälfte des 18. Jahrhunderts" (pp. 62-66), discusses
Benda's methods of ornamentation based on his manuscript in Berlin (Staatsbibliothek) and gives examples.
Uncertain if the 2 versions of Benda's ornaments are by
Benda himself or a friend or pupil, but in any case
contemporaneous with Benda.   9) Peter Damm, "Bemerkungen zu zwei Kammermusikwerken mit Corno da Caccia von
J.J. Fux und Chr. Petzold" (pp. 67-76), shows that by
the early 18th century hornists in Germany and Bohemia
began to develop a technique distinct from trumpet
music.   10) Günter Fleischhauer, "Bemerkungen zum
'Telemannischen Geschmack' in der Sonata a Cinque e-
Moll" (pp. 77-90).

The following books, in discussing the history of so many
masterworks of chamber music, do achieve some sort of
overall picture.

162. Renner, Hans, ed.   *Reclams Kammermusikführer.*   9th ed.
     Stuttgart: Reclam, 1980.   MT 140.R43.1980.   928
     pages.   6th ed. 1966, 7th ed. 1974, 8th ed. 1976.
     Mostly a chronological presentation (from Lassus! to
     Jean Françaix) of the masterpieces of chamber music.
     A brief biography of the composer, a brief analysis of
     each piece or representative pieces, and a survey of
     the composer's chamber music.   Also includes a brief
     history of chamber music, with a special section on
     music since 1945, and separate discussions of the cham-
     ber music of 20 countries or regions of the world.
     Useful index.   An excellent, handy guide for the lay-
     person who can read German, similar to Berger {163} but
     much vaster in scope, much more concise yet pithier,
     and basically benefiting from years of re-editing.   The
     small print and thin paper, however, do not make as
     physically durable and readable a book.

163. Berger, Melvin.   *Guide to Chamber Music.*   New York:
     Dodd, Mead & Co., 1985.   ML 1100.B45.   ISBN 0-396-
     08385-4.   xx + 470 pages.
     Non-technical discussion of 231 chamber works for 3 to
     8 players by 55 composers, from the late 18th century

to the present, arranged alphabetically by composer.
Besides the basic composers are a few 20th-century ones
much less often represented in general discussions (for
example Barber, Crumb, Dahl, Druckman, Fine, Kirchner,
Kraft, Laderman, Nielson, Piston, Rochberg, Schuller,
Sibelius, and Siegmeister). Gives composer's biography
and chief stylistic characteristics, followed by useful
information on the chosen pieces. Written by a performer who is insecure with scholarship, which leads to
some serious errors and omissions. Nonetheless a very
useful book for program annotators, lower level
teachers, laypersons, and performers.

*Despite the weaknesses in the above-mentioned works, they
are a vast improvement over what existed much earlier in
this century. The following is one of the worst.*

164. Walthew, Richard Henry. *The Development of Chamber
Music: three Lectures Delivered at South Place Institute 1909.* London/New York: Boosey & Co., 1909. ML
1106.W4.1909. 48 pages.
An amateurish, unsophisticated, prejudiced misrepre-
sentation of the development of sonata form and other
elements of chamber music. Confuses genres and basic
concepts and is depressingly short on facts. Of interest only to period scholars who need evidence of how
ignorant the English aristocrat was in regards to chamber music in 1909.

*In the light of the above, the following was a major break-
through (especially since it appeared before {164}):*

165. Kilburn, Nicholas. *Chamber Music and its Masters in
the Past and in the Present.* New and enlarged ed.
Gerald Abraham, in *The Music Story Series.* London:
William Reeves Bookseller/New York: Charles Scribner's Sons, [1932]. ML 1154.K48.1932. vii + 222
pages, 12 photos, 70 musical examples, discography.
Original title: *The Story of Chamber Music.* London:
Walter Scott Publishing Co./New York: Charles Scribner, 1904. ML 1154.K48. Reprint 1932 ed.: Boston:
Longwood Press, 1977.
A history of chamber music that is dated but which has
useful information on English chamber music and an
important discussion (by Abraham) of Russian chamber
music from Glinka to Arensky. General discussions of
composers's oeuvre rather than detailed discussions of
individual pieces.

*A special topic within the general history of chamber music
is the history of Hausmusik. The most valuable overview is:*

166. Finscher, Ludwig. "Hausmusik und Kammermusik," in
Musica, xxii (1968), 325-9. Also in Richard Baum and

Wolfgang Rehm, eds., *Musik und Verlag: Karl Vötterle
zum 65. Geburtstag am 12. April 1968* (Kassel: Bärenreiter, 1968), pages 67-76.   ML 55.V537M9.
A historical account of the functions of Hausmusik and
chamber music.   Defines chamber music as solo instrumental music for 2 to 9 voices, and Hausmusik as that
chamber music technically and spiritually easy enough
for the lay musician to play in his own social milieu.
Explores the possibility of structural as well as functional distinctions.   Until c.1700 function was the
primary distinction.   Then both Mattheson and Scheibe
recognize the greater development of material in chamber music.   By 1800 a new distinction developed between
concert and chamber music.   By mid-19th century Hausmusik becomes clearly distinct, but as a subculture it
already existed back in the 16th century and especially
after 1800.   Wilhelm Heinrich Riehl makes this salon
music worthy of study in the 1950's.   Studies the
Bärenreiter catalogues of the 20th century to ascertain
what is considered Haus- and what chamber music.

*A specialized history of Hausmusik in Berlin gives a general
impression of the history of Hausmusik throughout Europe:*

167. Höcker, Karla.   *Hauskonzerte in Berlin.*   Berlin: Rembrandt, 1970.   ML 279.8 B2H6.   192 pages, 26 photos.
A historical account of Hausmusik in Berlin beginning
with Sophie Charlotte, first Prussian Queen, and after
1740 Frederick the Great.   Hausmusik can be orchestral
or vocal (solo, choral, opera) as well as chamber; it
is performed with or without an audience, usually in
private homes or halls.   Early Hausmusik (late 18th
century) is chamber music or other music meant for
amateurs and professionals with a middle-class status
(replacing royal concerts in palaces).   Some groups
were very informal, others strictly organized.   Later
Hausmusik (early 19th century to immediately after
World War II) developed more into a private concert
without audience, such as Joachim and Mendelssohn's
family music.   Stresses the personalities and locales
of chamber music in Berlin, including the large Jewish
impact, but never seems to distinguish Hausmusik from
chamber music.   Hausmusik has 5 characteristics: an
artistic niveau, only invited guests for an audience,
no commercial aspects, a certain regularity in meeting,
and an aim at enjoyment in music.   Written for popular
audiences, but of use to scholars as well in understanding an important aspect of the performance of
chamber music.

*See also {478-484}. For a contemporary view of Hausmusik by
an English writer of the 19th century see the next work.*

168. Hullah, John Pyke. *Music in the House*, in *Art and Home
     Series*. 3rd (?) ed. London: Macmillan, 1877. ML 67.
     H91. 4th ed. London: Macmillan, 1878. Ed. used:
     Philadelphia: Porter & Coates, n.d. [frontispiece has
     1876]. ML 67.H8M8. vii + 79 pages.
     An early English treatise on Hausmusik which includes
     unaccompanied and accompanied vocal music along with
     instrumental music (where the piano is central). Writ-
     ten for the layperson, it is useful today as an histor-
     ical document on taste, on the state of the art, and on
     the levels of misconceptions the intelligent layperson
     of the 1870's possessed concerning the history of cham-
     ber music and all other music as well. Especially in-
     teresting is a chapter on "Practice and Rehearsal"
     where the former is first and private, the latter later
     and with the others who make up the ensemble. Con-
     trasts an opera rehearsal with a home rehearsal and
     gives some relevant advice: "Practice is only of use
     when concentrated on that which we cannot yet do."

*For an overall, non-technical study of ensemble music of all
kinds, see Wessem's* Het Musiceeren *{401}. General histories
of a particular instrument or family of instruments in regard to chamber music will be found in {319}-{337}. For a
discussion of chamber music in the 1960's, see Milos
Stedron's essay {457}.*

THE STRING QUARTET

*The string quartet has frequently been extolled as the
perfect art genre, and many equate chamber music with the
string quartet. The truth of the former is a subjective
matter, but clearly the latter is a gross oversimplification
and much too narrow. Many writings on the string quartet
suffer from these assumptions and must be put into perspective: they contain valuable information on the quartet
even if presented in blind adulation.*

*The only overall history of the string quartet in a full
volume is:*

169. Griffiths, Paul. *The String Quartet*. [London]: Thames
     and Hudson, 1983. ML 1160.G74.1983. 240 pages.
     Technical, detailed analyses of some of the most impor-
     tant quartets and many not so important, presented in
     historical sequence and with consideration of stylis-
     tic, formal and harmonic developments from composer to
     composer and from period to period. Useful index and
     chronology of works from 1759 to 1982. Conversational,
     non-scholarly tone seemingly aimed at the concert-goer
     and amateur player but a bit too technical for them.

A limited history is:

170. Konold, Wulf. The String Quartet from its Beginnings
    to Franz Schubert, in Paperbacks on Musicology, No.
    6. Trl. Susan Hellauer. New York: Heinrichshofen
    Edition, 1983. ML 1160.K6513.1983. ISBN 3-7959-
    0345-9. 209 pages. Original Das Streichquartett,
    von den Anfängen bis Franz Schubert. Wilhelmshaven:
    Heinrichshofens Verlag, 1980.
    The first in what is proposed as a multi-volume history
    of the string quartet, emphasizing the high and main
    points rather than the minor ones. Concentrates on
    Haydn, Boccherini, Mozart, Beethoven and Schubert
    (dwells on the earliest quartets, not the master-
    pieces), with no mention of others. For the layperson;
    greatly dependent on Finscher {173} and other scholars
    for data but misleading by omission and by emphasis.
    The English translation is horrendous. A good, though
    by no means complete or fully representative, biblio-
    graphy in the German version; the bibliography in the
    English version is riddled with errors.

A very simple, unsystematic history is:

171. Kramarz, Joachim. Das Streichquartett, in Martens-
    Münnich, Beiträge zur Schulmusik, Heft 9. Wolfen-
    büttel: Möseler, 1961. ML 1160.K89. 78 pages. 77
    musical examples. Companion volume Musikalische
    Formen in historischen Reihen, von Haydn bis Hinde-
    mith: das Streichquartett in Beispielen with complete
    musical examples. In German.
    A text for German high school teachers with a minimum
    of musical knowledge, so that they can convey to their
    students those subtleties of quartets which are not so
    obvious as in symphonies. It does not give methods but
    scholarly and artistic facts. Not a systematic history
    of the quartet but, through examples, a general presen-
    tation. The early history is based on Lehmann {175},
    Sandberger {176}, and Torrefranca {185} and therefore
    is now outdated. The rest of the book runs through
    specific quartet examples by famous composers, with a
    final chapter on special sound effects in quartet
    writing. Each discussed quartet is treated briefly,
    with a few characteristics of each movement including
    form, special thematic relationships, chords, and so
    on. Useful at the level for which it was written.

A biographical-bibliographical history is Wilhelm Altmann's
Kleiner Führer durch die Streichquartette für Haus und
Schule {62}. Several other older histories are so bad they
should be avoided: Marc Pincherle's Les Instruments du
Quatuor {1520} is out of date in its history of the music of
the string quartet but is useful for its history of string
quartet groups; and:

172. Stoeving, Paul. *The Violin, 'Cello and String Quartet,*
in *Fundaments of Musical Art,* Band 10. New York: The
Caxton Institute, 1927. MT 6.F9 vol.10. vi + 135
pages.
A bad source for information on the string quartet,
riddled with misconceptions, historical inaccuracies,
and false assumptions. Typical of the misinformation
among many devotées of the string quartet which should
be corrected by the other writings in this bibliography.

The meteoric rise of the string quartet to Olympian heights
during the second half of the 18th century has fascinated
numerous performers and scholars. The best account is:

173. Finscher, Ludwig. *Studien zur Geschichte des Streich-*
quartetts, i: Die Entstehung des klassischen Streich-
quartetts von den Vorformen zur Grundlegung durch
Joseph Haydn, in *Saarbrücker Studien zur Musikwissen-*
schaft, Band 3. Kassel: Bärenreiter, 1974. ML 1160.
F58.1. ISBN 3-7618-0419-9. 388 pages (pp.303-388
musical examples). Habilitation dissertation.
University of Saarland, 1967.
An important scholarly study of the origins of the
string quartet. It suffers from profuseness, lack of
an index, and appearing just before Webster's dissertation and important essays on the earliest Viennese
quartets {177, 178, 179}. The two earliest composers
of real quartets are Haydn in 1760 (composed in the
1750's; see Webster {939}) and Boccherini in 1761. The
second half of the book traces Haydn's development from
the Opus 1 divertimenti to the mature Opus 33 quartets
(1782), the latter being the first fully formed classical string quartets and therefore the basis for defining "string quartet." The first half of the book attempts to study what relationship if any certain musical types of composition of the 17th and 18th centuries
have with the classical string quartet. Avoids the
mistaken idea that the development of a genre of composition is historically connected with the development
of a form of a movement, or that a 4-voice sonata or
canzone *per se* is a string quartet (a 4-voice string
work of an earlier period is a relevant precursor).
What characterizes the classical string quartet (and
these elements are what one seeks in its forebears) are
a 4-voice setting; the homogeneous sound of an ensemble
of solo strings of the same family; the juxtaposition
of different textures while maintaining the ideal balance of the 4 voices; the cyclic sonata form in its
differing guises; the classical predilection for sensitive yet simple movement forms and different levels of
meaning; the principle of thematic-motivic development;
and the intimacy of chamber music. In his progression
from Opus 1 to Opus 33 Haydn strives after both loftier

spiritual goals as well as more advanced structural
possibilities. The quartets of Opus 33 are classical
both in the sense of perfect balance of harmony and
organization and also in the sense that they are the
first manifestation of the mature Viennese style --
before opera, symphony or piano sonata. In tracing the
quartet's forebears, consideration of 1) different nationalities (Italy, Paris, Vienna-South Germany-Bohem-
ia, England, North and Middle Germany) and the different lines of development even from town to town; 2) the
genres of pre-string quartet music (sinfonia and sonata
a quattro, concerto and concertino a quattro, sonate-
concert and symphonie en quatuor, Quartett-symphonie,
quadro or quartet divertimento); and 3) stylistic changes (disappearance of the continuo, orchestral and solo
settings, the 4-voice setting and the violin family).
Concludes with an essay on "The Theory of the String
Quartet," understanding a perfect art type, in which
the 4-part setting becomes the ideal both *per se* and as
a conversation among 4 persons (a concept first expressed by Johann Friedrich Reichardt, *Vermischten Musika-
lien* [Riga: 1773], p. 204, and here traced into the
19th century to Mendelssohn). See also {939}.

The best pioneering studies are the next 3:

174. Pincherle, Marc. "On the Origins of the String-
     Quartet," trl. M.D. Herter Norton, in *The Musical
     Quarterly*, xv (1929), 77-87.
     Presents some of the basic questions and a few possible
     answers on the origin of the string quartet. The ori-
     ginality of the string quartet does not lie in its form
     but in its combination of two violins, viola and cello.
     The precursors include the various Renaissance consorts
     which possessed "the spirit of the quartet": 4 homoge-
     neous string instruments. Mentions such works by Ben-
     jamin Rogers (1653), Purcell, Florentio Maschera
     (1593), Adriano Banchieri (1603), Giovanni Gabrieli
     (1615), Gregorio Allegri (before 1650), and others.
     Assumes that the harpsichord or other keyboard-harmony
     instruments would not be used. Specifically, Giuseppe
     San Martini (1743) and Guillemain (1739) allow for
     performance without harpsichord.

175. Lehmann, Ursula. *Deutsches und italienisches Wesen in
     der Vorgeschichte des klassischen Streichquartetts.*
     Würzburg-Aumühle: Konrad Triltsch, 1939. iii + 110
     pages. 785.74 L523d. PhD dissertation, Berlin.
     Seeks German and Italian elements in the development of
     the string quartet out of continuo-accompanied works of
     the Baroque for 2 treble instruments + 1 alto instru-
     ment + continuo. Considers the relationship of the in-
     struments to each other, the nature of the themes and
     expositions of the first movements, the processes of

development, and the forms of the whole piece as well
as the sonata form of the first movement. Studies
works written 1700-1770, though some forerunners of the
quartet go back into the 17th century. Begins with
a labored discussion of German versus foreign musical
characteristics of the 17th and 18th centuries as reflected in writings of the time, and tries to distinguish Italian from German concepts of melody (Italian
is more flowing, elegant, as evinced in 17th-century
trios, suites, sonatas), and Italian from German harmony (Germans more frequently mix modes). The 18th-
century North German builds a flowing, sequential melody, while the Italian uses a short head-motive and periodization. The early South German and Austrian quartets have a buffoonlike melodic style similar to divertimenti. Intricate analyses and comparisons of 17th-
and 18th-century Italian and German chamber music. *See
Finscher's critique in {173}.*

176. Sandberger, Adolf. "Zur Geschichte des Haydnschen
Streichquartetts," in *Ausgewählte Aufsätze zur Musikgeschichte* (Munich: Drei Masken Verlag, 1921; reprint
Hildesheim/New York: Georg Olms Verlag, 1973; original in *Altbayerische Monatsschrift* [1900], pages 1-
24), i, 224-265. ML 60.S26. ISBN 3-487-04900-7.
Possibly the most famous single essay on the history of
chamber music and the most often cited, especially in
the history of the string quartet. A scholarly, well-
documented study of the beginnings of the quartet which
serves as the basis for all subsequent studies. Seeks
origins of the quartet in Haydn's "cassation" and "quadro" and explains that Haydn's later statement on Opus
33 as a new kind of quartet is based on his new conception of thematic development. The forebears of the
quartet include cassation, divertimento, and serenade.
The old German orchestral suite and sonata united in
the homophonic cassation, with no continuo; folk music
influenced the art dances toward homophony, simplicity
and gaiety. The old orchestral sonata and chamber sonata led to the modern Italian symphony; movements 1
and 3 are light allegros in sonata form, while movement
2 is an andante. The Italians also developed the divertimento for winds and strings, similar to the opera
sinfonia and derived from the old divertimento da camera, with 3 movements -- the last a minuet. Some Germans (Placidus Cajetan von Camerloher [1718-1782],
Franz Aspelmayer [= Asplmayr, 1728-1786], and Franz
Josef Aumann [= Aumon, 1728-1797]) combine these Italian elements with a German folk spirit. The string
writing is usually simple and is the starting point for
Haydn's quartets. Also discusses the quadro of 4
voices -- quotes Scheibe, *Criticus musicus* (1745), p.

679: 2 types: Slow-Fast-Slow-Fast (da chiesa sonatas)
and Fast-Slow-Fast (concertante). The neapolitan influence here eventually favored the concertante in
form. Biggest problem: when did the continuo give way?
Since many cases are doubtful, looks for internal evidence. Studies a large number of specific quadros,
where old and new elements mix. Notes the differences
in national styles. Finally returns to Haydn's quadros
and cassations. The early quartets mix suite, chamber
trios, chamber quartets (and opera sinfonias, keyboard
sonata and concerto); Haydn's genius makes something
unusual with all these. Traces development of the
quartet to Opus 33 and Mozart's involvement.

The important question of the bass part of the quartet is
dealt with in:

177. Webster, James Carson, Jr. "The Bass Part in Haydn's
Early String Quartets and in Austrian Chamber Music,
1750-1780." PhD dissertation. Princeton University,
1973. UM 74-17499. DA xxxv.2A, pp. 1149-50. 429
pages.
An important study of the nature of the bass part of
chamber music as the string quartet emerges. Austrian
divertimenti 1750-1780 were soloistic works with "Basso"
designating the bass line but not implying instrumentation or orchestral performance. Both the cello (often
termed bassetl) and a 5-string string bass were commonly used in soloistic music. After 1780 the bass instruments were specifically called for. Webster picks the
instruments for many works on the basis of the range of
the instrument and includes "the first complete survey
of authentic sources for Haydn's 68 string quartets."
Documents show that all quartets of Haydn from Opus 17
(1771) on were soloistic, with cello as the bass; for
the earlier quartets anecdotal evidence indicates the
same. Op. 9 demands the solo cello on stylistic
grounds; the 10 early quartets probably do too, but the
evidence is inconclusive. Cites over 1000 Austrian
multi-movement ensemble works from the years 1750-1780.

178. _____. "Violoncello and Double Bass in the
Chamber Music of Haydn and his Viennese Contemporaries 1750-1780," in Journal of the American
Musicological Society, xxix (1977), 413-438.
An important scholarly study of the meaning of the basso part in classical Austrian chamber music. It did
not mean double bass but "bass part." After a detailed
discussion of 18th-century descriptions of the cello
and bass based largely on Leopold Mozart, Webster
identifies specific players of these instruments at
Esterhaz and, from Esterhazy documents, the exact
nature of their instruments. While the cello is much
like the modern instrument, the bass was tuned dif-

ferently: F_1, A_1, D, F#, A (the low F is open to
question at Esterhaz). The question remains: in
chamber music there is little evidence to support that
either the cello or the bass or both were used for
"bass" in the early Haydn chamber music. But in the
majority of cases, especially when low C is used, the
solo cello is the probable instrument.

and:

179. _____. "The Bass Part in Haydn's Early String
   Quartets," in *The Musical Quarterly*, lxiii (1977),
   390-424.
   A scholarly answer to two basic questions in the performance of Haydn's early string quartets: 1) Were they
   written exclusively for solo or for solo with *ad libitum* orchestral performance? Answer: for 4 solo string
   instruments. 2) What was the instrumentation of the
   "Bass" part? Answer: "From Opus 9 on, the scoring of
   the bass is certainly the solo violoncello; in the
   early quartets it probably was the cello, but other
   scorings cannot be definitely excluded."

And the question of doubling of parts is treated further in:

180. Hickman, Roger. "The Nascent Viennese String Quartet,"
   in *The Musical Quarterly*, lxvii (1981), 193-212.
   An attempt to distinguish orchestrally conceived "divertimenti" a4 from soloistically conceived "divertimenti" a4 on the basis of stylistic elements. The
   emergence of the solo versions in the late 1760's can
   be seen in the transition from Haydn's opera 1 and 2 to
   opus 9 and in the quartets of Vanhal and Gassmann.
   Many earlier works were titled "symphonies ou quatuors." Proposes that "string quartet" be used for the
   specific genre that flourished from the late 1760's on,
   and all precursors and hybrids before the late 1760's
   be termed "divertimenti a quatro." This way the earlier types can be treated as "masterly examples of the
   then prevailing forms" rather than as pale forebears of
   the classical quartet.

*The question of the earliest quartet is mistakenly treated
in:*

181. Dent, Edward J. "The Earliest String Quartets," in
   The Monthly Musical Record, xxxiii (1903), 202-204.
   Claims Alessandro Scarlatti's *Sonatas a Quattro* (2
   violins + Viola + Cello), written sometime between 1715
   and 1725, are the first string quartets. Analysis of
   form and comparison continually to Corelli. See Finscher's refutation {173}.

and:

182. Hull, A. Eaglefield. "The Earliest Known String Quartet," in *The Musical Quarterly*, xv (1929), 72-76, + xii pages musical insert and 1 unnumbered facsimile page.
Picks Gregorio Allegri's "Symphonia pro chelybus omnibus numeris absolutissima" as the first string quartet and reproduces it here. The piece, for "Duoi Violini, Alto, & Basso di Viola," was first printed by A. Kircher, *Musurgia Universalis* [Rome: 1650], i, libro vi, "De Musica Instrumentali," pp. 487-494. Dent's consideration of A. Scarlatti's chamber music is discussed. This article is extracted from Cobbett {7}.

Many others deal with the precursors; besides those above, see Vit on some quartet-symphonies {457} and:

183. Rothweiler, Hugo. *Zur Entwicklung des Streichquartetts in Rahmen der Kammermusik des 18. Jahrhunderts.* Reproduction of unedited typescript, [1935]. ML 1160. R6Z8. Apparently a final draft of Inaugural dissertation. University of Tübingen, 1934. ii + 71 pages, 47 musical examples.
A loose definition of chamber music, a brief discussion of gallant versus effective styles, and then a thematic analysis of Tartini's Sonata a Quattro in D and Haydn's Opus 33, no. 3, in order to determine the sound of the classical quartet. An annotated list of composers whose works are important for the pre-history of the string quartet (Tartini, Sammartini, Sacchini, Pugnani, Boccherini, Cambini, Giov. Batt. Cirri, Tom. and Gius. Giordani, J.C. Bach, Ant. Kammel, Joh. Stamitz, Franz Xaver Richter, Jean Baptist Wendling, Toeschi, Filtz, Franz Beck, Cannabich, Ernst Eichner, Willielm Cramer, Schobert, Abel, Wagenseil, Georg Matthias Monn, Aspelmeyer, Starzer, Gassmann, Albrechtsberger, Vanhal, E.Al. Förster, Ignaz Pleyel, Wranizky, Joh. Gottl. Graun, Scheibe, Chr. Schaffrath, C.P.E. Bach, Joh. Zach, Placidus Camerloher, Telemann, Graupner, E.F. dall' Abaco, and J.F. Fasch). Considers style, and the dichotomy between polyphony of 4 independent parts and the accompanied melody of 4 simultaneously sounding instruments in coordination. Finscher discredits this thesis since Rothweiler has built his whole premise of what constitutes the string quartet sound and style on 2 "arbitrarily chosen" works which for chronology and style are scarcely comparable.

184. Olleson, Philip. *The Rise of the String Quartet,* in *Arts: a Third Level Course, The Development of Instruments and their Music,* unit 18. Milton Keynes: Open University Press, 1974. ML 1160.044. ISBN 0-335-00862-3. 48 pages, 57 musical examples. Supplemented by Unit 19: the scores of the movements discussed in unit 18.

Concentrates on the string quartet from its beginnings
in the "late" 1750's through Haydn's Opus 33 and all of
Mozart's quartets (especially K.387 in G, 1782). Designed for the layperson who can read music as an
introduction to the early quartet and a teach-yourself
text. Accurate if shallow account. Each chapter with
question and answer exercises. Facsimile of the "Opus
3" Hoffstetter quartets clearly showing his name.
Basic principles of texture, form, keys, and comparison
of Haydn and Mozart.

*Adelmo Damerini, in "I Concerti a Tre di G. Antonio Brescia-
nello" {758}, cites these works as precursors of the string
quartet:*

185. Torrefranca, Fausto. "Avviamento alla Storia del Quartetto Italiano, con Introduzione e Note a Cura di A.
Bonaccorsi," in *L'Approdo Musicale*, xii (1966), 6-
181. Published posthumously by Bonaccorsi.
A lengthy attempt to prove the Italian origins of the
quartet through Italian stylistic achievements of the
18th century. Assails German attempts to consider
Haydn and Mozart as interacting to create the quartet
with no or little heed to Italian and French composers.
Emphasizes Boccherini and Sammartini, as well as
Galuppi, Cambini, Tommaso Giordani, Sacchini, and
Rauzzini. Detailed style analyses of these composers.
The Italian revolution in the 1700's is an "insurre-
zione di dilettanti contro la tradizione e l'Accademia"
which leads to Italian romanticism eventually, with
Mozart (schooled in Italy) as one of its main prota-
gonists. Cites Sandberger on the origins of the quartet in the divertimento, but believes the quartet has
its origins in the concerto in Paris and London as well
as in Italy. At the end, a list of terms for quartets
or similar pieces, with sources using those names (late
17th - 18th centuries), a grouping of Italian quartet
composers by generation, and an alphabetical list of
Italian quartet composers of the 18th century.

186. _____. "Mozart e il Quartetto Italiano,"
in Erich Schenk, ed., *Bericht über die musikwissenschaftliche Tagung der Internationalen Stiftung
Mozarteum in Salzburg vom 2. bis 5. August 1931.*
Leipzig: Breitkopf & Härtel, 1932. NYPL *MEC
(Mozart). Pages 79-102.
Cites the Italian concerto as a source for the string
quartet and Italians as important composers of the early string quartet. Dwells on Mozart's having heard
Boccherini's music just before Mozart wrote his first
quartets, and also Giordani and Sammartini.

A much more accurate and recent study is Salvetti's {719}.

187. Finscher, Ludwig. "Joseph Haydn und das italienische
     Streichquartett," in *Studien zur italienisch-
     deutschen Musikgeschichte*, iv, in *Analecta
     Musicologica*, iv (1967), 13-37.
     Dismisses Torrefranca's article {185} as unimportant,
     and reviews the failure of Italian string quartets at
     the time of the emergence of the great Viennese quar-
     tets of Haydn. The Italian quartet in the second half
     of the 18th century was weaker than the Viennese,
     Parisian and English ones. Italy was economically weak
     and in political disarray; it stuck to traditional ope-
     ra and church music rather than public subscription
     concerts and Hausmusik as in the North. In Italy
     string quartets were rare, isolated compositions. Re-
     views the Italian publishers's catalogues of the time
     and finds very little chamber music and very few impor-
     ted quartets except by Haydn and Cambini. Only the
     Tartini circle in Padua and the Doria-Pamphilj family
     in Rome enjoyed Hausmusik. The numerous Padua composi-
     tions, the originals of which are housed mostly in
     Berkeley today, are from the 1760's on and were played
     by professionals and connoisseurs; the Rome collection
     is strong on quartets and trios 1760-1780. But Venice
     must have had a lot of chamber music c.1775, and Fin-
     scher uses Michael Esser's quartets as evidence of
     this. Yet the most famous Italians (such as Boccherini
     and Cambini) went to Paris, others to Vienna, though
     Boccherini kept his individuality while in Spain. Dis-
     cusses Felice Radicate (1775-1820), Angelo Benincori
     (1779-1821), and Luigi Tomasini (1741-1808), 3 Italians
     who lived in Vienna in Haydn's time (the last, of
     course, as Haydn's concertmaster).

     *Klaus Fischer's "Die Streichquartette Gaetano Brunettis
     (1744-1798)" {772} draws the relationship between Italian
     and Viennese quartets of the late 18th century.*

188. Klein, D. "Le Quatuor à Cordes Français en 18e Siè-
     cle." PhD dissertation. University of Paris, 1970.
     Not seen.

189. Levy, Janet Muriel. "The *Quatuor Concertant* in Paris
     in the Latter Half of the Eighteenth Century." PhD
     dissertation. Stanford University, 1971. UM 71-
     23531. DAI xxxii.3A, pp. 1552-3. x + 346 pages +
     lxvi pages of music.
     Examination of a representative nucleus of the several
     thousand *quatuors concertants* of Paris 1770-1800. [A
     quatuor concertante is a string quartet in which the
     first violin is virtuosic and dominates the ensemble.]
     Composers include Cambini, Dalayrac, I.J. Pleyel, F.
     Fiorillo, L.E. Jadin, J.B. Le Chevalier de Saint-
     Georges, P. Vachon, G.B. Viotti, among others. Inves-
     tigates the meaning of the term and concludes that,
     principally, the number of parts indicates the number
     of players, all parts are in dialogue (mutually impor-

tant), and texture is the focus. Then goes into the
style of the repertoire, with an emphasis on rhetoric
and expression in the first movements and a consideration of basic musical components. The quartets "ca-
tered to dilettantism and/or showmanship." An excellent overview of the genre.

Dieter Trimpert's Die Quatuors Concertants von Giuseppe
Cambini *{782} is an extremely important study of French
quartet practice at the same time as the maturing of the
Viennese quartets.*

190. Hickman, Roger Charles. "Six Bohemian Masters of the
String Quartet in the late Eighteenth Century. PhD
dissertation. University of California at Berkeley,
1979. UMI 80-00378. DAI xl.7A, p. 3616. 512 pages.
A historical appreciation of Bohemian contributions to
the development of the Viennese string quartet 1770's -
1790's. The 6 Bohemians are Gassmann, Vanhal, Koželuch, Paul and Anton Wranizky, and Gyrowetz. Gassmann's are "divertimenti a quattro" and use fugues and
minor modes. Koželuch writes *quatuors concertants.*
The Wranizkys are more theatrical, and Gyrowetz points
to the Romantic quartet.

*For the early Russian string quartet, see Carol Greene, "The
String Quartets of Alexander Alexandrovich Aliabev" {524}.
For the history of Swedish quartets from the 18th to 20th
centuries, see Wallner {422}.*

191. Schaffner, Anne. "The Modern String Quartet in America
before 1800," in *The Music Review,* xl (1979), 165-7.
An important historical study of the existence of
string quartet performances in the United States from
1786 on (46 different concerts containing string quartet pieces in 7 major East Coast cities from 1786 to
1800). European as well as American composers are
represented.

192. Finscher, Ludwig. "Zur Sozialgeschichte des klassischen Streichquartetts," in Gesellschaft für Musikforschung, Georg Reichert and Martin Just, ed., *Bericht über den internationalen musikwissenschaftlichen Kongress Kassel 1962* (Kassel: Bärenreiter,
1963), pages 37-39.
An attempt to dispel earlier notions that the classical
string quartet was the province primarily of middle-
class music rooms and to a far less extent of courtly
music rooms. In all courts the nobility wanted to take
part, but when the music became too difficult c.1800,
the nobility changed to a listening audience. Only in
Vienna did the nobility continue to play. The flood of
easy quartet music designed for the middle classes was
not acceptable to the higher tastes of the nobility,

yet eventually, with the fall of the nobility, the middle class did inherit the best chamber music. This dichotomy between concert quartets of great difficulty for professionals and connoisseurs and easy quartets for the middle class and unskilled amateurs grew wider. The former grew more difficult, more esoteric. The middle class quartets were easier even in the heyday of the classical quartet -- 1780-1810 -- provided by Pleyel, Fränzl, Gyrowetz, Wranitzky, Koželuch, and Krommer; Mozart and Haydn at this period were beyond the middle class. Especially the first violin dominates, so that 3 mediocre players can enjoy playing a quartet with only 1 violinist who is any good (the *quatuor concertante*). After 1810 it was replaced by *quatuor brillant* performed by traveling virtuosi (often a great violinist with pick-up musicians on the other parts). Also arrangements from opera and orchestral music for string quartet. C.1815 concert series began in Paris, Vienna, Leipzig, and Prague for traveling professional quartets -- the basis for the modern quartet concert. Also semi-private house concerts where a traveling group is asked to perform. Serious quartet composition was designed and performed for and by the nobility; easy, artistically debased quartets were designed for the middle class 1780-1810.

Individual studies of Haydn, Mozart, and Beethoven are in Chapter 3, but {193} and {194} deal with the phenomenon of 3 such geniuses of chamber music collectively.

193. Wolff, Christoph, ed. *The String Quartets of Haydn, Mozart, and Beethoven: Studies of the Autograph Manuscripts. Isham Library Papers, no. 3.* Cambridge: Harvard University Press, 1981. ML 38. C17I86.1979. ISBN 0-674-84331-2. 368 pages, 117 facs., 40 musical examples.
"The proceedings of an international musicological colloquium held at Harvard in 1979," includes contributions by Lászlo Somfai, Jens Peter Larsen, James Webster, Georg Feder, Ludwig Finscher, Marius Flothuis, Alan Tyson, Christoph Wolff, Richard Kramer, Robert Winter, Sieghard Brandenburg, and Martin Staehelin. See separate entries in Chapter 3.

194. Sauzay, Eugène. *Haydn, Mozart, Beethoven: Étude sur le Quatuor.* 1st ed. Paris: Sauzay, 1861. ML1160.S24. 2nd ed. Paris: Firmin-Didot et Cie., 1884. ML 1160. S25. vi + 173 pages.
Haydn, Mozart and Beethoven perfected the string quartet, each in his own way but dependent initially on the previous one. Progress of the genre from simplicity to complexity -- the ultimate complexity is again simplicity. The appearance of organic unity in the complete oeuvre of the 3 composers with individual variety.

String quartets are perfect, trios and quintets less perfect. A thematic index of the oeuvre, with brief biographies of each composer, reasonably accurate and detailed for the time. Sauzay is an intelligent writer, and while the scholarship is dated, this is an excellent source for European attitudes towards and knowledge of chamber music in the 1860's-1880's.

195. Schumann, Robert. "Erster Quartett-Morgen: Quartette von J. Verhulst, L. Spohr und L. Fuchs," in *Neue Zeitschrift für Musik (1836)* in *Gesammelte Schriften*, ii (Leipzig: Georg Wigland, 1854), pp. 245-250. ML 410.S4A1. Continues with 5 more quartet mornings, pp. 251-272.
Schumann has much to say about chamber music of his time, and these criticisms can serve as typical. They discuss new works -- mostly string quartets -- by his contemporaries.

196. Altmann, Wilhelm. "Über einige mit Unrecht vergessene Streichquartette," in *Juhlakirja Ilmari Krohn'ille 8.XI.1927* (Helsinki: Musikvetenskapliga Sällskapel i Finland, 1927), pp. 1-5. ML 60.K95.
Discusses briefly 7 string quartets by 6 obscure composers of the late 19th and early 20th centuries: Karol Bendl (1838-1897), Alexander Faminzin (1841-1896), Friedrich Kiels (1821-1885), Friedrich Lux (1820-1895), Ludwig Neuhof (1859-?1909), and Leander Schlegel (1844-1913). They deserve to be performed alongside the usual masters (includes Sgambati's and Verdi's quartets among the popular masterworks of the time).

197. Wilke, Rainer. *Brahms, Reger, Schönberg Streichquartette: motivisch-thematische Prozesse und formale Gestalt*, in *Schriftenreihe zur Musik*, Band 18. Hamburg: Karl Dieter Wagner, 1980. HML 1736.460. ISBN 3-921-029-77-5. 233 pages. "Formale Untersuchungen an ausgewählten Streichquartetten des späten 19. und frühen 20. Jahrhunderts." PhD dissertation. University of Hamburg.
Analyzes specific movements of all 3 Brahms quartets, Schoenberg's 1897 and Op. 7, and Reger's Op. 74 with comments on Op. 54 and Op. 121. Defines "motive" and then studies how these 3 composers use motives and variation and build form out of them. Very technical, picky analyses, but the conclusions (pp. 180-191) are clear: Schoenberg started from Brahms and then went his own way by Op. 7, there are similarities and differences in cyclic procedures among all 3, and so on.

198. Goosens, Eugene. "The String Quartet since Brahms," in *Music and Letters*, iii (1922), 335-348.
Both Brahms and Tchaikovsky wrote their last string quartets in 1876. A list of string quartets after 1876

in Russia (Borodin, Taneiev, Glière), France (Saint-
Saëns, Fauré, D'Indy, Debussy, Ravel, Chausson, and
some of Les Sixes), Central Europe (Bartók, Schoenberg,
Wellesz, Haba, Kodály, Dohnányi), Germany (Reger,
Strauss), Italy (Pizzetti, Respighi, Casella, Malipiero, Tommasini), Scandinavia (Grieg), U.S.A. (Bloch!),
and especially England (Bridge, Bax, Holbrooke, Scott,
Ethel Smyth). The features that set the modern quartet
off from its predecessors are chromatic harmony and a
passion for color.

199. Walker, Mary Beth. "Selected Twentieth-Century String
     Quartets: an Approach to Understanding Style and
     Form." AMD dissertation. University of Arizona,
     1977. UMI 77-20621. DAI xxxviii.4A, p. 1734. 164
     pages.
     Analysis of 4 quartets by Ravel, Bartók (no. 4), Berg
     (*Lyric Suite*) and Weber, (Op. 28) in order to assist
     the student in listening to these works and to all
     20th-century string quartets.

200. Oberkogler, Wolfgang. *Das Streichquartettschaffen in
     Wien von 1910 bis 1925*, in *Wiener Veröffentlichungen
     zur Musikwissenschaft*, Band 22. Tutzing: Hans
     Schneider, 1982. MT 140.023.1982. ISBN 3-7592-0352-
     X. 383 pages.
     Finds 3 types of quartets: conservative ones (14 compo-
     sers including Felix Weingartner, Alexander Zemlinsky,
     Julius Bittner, Karl Weigl, Hans Gál, and Erich Korn-
     gold); those by the Schoenberg circle (Berg, Webern,
     Wellesz, and Pisk); and those by foreigners (Hauer and
     Hába). After a good introduction on the music scene in
     Vienna at the time, discusses each composer in turn.
     Gives important biographical information and -- the
     main material of the book -- analyzes thematic treat-
     ment and its contribution to the form of the composer's
     quartets. Deals also with Skriabin, Franz Schreker,
     the Verein für musikalische Privataufführungen with
     Rudolf Serkin, Eduard Steuermann and the Kolisch Quar-
     tet. Extensive bibliography, 397 musical examples.

201. Rauchhaupt, Ursula von. *Schoenberg, Berg, Webern: the
     String Quartets, a Documentary Study*. Trl. by
     Eugene Hartzell. Hamburg: Deutsche Grammophon
     Gesellschaft, 1971. MT 140.R3. 157 pages, 21
     facsimiles, 8 photos, musical examples. Original
     German *Die Streichquartette der Wiener-Schule:
     Schoenberg, Berg, Webern: eine Dokumentation*.
     Munich: H. Ellermann, 1971(?).
     Letters, reviews, and analyses by, from or to Schoen-
     berg, Berg and Webern concerning their string quartets.
     Editorial Commentary limited to 2-page preface. Docu-
     ments dated, sources cited. All trl. to English.
     Especially important: Schoenberg's lengthy "Notes on

the Four String Quartets" (1936), Berg's "Why is
Schoenberg's Music so Hard to Comprehend" (1924),
Webern's communications with Erwin Stein (1939), and
many letters among the 3 composers.

For technical studies of string quartets see, for example,
{514-515}. For studies of American string quartets, see
{191, 443, 444, 452, and 525}.

202. Griller, Sidney. "Some Notes on the Current Status of
    Chamber Music," in Music of the West Magazine, xiv
    (April 1959), 5.
    Notes the striking increase in interest in chamber mu-
    sic in America and abroad during the 30 years of the
    Griller Quartet and an upsurge in both professional and
    amateur quartets. A large amount of new, though diffi-
    cult, compositions (but Beethoven's last quartets are
    hard, too!). The author is heartened by the music stu-
    dent who is the amateur player and audience of the future.

                            Sonata

The basic historical study of the sonata as a genre of
chamber music is:

203. Newman, William S. The Sonata in the Baroque Era.
    Chapel Hill: University of North Carolina Press,
    1959. Rev. ed. 1966. ML 1156.N4S6.1966. Rev. ed.
    paperback, New York: W.W. Norton, 1972. SBN 393-
    00622-0. xiv + 468 pages, 85 musical examples.
    The Sonata in the Classic Era. Chapel Hill:
    University of North Carolina Press, 1963. 2nd ed.
    New York: W.W. Norton, 1972. ML 1156.N4S62.1972.
    SBN 393-00623-9. xxiii + 917 pages, 133 musical
    examples. The Sonata since Beethoven. Chapel Hill:
    University of North Carolina Press, 1969. 2nd ed.
    New York: W.W. Norton, 1972. 3rd ed. 1983. ML
    1156.N44.1983. ISBN 0-393-95290-8. xxvi + 870
    pages, 129 musical examples.
    The basic comprehensive history of works called
    "sonata" from c.1600 to c.1750 (vol. I), from c.1735 to
    c.1830 (vol. II), and from c.1830 to c.1915 (vol. III).
    The historical position of many chamber pieces as well
    as works for solo keyboard and other non-chamber music
    genres. Deals with general concepts (especially the
    meaning of "sonata" and the uses of the sonata), with
    sociological, stylistic and conceptual issues, and with
    specific composers grouped by nationality and date.
    Countries include not only the mainstream (Italy,

France, Germany, Austria, England) but also the ones
often neglected (Holland, Denmark, Sweden, Bohemia,
Poland, Switzerland, Russia, Iberia, the Americas).
Ensemble sonatas are treated about equally with solo
(keyboard) sonatas. Scholarly and well documented.
Huge bibliographies of books, articles, and scores.

204. Borrel, Eugène. *La Sonate*. Paris: Larousse, 1951. ML
1156.B7. 153 pages. In French.
An intelligent, comprehensive history of sonatas from
the end of the 16th century to the 20th. Considers the
uses of the term and "sonatas" which are not so designated. Concentrates on the 17th century and first half
of the 20th. His thoughts and historical points make
this study an important second reader after Newman's
books. Includes a sizable bibliography of sonatas arranged chronologically, by scoring, by nationality
(usually), and finally alphabetically by composer.

205. Bughici, Dumitru. *Suita si Sonata*. Bucharest: Editu-
ra Muzicala, 1965. ML 1158.B83. 342 pages. In
Romanian.
Intense discussion of the chamber suite but limited to
Bach and Rameau. The modern suite is orchestral. Sonata includes all solo and ensemble sonatas, the form
as well as the genre.

206. Selva, Blanche. *Quelques Mots sur la Sonate (Évolution
du Genre)*. Paris: Paul Delaplane, 1914. ML
1156.S35. 225 pages. In French.
A fanciful, outdated history and discussion of sonatas
which should be avoided by the audience for which it
was intended: amateurs, professional performers, and
students. It could be of some value for scholars who
need to document French Germanophobia and lack of
standards in chamber music c.1900. On the other hand,
the brief two-page forward by Paul Landormy presents a
thought-provoking exposé of the contradictions and
other weaknesses inherent in any choice of methodology
for a musical history such as that of the sonata. For
example, a chronological approach obscures development
of specific genres, a generic approach obscures
history; a generic approach also obscures unique contributions of individuals or that of schools, but to
deal with exceptional persons or schools obscures the
species in its normal occurrences.

*The term "sonata" has other meanings besides chamber music.
Sometimes it refers to a form. In many discussions of the
sonata the confusion in terminology is so severe as to
render the studies useless. Yet in some other such cases
(Nohl {461}, Riemann {214}) there is some value to the
studies. The types of chamber music called "sonata" undergo*

*changes from the beginning of the 17th century to the
present. One issue is to define sonata in the 17th century
-- an instrumental piece for an ensemble -- and to trace its
origins.*

207. Crocker, Eunice Chandler. "An Introductory Study of
the Italian Canzona for Instrumental Ensembles and
its Influence upon the Baroque Sonata." PhD
dissertation. Radcliffe College, 1943. DD x (1943),
p. 88. vi + 497 pages + 43 pages of music + [66]
pages + [60] pages of music.
A detailed consideration of these instrumental ensembles at the important moment when they became sonatas.
Careful definitions, review of pre-canzona vocal types
in the 16th century, and then the canzona in two e-
pochs: 1572-1608 and 1608-1621. Regards the problem of
nomenclature and the distinction between "sonata style"
and "canzona style" (which are contrasted in terms of
melody -- the canzona being more limited; rhythm --
canzona much more regular; texture -- canzona imitative
and sonata top dominated; medium -- canzona not in any
precise medium while sonata is written to show off the
instrument). Finally a review of the sonata and canzona after 1621. The canzona was thoroughly established
in the 16th century and it is that type of canzona
which is regarded as canzona-style after 1608.

208. Bonta, Stephen. "The Church Sonatas of Giovanni
Legrenzi." PhD dissertation. Harvard University,
1964. 2 vols. x + 638 pages. Vol. 2 contains
documents and musical examples.
After an extensive biography of Legrenzi primarily in
Ferrara and Venice, a penetrating study of the church
sonata in the 17th century beginning with its
liturgical function. Goes into the instruments used
for such sonatas, especially in Legrenzi's case, then
into performance practice. Church sonatas in the
church were probably orchestral, but the same sonata
performed in a chamber would be soloistic. Therefore
this optional situation is part of Legrenzi's style and
probably affects all church sonatas of the 17th
century. A detailed analysis of the sonatas including
sources, forms, harmony, and thematic treatment. See
also Bonta's "The Uses of the *Sonata da Chiesa*," in
Journal of the American Musicological Society, xxii
(1969), 54-84, which is an exhaustive study of the
liturgical position of the sonata da chiesa in Masses
and Vespers in the 17th century.

*An important clarification of early terminology appears in
the following:*

209. Daverio, John. "In Search of the Sonata da Camera
     before Corelli," in *Acta Musicologica*, lvii (1985),
     195-214.
     An important scholarly discussion of the Austro-German
     ensemble suite and its interaction with the Italian
     sonata idea. The "sonata" idea comes into its own in
     the 1630's "to replace *canzona* as the most popular term
     for abstract, multi-sectional ensemble works."
     "Sonata" meant sonata da chiesa, and in Italy sonata da
     camera "refers primarily to the *single dance*, and not
     to the dance group" before Corelli's Op. 2 extended it
     to a group of dances -- the suite. Corelli got *his*
     idea from Georg Muffat, who is a representative of the
     Austro-German school; the Austro-Germans, in turn, got
     this idea from England. Muffat was a younger colleague
     in Salzburg of Heinrich Biber and in the early 1680's
     worked with Corelli in Rome. Muffat's *Armonico Tributo*
     (Salzburg: 1682), a set of 5 sonatas for 2 violins + 2
     optional violas + violone + basso continuo probably
     composed in Rome and later partially republished as
     concerti in *Auserlesene...Instrumental-music* (Passau:
     1701), are basically Austro-German suites and were
     specifically performed for Corelli by Muffat. This
     counters the oft-held view that all new ideas in
     Baroque instrumental music came from Italy; Corelli
     seems clearly to have copied Muffat. Includes 4 tables
     to support the argument: a list of Italian dance and
     sonata (da camera) publications 1645-1684, contents of
     G.M. Bononcini's *Sonate da Camera, e da Ballo*, Op.2
     (1667), overall titles for dance groups in pre-Corel-
     lian Italian publications, and movement disposition in
     the sonatas of Muffat's *Armonico Tributo*. This article
     is an outgrowth of Daverio's dissertation "Formal De-
     sign and Terminology in the Pre-Corellian 'Sonata' and
     Related Instrumental Forms in the Printed Sources."
     Boston University, 1983. UMI DA8319967. DAI xliv.5A,
     p. 1234. 322 pages.

210. Klauwell, Otto. *Geschichte der Sonata von ihren
     Anfängen bis zur Gegenwart*. Köln/Leipzig: H. vom
     Ende, 1899. ML 1156.K63. iii + 128 pages.
     Four essays, of which only the first, on the old Ita-
     lian sonata from G. Gabrieli to A. Corelli, is rele-
     vant. A dated book to be avoided by the uninitiated
     but of use to scholars as a reflection on the state of
     musicological knowledge c.1900. Primary interest in
     solo keyboard sonatas. Traces the origins of the Ita-
     lian sonata to vocal music in the 16th century and to
     dance music. Credits Gabrieli with the first indepen-
     dent sonata. Sonata (Speer, M. Praetorius) is heavier
     than canzona, but eventually there was no distinction
     (Massimiliano Neri and Giov. Legrenzi).

211. Zingler, Ute. "Studien zur Entwicklung der italien-
     ischen Violoncellsonate von den Anfängen bis zur Mit-
     te des 18. Jahrhunderts." Inaugural dissertation.
     Frankfurt a/M, 1967. RILM 70-1790. iii + 248 pages.
     Traces first the probable origins of the modern cello
     to the mid-16th century and then the cello sonata from
     c.1689 when the first ones appear in Bologna by Domen-
     ico Gabrielli (1659-1690), who taught Legrenzi composi-
     tion, to the mid-18th century with Francesco Saverio
     Geminiani (1687-1762), Andrea Caporale (d.1756), and
     Pasqualino de Marzis (fl. 1740's). Presents collec-
     tions historically, chronologically, with analysis of
     representative pieces. The sonatas are homogeneous,
     with continuo accompaniment. After c.1750 the cello
     sonatas become virtuoso pieces or obligato keyboard
     pieces. The earliest examples still show canzone
     features -- frequent change of tempo in a single
     movement. But mostly all these sonatas are slow-fast-
     slow-fast or in 3 movements, with nascent sonata form
     not yet present in the fast second movements except in
     rare cases. Until 1720 the emphasis was on the slow
     movements, especially the third movement, but the
     emphasis then switched to the faster movements,
     especially when it is the second.

212. Schünemann, Georg. "Sonaten und Feldstücke der
     Hoftrompeter," in Zeitschrift für Musikwissenschaft,
     xvii (1935), 147-170.
     Description of manuscript books owned by Hendrich
     Lübeck and Magnus Thomsen, both German trumpeters at
     the turn of the 17th century, who served the Danish
     court. 483 sonatas, each usually in 6 to 8 sections.
     Composers rarely named; some are folk tunes or dances.
     Apparently unaccompanied.

For another discussion of the early sonata see Langley's
"Sonate concertate in stil moderno by Dario Castello: a
Transcription of Book One" {796}.

The trio sonata, "invented" by Salomone Rossi, became the
dominant type of ensemble sonata in the 17th and early 18th
centuries.

213. Apfel, Ernst. "Zur Vorgeschichte der Triosonate," in
     Die Musikforschung, xviii (1965), 33-36.
     The early trio sonata is either dance-like or church-
     like (with fugal fast movements). The former derive
     either from bicenium or dance-like arrangements of
     vocal polyphony of the 16th century.

214. Riemann, Hugo. "Die Triosonaten der Generalbass-
     Epoche" (originally 1897), in Präludien und Studien:
     Gesammelte Aufsätze zur Aesthetik, Theorie und

Geschichte der Musik (Leipzig: 1904; rep. Hildesheim: Georg Olm, 1967), iii, 129-156. ML 60.R56.1967. The source for many early 20th-century misconceptions about the early sonata. Its inaccuracies have been corrected over the past 90 years. Much of what Riemann considers sonatas are orchestral pieces. Claims the trio sonata is the source for the string quartet and the German orchestral suite the source for the sonata da camera (the latter is now accepted; see {209}).

215. Jensen, Niels Martin. "Solo Sonata, Duo Sonata and Trio Sonata: Some Problems of Terminology and Genre in 17th-Century Italian Instrumental Music," trl. from Danish by John Bergsagel, in *Festskrift Jens Peter Larsen 1902 14.VI 1972* (Copenhagen: Wilhelm Hansen Musik-Forlag, 1972), pages 73-101. ML 55.L215.1972. ISBN 87-7455-000-4. Challenges the use of 18th-century terminology for 17th-century violin + bass compositions and Riemann's and Newman's assumption that these works are instrumental monodies. These misconceptions obscure the evolutionary point of view; the early 17th-century sonatas were not parallel to monodies but had their own development from 16th-century types to 18th-century types. 17th-century terminology is consistent: it is determined by the number of melody instruments (violin + continuo or bass + continuo = sonata a une; 2 violins + continuo or 2 basses + continuo or violin + bass + continuo = sonata a due; 3 violins + continuo or 2 violins + bass + continuo or violin + 2 basses + continuo or 3 basses + continuo = sonata a tre). Challenges the concept of polarity between melody instrument(s) and continuo: melody lines are contrapuntal, homophonic or concertizing lines continuing in the 16th-century polyphonic tradition, with continuo merely an accompaniment. Cites collections by G.P. Cima, Giulio Belli, and Corelli. Concise, clearly written, well documented, of interest to students, scholars and performers.

216. Hogwood, Christopher. *The Trio Sonata*, in *BBC Music Guides*. London: British Broadcasting Corporation, 1979. HML 279.56. ISBN 0-563-17095-6. 128 pages. Designed for laypersons who read music, yet not written concisely enough for such an audience; some matters are of concern to the scholar, but most are not. Treats the highlights of Italian trio sonatas of the 17th and 18th centuries and the ground bass patterns used in some of them. Explains the difference between 3-part consort music and trio sonatas, and dwells on the many options in realization of the bass part. But the basic scoring is 2 violins + cello + keyboard. Covers a lot of territory but in crotchety, verbose language heavily

influenced by Burney. Also treats the trio sonata separately in Germany-Austria, England, and France.
See also Jiri Sehnal {457} on the distinction between da
chiesa and da camera in the second half of the 17th century.

217. Brockhoff, Maria-Elisabeth. "Studien zur Struktur der
italienischen und deutschen Triosonate im 17. Jahrhundert." Inaugural dissertation. Wilhelms University of Münster, 1944. HML Film 3237.63.1. vi + 130
pages.
Discusses the trio sonata from its beginnings to 4 distinctive late 17th-century composers: Legrenzi and Corelli in Italy and Matthias Weckmann and Buxtehude in
Germany. The beginnings in Italy go back to 16th-cen-
tury vocal polyphony and to the Gabrielis (orchestral
canzone) and S. Rossi. In Germany the Gabrieli orchestral canzona continues longer than in Italy with
Schein, Rosenmüller, Peuerl and others, and with the
English violinists and composers (especially William
Brade). Eventually native Germans, such as Caspar
Förster, write trio sonatas. The Italians have a chain
structure movement to movement; the Germans have a ring
structure (the end of the final movement leads back to
the opening of the first).

218. Schenk, Erich. Die italienische Triosonate, in Das
Musikwerk, Heft 7. Köln: Arno Volk, [1955]. The
Italian Trio Sonata, in Anthology of Music, vol. 7.
Köln: Arno Volk, 1955. M 2.M94512 no.7. 75 pages.
Basically a fine edition in score of 6 trio sonatas by
Giovanni Paolo Cima (1610), Francesco Turini (1621),
Giovanni Maria Bononcini (1672), Antonio Caldara
(1693), Francesco Antonio Bonporti (1703), and Gaetano
Pugnani (1754). Introduction is a history of the Italian trio sonata from c.1607 (Salomone Rossi) to c.1775
(F. Guerrini). The English is a bit stilted and in some
cases confusing, which limits its usefulness for the
non-scholarly performers who are most likely to want to
read it. Chronological discussion with a large amount
of information conveyed in just a few pages. No
attempt to show how the mid-18th-century trio sonata
developed into new classical chamber music types.
Sizeable bibliographies of modern editions and
secondary literature.

219. _____. The Trio Sonata outside Italy, trl.
from German by Robert Kolben, in Anthology of Music,
vol. 35. Köln: Arno Volk, 1970. M 2.M94512 no.35.
84 pages.
As in {218}, primarily a fine edition of 9 pieces for 3
instruments or trio sonatas by Joh. Stadlmayr, J.E.
Kindermann, J.H. Schmelzer, Dietrich Becker, Marin
Marais, John Ravenscroft, M.S. Biechteler, Joh. Gott-

lieb Graun, and Georg Christoph Wagenseil. Historical
introduction, arranged chronologically, with nationalities treated separately. Strong Italian influence
everywhere, but some Northern customs (such as the German preference for 5 or 6 lines rather than 3) affect
the Northern sonata's development in the North. Extensive bibliographies of reprints and secondary literature. Item {209} offers a different interpretation of
these works.

220. Hoffmann, Hans. *Die norddeutsche Triosonate des
     Kreises um Johann Gottlieb Graun und Carl Philipp
     Emanuel Bach.* Kiel: W.G. Mühlau, 1927. ML 1129.H7.
     188 pages. PhD dissertation. Kiel, 1924.
     Seeks the essence of the term "trio sonata" and the
     style of instrumental music of the Berlin circle of the
     mid-18th century. Studies form, means of expression,
     and performance practice in the trio sonatas of Graun
     and C.P.E. Bach as examples of the Berlin style and
     trio sonata concept. Includes a history of the trio
     sonata of the 17th and 18th centuries in general, which
     can still form a basis for newer research. Also dis-
     cusses J.S. Bach's trio sonatas. Mostly 3-movement
     trios (slow-fast-fast or fast-slow-fast) but also some
     in 4 movements (da chiesa). Expression tied to melody
     and rhythm. Reviews theorists of the time: Scheibe,
     Riedt, and Nichelmann. The Berlin trio sonata stands
     between 2 epochs, and the departure of C.P.E. Bach in
     1767 signals his need to enter the new period.

*See Marysue Barnes's dissertation "The Trio Sonatas of
Antonio Caldara" {780} for an historical summary of the
evolution of the trio sonata.*

The English had their own variety:

221. Johnson, Jane Troy. "The English Fantasia-Suite, *ca.*
     1620-1660." PhD dissertation. University of Cali-
     fornia at Berkeley, 1971. RILM 71-45. 526 pages.
     Studies 136 fantasia suites by major English composers
     of the mid-17th century (Giovanni Coperario, William
     Lawes, John Jenkins, John Hingston, John Birchensha,
     Christopher Gibbons, Christopher Simpson, and anony-
     mous). Preserved only in manuscript, each consists of
     3 movements: fantasia-almaine-galliard (Lawes expanded
     it to 4 movements). Scored for 1 or 2 violins, bass
     viol, and written-out continuo (a few late ones add a
     third or fourth violin). Analyzes the continuo parts,
     texture, and form. Historically important as "Eng-
     land's manifestation of the 'sonata' idea."

*The solo sonata is also important. The best general
descriptions and study of the solo violin sonata in the 17th
century are:*

222. Apel, Willi. "Studien über die frühe Violinmusik," in
     Archiv für Musikwissenschaft, xxx (1973), 153-174;
     xxxi (1974), 185-213; xxxii (1975), 272-297; xxxiii
     (1976), 213-239; xxxiv (1977), 117-147; xxxv (1978),
     104-134; xxxvi (1979), 183-213; xxxvii (1980), 206-
     235; xxxviii (1981), 110-141.
     The most important study of early Italian violin cham-
     ber music 1580-1700. Thoroughly documented analyses
     of each printed source chronologically presented.
     Segment I, 1582-1621; subsequent segments by decade.
     Index of composers in segment IX. Drawing on his 9
     articles "Studien..." {222}, Apel has reorganized the
     material into a single volume: *Die italienische Violin-
     musik im 17. Jahrhundert*, in *Beihefte zum Archiv für
     Musikwissenschaft*, vol. 21. Wiesbaden: Franz Steiner,
     1983. ML 5.A63 Suppl. Bd.2. ISBN 3-515-03786-1. ix +
     244 pages. Instead of the chronological order of
     sources in the articles, he deals here with one compo-
     ser at a time. He also corrects some errors and adds
     an opening essay on the earliest pieces for the violin.

223. Dunn, Thomas D. "The Sonatas of Biagio Marini:
     Structure and Style," in *The Music Review*, xxxvi
     (1975), 161-179.
     An overview of the sonata before Marini (especially
     Giovanni Paolo Cima's and Salomone Rossi's), a descrip-
     tion of the contents of Marini's *Affetti Musicali* Op. 1
     (1617), *Sonate* Op. 8 (1629) and *Sonate* Op. 22, and a
     discussion of the basic forms, textures, and styles of
     the sonatas. An important introduction to the begin-
     ning of the history of solo sonatas.

224. Mishkin, Henry G. "The Solo Violin Sonata of the
     Bologna School," in *The Musical Quarterly*, xxix
     (1943), 92-112.
     A scholarly study of the violinists and the violin
     sonatas of the Bologna school from 1670 to 1703, which
     includes Giuseppe Torelli, G.B. Vitali, and lesser
     ones. Includes also a list of solo violin sonatas
     published in Italy before 1670. Most illuminating
     violinist is Maurizio Cazzati, whose published sonatas
     of 1670 begin the Bologna school.

*Other solo instruments in the 17th and early 18th centuries
are treated in the following:*

225. Tennyson, Robert Scott. "Five Anonymous Seventeenth-
     Century Chamber Works with Trombone Parts, from the
     Castle Archives of Kromeriz." DMA dissertation.

University of Maryland, 1973. UM 73-28906. DAI
xxxiv.6A, p. 3459. 142 pages. A scholarly edition of 4 sonatas and 1 suite, preceded
by a historical and critical introduction. Two of the
pieces date from 1667 when Heinrich Biber was Capell-
meister in Kromeriz. All 5 works are scored for at
least 3 trombones and organ continuo; some have clarino
parts and strings (solo or orchestral?). The sonatas
are in subdivided single movements with antiphonal
choirs of sound; the suite dances are in binary form.

226. Anderson, Stephen Charles. "Selected Works from the
Seventeenth Century Music Collection of Prince-Bishop
Karl Liechtenstein-Kastelkorn: a Study of the
Soloistic Use of the Trombone and Modern Editions."
DMA dissertation. The University of Oklahoma, 1977.
DAI xxxviii.4A, pp.1722-3. 315 pages.
Modern edition of 12 pieces, some entitled "sonata,"
others with religious titles, by Giacomo Francesco
Libertini, Philipp Jakob Rittler, Johann Heinrich
Schmelzer(?), and Pavel Josef Vejvanovsky. A
historical analysis of these trombone pieces in which
the solo trombone is treated on an equal basis with
other common solo instruments such as the violin,
clarino, cornetto and bassoon.

227. Klitz, Brian Kent. "Solo Sonatas, Trio Sonatas, and
Duos for Bassoon before 1750." PhD dissertation.
University of North Carolina, 1961. UM 61-6125. DA
xxii.6, p. 2024. iv + 151 pages + 66 music pages.
Lists 159 such sonatas and analyzes representative
examples, especially by Bertoli (1645). Stresses the
Italian origins and development of bassoon sonatas.

See Loren Bartlett's "A Survey and Checklist of Representa-
tive Eighteenth-Century Concertos and Sonatas for Bassoon"
{66}.

228. Smithers, Don. "Seventeenth-Century English Trumpet
Music," in *Music and Letters*, xlviii (1967), 358-365.
Description of 10 trumpet sonatas of the seventeenth
century found in British Museum Music Ms. Add. 49,599,
the largest English collection of trumpet sonatas of
the time. Concerned with trumpet technique as revealed
in the manuscript.

229. McGowan, Richard Allen. "Italian Baroque Solo Sonatas
for the Recorder and the Flute." PhD dissertation.
The University of Michigan, 1974. UMI 75-756. DAI
xxxv.7A, p. 4594. 530 pages.
Historical analysis of recorder sonatas c.1710-1750
that shows parallels with historical analysis of violin
sonatas of the same period: 3 movements gradually replaced 4, single movements became more fully-developed,

contrapuntal styles are replaced by treble-dominated
homophonic dances, the minuet replaced the gigue as the
finale, and flute techniques changed with the transverse flute gradually replacing the recorder. *[Care-
less use of terminology in the abstract suggests
problems in the full dissertation.]*

230. Herbert, Ilse L. "Tipuri de Sonata de Camera din
     Secolul al Xviii-lea Privite din Punct de Vedere al
     Ansamblului Executant," in *Lucrari de Muzicologie*, ii
     (1966), 63-68. French, Russian and German Summaries.
     There are 3 types of instrumental ensemble performing
     sonatas in the (mid-)18th century: sonatas with contin-
     uo (the continuo line performed either by a harpsichord
     or by a deep melody instrument, rarely by both toge-
     ther), sonatas with concertant harpsichord (derives
     from trio sonatas), and sonatas for harpsichord accom-
     panied by other instruments.

*In the mid- and later 18th century a major topic is the
evolution of the trio sonata into the accompanied keyboard
sonata.*

231. Sheldon, David. "The Transition from Trio to Cembalo-
     Obbligato Sonata in the Works of J.G. and C.H.
     Graun," in *The Journal of the American Musicological
     Society*, xxiv (1971), 395-413.
     Explains a large collection of sonatas in Berlin which
     exist in two formats: 1) as flute and/or violin trio
     sonatas, and 2) as accompanied obligato sonatas in which
     one of the flute and/or violin parts is rescored for
     the right hand of the obligato keyboard.

232. Newman, William S. "Concerning the Accompanied Clavier
     Sonata," in *The Musical Quarterly*, xxxiii (1947),
     327-349.
     Recognizes the importance of this genre in 18th- and
     early 19th-century chamber music for its bulk, its
     position as transition from the Baroque to Classical
     sonata, and the gradual demise of the basso continuo.
     Primarily concerned with the textural problem: why the
     violin-dominated Baroque sonata would give way to the
     sonata with violin accompaniment of the Classical era.
     The changing role of the violin is largely due to the
     keyboard's rise as a solo instrument.

233. Fuller, David. "Accompanied Keyboard Music," in *The
     Musical Quarterly*, lx (1974), 222-245.
     A scholarly study carrying Newman {232} to greater
     depth, based on the huge musical repertory and on con-
     temporary reports. Despite ambiguity in terminology in
     the 18th century, all this music should be considered
     together as "chamber music with obbligato keyboard."
     The continuo accompaniment did not develop into the

obligato; rather the obligato keyboard replaced the
continuo. The Baroque keyboard in concerted music was
subordinated to the other instruments, whereas the
Classical keyboard was an equal partner or more. The 2
existed side by side during most of the 18th century.

234. Kidd, Ronald R. "The Emergence of Chamber Music with
     Obligato Keyboard in England," in *Acta Musicologica*,
     xliv (1972), 122-144. Based on "The Sonata for Key-
     board with Violin Accompaniment in England (1750-
     1790). PhD dissertation. Yale University, 1968.
     UMI 68-11199. DAI xxix.2A, pp. 626-7. 543 pages.
     Although Newman has already covered this topic, the au-
     thor has two additional historical points to make with
     detailed documentation: 1) there is no " 'progress' from
     an early optionally-accompanied style to the fully de-
     veloped concertante sonata of Mozart and Beethoven";
     they co-existed; 2) the English accompanied sonata
     like the French sonatas of Schobert, absorbed features
     from more elaborate Italian concertos. The accompanied
     keyboard sonata flourished equally in France and Eng-
     land. Among English composers are Charles Avison, Tho-
     mas Gladwin, and William Jackson.

235. Studeny, Bruno. *Beiträge zur Geschichte der Violin-
     sonate im 18. Jahrhundert*. Munich: Wunderhorn, 1911.
     Reduction of University of Munich PhD dissertation.
     ML 895.S8. 120 pages. In German.
     A dated scholarly study under the influence of Spitta,
     Wasielewski, Kretzschmar, Schering, and Sandberger.
     Asserts that the later violin-piano sonata grew out of
     the J.S. Bach trio sonata and accompanied solo sonata;
     draws attention to the Dresden school of violinists
     (Pisendel in particular) before 1750 and to the Berlin
     and Mannheim schools after mid-century. Most important
     statement: the homophonic style of South Germany mixes
     with the polyphonic style of North Germany in producing
     first Mozart's and Haydn's sonatas, then Beethoven's.

See also the articles and books on J.S. Bach in Chapter 3.
The French development gets special attention:

236. La Laurencie, Lionel de. *L'École Française de Violon
     de Lully à Viotti: Études d'Histoire et d'Esthétique*.
     3 vols. Paris: Librairie Delagrave, 1922-1924. ML
     874.L15. I: 440 pages, 28 reproductions, examples.
     II: iii + 516 pages, 44 reproductions, examples. III:
     iv + 319 pages, 15 reproductions, examples. In French.
     An exhaustive, scholarly study of French sonatas of the
     17th and 18th centuries which, despite its date, will
     continue as a principle starting point for any further
     study of French sonatas and chamber music for the
     foreseeable future. While the book is oriented toward
     the violin itself, the material presented is almost

entirely relevant to chamber music. Discussion of
specific performers, categories of sonatas, and
specific compositions. Chronologically presented, from
Lully to Viotti, with a chapter summarizing the
evolution of the French school, its compositions, and
criticism. Detailed biographies, well documented with
some documents quoted in full; artistic evaluation by
contemporaries and others; lists of works; overall
discussion of the works with detailed quotations and
supporting evidence (not a piece-by-piece, movement-by-
movement description). Summarized in La Laurencie, "La
Sonate de Clavecin et Violon en France," in *Le Courrier
Musical*, xxv, no. 7 (April 1, 1923), 119-120.

237. Beckmann, Gisela. *Die französische Violinsonate mit
Basso Continuo von Jean-Marie Leclair bis Pierre
Gaviniès*, in *Hamburger Beiträge zur Musikwissenschaft*, Band 15. Hamburg: Karl Dieter Wagner, 1975.
ML 874.B39. ISBN 3-921029-27-9. 353 pages.
Valuable for its background information on French
musical life in the second half of the 18th century,
which is gleaned primarily from French music periodicals of the time: *Mercure de France* (f.1724), *Journal
de Musique* (f.1773), *Almanach des Spectacles* (f.1752),
Almanach Musical (f.1775). Discusses a large repertory
of violin sonatas by 22 French violinists (1720-1769).
Brief biographies; survey of relevant works listing
key, movements, forms, tonalities, and meters; and
analyses of form, thematic character, development, bass
treatment, harmony and violin technique. A brief
exposé of intervals and ornaments by Mondonville.

238. Reeser, Eduard. *De Klaviersonate met Vioolbegeleiding
in het Parÿsche Muziekleven ten Tÿde van Mozart*.
Rotterdam: W.L. & J. Brusse's Uitgeversmaatschappÿ
N.V., 1939. ML 805.R43. Originally Rÿksuniversiteit
(Utrecht) PhD dissertation. I: 178 pages (history);
II: 102 pages (12 complete sonatas for piano and
violin). In Dutch. Summary in French and German.
An important scholarly study of the French sonata for
keyboard and violin accompaniment at the time of Mozart's visits to Paris (1763-1778). Background information on French taste, musical institutions (concerts
and publishers -- there were 23 music publishers in
Paris in 1775!), and performers. Emphasizes the key-
board-violin sonatas from Mondonville to Nikolaus Joseph Hüllmandel. General basic information as well as
specific, chronological study of the principal composers and their music (some works analyzed in detail).
Considers the changing relationship between violin and
keyboard, the forms moving from binary to sonata, and
the dichotomy after 1780 between the rare *violon obligé*
and the usual *violon ad libitum*. Notes that, in the
customary 3-movement scheme fast-slow-fast, the fast

movements are Italianate, the slow, French. Extensive
bibliography.

The obligato keyboard sonata developed in Germany, too:

239. Wierichs, Alfred. *Die Sonate für obligates Tasten-
instrument und Violine bis zum Beginn der Hochklassik
in Deutschland.* Kassel: Bärenreiter, 1981. ML
1156.W54. ISBN 3-7618-0672-8. vii + 220 pages +
xxvi pages. PhD dissertation. University of
Münster, 1981. xxxii + 220 pages.
Concentrates on the German manifestations of this
crucial problem of the combination of a melody and a
keyboard instrument in sonatas. Forty-nine composers
in turn are considered initially and then 12 composers
during the 1770's or final phase. The developments
occur in northeast Germany. Scholarly, well written,
carefully documented. A number of the composers are
not treated by Newman, and a number of the works discussed have not been treated by anyone until now.
Points to the origins of the keyboard-accompanied violin sonata in the Baroque trio sonata (already stated
by Mersmann in 1920) and in the principle of
concertizing.

240. Fischer, Wilhelm. "Mozarts Weg von der begleiteten
Klaviersonate zur Kammermusik mit Klavier," in
Mozart-Jahrbuch (1956), pages 16-34.
Since dilettantes were among the performers of the accompanied keyboard sonata, composers purposely wrote
parts easy enough for dilettantes to play. During a
15-year period Mozart took the sonata from here -- accompanied keyboard -- to real violin + piano sonatas as
well as to real piano + violin + cello trios. The
basic scholarly study of this phenomenon, well documented and clearly written. Proves its point by citing
titles of collections and by analysis of the music.

*Sonatas of the 18th century were written for other instru-
ments besides the violin.*

241. Shaw, Gertrude Jean. "The Violincello Sonata Literature in France during the Eighteenth Century." PhD
dissertation. Catholic University, 1963. UM 63-
6559. DA xxiv.2, p. 771. 346 (DA = 371) pages.
Lists this repertory (with modern editions) and analyzes its significance to the cello sonata repertory as
a whole. Most such sonatas were written by virtuoso
cellists, not general composers. They show nascent
sonata form and soloistic features of the instrument.

An important development in the mid-18th century was the
preference for flute over recorder in sonatas. See Buyse
{727} and:

242. Du Bois, Elizabeth Ann. *A Comparison of Georg Philipp
     Telemann's Use of the Recorder and the Transverse
     Flute as Seen in his Chamber Works*, in *The Emporia
     State Research Studies*, xxx, no. 3. Emporia
     (Kansas): Emporia State University, 1982. ML
     410.T26D8.1982. 72 pages.
     Telemann is an ideal composer for this question because
     he lived during the period of transition, he wrote an
     enormous amount of flute-recorder music, and he was im-
     mensely popular. A substantial biography and a detail-
     ed history of the 2 instruments in the 17th and parti-
     cularly 18th century (many illustrations). An assess-
     ment of Telemann's music for the 2 instruments and a
     detailed study of 3 pieces. Each instrument has pre-
     ferred keys and differences in timbre, technique, dyna-
     mics, range, and social status. Large bibliography.

243. Titus, Robert Austin. "The Solo Music for the Clarinet
     in the Eighteenth Century." PhD dissertation. State
     University of Iowa, 1962. UM 62-2412. DA xxii.12,
     pp. 4370-2. xiv + 604 pages.
     Discusses the development of the clarinet as an instru-
     ment in the 18th century and emphasizes its use in con-
     certos. Also includes references to clarinet sonatas
     and asserts that it lists all known ones to c.1800.

For bassoon sonatas of the 18th century see {66}.

Although there are more studies of specific 19th-century
ensemble sonatas than of those in previous centuries, there
are fewer studies of the genre as a whole in the 19th century. The genre is narrowly defined during this time: a
work for piano and one additional instrument, as in:

244. Selva, Blanche. *La Sonata: Étude de son Évolution
     Technique, Historique et Expressive en Vue de
     l'Interprétation et de l'Audition*. 3rd ed. Paris:
     Lerolle, 1913. ML 745.S5. viii + 250 pages.
     A short, dated, and inaccurate history of the sonata
     and sonata form and binary and ternary forms. A much
     longer, much more plausible essay on the function of
     the interpreter of music. Concentrates on the sonata
     before Beethoven, Beethoven's sonatas, and the sonata
     after Beethoven. Defines sonata as a piece for key-
     board with or without 1 other instrument, in 3 or 4
     movements. Mostly solo keyboard works. Surprising
     emphasis on the sonatas of Friedrich Wilhelm Rust.
     Of primary interest to the scholar who seeks French at-

titudes toward chamber music c.1900; avowedly under the
influence of d'Indy, to whom the book is dedicated.

Newman {203} is the best overall study of the period.
Another, though barely adequate, study is:

245. Shand, David Austin. "The Sonata for Violin and Piano
     from Schumann to Debussy (1851-1917)." PhD disser-
     tation. Boston University, 1948. DD xv (1948), p.
     111. 403 pages.
     An attempt to characterize a large number of violin +
     piano sonatas by European and American composers.
     Notes the balance between the 2 instruments, national-
     ism, and the influences of Wagner and Franck. The the-
     sis is of value for its scope, not its scholarship.

The best coverage in a brief format and an interesting study
of the phenomenon of arrangements of earlier editions is:

246. Freywald, Volker. *Violinsonaten der Generalbass-Epoche*
     in Bearbeitungen des späten 19. Jahrhunderts, in *Ham-*
     burger Beiträge zur Musikwissenschaft, Band 10.
     Hamburg: Karl Dieter Wagner, 1973. ML 895.F748V6.
     ISBN 3-921029-17-1. vii + 278 pages. Reprint of
     Hamburg University PhD dissertation, 1971.
     An attempt to understand the motivation and extent of
     interest of musicians 1850-1899 in 18th-century violin-
     basso continuo music. Reviews the revival of interest
     in older music in the 19th century; the low standing of
     violin sonatas vis-a-vis fantasy pieces and opera
     arrangements 1820-1840's; and the revival especially of
     Bach's *Chaconne*, Tartini's *Devil's Trill* and Corelli's
     Opus 5 in arrangements by Mendelssohn, Schumann,
     Vieuxtemps, Ferdinand David and others from the 1840's
     on. Some 18th-century sonatas of the Baroque remained
     known in the original and were used by violin students
     at the Paris Conservatoire and elsewhere, but not in
     public concerts. Arrangements in the middle of the
     19th century brought these pieces before the public,
     and many new editions appeared. A catalogue of edi-
     tions of such music 1849-1899, with complete title of
     original and basic title of 19th-century arrangement
     with date, arranger, publisher and commentary.

America enters the picture with:

247. Starr, James Alfred. "A Critical Evaluation of Perfor-
     mance Style in Selected Violin Works of Nineteenth
     Century American Composers." DMA dissertation.
     University of Illinois, 1978. DAI xxxix.5A, p. 2612.
     282 pages.
     Analyzes overall characteristics, performance style,
     and worth from a performance or compositional stand-

point in 7 violin + piano sonatas. Appendix has a performance edition of Horace Wadham Nicholl's sonata, as
well as some smaller pieces for violin and piano.

The overall picture of the 20th century has yet to be drawn.
For now there are numerous specialized studies:

248. Dresser, Mary Anne. "Twentieth-Century Russian Cello
     Sonatas." DMA dissertation. University of Texas,
     1983. UMI 83-19554. DAI xliv.5A, p. 1235.
     Concentrates on the relationship to communist theory of
     4 sonatas by Rachmaninov (1901), Shostakovich (1932),
     Prokofiev (1949), and Kabalevsky (1962). The first 2
     are Germanic and not communist; the latter 2 are commu-
     nist and follow the 1936 [and 1948] crackdowns. Also
     mentions other chamber music by these 4 composers.

249. Lister, William Warwick. "The Contemporary Sonata for
     Violin and Piano by Canadian Composers." MAD disser-
     tation. Boston University, 1970. UMI 71-13419. DAI
     xxxi.11A, p. 6099. 271 pages.
     Analysis of form, melody, harmony, rhythm, texture, and
     violinistics in 12 sonatas by 11 20th-century Canadian
     composers: Murry Adaskin, Istvan Anhalt, Jean
     Coulthard, Oskar Morawetz, Jean Papineau-Couture,
     Barbara Pentland, André Prévost, Harry Somers, Robert
     Turner, Jean Vallerand, and John Weinzweig.

250. Carlson, Paul Bollinger. "An Historical Background and
     Stylistic Analysis of Three Twentieth Century Compo-
     sitions for Violin and Piano." DMA dissertation.
     University of Missouri at Kansas City, 1965. UMI 67-
     10099. DA xxviii.2A, p. 706. 76 pages.
     Two chapters each to Stravinsky's *Duo Concertante*,
     Webern's *Four Pieces* Op. 7, and Ives' Sonata No. 2.

251. Tyska, Theodore Charles. "Technical Problems in Con-
     temporary American Violin Sonatas." MA thesis.
     American University, 1961. UM-321. MA I.1 (1962),
     p. 36. 61 pages.
     Not seen.

For contemporary flute sonatas see Mellott's "A Survey of
Contemporary Flute Solo Literature with Analyses of Repre-
sentative Compositions" {103}.

252. Theodore, Peter C. "A Survey of Published Sonatas and
     Sonatinas for Flute by American Composers since
     1920." MA thesis. Catholic University of America,
     1967. 87 pages.
     Not seen.

253. Geeting, Daniel Meredith. "A Comparative Study of
     Sonatas for Clarinet and Piano Published in the
     United States from 1950-1970." DMA dissertation.
     University of Oregon, 1974. UM 75-3875. DAI
     xxxv.10A, pp. 6750-1.
     A cursory study of 23 available sonatas and a compara-
     tive analysis of a more traditional one by Boris Pillin
     and a more innovative one by Howard Rovics.

*See also John Drew's dissertation on 20th-century American
sonatas for trombone + piano {505}.*

                      WOODWIND ENSEMBLES

*There is a small but fascinating literature about woodwind
ensembles:*

254. Niecks, Frederick. "Music for Wind Instruments
     Alone," in *Monthly Musical Record*, xlviii (1918),
     122-24, 148-49, and 170-71.
     One of the best early histories of wind ensemble music
     from the mid-18th to the end of the 19th century. The
     term "Harmonie" meant such ensembles serving in milita-
     ry or domestic music (accompanying dinners as in *Don
     Giovanni*). Commonly 1 oboe + 2 clarinets + 2 bassoons
     + 2 horns, but other combinations as well. Describes
     the careers of François Devienne (1759-1803) and Joseph
     Küffner (1776-1856), important wind players, and also
     the contributions of Mozart, Haydn, C.P.E. Bach, Beet-
     hoven, Schubert, Dittersdorf, Pleyel, Danzi, L.E. Jadin
     (1768-1853), Louis Javault, Gossec, Reicha, Onslow and
     others. Lists many woodwind ensemble works.

255. Fleury, Louis. "Chamber Music for Wind Instruments,"
     in *Chesterian,* new series, no. 36 (January, 1924),
     111-116; no. 37 (February 1924), 144-48.
     Considers only chamber music for winds alone or with
     piano (no strings). Deplores public's ignorance of
     wind chamber music and reviews the history of such
     music (Haydn, Mozart and Beethoven), noting the absence
     of the flute. The 19th century ignored the winds,
     except for minor composers like Spohr, Onslow and
     Reicha. Paul Taffanel's society in late-19th-century
     Paris revived such music in concerts of the classics
     together with new wind chamber music by the best compo-
     sers of the time including Saint-Saëns, Gounod, Lalo,
     Rubinstein, and Raff. This group was succeeded by La
     Société Moderne d'Instruments à Vent, first under Bar-
     rère 1895-1905 and still active in 1924. Lists newer
     works for wind chamber music, emphasizing *Les Sixes*.

256. Seay, Albert E. "Modern Composers and the Wind Ensemble," in *Music Educators Journal*, xxxv (Sept.-Oct. 1948), 27-28.
Assesses the bad performance of wind chamber music in America and the lack of professional American groups (only 2 short-lived professional wind quintets by 1948). Blames schools, which need to encourage American composers to write good wind chamber music. To do this the students's horizons must be extended -- more background and understanding of contemporary styles.

257. Hedlund, Harry Jean. "A Study of Certain Representative Compositions for Woodwind Ensemble, *ca.*1695-1815." PhD dissertation. University of Iowa, 1959. LC Mic 59-1683. DA xix.12, p. 3321. 223 pages.
Limited to works a3-a10, excluding recorder, string, keyboard, percussion, and brass instruments other than the French horn. Includes music from c.1695 (the "invention" of the clarinet by Denner) up to but not including the music of Anton Reicha; the music of Haydn, Mozart and Beethoven is also excluded. Works by 44 composers, c.120 titles, 21 18th-century music publishers. Discusses the music geographically (England, France and Germany-Austria), and lists in appendices all these pieces by composer and by scoring.

258. Kaplan, David Leon. "Stylistic Trends in the Small Woodwind Ensemble from 1750-1825." PhD (theory) dissertation. Indiana University, 1977. UMI 78-13164. DAI xxxix.2A, p. 532. 527 pages.
Analyzes melody, harmony, tonality, texture, and organizing features in 10 representative works.

259. Fitzgibbon, H. Macaulay. "Some Recent Chamber Music for Wind Instruments," in *Musical Opinion*, xxxiii (1910), 769-70.
A critical discussion and description of many new publications by Breitkopf & Härtel of chamber music involving winds, such as Rheinberger's *Nonet* Op. 139, Theodore Dubois's *Dixtuor* (double-quintet of strings and winds), Theodore Gouvy's *Petite Suite Gauloise* Op. 90 for 9 winds and *Octet* Op. 71 and *Serenades* Op. 82, and so on.

Specific types of woodwind ensembles have drawn more specialized study, especially the quintet:

260. Rush, Ralph Eugene. "The Classical Woodwind Quintet: its History, Literature, and Place in the Music Program of the American Schools." MA thesis. University of Southern California, 1946.
Not seen.

261. Sirker, Udo. *Die Entwicklung des Bläserquintetts in
     der ersten Hälfte des 19. Jahrhunderts*, in *Kölner
     Beiträge zur Musikforschung*, Band 50. Regensburg:
     Gustav Bosse, 1968. ML 1104.S57. PhD dissertation.
     1968.
     A scholarly historical study of the woodwind quintet
     (flute, oboe, clarinet, horn and bassoon). Gives 18th-
     century forebears and developments in the instruments
     themselves. Relationship of the woodwind quintet to
     other types of wind music and string chamber music
     (especially in Mozart and Beethoven). Considers socio-
     logical factors, structure of the instruments, and
     playing techniques. Especial attention to the earliest
     ensembles of flute, oboe, clarinet, English horn and
     bassoon by Franz Anton Rösler (= Rosetti), and the
     ripening of the genre under Reicha. Also discusses the
     music of Alexander Alexandrevitch Aljabjew, Siegfried
     Benzon, Henri Brod, Cambini, Danzi, Prosper Didier
     Deshayes, François-René Gebauer, Franz Paul Lachner,
     Johann Georg Lickl, Friedrich Lindner, H. Lindner,
     Wilhelm Mangold, Martin Mengal, Peter Müller, Onslow,
     and Nikolaus Schmitt.

262. Le Coat, Gérard. "Le Development de la Musique pour
     Quintette à Vent aux États-Unis," in *Revue Musicale
     de Suisse Romande*, xxiv (1971), no. 4, 10-12.
     A report to Europeans on the boom in woodwind quintets
     in America, where more such works have been written in
     the past 20 years than in Europe during the past 100
     years. Explains this after giving its history. The
     first such compositions in Paris by Cambini in 1802,
     then Reicha and Danzi, but after 1820 it is neglected,
     with only Paul Taffanel reviving it at the end of the
     19th century. Then neo-classicists (with Americans Co-
     well and Sowerby) bring it to new fruition in the
     1920's in Paris and elsewhere. The American explosion
     begins after 1950 with Samuel Baron organizing an
     independent quintet whose members are not part of an
     orchestra. It has succeeded because composers have
     found this combination vital and because it has become
     popular with school bands and ensembles, from grade
     school to college.

*See also Samuel Baron's "The Rebirth of the Woodwind Quintet
in America" {1525}.*

263. Kratochvíl, Jiří. "Nekolik Poznamek k Historii Decho-
     veho Kvinteta," in *Hudebni Veda*, vii (1970), 331-37.
     In Czech.
     Comments on the history of the woodwind quintet.

264. Wise, Ronald Eugene. "Scoring in the Neoclassic Wood-
     wind Quintets of Hindemith, Fine, Etler, and Wilder."

PhD dissertation. University of Wisconsin, 1967.
UMI 67-9026. DAI xxviii.4A, pp. 1462-3. 274 pages.
Analysis of scoring and its relationship to style and
musical quality. After background definitions and
history, analysis of 1 work by each of the 4 composers
which are neo-classic and of high quality. Discusses
idiomatic writing and difficulty, harmonic aspects of
scoring, and style. The pieces are idiomatic because
the ranges are mostly confined to standard ranges,
there are no unplayable parts, and there are no endur-
ance problems. Appendix II contains "the most complete
bibliography of woodwind quintets to date," over 800.

Other types of wind ensembles are also important:

265. Thomas, Orlan Earl. "Music for Double-Reed Ensembles
     from the Seventeenth and Eighteenth Centuries: 'Col-
     lection Philidor.'" DMA dissertation. University of
     Rochester, 1973. UMI 74-20475. DA xxxv.3A, pp. 1691-
     2. x + 91 pages + 103 pages of music.
     Concerned with instrumental pieces from the Philidor
     Collection a3-a6, which, it is assumed, were played by
     the double-reed instruments active at the court of
     Louis XIV. Documents the existence of such performers.
     Scoring of specific examples for oboe + bassoon +
     English horn is speculative.

266. Jones, Walter James. "The Unaccompanied Duet for
     Transverse Flutes by French Composers, *ca*.1708-1770."
     PhD dissertation. University of Iowa, 1970. UM 70-
     23908. DAI xxxi.6A, p. 2958. ix + 186 pages.
     List and discussion of c.450 duets in more than one
     movement by 32 French composers. Finds 3 chronological
     periods (1708-1723, 1724-1744, and 1745-1770) and notes
     the change in style from Rococo (La Barre and Hotte-
     terre) to Classical (virtuosic Italian style). Discus-
     ses ornaments and rhythmic alteration.

267. Fleury, Louis. "Music for Two Flutes without Bass,"
     trl. P. Wyatt Edgell, in *Music and Letters*, vi
     (1925), 110-118.
     A brief survey of duets for two flutes from the 17th
     century to 1925 (Koechlin's *Duet*). Special attention
     to Michel La Barre (1675-1743), Handel, Quantz, Michel
     Blavet (1700-1768), Boismortier, and Kuhlau. Opens up
     a subject that needs to be more thoroughly studied.

268. Gille, Harry, Jr. "The Clarinet in Chamber Music."
     MA thesis. University of Illinois, 1949.
     Not seen.

269. Schwadron, Abraham. "Idea Exchange: New Chamber In-
     strumentation for the Clarinet," in *The Instrumen-
     talist*, xxi (Jan. 1967), 16-18.

Discusses the various chamber music combinations in
which the clarinet is found, both to acquaint the
clarinetist with increased repertory and the composer
with new material.

270. Randall, David Max. "The Clarinet Duet from *ca.*1715 to
     *ca.*1825." DMA dissertation. University of Iowa,
     1970. UM 70-23961. DAI xxxi.6A, p. 2961. RILM 70-
     1540. v + 125 pages.
     Lists all the clarinet duets found in the time-period
     and analyzes specifically the duets of Michel Yost and
     Jean-Xavier Lefêvre. History of the genre. Omits
     arrangements of many opera airs. Does not discuss
     potpourris but includes them in the list.

271. Tuthill, Burnet C. "Bibliography of Clarinet Sona-
     tas," in *Woodwind Magazine,* ii (Dec. 1949), 9, and
     (Jan. 1950), 9.
     A list of sonatas for clarinet and piano, including a
     few arrangements. Gives title, publisher, and some-
     times useful, sometimes absurd, always opinionated com-
     ments. Updates article in Cobbett {7}. Useful for
     performers.

272. Klitz, Brian. "The Bassoon in Chamber Music of the Se-
     venteenth Century," in *Journal of the American Musi-
     cal Instrument Society*, ix (1983), 5-20.
     A survey of bassoons and bassoon-like instruments
     referred to or shown in 17th-century sources, and some
     of the earliest 17th-century compositions to call for
     a solo rather than supportive bassoon part. One of the
     earliest is Marini's "La Foscarina" (*Affetti Musica-
     li...Opus I*, Venice: 1617) where the trombone or bas-
     soon has tremolos. Another is by Giovanni Battista
     Riccio, "La Grimaneta" (*Terzo Libro della Divine Lodi
     Musicali*, Venice: 1620). Non-idiomatic bassoon writing
     is the rule, as in Francesco Usper's (= Sponga) *Batta-
     glia per Cantar e Sonar à8* (Venice: 1619). Numerous
     others centered in Italy or Central Europe; almost
     nothing from France and England.

273. Hedlund, H. Jean. "Ensemble Music for Small Bassoons,"
     in *The Galpin Society Journal*, xi (1958), 78-84.
     Describes briefly an 18th-century "parthia" for 2 horns
     + 2 fagottini (= bassoons sounding an octave higher
     than regular bassoons) + 2 quart-bassoons (smaller bas-
     soons sounding a fourth above the regular bassoon;
     sometimes called the tenoroon) + 2 regular bassoons.
     This is the only known chamber music for such bassoons.
     Analyzes form; the first movement (of 4) is binary with
     only a few suggestions of nascent sonata form, but the
     use of crescendo and decrescendo signs (first used by
     Geminani in 1739) helps date the piece c.1750.
     Possibly written by J.C.M. Trost.

BRASS ENSEMBLES

274. Husted, Benjamin F. "The Brass Ensemble: its History
     and Music." PhD dissertation. University of Roches-
     ter, 1955. D.D. xxii (1955), p. 247. ix + 930
     pages.
     Extensive history of brass ensemble music from the
     Renaissance to the 1950's, which notes its changing
     function from social *Gebrauchsmusik* (16th-17th centur-
     ies) to amateur arrangments of opera ditties (19th cen-
     tury). Analysis of the basic characteristics of con-
     temporary American brass music and, to a lesser extent,
     foreign brass music. One of the earliest histories and
     theoretical studies of 20th-century brass music.

275. Swift, Arthur Goodlow. "Twentieth-Century Brass En-
     semble Music: a Survey with Analayses of Representa-
     tive Compositions." PhD dissertation. University of
     Iowa, 1969. UM 70-4428. DAI xxx.9A, pp. 3978-79. 2
     vols. 569 pages.
     Traces the development of brass ensemble music 1900-
     1966, determines those factors which have most influ-
     enced that development, and provides a comprehensive
     (representative, not complete) list of original pub-
     lished brass ensemble works. Four specific, represen-
     tative works analyzed in detail: Ewald's Quintet, opus
     5; Ingolf Dahl's *Music for Brass Instruments*; Eino Rau-
     tavaara's *A Requiem for Our Time*; and Schuller's *Music
     for Brass Quintet*. This kind of chamber music is
     linked to the growth of such groups in secondary
     schools.

276. Van Ess, Donald Harrison. "The Stylistic Evolution of
     the English Brass Ensemble." PhD dissertation.
     Boston University, 1963. UMI 63-6645. DA xxiv.5,
     pp. 2074-5. 550 pages.
     Seeks the characteristics of style in English brass
     ensemble music, the significant stages of the develop-
     ment of the brass instruments, and the contribution
     made by the medium to English musical culture. His-
     torical discussion and analysis. Never specified
     whether chamber or orchestral band music.

*For Polish brass chamber music see Juliusz Pietrachowicz's
article {410}.*

277. Baer, Douglas Milton. "The Brass Trio: a Comparative
     Analysis of Works Published from 1924 to 1970." PhD
     dissertation. Florida State University, 1970. UM
     71-6959. DAI xxxi.9A, p. 4812. 135 pages.
     Reviews 53 brass trios. Finds the pieces conservative
     in form, harmony, rhythm and style.

278. Janetzky, Kurt. "Das Waldhorn-Quartett: von der Kurio-
     sität zur künstlerischen Erfüllung," in *Musica*, viii
     (April 1954), 142-4. In German.
     A brief history of the Waldhorn quartet as it appears
     in a description of 1806 and in a photograph in the
     mid-19th century. Its repertory (mostly arrangements
     of folksongs, chorales, opera excerpts) and its func-
     tion. Also contains a brief list of available pieces
     for Waldhorn quartet by Hindemith and others.

279. Van Norman, Clarendon Ess, Jr. "The French Horn: its
     Use and Development in Musical Literature." EdD
     dissertation. Columbia University, 1965. 74 pages.
     UMI 65-11714. DA xxvi.5, p. 2798. 74 pages.
     A historical approach to the use of horn in orchestral
     and solo (chamber) music from the 18th century to the
     1960's. Special detailed attention given to Mozart's
     Horn Concerto K.447, Beethoven's Sonata for Horn and
     Piano, Opus 17; Brahms's Trio for Horn, Violin and
     Piano, Opus 40; and Henry Cowell's *Hymn and Fuguing
     Tune No. 12 for Three Horns*.

For the trombone in 17th-century chamber music see Robert
Tennyson's dissertation {225}.

280. Tucker, Wallace E. "The Trombone Quartet, its Appear-
     ance and Development throughout History," in *Journal
     of the International Trombone Association*, vii
     (1979), 2-7, and viii (1980), 2-5.
     A survey of the history of the trombone quartet from
     the 16th century to the 20th. Considers the trombone
     quartet (works like Beethoven's *Funeral Equale*, 1812),
     also in combination with voices and in orchestral
     pieces. Bibliography of compositions for and of works
     about the trombone quartet.

281. Keathley, Gilbert Harrell. "The Tuba Ensemble." DMA
     dissertation. University of Rochester, Eastman
     School of Music, 1982. DAI xliii.8A, p. 2488. 145
     pages.
     Primarily a guide for composers who wish to write for
     the tuba ensemble, with information on range, orches-
     tration, acoustics, and the variety of tubas available
     historically and today.

282. Lonnman, Gregory George. "The Tuba Ensemble: its Or-
     ganization and Literature." DMA dissertation. Uni-
     versity of Miami, 1974. UMI 75-12870. DAI xxxv.12A,
     p. 7947. 63 pages.
     A history of the spread of the tuba ensemble in the
     United States since c.1970, with the objectives and
     literature for such groups. A survey of American
     colleges and universities finds 26 with tuba groups.
     Includes performance and program suggestions.

283. Boone, Dalvin Lee. "The Treatment of the Trumpet in
     Six Published Chamber Works Composed between 1920 and
     1929." EdD dissertation. University of Illinois,
     1972. UM 73-9885. DAI xxxiii.10A, p. 5762. 244
     pages.
     Analysis of basic elements of Stravinsky's *Octet*,
     Varèse's *Octandre*, Hindemith's *Drei Stücke*, Walton's
     Façade, Casella's *Serenata*, and Martinů's *La Revue de
     Cuisine* and the performance problems for the trumpet or
     trumpets in them. In all 6 the trumpet is less active
     and interesting than the woodwinds and/or strings.

284. Coleman, Jack. "The Trumpet: its Use in Selected Works
     of Stravinsky, Hindemith, Shostakovich, and Copland."
     DMA dissertation. University of Southern California,
     1965. UMI 65-12257. DA xxvi.6, p. 3389. 268 pages.
     The technical uses of the trumpet in the chamber as
     well as other music of these 4 composers. Finds Stra-
     vinsky has complete understanding of the trumpet's
     color and idiosyncrasies, but finds Hindemith non-
     idiomatic, drab, mechanical. Shostakovich uses only a
     very simple, limited trumpet technique, and Copland is
     complex in style, not in technique. Only a small part
     of the discussion concerns chamber music.

285. Tunnell, Michael Hilton. "A Comprehensive Performance
     Project in Trumpet Literature: an Essay on Selected
     Trumpet Excerpts from Brass Quintets by Ingolf Dahl,
     Gunther Schuller, Alvin Etler, and Jan Bach: and a
     Bibliography of Brass Quintets written by American
     Composers from 1938 to 1980." DMA dissertation.
     University of Southern Mississippi, 1982. DAI xliv.
     1A, p. 12. 242 pages.
     While the bulk of the dissertation concentrates on
     trumpet techniques, style and performance problems in
     the 4 brass quintets, there is a brief history of the
     brass quintet in America and a list of 293 such pieces
     by Americans from 1938 to 1980. An excerpt is pub-
     lished as "An Essay on Selected Trumpet Excerpts from
     Brass Quintets by Ingolf Dahl, Gunther Schuller, Alvin
     Etler, and Jan Bach," in the *Journal of the Interna-
     tional Trumpet Guild*, viii (1984), 14-38.

286. Tuozzolo, James Michael. "Trumpet Techniques in
     Selected Works of Four Contemporary American Compo-
     sers: Gunther Schuller, Meyer Kupferman, William
     Sydeman, and William Frabizio." DMA dissertation.
     University of Miami, 1972. UMI 72-31896. DAI
     xxxiii.6A, pp. 2972-3. 63 pages, 71 examples.
     Discusses the various new technical devices required by
     the four composers in the trumpet parts in 10 of their
     works, among which are 3 brass quintets, a duo for
     trumpet and double bass, a piece for trumpet with wind
     ensemble, 2 duets for trumpet and piano, and non-cham-

ber works. Brief analyses of the whole pieces before
being dissected into specific examples which are
categorized.

*See Georg Schünemann's "Sonaten und Feldstücke der Hoftrom-
peter" {212} for trumpet sonatas c.1600.*

287. Bolen, Charles Warren. "Open-Air Music of the Baroque:
      a Study of Selected Examples of Wind Music." PhD
      dissertation. Indiana University, 1954. UM 54-1806.
      DA xiv.8, p. 1232. 264 pages.
      Study of the equestrian ballet and other types of open-
      air music including tower music by Pezel, Gottfried
      Reiche, Johann Phillip Krieger, and Johann Georg Chris-
      tian Störl. Brief analyses of the brass music.

              MIXED ENSEMBLES OF WOODWINDS AND BRASS

288. Kurtz, Saul James. "A Study and Catalog of Ensemble
      Music for Woodwinds Alone or with Brass from *ca.*1700
      to *ca.*1825." PhD dissertation. University of Iowa,
      1971. UM 72-8273. DAI xxxii.9A, p. 5269. RILM 71-
      63. v + 243 pages.
      A historical analysis of woodwind repertory and ensem-
      bles and the terminology associated with them, followed
      by a catalogue. Includes a3 to a10 but excludes key-
      board and strings other than double bass. Also ex-
      cludes recorder, lighter works, and most band music.
      Popular combinations are 3 flutes; 2 oboes + bassoon +
      2 horns; 2 clarinets + 2 bassoon + 2 horns; 2 oboes +
      2 clarinets + 2 bassoons + 2 horns; 2 oboes + 2 bas-
      soons + 2 horns; and 2 clarinets + bassoon + 2 horns.
      This is presented as a preliminary, not a final, list.

289. Lewis, Edgar Jay, Jr. "The Use of Wind Instruments in
      Seventeenth-Century Instrumental Music." PhD disser-
      tation. University of Wisconsin, 1964. UM 64-3928.
      DA xxiv.10, pp. 4223-4. 538 pages.
      Assesses the significance of the solo parts for cor-
      netts, trombones, bassoons, trumpets, flutes and oboes
      in 176 instrumental works. Most significant trumpet
      music is sonatas for 1 or 2 trumpets and strings (solo
      or orchestral?).

290. Piersol, Jon Ross. "The Oettingen-Wallerstein Hofka-
      pelle and its Wind Music." PhD dissertation.
      University of Iowa, 1972. UMI 73-13583. DAI
      xxxiii.12A, p. 6954. 853 pages.
      A detailed history of this late-18th-century court or-
      chestra and its wind ensembles and chamber music. The
      orchestra was famous at the time and had the respect of
      Haydn. Appendix A gives biographies of all the 18th-

century wind musicians at court including Joseph Beder, Franz Czerwenka, Johann Feldmayr, Joseph Fiala, Johann Nisle, and Johann Türrschmidt. Appendix B gives incipits for and discussion of wind ensemble music a5 or larger in the court library (by Reicha, Rosetti, Feldmayr and Paul Winneberger). Appendix C is an annotated list with incipits of all other compositions in the library with winds, either solo or with strings.

291. Starkey, Willard A. "The History and Practice of Ensemble Music for Lip-Reed Instruments." PhD dissertation. University of Iowa, 1954. UMI 00-10246. DD xxii (1955), p. 246. DA xv.1, p. 131. 610 pages.
A history of ensembles of brass instruments and some related non-brass ones (such as zink and cornett), the social situation of such ensembles, performance practices, and a large survey of the literature.

292. Wahl, Ralph Victor. "Mixed-Wind Chamber Music in American Universities." AMD dissertation. University of Arizona, 1977. UMI 77-20632. DAI xxxviii.4A, p. 1734. 480 pages.
Discusses specific performing groups (American Wind Symphony Orchestra, Eastman Wind Ensemble, the Netherlands Wind Ensemble), specific college curricula, recordings, publications, and compositions (chapter 3 discusses 70 representative pieces for university-level concert mixed-wind chamber groups). Appendix includes a list of 861 pieces of all styles (18th-20th centuries) by more than 300 composers.

293. Hall, Harry Hobart. "The Moravian Wind Ensemble: Distinctive Chapter in America's Music." PhD dissertation. George Peabody College, 1967. UM 67-15007. DA xxviii.7A, pp. 2712-13. 2 vols. 568 pages.
Unclear if band or chamber music. History of its origins in Germany c.1731, its American start in Georgia 1735-40, and continues up to 1967. Discusses religious as well as secular aspects, including chorales, marches, dances, and collegia musica (virtuosic woodwind + ensembles); includes institutions, persons, and the music (especially that by David Moritz Michael [1751-1827]).

294. Oneglia, Mario Francesco. "The Trumpet in Chamber Music other than Brass Ensemble." EdD dissertation. Columbia University, 1966. UMI 67-5543. DA xxvii. 12A, pp. 4287-8. 232 pages.
A general discussion of the repertory in the Baroque, Classical, Romantic, and Modern periods, with detailed analysis of one work from each period by a representative composer. Also lists the repertory for students, teachers, and performers, with publishing data.

OTHER GENRES

*Of the remaining genres of chamber music in historical
studies, the piano trio receives the most attention:*

295. Flamm, Christa. "Leopold Koželuch: Biographie und
     stilkritische Untersuchung der Sonaten für Klavier,
     Violine und Violoncello nebst einem Beitrag zur Ent-
     wicklungsgeschichte des Klaviertrios." PhD disserta-
     tion. University of Vienna, 1968. 3 vols. 471
     pages.
     Well-written, scholarly study. Follows Erich Schenk
     (*Die italienische Triosonate* {218}; see also {240}) in
     pointing out that the classical trio came not from the
     Baroque trio sonata but from the solo piano sonata with
     obligato accompaniment; therefore specifically differs
     from Karsch {300} and Blume {296} who see the Classi-
     cal trio developing from the Baroque trio sonata.
     Believes the basic issue is the separation of the con-
     tinuo from obligato accompaniment instruments; only
     when the keyboard is written out is there a basis for
     the piano trio (therefore not trio sonatas with figured
     bass but sonatas with obligato bass that shares some of
     the motives). J.S. Bach emancipates the keyboard, but
     the gamba still just doubles the bass line. Rameau is
     the first to give 2 separate string parts from the key-
     board: a violin and a viola with keyboard in which all
     3 instruments play a separate but equal role. Mozart
     is the first to give the cello complete melodic identi-
     ty with and freedom from the piano and violin. Also
     considers the French sonata for keyboard with violin
     accompaniment to be a source for the piano trio, but
     not the Italian violin sonata with continuo accompani-
     ment and German violin sonata with obligato accompani-
     ment. Discusses much more of crucial importance to the
     development of the piano trio genre and includes the
     role of Koželuch's piano trios.

296. Blume, Ruth Christiane. "Studien zur Entwicklungs-
     geschichte des Klaviertrios im 18. Jahrhundert." PhD
     dissertation. University of Kiel, 1962.
     Not seen.

297. Dunn, Nancy Rose. "The Piano Trio from its Origins to
     Mozart's Death." DMA dissertation. University of
     Oregon, 1975. UMI 76-00923. DAI xxxvi.7A, p. 4094.
     97 pages.
     Discusses a few compositions by Schobert (c.1767),
     Mozart, Haydn, and Beethoven that can be convincingly
     labeled piano trios (as opposed to accompanied keyboard
     sonatas or anything else). Considers the independence
     of the cello, the independence of the violin, and the

technical and musical demands made upon the 3 performers. A brief, to the point dissertation.

298. Abbiati, Franco. "Origini del Trio con Pianoforte," in *Storia della Musica*, iii (Milan: Garzanti, 1941) pages 465-474. ML 160.A2. In Italian.
An outdated treatise that was important in its day. Traces the development of the piano trio from the trio sonata of the 17th century with its 3 lines of music to the solo sonata of the mid-18th century, to the freeing of the keyboard from the continuo, to the keyboard (trio) sonata with accompanied or obligato violin + cello (Wagenseil and Haydn) or harpsichord with violin + bass (Schobert). These were sometimes called divertimenti -- it took Beethoven to free the trio from the frivolous divertimento.

299. Cesari, Gaetano. "Origini del Trio con Pianoforte," in Franco Abbiati, ed., *Scritti inediti* (Milan: Carisch S.A., 1937) pages 183-198. ML 60.C35S43.
Similar to Abbiati's article with the same title {298}. The emancipation of the harpsichord from the continuo was necessary for the piano trio to emerge from the trio sonata; sees this emancipation in the sonatas of J.S. Bach with obligato continuo rather than basso continuo. A sonata a tre means 3 lines of music, not 3 instruments, so when the right hand has its own written-out counterpoint, 1 violin + harpsichord + cello = trio sonata (cello = harpsichord left hand). At this point the keyboard is the principle instrument; the cello continues as a bass support and the violin becomes accompaniment (Wagenseil's divertimenti, Haydn's *Sei Sonate per Clavicembalo con Accompagnamento d'un Violino e Violoncello*, 1776, and Schobert).

300. Karsch, Albert. *Untersuchungen zur Frühgeschichte des Klaviertrios in Deutschland*. PhD dissertation. University of Köln, 1943. Film copy at University of Virginia. 108 + 11 pages.
Traces the beginning of the piano trio from Franz Xaver Richter (who transferred Classical style to the medium), Johann Schobert, J.S. Bach (who freed the keyboard from merely accompanying), J.C. Bach (who was the first to create equality among all 3 instruments), J.C. Bach's circle (Johann Samuel Schröter, 1750-1788, and others), and Mozart. The emancipation of the cello and keyboard are decisive for this genre and receive the bulk of the attention; the violin already had achieved concertante status. The cello is emancipated with the gradual acceptance of improvised ornaments in and variation of the bass in the 1730's and after. Goes into the 16th century to trace the keyboard as accompaniment and as doubling instrument; then with Marini's *Sonata per l'organo e violino o cornetto* (from Opus 8)

the violin and organ right hand form a trio sonata over
the organ left hand. Other milestones are the obligato
keyboard sonata with accompanied violin of J.S. Bach
and the French keyboard sonata with accompanied violin
of Mondonville and Guillemain. Brief analysis of a
group of early trios or pre-classical trios by Ernst
Eichner (1740-1777), J.C. Bach, Johann Georg Lang
(1724-1794), Schobert, Vanhal, Otto Konrad Zink (1746-
1832) and Nathanael Gottfried Gruner.

301. Irving, Howard Lee. "The Piano Trio in London from
     1791 to 1800." PhD dissertation. Louisiana State
     University, 1980. UMI 81-10417. DAI xli.11A, pp.
     4535-6. 304 pages.
     A comparison of Haydn's trios published in London in
     1791 and 1794 with trios by other composers published
     in London at the same time (especially by Clementi,
     Johann Baptist Cramer, Adalbert Gyrowetz, Leopold
     Koželuch, and Ignaz Pleyel). Basically, the advanced
     compositional techniques used by Haydn were ignored by
     the others. Examines phrase structures, number of
     movements, tempo, meter, tonality, mode and form. The
     173 trios are either sonatas with optional violin and
     cello or concertante sonatas.

302. Horan, Catherine Anne. "A Survey of the Piano Trio
     from 1800 to 1860." PhD dissertation. Northwestern
     University, 1983. UMI 84-3432. DAI xliv.11A, p.
     3200. 867 pages.
     Detailed analyses of form, tonality, and instrumental
     relationships in 20 piano trios. Systematically deals
     with various definitions of the word trio in contempor-
     ary sources, and gives 2 catalogues of the entire re-
     pertory: thematic and by composer. Limited to trios
     for violin + cello + piano by composers who wrote at
     least 3 such works from 1800 to 1860. Most are Haus-
     musik pieces.

303. Drucker, Arno Paul. "A Chronological Survey and Styl-
     istic Analysis of Selected Trios for Piano, Violin,
     and 'Cello Composed by Native-born United States Com-
     posers during the Period 1920 to 1945." DMA disser-
     tation. Peabody Conservatory of Music, 1970. UMI
     77-17294. DAI xxxviii.2A, p. 4536. 275 pages.
     A survey of the American piano trio, its sources, and
     its publications, and a list of 30 trios by Americans,
     with a biography of each composer, bibliography, and a
     stylistic analysis of each trio by each composer.
     Chapter 2 contains a detailed analysis of the trios of
     Riegger, Luening, Copland, Harris, Piston, and Finney.
     Appendix lists 125 trios by native-born American compo-
     sers with dates, publishers, and sources.

As we have seen, of particular concern to historians is the
changing role of the keyboard from the continuo to the obligato keyboard to the equal partner in chamber music. This
is important not only for the piano trio.

304. Fillion, Michelle Marie. "The Accompanied Keyboard
     Divertimenti of Haydn and his Viennese Contemporaries
     (c.1750-1780)." PhD dissertation. Cornell Universi-
     ty, 1982. DAI xliii.12A, p. 1740. 2 vols. 573
     pages.
     "The first full-length study of Viennese chamber music
     with obligato keyboard before 1780" -- primarily trios
     for harpsichord + violin or flute + bass, and quartets
     for harpsichord + 2 violins + bass. Analyzes 93 such
     divertimenti: scoring, authenticity, chronology, and
     definition of repertory; and analyzes forms, textures
     and styles with historical and aesthetic significance.
     Vol. 2 contains thematic catalogue and presents full or
     partial editions of 15 previously unpublished pieces.

305. Hering, Hans. "Das Klavier in der Kammermusik des 18.
     Jahrhunderts," in *Die Musikforschung*, xxiii (1970),
     22-37. In German.
     Starts with the sonatas in which J.S. Bach used the
     keyboard either as obligato or as continuo; considers
     the accompanied keyboard sonatas of Bach's sons, the
     Mozarts, Mondonville, and others; and concludes with
     the equality of the keyboard and other instruments in
     sonatas and trios by W.A. Mozart and Haydn. Aims to
     correct false titles in modern editions, such as *The
     Violin Sonatas of Mozart* (Mozart wrote no violin
     sonatas but sonatas for Klavier and Violin).

In addition to the piano trio, the piano quartet and piano
quintet are significant genres.

306. Stern, Marion Goertzel. "Keyboard Quartets and Quin-
     tets Published in London, 1756-1775: a Contribution
     to the History of Chamber Music with Obbligato Key-
     board." PhD dissertation. University of Pennsylva-
     nia, 1979. UMI 79-19522. DAI xl.3A, p. 1147. 339
     pages.
     Survey of the repertory of accompanied keyboard sona-
     tas. Three textures: trio sonata, accompanied sonata,
     and concertante sonata. Historical background. Finds
     70 quartets and 21 quintets published in London 1756-
     1775 by native English, Italians living in London,
     French (Schobert), and German composers. These were
     performed by professionals at public and private
     concerts. Use of sonata-rondos for finales, predating
     Mozart K.157. Discussion of the relative importance of
     the keyboard vis-a-vis the strings.

307. Fuhrmann, Roderich. *Mannheimer Klavier-Kammermusik.*
     Marburg: Erich Mauersberger (typewriter photocopy),
     1963. ML 1129.F84. iv + 197 pages.
     A scholarly study of keyboard chamber music from Mann-
     heim exclusive of continuo chamber music and inclusive
     of sonata form. Divides Mannheim composers into 4
     groups: older generation of orchestral players (J.W.A.
     Stamitz, F.X. Richter, I.J. Holzbauer, C.G. Toeschi,
     and Anton Filtz), younger generation of orchestral
     players (C.P. Stamitz, Abbé Vogler, and Franziska Doro-
     thea Lebrun), non-orchestral players (Ernst Eichner and
     L. Tautz), and foreign composers (Andreas E. Forst-
     mayer, ? Liber, and Joh. Franz Xaver Sterkel). Discus-
     ses each composer's biography and relevant chamber mu-
     sic. Analyzes form, motivic development, number of
     movements (usually 3, sometimes 2, rarely 4), Italian
     and French versus Viennese influences, and function of
     the music. Wide-ranging discussion, based primarily on
     the music itself and not on secondary literature.

308. Saam, Joseph. *Zur Geschichte des Klavierquartetts bis
     in die Romantik,* in *Sammlung musikwissenschaftler
     Abhandlungen,* No. 9. Strassburg: Heitz, 1932. ML
     1165.S2. Inaugural dissertation. Ludwig-Maximil-
     lians-Universität Munich, 1931. iii + 170 pages.
     Opens with a short chapter on the precursors of the
     piano quartet (trio sonatas, piano concertos, string
     quartets). Then a discussion of the piano quartet with
     two discant instruments (piano rather than continuo;
     symphonic structure and its influences; Schobert, J.A.
     Bauer and many others). Most of the discussion focuses
     on the piano quartet with string trio (violin + viola +
     cello) by Georg Joseph Vogel (1749-1814), Mozart and
     Beethoven, then Pleyel, Wranizky, Tomaschek, Danzi,
     A.J. Romberg, finally the romantic generation of Dus-
     sek, Prince Louis-Ferdinand, Cramer, Hummel, Moscheles,
     Bernhard Romberg, Ferdinand Ries, and Czerny. Briefly
     discusses thematic development, tonality, and form in
     each of their quartets. The piano quartet's forebears
     were two kinds of trio sonatas: 2 treble instruments +
     continuo (cello + equivalent harpsichord) and 2 treble
     instruments + independent cello or viola + continuo.
     Telemann's suites exemplify the latter. Christoph
     Schaffrath's sonatas for viola da gamba + violin +
     cello + harpsichord lead to the string quartet, not the
     piano quartet. Johann Schobert wrote the first real
     piano quartet (its precursors were trio sonatas, cham-
     ber trios, chamber quartets and piano concertos) where
     there is a new spirit and the cello is separate from
     the keyboard.

309. Staples, James Gwynn, III. "Six Lesser-Known Piano
     Quintets of the Twentieth Century." DMA disserta-
     tion. University of Rochester, Eastman School of

Music, 1972. UM 73-984. DAI xxxiii.7A, pp. 3701-2.
v + 272 pages.
A detailed description and a performer's analysis of 6
piano quintets covering a wide range of countries and
styles: Webern (1907), Louis Vierne (1917), Elgar
(1918), Martinú (1944), Nicolas Medtner (1950), and
Ross Lee Finney (1953).

*Other combinations of string instruments are also studied
historically as genres.*

String Duos

310. Mazurowicz, Ulrich. *Das Streichduett in Wien von 1760
     bis zum Tode Joseph Haydns*, in *Eichstätter Abhand-
     lungen zur Musikwissenschaft*, Vol. I. Tutzing: Hans
     Schneider, 1982. ML 1122.M4.1982. ISBN 3-7952-0350-
     3. vii + 366 pages.
     The most important study of string duets. Includes an
     extensive thematic catalogue of such duets, organized
     by scoring (2 violins, violin + viola, violin + cello,
     alternate scoring, variations, dances, studies). Opens
     with a careful delineation of this repertory, including
     definition, categorization, and history. Compares the
     concepts dialogue, concertant, and duet in terms sug-
     gested by Finscher, Trimpert, and Unverricht but re-
     duced to 2 instruments. It is the alternation of dia-
     logue and concertant in duets that is a characteristic
     here of Viennese duets. Includes Mozart's and Michael
     Haydn's duets as well as Pleyel's, Vanhal's, Wrani-
     zky's, Boccherini's, Albrechtsberger's, and others.

311. Hausswald, Günter. "Barocke Kammermusik ohne General-
     bass," in *Hausmusik*, xxi (1957), 74-79.
     Considers Baroque duets where solo instruments play
     together without continuo. Looks at French, English as
     well as German examples. Stops at 1750 since after the
     mid-18th century other types of chamber music without
     keyboard developed which are much better known: violin
     duets, string trios, and string quartets.

312. Riehl, Wilhelm Heinrich von. "Viotti und das Geigen-
     duett," in *Musikalische Charakterköpfe: ein kunstge-
     schichtliches Skizzenbuch*, band 2, 7th ed. (Stutt-
     gart: J.G. Cotta-sche Buchhandlung, 1899), pages 151-
     182. ML 60.R551 (1st ed. 1853; 2nd ed. in 2 vols
     1857; 4th ed. in 2 vols 1868.) (2nd ed. in 3 vols
     1881), iii, 51-92.
     Points out how Viotti wrote these duets to express his
     pain at having been exiled twice -- from revolutionary
     Paris and from anti-French London. In Riehl's day the
     duets were used for teaching, played by teacher and
     student together, but Viotti did not write them as

exercises. He wrote them for himself, for artists and
amateurs, as Hausmusik. Points out the prevalence of
duets in the late 18th century, even arrangements of
whole quartets for 2 flutes. Considers also duets by
Spohr, Moritz Hauptmann, and others. The last 4 pages
deal with the role of women in Hausmusik -- the necessity of women playing violin rather than piano.

*See also Daniel Mellado's "A Study of 20th-Century Duets for
Violin and Violoncello" {85}.*

For guitar duets, see Guitar Review, *No. 31 (May 1969),
which includes Graham Wade, "An Historical Perspective of
the Guitar Duo" (pp. 7-8), John W. Duarte's "Rational of the
Guitar-Duo Form" (pp. 9-11), and Duarte's "The Future of the
Guitar Duo" (pp. 12-13).*

String Trios

313. Unverricht, Hubert. *Geschichte des Streichtrios*, in
     Mainzer Studien zur Musikwissenschaft, Band 2.
     Tutzing: Hans Schneider, 1969. ML 1165.U6. 363
     pages, 36 facsimiles.
     Lengthy, well-documented, scholarly study of the string
     trio. The first concern is to distinguish it from the
     trio sonata of the mid-18th century and not to consider
     it merely (and incorrectly) the source for the string
     quartet. Uses aesthetic and social study to determine
     the historical importance of the genre. Studies the
     term "string trio" as it is used and the compositions
     themselves. Considers the end of the trio sonata, the
     dialogue trio, special scorings and performance prac-
     tices of the string trios 1750-1775. Then proceeds to
     the main period (end of the 18th and 19th centuries)
     characterized by the grand trio, the concertante trio
     (one or two upper instruments dominate), the brillante
     trio (virtuoso display), and Hausmusik or pedagogic
     trio (easy). Considers the social setting, including
     the trio as background to conversation, its elevation
     into art music for quiet audiences, and Hausmusik;
     cites contemporary descriptions of performances.
     Follows the trio as either Hausmusik or virtuosic music
     in the later 19th century, and the revival of string
     trios in the 20th century with radio and interest in
     early music. The large number of trios cited and large
     bibliography (38 pages) make this a major reference for
     the non-keyboard trio, and its discussions of the
     social roles of the trio make it also important for the
     history of chamber music in general.

314. Lippmann, Friedrich, and Hubert Unverricht. "Die
     Streichtrio - Manuskripte der Bibliothek Doria -
     Pamphilj in Rom," in *Studien zur italienisch-*

deutschen Musikgeschichte, viii, in *Analecta
Musicologica*, ix (1970), 299-335.
An inventory of string trios (2 violins + cello) in
manuscripts from the last third of the 18th century,
with themes of all movements and concordances. Compo-
sers include Boccherini, Pugnani, Antonio Campioni,
Mysliveček, Giovanni Raimondi, Friedrich Schwindel,
Mattia Stabinger, and Francesco Zannetti.

315. Liew, Robert Chee Yee. "The Guitar Chamber Trio from
     1780-1830: its Style and Structure." PhD disserta-
     tion. Texas Technical University, 1983. UM 83-1460.
     DAI xliii.8A, p. 2489. vii + 176 pages.
     Shows the importance of the 6-string guitar c.1800,
     especially in chamber music and in trios. Trios rather
     than larger ensembles for reasons of balance. Formally
     conservative pieces.

316. Fruchtman, Efrim. "The Baryton Trios of Tomasini,
     Burgksteiner, and Neumann." PhD dissertation. Uni-
     versity of North Carolina, 1960. LC Mic.60-6986. DA
     xxi.11, p. 3477-8. 118 pages + 105 pages of music.
     A detailed analysis of 3 sets of divertimenti, each
     containing 24 trios for barytone or violin, viola or
     violin, and cello, by Luigi Tomasini (1741-1808), and
     the 2 others. Compares these to such trios at other
     courts; they are stylistically similar to other
     compositions of the time.

Other String Chamber Music

317. Drüner, Ulrich. "Eine Sonderform des klassischen
     Streichquartetts: Quartette für Violine, zwei
     Bratsche und Cello," in *Das Orchester*, xxvii (1979),
     644-45.
     More than 60 quartets for violin + 2 violas + cello,
     written c.1760-c.1830 by such eminent composers as Al-
     brechtsberger, Cambini, Giardini, Pleyel and Carl Sta-
     mitz, are unknown today. Traces this scoring to many
     sonatas à quatro in 17th-century Austria and Germany
     (continuo instead of cello, sometimes a wind substitut-
     ing for the violin). They may have been the source for
     the standard string quartet as well; the shortage of
     violists vis-a-vis violinists may have encouraged a
     violin to substitute for 1 of the violas. Gassmann may
     have been the first to adapt the 2-viola sonata to pre-
     classical style.

318. Sieber, Tilman. *Das klassische Streichquintett: quel-
     lenkundliche und gattungsgeschichtliche Studien*, in
     Neue Heidelberger Studien zur Musikwissenschaft, Band
     10. Bern: Francke Verlag, 1983. ML 1160.S54.1983.
     ISBN 3-7720-1526-3. 223 pages, 118 examples.

Major though flawed study of the classical string quintet and to what extent it represents a genre distinct
from the string quartet (but see negative review by
George R. Hill, *Notes*, June 1985, pp. 723-4). Uses the
works of over 40 composers of the time to establish its
characteristics (besides Boccherini, Cambini, Brunetti,
Pleyel, Beethoven and especially Mozart there are many
less-well-known composers represented). The quintet is
more varied, has thicker texture, and more contrast in
tone color than the quartet. Traces the Italian quintet from the Italian concerto and the Austrian quintet
from the divertimento (but Hill points to errors in
listing as string quintets works that are really something else). Recognizes also a dialogue quintet in
Italy, Austria and Mannheim. A great many composers,
quintets and their presumed forebears are discussed at
length in order to disprove pejorative descriptions of
the genre by Dahlhaus and Wiorra. Analysis subject to
errors. Extensive bibliography, which Hill criticizes
for its neglect of non-German scholarship after 1970.

Some studies deal with a particular string instrument or a
family of string instruments in relation to chamber music.
A few of these follow.

319. Caffarelli, Francisco di. *Gli Instrumenti ad Arco e la*
     Musica da Camera. Milan: Ulrico Hoepli, 1894. ML
     750.C12S7.1894. x + 235 pages.
     First considers the violin before 1600, then studies
     the basic types of 17th-century ensemble music (sonata,
     canzona, concerto, suite, various dances, chaconne and
     passacaglia) and those up to Mendelssohn. Mentions
     composers and their chief chamber works with several
     interesting lists (Italian violinists alphabetically up
     to Paganini's time, German compositions for the violin
     generically from solo to octet). Some brief, non-
     technical analyses (Beethoven quartets), and a biblio-
     graphy of violin treatises and Italian books on early
     music performance. Nothing here is unique or thorough,
     but it does show the extent to which Italians were
     aware of chamber music in 1894. Includes a somewhat
     fantasy-like history of music and aesthetics and the
     special characteristics of the violin (poses the anti-
     thesis of natural and learned qualities of violin per-
     formance and their application to music).

320. Tatton, Thomas James. "English Viola Music, 1890-
     1937." DMA dissertation. University of Illinois,
     1976. UMI 76-24188. DAI xxxvii.5A, p. 2489. 141
     pages.
     Lionel Tertis, English violist early in the 20th
     century, encouraged his English compatriots to write
     works for viola, an instrument largely neglected in the

19th century. Over 50 English composers responded.
Nearly all the works are chamber pieces. They fit into
the following categories: works of artistic and lasting
value, works of pedagogical interest, marginal works of
interest primarily to violists, and novelties. Discusses not only the pieces but performances, patrons,
violists, and ensembles. Special attention to Tertis,
and a list of viola works.

See also {1490-1495}.

321. Bacon, Analee Camp. "The Evolution of the Violoncello
     as a Solo Instrument." PhD dissertation. Syracuse
     University, 1962. UMI 63-6735. DA xxiv.4, pp. 1642-
     3. 192 pages.
     Shows the development of the role of the cello from its
     earliest experimental introduction to its acceptance as
     an indispensable instrument in chamber music. Further
     shows its evolution from a part of the continuo (where
     it arrived c.1600) to a solo instrument in the 18th
     century as the bass became more contrapuntal.

322. Planyavsky, Alfred. "Der Kontrabass in der Kammer-
     musik," in *Österreichische Musikzeitschrift*, xiii
     (1958), 57-63.
     Reviews the history of the string bass in instrumental
     music from c.1600 on, with special attention to the
     ambiguity of "bass" in the 17th and most of the 18th
     centuries (= cello or string bass?). The quartet for 2
     violins + viola + bass (= contrabass or string bass)
     occurs in Mozart's *Serenata Notturna* K.239. Also
     quintets for 2 violins + viola + cello + bass by Hoff-
     meister. Haydn's first symphony = cassation = 12 solo
     instruments including string bass. Mozart and Ditters-
     dorf wrote for Pichlberger = Pischlberger, a string
     bassist. The Bassettl does not mean cello or string
     bass in Vienna. See also Webster {177-178}. The
     string bass is important also in the early 19th cen-
     tury: Schubert's *Trout Quintet* and others influenced by
     Dragone. Then as the cello gained in popularity and
     virtuosity, the string bass is dropped from chamber
     music. Ends with a brief survey of chamber music for
     string bass of the post-Schubert period up to the
     1950's.

*There are also various combinations of winds and strings or
winds and keyboard which merit special studies.*

323. Alexander, Peter. "A Structural and Stylistic Study
     and Performance of Selected Twentieth-Century English
     Works for Clarinet and Piano." EdD dissertation.
     Columbia University, 1982. UMI 82-23091. DAI xliii.
     5A, p. 1337. 122 pages.

An analysis of 4 works for clarinet + piano by John
Ireland (*Fantasy-Sonata*), William Alwyn (Sonata), Alan
Rawsthorne (Concerto), and Arnold Bax (Sonata).
Different treatments of sonata form and technical
requirements for the clarinetist. Aimed at the pro-
fessional and collegiate clarinetist.

324. Rau, Ulrich. "Die Kammermusik für Klarinette und
     Streichinstrumente im Zeitalter der Wiener Klassik."
     PhD dissertation. University of Saarland, 1975. DAI
     (Eur), xlii.4, p. 692. 2 vols. 622 pages.
     Considers the clarinet quintets of Mannheim, Paris, and
     Vienna separately, and presents a history of the genre,
     its stylistic elements, and the role of the clarinet.

325. Osborn, Thomas Montgomery. "Sixty Years of Clarinet
     Chamber Music: a Survey of Music Employing Clarinet
     with Stringed Instruments Composed 1900-1960 for Two
     to Five Performers." DMA dissertation. University
     of Southern California, 1964. UMI 64-13504. DA
     xxv.9, pp. 5323-4. 404 pages.
     Classifies chamber music as Romantic (Classical-Roman-
     tic, late-Romantic, or post-Romantic), revolutionary
     (impressionistic or expressionistic), or anti-Romantic
     (national-folk, neo-Classic, neo-Baroque, composite, or
     abstract). Considers the repertory historically and
     notes unusual combinations of instruments as well as
     chamber vocal music with clarinet.

326. Anderson, Marcia Hilden. "A Survey of Twentieth-
     Century Finnish Clarinet Music and an Analysis of
     Selected Works." PhD dissertation. Michigan State
     University, 1975. UMI 75-20808. DAI xxxvi.3A, pp.
     1151-2. 172 pages.
     Examines the role of the clarinet in Finnish music
     (primarily a military band instrument until, c.1920, it
     found its way into classical music). Considers 22 of
     the over 60 clarinet works published and unpublished by
     Finnish composers and gives detailed analyses of 3
     which are typical: Erik Bergman (Three Fantasias, 1954,
     clarinet + piano), Pentti Raitio (*Elegia Sooloklari-
     netille*, 1966), and Aarre Merikento (*Konzert für
     Violine, Klarinette, Horn, und Streichsextett*, 1925),
     second movement. Most works considered are either part
     of woodwind quintets or for clarinet and piano.

327. Eagle, David William. "A Constant Passion and a Con-
     stant Pursuit: a Social History of Flute-Playing in
     England from 1800 to 1851." PhD dissertation.
     University of Minnesota, 1977. DAI xxxviii.12A, pp.
     7011-12. 241 pages.
     Shows the various social implications of flute playing
     by the middle and upper classes in England. Even
     George III was a flutist.

328. Harriss, Elaine Atkins. "Chamber Music for the Trio of
     Flute, Clarinet, and Piano: a Bibliographical and
     Analytical Study." PhD dissertation. University of
     Michigan, 1981. UMI 81-25122. DAI xlii.6A, p. 2353-
     4. 160 pages.
     Analyzes form, style, harmony, rhythm, melody, texture
     and scoring in 108 such works, which are graded accord-
     ing to technical difficulty. Some historical back-
     ground for each piece and composer. General discussion
     of the genre. The list includes arrangements.

*For a brief historical sketch of the flute quartet (flute +
violin + viola + cello) of the second half of the 18th
century, see Marion Valasek's dissertation {1506}.*

329. Meyer, W. Frederick. "Oboe Quartets from *ca.*1750-*ca.*
     1825." DMA dissertation. University of Rochester,
     Eastman School of Music, 1973. UM 73-24058. DAI
     xxxiv.4A, pp. 1953-4. xi + 116 pages.
     Examination of the oboe + violin + viola + cello reper-
     toire and its history, with analysis of 4 examples by
     Gassmann, Luigi Gatti, Jan Adam Frantisek Mica, and
     Mozart. A practical edition of the Gassmann piece.
     Considers the viability of the medium and different
     seating arrangements for the performers. One appendix
     provides a list of oboe quartets in modern editions.

*See Craig's dissertation {901} for another overall history
of the oboe quartet.*

*For chamber music with trumpet and other, non-brass instru-
ments, see {283-284} and {294}.*

*In the 17th and early 18th centuries there are special kinds
of chamber music which have received specialized historical
study:*

330. Swenson, Milton Allen. "The Four-part Italian Ensemble
     Ricercar from 1540 to 1619." PhD dissertation.
     Indiana University, 1971. UMI 71-21294. DAI
     xxxii.2A, p. 1004. 2 vols.: I: analysis and commen-
     tary, II: 94 ricercari in score. 1307 pages.
     A historical analysis of the chamber ensemble ricercar
     from the time of Adrian Willaert to that of Antonio
     Cifra. Defines "ricercar," surveys past literature on
     the subject, and traces the development of different
     kinds of ricercar (lute, keyboard, a2-a8, a1). Three
     kinds of ricercari among the 130 4-part pieces are
     studied: 1) spacious, conservative harmony, intricate
     counterpoint (Willaert's associates, Merulo), 2) con-

servative harmony but shorter and with livelier rhythm
(A. Gabrieli), 3) brief, lively rhythm, experimental
harmony, less intricate counterpoint, short motivic
themes (Malvezzi, Peri, Raval, and Quagliati).

331. Bartholomew, Leland Earl. *Alessandro Rauerij's Collec-*
     tion of Canzoni per sonare *(Venice, 1608).* Fort
     Hays: Fort Hays Kansas State College, 1965. ML 1133.
     B37. 2 vols. I: ix + 485 pages; II: x + 174 pages
     (mostly music). Print of typed dissertation, 1963.
     A historical, bibliographical, and analytical study of
     Canzoni per Sonare con Ogni Sorte di Stromenti (Venice:
     A. Rauerij, 1608), a collection of 36 works by 12 com-
     posers including G. Gabrieli, Claudio Merulo, Gioseffo
     Guami, Luzzasco Luzzaschi, and Frescobaldi. Scored for
     4, 5, 8 and 16 instruments + basso generale for organ
     (only 2 pieces have specific scoring: no. 33 for 8
     trombones + basso generale, and no. 34 for 4 viols + 4
     lutes + basso generale). History of the canzona in
     16th-century Italy, especially Venice, and points to
     private music making (chamber music) as one possible
     setting for these canzone. Most of the discussion cen-
     ters around editorial problems, analysis of the instru-
     mental ensemble forms and structure, and data on the 12
     composers. Vol. II is an edition of the 36 canzonas in
     score, an important collection of early Baroque chamber
     music representing the culmination of the ensemble
     canzona after more than a quarter century of develop-
     ment. The collection's importance for the early de-
     velopment of ensemble sonatas in the 17th century is
     discussed in Niels Jensen, "Solo Sonata..." {215}.

332. Cortner, Larry Lee. "Thirteen Chorale Preludes for
     Organ and Obbligato Instrument, Leipzig Poel. Mus.
     Ms. 364/2." MDA dissertation. Eastman School of
     Music, 1978. 124 pages.
     A history and scholarly edition of 12 organ trios with
     chorale cantus firmus in long notes by the obligato in-
     struments (oboe, oboe d'amore, horn, and trombone).
     Similar to works by Johann Ludwig Krebs and Gottfried
     August Homilius.

333. Meyer, Ernst Hermann. *English Chamber Music: the His-*
     tory of a Great Art from the Middle Ages to Purcell.
     London: Lawrence and Wishart, 1946. Reprint New
     York: Da Capo, 1971. ML 1131.M48.1971. German trl.
     by Gerda Becker, *Die Kammermusik Alt-Englands: vom*
     Mittelalter bis zum Tode Henry Purcells. Leipzig:
     Breitkopf & Härtel, 1958. xiv + 318 pages.
     The classic scholarly study of English consort music of
     the 16th and 17th centuries. Relates this music to
     other types (vocal and religious) and to the social
     environment (the popular element is most important -- a
     Marxist approach which colors but does not invalidate

much of the discussion). A social history with detailed analyses of representative pieces. "The main
stylistic developments of chamber music from Jenkins to
Purcell are the slow evolution from polyphony to homophony, and the final victory of dramatic and lyrical,
of subjectively emotional elements."

See Van der Meer in {457}.

334. Stoltzfus, Ila Hartzler. "The Lyra Viol in Consort
     with Other Instruments." PhD dissertation. Louisi-
     ana State University, 1982. DAI xliii.8A, p. 2491.
     248 pages.
     A historical and analytical study of English suites by
     five composers of the mid-17th century for a consort of
     a treble instrument, lyra viol, bass viol, and either a
     theorbo or harpsichord.

335. Coates, William. "English Two-Part Viol Music, 1590-
     1640," in *Music and Letters*, xxxiii (1952), 141-150.
     Discussion of 31 pieces for 2 viols in a Cambridge
     University manuscript of the 1630's. Reduces some of
     the analyses to charts.

336. Cohen, Albert. "The *Fantaisie* for Instrumental Ensem-
     ble in 17th-century France -- its Origin and Signifi-
     cance," in *The Musical Quarterly*, xlviii (1962), 234-
     243.
     The French *fantaisie* flourished in the first half of
     the 17th century, largely influenced by the English
     fancy but containing its own peculiarities. Sometimes
     for keyboard, sometimes for an ensemble of viols (solo
     or doubled?), it also was frequently performed simul-
     taneously by both. A scholarly article.

337. Sadie, Julie Anne. *The Bass Viol in French Baroque
     Chamber Music*, in *Studies in Musicology*, no. 26. Ann
     Arbor: University Microfilms International, 1980. ML
     760.V56582. ISBN 0-8357-1116-1. xiii + 189 pages,
     19 musical facsimiles, 6 pictures, 83 musical
     examples.
     A scholarly study aimed at acquainting bass viol
     players with the French repertoire c.1690's to 1740's.
     Defines chamber music as both instrumental and vocal.
     Considers the bass viol as a solo chamber instrument as
     well as part of the continuo. Compares the bass viol
     to the cello. Huge bibliography.

STUDIES OF THE CHAMBER MUSIC OF
PARTICULAR REGIONS OF THE WORLD

While many studies of particular genres, composers, and
individual works inevitably focus on a particular city or
country, there are some that dwell on the location as impor-
tant in itself. Especially Austria, Italy, Germany, and
France are the sites of much of the literature in this book;
only the most relevant in their cases will be listed below.
A few works discuss the chamber music of a number of differ-
ent countries as separate chapters (see Hemel {148} and
Reclam {162}).

ARMENIA

338. Ter-Simonyan, Margarita. *Kamerno-instrumental'naya*
     Ansamblevaya Muzyka Armenii. Erevan: Akademiya Nauk
     Armyanskoy SSR, 1974. ML 1151.A7T47. 155 pages.
     In Russian.
     Armenian chamber music both before and after merger
     with the Soviet Union. Names performers who perform
     standard classics and mid-20th-century Armenian compo-
     sers of chamber music such as Edward Merzoyan, Arno
     Babadzanian, and Edgar Oganesian (on whom the book
     concentrates). Discusses folk music influences on the
     chamber works by the 3. For scholars and laypersons.

AUSTRALIA

See {47}.

AUSTRIA

339. Biales, Albert. "Sonatas and Canzonas for Larger
     Ensembles in Seventeenth-Century Austria." PhD
     dissertation. UCLA, 1962. 2 vols. I: viii + 215
     pages; II: 31 pages of music.
     Concerned with ensembles larger than trio sonatas and
     with the music of Italian, Austrian, and other compo-
     sers writing in Austria in the 17th century. Unclear
     if chamber or orchestral -- perhaps the same music
     could be performed either way. Divides the composers
     into two periods: I: Period of Italian Dominance (1600-
     1678), with Giovanni Prioli, Francesco Stivori, Stef-
     fano Bernardi, Giovanni Valentini, Giovanni Battista
     Buonamente, Antonio Bertali, Paul Peurl, and William
     Young; and II: The Emergence of Austria as an Interna-
     tional Influence (1679-1700), with Johann Heinrich
     Schmelzer, Heinrich Biber, Georg Muffat, Alessandro
     Poglietti, Ferdinand Tobias Richter, and Pietro Andrea

Ziani. After history, analysis of form, instrumentation, concerto elements, harmony, melody, and rhythm.

The divertimento in 18th-century Austria is important for
future types of chamber music as well as in its own right:

340. Gibson, O. Lee. "The Serenades and Divertimenti of Mo-
     zart." PhD dissertation. North Texas State College,
     1960. UMI 60-1791. DA xxi.3, pp. 638-9. 394 pages.
     Study of the serenade and divertimento and their equi-
     valents in Vienna and Salzburg and to a lesser extent
     in Mannheim during the 18th century with reliance upon
     the works available in *Denkmäler der Tonkunst in Öster-*
     reich. Then concentrates on Mozart's contributions
     (including cassations, notturni, and marches as well).
     Considers scoring, title. Tries to understand the
     evolution of Austrian Gesellschaftsmusik in the second
     half of the 18th century.

341. Henrotte, Gayel Allen. "The Ensemble Divertimento in
     Pre-classic Vienna." PhD dissertation. University
     of North Carolina, 1967. UMI 68-6740. DAI xxviii.
     12A, p. 5091. 828 pages.
     Discusses 29 divertimenti by Giuseppe Porsile (1680-
     1750), Matthias Georg Monn (1717-1750), Johann Chris-
     toph Mann (1726-1782), and Franz Asplmayr (1728-1786).
     Regards these divertimenti as chamber music, not or-
     chestral, and considers them "as an adjunct to aristo-
     cratic social life, as a medium historically oriented
     between the suite and the string quartet, and as an
     instrumental cycle in the transition from Baroque to
     Classical music."

342. Meyer, Eve Rose. "Florian Gassmann and the Viennese
     Divertimento." PhD dissertation. University of
     Pennsylvania, 1963. UMI 63-7068. DA xxiv.12, pp.
     5453-4. 337 pages.
     Finds that the term "divertimento" was primarily a
     Viennese one, and that Gassmann's 32 divertimenti which
     are found in foreign sources are usually labelled in-
     stead sonata, trio, or quartet. Recognizes the chamber
     music quality of Gassmann's divertimenti, but also the
     possible small orchestral performance. Thirteen are
     trios for strings or flute + strings, 10 are string
     quartets, and 9 are for oboe + strings -- no continuo
     included or needed. All are in 3 movements, most start
     slow, and only 21 contain a minuet. In binary form and
     rudimentary sonata form. Compares Gassmann's works to
     those by the Haydn brothers, Mozart father and son,
     Mann, Dittersdorf, Starzer, and others.

See also {173, 174, 176, and 385}.

Vienna continues as a center of chamber music in the 19th and 20th centuries:

343. Hanslick, Eduard. *Geschichte des Concertwesens in Wien.* 2 vols. Vienna: Wilhelm Braumüller, 1869-1870. Reprint Westmead: Gregg International, 1971. ML 246.8.V6H2.1971. I: xv + 438 pages; II: xii + 534 pages.
     Invaluable historical descriptions of many facets of chamber music in one of the most important centers of chamber music in Europe. Includes such topics as the rise of dilettante concerts in rented rooms of inns in Germany and Vienna during the later 18th century, reviews of concerts by the Hellmesberger Quartet, Jansa's Quartet Evenings, comparison of the Müller and Hellmesberger Quartets, quartet evenings in 1856, chamber music by Rubinstein, Chopin, Beethoven (Op. 133), Schumann (Violin + Piano Sonata in D Minor), and much besides. Provides insight into Viennese tastes in the mid-19th century and the sensitive and sensible criticism of the leading music critic of the 19th century. Also includes some chamber music concerts in London (1862), Paris (1860 and 1867), and Switzerland (1857). Criticizes repertoire and performance practices. Continued in *Concerte, Componisten und Virtuosen der letzten fünfzehn Jahre 1870-1885.* 3rd ed. Berlin: Allgemeiner Verein für Deutsche Litteratur, 1896. 1st ed. 1885. 780.4 H24c. xvi + 448 pages. Includes reviews in Vienna 1870 to 1884, with premiers of Brahms's, Dvorák's, and others's famous chamber works.

344. Riedel, August. "Hausmusik in Wien vor 50 Jahren," in *Musikerziehung,* iii (1950), 232-235.
     Defines Hausmusik as chamber music a1-10 for friends who play music ("ausübende Musikfreunde"). Gives a good summary of the extraordinary cultivation of chamber music in Vienna 1900-1950: the outstanding professionals provided models for the Hausmusikanten. Names important amateurs, such as Theodor Hämmerle, cellist, whose circle played together 844 times.

345. Samohyl, Franz. "Kammermusik in Wien," in *Österreichische Musikzeitschrift,* xiii (1958), 187.
     A very brief comparison between Viennese chamber music groups and foreign ones. Foreign groups dedicate themselves to chamber music at an early age and begin their careers with government help. Viennese groups are formed by performers who first establish solo or orchestral careers and who struggle to get performances. The result is that Viennese groups are more musically universal.

For guitar chamber music in Vienna, see {134}.

346. Heller, Friedrich C. and Peter Revers. *Das Wiener
     Konzerthaus: Geschichte und Bedeutung 1913-1983.*
     Vienna: Wiener Konzerthausgesellschaft, 1983. ML
     246.8 V62W23.1983. 248 pages.
     A history of this important concert hall in Vienna,
     with appendices listing festivals and concerts with
     programs. Many chamber music concerts, some world
     premiers (including Hindemith's String Quartet Opus 32
     in 1932 and Sonata for 4 Horns in 1953), Viennese pre-
     miers, performance societies-series, and photos of
     floor plans of, among other things, the smaller chamber
     halls.

AZERBAIJAN

347. Kuliev, Tokhid. *Azerbaidzhanskaia Kamerno-Instrumen-
     tal'naia i Kontsertnaia Muzyka dlia Smychkovykh In-
     strumentov.* Baku: Azerneshr, 1971. ML 1137.K84.
     126 pages. In Russian.
     A study of chamber and concert music for string instru-
     ments in the Soviet state of Azerbaijan and a list of
     sonatas, piano quartets, string quartets, and other
     chamber music by Azerbaijanis. A history, concentrat-
     ing on genres (sonatas, piano trios, quartets and also
     string concertos). Analysis proves folk roots.

BRAZIL

See {7}.

BULGARIA

348. Krustev, Venelin. *Bulgarian Music.* Trl. Jean Patter-
     son-Alexieva. Sofia: Sofia Press, 1978. HML 196.
     60.6. 308 pages.
     Several chapters on Bulgarian chamber music in terms of
     communist ideology.

349. Stojanov, Penco. "Bulgarian Instrumental Chamber
     Music since 9 Sept. 1944," in Krum Angelov, ed.,
     Sovremennaja Bolgarskaja Muzyka. Moscow: Muzyka,
     1974. RILM 76-5961. In Russian.
     Not seen.

CANADA

350. Adeney, Marcus. "Chamber Music," in Ernest MacMillan,
     Music in Canada. Toronto: University of Toronto
     Press, 1955. ML 205.M3. Pages 114-125.
     Chronicle of 19th- and early 20th-century performance
     of chamber music in (mostly Eastern) Canada and the
     performers. Goes up to 1954. Without footnotes,
     bibliography or other documentation, it will be easy to
     read by the layperson but frustrating to the scholar.

351. Loudon, J.S. "Reminiscences of Chamber Music in
          Toronto during the Past Forty Years," in *Canadian
          Journal of Music*, i (1914), 52-53.
          Brief survey of chamber music in Toronto before 1871,
          then reminiscences from 1871 to 1914, by an amateur
          violinist, of the hardships in organizing chamber
          music. Cellists were hard to find, then became plenti-
          ful. Leads to the Toronto String Quartet (1908ff) --
          the first professional quartet in Upper Canada -- the
          Hambourg Concert Society Trio (1911), and the Academy
          String Quartet (1913). Recalls hearing United States
          quartets (Boston Quintet to the Flonzaley and Kneisel).

352. Bridle, Augustus. "Chamber Music in Toronto," in *The
          Year Book of Canadian Art 1913* (London/Toronto: J.M.
          Dent & Sons, [1913?]), pages 143-148. N 9.Y3.
          A history of chamber music in Toronto, which does not
          go back as far as in Montreal. String quartet playing
          begins only in c.1900, and only takes hold with the
          Toronto Quartet (whose repertory was Beethoven, Mozart,
          Haydn, Dvorak, Arensky, Tchaikovsky, Debussy and Hugo
          Wolf). It was a good, not great, ensemble and had a
          following by a discriminating audience.

353. Canadian Music Centre. *Canadian Chamber Music: Musique
          de Chambre Canadienne*. 2nd ed. Toronto/Montreal/
          Calgary/Vancouver: Canadian Music Centre, 1980. ML
          120.C2C28.1980. ISBN 0-9690836-4-5. No pagination
          (1738 items + indices). 1st ed. *Catalogue of Chamber
          Music Available on Loan from the Library of the Cana-
          dian Music Centre. Catalogue de Musique de Chambre
          Disponible à la Musicothèque du Centre Musical Cana-
          dien*. Toronto: Canadian Music Centre, 1967. 288
          pages, discography, bibliography. In French and
          English.
          A catalogue of chamber music scores, parts and a few
          recordings by Canadian composers, some published, some
          in manuscript. The scores and parts may be borrowed or
          rented but not the recordings. Gives brief biography
          of the composer, title, scoring, movement titles or
          tempos, difficulty, duration, date of composition,
          date, place and performers of premier, recording infor-
          mation (if any), publishing data or manuscript loca-
          tion, and several sentences describing the style,
          program, and/or techniques employed. Includes at the
          end a brief history of Canadian music.

*For a discussion of some Canadian string quartets, see
Horace McNeal's dissertation {514}. For a discussion of
contemporary Canadian sonatas for violin + piano, see
William Lister's dissertation {249}.*

CZECHOSLOVAKIA

See {457} and Fleischhauer {161}.

354. Schwarz, Erwin. "Quartette und Kammerorchester in der Tschechoslowakei," in *Das Orchester*, xv (1967), 197-200.
   Records the amazingly large number of Czech ensembles since World War II. By the early 1950's there were already 11 famous string quartets. Czechs are conservative performers, as opposed to Poles who are avant-garde composers. Starts with the quartets, trios and quintets, then deals with chamber orchestras.

355. Prochazka, Rudolph Ludwig Franz Ottokar, Freiherr von. *Der Kammermusikverein in Prag: Denkschrift zur fünfzigjährigen Gründungsfeier*. Prague: A. Haase, 1926. ML 247.8P6P62. 92 pages + 4 page addenda and corrections for the second printing in January, 1927.
   The history of this chamber music society from its forebears to its founding in 1876 to its 50th year. Discussion of the works and their interpreters: composers, soloists, and ensembles. The Rosé Quartet frequently performed, also Joachim, David Popper, Bohemian and Busch Quartets, Reger, Ševčik, and many others.

356. Boublik, Jan. "Czech Chamber Ensembles," in *Music News from Prague*, no. 6-7 (1977), 4-5.
   A listing in essay form of string chamber groups in Czechoslovakia since World War II. Among string quartets there have been the Czech, Ondricek, Smetana, Vlach, Janáček, Dvořák, Prague, Talich, Panocha, Kocian, and Dolezal. Also some trios listed.

See also Pilka {1526} and Bruun {146}.

DANZIG

357. Kessler, Franz. *Danziger Instrumental-Musik des 17. und 18. Jahrhunderts*. Stuttgart: Hänssler-Verlag, 1979. NYPL JMF81-207 ISBN 3-77510440-2. xiv + 217 (music) + xviii pages.
   The forward gives a history of instrumental music in Danzig, as performed publicly in halls, churches or towers, or privately for weddings, Tafelmusik or for enjoyment with professionals and amateurs mixing. Gives 10 pieces by Danzig composers: sonatas, canzonas, 1 concerto, and some other pieces of chamber music. Large and beautiful illustrations.

DENMARK

See Kai Bruun's Kammermusik {146}, vol. iii, pages 170-178.

358. Kammermusikforeningen. *Kammermusik i Hundrede ar: 1868
     - 5. December - 1968*. Copenhagen: Nyt Nordisk For-
     lag, 1968. ML 1142.K35. 204 pages.
     A history of the chamber music society of Copenhagen on
     its centennial with numerous photos and descriptions of
     its members, performers, concerts, programs, and organ-
     ization. A detailed list of all compositions played
     during the 100 years, alphabetically arranged by compo-
     ser, then title. Also other statistics -- most often
     played works and most often played composers -- no sur-
     prises here. Also a list of performers by instrument
     and alphabetically (includes Grieg, Schnabel, Fritz
     Busch, Anton Svendsen, Carl Nielsen, Hindemith, and
     numerous local persons) -- both members and guests.

359. Fabricus, Lars Borge. *Traek af Dansk Musiklivs His-
     torie m.m. Omkring etatsraad Jacob Christian Fabri-
     cus' Erindringer*. Copenhagen: Nyt Nordisk Forlag
     Arnold Busck, 1975. RILM 76-10405. xii + 603 pages.
     In Danish.
     Investigates mid-19th-century musical life in Copenha-
     gen as revealed in the memoires of Fabricus, Titular
     Councilor of State. Among others sheds light on the
     Vega Chamber Music Society c.1865-1870.

ENGLAND

*David Cox, in "English Chamber Music Since 1700," in Alec
Robertson, ed., Chamber Music {160}, pages 329-356, gives a
brief chronological history with some analysis.*

360. Coates, William. "Early English Chamber Music," in *The
     Canon: Australian Music Journal*, vii (April 1954),
     355-358.
     For the layperson, a brief introduction to English
     consort music c.1580-1628, which explains simply the *In
     Nomine* settings, fantasias, and the instruments they
     were meant to be played on.

See also Oliver Neighbour's The Consort and Keyboard Music
of William Byrd *{779}; Ernst Meyer's* English Chamber Music
{333}, and his Die mehrstimmige Spielmusik *{382}, where
there is also a review of English chamber music for 2 or
more instruments excluding solo and trio sonatas, which
served as a starting point for his study in {333}.*

361. Field, Christopher D.S. "The English Consort Suite of
     the Seventeenth Century." PhD dissertation. New
     College, Oxford, 1970. 3 vols. I: iii + 318 pages;
     II: thematic catalogue and 81 musical examples; III:
     14 fantazia-suites.
     Major scholarly study of this genre of 17th-century
     English music. Discusses the terms "suite" and "sett"
     used in 17th-century England and accepts the term "fan-

tazia-suite" as the modern term for 3-movement pieces
by William Lawes and others (fantasy-alman-galliard or
courante). Considers 3 generations of English consort
suite composers: Coprario (d.1626), William Lawes
(1602-1645), and John Jenkins (1592-1678) and Matthew
Locke (c.1622-1677), but also includes many others.
Criticizes Meyer's almost total neglect of the fan-
tazia-suite and distortions when he does mention them
in passing. Gives a summary of the history of the
suite in the early 17th century, keyboard as well as
consort, with William Brade receiving prominent attention. Gives abundant evidence that the violin was preferred even by Coprario to the treble viol (trios for
violin + bass viol + organ or for 2 violins + organ)
and discusses the organ or continuo part. Analyzes the
the structure and style of the individual movements and
the unity of the 3 movements. Also discusses court-
ayres ("slighter consort dances"). After Locke's *Consort of Fower Parts*, the consort suite declines rapid-
ly, replaced by the French or Lully suite.

*For a detailed analysis of the ensemble fantasias of John
Jenkins, see Robert Warner's dissertation {1037}.*

*The transfer from gamba to violin, mentioned above, is
discussed in more detail in the following:*

362. Evans, Peter. "Seventeenth-Century Chamber Music Manu-
      scripts at Durham," in *Music and Letters*, xxxvi
      (1955), 205-23.
      Eighty different compositions for gamba + continuo, 2
      or 3 gambas + continuo, and 2 violins + continuo. Half
      are anonymous, the rest by Jenkins, Henry Butler, Zam-
      poni and others. While none of the pieces is a master-
      piece, they show collectively the transition from gamba
      to violin in England in the 17th century.

363. Chazanoff, Daniel. "Early English String Chamber Music
      from William Byrd to Henry Purcell." EdD disserta-
      tion. Columbia University, 1964. UMI 65-4720. DA
      xxv.11, pp. 6673-4. 287 pages.
      Uncovers this repertory, traces its stylistic develop-
      ment, and reorients its place in music history. Limit-
      ed to music without keyboard, a3-6. Emphasis on the
      history of the music, its forms and styles, its social
      contexts, the most important composers, and the status
      of viols and violins as performing media. Also consi-
      ders the influence of this music on continental music.

364. Ashbee, Andrew. "Instrumental Music from the Library
      of John Browne (1608-1691), Clerk of the Parlia-
      ments," in *Music and Letters*, lviii (1977), 43-59.
      A scholarly report on 474 consort pieces a2 to a6 by

numerous English composers of the 17th century now in
the library of Christ Church, Oxford.

365. Meredith, Margaret. "Christopher Simpson and the Con-
     sort of Viols." PhD dissertation. University of
     Wales, 1969. RILM 70-1722. 3 vols.: I: x + 157
     pages; II: 238 pages (music); III: 217 pages (music).
     Scholarly, well-documented edition of music. Biography
     of Simpson (c.1605-1669), a detailed account of the re-
     volutionary times in which he lived (a Catholic, Simp-
     son had no position at court), and the musical institu-
     tions in London performing instrumental music. Discus-
     ses the close relationship of instrumental and vocal
     forms in the 16th century but their independence in the
     17th. Considers the fancy by Simpson, Jenkins, Pur-
     cell, Christopher Gibbons, Charles Coleman, and John
     Hingeston; the dances and divisions in which Simpson
     excelled; the viol family of instruments; and the organ
     and other continuo. Although Simpson does not specify
     "viol" in his music, it seems likely that he had this
     instrument in mind since he himself was a virtuoso on
     the instrument and no violin player. The consort is
     solo chamber music.

*See also Don Smithers's "Seventeenth-century English Trumpet
Music" {228}.*

366. Dart, Thurston. "Jacobean Consort Music," in *Proceed-
     ings of the Royal Musical Association*, lxxxi (1954-
     55), 63-75.
     History of viol consort music in England c.1530-c.1680.
     Concentrates on the years 1600-1625, which corresponds
     to *Musica Britannica*, vol. ix. Discusses the fantasy,
     In Nomine, and dances, and the major composers.

*See Ronald Kidd's "The Sonata for Keyboard with Violin
Accompaniment in England (1750-1790)" {234}.*

367. Scott, Hugh Arthur. "London's First Consort Room," in
     Music and Letters, xviii (1937), 379-390.
     Documented history of the first room (in the York
     Buildings on Villiers Street) regularly used for cham-
     ber concerts (vocal and instrumental) and operas.
     While most concerts were primarily vocal, some were
     purely instrumental chamber concerts. Concerts often
     included spoken readings from the classics and dancing.

368. Banfield, Stephen. "British Chamber Music at the Turn
     of the Century: Parry, Stanford, Mackenzie," in *The
     Musical Times*, cxv (1974), 211-13.
     A brief but good introduction to the chamber works of
     Parry (1848-1918), Stanford (1852-1924) and Mackenzie
     (1847-1935) placed in the historical and cultural set-

ting of England from the 1860's. Shows the then
English attitudes to chamber music and the state of the
art.

369. Henderson, Archibald Martin. "Chamber Music in
  Glasgow," in *Musical Memories* (London/Glasgow: The
  Grant Educational Co., 1938), pages 105-112. ML
  416.H475M9.
  Reminiscences of chamber music in Glasgow 1889-1914 by
  an accomplished pianist, professor of music, and lifelong resident of Glasgow. Describes concerts, performers, repertory, and the concert halls. Organized his
  own concerts there.

370. Antcliffe, Herbert. "The Recent Rise of Chamber Music
  in England," in *The Musical Quarterly*, vi (1920), 12-
  23. 4 portraits.
  Notes the increased interest in chamber music over the
  preceding 20 years owing to the development of local
  rather than foreign talent (caused by the World War).
  Establishment of clubs at Oxford and Cambridge as well
  as several in London, and their awarding annual prizes
  in composition of chamber music for strings. Creation
  of a Free Library of Chamber Music. Brief discussion
  of some new English chamber works by Frank Bridge, H.
  Waldo Warner, John B. McEwen, Eugene Goosens, and
  others. Emphasis on string quartets.

371. Stonequist, Martha Elisabeth. "The Musical Entente
  Cordiale: 1905-1916." PhD dissertation. University
  of Colorado, 1972. UMI 73-18597. DAI xxxiv.3A, p.
  1317. 384 pages.
  A detailed account of this English concert society's
  activities in promoting early 20th-century French music
  in Manchester and other English cities. Written by the
  granddaughter of the Executive Secretary of the society
  in Manchester, it contains many documents (programs,
  letters) to show the extent of French music performances in England and to evaluate the influence which
  it has had in England. No specific mention of chamber
  music in the abstract, but presumably chamber music was
  an important feature.

For other studies of English chamber music in the 20th cen-
tury see Peter Alexander's article {323}, and Tatton's
dissertation {320}.

FINLAND

See Marcia Anderson's "A Survey of Twentieth-Century Finnish
Clarinet Music..." {326}.

FRANCE

*See Edward Lockspeiser's "French Chamber Music since 1700,"
in Alec Robertson, ed.*, Chamber Music *{160}, pages 357-389;
Lionel de La Laurencie's* L'École Française de Violon de
Lully à Viotti *{236}; and Gisela Beckmann's* Die franzö-
sische Violinsonate mit Basso Continuo von Jean-Marie
Leclair bis Pièrre Gaviniès *{237}. For the history of the
Clarinet sonata in France in the late 18th century, see Dale
Kennedy's "The Clarinet Sonata..." {846}.*

372. Mellers, Wilfrid. "The String Quartet in France," in
     The Listener, lxi (1959), 570.
     An attempt to explain French string quartets of the
     19th and 20th centuries in terms of the social-politico
     aspects of French history. Many interesting, novel
     ideas are suggested, but because of the brevity of the
     article and the absence of any analysis of the pieces
     mentioned, the ideas are underdeveloped, seemingly in-
     accurate, and sometimes confusing. For example, the
     political climate of Austria was more conducive to the
     egalitarianism of the string quartet than was that of
     France, which explains why there are so many Austrian
     and so few French quartets; Austrian aristocratic auto-
     cracy was partially "undermined by war and foreign
     domination" while the French aristocracy "exploded in
     action rather than in art."

373. Schwarz, Boris. "French Instrumental Music between the
     Revolutions (1789-1830)." PhD dissertation. Colum-
     bia University, 1950. UM 50-366. DA x.4, p. 250.
     370 pages.
     Discusses musical life in Paris 1789-1830. Concen-
     trates on the mostly neglected symphony, the brilliant
     violin concerto, the shallow virtuosic piano piece, and
     finally chamber music. French chamber music was pri-
     marily the *quatuors brillants* dominated by the virtuo-
     sic first violin and piano works accompanied by other
     instruments. Boieldieu's piano trio (c.1800), Cherubi-
     ni's string quartets as well as Reicha's quintets for
     winds (1818-1820) were the exceptions.

374. Cooper, Jeffrey. *The Rise of Instrumental Music and
     Concert Series in Paris 1828-1871.* Ann Arbor: Uni-
     versity Microfilms International Research Press,
     1983. ML 497.8P4C6. ISBN 0-8357-1403-9. xiv + 387
     pages. PhD dissertation. Cornell University, 1981.
     A major source book for information on 19th-century
     French performers and performances of chamber music.
     Through discussion and charts, documents the concert
     halls, programs, seasons and audiences, performers,
     concert conditions, and concert series in France.
     Special attention given to the major concert series,
     among which Société Alard-Franchomme (= Société de

Musique de Chambre), Société des Derniers Quatuors de
Beethoven, Société des Quatuors de Mendelssohn, Séances
Populaires, Gouffé Séances, Lebouc Séances and to a
much lesser extent Société Sainte-Cécile are of special
importance for the history of chamber music. Draws
from the newspapers. Beethoven predominates. Of music
before 1800 only Haydn, Mozart and Boccherini get much
attention.

375. Landormy, Paul. "La Musique de Chambre en France de
     1850 à 1871," in *Le Mercure Musical*, nos. 8-9 (1911),
     37-50.
     Saint-Saëns (*Harmonie et Mélodie*) stated that before
     1871 there was no chamber music in Paris, but contrary
     to such popular belief there was considerable chamber
     music in Paris 1850-1871. Reviews in some detail the
     situation before 1850, listing numerous French compo-
     sers of chamber music (Baillot, Urhan, Dancla, Alard)
     and the interest in Mozart, Haydn, and Beethoven.
     Gives programs. Continues after 1850 with Lalo, Saint-
     Saëns himself, and many others). Describes chamber
     music societies.

Max Favre's Gabriel Fauré's Kammermusik *{878} gives a good*
summary of chamber music in 19th century France.

376. Augé de Lassur, Lucien. *La Trompette: un Demi-Siècle*
     de Musique de Chambre. Paris: Ch. Delagrave, 1911.
     ML 270.8P2L2. vii + 237 pages.
     An extraordinarily flowery chronicle of an amateur
     chamber music society "La Trompette" founded and direc-
     ted in Paris by Émile Lemoine. Amateurs and profes-
     sionals perform semi-privately for an invited audience.
     Repertory dwells on Beethoven, Mozart and Mendelssohn,
     gradually on others also. Saint-Saëns was an active
     participant. Enthusiasm and devotion carried when
     technique was wanting. Singers also included. A good
     source for the practice of chamber music in Paris at
     the time (1860-1910), who attended, who performed, what
     they played -- detailed names and some personal com-
     ments on the persons. Later performers included Pablo
     Casals, Harold Bauer, Wanda Landowska, Alfred Cortot,
     Serge Koussevitsky (on bass), and as always Saint-Saëns
     (who is a subscriber to the book). Promotes contem-
     porary chamber music by Debussy, Koechlin, and D'Indy.

377. Gut, Serge. *La Musique de Chambre en France de 1870 à*
     1918. Paris: Honoré Champion, 1978. ML 1127.G9.
     ISBN 2-85203-048-9. 239 pages.
     A well-documented history of French chamber music of
     this period, with strong emphasis on the social-eco-
     nomic position of the genre and on the individuals who
     were important. Appendix includes a list of winners of
     the chamber music prize of the Academy of Beaux Arts

1860-1918 and a list of most of the composers of chamber music in France 1870-1918 and their most important chamber works. Full of facts and details. Limited to music a2-a10. The main figures: Franck, Fauré, Saint-Saëns, and Debussy. Lists the principle political, social, economic, philosophical and musical reasons why 1870-1918 was a particularly good time for chamber music. Compares French to foreign situations. Considers French concert societies and professional chamber ensembles, concert halls, schools, and genres (sonatas, trios, quartets, and so on). Useful bibliography organized by topics.

378. Pleyel, Wolff et Cie, Maison. *La Musique de Chambre: Seances Musicales Donnés dans les Salons de...* I: Paris: Gautherin & Cie, 1893; II-X: Paris: Pleyel, Wolff, 1894-1903. NL V415.6. 10 vols. 1894 is the smallest: xxv + 207 pages; 1900-1901 combined volume the largest: iv + 413 pages.
A huge collection of concert programs published with index giving a clear picture of public chamber music in Paris 1894-1903.

379. Mari, Pierrette. "La Musique de Chambre," in *La Revue Musicale*, no. 316-317 (1978), 145-151.
Considers chamber music in France since the end of World War II. Characterized by unlimited exploitation of complexities to the detriment of expression, but at the same time it is vibrant and diverse. It has flourished because orchestras have shut themselves off to modern composers. Among composers briefly discussed are Messiaen, Alfred Déseclos, Jean-Louis Martinet, Serge Nigy, André Casanova, Honegger, Koechlin, Boulez, Jolivet, Daniel Lesur, and Alexandre Tansman. A selective list of chamber music by post-war Frenchmen.

GEORGIA SSR

380. Taktakisvili, Georgij. *K Istorii Strunnogo Kvarteta i Fortepiannogo Trio v Gruzzi.* Tbilisi: Ganatlebn, 1973. RILM 74-2977. 127 pages. In Russian.
A contribution to the history of the string quartet and piano trio in Georgia. Describes the rise of instrumental chamber music and the formation of chamber ensembles in Georgia up to 1966. Includes analysis of the music and stylistic traits of the ensembles.

381. Saverzasvili, Aleksandr, ed. *Sbornik Trudov Tbilisskoj Konservatorii*, vol. 5. Tbilisi: Konservatorija, 1977. RILM 77-2276. 296 pages.
Two articles in this collection from the Tbilisi Conservatory discuss chamber music: M. Kanceli, "Form in the String Quartets of Dmitrij Sostakovic" and D. Oj-

kasvili, "The Laws of Harmony and their Relationship to
the Chamber Works of Georgian Composers." Not seen.

GERMANY

*For an overview see Andrew Porter's "Modern German Chamber
Music," in Alec Robertson, ed., Chamber Music, {160}, pages
390-409.*

382. Meyer, Ernst Hermann. *Die mehrstimmige Spielmusik des
     17. Jahrhunderts in Nord- und Mitteleuropa, mit einem
     Verzeichnis der deutschen Kammer- und Orchestermusik-
     werk des 17. Jahrhunderts,* in *Heidelberger Studien
     zur Musikwissenschaft,* Band II. Kassel: Bärenreiter,
     1934. ML 467.M4M4. 258 pages. Expansion of PhD
     dissertation. University of Heidelberg, 1930.
     A scholarly study of the genres of chamber and orches-
     tral music of the 17th century in 3 regions of Europe:
     England, France-The Netherlands, and Germany, with the
     first two serving as prelude to the study of Germany.
     Excluded are pieces for 1 or 2 treble instruments with
     continuo. Notes strong English influence in northern
     Germany and Italian influence in southern Germany. At
     the beginning of the century German ensemble music was
     primarily suites, whereas after 1648 the number of Ger-
     man collections of polyphonic sonatas spectacularly
     grows to satisfy the new surge of collegia musica out-
     side religious circles. A history of the German sonata
     and its structure. Two types: organically unified ones
     as in Rosenmüller, and inorganically, ununified ones as
     in Weckmann. The latter are clearly chamber music, not
     orchestral. By c.1675 the sonata was the leading form
     of multi-instrument music in Germany, but then a de-
     cline set in as the Italian trio and solo sonata took
     over. The German sonata had a dominating top voice,
     but still an equal voice among equals, whereas in the
     Italian trio or solo sonata the top voice was *the*
     voice, the others not at all equal to it. Also, the
     instrumental concerto idea, occasionally present before
     in Germany, becomes common by the end of the 17th cen-
     tury. Gives ample proof that the vast majority of Ger-
     man sonatas until the 1670's was chamber music and only
     afterwards, under French overture and Italian concerto
     grosso influences, became orchestral. The fugue is an
     outgrowth of middle- and north-German sonata types of
     both Weckmann and Rosenmüller. Concludes with 3 exten-
     sive catalogues of multi-instrumental music in 16th-
     and 17th-century England, in 17th-century Belgium-The
     Netherlands-France-Poland-Scandinavia, and in Germanic
     countries 1590-1710.

383. Gottron, Adam. *Mainzer Musikgeschichte von 1500 bis
     1800,* in *Beiträge zur Geschichte der Stadt Mainz,*

Band 18. Mainz: Stadtbibliothek, 1959. ML 278.8
M35G6. vii + 236 pages.
Provides information on chamber musicians with a Mainz
connection, such as Philipp Friedrich Buchner (1614-
1669), Pachelbel, Froberger, Heinrich Anton Hoffmann
(1770-1842), Georg Friedrich Fuchs (1752-1821), and
Johann Franz Xaver Sterkel (1750-1817). Much chamber
music of the 18th century survives in archives in Rome,
Uppsala, and elsewhere.

*For a special study on the important Mannheim region of
Germany, see Roderich Fuhrmann's* Mannheimer Klavier-
Kammermusik *{307}.*

384. Riemann, Hugo. "Mannheimer Kammermusik des 18. Jahrhunderts," in *Mannheimer Kammermusik des 18. Jahrhunderts: I. Teil: Quartette und Quintette (ohne Klavier),* in *Denkmäler der Tonkunst in Bayern,* Jg. 15,
Bd. 27. (Leipzig: Breitkopf & Härtel, 1914), pages
ix-xxiii. M 2.D4.
Points out that symphonies are only one development
from orchestral trios or quartets, and chamber trios
and quartets could be played solo or orchestrally.
Demonstrates Stamitz's leading role in his 6 Opus 1
trios, then discusses each of the other principle composers: Richter, Filtz, Toëschi (whose quartets develop
from the trio sonata), Johann Baptist Wendling (flutist, 1720-1797), Schobert (use of a cantabile keyboard), and many others. Considers different genres,
the subordinate role of the keyboard, the special
importance of woodwind chamber music for England, and
the growth of idiomatic cello parts.
    *II. Teil: Trios und Duos (ohne Klavier und mit obli-
gatem Klavier),* in *Denkmäler der Tonkunst in Bayern,*
Jg. 16, Bd. 28. Leipzig: Breitkopf & Härtel, 1915.
A catalogue (pages xi-xxv) of published chamber music
by Mannheim composers, beginning with anthologies, then
listed by composer, then by date or opus number. Includes scoring, keys, publishing data, and locations.
Followed by a thematic catalogue (pages xxvii-lxiii),
alphabetically by composer.

*The discussion of the importance and history of divertimenti
is mostly found under Austria, but the following is a
contribution:*

385. Hausswald, Günter. "Der Divertimento-Begriff bei
Georg Christoph Wagenseil," in *Archiv für Musikwissenschaft,* ix (1952), 45-50.
Discusses a group of keyboard divertimenti in Dresden
manuscripts. Not concerned with chamber music *per se,*
but since divertimenti are important for the development of classical chamber music types, this discussion
is relevant.

386. Engländer, Richard. *Die Dresdner Instrumentalmusik in der Zeit der Wiener Klassik*, in *Uppsala Universitets Arsskrift 1956:5*. Uppsala: A.-B. Lundequistska Bokhandeln/ Wiesbaden: Otto Harrassowitz, [1956]. AS 284.U7.1956 no.5.
   Dresden experienced an upswing in interest in chamber music in the 1780's, partly as middle-class music and partly as court music (both mostly in private concerts and Hausmusik). Important musicians played there, such as Carl Stamitz (1787) and Mozart (1789). Gives a list of 126 composers and many works in the court records 1777-1810. Singles out the Swedish-German Johann Gottlieb Naumann for a special study; a pupil of Tartini, Naumann was a violist and wrote especially string duos and trios in Italy, then operas, but from 1786 on published chamber music in Dresden. Also considers Naumann's pupils Joseph Schuster (1748-1812), Franz Seydelmann (1748-1806), and Anton Teyber (1754-1822), who explored new dimensions of sonata form in chamber music and approached Beethoven's style (Neefe, Beethoven's teacher in Bonn, was first the teacher of Seydelmann in Dresden). Discusses piano music and the chamber music of Hasse and Christlieb Siegmund Binder (1723-1789). Scholarly book but also for the layperson.

For a discussion of chamber music in Berlin see Karla Höcker's Hauskonzerte in Berlin *{167}.*

387. Krause, Emil. *Die Entwicklung der Kammermusik*. Hamburg: C. Boysen, 1904. 785.7 K868e. vi + 53 pages.
   Mostly outdated but valuable for a history of chamber music in Hamburg 1800-1904. Cites specific performers and dates and gives sample programs. Divides the 19th century into 3 periods: 1800-1863; 1863-1874; and 1874-1904, based on local personalities and societies.

388. Sievers, Heinrich. *Kammermusik in Hannover: Historisches, Gegenwärtiges -- Kritiken, Meinungen: unter besonderer Berücksichtigung des Wirkens der Hannoverschen Kammermusik-Gemeinde 1929-1979*. Tutzing: Hans Schneider, 1980. ML 1129.S54. xiv + 213 pages + 9 pages of photos.
   A history of chamber music in Hannover from the 18th century to the present, with emphasis on the last 50 years. Recalls the numerous traveling virtuosos and chamber musicians in the very active musical life of the city, and gives many programs. Discusses the problems caused by the Nazis and gives a picture of musical life in Germany during World War II. Lists of performances of the chamber works of Hindemith, Berg, Schoenberg, Webern and Bartók in Hannover. Hannover was not a provincial city but in the center of chamber music activity in Germany. Many visiting chamber ensembles, after having performed live in Hannover,

were then recorded in the same hall by Deutsche Gramo-
phon Gesellschaft, which is located in Hannover.

389. Stütz, Gerhart, ed.   "Kammermusik," in *Musikpflege in
     Stadt und Bezirk Gablonz an der Neisse* (Schwäbisch-
     Gmünd: Lentelt-Gesellschaft, 1975), pages 56-60.   HML
     196.45.83.
     Traces string quartets from 1891 to 1940, including the
     Podwesky Quartet.

390. Hofmeyer, Günter.   *Kammermusik des 20. Jahrhunderts.
     1. Zyklus: Deutsche Kammermusik 1918-1933*.   Berlin:
     Deutsche Akademie der Künste zu Berlin, Sektion
     Musik, [1967].   ML 1129.H72.   22 pages, 9 portraits,
     3 facsimiles of programs.
     A good introduction to the history of German chamber
     music 1918-1933 reflected in the battle of the social
     classes of the time.   A Marxist interpretation of Ger-
     man history since the end of the 19th century: a compo-
     ser is judged on his awareness of the sufferings of the
     masses and his ability to demonstrate that in his crea-
     tive output.   Considers historical climates, sources of
     20th-century music (Wagner-Brahms influence, Strauss,
     Reger, Mahler, Debussy, who did not understand Marxist
     reality; and Stravinsky, Bartók, Busoni and non-musi-
     cians Picasso and Cocteau, who did), music and society,
     and the personalities and schools of 1918-1933 (special
     emphasis on Hans Eisler, and Schönberg).   Chamber music
     was the main vehicle of new music in the 1920's, not
     because orchestras and other concert groups were hos-
     tile to new music or could not afford it but mainly
     because the new composers, disgusted with the capital-
     istic world, sought new expressions where content was
     most important -- the inner substance of music, which
     traditionally is the realm of pure chamber music.

391. Bennwitz, Hanspeter.   "Die Donaueschinger Kammermusik-
     tage von 1921 - 1926."   PhD dissertation.   Freiburg
     i.B.: 1962.   247 pages.
     Not seen.

392. McCredie, Andrew.   "Modern Chamber Music from Strauss
     to Stockhausen," in *Canon: Australian Music Journal*,
     xvi (1962-1963), 3-12.
     A survey of the chamber works of Richard Strauss, Hans
     Pfitzner, Max Reger, Paul Hindemith, Wolfgang Fortner,
     Hans Werner Henze, Giselher Klebe, and Karlheinz Stock-
     hausen, with passing reference to a number of others.
     For the student or layperson.

393. Schneider, Frank.   *Das Streichquartettschaffen in der
     DDR bis 1970*, in *Beiträge zur musikwissenschaftlichen*

Forschung in der DDR, Band 12. Leipzig: VEB Deutscher Verlag für Musik, 1980. ML 1160.S3. 178 pages.
Includes lists of East German string quartet compositions 1945-1970 (including earlier quartets dating back
to 1914 by composers in the DDR after 1945). After
aesthetic, methodological and sociological background
to the subject, a collection of historical essays in 5-
year time segments on string quartet writing in the DDR
from Max Butting to Friedrich Goldmann and other
"moderns." Analyzes their principal string quartets
primarily to find to which school or type the piece
belongs. Ends with a thesis on why string quartets
have been popular and successful in the DDR -- its
transition from a middle-class to a socialistic art.

394. Nündel, Heinz. "Kammermusik," in *Forum: Musik in der
DDR*, in *Deutsche Akademie der Künste,* Arbeitshefte
ix, ii (Berlin: Henschelverlag, 1972), 77-94. RILM
73-2098.
"Surveys the development of chamber music and the impe-
tus it received from the principles of socialist realism in terms of its expressive means and formal outlines. Chamber music is no longer the province of the
privileged class. The strength of its bonds to socialist music culture lies in amateur, domestic, and school
performances."

*See also Manfred Vetter's remarks on chamber music in the
DDR {457}.*

ITALY

*For some aspects of early Italian chamber music, see Milton
Swenson's "The Four-part Italian Ensemble Ricercar from 1540
to 1619" {330}. For an outline of Italian violin sonatas in
the 17th century, see Willi Apel, "Studien über die frühe
Violinmusik" {222}.*

395. Schlossberg, A. "Die mehrstimmige Spielmusik des 17.
Jahrhunderts in Italian." PhD dissertation. Univer-
sity of Heidelberg, 1932.
No description available.

396. Schenk, Erich. "Beobachtungen über die modenesische
Instrumentalmusikschule des 17. Jahrhunderts," in
*Studien zur Musikwissenschaft: Beihefte der Denkmäler
der Tonkunst in Österreich*, xxvi (1964), 25-46.
Demonstrates that there was indeed an independent Modena School. Shows that this Modena School of instrumental music extends back to the beginning of the 17th
century. But with Uccellini's tenure there (1641-1665)
it is really a school. Important for trio sonatas.
Thereafter Giovanni Maria Bononcini (1673ff), G.B.

Vitali (1674ff) and others who became their pupils led
Modena. Analyzes some of their works.

397. Bridges, David Merrell. "Musica da Camera in Rome:
     1667-1700." PhD dissertation. George Peabody
     College, 1976. UM 76-21617. DAI xxxvii.4A, p. 1861.
     203 pages.
     Concerned with "all types of music that are not litur-
     gical or not a part of a large dramatic work," and
     finds an abundance of such music in Rome 1667-1700.

*The most nationalistic study of Italian string quartets is
Fausto Torrefranca's "Avviamento alla Storia del Quartetto
Italiano" {185}.*

398. Untersteiner, Alfredo. "Musica Istrumentale da Came-
     ra," in *Gazetta Musicale di Milano*, 1 (1895), 76-78.
     Points to the lack of interest in chamber music in
     Italy because of a preoccupation with opera, and notes
     that only 1 Italian publisher, no longer in business,
     had published chamber music scores. Yet such works are
     extremely important, and German publishers have pro-
     vided scores. Lists important works, mentioning that
     Verdi's quartet is frequently performed in Germany and
     almost never in Italy.

399. Oleson, Orval B. "Italian Solo and Chamber Music for
     the Clarinet -- 1900-1973: an Annotated Bibliogra-
     phy." DMA dissertation. University of Missouri at
     Kansas City, 1980. UMI 81-07086. ix + 176 pages.
     A list by composer of pieces for clarinet a1 to a8 by
     Italian composers. Appendices give the list by title,
     by scoring, and chronologically. Introduction explains
     methodology. Annotations include the composer, title,
     publishing data, range, duration, and further commen-
     tary. 88 chamber pieces (+ 8 solo clarinet works).

MOLDAVIA SSR

400. Miljutina, Izol'da. "Instrumental Chamber Music:
     Concerning a National Style," in *Evgenij Kletinič,
     ed., Muzykal'naya Kul'tura Moldavskoi*. Moscow:
     Muzyka, 1978. RILM 78-894. In Russian.
     Not seen.

THE NETHERLANDS

401. Wessem, Constant van. *Het Musiceeren en Concerteeren
     in den Loop der Tÿden*. Amsterdam: De Spieghel, 1929.
     ML 60.W468. 159 pages.
     A well-written, undocumented study of the development
     of ensemble music from the 16th to the 20th centuries,
     with special emphasis on the Netherlands. A few refer-
     ences to music before 1500. Not confined to our defi-

nition of chamber music; includes any situation when 2 or more persons get together to make music, and this entails vocal as well as instrumental music, chamber as well as orchestral, and such different genres as string quartet and jazz. Emphasizes the different private and public locales for such groups and the influences of England, Germany, Italy and France on Holland.

402. Caughill, Donald I. "A History of Instrumental Chamber Music in the Netherlands during the Early Baroque Era." PhD dissertation. Indiana University, 1983. UMI 84-6785. DAI xliv.12A, p. 3534. 561 pages. Identifies and evaluates "the constituents of the Dutch repertory for instrumental chamber ensembles produced during the early portion of the seventeenth century." Finds 68 works, of which 48 survive, which are described, classified, and analyzed. Includes the sociological nature of chamber music at the time, and concludes that this repertory is a combination of foreign and domestic stylistic elements.

403. [Bunge, Sas, + Rutger Schoute.] *60 Years of Dutch Chamber Music: 1913-1973*. Amsterdam: Stichting Cultuurfonds Buma en Stichting Nederlandse Muziekbelangen, 1974. ML 120.N4B85. 32 pages. In English, Dutch, and German.
List of chamber works organized by genre from trios to sextets, with title, scoring, date of writing, duration, publisher, recordings, premier, a facsimile of 2 pages of the score, titles of the movements, and commissions or prizes. Comments on the origins and basic structure of each piece. Biographies of each of the 50 composers, with portraits. Summary index at end.

NEW ZEALAND

404. Turnovsky, Fred. "Chamber Music in New Zealand," in *The Canon: Australian Music Journal*, vi (Dec. 1952- Jan. 1953), 229-32.
An overview of the flourishing of chamber music in New Zealand after 1948. Points out the problems facing the continued visits of foreign chamber music artists and the lack of local performers. Concerned only with public performances and its wide audience appeal.

NORWAY

405. Kortsen, Bjarne. *Modern Norwegian Chamber Music*. Haugesund: n.pub., 1965. 2nd ed. 1969. MT 140.K657. 1969. xiii + 174 pages.
Includes solo as well as ensemble instrumental music. Presents biographies of 10 composers, an assessment of their total output, bibliography, and analysis of the more important chamber works. An opening essay "A

Brief History of Chamber Music in Norway" from the
early 19th century shows how women were barred from
participating and the influence of Grieg and Ole Bull.

406. _____. *Contemporary Norwegian Chamber Music*.
Bergen: Edition Norvegica, 1971. MT 140.K654. iv +
235 pages. Reproduced typescript with typing
mistakes.
A continuation of the author's *Modern Norwegian Chamber
Music*. An essay on the four generations of contemporary Norwegian composers, then an exposé on 20 such composers arranged alphabetically, with biographies,
bibliographies, and analysis of one or two important
chamber compositions. The lengthy analyses are of motives, rhythms and tonality. Nineteen of the composers
also in {407}.

407. Norsk Komponistforeing (The Society of Norwegian Composers). *Contemporary Norwegian Orchestral and Chamber Music*. Oslo: Johan Grundt Tanum Forlag, 1970.
ML 120.N6N7. 386 pages. Supplement I, 1972. ML
120.N6N7.suppl. 88 pages.
List of the works of 76 Norwegian composers who belong
to Norsk Komponistforeing, many of whom have written
chamber music. Information includes composer's dates
and a very brief biography, most composers's portraits,
titles, scoring, publisher (or manuscript), number of
movements, duration, first performance, and recording.
Chamber works listed collectively on pages 324-344.

POLAND

408. Poszowski, Antoni. "Polnische Instrumentale Kammermusik in der ersten Hälfte des 18. Jahrhunderts,
dargestellt am Beispiel der 'Sonata' von S.S.
Szarzynski," in Eitelfriedrich Thom, ed., *Musikzen-
tren in der ersten Hälfte des 18. Jahrhunderts* (Magdeburg: Rat des Bezirkes, 1979), pages 15-23.
Not seen.

409. Spóz, Andrzej, ed. *Kultura Muzyczna Warszawy Drugiej
Polowy xix Wieku*. Warsaw: Pánstwowe Wydawnicturo
Naukowe, 1980. ISBN 83-01-00491-6. In Polish.
In an account of music life in Warsaw in the 19th cen-
tury, gives a few pages to chamber music (pages 234-
38). Names some composers and performers and gives
photos of the Trio Wirtuozów Polskich (1897) and
Quartet Smyczkowy Stanislava Barcewicza (1892).

410. Pietrachowicz, Juliusz. "Polish Chamber Music for
Brass Instruments since 1945," in *Journal of the
International Trombone Association*, vi (1978), 3-5.
After a brief history of Polish brass chamber music
from ancient times (12th century) to the present, a

list of contemporary works. Composers names and
addresses at end.

ROMANIA

411. Berger, Wilhelm Georg. *Ghid Pentru Muzica Instrumen-
    tala de Camera.* Bucharest: Editura Muzicale a
    Uniunii Compozitorilor din Republica Socialista
    Romania, 1965. ML 1100.B47. 415 pages. In
    Romanian.
    An overall history of chamber music from the early
    Renaissance (briefly) to 1965, with a final chapter
    devoted to the history of Romanian chamber music in the
    19th and 20th centuries.

RUSSIA
See also U.S.S.R.

*For an overview see Andrew Porter's "Russian Chamber
Music," in Alec Robertson, ed., Chamber Music {160}, pages
410-421. For an important discussion of Russian chamber
music by Gerald Abraham, see Nicholas Kilburn's Chamber
Music and its Masters in the Past and in the Present {165}.
See also Bruun's Kammermusik {146}, iii, 153-169.*

412. Raaben, Lev Nikolaevich. *Instrumental'-nyi ansambl' v
    Russkoi Muzyke.* Moscow: Muzyka, 1961. ML 1137.R2.
    476 pages. 164 musical examples. In Russian.
    A basic history of Russian chamber music from 1800 to
    1917. [See {423} for the same author's history of
    Soviet music.] Includes all types of chamber music as
    well as vocal chamber music from pre-Glinka to the re-
    volution. Mentions also performers, but the main in-
    terest is with composers and the place of their chamber
    music in 19th-century Russia. Glinka, Tchaikovsky,
    Glazunov, Arensky, Rachmoninof, and Taneiev get the
    most attention.

413. Seaman, Gerald. "The First Russian Chamber Music," in
    The Music Review, xxvi (1965), 326-37.
    An analysis of some early Russian chamber music (mostly
    string quartets) from the end of the 18th century into
    the mid-19th century, including works of Ivan Ivanovich
    Vorobёv (1776-1838), Ferdinand Titz (1742-1810), D.S.
    Bortnyansky, and A.A. Aliabev. All were influenced
    primarily by foreign art forms, but all also incorpor-
    ated Russian folk tunes and romances. Well documented,
    with leads for the scholar who wishes to go more deeply
    into the subject.

414. _____. "Amateur Music-Making in Russia," in
    Music and Letters, xlvii (1966), 249-259.
    Documents a very active chamber music life in the noble
    homes of 18th-century Russia. The classical chamber

music of Italy, France, Germany and England was very
popular, especially string quartets, and also popular
were chamber music arrangements of opera arias.
Mentions many composers of chamber music popular in
Russia -- the Mannheimers, Pugnani, C.P.E. Bach,
Giardini, Abel, Vanhal, among others -- and dwells
somewhat on the chamber music of Mozart, Haydn, and
Beethoven in Russia. Landowners had their own chamber
music performed by serfs whom they had trained in the
art by sending them to Italy as youngsters. Chamber
music also performed at the homes of poets and artists,
professors and writers. Glinka and his successors were
brought up on this rich enthusiasm for chamber music.

415. Sinjavskaya, L. "The Origin of the Russian Quartet,"
     in Nina Vol'per, ed., *Tradicii Russkoi Muzyki xvii-
     xix vv* (Moscow: Gosudarstvennyi Muzykal'no-Pedagogi-
     ceskii Institut Imeni Gnesinyh, 1978). RILM 78-2444.
     Not seen.

*A description of chamber music clubs and concerts in Russia
1760's-1804 is in Anne Mischakoff's book {1048}. For a
description of the Russian Chamber Brass School, see David
Reed's dissertation {873}, and for a study of 20th-century
Russian cello music see Mary Dresser's dissertation {248}.*

416. Altmann, Wilhelm. "Die Kammermusik der Russen," in
     Die Musik, vi.3 (1906-1907), 28-40.
     Points to the huge amount of chamber music coming out
     of Russia -- almost more than out of Germany and France
     together. Gives a survey, mentioning Glinka and ex-
     cluding almost all of Anton Rubinstein (as being too
     non-Russian). Starts really with Nicolaus Afanasieff
     in 1860, who evokes a Russian character (melancholy
     from folk music, tenderness from quick changes in emo-
     tions, and dance rhythms in unusual meters). Prefer-
     ence for variations and string quartets. Discusses
     chamber music from 1860 to 1905 by genre (string quar-
     tets, string trios, string quintets, and so on,
     including sonatas and 1 work with winds).

417. Nerody, Ivan. "Russia's Work in Chamber Music," in
     Musical America, xiv (May 18, 1912), 23.
     Notes that Russian chamber music dominates the field of
     international composition. Not a history but an out-
     line of its general character. Dismisses Glinka's and
     A. Rubinstein's chamber music as either inferior or not
     Russian, then goes into detail with Nicolas Afanasi-
     eff's first string quartet "Volga" (1860), a tone poem,
     which is more impressive for its rhythm than its har-
     mony. Contrasts the Moscow and St. Petersburg schools.

SOUTH AFRICA

See {49}.

SPAIN

418. Russell, Craig H. "An Investigation into Arcangelo
Corelli's Influence on Eighteenth-Century Spain," in
Current Musicology, no. 34 (1982), 42-52.
A scholarly study demonstrating the popularity of
Corelli's music in 18th-century Spain and showing
specific Spanish arrangements of Corelli sonatas.
Draws on Spanish theoretical writings.

419. Sanchez, Richard Xavier. "Spanish Chamber Music of the
Eighteenth Century." PhD dissertation. Louisiana
State University, 1975. UMI 76-12938. DAI xxxvi.
12A, p. 7725. xiii + 298 pages.
First, a discussion of the history of Spain in the 18th
century and of Farinelli, D. Scarlatti, and Boccherini,
all of whom lived extensively in Spain. Then a discussion of Spanish composers of chamber music during the
second half of the 18th century. The principal types
were solo and trio sonatas, duets for treble instruments, and string quartets. The leading composers were
Manual Canales, José Herrando, Francisco Manalt, Juan
Oliver y Astorga, Juan Pla, José Pla, Manual Pla,
Antonio Soler, Antonio Ximenez, and Nicolas Ximenez.
Their works compared with the prevailing Viennese works
of the time: the Spanish reveal a mixture of Baroque
and Classical styles but only rarely any typical
Spanish folk idioms. Appendix contains a list of all
known Spanish composers of chamber music, their works,
and where the music can be found.

*For chamber music as practiced in the House of Alba, see
Subirá's study {1575}.*

420. Subirá, José. "La Música de Cámera en la Corte
Madrileña durante el Siglo XVIII y Principios del
XIX," in *Anuario Musical*, i (1946), 181-194.
A brief account of chamber music at the courts of Fer-
nando VI, Carlos III and Carlos IV in the second half
of the 18th century where chamber music flourished.
The Spaniards there are basically forgotten, but not so
the foreigner Boccherini. In 1769 he dedicated his
Opus 8 quartets to Carlos's brother Luis and in 1770
his Opus 9 quartets to Messieurs les dilettantes de
Madrid. Gives other documentation to show an active
chamber music life at court and among Madrid society.
Discusses Boccherini's rival Gaetano Brunetti. Gives
many names and some brief biographical information of
18th-century Spanish composers and publishers whose
works are in the Biblioteca Nacional in Madrid and in

the Palacio Nacional de Madrid. An introduction, since many details are omitted from the study.

421. Castro y Serrano, José de. *Los Cuartetos del Conservatorio: Breves Consideraciones sobre la Música Clássica.* Madrid: Centro General de Administracion, 1866. ML 315.8M13C18. 220 pages.
An introduction to chamber music, especially string quartets, for mid-19th-century Spaniards who have become aware of it through a series of concerts of quartets at the conservatory in Madrid. Discusses the structure, form, essence and history (Haydn, Mozart and Beethoven) of the quartet and compares these 3 composers in an essay to Leonardo da Vinci, Rafael, and Michelangelo. A final chapter considers the future of Spanish music, which must be firmly rooted in the science and tradition of Western music. A good picture of the state of chamber music in mid-19th-century Spain by an intelligent and probing writer.

For discussion of 3 20th-century Spanish violin + piano sonatas, see Laura Klugherz's dissertation {1122}.

SWEDEN

422. Wallner, Bo. *Den Svenska Sträkkvartetten: Del I: Klassicism och Romantik,* in *Kungl. Musikaliska Akademiens Skriftserie,* No. 24. Stockholm: Kungl. Musikaliska Akademien, 1979. ML 1160.W34. ISBN 91-85428-12-4. 170 pages. 55 musical examples.
A history of Swedish quartets, from Anders Wesström (c.1720-1781) and Joseph Martin Kraus (1756-1792) to Algot Haquinius (1886-1966) and Edvin Kallstenius (1881-1967), with analyses of their music.

423. Brodin, Gereon. "Svensk Kammarmusikbibliografi," in *Ur Nutidens Musikliv,* v (1924), 24-31, 66-68, 94-102, and 120-123.
A catalogue of 18th- to 20th-century Swedish chamber music systematically organized by whether it is without or with piano, then by size of the ensemble, instrumentation, and finally alphabetically by composer. Gives title, scoring, and publisher (in those few cases when not in manuscript). Items are in the Musikaliska Akademiens Library, the Royal Library, and the Uppsala Library, but items in Lund are not included. Includes winds and strings. At the end a brief listing of less-well-known composers.

424. Hedin, Einar. *Mazerska Kvartettsällskapet 1849-1949: Minnesskrift pa Uppdrag av Sällskapets Styrelse.* Stockholm: Lindbergs, 1949. ML 1142.8.S8M35. 129 pages.

A detailed history of a quartet society in Stockholm named after Johan Mazer (1790-1847), written to commemorate the society's centennial in 1949. The membership performed the music itself, but on rare occasions outside professionals would come to give concerts, such as Leopold Auer in the 1860's. Discusses the programs, the membership, and the organization of the society.

425. Föreningen Svenska Tonsättare. *Förteckning över Svenska Kammarmusikverk.* Mimeographed, 1940. ML 120.S8 F52. 16 pages + supplement of 3 pages.
   Alphabetical list of Swedish composers of chamber music born from the mid-19th century to the early 20th century and a chronological list of the titles under genre under each composer. Includes title, publisher, and duration.

426. Broman, Sten. "Salomon Smiths Kammarmusikförening," in *Musikrevy*, xv (1960), no. 7, 231-232.
   In the season 1959-1960 the Smiths Kammarmusikförening was the oldest continual concert society for chamber music in Scandinavia. Started in 1909 in Malmö, it was originally called Malmö Kammarmusikförening, from 1920 to 1928 the Sydovenska Kammarmusikförening, and named after Smith in 1928. Smith was a patron (a pharmicist) who played second violin or viola. Contains a brief account of the various foreign and domestic groups which the society brought to Malmö and Lund.

427. Hellquist, Pers-Anders. "Svensk Kammarmusik i Dag," in *Musikrevy*, xvi (1961), no. 7, 239-41.
   Not seen.

SWITZERLAND

428. Eder, Leo. "Hausmusik in Basel," in *Schweizerische Musikzeitung*, xciv (1954), 230-233.
   Reminiscences of personal experiences of playing Hausmusik (chamber music) over a 50-year period in Basel. Reveals customs (such as, it was considered rude for many years to play without a jacket on) and gives some advice.

429. Staehelin, Martin. "Basels Musikleben im 18. Jahrhundert," in *Die Ernte: Schweizerisches Jahrbuch*, xliv (1963), 116-141.
   Points out that although famous Swiss composers and concerts are a matter of the present, they did not exist in the past. Basel, for one, had a flourishing Hausmusik in the 18th century. It grew out of the strong tradition of singing of psalms at home and in school. Students organized Collegia Musica in the 17th century before Germans did, and these developed in some cases into concert societies. Goes into detail on

groups found in 1692 and following, where singing was
important. In 1708 professionals were admitted to it.
Singing seems less important later in the 18th century,
when orchestras and trios were in the private homes.
Evidence of considerable taste and awareness of the
best music of the day, even if in other cases the
quality was not so good.

430. Schanzlin, Hans Peter. *Basels private Musikpflege im
     19. Jahrhundert*, in *Basler Neujahrsblatt*, no. 139.
     Basel: Helbing & Lichtenhaln, 1961. Harvard Swi
     28.1.3. 58 pages.
     After a brief survey of Hausmusik in Basel from the
     Middle Ages to 1800, a detailed study of its practice
     there in the 19th century. While in the past the
     church, the few educated people and the privileged ones
     furthered musical life, in the 19th century it was
     democratized -- for everyone -- thus public concerts,
     music societies, public music schools, and middle-class
     Hausmusik. As Hausmusik grew in the early 19th cen-
     tury, so did a new repertory for it: simple pieces and
     arrangements. At first Haydn and Mozart were popular,
     but not Beethoven. Shows vocal and piano as well as
     chamber music and discusses specific professional and
     amateur musicians and homes where chamber music was
     performed and describes repertory and audiences. Based
     on many documents. Male-dominated, except for female
     singers and a special visit by Clara Schumann.

                        UKRAINE S.S.R.

431. Kon'kova, Galina. "Certy Novogo v Prelomlenii i Raz-
     vitii Zanrov v Ukrainskoi Muzyke 60-70 Godov." PhD
     dissertation (theory). Kiev, Institut Iskusstvo-
     vedenija, Fol'klova i Etnografii Akademii, 1978.
     RILM 78-3052. 28 pages. In Russian.
     Discusses symphony, chamber, cantata, and oratorio in
     Ukrainian music 1960-1978, with special attention to
     the use of folk material.

432. Borovik, Nokolai. "Development Trends in Instrumental
     Chamber Music," in Ivan Ljašenko, ed., *Muzykal'naya
     Kul'tura Ukrainskoi SSR* (Moscow: Muzyka, 1979). RILM
     79-849. In Russian.
     Not seen.

                          U.S.S.R.

     *See also Armenia, Azerbaijan, Georgia, Moldavia, Russia,
               Ukraine, and Uzbek.*

433. Raaben, Lev Nikolaevich. *Sovetskaia Kamerno-Instru-*
     mental'naia Muzyka. Leningrad: Muzyka, 1963. ML
     1137.R23. 340 pages. 47 musical examples.
     A history of Soviet chamber compositions from 1917 to
     1963. Treats Russia first, then many of the republics
     individually: Ukraine, Belorussia, Moldavia, Georgia,
     Armenia, Azerbaijan, and so on. A continuation of
     {412}.

434. _____. *Mastera Sovetskogo Kamerno-*
     Instrumental'nogo Ansambliia. Leningrad: Muzyka,
     1964. ML 1137.R22. 180 pages. 16 portraits of
     chamber groups.
     A history of Soviet chamber performing ensembles from
     1917 to 1964, including chamber orchestras. Deals with
     4 different periods and the major groups in each:
     period of revolution, 1920's, 1930's-1940's, and after
     1945 to 1964. String quartets were the most popular,
     so the author concentrates on them.

435. Leszczyńska, Elzbieta. "Radziecka Muzyka Kameralna,"
     in *Prace Specjalne Państwowa Wyzsza Szkola Muzyczna w*
     Gdanásku, viii (1975), 43-52. RILM 78-5304. In
     Polish, with Russian summary.
     Notes the decline in interest for chamber music in the
     U.S.S.R. following the revolution, then studies some
     chamber music by Myaskovsky, Prokofiev, Shebalin, and
     Shostakovich.

436. Ratskaia, TSetsiliia Samoilovna. *Sovetskaia Kamernaia*
     Muzyka. Moscow: Znanye, 1965. ML 1137.R3. 80
     pages.
     First gives the West European roots of U.S.S.R. chamber
     music, then goes into the Soviet period. Stresses the
     necessity of lyricism and the importance of chamber
     music as a link between nations. Concentrates on
     Myaskovsky and Shostakovich. A third of the book deals
     with vocal chamber music. For the layperson.

437. Petrushanskaia, Remma Eosefovna. *Kamernaia Muzyka,* in
     Novoe v Zhizni, Nanke, Tekhnike, seria "Iskustvo,"
     No. 9. Moscow: Znaneia, 1981. NX 6.N6.1981. no.9.
     48 pages.
     For the layperson, an introduction to the history of
     chamber music in the West, in 18th-century and 19th-
     century Russia, and in the Soviet Union (half the
     book). Defines chamber music as musica da camera, by a
     limited number of performers, intimate, opposed to
     opera and church music.

See Lev Ginsburg's "Die Kammermusik in der modernen Musik-
praxis: nach dem Erfahrungen der sowjetischen Interpreta-
tionsschule" in {457}, pages 23-35.

438. Boelza, Igor. "New Soviet Chamber Music," in *Tempo*,
     xii (Sept. 1945), 40-41.
     Brief descriptions of Glière's String Quartet No. 4,
     Myaskovsky's String Quartet No. 9, Shebalin's String
     Quartet No. 6 and a Sonata for Violin + Cello (claims
     to be the first such work ever written by a Russian),
     and Shostakovich's String Quartet No. 2.

439. Uspenskij, Vladislav, and Abram Jusfin. "Sovremennaja
     Tema v Tvorcestva Leningradskih Kompozitorov," in
     Sovetskaja Muzyka, iv (April, 1975), 26-35. In
     Russian.
     Contemporary themes in the works of Leningrad compo-
     sers. Among other topics considers chamber genres in
     the music of Leningrad composers.

440. Blagoj, Dmitrij, "Trends in Performance Practice of
     Soviet Chamber Music," in Vladimir Grigor'ev and Vla-
     dimir Natanson, eds., *Muzykal'noe Ispolnitel'stro, X*
     (Moscow: Muzyka, 1979). RILM 79-1608. In Russian.
     Not seen.

               UNITED STATES OF AMERICA

General

*For a chronological history with some analysis for the lay-
person, see David Drew's "American Chamber Music," in Alec
Robertson, ed., Chamber Music {160}, pages 321-328.*

441. Phelps, Roger Paul. "The History and Practice of Cham-
     ber Music in the United States from Earliest Times up
     to 1875." PhD dissertation. University of Iowa,
     1951. DD xviii (1951), p. 220. 2 vols. xx + 991
     pages.
     In its day the most exhaustive study of American cham-
     ber music; it remains the only good overall history of
     early chamber music in the United States despite many
     details which need updating. Three epochs: before
     1800, 1800-1849, and 1850-1875. Each epoch divided
     into regional studies (I: New England, South Atlantic
     Coast, and Middle Atlantic states; II: the same, with
     Middle West; III: same as II, with South extended to
     Texas). Appendices include valuable documentation,
     such as catalogues of important collections, represen-
     tative programs, 12 musical examples by Americans,
     bibliography (extensive, though dated, and includes
     many important non-musical sources), and indices of
     composers, performers and titles. Shows that chamber
     music existed in New England in the 17th century.

18th Century

Other important introductions to early American chamber
music are Anne Schaffner's "The Modern String Quartet in
American before 1800" {191}, Marie Stolba's "Evidence for
Quartets by John Antes, American-Born Moravian Composer"
{525}, John Barker's "The Birth of Chamber Music in Ameri-
ca," in The American Record Guide, *xxxii (1965), 34-6, and*
Harry Hall's "The Moravian Wind Ensemble: Distinctive
Chapter in America's Music" {293}.

18th to 19th Centuries

442. Hermann, Myrl Duncan. "Chamber Music by Philadelphia
     Composers 1750 to 1850." PhD dissertation. Bryn
     Mawr College, 1977. UMI 78-01379. DAI xxxviii.9A,
     p. 5114. 334 pages.
     A historical and biographical account of chamber music
     in Philadelphia 1750-1850. Among the composers are na-
     tives Charles Hommann and William Henry Fry, non-Phila-
     delphian Benjamin Franklin, and foreigners John Gualdo,
     Jean Gehot, John Christopher Moller, Raynor Taylor,
     Benjamin Carr, Philippo Trajetta, Leopold Meignen,
     Robert Bremner, J.C. Schetky and R. Shaw. Also in-
     cludes patrons, performers and critics.

18th to 20th Centuries

443. Warburton, Thomas. "Historical Perspective of the
     String Quartet in the United States," in *American*
     Music Teacher, xxi (January 1972), no. 3, 20-22, 37.
     An interesting, yet unscholarly and inconsistent ac-
     count of American quartets and quintets from the late
     18th century to 1960's. Concerned with acceptance of
     quartets by the public and with the compositions them-
     selves. Full of names of composers, performers and
     reviewers. Shows the growth of the American string
     quartet from a European-dependent to an American work.
     Describes a few compositions in detail by Chadwick,
     Mason, Griffes, Ives, Gershwin, Cowell, Carter, and Mel
     Powell.

444. Smith, Nancy Page. "The American String Quartet, 1850-
     1918." MA thesis. University of North Carolina at
     Chapel Hill, 1949. 143 pages.
     Not seen.

445. Shirey, Betty. "String Quartets by American Born Com-
     posers." MM thesis. University of Cincinnati, 1949.
     74 pages.
     Not seen.

19th Century

446. Olsen, Deborah M. "Music in an American Frontier Com-
     munal Society," in *Brass Bulletin*, No. 33 (1981), 49-
     58, No. 34 (1981), 13-22, and No. 36 (1981), 64-77.
     In English with French and German translations.
     An interesting chronicle of the city of Aurora, Oregon,
     founded in 1856 by the religious leader William Keil.
     Music was important from the start, and although only a
     small portion of the article concerns chamber music, it
     is testimony to the diffusion of high level chamber
     music in frontier North America in the 1860's.

*See James Starr's "A Critical Evaluation of Performance
Style in Selected Violin Works of Nineteenth Century American Composers" {247}.*

19th to 20th Centuries

447. Tuthill, Burnet Corwin. "Fifty Years of Chamber Music
     in the United States 1876-1926," in *The Musical
     Courier*, xcix (Aug. 17, 1929), 8, (Aug. 24), 15, 20,
     (Aug. 31), 10.
     A review of this important phase of American chamber
     music, beginning with a brief account of groups before
     1876: the Mason-Thomas Quintet of New York (1855-1868)
     and the Mendelssohn Quintet Club of Boston (1849-1898).
     Then the Kneisel Quartet (1885-1917) of Boston, the
     Flonzaley Quartet, Berkshire Quartet (= Kortschak
     Quartet of Chicago), the Elshuco Trio, Gustav
     Dannreuther Quartet, New York String Quartet, Chicago
     Quartet, Gordon Quartet of Chicago, Musical Art Quar-
     tet, Zoellner Quartet of Los Angeles, Olive Meade Quar-
     tet (all female), Marianne Kneisel Quartet, Margulies
     Trio, Sittig Trio, Tollefsen Trio, Barrere Ensemble,
     Longy Club, New York Chamber Music Society, and more.
     Gives members's names and some dates. Also describes
     some amateur home chamber music in New York, Washing-
     ton, D.C., Cincinnati, and Mt. Airy, N.C. Unaware of
     chamber music before George Chadwick's Quartet No. 1
     (1878), but discusses American compositions for chamber
     groups by Arthur Foote, Mrs. H.H.A. Beach, Camille
     Zeckwer, Jacobi, Carpenter, Griffes, John Powell,
     Loeffler, Rubin Goldmark, and the expatriots Roy
     Harris, Roger Sessions, and Aaron Copland (then living
     in France).

448. Rice, Edwin T. *Musical Reminiscences*, ed. Margaret
     and Helen Rice. New York: Friebele Press, 1943. ML
     429.R5A3. 123 pages.
     A collection of finished and not-so-finished essays by
     a leading patron and witness of chamber music in the
     northeast United States during the first 3 decades of
     the 20th century. Includes information on the Kneisel

Quartet, Edward J. de Coppet, and the Flonzaley Quartet
(especially about a legal battle between the violist
Bailly and the Flonzaleys). The New York Public Library contains this volume together with 5 volumes of
manuscript notes taken at chamber music meetings 1887-
c.1915 in New York (JOG.73-198-Rice-Diaries, in the
Music Special Collections).

20th Century

449. Cadzow, Dorothy. "Contemporary American Chamber
      Music," in *International Musician*, xlvii, no. 10
      (April 1949), 31-33.
      A description of the leading American composers of
      chamber music in the 1940's and mentions some of the
      Europeans who came here before then who have had an
      impact. Mentions support groups: League of Composers,
      Society for the Publication of American Music, National
      Association for American Composers and Conductors,
      Composers' Forum, and National Federation of Music
      Clubs. Lists representative American chamber music.

450. Anon. "Chamber Music by Contemporary American Com-
      posers," in *National Music Council Bulletin*, xiii
      (Jan. 1953), 18-20.
      A modest list of chamber music by Americans available
      in 1953 in print. Organized by genres (strings, wood-
      winds, brass, combinations with piano, and other combi-
      nations) with author, title, scoring, and publisher.

451. United States Information Agency. *Catalogue of Pub-
      lished Concert Music by American Composers.* Washing-
      ton, D.C.: U.S. Government Printing Office, 1964. ML
      120.U5I45. 175 pages; chamber music pp. 91-120.
      Lists by instrument, solo or ensemble, then alphabeti-
      cally by composer. Includes title, scoring, publisher.
      75 composers of string quartets, 37 composers of wood-
      wind quintets, 28 composers of brass duets, trios and
      quartets, and more.

Other aspects of 20th-century American chamber music are
listed or studied in William Bedford's "Elizabeth Sprague
Coolidge..." {1577}, Daniel Gregory Mason's "The Flonzaley
Quartet" {1534}, Roger Chapman's "The American String
Quartet: 1924-1949" {63}, Arno Drucker's "A Chronological
Survey...Trios for Piano, Violin, and 'Cello..." {303},
Theodore Tyska's "Technical Problems in Contemporary
American Violin Sonatas" {251}, Peter Theodore's "A Survey
of Published Sonatas and Sonatinas for Flute by American
Composers since 1920" {252}, Daniel Geeting's "A Comparative
Study of Sonatas for Clarinet and Piano Published in the
United States from 1950-1970" {253}, Mari Hammer's "History
of Louisville's Chamber Music Society" {1580}, and Brian

Walls's "Chamber Music in Los Angeles, 1922-1954: a History
of Concert Series, Ensembles and Repertoire" {1581}.

452. Silliman, A. Cutler. "A Study of Musical Practices in
     Selected American String Quartets, 1930-1950." PhD
     dissertation. University of Rochester, 1954. DD xxi
     (1954), p. 255. 215 pages.
     Discussion of specific structural elements in 19 quar-
     tets by Samuel Barber, William Bergsma, Ross Lee Fin-
     ney, Roy Harris, Walter Piston, Quincy Porter, Walling-
     ford Riegger, Roger Sessions, William Schuman, and Ran-
     dall Thompson. The elements are harmonic texture, to-
     nal texture, cadences, linear procedures, internal form
     and larger forms. These quartets do not depart radi-
     cally from earlier quartets and display "the character-
     istics of contemporary music which are likely to en-
     dure." All are tonal, tertial and quartal harmonies
     prevail, the texture is mainly contrapuntal, continual
     cyclic and organic growth are featured, most movements
     are in traditional large forms, and the frequent use of
     a third progression at cadences is typically American.

                         UZBEK SSR

453. Golovjanc, T. "The History of Chamber Music Perfor-
     mance Practice in Uzbekistan," in Vladimir Plungjan,
     ed., Teoretičeskie Problemy Uzbekskoj Muzyki. Tash-
     kent: University of Tashkent, 1976. RILM 76-4947.
     Not seen.

                         YUGOSLAVIA

454. Rijavec, Andrej. "Novejši Slovenski Godalni Kvartet,"
     in Muzikološki Zbornik-Musicological Annual, ix
     (1973), 87-107. Summary in English.
     Notes that Slovanic composers have made significant
     contributions to 20th-century string quartets, begin-
     ning with Slavko Osterc's Second Quartet (1934), but
     more importantly with Lucijan Marija Škerjanc's Fifth
     Quartet (1945), Ivo Petrič's Quartet (1956), Vilko
     Ukmar's Third String Quartet (1959), and others. These
     quartets demonstrate a wide variety of styles and tech-
     niques including neo-romanticism, neo-classicism and
     much more modern improvising types. Analysis of impor-
     tant characteristics of each of these works.

455. Mětšk, Juro. "Das Streichquartett der sorbischen
     Musikkultur vor 1945: historisch-analytischer
     Überblick," in Beiträge zur Musikwissenschaft, xx
     (1978), 199-218.
     A general explanation of the dearth of great Serbian
     art music and especially chamber music before the 19th
     century and even afterwards. Then discusses and des-
     cribes the string quartet of Korla August Kocor (1822-

1904), the founder of Serbian art music, and the 3
string quartet works of Bjarnat Krawc (1861-1948).
Their absolute worth and nationalistic significance are
also discussed from a Marxist standpoint.

456. Andreis, Josip. *Music in Croatia*, trl. Valdimir Ivir.
Zagreb: Institute of Musicology-Academy of Music,
1974. HML. xv + 416 pages.
Most of the book deals with the 19th and 20th centuries. Includes frequent references to the chamber
music of important Croatian composers such as Milo
Cipra (b.1906), Josíp Slavenski (1896-1955), Krsto Odak
(1888-1965), the violinist Djuro Eisenhuth (1841-1891),
and Ivan Zajc (1832-1914).

CHAPTER III. ANALYTIC STUDIES

AESTHETICS AND DEFINITIONS

Some studies attempt to deal with chamber music's role in aesthetics, or at least to justify chamber music as a proper form of art for humankind. In the course of some of these discussions, basic definitions of the concepts "chamber music," "Hausmusik," "ensemble music" are grappled with.

Definition of chamber music:

457. Pečman, Rudolf, ed. *Colloquium Musica Cameralis Brno 1971*, in *Colloquia on the History and Theory of Music at the International Music Festival in Brno*, Vol. 6. Brno: Cesky Hudebni Fond, 1977. NYPL JMK 75-20 vol. 6. 568 pages.
An important collection of 41 essays, 38 in German and 1 each in English, Russian and French. 5 overall topics: theory, aesthetics and sociology of chamber music; Bohemian chamber music; definition of chamber music; European chamber music; and 20th-century chamber music. Most fit into my definition but some do not. Essentially chamber music is intimate music. All the participants debated the meaning of chamber music, some on the basis of surveys of commonly held definitions of the term by ordinary people.

458. Alain, Olivier. *La Musique de Chambre*, in *Cahiers du Journal Musical Français*, No. 13. Paris: Société Française de Diffusion Musicale, [1955]. NYPL *MG/p.v.273. 48 pages.
Opens with an essay on the essence of the intimacy of chamber music. Then discusses chamber music of the kings of France, the distinction between da camera and da chiesa, and the 20th-century concept of chamber music as secular works for 10 or fewer solo instruments. Finds the listener "imprisoned" by the professional performer and the professional performer "imprisoned" by the listener, rather than the performer and listener as one. The professional depends on mass taste and mass taste is not toward chamber music; therefore one must courageously invite youth to discover chamber music, where the highest realizations of the human spirit are to be found. Reviews instruments used in chamber music and the history of chamber music from the 16th century to 1950. Ends with a systematic list of possible combinations of instruments in chamber music and mentions a few composers who have written for them.

459. Genin, R.E. "Essai d'une Definition de la Musique de
     Chambre," in *La Revue Musicale*, no. 232 (1956), 4-14.
     Brief definition of chamber music as secular, intimate,
     instrumental music distinguished by purity, autonomy,
     and evocation. Included are 19 portraits of chamber
     ensembles (Loewenguth, Barylli, New-Music, Parrenin,
     Pasqual quartets and Quartetto Italiano, and several
     trios, duos and soloists).

Ernst Schmid, in Carl Philipp Emanuel Bach und seine Kammermusik *{535}, defines chamber music as all pieces for 1 or
more melody instruments with or without basso continuo as
well as obligato keyboard with 1 or more melody instruments.
Excludes pieces for 1 or more keyboards, concertos, sinfonias, marches and dance music. Describes musical aesthetics
in Italy, France, Poland and Germany 1730-1780.*

460. Rowen, Ruth Halle. "Some 18th Century Classifications
     of Musical Style," in *The Musical Quarterly*, xxxiii
     (1947), 90-101.
     An important though limited attempt to define the term
     "chamber music," first by location (in which both the
     nature and size of the hall are considered and the kind
     of people who perform and listen are classified), then
     by style (Mattheson used the term "domestic" music no
     matter where it is performed; Scheibe: "it must be
     above all lively and penetrating"; Mattheson continues
     that the most important aspect of chamber music is that
     it is instrumental, whether concerto grosso, overture,
     sonata or suite). Style is much less carefully de-
     fined, and at the end location is regarded as the most
     important. Uses writers almost entirely before 1754
     (Koch, 1802, is the only real exception).

461. Nohl, Ludwig. *Die geschichtliche Entwickelung der Kam-
     mermusik und ihre Bedeutung für den Musiker.* Braun-
     schweig: Friedr. Vieweg, 1885. 2nd ed. Wiesbaden: M.
     Sändig, 1969. ML 1100.N74.1969. v + 140 pages.
     Classic 19th-century study of chamber music. The
     greatest accomplishments in music are symphony, quartet
     and sonata, and Beethoven's examples are the best --
     even carrying respect for German music over the Alps to
     Rome. Everything leads to Beethoven via Mozart and
     Haydn; melody and its expression are the most important
     things in music and clearest in chamber music.

462. Schubert, F.L. "Die Formen der Kammermusik," in *Die
     Instrumentalmusik in ihrer Theorie und ihrer Praxis
     oder die Hauptformen und Tonwerkzeuge der Concert-,
     Kammer-, Militär- und Tanzmusik wissenschaftlich und
     historisch erläutert für Tonkünstler und Musikfreunde*
     (Leipzig: Moritz Schäfer, 1865), pages 129-154. NYPL
     Drexel 3304.

An attempt to present a systematic description of chamber music. Includes solo music and prefers the piano. The main forms correspond to the 4-movement symphony, especially sonata form. Color is important. Considers the aesthetic significance of each of the movements of a 4-movement sonata.

463. Scott, Cyril. "Chamber Music: its Past and Future," in *The Musical Quarterly*, vii (1921), 8-19.
A personal, amusing definition of what is true chamber music by an important English composer. Dislikes Haydn's piano trios and Beethoven's string trios, Brahms's chamber music and Mendelssohn's. Prefers instead the French, Russians, and Chopin for color effects combined with novel musical content. Thus he concludes Ravel's chamber music is the best.

464. Pierce, Edwin Hall. "Certain Questionable Tendencies in Modern Chamber Music," in *The Musical Quarterly*, xi (1925), 261-270.
A somewhat confusing tirade against modern composers who write extremely difficult ensemble music which can be played only by top professionals who work together at it for a long time. Considers the modern piano suitable for chamber music in the large concert hall if it does not conflict with the flow of the strings, but Reger and other moderns obscure the music with piano parts that are too thick. Also, composers have neglected duets and trios without piano. Calls for the modern composer to write true chamber music with modernisms but without absurd technical difficulties.

465. Lemacher, Heinrich, and Hugo Wolfram Schmidt. *Almanach der Hausmusik für Kenner und Liebhaber*. Köln: Hans Gerig, 1958. ML 128.C4L4. 152 pages.
A collection of 31 radio lectures given on Westdeutschen Rundfunk for the layperson, with list of repertory. Of value for aesthetics is his discussion of humor in string chamber music; quotes Goethe and "the philosophers" and then brings in Boccherini's Quintet "La Musica Notturna di Madrid," where the imitation of a serenading guitar by the cellist is cited as humor, and M. Käsmeyer's "Fuge für Streichquartet über 'O du lieber Augustin,'" where the quotation is another instance of humor. See also {752}.

466. Dahlhaus, Carl. *Die Idee der absoluten Musik*. Kassel: Bärenreiter, 1978. ML 3854.D34. ISBN 3-7618-0599-3.
A thorough study of the prevailing 19th- and early 20th-century belief in absolute music, which was not possible before and which is no longer accepted. The chief absolute music c.1800 was the symphony, but by 1870 it was the string quartet -- especially Beetho-

ven's last ones. Considers the ideas of Hanslick,
Wagner, and many German philosophers and writers of the
19th century. Form is essential to absolute music, and
so is a model of what is then expected. Considers the
meaning of the term and its relationship to "program"
music, words, and philosophical concepts.

Chamber music justified:

467. Queux de Saint-Hilaire, L.M.D. *Lettre á M. Adolphe
     Blanc, Membre de la Société Académique des Enfants
     d'Apollon sur la Musique de Chambre.* Paris: Jouaust,
     1870. ML 1100.Q93. 31 pages.
     An essay in tribute to chamber music, a justification
     of it in spite of its lack of glamor, its sustained
     concentration, and its frequent performance by ama-
     teurs. Pays tribute especially to Haydn, Mozart and
     Beethoven, all of whom devoted supreme effort to
     chamber music. Evaluates their instrumental styles
     from a personal, emotional reaction to them: prefers
     Haydn's quartets, Beethoven's symphonies, and Mozart's
     opera arias. Calls on modern composers to return to
     the true art: instrumental music, especially chamber
     music.

468. Boughton, Rutland. "The Future of Chamber Music," in
     The Musical Times, liii (September, 1912), 570-572.
     Notes the absence of really new chamber music (= string
     quartets) since Beethoven and tries to formulate how
     and why chamber music should be revived. Believes
     Wagner was right when he stated that with the choral
     movement of the Ninth Symphony pure instrumental music
     died. Proposes programs and dramatic values be given
     to chamber music.

469. Honegger, Arthur. "In Behalf of Chamber Music," in
     Boston Symphony Orchestra Concert Bulletin (1950-
     1951), 352-4. Originally "Pour la Musique de
     chambre," in *Incantation aux Fossiles.*
     Sees music in its pure state in chamber music: "it is
     there that musical thinking can unfold most truthfully,
     and bring to the one who loves this form of art the
     subtlest and noblest of emotion." Sees more in 2 pages
     of Fauré's string quartet than in all of Berlioz's *Re-
     quiem.* Attacks radio, which ruins youth, music critics
     who shun chamber music reviews, and composers who make
     it too difficult. Proposes that chamber ensembles
     receive grants to encourage new chamber music.

470. Bonavia, Ferruccio. "For Lovers of Chamber Music," in
     Music and Letters, xv (1934), 153-156.
     A brief but passionate statement on the value of cham-
     ber music.

471. Ritter, Frederic Louis. "Chamber Music," in *Musical Bulletin*, i (November, 1880), 184.
A very short but interesting appeal for more chamber music which allows individual expression and imagination. "The ideal symmetry, harmony and unity of the whole form binds [the individual performers] all naturally together without tampering with the necessary, spontaneous free life of the spirit." Condemns orchestral transcriptions of chamber music and sensational pianistic displays as antithetical to the chamber music ideal. The same author, a teacher at Vassar College, appeals in *Musical Standard*, xviii (1880), 378-379, for Americans to put aside their love of the sensational and concentrate on "a more solid, refined and substantial aesthetical development of music," namely chamber music.

472. Betti, Adolfo. "Why Chamber Music?" in *Musical America*, lviii (Feb. 10, 1938), 22-23.
Refutes the assertion that chamber music is music for museums or for old players who, having lost their vitality, can only play in a dull way. Shows that technical problems abound in chamber music, especially bowing which is more difficult than in the virtuosic solo repertory. The young artist can learn more about shading, rhythm, tempo, style, and interpretation from chamber music (primarily string quartets) than from concertos. And most important, the virtuoso learns humility in chamber music. Includes photos of 8 late-19th-century and early 20th-century chamber groups (St. Petersburg Quartet, Bohemian Quartet, Joachim Quartet, Flonzaley Quartet, Danreuther Quartet, Mendelssohn Quintette Club [1849], Mason-Thomas Quintette, and Kneisel Quartet).

The string quartet as the ideal chamber music:

473. Antcliffe, Herbert. "Why Quartets?" in *The Musical Times*, xci (1950), 233-234.
Considers why string quartets take precedence over other chamber combinations. Discusses snobbery and proposes several more important reasons why they are preferred: the ideal of 4-voice writing, the intimacy of solo string music without orchestrally extraneous sounds, and the family of string sound from soprano - alto - tenor - bass not duplicated in other instruments. Not every quartet is perfect, but in its highest manifestations, the string quartet is perfection.

474. Stahmer, Klaus. "Anmerkungen zur Streichquartettkomposition seit 1945," in *Hamburger Jahrbuch für Musikwissenschaft*, iv, *Zur Musik des 20. Jahrhunderts* (Hamburg: Karl Dieter Wagner, 1980), pages 7-32.

The string quartet has undergone many changes since
1945, but it is wrong to define the genre by one style
alone, that of the 19th century. The essential character of the string quartet has not changed: its unification of 4 like instruments into a totality greater than
its parts, and its privacy, exclusivity and autonim-
ity.

475. Redfield, John. "A Wider Range for Chamber Music," in
     Modern Music, iv (March-April, 1927), 22-28.
     Explains that the relative primitiveness of wind in-
     struments and the perfection of string instruments in
     Haydn's to Beethoven's day inevitably led to string
     chamber music as the highest form of chamber music.
     But since wind instruments have been perfected, they
     too should be used by serious composers of chamber
     music. Discusses various possibilities and points to
     the growth of wind chamber music societies around the
     world. Then goes on to chamber orchestra where winds
     share with strings.

H. Wiley Hitchcock's "The Chamber Music," in Ives: a Survey
of the Music *{1018}, expands the conversation idea into
argumentation of 4 players (in reference to Ives's String
Quartet No. 2).*

Hausmusik:

476. Cherbuliez, Antoine-Elisée. "Hausmusik" in Gottfried
     Schmid, ed., *Musica Aeterna* (Zurich: Verlag Max S.
     Metz, 1948), i, 343-356. NYPL *MD 1948.
     A long essay glorifying the basic concepts of Haus-
     musik. The love of music is the prerequisite for
     Hausmusik, just as the cultivation of Hausmusik
     nourishes the love of music. It takes place in private
     homes no matter what class of people, it involves
     active participation. It is not required to forget
     artistic standards in Hausmusik; indeed, some great
     composers have written it. No one stands out in Haus-
     musik; all are equals. The same writer is more precise
     in his "Hausmusik," in Gesellschaft der Musikfreunde
     Braunwald, ed., *Die Musik im Leben des Menschen* (Basel:
     Gaiser & Haldimann, 1941), pages 218-250. In Hausmusik
     the listener and player are one and the same, which
     eliminates the dichotomy in public performances. Cham-
     ber music and Hausmusik are related: both use small,
     intimate ensembles; but they differ in that chamber
     music is more soloistically oriented, Hausmusik is more
     choral; chamber music is sometimes distinguished from
     theatrical, orchestral and church music, which is more
     important to it than to Hausmusik, where the location
     remains essential. Thus chamber music can be public,
     while Hausmusik cannot.

477. Mies, Paul. "Rund um die Hausmusik," in *Musikhandel*, xvii (1966), 261-262, 317-319, 379-380.
Considers the definition, history and contemporary state of Hausmusik. It is all that is not theatrical or liturgical. It is inevitably a many-faceted type of music satisfying so many different kinds of people -- no longer limited to a few aristocratic Kenner and Liebhaber. Shows that Hausmusik is defined by its location and performers, while "chamber music" is much more ambiguous. "Chamber music style is more free and lively than church style and, since there is no action, more carefully worked out and artistic than theater style." This is a distinction by Quantz, who does not consider "concert style." Form and style, rather than location, determine chamber music.

478. Hayward, John Davey. *Chamber Music for Amateurs: Notes from a Library*, in *The Strad Library*, no. 22. London: The Strad/New York: C. Scribner's Sons, 1923. ML 128.C4H2. vi + 81 pages.
An informal, non-technical, non-scholarly study of chamber music by an amateur musician (physician). Defines chamber music as "compositions for a few instruments, and it does not include music for the voice" (also excludes all solos and duets with piano or organ and all works for more than 8 instruments). Draws on his personal library to guide the reasonably skilled amateur in repertory. Contrasts professionalism and amateurism in chamber music and shows the special place for amateurs.

479. Reissmann, August. *Die Hausmusik: in ihrer Organisation und Kulturgeschichtlichen Bedeutung*. Berlin: Robert Oppenheim, 1884. ML 67.R34. vii + 322 pages.
Explores how music in the home can educate mankind to nobility. To this end first explores how music educates people and then deals with music in the home. Hausmusik includes song, instrumental music, and piano music. The first chapter deals with musical aesthetics; the physical phenomenon of tone and sound are necessary for people's perceptions of the artist's organization of tone and sound, but the latter (perceptions) are independent. Song, because it has greater meaning, is more important for education than instrumental music, which appeals to phantasy. In the latter, a row of beautiful sounds is irritating if it is not controlled by form. A chapter on instrumental music ranks instruments on their proximity in sound and sound production to the human voice; then discusses forms -- the highest is sonata form in duos, sonatas, trios, and quartets, and the lower forms are suites. understand art works, education is necessary. Most effort is spent on vocal music, but in a chapter at the end on instrumental music in the house, concentrates on

marches and dances, which *can* have poetic meaning, then
on variations, and at last on chamber music (as well as
concertos and symphonies and solo piano sonatas). Allows that man's perceptions of the beautiful in music
vary from person to person, but then proceeds to discuss music under the assumption that German art music
is the ultimate. An interesting, intelligent, even if
biased and now dated, book on musical aesthetics as it
relates to Hausmusik and the proper education for
children if they are to come to benefit most from this
conception of what is art music.

480. Salmen, Walter. "W.H. Riehls Gedanken zur Gesundung
     der Hausmusik," in *Hausmusik*, xvii (1953), 169-170,
     172.
     A brief analysis of Riehl's (1823-1897) thought about
     the state of Hausmusik in his own day. Shows how
     Riehl, brought up with chamber music in the home, con-
     sidered Hausmusik in a larger sociological framework of
     the state of the German family and its home. There was
     great danger to the family structure evident in his own
     time, and its disintegration was feared. This would
     lead to national disintegration. Hausmusik was also
     disintegrating into being too virtuosic or too esoteric
     -- too separate from the folk. Thus the state of music
     in the home -- chamber music to a large extent -- mir-
     rors the whole society. Haydn's quartets are the ideal
     Hausmusik since they are the perfect balance between
     simplicity, feeling, and nature. Purity of form and
     thought are the composer's goals, and the modern world
     must be built on those ideals.

481. Dechant, Rudolf. "Besinnliche Gedanken zur Haus-
     musik," in *Musikerziehung*, iii (1949-1950), 134-137.
     The location is not the main criterion of Hausmusik; it
     is the ordinary individual's participation that makes
     it so. The choice of what to play is important --
     something denied when listening is confined to a con-
     cert or radio. Mostly a song to glorify Hausmusik.

482. Valentin, Erich. *Musica Domestica: von Geschichte und
     Wesen der Hausmusik*. Trossingen: Hohner, 1959. ML
     67.V234M. 154 pages, 7 reproductions of paintings.
     An excellent introduction to the history of Hausmusik
     (the term) and its implications, including distinctions
     between salon music (primarily for the piano) and Haus-
     musik and between *Dilettanten* (does not care about pro-
     fessionals and receives enjoyment from the playing, not
     from the music in an abstract sense) and *Liebhaber*
     (concerned with the essence of music and strives for
     professional perfection). In the history of Hausmusik
     shows that although the term was coined by Johann Rist,
     Frommer gottseliger Christen alltägliche Hausmusik
     (Lüneburg: 1654), it does not recur until the 19th

century. Music serving the function of Hausmusik before then was performed by *Liebhaber*; Goethe introduces the terms *Hausgesang* and *musikalische Hausübung* c.1807. Hausmusik is mentioned in the 1830's, though not with the identical meaning it assumed later; W.H. Riehl (in works like {312} and {1061}; see {480}) is the first to treat it in its modern sense: music for private homes, no audiences. It is exclusively a German concept. Concerned with the present situation where people have become passive listeners instead of active performers.

See Ludwig Finscher's "Hausmusik und Kammermusik" {166}.

483. Vetter, Oskar. *Warum and wie spielen wir Kammermusik? Fragen und Antworten eines Dilettanten.* Vienna: Ludwig Doblinger, 1938. ML 1100.V48 87 pages.
A defense of dilettantism. The dilettante does not recognize difficulties inherent in things and always tries to do what he or she does not have the ability to do (Goethe). Expression is the most important thing in music -- the more intense the expression, the better the music. Pure instrumental music grew in expression from the canzona to the post-Haydn quartet. Melody is the principle vehicle of expression, but rhythm and harmony also serve. This expression the dilettante appreciates and is achievable in chamber music. Melody is absent in old polyphony, individuals do not express but only join a group to express (ceremonial music); different from Haydn, Mozart and Beethoven where homophony conquers polyphony, dynamic conquers static, active listening replaces passive listening. This classical chamber music is good for dilettantes who have the possibility to express personal feelings by recreating the emotional melodies of Haydn and his successors's chamber music. This is the one chance to become artists, creators of art. The dilettante plays with the freshness of inspiration, while the professional tames the inspiration with technical controls. This is especially so in string quartets, not so much in piano + another instrument (sonatas), because of the equality in importance and expression of each of the 4 players. This answers the "Why" ("Warum"). "How" ("Wie") is answered by the expression, which is equally important with the musical thought. Concerned only with string trios, quartets, quintets, sextets, and octets. Cites Hans von Bülow: interpretation should be correct, beautiful and interesting. Correct means rhythmically coordinated with the others. The first violin must determine tempos after studying the piece enough to know what tempos bring the melody to full expression. Gives other advice to players, also when a piano is present; dilettantism does not mean ignorance and unpreparedness. The more experienced the player, the more he/she knows how to phrase properly and

balance properly. Beautiful means good intonation, clean technique, and full tone. Correct depends on understanding, intelligence, but beautiful does not -- stupid people can play beautifully. To play beautifully one needs training of muscles, exercise, yet intelligence can assist in it up to a point. Beautiful requires intonation and attention to the other players. Only when the technical things are certain can the players concentrate on musical matters: the ideal is not always obtainable. Therefore, it is best to play easier pieces. Interestingly, the personality of the player is expressed. The dilettante has a duty -- in Vienna especially in 1938 -- to carry on "the spirit of German chamber music."

484. Spranger, Eduard. *Rede über die Hausmusik.* Kassel: Bärenreiter, 1955. 780.13 Sp75. 41 pages.
A lecture by a philosophy professor on the essence of Hausmusik. Hausmusik has 3 requisites: lovers (Liebhaber) of art, an intimate circle of friends or relatives, and good feeling. A charming, amusing book, which champions the concept and practice of Hausmusik. Conscious of the changing home conditions of the 20th century, emphasizes the importance of bringing young people into the fold, and stresses that Hausmusik is played by Liebhaber for the sheer enjoyment of the playing and not for any possible extra-musical meanings.

Sociology of chamber music:

485. Ferguson, Donald N. *Image and Structure in Chamber Music.* 1st ed. Minneapolis: University of Minnesota Press, 1964. Reprint New York: Da Capo, 1977. ML 1100.F47.1977. ISBN 0-306-77415-1. xiii + 339 pages, 49 musical examples.
Thought-provoking psychological analyses of the effect of music on people (as in the author's *Music as Metaphor*), concentrates here on the chamber works of Haydn, Mozart, Beethoven, Schubert, Mendelssohn, Schumann, and Brahms (but also confronts briefly nationalistic, American, 20th-century, and pre-Haydn chamber music). Despite misinformation and misconceptions on structural and historical facts as well as a strong personal bias, there are many ideas here that a scholar could develop further, such as what constitutes emotion or image in intimate music, or expression versus design (Romanticism versus Classicism).

486. Adorno, Theodor W. "Kammermusik," in *Einleitung in die Musiksoziologie, zwölf theoretische Vorlesungen* (Frankfurt/M: Suhrkamp Verlag, 1962), English trl. by E.B. Ashton, "Chapter 6: Chamber Music," in *Introduction to the Sociology of Music* (New York: The Seabury

Press; a Continuum Book, 1976), pp. 85-103. ML 3797.
1.A3413. ISBN 0-8164-9266-2.
Studies the social role of chamber music, which is
antithetical to bourgeois life-style of self-indulgence
and competition. Chamber music assumes a polite relationship with each musician subservient to the whole,
and as long as noblemen and the bourgeoisie avoided
money-making occupations outside working hours, chamber
music was possible. The physician is a significant
example of this; he shuts out his medical practice when
he is at home so that he can enjoy chamber music.
Considers chamber music in light of German idealism,
and attacks subjective ideas in chamber music. The
dichotomy is between external and private aspects of
chamber music. As a private medium the composer (especially Beethoven, Brahms and Schönberg) could concentrate on structure without regard to monumentality;
chamber music is critical, unemotional, and anti-ideo-
logical. Believes that Schönberg's First Chamber Symphony is introvertial chamber music turned against
extrovertial concert audiences; its success, based on
the development of single tunes and their parameters,
led to the end of the hegemony of the string quartet,
dependent on themes and motives. This corresponds to a
change in social conditions. Nowadays white-collar institutions have replaced middle-class leisure; thinks
the new society is anti-intellectual, plastic, anti-
chamber music, though statistics are not actually
known. A penetrating essay for layperson and scholar,
student and performer.

See Wolfgang Ruf's "Die Kammermusik in der Musiklehre der
18. Jahrhunderts" in Fleischhauer {161}, pages 17-22, which
traces the change from the aristocratic concept of music as
handiwork to the middle-class idea of a work of genius, as
evinced in Mattheson's writings and resulting in the string
quartet as perfect synthesis. See also Klaus Stahmer, "Zur
Frage der Interpretation von Musik: eine musiksoziologische
Modellstudie dargestellt an dem 1. Satz von Beethovens
Streichquartett op. 130" in Pečman {457}, pages 81-99.

487. Dahlhaus, Carl. "Brahms und die Idee der Kammer-
      musik," in *Neue Zeitschrift für Musik*, cxxxiv (1973),
      559-563.
      "The idea of chamber music originated in the aristo-
      cratic culture of the 16th-18th centuries and was taken
      over by the middle-class culture of the 19th century."

488. [Schaul, J.B.] *Ueber Tonkunst, die berühmtesten Ton-*
      künstler und ihre Werke, in Briefen zur Bildung des
      Geschmacks in der Musik. Karlsruhe: Gottlieb Braun,
      1818. ML 60.U32. Erster Brief, pages 1-19.
      On chamber music (= string quartets), discusses Pleyel,
      Boccherini, Mozart, and Haydn. There are 6 kinds of

audiences for chamber music: those who like any kind of
music, those who think of themselves as well-travelled
and therefore have more experienced ears, superficial
players of instruments, those who specialize in one
genre of music and are of not bad taste but who are too
critical, doctors of music who play reasonably well and
who are always ready to explain and give their opinion
about the music, and those who without prejudice or
suffering enjoy the honor and joy of art without
showing off how much they know unless it is well researched and thought-out. Prefers the last. Interesting especially for its date; for example, states that
to hear Pleyel play his own chamber music is much
better than to hear others play it.

489. Dahlhaus, Carl, editor. *Studien zur Trivialmusik des*
     19. Jahrhunderts, in *Studien zur Musikgeschichte des*
     19. Jahrhunderts, Band 8. Regensburg: Gustav Bosse
     Verlag, 1967. ML 196.D32. 227 pages.
     A collection of 14 essays by different authors (the
     forward and 2 essays by Dahlhaus himself) on trivial
     music, which is the repertory of 19th-century dance
     halls, promenade concerts, salons and variety theatres.
     It was music of the day -- direct, without deep emo-
     tions, perfect for the new 19th-century industrial
     middle class. It implies a negatived value, and this
     prejudice against it has led to neglect in musicologi-
     cal studies until this volume, where it is analyzed in
     great depth. It becomes difficult to precisely define
     and evaluate kitsch vs. art, yet "aesthetic judgments
     are insupportable if they are not buttressed through
     technical analyses of compositions." Trivial is a
     necessary but not sufficient condition of kitsch. The
     progression V-I is trivial (banal) if emphasized, but
     kitsch when it is made too dramatic, too pretentious.
     Careful theorizing about salon music (which includes
     the deep, true expressive music of the masters) and
     Hausmusik (where trivial music is more important) in
     the 19th century.

490. Bujic, Bojan. "Chamber Music in the Twentieth Century:
     Cultural and Compositional Crisis of a Genre," in *The*
     British Journal of Aesthetics, xxii (1982), 115-125.
     Composers of the 19th and 20th centuries turned to
     chamber music to escape from the requirements of con-
     temporary bourgeois society for concert, symphonic, and
     operatic music. Recognizes some validity in Adorno's
     criticisms of contemporary music but finds he goes too
     far. Considers Schoenberg, Berg and Bartók in detail.
     After the war the essentials of chamber music -- in-
     wardness, absence of rhetorical accent, complexity of
     compositional means -- have been reduced to only the
     third: complexity. Since 1945, chamber music has been
     used for ideological purpose, denying the intimacy and
     independence essential to it. Composers have tried too

hard to communicate in chamber music and thereby have become enslaved in the ideas they try to communicate. Only Milton Babbitt and Ligetti have survived as chamber composers.

491. Heuss, Alfred Valentin. *Kammermusikabende: auf welche Weise kann Kammermusik dem Volk geboten werden? Erläuterungen von Werken der Kammermusikliteratur.* Leipzig: Breitkopf & Härtel, 1919. MT 140.H29. xxiv + 152 pages.
A collection of 24 program notes written during World War I for concerts of chamber music in Alberthalle in Leipzig. Published here for people who, for lack of opportunity to hear orchestral concerts, will be hearing chamber music instead. An introductory chapter tackles the question: Is chamber music possible for the masses? The surprisingly successful concerts in Leipzig suggest an affirmative answer. If one gives the central ideas or images of a work to the masses, the masses grab on to such ideas and images and come to like the music, no matter how difficult. Their ears are honed through regular listening, so that chamber music is as accessible as orchestral music. The rest of the book deals with notes to the Leipzig programs.

492. Fellerer, Karl Gustav. "Carl Reinecke und die Hausmusik," in Ursula Eckart-Bäcker, ed., *Studien zur Musikgeschichte des Rheinlandes,* iii, *Beiträge zur rheinischen Musikgeschichte,* Heft 62 (Köln: Arno Volk, 1965), pp. 103-109. ML 55.S88.
First explains Reinecke's (1824-1910) lifelong concern for education for the Hausmusikanten and then goes into some detail into the actual instruction Reinecke used to educate students who were not to become professional but rather to become proficient enough to enjoy Hausmusik. Based on his *Die Musik im Hause: was wollen wir spielen?* (Leipzig: F.E.C. Leuckart, 1886). Reinecke believed piano instruction to be essential but also recognized the importance of string instruments in their concern with intonation. Students must learn techniques, musicianship, and sight-reading. Warns against using Haydn and Mozart for teaching pieces since the student is likely to forever after have a block against them as great music. He is generally against salon music as tasteless but prefers elegant movements to teach children how to play and appreciate elegance. Reinecke's recommended pieces and methods remained basic in Germany c.1860-1914, when other kinds of music (return to Baroque, for example) and recordings and radio began to change the nature of Hausmusik. Reinecke recognizes chamber music as important for Hausmusik and he recommends graded works for violin + piano, cello + piano, and piano + violin + cello. He avoids string quartets, however, and chamber music with

winds. Vocal music decreases in importance as the
Sangvereins increase; he limits it to duets for women.
In this last Reinecke differs from August Reissmann,
*Die Hausmusik in ihrer Organisation und kulturge-
schichtlichen Bedeutung* {479}, who considers song an
essential ingredient of education for Hausmusik.

ANALYTIC METHODS

*Studies that are primarily written to codify or verify a
particular analytic method sometimes use a specific chamber
work or group of chamber works as the vehicle for the exposé. Since most of these studies can also be included in
the next section under the study of specific works, only a
representative sampling is given here. For additional
analyses of 19th- and 20th-century chamber music, see Arthur
Wenk's* Analyses of Nineteenth-Century Music, *in MLA Index
and Bibliography Series, No. 15 Second Edition: 1940-1980
(Boston: Music Library Association, 1984), 83 pages. ML
118.W43.1984. ISBN 0-914954-29-6. 1st ed, 1976. And*
Analyses of Twentieth-Century Music: Supplement to Second
Edition, *in MLA Index and Bibliography Series, No. 14
(1984), 132 pages. ML 118.W462.1984. ISBN 0-914954-28-8.*

Traditional, pre-20th-century theory:

493. Daube, Johann Friedrich. *Der musikalische Dilettant:
     eine Abhandlung der Kompositionen.* Vienna: Johann
     Thomas Edlen von Trattnern, 1773. English trl. by
     Susan Pauline Snook, "J.F. Daube's *Der musikalische
     Dilettant, eine Abhandlung der Komposition* (1773): a
     Translation and Commentary. PhD dissertation.
     Stanford University, 1978. UMI 78-22576. MT 40.
     D381.1978a. 2 vols. I: vii + 426 pages (transla-
     tion); II: iii + 467 pages (commentary).
     A textbook on how to compose, designed for dilettantes
     (music lovers of the leisure classes of whatever abil-
     ity and training who make music together). Six chap-
     ters deal with galant-style music and 6 others with
     strict style (canon, fugue, and so on). Since chamber
     music is the music of the dilettante in 1773, this book
     is of special relevancy to chamber music at that time.
     Gives biography of Daube (before 1730-1797) and back-
     ground on his times and works (makes much use of
     Michael Karbaum, "Das theoretische Werk J.F. Daubes,"
     PhD dissertation, University of Vienna, 1968). Many
     references to specific chamber types, such as trios and
     trio sonatas ("Combining Three Voices"), string quin-
     tets and mixed winds and strings ("Composition in Five
     and More Parts"), and much more. Defines terms like
     "galant," gives chamber music illustrations of harmony

lessons, discusses ornamentation and variation (written and improvised), and anticipates Goethe's description of chamber music as conversation or dialogue among instruments with motives as speech.

Louise Cuyler, in "Tonal Exploitation in the Later Quartets of Haydn" {953}, demonstrates Haydn's bimodality and shows that he "explored ... [tonal] resources that were not fully realized until a century after his death."

Pleasants Parsons, in "Dissonance in the Fantasias and Sonatas of Henry Purcell" {1223}, analyses the Purcell works on the basis of how "dissonance" is described in 17th-century treatises.

494. Gressang, Jean C. "Textural Procedures in Instrumental Ensemble Music and Chamber Music Prior to the Classic Period." PhD dissertation. Florida State University, 1978. UMI 78-22170. DAI xxxix.6A, p. 3211. 187 pages.
"An inquiry into the identification of, the nature of, and factors contributing to the prominence of dominant textural procedures in chamber music prior to its evolution in the 'classic' or modern sense." Starts with the middle ages; chapter 3 is devoted to chamber music of the Baroque and chapter 4 to the transition to Classic-period stylistic changes in chamber music.

495. Kirkendale, Warren. *Fuge und Fugato in der Kammermusik des Rokoko und der Klassik.* Tutzing: Hans Schneider, 1966. ML 448.K87. 378 pages. 2nd, rev., and trl. ed. *Fugue and Fugato in Rococo and Classical Chamber Music.* Durham, N.C.: Duke University Press, 1979. ML 195.K5713.1979. ISBN 0-8223-0416-3. xxvii + 383 pages.
Exhaustive scholarly study of the use of fugues and fugatos, and an attempt to place the famous fugue movements of Haydn's Opus 20, Mozart's K.387, and Beethoven's Op. 59 no. 3, 131, and 133 in context. Part I (Rococo) concentrates on 737 fugal movements by 83 composers from Vienna, Italy, England and several regions of Germany; many chamber works hitherto neglected show this phenomenon to be much more common than heretofore believed. Part II (Classical) concentrates on Haydn, Mozart, Beethoven, and Beethoven's contemporaries (though numerous references are made to Brahms, Mendelssohn and other later Romantics). The fugue as a separate entity is analyzed as well as the nature of subject, development, cadence, and sequence. Considers many types of chamber composition.

496. Emerson, Isabelle Putnam. "The Role of Counterpoint in the Formation of Mozart's Late Style." PhD dissertation. Columbia University, 1977. DAI xxxviii. 2A, pp. 536-7. 330 pages.

Studies the development of Mozart's contrapuntal writing in his Vienna years 1781-1791, which is the result
of his contact with the music of J.S. Bach and his contrapuntal studies 1781-1783. Chooses 5 pieces, 3 of
which are chamber: string quartet K.387, and string
quintets K.593 and 614. Mozart's new conceptions are
based on unification of a small amount of material.

*László Somfai, in "A Bold Enharmonic Modulatory Model in
Joseph Haydn's String Quartets" {962}, demonstrates Haydn's
use of enharmonic spellings. See also Michael Montgomery's
"A Critical Analysis of the Modulations of W.A. Mozart in
Selected Late Instrumental Works" {1163}.*

*Hartmut Fladt {569} deals with the flexible sonata form from
Beethoven's Op. 59 on and inherited by Bartók.*

497. Fairleigh, James Parkinson. "Transition and Retransi-
        tion in Selected Examples of Mozart's Sonata-Type
        Movements." PhD dissertation. University of Michi-
        gan, 1973. UMI 74-3620. DAI xxxiv.10A, p. 6684.
        276 pages.
     Includes movements from string quintets, string quar-
     tets, duo sonatas, piano trios, piano quartets, as well
     as non-chamber music types.

498. Nicolosi, Robert Joseph. "Formal Aspects of the Minuet
        and *Tempo di Minuetto* Finale in Instrumental Music of
        the Eighteenth Century." PhD dissertation. Washing-
        ton University, 1971. UMI 72-9360. DAI xxxii.9A, p.
        5273. 202 pages.
     An important study of the last movement minuet found in
     so many 18th-century instrumental works, among them
     many chamber pieces (especially violin + piano sona-
     tas). While emphasis is on Haydn, Mozart and Beetho-
     ven, others in other areas of Europe are considered as
     well. The minuet was expanded in form when it became
     such a final movement, and the term "tempo di minuetto"
     usually was a sign of such expansion.

499. Frisch, Walter. *Brahms and the Principle of Developing
        Variation.* Berkeley/Los Angeles/London: University
        of California Press, 1984. MT 92.B81F7.1983. ISBN
        0-520-04700-1. xv + 217 pages.
     An analysis of Brahms's works in general from the
     standpoint of an expanded interpretation of Schoen-
     berg's approach. Schoenberg's concept of developing
     variation is regarded as essential to Brahms, and
     Schoenberg considered it a major compositional concept.
     It "is primarily a thematic or melodic procedure,"
     whereby the whole piece evolves out of a continual
     reshaping of a theme or melody. In demonstrating this,
     uses most of Brahms's chamber music (as well as sym-
     phonies and piano music) as examples, showing how

Brahms altered his idea of variation. For example, the chapter "Song and Chamber Music, 1864-1879" stresses Brahms's development of the developing variation principle in songs 1865-1873 and then in the 2 op. 51 quartets. The songs come between 2 outpourings of chamber music in 1862-1865 and 1873.

Robert Moevs's "Intervallic Procedures in Debussy: Serenade from the Sonata for Cello and Piano, 1915" {840} is a concentrated analysis of the opening 2 intervals in the movement and how they generate the entire movement.

William Hymanson, in "Hindemith's Variations: a Comparison of Early and Recent Works" {993}, is a study of Hindemith's concept of theme and variations and how that concept changed during his career.

Friedhelm Krummacher, in "Kantabilität als Konstruktion: zum langsamen Satz aus Mozarts Streichquartett KV 465" {1148}, shows that the structure of the slow movements evolves out of the cantabile of the opening theme and continues to evolve until the end of the movement. This is quite different from forms based on contrast. The form is not transferable; it depends on the particular cantabile melody. Such structure is hard to analyze with words.

500. Altmann, Wilhelm. "Zur weiteren Entwicklung der Kammermusik," in *Zeitschrift der Internationalen Musikgesellschaft*, iv (1902-1903), 257-258.
An important statement on the use of cyclic form by Schubert, Anton Rubinstein, and others in their chamber music. Rubinstein even goes so far as to repeat the first themes of his first 2 violin + piano sonatas at the beginning of his third violin + piano sonata.

501. Fisher, John Frederic. "Cyclic Procedures in the String Quartet from Beethoven to Bartok." PhD dissertation. The University of Iowa, 1981. UMI 81-23319. DAI xlii.5A, p. 1844. 235 pages.
After discussion of the cyclic idea from the Middle Ages to the 18th century, an analysis of that idea in the middle and late quartets of Beethoven, the quartets of Schubert, Mendelssohn, Schumann, Brahms, Dvořák, Grieg, Franck, Debussy, Ravel, Schoenberg and Bartók. "Cyclic" is considered in different ways; earlier quartets have implicit cyclic levels, later ones explicit ones.

502. Sharp, J. Wharton. "The Introduction in Relation to the String Quartet," in *The Strad*, xxiii (1913), 359-61, 415-16, 458-460, xxiv (1914), 17-19, 54-55.
Discusses the use of "introductions" to quartets or quartet movements from Haydn to Cesar Franck but with emphasis on the classical composers. Shows how they do

not simply quiet the audience down but provide vital
material for what follows. Much more up-to-date and
thorough discussions of the same topic (but not limited
to chamber music) are found in Rudolf Klinkhammer, *Die
langsame Einleitung in der Instrumentalmusik der
Klassik und Romantik* (Regensburg: 1971) and Klaus
Kropfinger, "Zur thematischen Funktion der langsamen
Einleitung bei Beethoven," in *Festschrift J. Schmidt-
Görg* (Bonn: 1967), pages 197-216.

503. Moe, Orin, Jr. "The Implied Model in Classical Music,"
     in *Current Musicology*, no. 23 (1977), 46-55.
     While many compositions of the classical period are
     based explicitly on earlier pieces, finds that many
     more are based on implied models -- not on a specific
     example but on what is perceived by the listener as the
     norm for a particular practice. The examples used to
     demonstrate this are primarily Haydn string quartets.

504. Coonrod, Michael McGill. "Aspects of Form in Selected
     String Quartets of the Twentieth Century." DMA
     dissertation. Peabody Institute of the Johns
     Hopkins University, 1984. UMI 84-17659. DAI xlv.5A,
     p. 1233. 219 pages.
     Analyzes structure in general in string quartets from
     1900 to 1971 and styles, pitch organization, harmony,
     rhythms, texture and overall shape in Berg's *Lyric
     Suite* (1926), Bartók's Fourth Quartet (1928), Seeger's
     Quartet (1931), Lutoslawski's Quartet (1964), Carter's
     Third Quartet (1971), and Xenakis's First Quartet *St/4-
     1,080262* (1962). Notes the similarities in their
     structure as well as their differences. An appendix
     gives "a complete serial analysis of the *Lyric Suite*."

505. Drew, John Robert. "Classic Elements in Selected Sona-
     tas for Trombone and Piano by Twentieth-Century Amer-
     ican Composers." DMA dissertation. University of
     Kentucky, 1978. UMI 78-24393. DAI xxxix.6A, p.
     3208. 97 pages.
     Analysis of 9 sonatas by Halsey Stevens, Richard Mona-
     co, Klaus George Roy, John Davison, Paul Hindemith,
     George F. McKay, Robert W. Jones, Walter Watson, and
     Henry Cowell. The abstract does not define "classic."

20th-century theories.

*For an early demonstration of the 12-tone technique, see
Erwin Stein"s "Schoenberg's New Structural Form" {1270}.*

506. Stein, Erwin. "Schönberg's Bläserquintett," in *Pult
     und Taktstock*, iii (1926), 103-107.
     Use of the wind quintet to explain the basic principles
     of 12-tone, atonal composition. Analyzes the form of

the 4 movements and only generalizes about other matters including the virtuosity required of the players.
Norbert Dietrich in Arnold Schönbergs Drittes Streichquartett op. 30: seine Form und sein Verhältnis zur Geschichte
der Gattung *{1268}, discusses the problem of sustaining
longer movements when the use of shifting tonal centers is
no longer relevant. Believes there is a connection between
the row and form, and seeks to find what remains of traditional form in this piece. Considers rhythmic contribution
to form as well. Stephen Peles, in "Interpretations of Sets
in Multiple Dimensions: Notes on the Second Movement of
Arnold Schoenberg's String Quartet #3" {1269}, presents a
complicated, highly technical discussion of the interaction
of the particular row (set) on the movement as a whole.*

507. Corson, Langdon. *Arnold Schoenberg's Woodwind Quin-
     tet, Op. 26: Background and Analysis*, ed. by Roy
     Christensen. Nashville: Gasparo Co., [1984]. MT
     145.S26C67. iii + 87 pages, 3 oversized inserts
     (analyzed examples, bar graphs, and row chart).
     Intended as a companion to the Gasparo GS-204 recording
     of the quintet by the Oberlin Woodwind Quintet, serves
     as an excellent introduction to Schoenberg's methodolo-
     gy and the structure of the piece. Begins with a his-
     torical background, continues with technical analyses
     of the handling of the row and form, and ends with a
     critique of Schoenberg's music by George Rochberg. The
     Quintet (1924) was Schoenberg's first full-length com-
     position using the 12-tone technique. Schoenberg's
     primary aim was to seek unity without tonality; the
     method was not important in and of itself but as a
     means to good-sounding music.

*See Richard Hill, "Arnold Schoenberg: String Trio" {1278}.
Bruce Archibald, in "Some Thoughts on Symmetry in Early
Webern: Op. 5, No. 2" {1400}, demonstrates how Webern con-
structs chords symmetrically or nearly symmetrically and how
the former act on the latter.*

508. Pleasants, Henry, and Tibor Serly. "Bartók's Historic
     Contribution," in *Modern Music*, xvii (March-April,
     1939), 131-140.
     Cites Bartók's subordination of harmony to melodic line
     as his major contribution in breaking with 19th-century
     tradition. Briefly traces this concept in several
     pieces: the second sonata for violin + piano and string
     quartets nos. 3 and 4.

509. Kárpáti, János. "Alternative Structures in Bartók's
     'Contrasts,'" in *Studia Musicologica*, xxiii (1981),
     201-207.
     Not seen.

510. Thomas, Jennifer. "The Use of Color in Three Chamber
     Works of the Twentieth Century," in *Indiana Theory
     Review*, iv, no. 3 (1981), 24-40.
     Analysis of color in Webern's Quartet Op.
     22, Stravin-
     sky's *Abraham and Isaac*, and Crumb's *Eleven Echoes of
     Autumn*, and shows how in the last "color has reached a
     peak of importance."

*Herbert Ritsema, in "The Germ Cell Principle in the Works of
Willem Pÿper (1894-1947)" {1205}, defines the concept and
traces it in some chamber and other works by Pÿper. See
also Peter Dickinson's "The Instrumental Music of Willem
Pÿper (1897-1947)" {1204} for further discussion of the
germ-cell idea.*

511. Landau, Victor. "The Harmonic Theories of Paul Hinde-
     mith in Relation to his Practice as a Composer of
     Chamber Music." PhD (education) dissertation. New
     York University, 1957. UMI 58-664. DA xviii.3, pp.
     1062-3. 342 pages.
     Considers Hindemith's music a3-7, taken from 7 differ-
     ent creative periods (1917-1952). Selects 2 movements
     of pieces from each period and extracts an opening,
     middle and closing portion of each to analyze according
     to Hindemith's theories of harmony. Finds that Hinde-
     mith obeyed his own rules less than one would expect.

*See also William Hymanson's "Hindemith's Variations: a
Comparison of Early and Recent Works" {993}.*

*Ronald Henderson, "Tonality in the Pre-Serial Instrumental
Music of Roger Sessions" {1326}, studies tonality in the
light of Sessions's own comments and Hindemith's theories of
harmonic and melodic progression. Richard Derby, in "Carter's Duo for Violin and Piano" {795}, attempts to demonstrate Carter's theory of composition within this piece.
Highly technical.*

Newer approaches to theory of older music:

*Allen Forte, in "Bela Bartok: Fourth String Quartet (I)
1928," in Contemporary Tone Structures {580} gives a Schenkerian analysis of the first movement which serves to demonstrate Forte's approach to analysis. Werner Hümmeke, in
Versuch einer strukturwissenschaftlichen Darstellung der
ersten und vierten Sätze der zehn letzten Streichquartette
von W.A. Mozart {1149}, proposes to present scientifically
the structure of the first and fourth movements of Mozart's
string quartets in order to be able to properly compare them
to Haydn's. The scientific structure of a piece is determined by the actual appearance of the music and not in
reference to anything existing a priori, including forms.
For a similar study of Haydn's Op. 76 quartets, see Burck-*

hard Löher's book on Haydn {965}. Hans Keller, in "Functional Analysis of Mozart's G Minor Quintet" {1164}, analyzes without words. Jonathan Kramer, in "Multiple and Non-Linear Time in Beethoven's Opus 135" {665}, considers different concepts of time (clock time versus experiential time), with the Beethoven used as demonstration. Kopfermann {655} questions the meaning and logic of analysis and finds Reti's approach most effective.

Newer theories for 20th-century string quartets:

512. Hechtel, Herbert. "Untersuchungen zur Gestaltsanalyse, durchgeführt an Streichquartetten in der Neuen Musik nach 1950." PhD dissertation. University of Erlangen.
Not seen.

513. Schweitzer, Eugene William. "Generation in String Quartets of Carter, Sessions, Kirchner, and Schuller: a Concept of Forward Thrust and its Relationship to Structure in Aurally Complex Styles." PhD dissertation. University of Rochester, 1966. UM 66-2363. DA xxvii.6A, p. 1856. 202 pages (DA = 215 pages).
Picks Carter's Second, Session's Second, Kirchner"s First, and Schuller's First string quartets to study forward drive -- tension to relaxation; the mental functions of retrospection, synthesis, and expectation; and motor elements vs. intellectual elements.

514. McNeal, Horace Pitman. "A Method of Analysis Based on Concepts and Procedures Developed by Allen Forte and Applied to Selected Canadian String Quartets, 1953-1962." PhD dissertation. Ohio State University, 1979. UMI 79-22527. DAI xl.4A, p. 1742. 219 pages.
The quantitative measurement of unordered pitch class collections in four string quartets by Canadian composers Jean Coulthard, Harry Somers, Claude Champagne, and John Weinzweig. A highly technical study for the professional music theorist.

515. Salibian, Ohannes Sarkis. "String Quartet Process." PhD dissertation. University of Iowa, 1980. UMI 81-14297. DAI xlii.1A, p. 16. 16 pages.
An attempt to develop a new notational system for string quartet writing that allows for new musical ideas and, by the "elimination of unnecessary ambiguities," arrives at "more precise musical elements." Designed for the composer.

ANALYSIS OF SPECIFIC WORKS

The following is an alphabetical list of composers of
chamber music about whose music significant studies have
been written. The studies sometimes are of individual
compositions, at other times of groups of chamber works or
the composer's entire output of chamber music. Some of the
studies are analytical, either in a general sense or in a
highly technical sense. Other studies are more historical,
with an attempt to place the work or the composer in a
larger context or simply to place the piece in a time and
locale. The remaining are bibliographical, with emphasis on
the location, condition, and verification of sources. For
additional analyses in collections, see Renner {162}, Berger
{163}, many of the general histories and generic histories,
and the following:

516. *Der Musikführer*. Nos. 1-150: Frankfurt a/Main: H.
     Bechhold, late 19th century. Nos. 151 and following:
     Leipzig: Hermann Seemann, 1903.
     A collection of separate booklets each devoted to the
     analysis of a particular work or group of works, of
     which nos. 23, 45, 57, 160, 211, 225, 226, 228, 235,
     238, 244, 245, 248, 285, 289, 298, 360, 361, and 363
     are chamber works by Beethoven, Brahms, Volkmann, Paul
     Juon, Schubert, Schumann, and Smetana. Written by
     different German authors such as H. Riemann, Walter
     Niemann, Georg Riemenschneider, and others.

For thematic catalogues including chamber music of many
individual composers, see Barry Brook, Thematic Catalogues
in Music: an Annotated Bibliography *(Hillsdale [New York]:*
Pendragon Press, 1972), ML 113.B86.

Karl Friedrich Abel
1723-1787

517. Knape, Walter. *Karl Friedrich Abel: Leben und Werk*
     eines frühklassischen Komponisten. Bremen: Schüne-
     mann Universitätsverlag, 1973. ISBN 3-7961-3036-4.
     240 pages.
     A biography and then afterwards a discussion of the
     elements of Abel's music, including 21 string quartets,
     37 trio sonatas, 32 solo + keyboard sonatas, and 45
     gamba sonatas + basso continuo. Considers style, form,
     articulation, rhythm, and other matters. Abel lived in
     London from 1758 on and from 1763 was associated there
     in concerts with J.C. Bach.

Eugène D'Albert
1864-1932

518. Pangels, Charlotte. *Eugen D'Albert: Wunderpianist und
     Komponist: eine Biographie.* Zurich: Atlantis, 1981.
     HML 1250.15.68.   ISBN 3-7611-0595-9.
     List of works includes 2 string quartets. Events
     leading up to their composition and first performance
     are described; gives documents, especially letters.

Tomaso Albinoni
1671-1750

519. Giazotto, Remo. *Tomaso Albinoni: "Musico di Violino
     Dilettante Veneto" (1671-1750), con il Catalogo Tema-
     tico delle Musiche per Strumenti,* in *Storia della
     Musica,* Series 11.   Milan: Fratelli Bocca, 1945.   HML
     1256.33.   362 pages.
     After biography and historical background of the trio
     sonata in Venice 1650-1700, an analysis of each of
     Albinoni's 9 published collections (3 are labelled
     "sonatas") and some miscellaneous ones.   Includes a
     thematic catalogue.

520. Talbot, Michael.   "The Instrumental Music of Tomaso
     Albinoni (1671-1741)."   PhD dissertation.   Cambridge
     University, 1969.   RILM 70-1776.   3 vols.   707 pages.
     After a biography and general assessment of Albinoni
     the man, a historical, then analytical discussion of
     his chamber and orchestral music.   Assumes that all
     works with violas are symphonic, and all works without
     violas, chamber.   This gives 25 sonatas a tre (Op. 1
     1694 and Op. 8 1718-19), 18 balletti a tre (Op. 3 1701
     and Op. 8), and 30 "solo" sonatas (1709, c.1712, 1717,
     and 1741-2), plus a few other pieces.   Studies the
     original prints and their contents, considers authen-
     ticity and dating, and discusses concordances.
     Analysis of form and style.

521. Newman, William S.   "The Sonatas of Albinoni and
     Vivaldi," in *Journal of the American Musicological
     Society,* v (1952), 99-113.
     An attempt to characterize the 47 so-called sonatas of
     Albinoni and the 76 known sonatas of Vivaldi, with
     identification of sources and editions.   Comparison of
     the Albinoni and Vivaldi with each other and with the
     Corelli sonatas.   An excellent general description of
     these works based on solid scholarship.

Johann Georg Albrechtsberger
1736-1809

522. Harpster, Richard William. "The String Quartets of
     Johann Georg Albrechtsberger: an Historical and For-
     mal Study." PhD dissertation. University of South-
     ern California, 1976. DAI xxxvi.11A, p. 7035.
     An examination of the 85 extant string quartets, which
     are influenced by C.P.E. Bach's generation of compo-
     sers, by contemporary Viennese composers (Mozart,
     Haydn, Beethoven), and by contrapuntalists (Fux, Mar-
     purg and Kirnberger). Albrechtsberger's sonatas are
     more archaic prelude-fugue type movements, while his
     quartets are more up-to-date. Considers form, theme
     contrast, developmental techniques, method of retransi-
     tion, and recapitulation. Includes an annotated thema-
     tic catalogue of the quartets with bibliographic data.

Franco Alfano
1875-1954

523. Pannain, Guido. "Sonata per Violoncello e Pianoforte
     di Franco Alfano," in *Rivista Musicale Italiana*,
     xxxiii (1926), 604-620.
     Extensive review and analysis of this sonata published
     1926 by Universal Editions, Vienna. Regards the work
     as very important in the history of contemporary Ital-
     ian music. The analysis is descriptive and subjective.

Alexander Nikolayevitch Aliabev
1787-1851

524. Greene, Carol. "The String Quartets of Alexander Alex-
     androvich Aliabev," in *The Music Review*, xxxiii
     (1972), 323-329.
     A biography and brief discussion of the basic forms and
     style of the 2 surviving string quartets by this pio-
     neer of Russian chamber music.

John Antes
1740-1811

525. Stolba, K. Marie. "Evidence for Quartets by John
     Antes, American-Born Moravian Composer," in *Journal
     of the American Musicological Society*, xxxiii (1980),
     565-74.
     Discovers letters in the Benjamin Franklin archives in
     Philadelphia to Franklin from Antes, the first Ameri-
     can-born composer to have written chamber music. The
     letters mention that Antes is sending Franklin a copy

of his 6 quartets, but the whereabouts of the music is
unknown.

Anton Stepanovitch Arensky
1861-1906

526. Chepin, G. *A.S. Arenskii*. Moscow: Muzyka, 1966. HML
1310.15.87. 180 pages. In Russian.
A discussion of Arensky's music (chamber music on pages
118-139), with ample musical examples. Concludes with
a list of his works by opus number and a chronology of
his life.

Thomas Arne
1710-1778

527. Sadie, Stanley. "The Chamber Music of Boyce and Arne,"
in *The Musical Quarterly*, xlvi (1960), 425-36.
The trio sonatas of each are their only chamber music:
Boyce's 12 in 1747 and Arne's 10 in 1757. Historical
account of their publication (Boyce's might also be
orchestrally performed) and analysis of their basic
forms, styles, meters. Boyce's published versions are
compared to manuscript copies with the composer's
corrections.

Milton Babbitt
b.1916

528. Borders, Barbara. "Formal Aspects in Selected Instrumental Works of Milton Babbitt." PhD dissertation.
University of Kansas, 1979. DAI xl.8A, p. 4290. 232
pages.
Analyzes certain formal characteristics of Babbitt's
Composition for Twelve Instruments (1948, 1954), *Sextet*
for piano and violin (1966), and *String Quartet No. 3*
(1970). Considers first "a formal overview, based primarily on audibly perceptible organization," then the
organization of pitch and rhythm, and finally how these
3 "totally organized" works compare with each other.

529. Sward, Rosalie La Grow. "An Examination of the Mathematical Systems Used in Selected Compositions of Milton Babbitt and Iannis Xenakis." PhD dissertation.
Northwestern University, 1981. DAI xlii.5A, p. 1848.
609 pages.
A highly technical study of the mathematical systems
used in Babbitt's *String Quartet No. 2* and Xenakis's
ST/4-1,080262 for String Quartet (as well as several
other works by the 2 men). Involves computer analysis
and comparison of their works.

530. Zuckerman, Mark Alan. "Derivation as an Articulation
       of Set Structure: a Study of the First Ninety-two
       Measures of Milton Babbitt's String Quartet No. 2."
       PhD dissertation. Princeton University, 1976. DAI
       xxxviii.7A, pp. 3799-3800. 164 pages.
     An analysis of 12-tone structure of these 92 measures.
     "In particular, structures derived from the background
     set are traced to their realizations at levels beneath
     and on the surface of the piece." After raising basic
     issues and analyzing the background set, consideration
     of 12 different aspects of the whole score, such as the
     large-scale episodic plan of the quartet. Highly tech-
     nical, theoretic discussion for professional theorists.

531. _____. "On Milton Babbitt's String
       Quartet No. 2," in *Perspectives of New Music*, xiv,
       no. 2, and xv, no. 1 (1976), 85-110.
     A detailed discussion of the row (set) of the quartet,
     its permutations and combinations, and its effect on
     dynamics, form, harmony, and orchestration. Then fol-
     lows a poetic-prose description of the successive
     events of the quartet based on technical theoretic
     analysis.

532. Arnold, Stephen, and Graham Hair. "An Introduction
       and Study: String Quartet No. 3," in *Perspectives of
       New Music*, xiv, no. 2, and xv, no. 1 (1976), 155-86.
     An introduction to Babbitt's terminology and methods of
     analysis and their application to his third string
     quartet. A detailed analysis of the row (set) and its
     bearing on the 4-part structure of the piece and its
     rhythm. Includes charts.

533. Hush, David. "Asynordinate Twelve-Tone Structures:
       Milton Babbitt's Composition for Twelve Instruments,"
       part 1, in *Perspectives of New Music*, xxi (1982-
       1983), 152-208.
     A highly technical, mathematical analysis for advanced
     music theorists of Babbitt's piece of 1948 for woodwind
     quintet, string trio, trumpet, harp, celesta, and
     string bass. Builds on Babbitt's own essay "Set Struc-
     ture as a Compositional Determinant" to show how Bab-
     bitt applies the example of Schoenberg's 12-tone system
     to his own music. Babbitt's analysis of Schoenberg's
     Fourth String Quartet results in a theoretical system
     for 12-tone music; goes on to show "how entire twelve-
     tone compositions may be seen to be consequences of the
     structure of the original sets on which they are
     based."

Grazyna Bacewicz
1909-1969

534. Rosen, Judith. *Grazyna Bacewicz: her Life and Works*,
     in *Polish Music History Series*, No. 2. Los Angeles:
     University of Southern California, 1984. ML 410.
     B08R7.1984. ISBN 0-916545-00-8. 70 pages.
     An extensive biography and categorical list of works of
     Bacewicz, a Polish violinist and composer. She wrote a
     great many chamber pieces, including 7 string quartets,
     sonatas, a wind quintet, and other pieces for various
     combinations of instruments. An analysis of this music
     awaits a proposed companion volume.

Carl Philipp Emanuel Bach
1714-1788

For a catalogue of Bach's chamber music, see Alfred Wot-
quenne, Thematisches Verzeichnis der Werke von Carl Philipp
Emanuel Bach (1714-1788), *(1905; reprint Wiesbaden: Breit-*
kopf & Härtel, 1964), pages 53-69. ML 134.B08W6.1964.

535. Schmid, Ernst Fritz. *Carl Philipp Emanuel Bach und*
     seine Kammermusik. Kassel: Bärenreiter, 1931. ML
     410.B16S3. xii + 189 pages + 71 pages of music (154
     examples) + 18 facsimiles of music, title pages and
     portraits.
     The basic study of this Bach's chamber music, a scho-
     larly, detailed, well-documented and well-written book.
     Defines chamber music as all pieces for 1 or more melo-
     dy instruments with or without continuo as well as ob-
     ligato keyboard + 1 or more melody instruments. Ex-
     cludes pieces for 1 or more keyboards, concertos, sin-
     fonias, marches and dance music. Begins with a des-
     cription of the aesthetics 1730-1780 in Italy, France,
     Poland and Germany, and bases much of the discussion on
     national differences in chamber music. Only by leaving
     Berlin and freeing himself from its music was Bach able
     to accept other nationalistic types (especially from
     Austria and South Germany). Reviews contemporary Ger-
     man attitudes toward chamber music from J.A. Scheibe,
     Chr.Fr.O. Schubart, and J.G. Sulzer, where it is in-
     ferior to programmatic and vocal music; chamber music
     is school music, study for more important things. De-
     tailed analyses. Rich in quotations by 18th-century
     theorists and commentators, and through Schmid's judi-
     cious selections and conclusions, the reader will gain
     an understanding of chamber music in the period far
     beyond the works of C.P.E. Bach. The North German
     supplement to studies of Viennese, French, Mannheimer
     and Italian chamber music of the time.

536. Schulenberg, David Louis. *The Instrumental Music of
     Carl Philipp Emanuel Bach*. Ann Arbor: UMI Research
     Press, 1984. ML 410.B16S35.1984. ISBN 8357-1564-7.
     202 pages. A corrected print of his PhD disserta-
     tion. State University of New York at Stony Brook,
     1982. DAI xliii.4A, p. 969. 427 pages.
     The ensemble sonatas are treated along with solo key-
     board works, concertos, and symphonies in the context
     of what contemporary theorists describe for form,
     rhythm, and the generation of melodic material. The
     emphasis is on Bach's whole instrumental output. It
     defines Bach's own standards he set for himself without
     imposing criteria of Classical or Baroque music that
     are irrelevant to Bach. Points to a kind of mannerism
     in his music, and to the probable influence of Telemann
     on Bach in the trio sonatas. This is the best account
     of Bach's instrumental music -- chamber music *en
     passant*.

537. Jacobs, Richard Morris. "The Chamber Ensembles of C.P.
     E. Bach Using Two or More Wind Instruments." PhD
     dissertation. University of Iowa, 1963. UM 64-7926.
     DA xxv.2, pp. 1248-9. xvii + 193 pages.
     After historical background on Bach and a chronological
     discussion of ensemble music with winds prior to him, a
     consideration of both orchestral and chamber music by
     Bach which includes at least two or more winds. Analy-
     zes the pieces and gives bibliographical information.

              Johann (= John) Christian Bach
                       1735-1782

538. Mekota, Beth Anna. "The Solo and Ensemble Keyboard
     Works of Johann Christian Bach." PhD dissertation.
     University of Michigan, 1969. UM 69-18059. DAI
     xxx.5A, p. 2063. 309 pages (DAI = 317 pages).
     Discusses mostly keyboard sonatas with flute or violin.
     Points out omissions and other weaknesses.

539. Roe, S.W. "The Keyboard Music of J.C. Bach: Source
     Problems and Stylistic Development in the Solo and
     Ensemble Works." PhD dissertation. Worcester
     College, Oxford University, 1982.
     Not seen.

540. Keahey, Delores Elaine Jerde. "The Genoa Manuscripts:
     Recently Rediscovered Trios of Johann Christian
     Bach." PhD dissertation. University of Texas, 1977.
     UMI 78-07332. DAI xxxviii.12A, p. 7014. 621 pages.
     Discusses 8 trios for 2 violins + bass and 3 for violin
     + cembalo + bass, preserved in a Genoa manuscript.
     Includes "the first watermark studies devoted to Bach's
     works," a thematic index of all his trios (some 40), an

updated biography, and a critical edition of the 11
analyzed trios.

Johann Christoph Friedrich Bach
1732-1795

541. Wohlfarth, Hannsdieter. *Johann Christoph Friedrich
Bach: ein Komponist im Vorfeld der Klassik*, in *Neue
Heidelberger Studien zur Musikwissenschaft*, Bd. 4.
Bern/Munich: Francke Verlag, 1971. HML 1373.60.95.
263 pages. PhD dissertation "Johann Christoph
Friedrich Bach als Instrumentalkomponist." University of Heidelberg, 1968. RILM 71-648.
The chamber music of this Bach takes up only pages 171-
184; the rest of the book deals with symphonies, concertos, keyboard works, biography and bibliography.
The second youngest son of J.S. Bach, J.C.F. worked in
Bückeburg and wrote 30 chamber pieces (27 survive): 15
for flute, violin or cello + piano or harpsichord, 3
trio sonatas, 4 keyboard trios, 6 flute quartets, a
sextet (2 horns + oboe + violin + cello + Hammerkla-
vier), and a lost septet. Considers the works historically, and analyzes several in more detail to discover
to what extent they fit into Baroque or newer Italian
practices. Finds that the chamber music parallels the
development of the symphony. It is important to remem-
ber for which type of keyboard the chamber music is
written so that the modern pianist can better balance
with the other players.

Johann Sebastian Bach
1685-1750

*For a catalogue of Bach's chamber music (= sonatas) see
Wolfgang Schmieder*, Thematisch-Systematisches Verzeichnis
der musikalischen Werke von Johann Sebastian Bach: Bach-
Werke-Verzeichnis (BWV) *(Wiesbaden: Breitkopf & Härtel,
1950; 3rd printing 1966), pages 559-579. ML 134.B1S1.1966.
For a bibliography of writings about Bach's chamber music
see Christoph Wolff*, Bach-Bibliographie: Nachdruck der Ver-
zeichnisse des Schriftums über Johann Sebastian Bach (Bach-
Jahrbuch 1905-1954), mit einem Supplement und Register *(Kassel: Merseburger, 1985), pages 462-464. ML 134.B1W64.1985.
ISBN 3-87537-197-6.*

542. Doflein, Erich. "Joh. Seb. Bach in der Haus- und Kammermusik," in *Hausmusik*, xiv (1950), 1-8, 29-34, and
63-72.
Notes that except for some keyboard works, Bach wrote
for accomplished performers; he did have music in his
home for his family, but they were well trained.
Today's Hausmusikanten should always go to Urtext

editions, and available editions in 1950 are evaluated.
Considers Bach's keyboard music and chamber music for
violin, viola, cello, viola da gamba, flute, recorder,
voice, and larger ensembles.

*See Rudolf Pečman's "Johann Sebastian Bach und der Stil der
italienischen Triosonate" in {457}, pages 337-343.*

543. Eppstein, Hans. *Studien über J.S. Bachs Sonaten für
ein Melodieinstrument und obligates Cembalo*, in *Acta
Universitatis Upsaliensis, Studia Musicologica
Upsaliensia*, Nova Series 2. Uppsala: Universität/
Stockholm: Almqvist u. Wiksells, 1966. MT 145.B14
E65. 199 pages, 44 musical examples. Publication of
PhD dissertation, Uppsala.
A detailed, specialized study of the Bach sonatas designed primarily for musicologists. Largely concerned
with proving several speculations about the origins of
the sonatas and their melodic-rhythmic structure. Considers the authenticity of these sonatas, their various
versions, the interrelationship of the 2 instruments,
the historical position of Bach's sonatas, and the
structure of each of the sonatas. Concentrates on the
authenticated sonatas and leaves the others for a final
chapter. Doubts if Bach really knew any French sonatas
with obligato keyboard; the idea was in the air.
Challenges the term "trio" for these pieces as they
stand (treble + obligato keyboard), though recognizes
the relationship of many other composers's trio sonatas
to their similarly scored obligato keyboard + treble
transcriptions. Bach conceived the 3-line sonata movements (most of them are 3-line) as 3 lines; there is no
continuo possible, no 2 trebles + continuo, with its
then resulting improvised additions of a fourth or
fourth and fifth parts. The Klavier is complete with 2
lines of music. The Klavier has 2 functions here: to
present the 2 remaining lines of a 3-voice work and as
an opposing player to the melody instrument. Draws attention to the Stimmtausch (exchange) of the 3 parts,
even when 2 of them are accompaniment to the third.
The violin is almost always higher than the right hand
of the keyboard. Considers the relationship of the instruments and their functions; and analyzes the sonatas
in detail. Considers the gamba sonata in G and its
trio version BWV 1039; both are based on another now
lost trio version but denies that this could have been
the case with the 6 violin + obligato keyboard sonatas
BWV 1014-1019.

544. _____. "Zur Problematik von J.S. Bachs Sonata
für Violine und Cembalo G-Dur (BWV 1019)," in *Archiv
für Musikwissenschaft*, xxi (1964), 217-242.
In trying to identify, authenticate, and describe
Bach's sonatas for solo instrument and keyboard, takes

one authentic work -- the sonata BWV 1019 -- as a point
of study of basic Bach stylistic traits in sonatas. A
scholarly approach. Compares 7 sources of this sonata,
which are quite different. Considers chronology and
assumes Cöthen as the location and time (1717-1723) for
the composition (see Marshall {550}).

545. _____. "J.S. Bach's Triosonate G-dur (BWV
1039) und ihre Beziehungen zur Sonate für Gambe und
Cembalo G-dur (BWV 1027)," in *Die Musikforschung*,
xviii (1965), 126-137.
Considers the questions: is the trio sonata (violin +
flute + continuo) or the solo sonata earlier (the 2
sonatas are the same except for scoring and numerous
details upon which Eppstein bases his case, and the
solo sonata survives in an authentic Bach-written
manuscript), and if the trio sonata is later, is it
authentic? On the basis of comparison of melodic lines
as characteristic of 1 instrument or another, it
answers the first question: the solo gamba sonata comes
first; and the second: the trio sonata is authentic.
Refutes Ulrich Siegele, "Kompositionsweise und Bear-
beitungstechnik in der Instrumentalmusik Johann
Sebastian Bachs" (PhD dissertation; University of
Tübingen, 1957). See {546-547}.

546. Dürr, Alfred. "Zu Hans Eppsteins 'Studien über J.S.
Bachs Sonaten für ein Melodieninstrument und obligates Cembalo,'" in *Die Musikforschung*, xxi (1968),
332-340.
Considers many of Eppstein's points and finds room for
further discussion without refuting those points.
Questions the nature of Ur-versions of gamba sonatas,
all of which are transcriptions.

547. _____. "Zu Hans Eppsteins Erwiderung," in *Die
Musikforschung*, xxii (1969), 209.
Believes that Eppstein has not proved that the trio
sonatas come from the cembalo sonatas and the latter
from some lost Ursonata.

548. Mackerness, E.D. "Bach's F Major Violin Sonata," in
The Music Review, xi (1950), 175-179.
A comparison of this sonata with its model, Bach's
earlier Trio Sonata in G for flute + violin + continuo,
and how the 3-instrument original is reduced to 2 instruments (actually the cembalo of the violin sonata is
obligato so the number of voices remains the same).

549. Blume, Friedrich. "Eine unbekannte Violinsonate von
J.S. Bach," in *Bach Jahrbuch*, xxv (1928), 96-118.
A detailed study of the manuscript source, the handwriting and the music of Bach's BWV 1021 sonata for
violin + continuo in G Major, which shows many simil-

arities to the trio for flute + violin + continuo in
G. Dates it without certainty c.1720 or 1727.
Includes a facsimile of 1 page of the manuscript.

550. Marshall, Robert L. "J.S. Bach's Compositions for Solo
Flute: a Reconsideration of their Authenticity and
Chronology," in *Journal of the American Musicological
Society*, xxxii (1979), 463-498.
Only 5 flute solo works appear in the *Neue-Ausgabe*.
Considers 3 additional sonatas that others (Dürr and
Eppstein) have eliminated as not by J.S. Bach and de-
cides they are indeed at least partially by J.S. Bach.
Then turns around to challenge the authenticity and
dating of the 5 others and, on the way, the long-
accepted myth that Bach composed most of his keyboard
and chamber works in Cöthen. All are allowed some
degree of authenticity, but the conjectures as to their
origins (arrangements of other works, dates of composition) are scrutinized.

551. Addington, Christopher. "The Bach Flute," in *The
Musical Quarterly*, lxxi (1985), 264-280.
An expert on baroque flutes analyzes the Bach sonatas
from the standpoint of the kind of instrument for which
they were written.

552. Nitschke, Wolfgang. "Zu Johann Sebastian Bachs Flöten-
sonate in h-Moll: Versuch einer Analyse des ersten
Satzes," in Heinrich Poos, ed., *Festschrift Ernst
Pepping zu seinem 70. Geburtstag am 12. September
1971* (Berlin: Verlag Merseburger, 1971), pp. 240-246.
ML 55.P47F5. ISBN 3-87537-003-1.
Concerned with the sonata for flute and obligato harpsichord in B Minor (BWV 1030), which is apparently an
arrangement (in Leipzig) of an earlier sonata in G Minor for flute + continuo (in Cöthen), based on research
of Hans-Peter Schmitz, *Kritischer Bericht* to Johann Sebastian Bach, *Neue Ausgabe sämtlicher Werke*, Series VI,
Band 3, *Werke für Flöte* (Kassel: Bärenreiter, 1963), p.
32. Analyzes the first movement, Andante, the longest
and most complicated first movement in any Bach sonata,
to show its basic da capo form and its suggestions of
contrasting themes as in sonata form (albeit here both
are in the same key). The movement is divided into 3
sections which are subdivided into periods and motives,
with the tonal centers outlined. The third section is
a development of the first section, not simply an ornamented recapitulation.

553. Claypool, Richard D. "J.S. Bach's Sonatas for Melody
Instrument and Cembalo Concertato: an Evaluation of
all Related Manuscript Sources." PhD dissertation.
Northwestern University, 1975. UM 76-11878. DA

xxxvi.11A, p. 7034. 2 vols. I: v + 183 pages; II: 363 pages.
A bibliographic and source analysis of these sonatas, with a collation of discrepancies among the sources. Attempts to date the sources. For the advanced researcher in Bach scholarship.

See also Jürgen Eppelsheim, "Funktionen des Tasteninstruments in J.S. Bachs Sonaten mit obligatem Cembalo," in {161}, pages 23-33.

Heinrich Joseph Baermann
1784-1847

554. Rau, Ulrich. "Von Wagner, von Weber? Zwei Kammermusikwerke für Klarinette und Streichinstrumente unter falscher Autorschaft," in *Die Musikforschung*, xxix (1976), 170-175.
Conclusively shows that the Adagio for clarinet and string quintet, assumed to be an early work of Wagner's, is in fact the second movement of a clarinet quintet, Op. 23, by Baermann, and that the Introduction, Theme and Variations for clarinet + string quartet, assumed to be by C.M. von Weber, is in fact a clarinet quintet by Joseph Küffner (1777-1856).

Tadeusz Baird
1928-1981

555. Jazwinski, Barbara. "Four Compositions by Tadeusz Baird." PhD dissertation. City University of New York, 1984. UMI 85--1144. DAI xlv.8A, p. 1369. viii + 105 pages.
After a brief biography, an analysis of 4 atonal pieces: *String Quartet No. 1* (1957), *Four Essays for Orchestra* (1958), *Exhortation for Orchestra* (1959-60), and *Elegeia for Orchestra* (1973). Discusses pitch-structure, texture, and form.

Adriano Banchieri
1568-1634

556. Kelly, David Terrence. "The Instrumental Ensemble Fantasias of Adriano Banchieri." PhD (education) dissertation. Florida State University, 1962. UM 62-4615. DA xxiii.5, p. 1732. 300 pages (DA = 310 pages).
A biography and a history of the instrumental canzona and Banchieri's role in it. Of special concern is his *Fantasie overo Canzoni Francese per Suonare nell'Organo*

et Altri Stromenti Musicali, à Quattro Voci (Venice: 1603), which is also given as a performing edition.

Samuel Barber
1910-1981

For a catalogue of Barber's chamber music, see Don A. Hennessee, Samuel Barber: a Bio-Bibliography, in Bio-Bibliographies in Music, No. 3 (Westport [Connecticut]/London: Greenwood Press, 1985), pages 66-74. ML 134.B175H4.1985. ISBN 0-313-24026-4.

Béla Bartók
1881-1945

For a general introduction to Bartók's chamber music, see Mosco Carner's essay in Alec Robertson, ed., Chamber Music *{160}.*

Another general introduction is:

557. Walsh, Stephen. *Bartók Chamber Music, in BBC Music Guides.* London: BBC, 1982. MT 145.B25W34.1982. ISBN 0-563-12465-2. 88 pages, 25 musical examples. Designed for the student and informed layperson, the best non-technical exposé of the chamber music in English. Presents its subject in light of Bartók's career, thoughts, outside influences (other composers and folk music), and total oeuvre. Traces early development from late Romantic to his own style based on Hungarian folk music; shows events leading up to the composition of each important chamber work and discusses the principal rhythmic, thematic and harmonic elements of each movement. Continually tries to understand what motivated Bartók aesthetically to do what he did and to find overall consistencies and compositional principles that can explain the music. Not to be read for information on a single piece but for the total picture.

558. Haraszti, Émile. "La Musique de Chambre de Béla Bartók," in *La Revue Musicale,* xi.2, no. 107 (1930), 114-125.
     Bartók's works evince all the problems facing contemporary music: exaltation of Russian dynamism, objectivism of the geometric French, and atonal and polytonal polyphony of the horizontal Germans. Contrasts Stravinsky -- cosmopolitan dweller -- with the peasant Bartók. Both have developed from nationalism to individualism, from general to abstract. Divides Bartók's music into 3 periods. Stresses nationalism in the first (piano quintet and string quartet no. 1), return to classicism in the second (2 sonatas for violin +

piano, string quartet no. 2), and maturity in the third
(string quartets nos. 3 and 4).

559. Stevens, Halsey. "The Chamber Music," in *The Life and
     Music of Béla Bartók* (New York: Oxford University
     Press, 1953), pp. 170-226. ML 410.B26S8. Rev. ed.
     1964.
     An analysis of Bartók's chamber music, with the first
     33 pages devoted to the 6 quartets. After general
     remarks, considers each of the quartets in turn, stres-
     sing Bartók's symmetry of form, motivic development,
     and, in a general way, his tonalities. Less attention
     is given to the folk elements, harmony, and coloristic
     effects, and only passing attention to rhythm. The
     remaining 23 pages concentrate on the violin + piano
     sonatas, the duos for 2 violins, sonata for 2 pianos +
     percussion, *Contrasts*, and the solo violin sonata.
     Gives historical data and then concentrates on form
     with other aspects more lightly touched upon (if at
     all). A good general introduction, in English, to the
     chamber music of Bartók, even if some aspects are
     short-changed and some other aspects (tonality,
     harmony) might be too technical for the beginner.

560. Seiber, Mátyás. "Béla Bartók's Chamber Music," in
     Tempo, no. 13 (Autumn, 1949), 19-31. Reprinted in
     Béla Bartók: a Memorial Review of his Life and Works
     (New York: Boosey and Hawkes, 1950), pages 23-35.
     A history of Bartók's chamber music that tries to show
     a continuous evolution from his student works in 1898
     to the sonata for solo violin (1944). Important works
     are briefly but cogently analyzed. A good introduction
     for the student.

561. _____. *Die Streichquartette von Béla Bartók.*
     1945. *The String Quartets of Béla Bartók*, trl. K.W.
     Bartlett. London/New York: Boosey & Hawkes, 1954.
     MT 145.B25S4. 22 pages, 72 musical examples.
     A general introduction to the quartets for the lay-
     person who reads music: not technical, not scholarly.
     A running description of thematic and other events,
     with the principal themes.

562. Abraham, Gerald. "The Bartók of the Quartets," in
     Music and Letters, xxvi (1945), 185-194.
     After proving that Bartók's 6 quartets are the most
     important set since Beethoven's, an analysis of each
     one in succession commenting on motives, tonalities and
     harmonies, folk tunes, color effects and form.

563. Kárpáti, János. *Bartók's String Quartets*, trl. Fred
     Macnicol. Budapest: Corvina Press, 1975. MT 145.
     B25K43. ISBN 963-13-3655-7. 279 pages, 254 musical

examples. Original *Bartók Vonósnégyesei*. Budapest:
Zenemúkiadó, 1967.
The most important study of Bartók's quartets. The
first half of the book deals with general elements in
Bartók's style and the quartet from Beethoven to
Bartók; the second half is an extremely detailed
analysis of each movement of the 6 quartets, with
several pages of historical data on each one. This is
a treasure house of information on these pieces and
should be basic to any research on them. An extremely
useful bibliography with good documentation and caution
exerted when called for. The analyses are concerned
with motives, tonalities, harmonies, form and only
slightly with new color effects. Considers folk music
influence and monothematicism, chromaticism, polytonal-
ity, scordatura, pentatonicism, quartal harmonies, and
much more. Bartók's harmonic system is a flexible com-
promise between the tonality of neo-classicism and the
atonality of Schoenberg; refutes rigid theoretical
systems in analyzing the quartets. Bartók is not
nationalistic but internationalistic since he did not
limit himself to one folk music tradition.

564. Siegmund-Schultze, W. "Tradition und Neuerertum in
     Bartóks Streichquartetten," in *Studia Musicologica*,
     iii (1962), 317-328. This volume also bears the
     title *Zoltano Kodály Octogenario Sacrum* (Budapest:
     Akadémiai Kiadó, 1962).
An extremely important essay in placing Bartók's quartets in a social and aesthetic context. Well written
for anyone who already has a working knowledge of the 6
quartets. No musical illustrations. Seeks to answer
the question: how much is in the classical tradition
and how much is new in Bartók's quartets. Contrasts
the social goals of Beethoven and Bartók (Beethoven
lives at the height of bourgeois humanism, Bartók at
its destruction). At the turn of the century the
classical tradition was going nowhere in Germany and
Austria; it took the nationalists Smetana, Borodin,
Debussy, Ravel and Roussel, drawing on their own folk
music, to point to a new direction for the string
quartet, and Bartók takes off from there. Considers
the basic elements of each quartet, with Beethoven
often serving as the only model. The last 2 quartets
are a positive awareness of life, progress, the victory
of humanity despite the antihumanistic dangers of his
time (1934 and 1939) -- themes already conceived by
Beethoven. Despite the tragedy and melancholy, an
inner indomitable spirit -- a Classical idea. Concludes with the observation that bridge-form applies to
the 6 quartets as a whole: 1 and 6, 2 and 5, and 3 and
4 are similar in character. *See {570} for a similar
treatment*.

*For a study of the organic unity in Bartók's quartets, see
Werner Pütz,* Studien zum Streichquartettschaffen bei Hindemith, Bartók, Schönberg und Webern *{995}.*

565. Babbitt, Milton. "The String Quartets of Bartók," in
     The Musical Quarterly, xxxv (1949), 377-385.
     The 6 quartets are recognized as a unity, "a single
     conceptual attitude," which reveals "a thorough aware-
     ness of the crucial problems confronting contemporary
     musical composition." The author points out thematic
     elements which generate polyphony and harmony and unify
     the movements.

566. Perle, George. "Symmetrical Formations in the String
     Quartets of Béla Bartók," in *The Music Review,* xvi
     (1955), 300-312.
     Points to the use of symmetrical scales in Debussy and
     the Russian nationalists. Then analyzes Bartók's use
     of symmetrical formations not as textural devices but
     as important functions of the total structures. A
     symmetrical formation can be a particular scale
     ascending in one instrument simultaneously with its
     descent in another, the scale itself frequently having
     symmetrical properties. An important analysis for
     anyone who wishes to comprehend the structure of the
     Bartók quartets.

567. Walker, Mark Fesler. "Thematic, Formal and Tonal
     Structure of the Bartók String Quartets." PhD dis-
     sertation. Indiana University, 1955. UM 55-1694.
     DA xv.12, p. 2543. 387 pages.
     Attempts to define Bartók's thematic material, to de-
     termine the formal plans at all levels, and to explain
     tonal organization of the 6 string quartets. Describes
     and analyzes the quartets, a separate chapter to each.

568. Traimer, Roswitha. *Béla Bartóks Kompositionstechnik
     dargestellt an seinen sechs Streichquartetten.* Re-
     gensburg: Gustav Bosse Verlag, 1956. ML 410.B26T7.
     vi + 91 pages, 198 musical examples. PhD disser-
     tation. University of Munich, 1953.
     A scholarly attempt to uncover a musical system in the
     works of Bartók by studying the music itself rather
     than imposing a system on the music. The quartets are
     a convenient and representative genre since they cover
     all his life and, with 4 equal instruments, depend on
     the structure rather than bravura. Even folk music
     elements are better represented in the quartets as an
     integrated part of his compositional style. Bartók's
     system involves motives; his peculiar harmonies and
     forms derive from motives. These in turn are based on
     his studies of and empathy for Hungarian and similar
     folk music.

569. Fladt, Hartmut. *Zur Problematik traditioneller Form-typen in der Musik des frühen zwanzigsten Jahrhunderts, dargestellt an Sonatensätzen in den Streich-quartetten Béla Bartóks*, in *Berliner musikwissenschaftliche Arbeiten*, Band 6. Munich: Musikverlag Emil Katzbichler, 1974. ML 448.F87. ISBN 3-87397-036-8. 182 pages.
An intense treatise on sonata form primarily for scholars, in which ideas of Adorno and Dahlhaus are adapted. Then the application of this treatise to string quartets and specifically Bartók's. Beethoven by his Op. 59 established sonata form in all movements, but it was a flexible sonata form that had different solutions in each use. This flexible sonata form, posing ever new problems, was inherited by Brahms, Schoenberg, and Bartók; therefore analysis of their works must assume a basic sonata form idea which they confronted, rather than the creation of a whole new form. Considers Brahms's C Minor String Quartet as basic for Bartók's starting point, then the folk element (emphasizes Bartók's anti-bourgeois sentiments) which is basic to all elements of the music. Always links political history to the shape of Bartók's works; this is especially evident in the 1930's when, as Bartók despaired because of fascism, he aimed at more communicability, new simplicity, classicism, clarity -- thematic arches rather than motives, more unaltered, sentimental uses of 19th-century Hungarian popular themes to symbolize the political crisis. *For a similar idea see {564}.*

570. Spinosa, Frank. "Beethoven and Bartók: a Comparative Study of Motivic Techniques in the Later Beethoven Quartets and the Six String Quartets of Béla Bartók." DMA dissertation. University of Illinois, 1969. RILM 69-3843. UMI 70-13499. DAI xxx.2A, p. 791. 214 pages.
Starts with a survey of string quartets written after Beethoven and before Bartók in which Beethoven's use of dramatic motives is abandoned in favor of extended lyric expression and orchestral string sonorities. Bartók, on the other hand, followed Beethoven's idea of motivic development. Analyzes Beethoven's Op. 95 - 135 as well as Bartók's 6 quartets in detail according to motivic aspects and finds many parallels in their compositional approaches.

571. Thomason, Leta Nelle. "Structural Significance of the Motive in the String Quartets of Béla Bartók." PhD dissertation. Michigan State University, 1965. UM 66-6876. DA xxvii.3A, pp. 793-4. 395 pages.
Sets out to prove "that the content of the melodic motives manifests itself in other elements of the quartets so that it becomes the most important factor." A detailed theoretic discussion of the motives.

572. Rands, Bernard. "The Use of Canon in Bartók's Quar-
     tets," in *The Music Review*, xviii (1957), 183-188.
     Points to the prominent position of canon and strettos
     in the quartets.

573. Gow, David. "Tonality and Structure in Bartók's First
     Two String Quartets," in *The Music Review*, xxxiv
     (1973), 259-271.
     A detailed analysis of these quartets based on con-
     sideration of harmony and assuming they still have
     vestiges of tonality.

574. Wellesz, Egon. "Die Streichquartette von Béla Bar-
     tók," in *Musikblätter des Anbruch*, iii (1921), 98-
     100.
     Recognition of Bartók's quartets as evolving from the
     contents, not from pre-conceived forms. It is a time
     when many are seeking a new expressive language by
     returning to the string quartet, and Bartók is one of
     the best. Brief analysis of the first 2 quartets but
     without musical illustrations.

575. Whittall, Arnold. "Bartók's Second String Quartet," in
     The Music Review, xxxii (1971), 265-270.
     Analysis of the quartet in harmonic terms: since the
     piece is neither tonal nor 12-tone, another harmonic
     criterion has to be found, either perfect fourths and
     tritones or major and minor thirds, where the second in
     each case (or tritone or minor third) acts as a tonic.

576. Breuer, Janós. "Die erste Bartók-Schallplatte: das
     ii. Streichquartett op. 17 in der Einspielung des
     Amar-Hindemith-Quartetts," in *Hindemith-Jahrbuch*, v
     (1976), 123-145.
     Account of a recording made on DGG in 1925 of Bartók's
     second string quartet performed by Hindemith's quartet
     -- the first recording ever made of a piece by Bartók.
     Reviews the close relationship of the 2 composers,
     gives information on the Amar-Hindemith Quartet -- who,
     when, where -- and details on the particular recording
     at hand. Reviews the piece as played.

577. Kartman, Myron Herbert. "Analysis and Performance
     Problems in the Second, Fourth and Sixth String
     Quartets by Béla Bartók." MAD dissertation. Boston
     University, 1970. UMI 71-13418. DAI xxxii.3A, p.
     1552. 253 pages.
     No abstract available.

578. Berry, Wallace. "Symmetrical Interval Sets and Deriva-
     tive Pitch Materials in Bartók's String Quartet No.
     3," in *Perspectives of New Music*, xviii (1979-1980),
     287-379.

Gives a highly technical analysis of the pitch organization in this quartet. Finds the fundamental hexa-
chord d up to b with interval patterns 2-2-1-2-2 and
its various implied tetrachords 2-2-1, 1-2-2, 2-1-2,
and 2-3 or 3-2 as the basis for the melodic and harmonic materials of the quartet.

579. Monelle, Raymond. "Bartók's Imagination in the Later
      Quartets," in *The Music Review*, xxxi (1970), 70-81.
      Bartók contrasts traditional, classical gestures with
      radical and astringent music. Treats quartets nos. 3-6
      from this contrast of simple (often folk) and familiar
      with the revolutionary sound of polymodality and
      serialism.

580. Forte, Allen. "Béla Bartók: Fourth String Quartet (I)
      1928," in *Contemporary Tone Structures* (New York:
      Columbia University Teachers College, 1955), pp. 139-
      143, 193-194 (charts). ML 197.F7.
      A Schenkerian analysis of the first movement of this
      piece. Very succinct approach to the overall tonal
      tendencies of the movement without further discussion
      of the other structural aspects found there. The work
      has 4 primary tones -- C, E, G, F# -- and the "general
      structural concept" is the adjacent tone postulate;
      in short, Bartók uses seconds. This analysis is an
      example of Forte's approach to analysis as presented in
      detail in the earlier part of the book.

581. _____. "Bartók's 'Serial' Composition," in *The
      Musical Quarterly*, xlvi (1960), 233-245.
      A highly technical analysis of the third movement of
      Bartók's Fourth String Quartet in which he experiments
      with serial devices without sacrificing his own charac-
      ter. He uses complementation -- "the basis of trichor-
      dal and hexachordal combination within each section and
      of progression from section to section." In addition,
      Bartók follows through on the system at the level of
      melodic detail.

582. Antokoletz, Elliott Maxim. "Principles of Pitch Organ-
      ization in Bartók's Fourth String Quartet." PhD dis-
      sertation. City University of New York, 1975. UM
      75-21334. DAI xxxvi.4A, p. 1885. xii + 152 pages.
      Based on George Perle's theories, a highly technical
      analysis of the quartet. Starts with subdividing the
      octave into the total complex of interval cycles, then
      selecting tetrachordal segments from each of these
      cycles; the quartet uses two of these 4-note cycles in
      a significant way. Also considers rhythm, which grows
      from two elementary rhythmic cells and which reveals
      various mathematical patterns. For the advanced music
      theorist.

For a discussion of the 4th String Quartet see also Michael Coonrod's dissertation {504}.

583. Mason, Colin. "An Essay in Analysis: Tonality, Symmetry and Latent Serialism in Bartók's Fourth Quartet," in *The Music Review*, xviii (1957), 189-201. A detailed, thorough examination of tonality and motivic structure in the fourth quartet.

584. Monelle, Raymond. "Notes on Bartók's Fourth Quartet," in *The Music Review*, xxix (1968), 123-129. A challenge to those who would consider this quartet in traditional forms; at most, sonata form and scherzo form are treated as parodies. An imaginary Hungarian folk song in the finale is in the earlier movements as a germ motive.

585. Chapman, Roger E. "The Fifth Quartet of Béla Bartók," in *The Music Review*, xii (1951), 296-303. A formal analysis that points to the "arch" structure of the whole. Not too detailed in terms of thematic and rhythmic structure.

586. Jemnitz, Alexander. "Béla Bartók: V. Streichquartett," in *Musica Viva*, i (April, 1936), 19-33. A sizable review of the Fifth quartet in German, with summaries in English, French and Italian. Considers the difference between "being" and "becoming." In a static aesthetic, "being" is the accepted state; therefore sonata form, with its exact or nearly exact repetition of the exposition in the recapitulation, is perfectly acceptable. But since Beethoven evolution or drama is more important -- objects are always growing, evolving, "becoming" -- and recaps are no longer acceptable. Bartók's *Fifth String Quartet* is a synthesis of these 2 concepts. The piece is not only a cyclic sonata but a continual evolution. The first movement has an exposition that continually grows -- early motives evolve into them, the first theme evolves into the second, likewise in the recapitulation the second theme comes first -- a continual evolution that doesn't stop here but goes on in subsequent movements.

For consideration of Bartók's Quartet No. 2, movement 1, and Quartet No. 5, movement 1, see Robert Donahue's "A Comparative Analysis of Phrase Structure in Selected Movements of the String Quartets of Béla Bartók and Walter Piston" {1210}. For important information on how to play the Fifth String Quartet, see Gertler {1508}.

587. Vinton, John. "New Light on Bartók's Sixth Quartet," in *The Music Review*, xxv (1964), 224-238. One of many articles on this quartet by important theorists and musicologists, this is based on documen-

tation newly available. A detailed analysis of rhythm and motives. Includes plates of 2 pages of Bartók's manuscript, described and discussed, which show that some material was an afterthought but an extremely important unifying factor in the whole quartet.

588. Suchoff, Benjamin. "Structure and Concept in Bartók's Sixth Quartet," in *Tempo*, no. 83 (Winter, 1967-1968), 2-11, with 6 facsimiles of Bartók's manuscript. An analysis of the sketches for the quartet in order to ascertain how the introductory motive developed into the cyclic unifier for the whole piece. Bartók changed his original ideas for this quartet written at the outbreak of World War II.

589. Oramo, Ilkka. "Marcia und Burletta: zur Tradition der Rhapsodie in zwei Quartettsätzen Bartóks," in *Die Musikforschung*, xxx (1977), 14-25. Considers the similarity between the 4-note motive in the *Marcia* of the Sixth Quartet (1939) and in the *Verbunkes* of *Contrasts* for violin + clarinet + piano (1938), and the similarity between the motives of the *Burletta* in the same quartet and *Sebes* in *Contrasts*. Assumes these similarities to be intended; thereupon analyzes the various movements and concludes that *Contrasts* was a model for the quartet.

590. Sidoti, Raymond Benjamin. "The Violin Sonatas of Béla Bartók: an Epitome of the Composer's Development." DMA dissertation. Ohio State University, 1972. UMI 72-26963. DAI xxxiii.4A, p. 1773. 55 pages. An analysis of 4 violin sonatas, including the early, unnumbered 1903 sonata influenced by Strauss's *Also sprach Zarathustra*, the first and second sonatas (1921 and 1922) which show Bartók's own highly developed style with folk music influences, and the unaccompanied sonata (1944), his last completed work.

591. Groth, Clause Robert, Jr. "A Study of the Technical and Interpretive Problems Inherent in Bartók's Violin Sonatas." DMA dissertation. University of Oregon, 1971. UMI 72-8536. DAI xxxii.9A, p. 5266. 147 pages. Omits the early violin-piano sonata. Designed "as a guide for the violinist wishing to study and perform these works." Analyzes 3 sonatas in detail and helps in solving some specific technical and interpretive problems.

592. Szentkirályi, András. "Bartók's Second Sonata for Violin and Piano (1922)." PhD dissertation. Princeton University, 1976. UMI 76-25120. DAI xxxvii.5A, pp. 2488-9. 236 pages.

A highly technical, mathematical analysis of the 2 movements of this sonata. Three basic relationships govern it: the "axis system" (tonic, dominant, subdominant), the "golden section" (a:b = b:[a+b], with a = 0.618, b = 0.382), and the "principle of duality" (symmetry versus asymmetry, chromatic versus diatonic, macro- verus microstructures, and so on, whereby opposites simultaneously complement one another).

593. Leichtentritt, Hugo. "On the Art of Béla Bartók," in *Modern Music*, vi, no. 3 (March-April, 1929), 3-11.
After discussing Bartók's *Allegro Barbaro* and the *Dance Suite for Orchestra*, an analysis of the second sonata for violin + piano. Notes the influences of Hungarian folk song on the rhythm and tonality of the piece and analyzes the 2 scales found in it.

594. Mason, Colin. "Bartók's Rhapsodies," in *Music and Letters*, xxx (1949), 26-36.
A discussion of the 3 rhapsodies and their various versions. Nos. 2 and 3 (violin + piano versions) are virtuosic, relatively shallow pieces compared to the works immediately before and after them. They use folk themes. Mostly concerned with origins and form.

595. Doflein, Erich. "A propos des '44 Duos pour Deux Violons' de Bartok," in *Revue Musicale*, no. 224 (1955), 110-112.
Recounts how he solicited these duos from Bartók in 1930-1931 in order to have contemporary art music easy enough for students.

Arnold Bax
1883-1953

596. Foreman, Lewis. *Bax: a Composer and his Times*. London/Berkeley: Scholar Press, 1983. ML 410.B275. ISBN 0-85967-643-9. xix + 491 pages.
A biography that mentions chamber music in the course of events (see index). List of works shows 5 string quartets, 5 quintets for various scorings, 1 piano quartet, various sonatas, trios and others.

597. Scott-Sutherland, Colin. *Arnold Bax*. London: J.M. Dent & Sons, 1973. ISBN 0-460-03861-3. xviii + 214 pages.
A brief discussion of 2 string quartets, a nonet, a sonata for flute + harp, "Threnody and Scherzo" (bassoon + harp + string sextet), 3 sonatas for violin + piano, a cello sonata, and others.

Amy Beach
1867-1944

598. Flatt, Rose Marie Chisholm. "Analytical Approaches to
      Chromaticism in Amy Beach's Piano Quintet in F#
      Minor," in *Indiana Theory Review*, iv, no. 3 (1981),
      41-58.
      A brief biography, a theoretical consideration of
      "chromaticism" in late-19th-century traditional tonali-
      ty, and application of concepts of chromaticism to
      measures 1-34 of the second movement of the quintet.

599. Piscitelli, Felicia. "The Chamber Music of Mrs. H.H.
      Beach (1867-1944)." MM thesis. University of New
      Mexico, 1983. MAI 322765. MAI xx (1984), p. 384.
      85 pages.
      Analysis of the chamber works shows that, while she
      composed in a basically late-Romantic style, Mrs. Beach
      tended to incorporate impressionistic harmonies, a
      leaner texture, and more concise motivic development
      into her music in her later years.

Ludwig van Beethoven
1770-1827

*For a list of all the chamber music by Beethoven, see The
New Grove {1}; Georg Kinsky and Hans Halm, eds., Das Werk
Beethovens: thematisch-bibliographisches Verzeichnis seiner
sämtlichen vollendeten Kompositionen (Munich-Duisburg: G.
Henle, 1955), systematic index pages 736-737 (ML 134.B4K5);
and the following:*

600. MacArdle, Donald W. "A Check-list of Beethoven's Cham-
      ber Music," in *Music and Letters*, xxvii (1946), 44-
      59, 83-101, 156-174, and 251-257.
      A systematic list of all chamber works attributed to
      Beethoven, according to number of instruments, scoring,
      opus number (if any), with basic data (key, title,
      dates). A lengthy discussion of each of the chamber
      pieces, including sources, first publications, and
      authentication. There is an exhaustive, annotated
      bibliography. At the end is "Addenda and Corrigenda."

*For a non-technical introduction to Beethoven's chamber
music, see Roger Fiske's essay in Alec Robertson, ed.,
Chamber Music {160}.*

601. Gysi, Fritz. "Beethovens Kammermusik," in Gustav
      Bosse, ed., *Beethoven-Almanach der Deutschen Musik-
      bücherei auf das Jahr 1927* (Regensburg: Gustav Bosse,
      1927), pages 270-282. ML 21.A463B6.
      An essay that probes Beethoven's musical intentions in
      moving from a popular "conversation style" in his

earliest chamber music to an independent "diction" in
his last chamber works. Divides Beethoven's chamber
pieces into works for winds with or without piano,
works with 1 or more strings with piano, and works only
for strings; then tries to place the first group before
1800, the second 1800-1815, and the third after 1815.

602. Kerman, Joseph. *The Beethoven Quartets*. New York:
     Alfred A. Knopf, 1967. MT 145.B425K47. 386 pages,
     184 musical examples.
     The outstanding modern critical study of the quartets.
     Scholarly yet readable history and analysis, with fre-
     quent discussion of others's analyses. Since anyone
     who wishes to understand Beethoven's quartets must read
     this, no summary is needed here.

603. Marliave, Joseph de. *Les Quatuors de Beethoven*, ed.
     Jean Escarra. Paris: Librairie Félix Alcan, 1925.
     MT 145.B425M3. *Beethoven's Quartets,* trl. into
     English by Hilda Andrews. London: John Johnson for
     Oxford University Press, 1928. MT 415 B425.M33.1928.
     Reprint: New York: Dover Publications, 1961. MT 145.
     B425M33.1961. xxiii + 379 pages, 321 examples.
     Extensive, detailed history of Beethoven's string quar-
     tets, with attention to his notebooks, early editions,
     and contemporary accounts. Frequent citations of 19th-
     century and early 20th-century scholars to explain
     historical data and stylistic generalizations. Discus-
     sions of individual quartets are romanticized descrip-
     tions with little significant analysis (see Kerman's
     critique in his study); looks for "deeper meaning,"
     often in biography rather than in the music.

604. Mason, Daniel Gregory. *The Quartets of Beethoven*. New
     York: Oxford University Press, 1947. MT 145.B425M35.
     x + 294 pages.
     An analysis of each of the quartets on a non-technical
     level with an attempt to discover the most important
     rhythmic or motivic ideas that give unity and form to
     each movement and each quartet. Well written for the
     non-scholar, informed layperson.

605. Radcliffe, Philip. *Beethoven's String Quartets*. Lon-
     don: Hutchinson University Library, 1965. MT 145.
     B425R3. 2nd ed. Cambridge/New York: Cambridge Uni-
     versity Press, 1978. MT 145.B425R3.1978. ISBN
     0521219639. 192 pages, 102 musical examples.
     A non-technical discussion of the quartets in context
     of all of Beethoven's works and the works of Mozart,
     Haydn and Schubert. Each quartet treated separately
     but also in comparison with the others.

606. Lam, Basil. *Beethoven String Quartets*, i, in *BBC Music
     Guides*, nos. 32-33. Seattle: University of Washing-

ton Press, 1975. MT 145.B425L35. ISBN 0-295-95423.
68 pages, 43 musical examples.
Introductions to and critical analyses of Op. 18, 59
and 74, as well as Trios Op. 3 and 9, and Quintet Op.
29.

607. Shepherd, Arthur. *The String Quartets of Ludwig van*
Beethoven: Historic and Analytic Commentaries.
Cleveland, Ohio: Horace Carr, 1935. MT 145.B42S42.
91 pages.
Program notes for a performance of the cycle at Sever-
ance Hall, Cleveland, Spring, 1935, by Joseph Fuchs,
Rudolph Ringwall, Carlton Cooley and Victor de Gomez.
Written for the layperson. Mixes history, fantasy,
anecdote; not much originality, but entertaining. Considers the evolution of themes from the sketch books to
the printed edition and the "poetic idea" in the late
quartets.

608. Valetta, Ippolito. *I Quartetti di Beethoven,* in *Bib-*
liotheca Artistica, Band 33. Milan: Fratelli Bocca,
1943. 2nd ed. 1948. MT 145.B425V47.1948. 80 pages.
In Italian.
Program notes for a performance of the cycle in Rome in
March, 1905, by the Joachim Quartet. Written for the
general Italian public, discusses briefly each quartet,
the order of movements, and the architecture of the
whole. An introductory essay points to the quartets as
Beethoven's "most profound, intimate, and artistic,"
works and divides them into 3 maniera.

609. Guardia, Ernesto de la. *Los Cuartetos de Beethoven:*
su Historia y Anàlisis. Buenos Aires: Ricordi
Americana, 1952. MT 145.B425G8. 245 pages.
Notes for the first complete cycle in Buenos Aires in
1925 and repeated in 1927. A good introduction for the
Spanish-reading layperson. Short analyses mix relatively few technical concepts with general emotive
descriptions. Lists the quartet themes.

610. Helm, Theodor. *Beethoven's Streichquartette: Versuch*
einer technischen Analyse dieser Werke im Zusammen-
hange mit ihrem geistigen Gehalt: mit Vielen in den
Text gedruckten Notenbeispielen. Leipzig: Siegel,
1885. 2nd enlarged ed. 1910. 3rd ed. (reprint of
1910 ed.) 1921. 4th ed. (reprint of 1921 ed.) Nie-
derwalluf b. Wiesbaden: M. Sändig, 1971. MT 145.
B425H5.1971. ISBN 3-500-23600-6. vii + 355 pages.
Originally appeared in *Musikalische Wochenblatt* iv
(1873).
Primarily for the non-scholar, younger reader who needs
to study the scores intimately before reading the book.
Seeks both the musical structure and the spiritual
values. The final section of the book, expanded in the
second edition, deals with quartets after Beethoven.

The author is awe-struck, but does also provide basic
historical data (as known in 1885). Points out principal themes, tonalities and some other details but does
not dwell on technical matters. Far more useful than
Desmarais's description {613} but not yet underscoring
the complicated interrelationships of the quartets as
expounded by later writers. (Criticizes Mahler for an
1899 orchestral performance of Op. 95 in Vienna.)

611. Riemann, Hugo. *Beethoven's Streichquartette erläutert.*
     Berlin: Schlesinger (R. Lienau), 1910. MT 145.B425
     R5. 188 pages.
     A detailed theoretic analysis of each of the quartets
     based on Riemann's *Handbuch der Harmonielehre.* Each
     group of quartets starts with a brief historical sketch
     of when written, published and first performed.
     Analyzes motives and harmonic progressions. Avoids
     subjective statements, but at the same time often lacks
     a sense of the whole of each quartet (whether harmonic
     or extramusical or formal). Also gives performance
     suggestions based on theory (for example, in Op. 18 No.
     1, warns the performers not to rush the second movement
     since the quarters of the melody are more crucial than
     the eighths of the accompaniment).

612. Lonchampt, Jacques. *Les Quatuors à Cordes de Beetho-
     ven,* in *Les Cahiers du Journal Musical Français,* Vol.
     15. Paris: Société Française de Diffusion Musicale
     et Artistique, 1956. NYPL *MEC. 119 pages.
     A quartet-by-quartet description and analysis designed
     for the intensely involved layperson. Gives biograph-
     ical information affecting the creation of the quartet
     and quotes freely from a host of 19th- and 20th-century
     writers (including Wagner). Useful for a more cultur-
     ally oriented interpretation rather than a musicologi-
     cal or theoretic one.

613. Desmarais, Cyprien. *Les Dix-huit Poèmes de Beethoven,
     Essai sur le Romantisme Musical.* Paris: Société pour
     la Propagation du Catholicisme, des Sciences et des
     Artes, 1839. MT 145.B425D48. Reprint in part 3 of
     Essai sur les classiques et les Romantiques (1824);
     Le Roman: Etudes artistiques et littéraires (1837);
     and *Les Dix-Huit Poèmes de Beethoven* (1839). Geneva:
     Slatkine Reprints, 1973. PN 710.DA70.1973. xiv +
     147 pages.
     A very early discussion of Beethoven's string quartets.
     Gives poetic, extra-musical interpretations of each:
     no. 1 is "la vision," no. 2 is "la rêve du bonheur,"
     no. 3 is "le poète," no. 4 is "les passions, la jalou-
     sie," and so on. No theory or history.

614. Ciortea, Tudor. *Cvartetele de Beethoven.* Bucharest:
     Editura Muzicalá a Uniunii Compozitorilor dìu

Republica Socialistá Romãnia, 1968. MT 145.B415.C6.
309 pages, 488 musical examples. In Romanian.
After a 12-page historical introduction, each quartet
receives a chapter-long analysis primarily of themes,
with some extra-musical references. Despite its great
length, the book seems superficial, the descriptions
and references unoriginal. Ciortea is a distinguished
Romanian composer.

615. Mila, Massimo. *I Quartetti di Beethoven (Parte Prima:*
     1798-1810): Corso Monografico di Storia della Musica.
     Turin: G. Giappichelli, 1968. MT 145.B425M54. 129
     pages. In Italian.
     Designed as a college course for non-music students at
     the University of Turin. After a brief opening chapter
     on bibliography (Kerman's book was received too late
     for inclusion), a discussion of the quartets, one by
     one, from Op. 18 to Op. 95. Historical background,
     analyses of tonalities, form, emotion. See {640}.

616. Biamonti, Giovanni. *I Quartetti di Beethoven.* Rome: G
     Glingler, 1924. NL V49.095. 40 pages.
     A quartet-by-quartet discussion ending with Op. 133.
     Compares the spirit of the quartets with other works
     Beethoven was writing at the time. Subjective, with
     some structural facts.

617. Wolff, Christoph, ed. *The String Quartets of Haydn,*
     Mozart, and Beethoven: Studies of the Autograph Manu-
     scripts: a Conference at Isham Memorial Library,
     March 15-17, 1979, in *Isham Library Papers,* no. 3.
     Cambridge, MA: Harvard University, Department of
     Music, 1980. ML 38.C17I86.1979. ISBN 0-674-84331-2.
     xi + 357 pages, 177 facsimiles, 40 examples.
     The proceedings of an international musicological col-
     loquium at Harvard in 1979, in which some of the
     world's leading scholars of Haydn, Mozart and Beethoven
     assembled to find meaning in the autograph manuscripts
     of the string quartets of these 3 composers. Contents
     include: Haydn: László Somfai, "An Introduction to the
     Study of Haydn's Quartet Autographs (with Special At-
     tention to Opus 77/6" (pp.1-51), with response by Jens
     Peter Larsen (pp.52-57) and discussion (pp.57-61).
     James Webster, "The Significance of Haydn's String
     Quartet Autographs for Performance Practice" (pp. 62-
     95), with discussion (pp.96-99). Georg Feder, "Haydn's
     Corrections in the Autographs of the Quartets Opus 64
     and Opus 71/74" (pp.99-110) and discussion (pp.111-
     119). Mozart: Ludwig Finscher, "Aspects of Mozart's
     Compositional Process in the Quartet Autographs: I. The
     Early Quartets, II. The Genesis of K.387" (pp.121-153).
     Marius Flothuis, "A Close Reading of the Autographs of
     Mozart's Ten Late Quartets" (pp.154-173) and discussion

(pp.174-178). Alan Tyson, "Mozart's 'Haydn' Quartets: the Contribution of Paper Studies" (pp.179-190). Christoph Wolff, "Creative Exuberance vs. Critical Choice: Thoughts on Mozart's Quartet Fragments" (pp.191-210) and discussion (pp.211-221). <u>Beethoven</u>: Richard Kramer, "'Das Organische der Fuge': On the Autograph of Beethoven's String Quartet in F Major, Opus 59, No.1" (pp.223-265), with response by Robert Winter (pp.266-272) and discussion (pp.273-277). Sieghard Brandenburg, "The Autograph of Beethoven's String Quartet in A Minor, Opus 132: the Structure of the Manuscript and its Relevance for the Study of the Genesis of the Work" (pp.278-300), with discussion (p.301). Martin Staehelin, "Another Approach to Beethoven's Last String Quartet Oeuvre: the Unfinished String Quintet of 1826/7" (pp.302-323), with discussion (pp.324-326). General discussion (pp.327-328). An appendix lists all the quartets of Haydn, Mozart, and Beethoven chronologically, with dates of composition and first publication and with a separate list of autograph sources.

618. Brusatti, Otto. "Klangexperimente in Beethovens Streichquartetten," in *Studien zur Musikwissenschaft: Beihefte der Denkmäler der Tonkunst in Österreich*, xxix (Tutzing: Hans Schneider, 1978), 69-87.
Compares sounds of the late quartets with sounds from Beethoven's other pieces (piano sonatas, violin + piano sonatas, symphonies). Beethoven's influence on later quartets is not only in form and motivic development but also in color effects: pizzicato in Op. 74, sul ponticello in Op. 131, and the bagpipe effect as in second movements in the late quartets.

619. Clarke, Rebecca. "The Beethoven Quartets as a Player Sees Them," in *Music and Letters*, viii (1927), 178-190.
Starting from the premise that it is more satisfying and more edifying to play a quartet by Beethoven than to listen to one, the author (a distinguished violist) characterizes each of the quartets. Little, momentary details are more important than formal design.

620. Ginsburg, Lev S. "Zur Geschichte der Aufführung der Streichquartette Beethovens in Russland," in *Gesellschaft für Musikforschung, Bericht über den internationalen musikwissenschaftlichen Kongress Bonn 1970* (Kassel: Bärenreiter, 1971), pages 135-140. ISBN 3-7618-0146-7.
Briefly traces the history of the performance of Beethoven's quartets in Russia, starting with the violinist Karl Amenda who in 1799 brought the first version of Op. 18 No. 1 to Latvia and Russia. Indeed, Latvia heard Beethoven's Op. 18 early and often. The Op. 59

were of course popular from the start (1806) for their
use of Russian folk tunes, and the dedicatee of Opera
127, 130, and 132 was also Russian -- the cellist Niko-
lei Golizin (1794-1866). Even if these late quartets
were not popular in Russia, they had their admirers who
played them often. Cites their reception by Glinka,
Balakirev, and other famous Russian musicians. After
1918, when concerts were open to all classes, the performance of string quartets in general increased and
the audience for Beethoven also grew. Mentions many
amateur and professional quartet ensembles in Russia.

621. Judenič, Nina. "Beethoven und die Volksmusik: darge-
     stellt an seinen Streichquartetten," in Ladislav Bur-
     las, ed., *Feiern zum 200. Jahrestag der Geburt Ludwig
     van Beethovens in der ČSSR: Tagungsbericht des ii.
     internationalen musikologischen Symposiums* (Piešťany:
     Moravany, 1970), 191-215.
     Not seen.

622. Beeson, Colin. "Rhythm in Beethoven's String Quar-
     tets." PhD dissertation. University of Reading,
     1976. RILM 76-5485. 181 pages.
     Considers the conflict for performers between meter and
     both harmonic and melodic rhythm, hemiola, syncopation,
     notational problems and changes of tempo within single
     movements.

623. Hadow, William Henry. *Beethoven's Op. 18 Quartets*, in
     The Musical Pilgrim. London: H. Milford for Oxford
     University Press, 1926. Reprints 1942 and 1948. MT
     145.B425H12. 64 pages.
     For the layperson, describes the forms, basic keys and
     chief melodies of each of the 6 quartets. Also at-
     tempts to deal with the dramatic elements. Attributes
     some of the revolutionary expression and balance of Op.
     18 to Beethoven's access to outstanding string players
     (Schuppanzigh, Linke, Weiss).

624. Levy, Janet M. *Beethoven's Compositional Choices: the
     Two Versions of Opus 18, No. 1, First Movement*, in
     Studies in the Criticism and Theory of Music, ed.
     Leonard B. Meyer. Philadelphia: University of
     Pennsylvania Press, 1982. ML 410.B4L5345.1982. ISBN
     0-8122-7850-X. x + 101 pages.
     Trys to explain Beethoven's remark that with the second
     version of Op. 18 No. 1 (the accepted version, as pub-
     lished) he had "learned to write quartets properly."
     Since both versions exist complete, this is not a his-
     torical study (what outside influences caused Beethoven
     to do what he did) but a comparison of some details
     of the 2 complete artistic pieces. Considers how
     changes in details (for example, elimination of many
     uses of the turn motive) affect syntax and tighten the

structure. Does not consider every change in detail and does not necessarily discuss fully all the changes that are considered. Frequently juxtaposes scores of the 2 versions so that the differences are clear. Conclusion is that Beethoven meant numerous scoring changes to enhance continuity and coherence and a tightening and telescoping of ideas for the same goal. An important study for understanding the extent of Beethoven's skill and in particular how Op. 18 No. 1 in version 2 achieves some of its greatness.

625. Wedig, Hans Josef. *Beethovens Streichquartett op. 18 Nr. 1 und seine erste Fassung: erste vollständige Veröffentlichung des Werkes aus dem Beethovenhaus mit Untersuchungen*, in *Veröffentlichungen des Beethovenhauses in Bonn*, Band 2. Bonn: Beethovenhaus, 1922. ML 410.B42B42.no. 2. 23 pages + 39 pages of the complete score of the first version.
An amazingly accurate and well-written essay on the string quartet of the 1780's and 1790's: Haydn, Mozart, Ferdinand Fränzl, Leopold Koželuch, Pleyel and Emanuel Aloys Förster, all of whom had a big influence on Beethoven's quartet writing. Förster in Op. 16 (1798) is a model for harmonic richness, varied return of themes, sharp dynamic contrasts, surprising rhythmic freedom, and dramatic curve of the development sections. A well-documented account of Beethoven's writing of Op. 18 No. 1, its thematic relationship to other Beethoven works and works by other composers, and the special historical situation of the 2 versions. Does not enter into how the 2 versions came about, but concentrates on comparing the first movements.

626. Greenfield, Donald Tobias. "Sketch Studies for Three Movements of Beethoven's String Quartets, Opus 18 #1 and 2." PhD dissertation. Princeton University, 1983. UMI 83-03994. DAI xliii.9A, p. 2825. 514 pages.
Studies the sketches for movements 1 and 4 of no. 1 and movement 2 of no. 2 to see how Beethoven composed in individual, specific cases. Transcribes nearly every sketch for these 3 movements. Considers a Prague manuscript copy with variants separately.

627. Brandenburg, Sieghard. "The First Version of Beethoven's G Major String Quartet, Op. 18 No. 2," in *Music and Letters*, lviii (1977), 127-152.
Since Beethoven revised important details of Op. 18 No. 1 between 1799 and 1801, presumes the same kind of revisions took place with Op. 18 No. 2. Supports this with evidence from sketch books.

628. Johnson, Douglas. "Beethoven's Sketches for the Scherzo of the Quartet Op. 18, No. 6," in *Journal of the*

American Musicological Society, xxiii (1970), 385-
404.
A detailed scholarly account of the isolated sketch
manuscript for the scherzo movement now in the University of California at Berkeley. Compares it to
sketches of the other movements in manuscripts located
elsewhere and to the finished product. Tries to recreate Beethoven's process of composition by analyzing
the discarded notes.

629. Abraham, Gerald Ernst Heal. *Beethoven's Second-Period
     Quartets*, in *The Musical Pilgrim*. London: Milford
     for Oxford University Press, 1942. Reprint: St.
     Clair Shores (Michigan): Scholarly Press, 1978. MT
     145.B425A12. ISBN 0-403-01500-6. 79 pages, 43
     examples.
     A brief introduction to Op. 59, 74 and 95 for students,
     scholars, and laypersons. A historical introduction
     reveals the author's keen wit, musicality and excep-
     tional knowledge of music history. A movement-by-move-
     ment analysis, first outlining the basic themes and
     forms and then tying everything together with lucid and
     cleverly stated commentary.

630. Vetter, Walter. "Das Stilproblem in Beethovens
     Streichquartetten, op. 59," in *Musikleben*, i (1948),
     177-180.
     Notes the cyclic unity of each of the quartets and the
     organic and architectural unity of the 3 together. The
     old sonata form disappears -- no repetition of the ex-
     position, long, flowing melodies replace simple first
     or second themes, and repetition of long lines in coun-
     terpoint replaces dramatic development of motives.
     Mersmann stresses linear aspects while Riemann looked
     for sonata form and harmony in everything.

631. Hübsch, Lini. *Ludwig van Beethoven: die Rasumowsky-
     Quartette op. 59 Nr. 1 F-dur, Nr. 2 e-moll, Nr. 3 C-
     dur*, in *Meisterwerke der Musik*, Heft 40. Munich:
     Wilhelm-Fink-Verlag, 1983. MT 145.B425H8.1983. ISBN
     3-7705-2165-X. 126 pages.
     A highly concentrated study of these 3 quartets: their
     history, origins, reception, position in Beethoven's
     output, cyclic features as a group, and thematic analy-
     sis. Contains fussy details; see condemning review by
     Peter Cahn (*Neue Zeitschrift für Musik*, cxlvi [Jan.
     1985], 41).

*See {642}, part v: "Sketches for the String Quartets, Opus
59 (1806)."*

632. Tyson, Alan. "The 'Razumovsky' Quartets: Some Aspects
     of the Sources," in Alan Tyson, ed., *Beethoven
     Studies 3* (Cambridge: Cambridge University Press,
     1982), pp. 107-140. ML 410.B4. ISBN 0-521-24131-6.

A highly technical analysis of the manuscripts of primary interest to scholars. Easily dates and shows the
order of composition of the 3 quartets based on known
sources and watermarks. Then turns to new, special
problems in the sketches and autographs. Shows that a
major source of sketches for Op. 59 was at one time
bound as a collection but the folios were not in a
bound collection when Beethoven wrote on them; therefore the present order of the sketches does not have to
be considered when tracing the order of composition.
Sketches for the F Major and E Minor quartets are too
incomplete to reveal any compositional process, but the
C Major first movement is nearly complete, as are the
minuet and trio as well. These sketches show clearly
that the C Major quartet was no. 3 and that it was
influenced by Mozart's chamber music, especially K.465.
A number of other details are touched upon, such as the
temporary rededication of the Op. 59 to Prince Lichnow-
sky rather than Razumovsky, and the use of development-
recap repetition as well as exposition repetition --
considered but, in the long run, rejected.

633. Salmen, Walter. "Zur Gestaltung der 'Thèmes Russes' in
Beethoven's op. 59," in Ludwig Finscher and Christoph-Hellmut Mahling, eds., *Festschrift für Walter
Wiora zum 30. Dezember 1966* (Kassel: Bärenreiter,
1967), pp. 397-404. ML 55.W46F5.
Beethoven combines pure music with simple folk tunes.
Since the middle of the 18th century there were artistic arrangements of Russian tunes and other national
folk tunes -- a rediscovered naivité. Beethoven owned
a collection of Russian tunes collected by Johann Gottfried Pratsch (St. Petersburg: 1790), from which came
the Russian tunes in Op. 59. The tune symbolizes the
simple, common man; the work of art is complicated and
removes itself from Hausmusik, yet is here bound to a
folk tradition.

*For a discussion of the revolutionary nature of and possible
Masonic influences on Beethoven's Op. 59 No. 1 quartet, see
Jacques Chailley's "Sur la Signification du Quatuor de
Mozart K.465..." {1146}.*

634. Headlam, Dave. "A Rhythmic Study of the Exposition in
the Second Movement of Beethoven's Quartet Op. 59,
No. 1," in *Music Theory Spectrum*, vii (1985), 114-
138.
Traces the rhythmic organization of this exposition to
the rhythm in the cello of the first 4 measures. Based
on studies by William Rothstein and Carl Schachter --
the latter's distinction between tonal rhythm ("derives
from articulations of tonal structure") and durational
rhythm ("derives from patterns of stress and duration

that produce pulse and meter"). Highly technical but
clearly written for the professional theorist.

635. Finscher, Ludwig. "Beethovens Streichquartett op. 59,
     3: Versuch einer Interpretation," in Gerhard Schuh-
     macher, ed., *Zur musikalischen Analyse*, in *Wege der
     Forschung*, Band 257 (Darmstadt: Wissenschaftliche
     Buchgesellschaft, 1924), 122-160. MT 6.S352Z8.
     The 3 Op. 59 quartets form a unity in conception when
     as a group they are compared to earlier quartets by
     Beethoven, Haydn, and others. Compares and contrasts
     the 3 quartets to each other, then concentrates on the
     third. A very complicated analysis of the entire
     piece, which relates the symphonic tone to the result
     of the impression on Beethoven of Schuppanzigh's public
     concerts. Symphonic is not just in the treatment of
     the instruments but in the use as well of symphonic
     stylistic and formal devices such as cyclic unity.

636. Livingstone, Ernest. "The Final Coda in Beethoven's
     String Quartet in F Minor, Opus 95," in Jerald C.
     Graue, ed., *Essays on Music for Charles Warren Fox*
     (Rochester: Eastman School of Music Press, 1979), pp.
     132-144. ML 55.F69. ISBN 0-9603-186-07.
     An attempt to explain the coda's relationship to the
     rest of the quartet based on motivic and intervallic
     similarities with the earlier movements. At the very
     end mentions the contrast in mood which the F Major
     coda presents to the overriding melancholy of the rest
     of the quartet, but ignores the coda as the culmination
     of a continual struggle between F Minor and D Major
     throughout the quartet.

*The late quartets were largely misunderstood in the 19th
century but have become especially valued in the 20th. The
following is a mechanical analysis or description without
any insight, typical of the 19th century and quite different
from 20th-century analyses.*

637. Bargheer, Carl Louis. *L. von Beethoven's fünf letzte
     Quartette für die Kammermusik-Abende der Philhar-
     monischen Gesellschaft in Hamburg.* Hamburg: J.F.
     Richter, 1883. 787.B39qYb. iv + 56 pages.
     A brief introduction which quotes Carl Holz (Schup-
     panzigh's second violinist) on how Beethoven regarded
     the composition of the 5 quartets. Describes the order
     of themes and, in some cases, their development.
     Tonalities are mentioned in passing. No historical
     insight, no mention of the generative 4-note motive.

*On the other hand, respected 20th-century musicians have not
always respected the pieces:*

638. Moldenhauer, Hans. "Busoni's Kritik an Beethovens
     letzten Quartetten," in *Neue Zeitschrift für Musik*,
     cxxi (1960), 416-417.
     Prints and comments on a letter by Busoni of November
     15, 1917, now owned by Ludwig Finscher. Busoni is dis-
     appointed with the last 5 quartets of Beethoven which
     are too incomprehensible; the contents are noble but
     they often get lost in dry, dull formulas. Also prints
     Mario Castelnuovo-Tedesco's response upon reading
     Busoni's letter; he agrees with Busoni -- the Op. 59
     quartets were the last to balance form and ideas.

*A good, uncomplicated introduction to the late quartets is
the following:*

639. Fiske, Roger. *Beethoven's Last Quartets*, in *The Musi-
     cal Pilgrim*. London: Geoffrey Cumberlege for Oxford
     University Press, 1940. MT 145.B425.F56. 77 pages,
     67 musical examples.
     A brief but in-depth analysis of the last 5 quartets
     and *Der Grosse Fuge* for the non-specialist. In the in-
     troduction places the quartets within Beethoven's bio-
     graphy. Then concentrates on motivic and rhythmic
     structure. Brief historical data.

640. Mila, Massimo. *Beethoven: I Quartetti Galitzine e la
     Grande Fuga: Corso Monografico de Storia della Musi-
     ca*. Turin: G. Giappichelli, 1969. ML 410.B42M64.
     iii + 161 pages. In Italian. A sequel to {615}.
     A popular, intelligent history of the quartets, their
     cool reception at first, the late style of Beethoven,
     and his place among the visionaries of the 19th cen-
     tury who explore the frontier of consciousness. Based
     on Marliave, Fiske, Ulrich and others. Analyses are
     non-technical and in essay form, with frequent quota-
     tions from Rolland, Bekker, Kerman, and others.

Somewhat more technical but still for the layperson is:

641. Truscott, Harold. *Beethoven's Late String Quartets*.
     London: Dennis Dobson, 1968. MT 145.B425T8. SBN
     234-77973-X. vii + 148 pages.
     Expansion of 6 radio talks in 1964, assumes that the
     reader has the scores in hand but it includes, never-
     theless, 53 musical examples. Intended for the in-
     formed layperson who wants to understand music. An
     intelligent introduction shows Beethoven's treatment of
     sonata form, especially in his third period. Then
     analyzes style, texture, harmony, treatment of melody
     and rhythm in the quartets, including Op. 133. Not
     extra-musical or philosophical.

*For motivic analysis of Op. 95 - 135, in comparison with
Bartók's 6 quartets, see Frank Spinosa's dissertation {570}.*

642. Johnson, Douglas P., Alan Tyson, and Robert Winter, ed.
     *The Beethoven Sketchbooks: History, Reconstruction,
     Inventory*. Berkeley/Los Angeles: University of Cali-
     fornia Press, 1985. ML 410.B4J58.1985. ISBN 0-520-
     04835.
     See part iv: "Sketches in Score for the Late Quartets"
     (pages 463-508), and part v: "Some Problematical Cases:
     Sketches for the String Quartets, Opus 59 (1806)"
     (pages 524-526).

643. Kreft, Ekkehard. *Die späten Quartette Beethovens: Sub-
     stanz und Substanzverarbeitung*. Bonn: H. Bouvier,
     1969. MT 145.B425K7. 279 pages.
     A detailed, theoretical analysis for music theorists of
     the motivic, harmonic and formal concepts of the late
     quartets, including Op. 133. Not as concerned with the
     superficial elements of form as with its "substance."
     Dissects themes and motives and traces them in differ-
     ent guises. Much of this study is through charts and
     formulas. After a quartet-by-quartet analysis, a sum-
     mary of the substance of themes, development of sub-
     stance, substance in non-sonata-form movements, and
     variation.

644. Cooke, Deryck. "The Unity of Beethoven's Late Quar-
     tets," in *The Music Review*, xxiv (1963), 30-49.
     Based on the author's *The Language of Music* (London:
     Oxford University Press, 1959). Analyzes the "motivic
     evolution" of the 5 quartets, with stress on the extra-
     musical significance of the motives.

645. Sekine, Kazue. "Beethoven Bannen No Gengakushijusokyo-
     ku." MA thesis. Tokyo National University of Fine
     Arts and Music, 1976. RILM 76-5632. 197 pages. In
     Japanese.
     Analyzes the idea of motivic unity in the last quartets
     and considers them also from a biographical viewpoint.

646. Riseling, Robert A. "Motivic Structures in Beethoven's
     Late Quartets," in Johan Glowacki, ed. *Paul A. Pisk:
     Essays in his Honor* (Austin: University of Texas,
     1966), pages 141-162. ML 55.P6G6.
     A technical study that attempts to show the unity in
     Beethoven's late quartets by motivic structure (not
     only the B-A-C-H theme but also a basic fourth and
     third interval), rhythm, and spatial organization.

647. Wildberger, Jacques. "Versuch über Beethovens späte
     Streichquartette," in *Schweizerische Musikzeitung*, cx
     (1970), 1-8.
     Seeks to correlate Beethoven's psychological state of
     mind with the happenings in his late quartets. His
     fixation on his nephew corresponds to his fixation on
     the 4-note unifying motive. Suppositions, not facts.

648. Müller-Blattau, Joseph. "Beethoven im Spätwerk," in Walther Vetter, ed., *Festschrift Max Schneider zum achtigsten Geburtstage* (Leipzig: Deutscher Verlag für Musik, 1955), pp. 215-225. ML 55.V4.
A good, general, not very technical introduction to the late quartets for layperson and student. Believes all the late works are interrelated, not so much for their expression of events in Beethoven's life but for their cyclic expression of his most mature thoughts on art, mankind and the world. Three genres: piano music, symphony, and quartet. Devotes most of the article to the quartets. Reviews the first century of writings on them and then takes a new look. Finds initially different principles of construction from the earlier quartets: for example, individual forms of movements give way to cyclic, motivic structure, 4 movements give way to 5, 6, 7 movements, but they are always unified.

649. Stephan, Rudolf. "Zu Beethovens letzten Quartetten," in *Die Musikforschung*, xxiii (1970), 245-256.
A few remarks on the quartets. Relates them thematically to many other pieces by Beethoven. Emphasizes the form of Op. 131.

650. Mahaim, Ivan. *Beethoven*. Paris: Desclée De Brouwer, 1964. MT 145.B425M5. 2 vols. I: *Beethoven: Naissance et Renaissance des Derniers Quatuors*, 280 pages, 16 charts, 229 illustrations (including programs, portraits, letters, postcards, and music); II: *Beethoven: La Terre Natale et la Trilogie*, 298 pages, 40 illustrations.
An exhaustive, exciting, beautiful book on the performers and performances of Beethoven's late quartets (including Op. 133) from their premiers until the end of the Capet Quartet in 1928, with primary emphasis on the 19th century. Handsomely illustrated with portraits and programs of the concerts, documented with numerous additional bits of information (for example, in chart no. 7, what Beethoven quartets were played by the Quatuor Millout 1849-1881; in chart no. 8, what Beethoven quartets were played by the Quatuor Schwaederlé in Strassburg 1855-1867). Draws from newspapers, journals, autobiographies, and diaries. America is included, beginning with the Theodor Thomas Quartet of New York 1855-1868 (chart no. 10), as well as Russia, Poland, Hungary, Denmark, Italy, and other places. Vol. II has extensive bibliography, indices, biographical data, a discussion of the B-A-C-H motive, and special attention to Op. 133.

651. Krummacher, Friedhelm. "Synthesis des Disparaten: zu Beethovens späten Quartetten und ihrer frühen Rezep-

tion," in *Archiv für Musikwissenschaft*, xxxvii
(1980), 99-134.
Scholarly, thought-provoking discussion, with reference
to the most important literature on these quartets from
the 1950's to the late 1970's. Challenges the idea
that there is nothing new to be said about them; are
they not much easier and better received by audiences
today than 85 years ago? But they may have lost some
of their purpose by being so readily accepted today
rather than by posing enormous difficulties to the
listener. What did Beethoven intend? The confusion of
the early listeners should not be taken simply as their
stupidity. Reviews various analytical studies, and
spends much time with Mendelssohn's reaction to the
quartets. Considers whether or not the contrast of
Classical and Romantic has any bearing on how one
listens to the quartets.

652. Ebert, Alfred. "Die ersten Aufführung von Beethovens
     Es-Dur Quartett (op. 127) im Frühling 1825," in *Die
     Musik*, ix.3 (1909-1910), 42-63 and 90-106.
     Reviews Beethoven's writing of the quartet in 1824-
     1825, and then places in order all the documents (let-
     ters and notebooks) describing its first performance.
     Reveals how Schuppanzigh worked, the concerts he gave
     regularly at the old Musikverein, as well as his parti-
     cularly close relationship with Beethoven. The quartet
     was premiered by Schuppanzigh unsuccessfully on March
     6, 1825. Played privately by Boehm's quartet c.March
     20-22, 1825, and publicly on Wednesday, March 23, 1825,
     both with great success. Also played soon thereafter
     by Joseph Mayseder.

653. De Kenessey, Stefania Maria. "The Quartet, the Finale
     and the Fugue: a Study of Beethoven's Opus 130/133."
     PhD dissertation. Princeton University, 1984. UMI
     84-05109. DAI xliv.11A, p. 3198. 341 pages.
     Analyzes the quartet and shows that the motivic materi-
     al of the first movement is organized about the chroma-
     tic hexachord F up to B-flat. This hexachord also go-
     verns the entire quartet, with each half-step ascending
     through each pair of movements and reaching its climax
     in the present Finale. The original fugue movement
     radically expanded the ascent from G up to B-flat,
     whereas the present Finale emphasizes the smaller
     trichord F to G.

654. MacArdle, Donald W. "Beethoven's Quartet in B-Flat,
     Op. 130: an Analysis," in *The Music Review*, viii
     (1947), 11-24.
     A detailed description of the quartet outlining the ba-
     sic themes, harmonies, forms and styles of each move-
     ment. A schematic "analysis" at the end.

See Stahmer's "Zur Frage der Interpretation von Musik: eine musiksoziologische Modellstudie dargestellt an dem 1. Satz von Beethovens Streichquartett op. 130," in {457}, pages 81-99.

655. Kopfermann, Michael. *Beiträge zur musikalischen Analyse später Werke Ludwig van Beethovens*, in *Berliner musikwissenschaftliche Arbeiten*, Bd. 10. Munich/Salzburg: Musikverlag Emil Katzbichler, 1975. ML 410.B42K66.1975. ISBN 3-87397-040-6. 150 pages.
A thought-provoking treatise on the meaning of analysis with special attention to Rudolph Reti. A study of the relationship of form and harmony (the musical logic in a piece) in late Beethoven, with most of the discussion centering around the first movement of Op. 130.

656. Tovey, Donald Francis. "Some Aspects of Beethoven's Art Forms," in *Music and Letters*, iii (1927), and in Hubert Foss, ed., *Essays and Lectures on Music* (London/New York/Toronto: Oxford University Press, 1949), pages 271-297.
On pages 288-297 is an analysis of Beethoven's Op. 131 that is written in marvelous prose. Primarily concerned with tonalities. Warns against referring to forms as moulds and campaigns for the appreciation of the individuality of great works.

657. Winter, Robert S., III. *Compositional Origins of Beethoven's Opus 131*, in *Studies in Musicology*, no. 54. Ann Arbor: UMI Research Press, 1982. MT 145.B425W5. 1982. ISBN 8357-1289-3. xxiv + 385 pages. "Compositional Origins of Beethoven's String Quartet in C#-Minor, Op. 131." PhD dissertation. University of Chicago, 1978. DAI xxxix.4A, p. 1923.
An attempt to recreate Beethoven's creative process by analysis of some 350 pages of score sketches for Op. 131 and a comparison of them with the final version. Evaluates the Beethoven sketch books and deals with watermarks, the sequence of the original books, autographs compared to first editions, and the "evolution of the finale." One of the finest critical analyses of any Beethoven Quartet.

658. _____. "Plans for the Structure of the String Quartet in C Sharp Minor, Op. 131," in Alan Tyson, ed., *Beethoven Studies*, ii (London/Oxford/New York: Oxford University Press, 1977), pp. 106-137. ML 410.B4. ISBN 0-19-315315-7.
A scholarly analysis of the "Kullak" Sketchbook's "telescoped draft" of the overall tonal plan of Op. 131. A brief review of the various types of sketches, then concentration on how Beethoven planned this quartet: first in 4 movements, then in 3, finally in 7. Also considers the opening fugue movement which follows di-

rectly on Op. 133, and the key of C♯ and various related keys for fugue answers (especially subdominant) and
subsequent movements including an aborted "D-flat postscript" -- mainly from the "Kullak" sketches but also
utilizing other sketches and drafts. Fascinated with
the "tug-of-war between large-scale design and its
ramifications for specific movements." By the fourth
and fifth tonal overviews the emphasis on subdominant
and neopolitan is clear. The final version alters this
emphasis, especially by bringing in more dominant and
by moving the Scherzo from F♯ minor to E major. Thus
it is only by knowing the tonal overviews that we can
trace Beethoven's struggle with new tonal conceptions
-- not between the tonalities of sections of a movement
but among whole movements.

659. Brandenburg, Sieghard. "The Historical Background to
the 'Heiliger Dankgesang' in Beethoven's A-Minor
Quartet Op. 132," in Alan Tyson, ed., *Beethoven
Studies* iii (Cambridge/London/New York: Cambridge
University Press, 1982), pp. 161-191. ML 410.B4.
ISBN 0-521-24131-6.
The most important scholarly study of the origins and
meaning of Beethoven's use of a chorale for movement 3
of Op. 132 -- a study derived from the sketches. Beethoven achieves an integration of church music elements
with classical form. Explores the influence on Beethoven of treatises and articles on church music which
Beethoven probably read (books in his possession, periodicals he received); the 19th-century conception of
church-like music is manifested in the adagio molto tempo, uniform minim rhythm, uncertainty of meter, simplicity, no ornaments, and note-against-note rhythm. The
accompaniment of a chorale can vary, but the tune remains "pure"; Türk discusses contrapuntal variation in
the 3 lower parts, which serves as a model for the second strophe of the Dankgesang. Türk is a major influence, as are also Kirnberger, Knecht and Vogler, rather
than Gafurius or Zarlino directly. The sketches disprove Kerman's program for the quartet as a whole.
From the start Beethoven intended the alternation of a
chorale and "interludes," but the idea of "lydian" was
not indicated in the music or by rubric until after the
completion of the autograph. He only gradually arrived
at a lydian sound. Continual changes in the sketches
also rule out a pre-existent chorale tune as a model as
well as a polyphonic model.

660. Grew, Sidney. "The 'Grosse Fuge': the Hundred Years of
its History," in *Music and Letters*, xii (1931), 140-
147.

Except for the Joachim and Heckmann (1848-1891) Quartets, nobody performed Op. 133 in public from 1825 to 1925 and the score was not readily available to students. Thus it could hardly be analyzed or understood properly. Yet it was continually condemned. Explains its history, including the first apparently successful readings by Ferdinand David (1810-1873), and reviews Joachim's and Heckmann's performances, the major revival by both the Léner and Brodsky Quartets (1927), and the earliest recording. Points to the continual misunderstanding by important critics, yet is appreciated by the average audience.

661. _____. "The 'Grosse Fuge': an Analysis," in *Music and Letters*, xii (1931), 253-261. Characterizes Op. 133 as a "sonata fugata." After admitting the difficulty in finding form in the piece, notes that it consists basically of 3 movements distinguished by tonality B-flat to A-flat to B-flat, with the first similar to exposition, the second similar to development, and the third similar to coda. It is a double fugue that does not follow the rule of double fugues: fugue 1, fugue 2, then a combination of 1 and 2. Explains the scherzo movements before and after the A-flat movement.

662. _____. "Beethoven's Grosse Fuge," in *The Musical Quarterly*, xvii (1931), 497-508. A summary of the 2 articles in *Music and Letters*.

663. Scherchen, Hermann. "Beethovens Grosse Fuge opus 133," in *Die Musik*, xx (1927-1928), 401-420. Reprinted in Gerhard Schuhmacher, *Zur musikalischen Analyse*, in *Wege der Forschung*, Band 257 (Darmstadt: Wissenschaftliche Buchgesellschaft, 1974), 161-185. MT 6.S3529Z8.
Contrasts the relationship of law to freedom, the materials of composition to fantasy, which Beethoven himself states on his score: "Tantôt libre, tantôt recherchée." Considers the importance of the fugue for Op. 130 as the second part of a dualism also apparent in other great works of art by Beethoven and others. But within the fugue the dualism remains: freedom versus law. A detailed motivic, rhythmic, and formal analysis of the piece.

664. Kirkendale, Warren. "The 'Great Fugue' Op. 133: Beethoven's 'Art of Fugue,'" in *Acta Musicologica*, xxxv (1963), 14-24.
Discredits metaphysical and formalistic analyses of Op. 133 and concentrates instead on the composer's point of departure and intention, which are found in the nature of the counterpoint and historical, biographical, and

philological facts. Looks at Fux and Albrechtsberger, who were Beethoven's models in fugues, and finds direct sources for Beethoven's fugue. Also shows how this influence extended to other late works besides Op. 133. Scholarly, well-documented, with musical examples. See also {495}.

665. Kramer, Jonathan D. "Multiple and Non-Linear Time in Beethoven's Opus 135," in *Perspectives of New Music*, xi, no. 2 (1973), 122-145. Listens to Beethoven's Opus 135, first movement, on the basis of some modern conceptions of time. For example, free of clock-time (measured time), the Beethoven movement starts with a very strong final cadence (mm. 5-10), after which the contents of the movement are revealed. But also 2 other strong cadences (mm. 104-109 and 188-193): the movement has 3 endings -- 3 times experiencing the same moment of time. Music can be listened to simultaneously as linear (clock) time and as gestural (experience) time. Contemporary life scrambles time in art -- a common occurrence -- so that we look back on previous art in the same way. Uses the Beethoven as a starting point and then goes off into theories about time.

666. Bumpas, L. Kathryn. "Beethoven's Last Quartet." PhD dissertation. University of Illinois, 1982. UMI 83-02817. DA xliii.9A, p. 2824. 2 vols. 713 pages. A study of Opus 135, which gives biographical information on Beethoven's last year, his working habits, analysis of the 4 main manuscript sources, and this quartet's relationship to the other late quartets.

After the string quartets, the most intensely studied chamber music by Beethoven is the violin + piano sonatas. Here, too, the changes in attitudes and methods of study over nearly a century are extensive.

667. Midgley, Samuel. *Handbook to Beethoven's Sonatas for Violin and Pianoforte*. London: Breitkopf & Härtel/ The Vincent Co., 1911. MT 145.B422M5. 68 pages. Eloquent rhapsody on the greatness of Beethoven and the sonatas. For the layperson who needs to become superficially acquainted with the pieces. Analyzes each movement from the standpoint of emotive content and principal themes. Dated, sometimes inaccurate, brief overview.

668. Rupertus, Otto. *Erläuterungen zu Beethovens Violin-sonaten*, in *Tongers Musikbücherei*, Band 7. Köln: P.J. Tonger, 1915. MT 145.B422R8. 3rd improved ed. 1920. MT 145.B42R8.1920. In German.

An amateurish description of each movement. Relates the A Minor Sonata Op. 23 to Beethoven"s "Immortal Beloved" and the Rondo of the Spring Sonata to quiet joy speaking innocently in the sunshine about the spirit imbued in the present moment.

669. Engelsmann, Walter. *Beethovens Kompositionspläne dargestellt in den Sonaten für Klavier und Violine.* Augsburg: Benno Filser, 1931. MT 145.B422E7. 208 pages. In German.
A highly technical, theoretic book that tries to understand Beethoven's approach (conscious or unconscious) to multi-movement sonatas from an objective, not subjective, standpoint. Based on Riemann's analyses of the piano sonatas and string quartets that show a continual variation or developmental technique of head motives throughout multi-movement works. Analyses of the violin + piano sonatas avoid simple theme-by-theme description. In the opening chapter reviews some early 20th-century attempts to show unity in classical compositions, builds on them, but goes in a new direction: "die Einbeziehung des bewusst gestaltenden Willens - Formwillens - als eines ethischen Prinzips." A single lead motive is the source of each sonata in all its parts, movements and themes. Does not cover the sonatas in chronological order but as they fit into the discussion.

670. Wetzel, Justus Hermann. *Beethovens Violinsonaten, nebst den Romanzen und dem Konzert.* Berlin: Max Hesse, 1924. MT 145.B425W3. 2 vols. but only vol. II located. Vol. II: ix + 402 pages. In German.
Deals with sonatas 1 - 5 and the 2 Romances. Too technical for the layperson, designed for the theorist as an alternative kind of analysis to Schenker. A purely theoretic, not hermeneutic study; concerned with the musical events and not aesthetics. The introduction covers the basic questions of theoretic analysis, followed by analyses of the 5 sonatas and romances. Complicates a rigid conception of meter and form. Detailed charts. Main point is the rhythmic drive of the motives and how these motives form the whole movement and piece; also important is the rhythm of the harmony and the tonal centers.

For performance suggestions of the sonatas, see Joseph Szigeti's The Ten Beethoven Sonatas for Piano and Violin, ed. Paul Rolland {1472} and Marcel Herwegh's Technique d'Interprétation sous Forme d'Essai... {1473}.

671. D'Aranyi, Jelly. "The Violin Sonatas," in *Music and Letters*, viii (1927), 191-197.
A personal feeling of the Beethoven sonatas, especially Op. 96, by an important violinist.

672. Johansen, Gail Nelson. "Beethoven's Sonatas for Piano
     and Violin, Op. 12, No. 1 and Op. 96: a Performance
     Practice Study." DMA dissertation. Stanford Univer-
     sity, 1981. DAI xlii.2A, p. 445. 120 pages.
     Studies principle violin treatises by Beethoven's con-
     temporaries (Spohr, Baillot, Rode, and Kreutzer) to
     determine more precisely the form, topic, periodicity,
     harmony, rhythm, scansion, melody and texture of these
     2 sonatas so as to enable the performer to better rea-
     lize their "unique character and effect." Considers
     new happenings in bow construction and related develop-
     ments in keyboard music.

673. Kramer, Richard A. "The Sketches for Beethoven's Vio-
     lin Sonatas, Opus 30: History, Transcription, Analy-
     sis." PhD dissertation. Princeton University, 1974.
     UMI 74-17468. DAI xxxv.2A, pp. 1144-5. 3 vols. 659
     pages.
     A detailed, penetrating study of Beethoven's sketches
     in general and sketches for these 3 sonatas in particu-
     lar. Includes transcriptions. The longer sketches re-
     flect a sense of time which is affected by changes.
     They reveal the two sides of composition: natural, un-
     impeded, improvisational, and rational, editorial,
     critical -- and how Beethoven juxtaposed the two.

674. Obelkevich, Mary Rowen. "The Growth of a Musical Idea
     -- Beethoven's Opus 96," in *Current Musicology*, no.
     11 (1971), 91-114.
     Carefully traces the evolution of this last sonata
     through 4 different manuscript stages to the final
     printed version. Shows the tune from which Beethoven
     borrowed the theme for the finale and how he gradually
     changed it. Considers the different positions of the
     movements and numerous other important details.

675. Henle, Günther. "Ein Fehler in Beethovens letzter Vio-
     lin-Sonate?" in *Die Musikforschung*, v (1952), 53-54.
     Shows that the "a" in m. 158 of Op. 96, fifth eighth-
     note, should really be "a-flat." Corroborated in Lud-
     wig Misch, "Zur Frage 'Ein Fehler in Beethovens letzter
     Violinsonate?'" in *Die Musikforschung*, v (1952), 367-
     368.

*The remaining Beethoven chamber music also receives consid-
erable attention:*

676. Szabo, Edward Joseph. "The Violoncello-Piano Sonatas
     of Ludwig van Beethoven." EdD dissertation. Colum-
     bia University, 1966. UMI 70-12530. DAI xxxi.1A, p.
     418. 149 pages.

For laypersons, a historical, analytical and stylistic
examination of the 5 cello sonatas. After a brief history of the instrument's construction, a measure-by-
measure analysis seeking form, melody, rhythm, harmony,
tonality, dynamics, and special devices.

677. Orrego Salas, Juan. "La Obra para Violoncello de Beethoven," in *Revista Musical Chilena*, xiv (May-June,
1960), 34-50. In Spanish.
Studies the 5 sonatas and 3 sets of variations first by
placing them in the context of Beethoven's 3 periods
and then by comparing them to other works of Beethoven.
Superficial, unoriginal, dramatic analyses. The article will entertain the uninitiated layperson and bore
everyone else.

678. Dahlhaus, Carl. "'Von zwei Kulturen der Musik': die
Schlussfuge aus Beethovens Cellosonate opus 102,2,"
in *Die Musikforschung*, xxxi (1978), 397-405.
An essay on the relationship of Beethoven's conception
of fugue writing, as exemplified in the final movement
of this sonata, to the model of fugue writing he
learned as a child studying Bach's *Well-Tempered Klavier*. Whereas the model (Bach) is a growing contrapuntal configuration around a ubiquitous theme, the Beethoven example is development of the theme, which allows
irregularities not tolerated in "school-book" fugues.

679. Hiebert, Elfrieda Franz. "The Piano Trios of Beethoven: an Historical and Analytical Study." PhD dissertation. University of Wisconsin, 1970. RILM 70-
482. UM 70-22652. DA xxxi.10A, p. 5447. 407 pages.
A critical study of the sources of the original, doubtful, and arranged piano trios of Beethoven; a textural
study of the piano's changing roles in the trios; and
a practical study of performance problems. Scholarly,
but aimed at performers.

680. Smith, Robert Ludwig. "A Study of Instrumental Rela-
tions: the Piano Trios of Beethoven." PhD dissertation. Florida State University, 1971. UMI 72-21331.
DAI xxxiii.2A, p. 779.
Studies the leading and accompanying roles of each instrument in the trios in different stylistic situations: accompanied melody, counterpoint, unaccompanied
solo voice, chordal style. Also considers tutti, concertino, and solo. Finds the majority of solo passages
goes to the piano.

681. Engel, Carl. "Beethoven's Opus 3: an 'Envoi de Vien-
ne'?" in *The Musical Quarterly*, xiii (1927), 261-279.
On a working manuscript of the last movement of Beethoven's Opus 3 string trio now in the Library of Congress. Explains how the Library obtained it, and pro-

ceeds to date it 1793 or 1794 in Vienna, contrary to
the dates (by an unknown hand) on the manuscript and in
Thayer.

682. Platen, Emil. "Beethovens Steichtrio D-Dur, opus 9 Nr.
    2: zum Problem der thematischen Einheit mehrsätziger
    Formen," in Siegfried Kross and Hans Schmidt, eds.,
    *Colloquium Amicorum: Joseph Schmidt-Görg zum 70.
    Geburtstag* (Bonn: Beethovenhaus, 1967), pp. 260-282.
    ML 55.S35C6.
    Considers a previously unnoticed case of thematic unity
    in Beethoven's Trio Op. 9, no. 2. A technical, detail-
    ed analysis designed for scholars and theorists. The
    themes and motives used in Op. 9, no. 2, are common to
    Beethoven's chamber music in the period 1796-1800 and
    can be found in Op. 12, no. 1, Op. 14, no. 1, Op. 18,
    no. 3, Op. 26 and Op. 50. Briefly discusses the valid-
    ity of studying thematic or other unity in multi-
    movement works.

683. Altmann, Wilhelm. "Beethovens Umarbeitung seines
    Streichtrios Op. 3 zu einem Klaviertrio," in *Zeit-
    schrift für Musikwissenschaft*, iii (1920-1921), 124-
    158.
    Discusses the authenticity, dating, and interpretation
    of a manuscript (apparently in Beethoven's hand) in
    which the first movement and part of the second of Op.
    3 designates a "cembalo" (in no way a figured bass)
    over the cello part and adds a new cello line. As-
    sumes the old cello line is the left hand of the
    "cembalo" and the viola part becomes an improvised
    right hand; the violin stays the same.

684. Toens, George. "Beethoven Used the Clarinet Often in
    his Chamber Music Works," in *Woodwind World*, i (Nov.
    1957), 5.
    A brief survey of Beethoven's chamber music including
    the clarinet.

685. Ohlsson, Eric Paul. "The Quintets for Piano, Oboe,
    Clarinet, Horn and Bassoon by Wolfgang Amadeus Mozart
    and Ludwig van Beethoven." DMA dissertation. Ohio
    State University, 1980. UMI 81-00098. DAI xli.7A,
    pp. 2823-4. 130 pages.
    A history, analysis and comparison of Mozart's K.452
    and Beethoven's Op. 16 quintets.

686. MacArdle, Donald W. "Beethoven, Artaria, and the C
    Major Quintet," in *The Musical Quarterly*, xxxiv
    (1948), 567-574.
    Artaria published Beethoven's Op. 29 quintet just as
    he wanted it, complete and correct. A brief, scholarly
    account correcting errors in later publications.

687. Tyson, Alan. "The Authors of the Op. 104 String Quin-
     tet," in Alan Tyson, ed., *Beethoven Studies,* i (New
     York: W.W. Norton, 1973), pp. 158-173. ML 410.B42T9.
     ISBN 0-393-02168-8.
     Scholarly study of Beethoven's arrangement of his Piano
     Trio in C Minor, Op. 1 No. 3 for string quintet (2
     violins + 2 violas + cello). Presents the known facts
     and assumptions on how this piece came into being and
     then interprets them differently from Thayer and
     others. The surviving fair copy by Beethoven's chief
     copyist is apparently an arrangement of the trio by an
     unknown Herr Kaufmann, on which Beethoven has made ex-
     tensive, substantial changes. Therefore before anyone
     criticizes Beethoven for some aspect of the printed
     score, the critic should know what portion of the score
     is Kaufmann's and what is truly Beethoven's effort to
     make the transcription passable. There remain some
     difficulties -- inconsistencies -- for the editor and
     for performers, some of which are pointed out. Also
     discusses briefly the early published editions of the
     score, each with changes, and authenticates the first
     London edition c.1819.

688. Orle, Alfred. "Beethovens Oktett op. 103 und seine
     Bearbeitung als Quintett op. 4," in *Zeitschrift für
     Musikwissenschaft,* iii (1920-1921), 159-179.
     Despite its late opus number, Op. 103 was written
     c.1792 and rewritten (not just transcribed) as a quin-
     tet Op. 4 not later than February, 1797. Thus the
     later work will show the extent to which Beethoven
     developed as a composer during his first few years in
     Vienna. Since the melodies are basically maintained,
     the differences are to be found in the overall struc-
     ture, the expanded dimensions, the increased develop-
     ment, coda, and transitions. For example, the first
     movement of the quintet is 99 beats longer than that of
     the octet, 27 in the development, 47 in the coda.
     Thoroughly compares the 2 works.

689. Wessely, Othmar. *"Zur Geschichte des Equals,"* in *Beet-
     hoven-Studien: Festgabe der österreichischen Akademie
     der Wissenschaften zum 200. Geburtstag von Ludwig van
     Beethoven,* in *Veröffentlichungen der Kommission für
     Musikforschung,* Heft 11 (Vienna: Hermann Böhlaus
     Nachf., 1970), pages 341-360. AS 142.V31.Bd.270.
     A history of the 3 works Beethoven wrote for trombone
     quartet while visiting his brother in Linz in 1812.
     Discusses the various eye-witnesses to Beethoven's
     composing them, especially Franz Xaver Glöggl, whose
     extraordinary career is described and who wrote his
     account of the episode in a letter to Robert Schumann.
     One of the Equals was played at Beethoven's funeral.

Considers the liturgical function of the pieces. Shows
that they are a mixture of pavan and Lied. Later
Bruckner had to write such pieces, which belong to an
old Linz tradition.

Franz Benda
1709-1786

*For a list of Benda's chamber music, see Douglas A. Lee,
Franz Benda (1709-1786): a Thematic Catalogue of his Works
in Thematic Catalogues, no. 10 (New York: Pendragon Press,
1984), xxii + 221 pages. ML 134.B442A2. 1984. ISBN 0-918-
72842-8.*

690. Lee, Douglas A. "Some Embellished Versions of Sonatas
     by Franz Benda," in *The Musical Quarterly*, lxii
     (1976), 58-71.
     Discusses embellishments of 32 sonatas for violin +
     bass by Benda found in a large manuscript in Berlin.
     Variation technique is common, and many sonatas seem
     intended for pedagogic purposes. The style is transi-
     tional from Baroque to Classical. Biographical infor-
     mation and Benda's importance as founder of the North
     German school of violinists.

*See Rudolf Zelenka's "Verzierungsmöglichkeiten in der
Violinsonate A-Dur von Frantisek Benda: ein Beitrag zur
Entwicklung der Kammermusik in der 1. Hälfte des 18.
Jahrhunderts" in {161}, pages 62-66. See also {1475}.*

William Sterndale Bennett
1816-1875

691. Bennett, J.R. Sterndale. *The Life of William Sterndale
     Bennett.* Cambridge: Cambridge University Press,
     1907. HML 1540.15. xii + 471 pages.
     A biography by the composer's son, which includes a
     list of works (pages 455-464), among which are a string
     quartet, a piano sextet, a piano trio, and a cello +
     piano sonata. The works are discussed historically in
     the course of the text.

Jörgen Bentzon
1897-1951

*Bentzon's works are catalogued in Mindeskrift over Jörgen
Bentzon: 14. Februar 1897/9. Juli 1951 (Udgivet af gamle
elever og venner, 1957), HML 1547.15. He wrote 5 string
quartets, a sonatina for flute + clarinet + bassoon, and
other chamber pieces.*

692. Monsen, Ronald Peter. "A Study of Selected Clarinet
     Solo and Chamber Music by Jörgen Bentzon: a Basis for
     Performance and Teaching." DMA dissertation. Uni-
     versity of Wisconsin-Madison, 1978. DAI xxxix.8A,
     p.4586. 240 pages.
     History and biography of the Danish composer. Analyzes
     performance problems (technique, balance, intonation,
     tonal matching, projection, articulation, fingerings,
     range) in 7 works. Designed for performers, not
     historians or theorists.

Niels Viggo Bentzon
b.1919

For a catalogue of the works of this Danish composer of 11
string quartets, 7 sonatas for violin + piano, 4 sonatas for
cello + piano, 3 piano trios, 2 string trios, 1 piano quar-
tet, 1 piano quintet, many duets, 3 quartets for 4 flutes, a
trio for trumpet + horn + trombone, and so on, see Klaus
Mollerhoj, Niels Vigg Bentzons Kompositioner: en Fortegnese
over Voerkerne med Opusnummer *(Copenhagen: Wilhelm Hansen,*
1980), ISBN 87-7455-009-8.

Alban Berg
1885-1935

693. Redlich, Hans F. *Alban Berg: the Man and his Music.*
     London: J. Calder/ New York: Abelard-Schuman, 1957.
     ML 410.B47R35. 316 pages, 185 examples.
     This definitive biography of Berg is in 3 parts; the
     chamber music is discussed in part 2, chapter 3, pp.
     49-58, which deals with early works (string quartet Op.
     3 and 4 pieces for clarinet + piano), and part 2, chap-
     ter 5, pp. 137-154, which deals with the development of
     serial technique (*Lyric Suite*). In the *Lyric Suite*
     stresses its structural and aesthetic affinity with
     Beethoven's late quartets, Mahler's *Das Lied von der*
     Erde, and Zemlinksy's *Lyric Symphony*. Points out di-
     rect quotations from Wagner and others and analyzes the
     serialism in those movements which have it. The early
     string quartet is in 2 movements, the second acting as
     a development of the first. Shows here the influence
     of Schoenberg, Strauss and Mahler. The clarinet pieces
     represent Berg as a miniaturist who was rebelling a-
     gainst the "symphony of thousands" syndrome.

For a documentary study of Berg's string quartets, see
Ursula von Rauchhaupt, Schoenberg, Berg, Webern *{201}.*

694. Parish, George David. "Motive and Cellular Structure
     in Alban Berg's *Lyric Suite*." PhD dissertation.

University of Michigan, 1970. UM 71-15262. DA
xxxi.12A, p. 6650. vi + 319 pages.
A detailed, technical analysis of the rows used by Berg
in the *Lyric Suite* and their effect on the character of
the music and its harmony. Studies the 4-note cells in
linear and vertical positions, and the rhythms of the
piece. Less concerned with form than with the pacing
of events in each movement.

695. Bouquet, Fritz. "Alban Bergs 'Lyrische Suite': eine
Studie über Gestalt, Klang und Ausdruck," in *Melos*,
xv (1948), 227-231.
A non-technical analysis of this string quartet, which
in 1948 was almost totally forgotten in Germany where
it had been banned since 1933. With the elimination of
symphonic and duet forms, the piece achieves its dramatic lyricism in the heightening expression of each
movement. Discusses tonality (F plays an important
role), use of the row and its motives, form, and the
character of each movement. Notes especially the
dynamic linearity of the whole piece.

696. Brindle, Reginald Smith. "The Symbolism in Berg's
Lyric Suite," in *The Score*, no. 21 (October 1957),
60-63.
Notes the symbolism of the number 23 in the *Lyric
Suite*. This is evident in a letter Berg wrote to
Schoenberg in connection with the *Kammerkonzert* written
just before, where the number 3 was important. 23
stands for the number of letters in Zemlinksy's name
(he is the dedicatee) + A.B. Metronome markings and
the number of measures in all movements (except the
second) are 23 or multiples of 23.

697. Floros, Constantin. "Das esoterische Programm der
Lyrischen Suite von Alban Berg: eine semantische
Analyse," in *Hamburger Jahrbuch für Musikwissen-
schaft*, I (Hamburg: Karl Dieter Wagner, 1974), 101-
145. Reprinted in Rainer Riehn and Heinz-Klaus
Metzger, eds., *Alban Berg Kammermusik I*, in *Musik-
Konzepte*, Heft 4 (Munich: Musik-Konzepte, 1978),
pages 5-48.
Justifies a programmatic approach as opposed to a pure
music one to Berg's purely instrumental music. Consi-
ders specifically the *Lyric Suite*: the character of
each movement, the number symbolism, Zemlinsky's
Lyrischer Symphonie, Wagner's *Tristan Liebestod*, and
Berg's autobiography.

698. Perle, George. "The Secret Programme of the Lyric
Suite," in *The Musical Times*, cxviii (1977), 629-632,
709-713, and 809-813. German trl. in Rainer Riehn
and Heinz-Klaus Metzger, eds., *Alban Berg Kammermusik*

I, in *Musik-Konzepte*, Heft 4 (Munich: Musik-Konzepte, 1978), pages 49-74, with a new bibliography. Discovers the program of the *Lyric Suite*. Locates the personal copy of the score that Berg presented to his secret love, Hanna Werfel (sister of Franz), with explanations written in by Berg of the significance of certain elements of form and meter in terms of their hidden love and with poems and verses attached.

699. Blankenship, Shirley Meyer. "Berg Lines: Opus 3, Lyrische Suite." DMA dissertation. University of Illinois, 1977. UMI 77-26633. DAI xxxviii.6A, p. 3126. 173 pages.
A comparison of Berg's 2 string quartets. Despite serialism in the *Lyric Suite* and not in Opus 3, the two quartets are stylistically linked. Compares them to those by Debussy and Schoenberg. Opus 3 was written to express a "type of dramatic conflict associated with classicism," while "in the Lyric Suite, Berg was preoccupied with the expression of romantic lyricism."

See Michael Coonrod's dissertation "Aspects of Form in Selected String Quartets of the Twentieth Century" {504}.

700. Tardif, Paul John. "Historical and Performance Aspects of Alban Berg's Chamber Concerto for Piano, Violin, and Thirteen Winds." DMA dissertation. Peabody Conservatory, 1976. UMI 77-13163. DAI xxxvii.12A, pp. 7399-7400. v + 210 pages (DAI = 217 pages).
A history of the conception and reception of this piece (1923-1929) and "a performance guide designed to assist musicians who attempt to play the work," with comments on tempo, melodic unity, dynamics, and staging.

Arthur Berger
b.1912

701. Barkin, Elaine. "Post Impressions: Arthur Berger's Trio for Guitar, Violin & Piano (1972)," in *Perspectives of New Music*, xvii (1978-1979), 23-37.
A poetic-prose rhapsody, with allusions to highly technical structural aspects of the piece. Subjective reaction to notes or phrases. This is quite different from the amateur description of music, since details of structure and outstanding sounds are precisely described in technical musical terms. Extensive musical illustrations pinpoint the passages. An amazing bit of analysis and description.

Leonard Bernstein
b.1918

For a catalogue of the chamber pieces, see Jack Gottlieb,
Leonard Bernstein: a Complete Catalogue of his Works:
Celebrating his 60th Birthday August 25, 1978 *(New York:*
Amberson Enterprises, Inc., 1978), 68 pages. ML 134.B51G7.
ISBN 0-913932-40X.

702. Del Rosso, Charles Francis. "A Study of Selected Solo
      Clarinet Literature of Four American Composers as a
      Basis for Performance and Teaching." EdD disserta-
      tion. Columbia University, 1969. UMI 70-4567. DAI
      xxx.9A, pp. 3969-70. 192 pages.
      For performers and clarinet teachers. Analyzes Bern-
      stein's sonata for clarinet + piano, Doran's sonata
      for clarinet + piano, Dello Joio's *Concertante* for
      Clarinet + Piano, and Copland's *Clarinet Concerto.*

Giovanni Antonio Bertoli
fl.c.1639-1645

703. Urbinato, Joseph Mario. "A Critical Edition and Analy-
      sis of Nine Sonatas for Bassoon and Continuo by Gio-
      vanni Antonio Bertoli." MAD dissertation. Boston
      University, 1969. UMI 71-30020. DAI xxxii.8A, p.
      4053. 400 pages.
      Bertoli's biography and the possible influence of the
      solo Venetian instrumentalists on him. Analyzes the
      form, harmony, melody and continuo of the 9 sonatas,
      which are virtuoso pieces.

Franz Berwald
1796-1868

For a list of the chamber works, see Erling Lomnäs, ed.,
Franz Berwald: die Dokumente seines Lebens, *supplement to*
Franz Berwald, Sämtliche Werke, *in* Monumenta Musicae
Svecicae *(Kassel: Bärenreiter, 1979), pages 705-708.*

704. Layton, Robert. *Franz Berwald.* London: Anthony
      Blond, 1959. HML 1591.15.48. 194 pages.
      A biography in which the chamber music is discussed
      both in terms of where it fits into Berwald's life and
      how it demonstrates his stylistic personality. His
      chamber works include 4 string quartets, 5 piano trios,
      1 quartet for piano + winds, 2 piano quintets, a sep-
      tet, and duos for piano + violin or cello.

Carlo Besozzi
1738-1791

705. Nimetz, Daniel. "The Wind Music of Carlo Besozzi."
     PhD dissertation. University of Rochester, Eastman
     School of Music, 1967. UMI 67-14773. DAI xxviii.8A,
     pp. 3212-3. 2 vols. 293 pages.
     A study and edition of 24 sonatas by this Dresden court
     oboist. Seventeen are for 2 oboes + 2 horns + bassoon;
     7 add 2 English horns. They survive in manuscript in
     Vienna's Musikfreunde Library, with a microfilm copy in
     the Sibley Library, Eastman School. Gives biographical
     data and analyzes in detail all the sonatas.

Heinrich Ignaz Franz von Biber
1644-1704

706. Dann, Elias. "Heinrich Biber and the Seventeenth Cen-
     tury Violin." PhD dissertation. Columbia Universi-
     ty, 1968. UMI 71-22435. DAI xxxii.3A, pp. 1547-8.
     419 pages.
     Extensive analysis of the style of Biber's sonatas, the
     history of violin technique on the all-gut violin, the
     capabilities of the old straight or slightly arched
     bow, the various tuning systems, and German polyphonic
     writing. Makes use of a then recently uncovered source
     of Biber autographs in Kromeriz, Czechoslovakia.

Christlieb Siegmund Binder
1723-1789

707. Fleischer, Heinrich. *Christlieb Siegmund Binder*
     (1723-1789): mit 74 Notenbeispielen und einem thema-
     tischen Verzeichnis sämtlicher Werke, in *Forschungs-*
     arbeiten des musikwissenschaftlichen Instituts der
     Universitäts Leipzig, Band 3. Regensburg: Gustav
     Bosse, 1941. HML 1494.15.
     Analyzes scoring, tonal relationships of the movements,
     and style (still contrapuntal in some, more modern in
     others) in Binder's chamber music (trio sonatas for
     flutes or flute and violin or violins + continuo, 2
     string quartets with continuo, 5 obligato trio diverti-
     menti, and so on). Important as transitional music
     from Baroque to Classical. Includes a thematic cata-
     logue, with chamber music on pages 141-146.

Johann Adam Birkenstock
1687-1733

708. Ostrow, Isaac M. "The Solo Violin Sonatas of Johann
     Adam Birkenstock: a Practical Edition." DMA disser-

tation. University of Rochester, 1970. 2 vols. I:
ii + 49 pages; II: 209 pages of music.
Biography, a brief account of the solo-accompanied
violin sonata in the early 18th century, critical
notes, and performance suggestions for the music in
vol. II: *Birkenstock's Sonate a Violino Solo e Violoncello o Basso Continuo, Opus I* (Amsterdam: 1722).

Mathieu-Frédéric Blasius
1758-1829

709. McCormick, Cathy Louise. "Mathieu-Frédéric Blasius
     (1758-1829): a Biographical Sketch, Catalog of Works,
     and Critical Performance Edition of the *Quatuor Con-
     certant in F*, Op. 1, No. 1." PhD dissertation.
     Michigan State University, 1983. UMI 84-00600. DAI
     xliv.10A, p. 2922. 158 pages.
     Discusses the sociological role of music during a dif-
     ficult period in French history and the biography of
     this versatile Alsatian musician. A detailed study of
     the quartet for clarinet + violin + viola + cello
     (1782).

Michel Blavet
1700-1768

710. Bauer, Carla Christine. *Michel Blavets Flötenmusik:
     eine Studie zur Entwicklung der französischen Instru-
     mentalmusik im 18. Jahrhundert*, in *Hochschulsammlung
     Philosophie Musikwissenschaft*, Band 2. Freiburg:
     Hochschulverlag, 1981. ISBN 3-8107-2149-2. viii +
     239. PhD dissertation. University of Freiburg,
     1981.
     A detailed analysis of Blavet's sonatas for transverse
     flute + continuo and 2 flutes without bass, as well as
     other pieces which are pedagogic and also art music.
     Considers tempo, inégalité, and ornaments. Also re-
     lates these works to the changing aesthetics in France
     in the 18th century.

Arthur Bliss
1891-1975

For a catalogue, see Louis Foreman, Arthur Bliss: Catalogue
of the Complete Works *(Sevenoaks [Kent]: Novello, 1980),
ISBN 0-85360-069-4, and* Supplement to Catalogue of the
Complete Works *(1982), ISBN 0-85360-116-X.*

711. Blom, Eric. "The Clarinet Quintet of Arthur Bliss,"
     in *The Musical Times*, lxxiv (1933), 424-427.
     A detailed structural analysis.

Ernest Bloch
1880-1956

For a list of Bloch's works including chamber music see Anon., Ernest Bloch [biography and list of works] (no publishing information) ML 134.B62S3.1960z. For a non-technical introduction to Bloch's chamber music, see Andrew Porter's essay in Alec Robertson, ed., Chamber Music {160}, and:

712. Chissell, Joan. "Style in Bloch's Chamber Music," in
     Music and Letters, xxiv (1943), 30-35.
     A non-technical analysis of Bloch's music pointing to
     intuitive forces rather than rational ones in genera-
     ting his basic sound. Thus the "primitive" music of
     Bali in his Quintet, and the Jewishness of his *Baal
     Shem Suite, Abodah* for Violin + Piano, and other works.
     Uses pentatonic scales (viola suite) and native instru-
     ments and dances (quartet piece "Tongataboo" and Quin-
     tet). Considers Bloch's forms, harmony, rhythm, and
     color effects.

713. Jones, William. "Ernest Bloch's Five String Quartets,"
     in *The Music Review*, xxviii (1967), 112-121.
     An intelligent analysis of melodies and scales and how
     Bloch moved from a Romantic (no. 1) to neo-Classic
     (nos. 2-5).

714. Guibbory, Yenoin Ephraim. "Thematic Treatment in the
     String Quartets of Ernest Bloch." PhD dissertation.
     University of West Virginia, 1970. UMI 71-4849. DAI
     xxxi.8A, pp. 4199-4200. RILM 76-15534. 443 pages.
     An analysis of the 5 string quartets (1916-1956) which
     reveals cyclic unity and the interrelationship of
     themes throughout each entire quartet. Observes "a
     progression towards greater economy of means and
     stricter control of form" from nos. 1 to 5.

715. Rimmer, Frederick. "Ernest Bloch's Second String
     Quartet," in *Tempo*, no. 52 (Fall, 1959), 11-16.
     A technical analysis of motivic transformation in what
     the author believes to be Bloch's best quartet.

716. Raditz, Edward. "An Analysis and Interpretation of the
     Violin and Piano Works of Ernest Bloch (1880-1959)."
     PhD dissertation. New York University, 1975. UM
     76-1750. DA xxxvi.7A, pp. 4099-4100. 230 pages.
     A Schenkerian analysis of *Melodie, Baal Shem Suite,
     Violin Sonata*, and *Poeme Mystique*, with the aim of
     helping the interpreter. Charts.

717. Newlin, Dika. "The Later Works of Ernest Bloch," in
     The Musical Quarterly, xxxiii (1947), 443-459.

Concentrates on the Piano Quintet (1923) and contrasts
the music of Bloch and Schoenberg.

Luigi Boccherini
1743-1805

For a general, non-technical introduction to Boccherini's
chamber music, see Maurice Lindsay's essay in Alec Robert-
son, ed., Chamber Music {160}. For a catalogue including
chamber pieces, see Yves Gérard, Thematic, Bibliographical
and Critical Catalogue of the Works of Luigi Boccherini,
trl. by Andreas Mayor (London: Oxford University Press,
1969), xix + xv + 716 pages. ML 1341.B63G5.

718. Lindsay, J. Maurice, and W. Leggat Smith. "Luigi
     Boccherini (1743-1805)," in *Music and Letters*, xxiv
     (1943), 74-81.
     An appreciation of Boccherini on his 200th birthday, a
     biography, and a brief characterization of his works
     including chamber music.

719. Salvetti, Guido. "Luigi Boccherini nell'Ambito del
     Quartetto Italiano del Secondo Settecento," in Fried-
     rich Lippmann, ed. *Studien zur italienisch-deutschen*
     Musikgeschichte, No. 8, in *Analecta Musicologica*,
     Band 12 (Köln: Arno Volk, 1973), pages 227-252.
     Traces Boccherini's precedents and preparation for his
     first string quartets (Op. 2). Boccherini is not so
     influenced by the Italian quartetto concertante (Duran-
     te and others), which did influence Cambini and Giardi-
     ni; rather he bears much more affinity to Alessandro
     Scarlatti in his "severe" style with its contrapuntal
     treatment of all 4 instruments without harpsichord.
     Scarlatti's example -- foreign to both concerto and
     sonata -- leads to the strong expressive and contrapun-
     tal style of Boccherini. Boccherini was a great cel-
     list who in his youth (1765) played quartets with
     Nardini and Manfredi (violins) and Cambini (viola), so
     that when he wrote his Op. 2, he was thoroughly ac-
     quainted with string quartet writing. What is new in
     Op. 2 is the equality of the instruments with the viola
     and cello taking full part in the "dialogue" (pairing
     not only the 2 violins but also violin with cello or
     violin with viola). After Op. 2 Boccherini went to
     Paris, where to publish he had to relinquish his severe
     style and follow the concertante mode in fashion there,
     though not entirely (Op. 8, nos. 4 and 6 still retain
     the equilibrium of Op. 2). Discusses the other quar-
     tets to Op. 58, his last collection. While Viotti at
     the time had created the quartetto brillante --
     excessive first violin virtuosity -- Cambini and
     Giardini never went that far and Boccherini stayed much
     closer to them. Shows how Boccherini kept his indi-

viduality even from Cambini and Giardini, let alone
from Haydn and Beethoven (the connections with Mozart
need further study).

720. Bonaccorsi, Alfredo. "Luigi Boccherini e il Quartetto," in Adelmo Damerini and Gino Roncaglia, eds.,
*Musiche Italiane Rare e Vive da Giovanni Gabrieli a
Giuseppe Verdi* (Sienna: Accademia Musicale Chigiana,
1962), pp. 301-306. ML 290.D29.
Considers the relationship of "expression" to "form"
and the ideal of the string quartet as "a happy equi-
librium, a harmony and fusion of its parts as sound and
as an amalgamation of sound." Finds Boccherini always
true to his style, whether in a slow cantabile or in a
very rapid movement: always a significant and healthy
rhythm; harmonious, light embellishments; clear, bright
atmosphere. The problem is getting to know the works
of Boccherini which are still largely unpublished in
modern edition. Analyzes the quartettinos and quintets, not the quartets. Closes with a plea for an
edition of Boccherini's works so that the historian can
properly judge Italian quartet history.

721. Smith, Alan Michael. "A Performance Edition and Historical Documentation of an Unpublished Cello Sonata
in E-flat Major by Luigi Boccherini." DMA dissertation. University of Texas, 1977. DAI xxxviii.7A, p.
3797. 106 pages.
Proposes that the bass of this sonata (no. 9) be performed by a second cello or double bass. Compares
cello performance practices of the 18th and 20th
centuries and discusses the cello sonatas of Boccherini
and their contribution to cello literature.

722. Amsterdam, Ellen Iris. "The String Quintets of Luigi
Boccherini." PhD Dissertation. University of California at Berkeley, 1968. RILM 69-1008. DAI xxx.3A,
pp. 1191-2. iv + 177 pages.
The quintets for 2 cellos are especially successful as
concertante pieces demonstrating Italian lyricism,
Spanish rhythmic vitality, French string technique, and
German counterpoint. Studies stylistic and formal
features of all the string quintets (including the few
not for 2 cellos but 2 violins + viola + cello + bass)
and compares them to those by Brunetti and Cambini.

723. Keller, Hans. "Mozart and Boccherini: a Supplementary
Note to Alfred Einstein's *Mozart: his Character - his
Work*," in *The Music Review*, viii (1947), 241-247.
Discusses the influence of Boccherini's Quintet in C on
several Mozart pieces (including the violin + piano
Sonata in D, K.306).

724. Salvetti, Guido. "I Sestetti di Luigi Boccherini," in
     Chigiana: Rassegna Annuale di Studi Musicologici,
     xxiv (1967), 209-220.
     Establishes the historical and aesthetic bases for
     Boccherini's sextets. Analyzes forms, harmony and
     rhythm of sextets Op. 15, 24, and 42 and notes their
     greater diversity in timbre than trios or quartets
     (Boccherini mixes winds and strings in all 3 sextets).

                    Joseph Bodin de Boismortier
                            1689-1755

725. Peterman, Lewis Emanuel. "The Instrumental Chamber
     Music of Joseph Bodin de Boismortier with Special
     Emphasis on the Trio Sonatas for Two Treble Instru-
     ments and Basso Continuo." PhD dissertation.
     University of Cincinnati, 1985. UMI 85-18112. DAI
     xlvi.6A, p. 1437. 1017 pages.
     Examines 47 of the 51 extant chamber music publications
     of Boismortier, an extremely productive composer of
     chamber music, most of it for flute with other instru-
     ments. Transcribes and analyzes the 40 surviving trio
     sonatas for 2 treble instruments + continuo, and "ana-
     lyzes" in charts the over 1300 movements of chamber
     music examined. A brief summary of Parisian musical
     life in the first half of the 18th century and Italian
     influences on it. Lists modern as well as original
     editions.

726. Burden, Ross Patrick. "The Wind Music of Joseph Bodin
     de Boismortier (1689-1755)." DMA dissertation.
     University of Iowa, 1971. RILM 72-1613. UM 71-
     30406. DA xxxii.5A, p. 2726. x + 262 pages.
     Considers French wind music of the first half of the
     18th century and discusses Boismortier's life and style
     in a few individual pieces. Thematic index of the wind
     music and a list of his other works.

727. Buyse, Leone Karena. *The French Rococo Flute Style
     Exemplified in Selected Chamber Works of Joseph Bodin
     de Boismortier (1689-1755)*, in *The Emporia State
     Research Studies*, xxvii, no. 4. Emporia (Kansas):
     Emporia State University, 1979. ML 410.B693B9. 25
     pages. MA thesis.
     Notes Boismortier's unusual preference for the trans-
     verse flute, though he was no flute player himself. A
     history of the instrument, a look at France and the
     Rococo style, and consideration of his special contri-
     butions. Analyzes 3 works: Sonata Op. 7 No. 5 (3
     flutes), Concerto Op. 15 No. 2 (5 flutes) -- in both
     cases without bass or any other instrument -- and Con-
     certo Op. 37 No. 6 (flute + violin + oboe + bassoon +
     continuo). Discusses numerous French flutists in the

first half of the 18th century. A brief biography.
Contrasts French and Italian styles. Buyse is a
flutist in the San Francisco Symphony.

Giovanni Maria Bononcini
1642-1678

728. Klenz, William. "Giovanni Maria Bononcini: a Chapter
in Baroque Instrumental Music." PhD dissertation.
University of North Carolina, 1958. UMI 59-50. DA
xix.11, pp. 2972-3. 575 pages.
A cultural and social history of Bononcini's pre-Corel-
li sonatas. Notes his importance at the Este Court in
Modena and his relationship to foreign courts and
Bologna.

Francesco Antonio Bonporti
1672-1749

729. Harris, Brian Lorne. "The Published Trio Sonatas of
Francesco Antonio Bonporti (1672-1748 [*sic!*])." PhD
dissertation. University of Washington, 1980. UMI
80-13532. DAI xl.12A, p. 6060. 572 pages.
A history of the trio sonata to the 1690's, Bonporti's
biography (Harris and Slonimsky differ on the date of
death), a list of works, early sources for the 40 trio
sonatas 1696-1705, styles of the da chiesa and da
camera sonatas, and an edition of the 40 sonatas (appendix). Bonporti is a pupil of Corelli.

Alexander Porfirievitch Borodin
1833-1887

730. Abraham, Gerald. "The Chamber Music Works," in *Borodin: the Composer and his Music* (London: William
Reeves, [1929]), pp. 119-143. ML 410.B73A4.
For the informed layperson and student, an analysis of
all Borodin's chamber music: 2 string quartets, another
isolated string quartet movement on the name Belaiev,
and an arrangement for string quartet of the Scherzo to
the incomplete third symphony. Emphasizes thematic material, color effects derived from harmony, and the pe-
culiarities of the instruments in the 2 complete quartets. While the first quartet has many clever technical achievements, the second is a perfect lyrical masterpiece (at least in the first 3 movements) where the
structural achievements are there because they are a
natural part of the lyricism. Draws parallels with
Beethoven.

731. Solovtsova, Liubov' Andreevna. *Kamerno-Instrumental'-*
     naia Muzyka A.P. Borodina. Moscow: Gos. Muzykalnoe
     Ejd-vo, 1952. MT 145.B7S6. 76 pages. In Russian.
     Analyzes for the layperson Borodin's 2 string quartets,
     trio, quintet, and *Melancholy Suite.* Points out the
     polyphonic and orchestral character of the quartets,
     but mostly talks about emotions. A description of
     Russian chamber music in the 19th century and Borodin's
     place in this.

732. Golovinskij, Grigorij. *Kamerne Ansembli Borodina.*
     Moscow: Muzyka, 1972. RILM 72-514. 310 pages. In
     Russian.
     "An analysis of stylistic development in the chamber
     music of Borodin. Discusses the relationship of his
     chamber works to their era with special reference to
     the general development of chamber music."

733. Poray-Kuczewski, Kasimir. "Die Orchesterwerke und
     Streichquartette Alexander Borodins." PhD disser-
     tation. University of Vienna, 1935.
     Not seen.

                         Pierre Boulez
                           b.1925

734. Baron, Carol K. "An Analysis of the Pitch Organization
     in Boulez's 'Sonatine' for Flute and Piano," in *Cur-*
     rent Musicology, no. 20 (1975), 87-95.
     Analyzes the row Boulez uses in this piece and how he
     derives themes or motives from it.

                        William Boyce
                          1710-1779

For a comparison of Boyce's and Arne's trio sonatas, see
Stanley Sadie's article {527}.

                        Martin Boykan
                          b.1931

735. Harbison, John, and Eleanor Cory. "Martin Boykan:
     String Quartet (1967): Two Views," in *Perspectives of*
     New Music, xi, no. 2 (1973), 204-209. Followed by
     the complete score.
     Harbison responds subjectively to hearing the score on
     different occasions, with specific remarks on pitch,
     rhythm, and polyphony. Cory analyzes pitch, phrase,
     cadences and gesture in detail; finds a chromatic
     hexachord as the basic structural material.

Johannes Brahms
1833-1897

*For a catalogue of Brahms's chamber music, see Margit L.
McCorkle, Johannes Brahms: thematisch-bibliographisches
Werkverzeichnis (Munich: G. Henle, 1984), systematic index
pages 773-774, 777, and 779. ML 134.B8M3.1984. ISBN 3-
87328-041-8.*

736. Drinker, Henry Sandwith. *The Chamber Music of Johannes
     Brahms*. Philadelphia: Elkan-Vogel, 1932. MT 145.B72
     D8. First reprint Westport: Greenwood Press, 1974.
     MT 145.B72D8.1974. ISBN 0-8371-6941-0. Second re-
     print Wilmington: International Academic Publishing
     Co., 1979. MT 145.B72D8.1979. v + 130 pages.
     Program notes for a performance of all Brahms's chamber
     music in Philadelphia in 1933. An assessment of the
     man and his music, a tabulation of his works, and an
     essay on the principal characteristics of his style.
     Much historical data on the composition of the pieces,
     a brief, non-technical summary of the emotional events
     of the movements, a few rhythmic peculiarities, and
     parallels in other works.

737. Mason, Daniel Gregory. *The Chamber Music of Brahms*.
     New York: Macmillan, 1933. Reprint Freeport (New
     York): Books for Libraries Press, 1970. Reprint New
     York: AMS Press, 1970. MT 145.B425M35. xiii + 276
     pages.
     Thorough description of all the chamber music, in chro-
     nological order but without any history. Emphasis on
     texture, rhythm, melodic motives, and tonal centers but
     not any detailed harmonic or formal analyses. Briefly
     pictures Brahms as being a simple, direct, unaffected
     man, a romantic but unsentimental genius, a thoughtful
     composer, whose chamber music reflects all these
     characteristics. Mason discusses much of Brahms's
     chamber music in a series of articles in *The Musical
     Times*, lxxiii (1932), and lxxiv (1933).

738. Colles, Henry Cope. *The Chamber Music of Brahms*, in
     The Musical Pilgrim. London: Humphrey Milford for
     Oxford University Press, 1933. MT 145.B72C6.
     Reprint: New York: AMS Press, 1976. MT 145.B72C6.
     1976. ISBN 0-404-1284-x. 64 pages, 22 musical
     examples.
     Originally program notes for concerts by the Isolde
     Menges String Quartet, Harold Samuels and assisting
     artists, in 1933; revised for the book. A brief his-
     tory of Brahms's chamber music including discarded or
     later-revised works; discussion of each piece in chro-
     nological order. Writes well for the layperson; cogent
     analyses of rhythm, form, melodic motives, and harmony;
     full of cross references to other Brahms compositions.

739. Keys, Ivor Christopher Barfield. *Brahms Chamber Music*,
     in *BBC Music Guides*, no. 26. London: BBC/Seattle:
     University of Washington Press, 1974. MT145.B72K5.
     1974b. 68 pages, 36 examples.
     A non-technical discussion, for the layperson, of the
     principal chamber works.

     See Peter Lathan on Brahms's chamber music in Alec Robert-
     son, ed., Chamber Music {160}.

740. Antecliffe, Herbert. "Chamber Music of Brahms," in
     Monthly Musical Record, xxxvi (July, 1906), 146-147.
     Reviews for the layperson Brahms's chamber music and
     points out its importance to his total output. Consi-
     ders briefly the role of the piano, and Brahms's unique
     position as the bridge between the classical past
     (Beethoven) and the uncertain future.

741. Evans, Edwin. *Handbook to the Chamber and Orchestral*
     Music of Johannes Brahms: Historical and Descriptive
     Account of Each Work with Exhaustive Structural, The-
     matic and Rhythmical Analyses, and a Complete Rhyth-
     mical Chart of Each Movement, Copiously Illustrated
     in Music-Type: Complete Guide for Student, Concert-
     goer and Pianist. London: William Reeves [1912].
     Facsimile reprint in Burt Franklin: *Research and*
     Source Works Series 557. New York: Lenox Hill (Burt
     Franklin), 1970. ML 410.B8E82.1970. SBN 8337-10885.
     viii + 304 pages, 435 examples.
     Arranged by opus number, each piece has a complete
     chapter. Some historical data and comments by Brahms
     and/or others on a particular work, analyses of each
     movement with special emphasis on rhythm, the lengths
     of phrases, sections and movements, and motivic and to-
     nal organization. Not particularly useful for perfor-
     mers and uninitiated concert-goers despite title. Dry,
     longwinded, technical reading. Shows how original and
     effective Brahms was in treatment of phraseology and
     rhythm and defends him against attacks by those who
     find fault with these 2 elements of his style.

742. Kohlhase, Hans. "Brahms und Mendelssohn: strukturelle
     Parallelen in der Kammermusik für Streicher," in *Ham-*
     burger Jahrbuch für Musikwissenschaft, vii, Brahms
     und seine Zeit (Hamburg: Laaber, 1984), pp. 59-85.
     Brahms and Mendelssohn wrote music, not words; were not
     eager for virtuosic fame; were highly self-critical;
     and had the same high regard for Bach, Handel and
     Beethoven without deprecating Mozart and Haydn -- all
     unusual for the 19th century. Sees if these similari-
     ties carry over into their string chamber music with
     similar structures.

743. Becker, Heinz. "Das volkstümliche Idiom in Brahmses

Kammermusik," in *Hamburger Jahrbuch für Musikwissen-schaft*, vii, *Brahms und seine Zeit* (Hamburg: Laaber, 1984), pp. 87-99.
Shows the continual importance of folk music for Brahms and specifically in his chamber music with the subdominant up to tonic to supertonic beginning of melodies.

744. Brand, Friedrich. *Wesen und Charackter der Thematik im Brahmsschen Kammermusik*. Berlin: Deutsche Brahms-Gesellschaft, 1937. ML 410.B8B7. xii + 155 pages, 120 examples. "Das Wesen der Kammermusik von Brahms." PhD dissertation. Berlin, 1937.
A thematic analysis of the chamber music. Characterizes first-movement themes, second-movements themes, and so on. Finds 2 kinds of opening themes in first movements of all periods: the symphonic (dynamic at the start) and sonata-like (cantabile at the start), with a few works that mix the 2. Also notes Hungarian and gypsy elements, and continually compares Brahms's themes with those by Beethoven, Mendelssohn, Schumann, Reger, Bartók and others. Considers the accompaniment to the themes. Dryly written for students, theorists and performers who already know the music.

745. Fenske, David Edward. "Texture in the Chamber Music of Johannes Brahms." PhD dissertation. University of Wisconsin, 1973. RILM 73-580. UM 73-28915. DA xxxiv.10A, pp. 6684-5. 540 pages (DAI = 546 pages).
Defines closely the various components of texture in Brahms's chamber music: tessitura, range, gap between parts, double-stopping, rhythmic activity and instrumentation. Statistics as well as narratives. A lot of effort to prove what every performer of Brahms's chamber music already knows: widest range and tessitura in the piano, the vertical density exceeds the norm approximately 8% of the time, the densest concentration occurs 40% of the time, the uppermost parts are more contrapuntal than the lowest, and the inner parts have percentages that are similar to the upper parts.

746. Czesla, Werner. *Studien zum Finale in der Kammermusik von Johannes Brahms*. Bonn: Rheinische Friedrich-Wilhelms-Universität, 1968. MT 145.B72C9. 252 pages. Inaugural dissertation. Rheinische Friedrich-Wilhelms Universität in Bonn, 1966.
Analyzes the finales of 2 quartets, 2 string quintets, the horn trio, 2 piano quartets, 2 piano trios, 2 sextets, the piano quintet, the cello sonata and 3 piano sonatas. Considers motivic-thematic treatment and form (for example how Brahms treats development and recapitulation sections) and the fact that Brahms's music is more organically unified than anyone else's. Considers also the introductions to finales, and in all cases the organic growth of themes from one part to another. Al-

though Schenker figures prominently in the bibliography, uses Schenkerian analysis only superficially.

747. Breslauer, Peter S. "Motivic and Rhythmic Contrapuntal Structure in the Chamber Music of Johannes Brahms." PhD dissertation. Yale University, 1984.
Based on Schenkerian principles, determines "the parts played by chromatic diminution and the bass" in the contrapuntal structure of Brahms's chamber music. This theory is then applied to the Piano Quartet Op. 25, the String Quartets Op. 51, and the Clarinet Quintet Op. 115, movement 2.

748. Hill, William G. "Brahms' Opus 51: a Diptych," in *The Music Review*, xiii (1952), 110-124.
Analyzes the cyclic unity of each of the 2 earlier string quartets and finds similarities between both in the opening motives, motivic treatment, and other mostly thematic and motivic factors. Despite Brahms's deception in describing these as not related, they were written at the same time and with many of the same ideas -- 2 externally different works that form a diptych -- 2 sides of the same picture.

See also {197}.

749. Forte, Allen. "Motivic Design and Structural Levels in the First Movement of Brahms's String Quartet in C Minor," in *The Musical Quarterly*, lxix (1983), 471-502.
A detailed Schenkerian analysis of the foreground motives and their "penetration of the middleground, a strong feature of this work and probably a structural aspect of widespread significance in all music of the later nineteenth century."

750. Fellinger, Imogen. "Brahms' Sonate für Pianoforte und Violine op. 78: ein Beitrag zum Schaffensprozess des Meisters," in *Die Musikforschung*, xviii (1965), 11-24.
A detailed description of the manuscript of this sonata (2 facsimiles are included) and differences, important and unimportant, from the accepted printed version.

751. Fischer, Richard Shaw. "Brahms' Technique of Motivic Development in his Sonata in D Minor Opus 108 for Piano and Violin." DMA dissertation. University of Arizona, 1964. UM 64-8763. DA xxv.3, p. 1956. 188 pages.
Attempts to show that the thematic material of a movement is derived from its principal subject, that these derivations result from the imitation, variation, and/ or transformation of motives which constitute the structure of that principal subject, that the opening 4

measures of the sonata generate the entire thematic
substance of all 4 movements, and that motivic development is related to dynamics and harmony.

752. Ravizza, Victor. "Möglichkeiten des Komischen in der
Musik: der letzte Satz des Streichquintetts in F dur,
op. 88 von Johannes Brahms," in *Archiv für Musikwissenschaft*, xxxi (1974), 137-150.
Explores humor (comedy) in the finale from Brahms's
quintet. Quotes various authors who define "comedy" as
the sudden solution of a serious dilemma into nothing-
ness. Brahms achieves this when he sets up a potential
fugue with its assumed high tension and then does
nothing with it.

753. Dunhill, Thomas F. "Brahms' Quintet for Pianoforte
and Strings," in *The Musical Times*, lxxii (1931),
319-322.
A history of this quintet: it was first a string quintet with 2 cellos, then for 2 pianos, and finally in
1866 in its present form. Analyzes melody.

*For a comparison of Brahms's Quintet in F and Bruckner's
Quintet in F, see Hans Redlich's article {770}.*

754. Häfner, Roland. *Johannes Brahms, Klarinettenquintett*,
in *Meisterwerke der Musik*, Heft 14. Munich: Wilhelm
Fink, 1978. MT 145.B7H3. ISBN 3-7705-1611-7. 54
pages, 22 examples + oversize chart with 9 tables.
A simple, direct, well-written and well-documented
study of this piece for student, layperson and scholar.
Analyzes form and thematic processes of each of the
movements wherein the organic unity is revealed. Considers variation form in chamber music. Opens with
historical background.

755. Dyson, George. "Brahms' Clarinet Quintet, Op. 115," in
The Musical Times, lxxvi (1935), 315-319.
Points out Brahms's debt to the clarinetist Richard
Mühlfeld. A non-technical analysis of keys, themes,
and form.

Johann Evangelist Brandl
1760-1837

756. Leinert, Friedrich Otto. *Johann Evangelist Brandl
(1760-1837) als Lieder- und Kammermusikkomponist.*
Wolfenbüttel: Verlag für musikalische Kultur und
Wissenschaft, 1937. ML 410.B83L4. 142 pages + 28
page musical supplement, 53 examples. PhD dissertation. University of Marburg, 1936.

Scholarly study of the vocal and chamber music of this
relatively obscure South German composer. Biography
and bibliography. Discusses Brandl's 6 string quintets
Op. 11 (1797); 3 string quartets Op. 23 (1803); flute
quartets Op. 15 and 40; flute quintets Op. 58 and 60;
sextet for violin + oboe + bassoon + 2 violas + cello,
Op. 52; and others. Brandl was influenced by Haydn and
Mozart and not at all by Beethoven. Historical context; analyses somewhat pedantic and shallow.

757. Danzer, Otto. *Johann Brandls Leben und Werke: ein*
     Beitrag zur Musikgeschichte von Karlsruhe. Brünn/
     Prague/Leipzig: Rudolf M. Rohrer, 1936. ML 140.B817
     D3. 95 pages.
     A biography and analysis of representative works, in-
     cluding chamber music (pages 70-82). Gives locations
     of the music (chamber music in Vienna and Berlin in
     1936). Less pedantic analyses than Leinert's.

Giuseppe Antonio Brescianello
c.1690-1757

758. Damerini, Adelmo. "I Concerti a Tre di G. Antonio Bre-
     scianello," in *Collectanea Historiae Musicae*, I, in
     Historiae Musicae Cultores, II (Florence: Leo S.
     Olschki, 1953), pp. 165-170. ML 55.C73 vol. 1.
     Briefly describes 12 trio concertos (2 violins + bass).
     Most are fast-slow-fast and display effective chroma-
     ticism and skillful counterpoint, even in the slow
     movements. The bass is treated equally with the vio-
     lins, not as a continuo part. They are important imme-
     diate precursors of the classical concerto, trio, quar-
     tet and symphony. For scholars, laypersons, performers
     and students.

Jean-Baptiste Bréval
1753-1823

759. Viano, Richard J. "Jean-Baptiste Bréval (1753-1823):
     Life, Milieu, and Chamber Works with Editions of Ten
     Compositions and Thematic Catalogue." PhD disser-
     tation. City University of New York, 1983. UMI 84 -
     1488. DAI xliv.10A, p. 2924. 465 pages.
     A biography, thematic catalogue, and bibliography of
     Bréval, whose many compositions are mostly chamber
     music for either the private salon or public concert
     hall, for amateurs or virtuosi. He also wrote a
     treatise on the cello (1804). Considers the forms, the
     principles of concertante and dialogue, and cello tech-
     nique in the chamber music.

Frank Bridge
1879-1941

760. Bray, Trevor Ian. "Bridge's Novelletten and Idylls,"
     in *The Musical Times*, cxvii (Nov. 1976), 905-6.
     Considers Bridge's earliest important published chamber
     music and its use of cyclic features.

Benjamin Britten
1913-1976

761. Evans, Peter. *The Music of Benjamin Britten*. Minnea-
     polis: University of Minnesota Press, 1979. ML 410.
     B853E9. ISBN 0-8166-0836-9. vii + 564 pages.
     Whatever insights Evans might have into Britten's cham-
     ber music are totally lost in a dreadfully profuse and
     incomprehensible style of writing. Analyzes all the
     chamber music with reference to his other works and to
     the major composers of his time.

762. Mitchell, Donald. "The Chamber Music: an Introduction,"
     in Christopher Palmer, ed., *The Britten Companion*
     (London/Boston: Faber and Faber, 1984), chapter 32,
     pp. 369-374. ML 410.B853B7.1984b. ISBN 0-571-13147-
     6. Originally the program book for the 1977 Benson &
     Hedges Musical Festival.
     "Concentrated, economical and demanding musical think-
     ing" which comes naturally from sparse or spare trans-
     parent textures -- precisely mixed and calculated
     sound -- is the element of chamber music found in most
     of Britten's work, even the operas. Points to Brit-
     ten's devotion to chamber music as listener and as per-
     former (on piano and viola), and his composition of
     chamber music for specific performers whose personali-
     ties figure in the music, beginning with the oboe quar-
     tet Op. 2 (1932) for Leon Goossens. Briefly surveys
     the chamber music, including the unnumbered juvenalia
     string quartets. Most attention is given to the 3
     mature quartets and especially to the poetic sense of
     the third -- Britten's recognition of impending death.

763. Matthews, David. "The String Quartets and Some Other
     Chamber Works," in Christopher Palmer, ed., *The Brit-
     ten Companion* (London/Boston: Faber and Faber, 1984),
     chapter 34, pages 383-392. ML 410.B853B7.1984b.
     ISBN 0-571-13147-6.
     A brief discussion of some solo works, then analyses of
     the 3 mature Britten quartets for the informed layper-
     son. Discusses form, melody, tonality (or lack there-
     of) and points out unusual or important treatments of
     these by Britten. Takes special note of the chacony -
     passacaglia movements and the influences of and simi-

larities with works by Beethoven, Schubert, Mahler,
Stravinsky, Bartók, and Shostakovich.

764. Brown, David. "Stimulus and Form in Britten's Work,"
in *Music and Letters*, xxxix (July, 1958), 218-226.
Discusses String Quartet No. 2 and "The Holy Sonnets of
John Donne" (both written 1945-1946). Assumes that the
reader has the scores in hand. In the quartet, discusses Bartók's influence and Britten's individuality.
Does not find Britten entirely successful in this quartet; a lack of certainty plagues the first 2 movements,
but the third (Chacony) is successful.

765. Keller, Hans. "Benjamin Britten's Second Quartet," in
Tempo, no. 3 (March, 1947), 6-8.
Brief but cogent analysis of form, motives and keys.

766. Matthews, David. "Britten's Third Quartet," in *Tempo*,
no. 125 (June, 1978), 21-24.
Formal analysis, with references to the previous 2
quartets and *Death in Venice*.

767. Evans, Peter. "Britten's Cello Sonata," in *Tempo*, no.
58 (Summer, 1961), 8-16, with facsimile of a manuscript page.
Detailed analysis of the tonal schemes and motives.

768. Wood, Hugh. "Britten's Latest Scores," in *The Musical
Times*, ciii (1962), 164-5.
Brief, interesting analysis of the sonata form of the
first movement of his cello + piano sonata. The whole
piece is monothematic under the influence of Bartók.

Max Bruch
1838-1920

769. Lauth, Wilhelm. *Max Bruchs Instrumentalmusik*, in *Beiträge zur rheinischen Musikgeschichte*, Heft 68.
Köln: reproduced typescript by Arno Volk-Verlag,
1967. MT 92.B88L4. 155 pages. PhD dissertation.
University of Köln, 1967. RILM 68-2086.
Bruch's chamber music is only a small amount of his
surviving instrumental music. A large number of chamber music manuscripts once owned by the Berlin publisher Rudolph Eichmann apparently was lost in the war.
Analyzes the chamber pieces one by one, starting with
the Trio for piano + violin + cello Op. 5 in C Minor
(1857). Relates the chamber music to contemporaneous
and immediately preceding works by others. The late
published chamber music is either wholly or partially
folksong arrangements or rearrangements of earlier
works. Most significant are some works for his son Max
Felix Bruch, a great clarinetist.

Anton Bruckner
1824-1896

For a catalogue of Bruckner's 4 pieces of chamber music, see Renate Grasberger, Werkverzeichnis Anton Bruckner (WAB) (Tutzing: Hans Schneider, 1977), pages 121-124. ML 134.B87 A18. ISBN 3-7952-0232-9.

770. Redlich, Hans Ferdinand. "Bruckner and Brahms Quintets in F," in *Music and Letters*, xxxvi (1955), 253-258. Brief analysis of Bruckner's only mature piece of chamber music in terms of suitability for the instruments and tonality. An even briefer exposé of Brahms's debt to Bruckner in his F Major Quintet.

771. Nowak, Leopold. "Form und Rhythmus im ersten Satz des Streichquintetts von Anton Bruckner," in Gerhard Schuhmacher, *Zur musikalischen Analyse*, in *Wege der Forschung*, Band 257 (Darmstadt: Wissenschaftliche Buchgesellschaft, 1974), pages 186-203. MT 6.S3529 Z8. ISBN 3-534-04791-5. Originally in Horst Heussner, ed., *Festschrift Hans Engel zum siebzigsten Geburtstag* (Kassel: Bärenreiter, 1964), pages 260-273. Shows Bruckner's care with form, as evinced in this quintet movement. Detailed analysis of the motives.

Gaetano Brunetti
c.1744-1798

772. Fischer, Klaus. "Die Streichquartette Gaetano Brunettis (1744-1798) in der Bibliothèque Nationale in Paris im Zusammenhang mit dem Streichquartett des 18. Jahrhunderts," in Christoph-Hellmut Mahling and Sigrid Wiesmann, eds., *Gesellschaft für Musikforschung, Bericht über den internationalen musikwissenschaftlichen Kongress Bayreuth 1981* (Kassel: Bärenreiter, 1984), pp. 350-359. ML 26.G49.1981. Brunetti was a prolific and important chamber music composer, who because of unfounded rumors that he plagiarized and hurt Boccherini has not received his due. Brunetti worked at the Spanish court with Boccherini. Detailed scholarly study of the manuscripts of 27 string quartets, an analysis of their form and texture, and comparisons to Haydn's Op. 9-33. Brunetti shows Italian characteristics (Op. 2, 1770's), French characteristics (Op. 3), and independence (the next 15 quartets). The 27 show Brunetti's growth as a quartet composer and the relationship between the Italian and Viennese quartets of the late 18th century.

773. Belgray, Alice Bunzl. "Gaetano Brunetti: an Exploratory Bio-Bibliographical Study." PhD dissertation.

University of Michigan, 1970. UMI 71-23693. DAI
xxxii.3A, p. 1546. 283 pages.
Uncovers sonatas for violin and bass by Brunetti, presents 1 complete sonata and an independent movement
Adagio Glosado, and includes a thematic index. Gives
court documents on his life.

Ferruccio Benvenuto Busoni
1866-1924

774. Beaumont, Antony. *Busoni the Composer.* Bloomington:
     Indiana University Press, 1985. ML 410.B98B4.1984.
     ISBN 0-253-31270-1. 408 pages.
     Describes Busoni's second violin + piano sonata (pp.
     53-58) and a few other works. Discusses tonalities,
     thematic treatment, mood, and the use of Bach's
     chorale "Wie wohl ist mir" and Beethoven's Op. 109.

Henry Butler
c.1590-1652

775. Phillips, Elizabeth Van Vorst. "The Divisions and
     Sonatas of Henry Butler." PhD dissertation. Wash-
     ington University, 1982. UM 83-2355. DA xliii.9A,
     p. 2826. viii + 253 pages (DA = 303 pages).
     Discusses the form and style of the string ensemble
     music and compares it with Italian works of the time.
     Butler wrote some of the earliest sonatas in England,
     and his sonata for bass viol + basso continuo may be
     the earliest such sonata in any country.

Max Butting
1888-1976

776. Brennecke, Dietrich. *Das Lebenswerk Max Buttings.*
     Leipzig: VEB Deutscher Verlag für Musik, 1973. HML
     1844.65.10. 372 pages.
     Lists Butting's 10 string quartets (1914-1971) and
     other chamber and Hausmusik. Discusses them as part of
     a biography.

Dietrich Buxtehude
1637-1707

*For a catalogue of Buxtehude's chamber music, see Georg Kar-
städt, Thematisch-systematisches Verzeichnis der musikalischen Werke von Dietrich Buxtehude: Buxtehude-Werke-Ver-
zeichnis (BuxWV) (Wiesbaden: Breitkopf & Härtel, 1974),
pages 195-215. ML 134.B95K3. ISBN 3-7651-0065-X.*

777. Defant, Christine. *Kammermusik und Stylus Phantasticus: Studien zu Dietrich Buxtehudes Triosonaten*, in *Europäische Hochschulschriften, Reihe 36, Musikwissenschaft*, No. 14. Frankfurt am Main/Bern/New York: Peter Lang, 1985. ISBN 3-8204-8514-7. 514 pages. PhD dissertation. University of Kiel.
A thorough analysis of 4 Buxtehude sonatas for violin + viola da gamba + continuo (Op. 1 nos. 3 and 6, Op. 2 nos. 5 and 6) on the basis of theories of style and genre by Mattheson and Kircher and of contemporary practice by Corelli, Marini, Rosenmüller, Schmelzer, Biber and others. Primarily concerned with form and melodic structure. "Stylus phantasticus" is Kircher's term for secular style. Particular attention to the chamber sonatas of the Hamburg school of organists.

778. Linfield, Eva. "Dietrich Buxtehude's Sonatas: a Historical and Analytical Study." PhD dissertation. Brandeis University, 1984. UMI 84-20780. DAI xlv.8A, pp. 2298-9. 432 pages.
Concerned with sonatas for violin + viola da gamba + harpsichord or similar scoring. Fourteen were published in 2 sets; others, in manuscript, were written over a period of 30 years. Places the sonatas in historic and geographic context and analyzes them.

William Byrd
1543-1623

779. Neighbour, Oliver. *The Consort and Keyboard Music of William Byrd*. Berkeley/Los Angeles: University of California Press, 1978. ML 410.B996M9.1978.vol.3. 272 pages.
A scholarly study of Byrd's viol consort music of the second half of the 16th century. Discusses sources, styles, and functions, and analyzes individual pieces. Considers the Byrd works in context of English chamber music of the time. The first 100 pages deal with consort music, the rest with keyboard music.

Antonio Caldara
1670-1736

780. Barnes, Marysue. "The Trio Sonatas of Antonio Caldara." PhD dissertation. Florida State University, 1960. LC Mic 60-1403. DA xx.11, pp. 4405-6. 2 vols. 509 pages. Edition of 15 sonatas in Vol. II.
Reviews the evolution of the trio sonata and biographical data on Caldara. Analyzes in detail Op. 1 and 2 trio sonatas (1693, 1699), some da chiesa and the rest da camera. They are typical of the time.

Giovanni Giuseppe Cambini
1746-1825

781. Roncaglia, Gino. "Giovanni Giuseppe Cambini Quartet-
     tista," in Adelmo Damerini and Gino Roncaglia, eds.,
     *Musiche Italiane Rare e Vive da Giovanni Gabrieli a
     Giuseppe Verdi* (Sienna: Accademia Musicale Chigiana,
     1962), pp. 293-299.
     Cambini, along with Boccherini, had established a con-
     trapuntal style for quartets before Haydn. Traces the
     quartet from sinfonias a4 of Giovanni Maria Bononcini
     and sonatas a4 by Tartini, Giordini, Galuppi, Latilla,
     Nardini, Rutini, Bertoni, Tommaso, Giordani, Boccher-
     ini, Manfredi, Zanetti, Cambini, and Bruni to Haydn,
     Mozart and Beethoven. Cambini wrote at least 144 quar-
     tets (see {782} for a different figure), and he is un-
     fortunately remembered as being facile and superficial.
     He wrote music to make money since he was quite inse-
     cure (he had been a slave in Barberia), but when he
     took the time to be careful, he was a master of style
     and inspired. The quartets are usually in 2 movements,
     a few in 3, rare early works in 4. The first is bina-
     ry, the second an inspired theme with variations, some
     virtuosic. He loves freedom and variety of timbre,
     rapid change of emotions, and occasionally titles or
     programs. Some quartets are for more unusual scorings:
     flute + violin + viola + cello or violin + 2 violas +
     cello. Dialogue or conversation effect. Much more
     dramatic and romantic than galant. Detailed analysis
     of Op. 20 No. 5, in 3 movements.

782. Trimpert, Dieter Lutz. *Die Quatuors Concertants von
     Giuseppe Cambini*, in *Mainzer Studien zur Musikwissen-
     schaft*, Band 1. Tutzing: Hans Schneider, 1967. MT
     145C33T7. 328 pages.
     A detailed, scholarly study of the chamber music, be-
     ginning with the biography of this Italian-born, French
     composer who flourished in Paris 1773-1804 and wrote an
     enormous amount of music, including 114 string quin-
     tets, 3 wind quintets, 174 string quartets, 33 or 39
     "quatuors d'airs" and 5 piano quartets. An extremely
     important study of French quartet practice at the same
     time as the maturing of Viennese quartet practice.
     Cambini is discussed in detail, but he is also used as
     a means for understanding the whole French practice of
     the time. Cambini's quartets were widespread during
     his lifetime -- known to Mozart and Gluck, concerts in
     Germany and even in Philadelphia (1786) and New York
     (1794). Also compares Cambini's quartets to Haydn's
     (especially Op. 17) not only in the concertant style
     but also in form and other considerations, and to
     Mozart's middle quartets (especially K.298, which is a
     quatuor d'airs). There is no talk of "influence," only
     of similarities. Concludes with a thematic catalogue

of all Cambini quartets, string quintets, quartets with flute or oboe with strings, quartets for violin + 2 violas + cello, and the quatuors d'airs.

Carlo Antonio Campioni
1720-1788

783. Floros, Constantin. "Un Compositore Livornese del xviii Secolo: l'Opera Strumentale di C. Antonio Campioni," in *Rivista di Livorno: Rassegna di Attività Municipale*, ix (1959), 27-39. PhD dissertation "Carlo Antonio Campioni als Instrumentalkomponist." University of Vienna, 1955.
Lists Campioni's 35 trio sonatas (2 violins + continuo), 6 violin duets, 6 duets for violin + cello or harpsichord, and various other sonatas. Deals with their importance in the history of 18th-century instrumental music. They were widely disseminated in England, France, and Holland and belong to a period of transition from the contrapuntal to the virtuosic sonata. More traditional than Pugnani's, there is more counterpoint and less domination by violin 1. Considers the instrumentation of the bass (can be played without keyboard). All are in 3 movements slow-fast-fast; some are binary, the rest in nascent sonata form. Campioni's biography is in an earlier article in the same periodical, v (1955), 134-150.

Christian Cannabich
1731-1798

784. Soutar, Marjorie Elizabeth. "Christian Cannabich (1731-1798): an Evaluation of his Instrumental Works." PhD dissertation. University of Aberdeen, 1972. 3 vols. RILM 72-1766.
Not seen.

John Alden Carpenter
1876-1951

785. Pike, Gregory Burnside. "The Three Versions of the *Quintet for Piano and Strings* by John Alden Carpenter: an Examination of Their Contrasting Musical Elements Based upon a Formal Analysis of the Original 1934 Version." DMA dissertation. University of Miami, 1981. UMI 82-11819. DAI xlii.12A, p. 4970. 136 pages.
A biography and overall assessment of Carpenter's oeuvre, followed by a detailed harmonic analysis of the

original and 1947 revised version and an incomplete
second revised version (undated) of the quintet.

Elliott Cook Carter
b.1908

786. Schiff, David. *The Music of Elliott Carter*. London:
Eulenburg Books/New York: Da Capo, 1983. ML 410.
C3293S34.1983. ISBN 0-903873-06-0.
Analysis of Carter's works in chronological order, including the 3 string quartets, sonatas, duos, brass
quintet and others. The analyses, which are shallow,
are prefaced by useful data on the piece. Designed for
the non-professional musical reader. Schiff studied
with Carter and includes here personal interviews.

787. Harris, Jane Duff. "Compositional Process in the
String Quartets of Elliot Carter." PhD dissertation.
Case Western Reserve University, 1983. UMI 83-28260.
DAI xliv.11A, p. 3200. 320 pages.
Shows how Carter's own criteria for composition (dis-
course, time, and texture) change from Quartet No. 1
(thematic), to No. 2 (characters texturally defined),
to No. 3 (2 textures).

788. Glock, William. "A Note on Elliott Carter," in *The
Score*, no. 12 (June 1955), 47-52.
An introduction to Carter's technique of metrical modulation whereby tempo changes are effected by metrical
change. Shows the progression of Carter's ideas from
the Cello + Piano Sonata to the String Quartet No. 1.
Compares Carter's overall polyphony of varying rhythms
to the mannerists of the late 14th century.

789. Headrick, Samuel Philip. "Thematic Elements in the
Variations Movement of Elliott Carter's 'String
Quartet Number One.'" PhD dissertation. University
of Rochester, 1981. UMI 81-16504. DAI xlii.3A, pp.
907-8. 149 pages.
Finds that Carter uses 3 themes, each introduced at a
different point in the movement and each gradually
accelerating until vanishing.

790. Stein, Don Allan. "The Function of Pitch in Elliott
Carter's 'String Quartet No. 1.'" PhD dissertation.
Washington University, 1981. UMI 81-22759. DAI
xlii.4A, p. 1371. 110 pages.
Considers pitch as a unifying factor in this piece, and
notes 3 sets of pitch complexes that recur with greatest frequency and at structurally significant points.
As this highly technical study unfolds, other factors
(such as harmony and motives) are considered as well.

791. Steinberg, Michael. "Elliott Carter's Second String
     Quartet," in *The Score*, no. 27 (July 1960), 22-26.
     Praises the 4-movement quartet, premiered March 25,
     1959, as entirely new, starting with its form of an
     introduction and conclusion and cadenzas linking each
     of the movements. Finds Carter concerned with the 4
     individuals in the quartet and their ever-changing
     relationship. A good analysis.

792. Gass, Glenn. "Elliot Carter's Second String Quartet:
     Aspects of Time and Rhythm," in *Indiana Theory Re-
     view*, iv, no. 3 (1981), 12-23.
     The interactions of the different time worlds of each
     of the 4 instruments gives form to the piece. The
     cello, for example, has a fluid free rhythm, while the
     second violin plays "even, rigid rhythmic figures"
     ("the metronome of the quartet"). The first violin
     goes between these extremes, and the viola "presents
     odd rhythmic figures" and uses special expressive
     devices like glissando. There are 4 main sections or
     movements to the piece, each given to the domination by
     a particular instrument.

793. Mead, Andrew W. "Pitch Structure in Elliott Carter's
     String Quartet No. 3," in *Perspectives of New Music*,
     xxii (1983-1984), 31-60.
     A clear, concise analysis and description for the pro-
     fessional theorist of a complicated composition. The
     viola and violin 2 are treated as a unit distinct from
     the cello and violin 1. The 2 units contrast in rhythm
     with the former in even rhythm and the latter in a
     free, irregular rhythm. There are 10 movements (6 for
     the former unit, 4 for the latter) distinguished by
     character, playing technique, and interval. The 6 + 4
     are combined in all possible ways (= 24) plus each
     alone (= 10) + coda (= 35 sections of the piece).
     Finds other structural factors within the above, and
     also traces 12-tone sets in the piece. The associa-
     tions and differentiations among the movements and duos
     provide "a hierarchical language whereby we might un-
     derstand the piece and eventually know it whole."

*For another discussion of the third string quartet, see
Michael Coonrod's dissertation {504}.*

794. Shinn, Randall Alan. "An Analysis of Elliott Carter's
     Sonata for Flute, Oboe, Cello, and Harpsichord
     (1952)." DMA dissertation. University of Illinois,
     1975. UM 76-6957. DA xxxvi.9A, p. 5631. 183 pages.
     A detailed thematic analysis for the professional
     theorist, with emphasis on the energy level of differ-
     ent moments of the sonata and on the tertial yet non-
     functional harmony.

795. Derby, Richard. "Carter's *Duo for Violin and Piano*,"
     in *Perspectives of New Music*, xx (1981-1982), 149-
     168.
     A detailed, technical analysis of some aspects of this
     1974 duo. Follows up Carter's statement "that the
     nature of the composition is based on the performance
     characteristics of each instrument, e.g., the violin is
     often changing moods suddenly while the piano remains
     more constant in demeanor," and the melodic intervals
     used on the 2 instruments differ. Carter uses 12-tone
     aggregates in a "fixed octave scheme." Also considers
     the effect of metric modulation -- the gradual reduc-
     tion of the ratio of violin notes to piano notes.

Dario Castello
early 17th century

796. Langley, Richard Douglas. "*Sonate Concertate in Stil
     Moderno* by Dario Castello: a Transcription of Book
     One." PhD dissertation. Washington University,
     1974. UM 75-6581. DA xxxv.9A, p. 6184. 211 pages.
     Biography and works, historical background, stylistic
     and other characteristics. Concludes with a transcrip-
     tion of the *Sonate* (Venice: 1621), which are similar to
     canzone and written for specifically denoted instru-
     ments (organ or spinet for the continuo).

Maurizio Cazzati
c.1620-1677

797. Suess, John. "The Ensemble Sonatas of Maurizio Caz-
     zati," in *Studien zur italienisch-deutschen Musik-
     geschichte*, xii, in *Analecta Musicologica*, xix
     (1979), 146-185.
     Basic discussion of the 5 collections of sonatas and
     canzoni a3 by Cazzati, the father of the Bologna
     School. Essential for students and scholars who wish
     for a more exact picture of 17th-century Baroque
     sonatas.

Giacomo Cervetto
c.1682-c.1783

798. Conable, William G., Jr. "The Instrumental Sonatas of
     Giacomo Cervetto." DMA dissertation. Boston Univer-
     sity, 1969. RILM 70-1670. UMI 70-22442. DAI
     xxxi.5A, p. 2418. 2 vols. 337 pages.
     Discusses the life of the cellist Cervetto, who was
     active in London in 1738 and who composed 12 trio
     sonatas (some for 3 cellos), 12 solo sonatas for cello
     + continuo, 6 sonatas for flute + continuo, and 6 di-
     vertimenti for 2 cellos. Analyzes all the sonatas and

notes their evolution from Baroque to Classical styles,
sometimes within the same piece. Vol. II is a critical
edition of the 12 solo cello + continuo sonatas.

Ernest Chausson
1855-1899

799. Grover, Ralph Scott. *Ernest Chausson: the Man and his
Music.* Lewisburg, PA: Bucknell University/London:
Associated University Press, 1980. ML 410.C455G76.
ISBN 0-8387-2128-2. 245 pages. Chapter 6: "Chamber
Music."
History of the 5 chamber works, discussion of the in-
fluences by Franck, Debussy and non-French music on
them, and an excellent formal analysis. Note: the only
other major chapter on Chausson's chamber music (Jean-
Pierre Barricelli and Leo Weinstein's "Chamber Music,"
in *Ernest Chausson: the Composer's Life and Works* [Nor-
man: University of Oklahoma Press, 1955; reprint Westport (Connecticut): Greenwood Press, 1973], pp. 140-58,
ML 410.C455B3.1973, ISBN 0-8371-6915-1) is inadequate.

Carlos Chávez
1899-1978

800. Parker, Robert L. *Carlos Chávez: Mexico's Modern-Day
Orpheus.* Boston: Twayne Publishers (G.K. Hall),
1983. ISBN 0-8057-9455-7. xiii + 166 pages.
Chapter 3: "Chamber Music."
The earlier chamber music is more traditional (piano
sextet 1919, string quartet 1921, and sonatinas for
violin + piano and cello + piano 1924), and some traditional chamber music continues to 1969 (such as 3 more
string quartets 1932, 1943, and 1964). Non-traditional
includes *Energía* 1925 for 9 mixed strings and winds,
Sonata for Four Horns 1929, Soli 1933 for oboe + clarinet + trumpet + bassoon, *Xochipilli* 1940 for piccolo +
flute + e-flat clarinet + trombone + percussion for 6
players, and several percussion ensembles pieces. Discusses each work. Excellent bibliography and discography, which supplant Rudolfo Halffter, *Carlos Chávez:
Catálogo Completo de sus Obras* (Mexico: Sociedad de
Autores y Compositores de Música, 1971).

Luigi Cherubini
1760-1842

801. Saak, Siegfried. *Studien zur Instrumentalmusik Luigi
Cherubinis*, in *Göttinger musikwissenschaftliche Arbeiten*, Band 8. Göttingen: Jürgen Kinzel, 1979. HML
2005.15.78. vii + 234 pages.

The fourth chapter "Untersuchungen zur Kammermusik"
(pages 106-226) is the most intensive study of Cherubini's chamber music available. The chamber music
consists of 6 string quartets, 1 string quintet (2
violins + 1 viola + 2 cellos), and "Souvenir...par
Baillot" (1928). Does not deal with them separately
but considers various conpositional aspects and then
uses the various sections of the chamber movements to
illustrate the point (slow introductions, second
themes, slow middle movements, scherzi, and so on).
Good bibliography.

802. Mansfield, Orlando A. "Cherubini's String Quartets,"
in *The Musical Quarterly*, xv (1929), 590-605.
Discusses each of the 6 quartets. Gives historical
data (without documentation) including first performances. Considers form, basic keys, some important
technical achievements, and insights for the performer.

803. Saak, Siegfried. "Ein unbekannter Streichquartettsatz
Luigi Cherubinis," in *Die Musikforschung*, xxxi
(1978), 46-51.
Discusses the phenomenon of Cherubini's long abstinence
from quartet-writing between 1814 and 1829 and considers this isolated movement -- the first, in G, of an
intended second quartet in 1814 -- which survives in
manuscript in the Bibliothèque Nationale in Paris.
Cherubini felt he could not compete with Beethoven.

Frédéric Chopin
1810-1849

*For a list of Chopin's chamber music, see Krystyna Koby-
lanska,* Frédéric Chopin: thematisch-bibliographisches
Werkverzeichnis *(Munich: G. Henle, 1979), p. 326, trl. by
Helmut Stolze from the Polish* Ougud Rekopisy utworów Chopina
Katalog *(Cracos: Polskie Wydawnictwo Muzyczne, 1977).* ML
134.C54A315. ISBN 3-87328-029-9.

804. Delgado, Imelda. "The Chamber Music of Chopin." PhD
dissertation. Indiana University, 1975. RILM 75-
1135. 112 pages.
History and analysis of Chopin's sonata for violin +
piano, piano trio, 2 other pieces for cello + piano,
and a flute + piano piece.

805. Gajewski, Ferdinand John. "The Work Sheets to Chopin's Violoncello Sonata." PhD dissertation.
Harvard University, 1980. 2 vols. I: v + 208 pages;
II: 113 pages of facsimiles of the worksheets.
The most extensive work sheets for any piece by Chopin
pertains to his Op. 65 cello + piano sonata, his last
published music. Gives historical and documentary

background to the writing of the sonata and to the
manuscript (first owned by Auguste Franchomme [1808-
1884], the cellist to whom the work is dedicated).
During 150 years numerous pages have been given away,
but a 1954 photograph of the whole allows it to be seen
in a much more complete state. A movement-by-movement,
section-by-section analysis of Chopin's process of composition of the sonata, with special attention to key
areas, harmony and motives.

Muzio Clementi
1752-1832

*For a catalogue of Clementi's chamber music, see Alan Tyson,
Thematic Catalogue of the Works of Muzio Clementi (Tutzing:
Hans Schneider, 1967), 136 pages. ML 134.C585T9.*

Samuel Coleridge-Taylor
1875-1912

806. Carter, Nathan M. "Samuel Coleridge-Taylor: His Life
     and Works." DMA dissertation. Peabody Institute of
     the Johns Hopkins University, 1984. UMI 84-17662.
     DAI xlv.6A, p. 1566. 392 pages.
     Part 4 of the dissertation includes a detailed analysis
     of selected chamber music.

Edward T. Cone
b.1917

807. Morgan, Robert P. "Edward T. Cone: String Sextet," in
     Perspectives of New Music, viii, no. 1 (1969), 112-
     125.
     A technical analysis of the prevailing hexachords
     (groups of 6-note semi-rows) in Cone's sextet (1966,
     for 2 violins + 2 violas + 2 cellos). Explains the
     forms of the 3 movements.

Paul Constantinescu
1909-1963

808. Berger, Wilhelm. "In Semnari despre Creatia de Camera
     a Eminentului Compozitor Paul Constantinescu," in
     Muzica, xxiii, no. 12 (Dec. 1973), 7-8. In Romanian.
     Characterizes Constantinescu's chamber music.

Arnold Cooke
b.1906

809. Gaulke, Stanley Jack. "The Published Solo and Chamber
     Works for Clarinet of Arnold Cooke." DMA disserta-
     tion. University of Rochester, Eastman School of
     Music, 1978. DAI xxxix.6A, pp. 3209-10. 292 pages.
     A brief biography of this contemporary British composer
     and pupil of Hindemith, followed by a discussion of
     style, form, texture, clarinet technique and ensemble
     problems in 6 works. Includes a list of Cooke's works
     and correspondence between Cooke and Gaulke.

Aaron Copland
b.1900

For a list of Copland's chamber music, see Joann Skowronski,
Aaron Copland: a Bio-Bibliography, *in* Bio-Bibliographies in
Music, *No. 2 (Westport [Connecticut]/London: Greenwood
Press, 1985), pages 238-239. ML 134.C66S55.1985. ISBN 0-
313-24091-4.*

810. Butterworth, Neil. *The Music of Aaron Copland.* New
     York: Universe Books/London: Toccata Press, 1985. ML
     410.C7. ISBN 0-87663-495-1. 262 pages.
     The music of Copland presented in biographical order,
     with information on each piece's origins and first per-
     formances and some brief commentary on the nature of
     the music. The Piano Quartet and Nonet receive a
     little more attention than the other chamber music.
     Includes a list of chamber music.

811. Smith, Julia Frances. *Aaron Copland: his Work and Con-
     tribution to American Music.* New York: E.P. Dutton,
     1955. ML 410.C756S5. 336 pages. PhD dissertation.
     New York University, 1950. 649 pages.
     En passant discussion of the few pieces of chamber
     music: *Allegro for String Quartet* (1921), *Piano Quartet*
     (1950), *Rondino for String Quartet* (1923), *Vitebsk* for
     piano + violin + cello (1929), *Two Pieces for String
     Quartet* (1923, 1928), *Sextet* (1937 arr. for string
     quartet + clarinet + piano of Short Symphony, 1933),
     Sonata for Violin + Piano (1944), and *2 Pieces* for
     violin + piano (1926). Their historical background and
     the principle influences on them: jazz, American West-
     ern songs, Jewish music, Stravinsky, and so on. Ana-
     lyzes in greater depth only the violin + piano sonata.

812. Plaistow, Stephen. "Some Notes on Copland's Nonet," in
     Tempo, no. 64 (Spring, 1963), 6-11.
     After a review of Copland's compositions and the expec-
     tations of his return to a more serious style in the
     1950's, the Nonet (1960) comes across as retreat into a

charming, well-written, but highly conservative style.
Brief technical discussion.

Roque Cordero
b. 1917

813. Brawand, John Edward. "The Violin Works of Roque Cordero." DMA dissertation. University of Texas at
Austin, 1985. UMI 85-27503. DAI xlvi.10A, p. 2849.
125 pages.
A study of Cordero's *Dos Piezas Cortas* (1945), *Sonatina*
for violin + piano (1946), and *Violin Concerto* (1962),
each in a different style: tonal, early 12-tone, and
mature 12-tone. Includes also an assessment of musical
life in Central America, a biography, and Cordero's
place in his native Panama.

Arcangelo Corelli
1653-1713

*For a catalogue and extensive bibliography of Corelli's
chamber music, see Hans Joachim Marx,* Die Überlieferung der
Werke Arcangelo Corellis: Catalogue Raisonné, *supplement
volume to* Arcangelo Corelli: historisch-kritische Gesamtaus-
gabe der musikalischen Werke *(Cologne: Arno Volk, 1980), 356
pages. ML 134.C67A25. ISBN 3-87252-121-7.*

814. Pincherle, Marc. *Corelli,* in *Les Maîtres de la Musique, nouvelle série.* Paris: Félix Alcan, 1933.
Rev. *Corelli et son Temps.* Paris: Éditions Le Bon
Plaisir, 1954. *Corelli: his Life, his Work,* trl. by
Hubert E.M. Russell. New York: Norton, 1956. ML
410.C78P52. 236 pages, 29 musical examples.
For the general reader as well as scholar. Clears up a
lot of biographical misinformation in previous studies
and clearly describes and defines the genres of Corelli's music. Discusses all the trio sonatas separately
from the solo sonatas and the concerti grossi. Considers form, tonality (29 of the 48 trio sonatas are each
entirely in 1 key; the 19 others change only for 1 slow
movement), texture, harmony, ornamentation (Op. 5),
violin technique (especially in *La Folia*), and much
more. Some historical discussion is outdated.
Bibliography lists the full title of each of the 6
opera and the many early editions of each, the arrangements of them by other composers, anthologies,
manuscripts and questionable works.

815. Libby, Dennis. "Interrelationships in Corelli," in
Journal of the American Musicological Society,
xxvi (1973), 263-287.

Studies Corelli's reuse of cliches in melody, tonal
structure, and form, from one piece to the next.

816. Deas, Stewart. "Arcangelo Corelli," in *Music and Letters*, xxxiv (1953), 1-10.
A naive and limited description of Corelli's works, including misunderstood anecdotes and questionable
opinions on the value of Op. 2 and 4.

817. Wintle, Christopher. "Corelli's Tonal Models: the
Trio-Sonata Op. 3, No. 1," in S. Durante and P. Pe-
trobelli, *Nuovissimi Studi Corelliani: Atti del Terzo
Congresso Internazionale (Fusignano, 1980)* (Florence:
Societè Italiana di Musicologia, 1982), pages 29-69.
ML 410.C78C6.1980. ISBN 88-222-3096-5.
Studies Corelli's significance to the history of theory
c.1700. That Schenker's 18th-century theory can apply
to late 17th-century Corelli shows "the fundamental
historical importance of this music." Corelli's music
is elaboration of cadential models, which *per se* fits
Schenker, but surface rhythmic configurations are also
important in determining genre.

*For an important historical study leading to Corelli's Op.
2, see John Daverios's article and dissertation {209}.*

818. Marx, Hans Joachim. "Some Unknown Embellishments of
Corelli's Violin Sonatas," in *The Musical Quarterly*, lxi (1975), 65-76.
An English manuscript of the mid-18th century, hitherto
unknown, adds another highly-ornamented version of the
Corelli solo sonatas to those already known (Marx lists
7 such versions including his new one). Demonstrates
the style and taste of ornamentation of the time and
how these oldest permanent pieces in the chamber
repertory have survived despite changes in taste and
style of different epochs.

819. Boyden, David D. "Corelli's Solo Violin sonatas
'Grac'd' by Dubourg," in *Festskrift Jens Peter Larsen
1902 14.VI.1972* (Copenhagen: Wilhelm Hansen Musik-
Forlag, 1972), pp. 113-125. ML 55.L215.1972.
An analysis of the ornaments of certain movements of
Corelli's solo violin sonatas by Matthew Dubourg (1703-
1767), pupil of Geminiani who was himself a pupil of
Corelli. While Corelli ornamented only slow movements,
Dubourg ornaments both slow and fast and also dance-
like movements. Dubourg's graces are rare examples by
an English violinist. Lists all known ornamented versions of Corelli's solo sonatas and then gives biographical information on Dubourg (who as concertmaster
of the Viceroy's Band in Dublin was involved in the
premier of Handel's *Messiah*). Describes the Dubourg
manuscript in detail, including watermarks, page sizes,

and so on. Goes into the actual graces themselves, from simple passing tones and appoggiaturas to extensive gorge; the simpler ones, less disruptive, are in the fast movements, while the fancier graces, often disrupting the rhythm, are in the slow movements. Only fugue passages are not graced.

820. Cherry, Norman. "A Corelli Sonata for Trumpet, Violins and *Basso Continuo*," in *Brass Quarterly*, iv (1960-1961), 103-113.
Authenticates this sonata in D Major found in 2 copies in Naples, Library of the Conservatorio. It has 5 movements, of which the fourth is scored for trumpet + continuo without violins. Speculates that Corelli may have written the sonata in 1689 when he visited Bologna and heard similar music composed for the Feast of San Petronio (October 27). See also Cherry, "A Corelli Sonata for Trumpet, Violins, and *Basso Continuo*: a Postscript," in *Brass Quarterly*, ii (1960-1961), 156-158. Incorporates findings by Michael Tilmouth, "Corelli's Trumpet Sonata," in *Monthly Musical Record*, xc (1960), 217-221, which corroborate Cherry's article. Tilmouth cites an incomplete copy in Trinity College Music Library, London, and quotes an announcement in the *The Daily Courant* (London newspaper), March 16, 1713, of a concert by Mr. Twiselton, trumpet, who is to play a Corelli sonata composed for him.

John Corigliano
b.1938

821. Bobetsky, Victor V. "An Analysis of Selected Works for Piano (1959-1978) and the Sonata for Violin and Piano (1964) by John Corigliano." DMA dissertation. University of Miami, 1982. DAI xliv.1A, p. 10. 109 pages.
Analyzes harmony, form, melody, and rhythm in the sonata.

François Couperin
1668-1733

822. Mellers, Wilfrid H. "Couperin's Suites for Two Viols," in *The Score*, ii (Jan. 1950), 10-17.
The last published works of Couperin, in 1728, these 2 suites are for 2 viols, one of which is figured. Reviews the viol's history as a virtuoso instrument in France from 1660 on and the chamber music for viol of other composers in France. Discusses these 2 pieces. 2 possible scorings: for 2 solo viols in duet, or for 1 solo viol accompanied by the second viol and continuo.

Analyzes briefly each of the movements and quotes in
full the "Pompe Funèbre" of the A Major Suite.

823. Beaussant, Philippe. "La Musique de Chambre," in *François Couperin* (Paris: Arthème Fayard, 1980), pp. 229-
324. ML 410.C855B4. ISBN 2-213-00896-5. In French.
For a lay audience, the chamber music section discusses
briefly the *sonatas en trio, les Nations (sonades et
suites de cimphonies en trio), Concerts Royaux* 1-14,
and *Pièces* for viol. Brief history of Couperin's chamber music in general and each collection in particular,
and brief, non-technical discussion of each movement.
Superficial remarks on viol technique and no discussion
of Couperin's handling of ensemble and the non-harpsi-
chord part(s).

824. Mellers, Wilfrid. "The Two-Violin Sonatas," and "The
Concerts Royaux and Suites for Viols," in *François
Couperin and the French Classical Tradition* (London:
D. Dobson, 1950; New York: Roy Publishers, 1951), pp.
97-127 and 234-271. ML 410.C855M4.
Discusses the dichotomies of voice and instrument
(polyphony versus homophony) and *da chiesa* and *da camera* in Couperin's trio sonatas. This broad approach to
the music would be effective if it were not founded on
errors of concept and history.

Henry Cowell
1897-1965

825. Manion, Martha. *Writings about Henry Cowell: an Annotated Bibliography,* in *Institute for Studies of American Music,* No. 16. Brooklyn: City University of
New York, 1982. ISBN 0-914678-17-5. xi + 369 pages.
Reference to studies and reviews of Cowell's chamber
music including such unusually titled works as *Quintet for String Quartet and Thundersticks, Quartet Pedantic, Solo for Violin with String Piano,* and *Solo for
Violin with Thunderstick,* as well as normally-titled
(but not necessarily normal sounding) works like 5
string quartets, *Suite for Violin and Piano, Suite for
Woodwind Quartet, Sonata No. 1 for Violin and Piano,*
and so on.

Paul Creston
1906-1985

826. Sibbing, Robert Virgil. "An Analytical Study of the
Published Sonatas for Saxophone by American Composers." EdD dissertation. University of Illinois,
1969. UMI 69-15389. DAI xxx.3A, p. 1197. 184
pages.

Analyzes the form, melodic and phrase structure, harmony, rhythm, counterpoint and other factors of sonatas for alto saxophone + piano by Creston, Heiden, Hindemith, Kanitz, and Tuthill. Special emphasis on performance and teaching problems of each work.

Henri-Jacques de Croes
1705-1786

827. Clercx, Suzanne. *Henri-Jacques de Croes: Compositeur et Maître de Musique du Prince Charles de Lorraine 1705-1786*, in *Beaux-Arts*, vii (1937), fasc. 3A-B. 2 vols. HML 2147.15.13. I: v + 92 pages; II: cxxvii pages (index, bibliography, thematic catalogue, letters and documents).
Describes the musical form, tonalities, tempos and meters in 3 collections of trio sonatas of this French composer: (Op.1 and 3: 2 violins or 2 flutes + continuo; Op. 4: 2 violins or 2 flutes + optional cello + continuo).

Bernhard Henrik Crusell
1775-1838

828. Spicknall, John Payne. "The Solo Clarinet Works of Bernhard Henrik Crusell (1775-1838)." DAM dissertation. University of Maryland, 1974. UM 74-29112. DAI xxxv.6A, pp. 3800-3801. 297 pages.
A catalogue of 33 works (some non-extant) by this Swedish court composer and clarinetist. Fourteen feature the clarinet (3 concertos, 3 quartets, duets, smaller solo pieces, and miscellaneous ones). Analyzes primarily 1 concerto, 1 clarinet quartet, and 1 clarinet duet. Crusell's style is early Romantic, and his clarinet technique has a wide tessitura, color effects, non-patterned articulations, disjunct leaps and deemphasis of the bar lines.

Franz Danzi
1763-1826

829. Hoff, Helen Arlene. "The Bassoon in Eight Quartets for Bassoon, Violin, Viola, and Cello Written c.1800." DMA dissertation. University of Oregon, 1976. DAI xxxvii.12A, p. 7393. xi + 200 pages.
Comparative analysis of form, keys, range, and so on, in 8 bassoon quartets by Danzi, Carl Stamitz, J.C. Vogel, Devienne, and Franz Krommer, from the standpoint of a bassoon player. Vogel, Krommer and Devienne treat the bassoon as a soloist; Stamitz treats it as an equal member of the ensemble without exploiting any of the instrument's special qualities; Danzi treats all in-

struments equally but takes advantage of unique bassoon
qualities. Stamitz's is the easiest and Danzi's the
hardest.

Peter Maxwell Davies
b.1934

*For a description and discography of Davies's chamber music,
see Davies's* The Complete Catalogue of Published Works
(London: Judy Arnold, 1981), pages 38-46. ML 134.D25P5.

830. Griffiths, Paul. *Peter Maxwell Davies,* in *The Contem-*
     porary Composers. London: Robson Books, 1982. ML
     410.D. ISBN 0-86051-138-3. 196 pages.
     Lists Davies chamber music for various instruments, and
     analyzes the string quartet (1961) in detail.

Claude Debussy
1862-1918

*For a catalogue of Debussy's chamber music, see François
Lesure,* Catalogue de l'Oeuvre de Claude Debussy, *in* Publi-
cations du Centre de Documentation Claude Debussy, *No. 3
(Geneva: Minkoff, 1977). ML 134.D26L5. ISBN 2-8266-0657-3.
For a bibliography of writings about Debussy's music, in-
cluding chamber music, see Claude Abravanel,* Claude Debussy:
a Bibliography, *in* Detroit Studies in Music Bibliography,
*No. 29 (Detroit: Information Coordinators, 1974), 214 pages.
ML 134.D26A2. ISBN 911772-49-9.*

831. Wilson, Eugene Norman. "Form and Texture in the Cham-
     ber Music of Debussy and Ravel." PhD dissertation.
     University of Washington, 1968. UM 68-12723. DA
     xxix.3A, p. 927. iv + 272 pages
     Contrasts the different paths Debussy and Ravel take
     after starting in nearly the same place. Compares form
     and harmony in their early string quartets: both are
     mainly tonal with some pentatonicism, and both regard
     sonata form as ternary without the traditional polarity
     of tonic-dominant. Late Debussy comes up with entirely
     new sounds, forms, and silences, while late Ravel re-
     tains much of his earlier style.

832. Seraphin, Hellmut. "Debussys Kammermusikwerke der
     mittleren Schaffenszeit: analytische und historische
     Untersuchung in Rahmen des Gesamtschaffens unter be-
     sonderer Berücksichtigung des Ganztongeschlechts."
     Inaugural dissertation. University of Erlangen,
     1962. HML 2236.188. 144 pages.
     Lengthy, technical analysis of harmony and especially
     the whole-tone scale's effect on the various aspects of
     Debussy's *Première Rhapsodie* (1910) for clarinet +

piano. Also considers the same question in *Petite
Piéce* for clarinet + piano, *Syrinx* for flute, and
briefly the string quartet and 3 late sonatas.

833. Krein, IUlian Grigor'evich. *Kamerno-instrumental'nye
     Ansembli Debussi i Ravelia*. Moscow: Muzyka, 1966.
     MT 140.K73. 112 pages. In Russian.
     A piece-by-piece analysis of structure and the use of
     different scales to achieve impressionistic effects in
     the major chamber works, first those by Debussy, then
     those by Ravel. For the general audience.

834. Shera, Frank Henry. "Quartet for Strings, Op. 10
     (1893, published 1895)," in *Debussy and Ravel* (Lon-
     don: Oxford University Press, 1925), pp. 29-35. MT
     92.D3S5.
     The 2 composers are basically miniaturists who think
     homophonically in colors. Their quartets are not of
     the same level as their shorter works, since quartets
     are long and basically contrapuntal. A measure-by-
     measure analysis of themes, rhythm, texture and form
     with occasionally appropriate, overblown adjectives
     ("murmuring arpeggios," "the second movement has a
     freakish, gnome-like character") but more often with
     pedestrian facts.

835. Hartke, Stephen Paul. "Comparative Aspects of the
     Treatment of the 'Harmonic Envelope' in the First
     Movements of Debussy's Quartet in G Minor and Ravel's
     Quartet in F Major." PhD dissertation. University
     of California in Santa Barbara, 1982. UMI 84-00037.
     DAI xliv.10A, p. 2921. 31 pages.
     Concerned with how Debussy and Ravel were able to
     create a sense of increasing and decreasing tension
     while employing static harmonic regions (= harmonic
     envelopes). Offers a new system to describe composi-
     tional procedures in such music, and through this new
     system finds that Debussy gains structural contrast by
     gradually shifting from complex, denser pitch-sets to
     simpler ones, whereas Ravel moves "from diatonic enve-
     lopes to octatonic pitch sets and back to diatonic
     again."

836. Hedges, Bonnie Lois. "The Structural Significance of
     Duration and Concepts of Linear and Cyclical Movement
     in Two Chamber Works of Claude Debussy." PhD disser-
     tation. University of Texas, 1976. UMI 77-3911.
     DAI xxxvii.8A, p. 4685. 171 pages.
     Concerned with the dynamic continuity of music as exem-
     plified in the String Quartet and the Sonata for Flute,
     Viola, and Harp. Finds the Quartet goal-oriented on a
     linear course, the Sonata (cyclic variations) a multi-
     layered texture of relatively independent rhythmic pat-
     terns. The Quartet is therefore traditional, while

the Sonata is a "link in the trend toward interacting
of world cultures and disciplines that distinguished
twentieth-century civilization in general" and new
musical expression in particular (Meyer's stasism).

837. Whitman, Ernestine. "Analysis and Performance Critique
of Debussy's Flute Works." DMA dissertation. University of Wisconsin, 1977. DAI xxxviii.11A, p.
6393. 126 pages.
Concentrates on *Syrinx* and the Sonata for Flute + Viola
+ Harp. Dynamics and rhythm create an increase of mo-
mentum from the first to the last movement of the sonata, which must be understood by the performer.

838. Allen, Judith Shatin. "Tonal Allusion and Illusion:
Debussy's Sonata for Flute, Viola and Harp," in
Cahiers Debussy, Nouvelle Série, no. 7 (1983), 38-48.
Traces the disintegration of traditional tonality
through the 3 movements of this sonata, where the
tritone relationship of F-B is stressed and where
assumptions of tonal expectancy are distorted. For
example, the usual tonic to dominant (linearly) is
replaced by tonic to submediant (linearly) in the tonic
traid. Despite the distortions, there is a linear
tonality (F) which is brought to a decisive conclusion
at the end of movement 3 in its coda.

839. Rauss, Denis-François. "*'Ce Terrible Finale'*: les
Sources Manuscrites de la Sonate pour Violon et Piano
de Claude Debussy et la Genèse du Troisième Mouve-
ment," in *Cahiers Debussy, Nouvelle Série*, no. 2
(1978), 30-62.
For the scholar, this is a detailed comparison of the
manuscript sources with each other and with the final
version. Refers to Debussy's own comments about the
piece in his letters. Shows how Debussy composed and
corrected himself. Speculates on the chronology of the
sources and on the internal order of the work.

840. Moevs, Robert. "Intervallic Procedures in Debussy:
Serenade from the Sonata for Cello and Piano, 1915,"
in *Perspectives of New Music*, viii, no. 1 (1969), 82-
101.
Shows that a pattern of intervals is presented by Debussy at the opening of this movement and that he then
builds his music out of these intervals. Three notes
ascending in half steps (A-flat - A - B-flat) are followed by 3 more (C# - D - E-flat) and then rounded off
by a whole step (G-flat - A-flat) that complete the octave. The first 2 groups of half steps are separated
by a minor third (in turn, 3 half steps) and then the
second group of 3 is likewise separated from the whole
step by a minor third. The expansion from half to
whole step is the next stage -- the juxtaposition of 2

sound systems -- and the 2 operate within antipodes of musical space delineated by perfect fifth and tritone.

841. Nygren, Dennis Quentin. "The Music for Accompanied Clarinet Solo of Claude Debussy: an Historical and Analytical Study of the *Première Rhapsodie* and *Petite Pièce*." DM dissertation. Northwestern University, 1982. UMI 84-00759. DAI xliv.10A, p. 2922. 183 pages.
Analyzes and compares these 2 works of 1910, which demonstrate important characteristics of Debussy's style. Rich in references and historical documentation. Gives a measure-by-measure master-class on performing the Rhapsodie.

Frederick Delius
1862-1934

842. Hutchings, A.J.B. "The Chamber Works of Delius," in *The Musical Times*, lxxvi (1935), 17-20, 214-216, 310-311, and 401-403.
A lengthy defense of Delius with analyses of the principle themes of the 3 violin + piano sonatas, the Sonata for cello + piano, the String Quartet, and piano pieces. Rhapsodizes on their beauties without much critical attention.

843. Bacon-Shone, Frederic. "Form in the Chamber Music of Frederick Delius." PhD dissertation. University of Southern California, 1976. RILM 76-15449.
Not seen.

844. Foss, Hubert. "The Instrumental Music of Frederick Delius," in *Tempo*, no. 26 (Winter, 1952-1953), 30-37.
Puts the 3 violin + piano sonatas and the cello + piano sonata in perspective of Delius's oeuvre. Compares Delius to Brahms: the former lacks the rhythmic verve of the latter, but Delius never pads his works whereas Brahms often does so to fill out predetermined forms.

845. Threlfall, Robert. "Delius's Violin Sonata (No. 1)," in *The Delius Society Journal*, no. 74 (Jan. 1982), 5-12.
Studies the large number of manuscripts, proofs and the first edition of this 1917 sonata and then the differences among them. Specifies notes and phrasings that are not correct in the printed score.

François Devienne
1759-1803

846. Kennedy, Dale Edwin. "The Clarinet Sonata in France
    before 1800 with a Modern Performance Edition of Two
    Works." PhD dissertation. University of Oklahoma,
    1979. UMI 80-12284. DAI xl.12A, pp. 6061-2. 247
    pages.
    Discusses late-18th-century clarinet performance prac-
    tice with special emphasis on Devienne. Biography, an
    edition of 2 of his sonatas, and the history of the
    clarinet sonata in France to 1800.

See also Helen Hoff's dissertation {829}.

David Diamond
b.1915

847. Binder, Daniel Ambrose. "A Formal and Stylistic Analy-
    sis of Selected Compositions for Solo Accordion with
    Accompanying Ensembles by Twentieth-Century American
    Composers with Implications of their Impact upon the
    Place of Accordion in the World of Serious Music."
    DA dissertation. Ball State University, 1981. DAI
    xlii.10A, p. 4194. 209 pages.
    One of the works discussed is Diamond's *Night Music for
    Accordion and String Quartet*.

Karl Ditters von Dittersdorf
1739-1799

848. Rigler, Gertrude. "Die Kammermusik Dittersdorfs," in
    *Studien zur Musikwissenschaft: Beihefte der Denkmäler
    der Tonkunst in Österreich*, Band 14 (Vienna: Univer-
    sal-Edition, 1927), pages 179-212 + xi-xiii.
    Seeks the roots of Dittersdorf's style in Vienna under
    Wagenseil rather than in Mannheim, and considers the
    importance of his style for the later Haydn and Mozart.
    Characterizes Dittersdorf's chamber music -- for exam-
    ple, most quartets and quintets are in 3 movements with
    a minuet as the second movement, first movements are in
    sonata form, also uses Lied-Romance, minuet, rondo, and
    variation forms. Spiritually Dittersdorf stands near
    Haydn, and he was more highly regarded than Mozart in
    his own day.

849. Altmann, Wilhelm. "Die Streichquintette Dittersdorf,"
    in *Studien zur Musikgeschichte: Festschrift für Guido
    Adler zum 75. Geburtstag* (Vienna/Leipzig: Universal
    Edition, 1930), pp. 187-189. ML 55.A2S8.
    Dittersdorf wrote these 6 quintets (2 violins + viola +
    2 cellos) for Fredrich Wilhelm II of Prussia (an

amateur cellist) but there is no evidence they were
performed in 1789 and they remained unpublished until
now. Each is in 3 movements. The technical demands of
the first violin and first cello are considerable, but
the viola and second cello are mere accompaniment.
Brief descriptions of each quintet. Influenced by
Mozart and Haydn, yet suggest early Beethoven.

Ernö Dohnányi
1877-1960

850. Tovey, Donald Francis. "Dohnányi's Chamber Music,"
     originally in Cobbett {7}, reprinted in *Essays and
     Lectures on Music*, ed. Hubert Foss (London/New York/
     Toronto: Oxford University Press, 1949), pages 302-
     310. ML 60.T665.1949.
     Notes Brahms's influence on Dohnányi, though in rhythm
     Dohnányi was his own master. Analyzes for layperson or
     scholar each of the first 8 chamber pieces: 2 quintets,
     3 string quartets, 1 string trio, and 2 sonatas (violin
     + piano and cello + piano). Contains rich prose rather
     than detailed analyses.

Gaetano Donizetti
1797-1848

*Apparently there is no study of Donizetti's 18 string quar-
tets, written for the ensemble in which his teacher Simon
Mayr was the violist. Useful but limited information in
William Ashbrook,* Donizetti and his Operas, *2nd ed. (Cambridge: Cambridge University Press, 1982), ML 410.D7A83.
1982, ISBN 0-521-23526-X.*

Matt Doran
b.1921

See Charles Del Rosso's "A Study of Selected Solo Clarinet
Literature of Four American Composers..." {702} *for a discussion of his Sonata for clarinet + piano.*

Jean Roger-Ducasse
1873-1954

851. Ceillier, Laurent. *Roger-Ducasse: le Musicien --
     l'Oeuvre.* Paris: A. Durand et Fils, 1920. HML
     2360.15.12.
     A brief discussion of his string quartet and piano
     quartet. Describes form, motives, and rhythm. In the
     string quartet notes the use of the principal motive of

movement 1 in the Scherzo in augmentation, and the use
of F.A.U.Ré as the theme of movement 4.

Antonin Dvořák
1841-1904

852. Šourek, Otakar. *Dvořákovy Skladby Komorní: Charak-
     teristika a Rozbory.* Prague: Hudebni matice Umelecke
     Besedy, 1949. MT 145.D8S7.1949. 213 pages. The
     Chamber Music of Antonin Dvořák, abridged English
     trl. by Roberta Finlayson Samsour. Prague: Artis,
     19[56]. MT 145.D8S72. 177 pages. Reprint of the
     English trl. Westport (Connecticut): Greenwood Press,
     1978. MT 145.D8S72.1978. ISBN 03-13205418.
     Discussion of the major chamber music by Dvořák, ar-
     ranged by genre. In the early chamber works, which are
     not analyzed, shows Dvořák's learning to control tradi-
     tional forms and balancing this control with imagina-
     tive invention. Each analysis of the later works opens
     with a brief but rich historical note (Šourek has also
     written the major Czech biography of Dvořák in 4 vol-
     umes). The analyses themselves are not technical, are
     often poetic, but also factual, concentrating on tonal-
     ity and the nature and location of themes. A basic
     handbook for Dvořák's chamber music and a basic work
     upon which more specialized and detailed studies need
     be based.

853. Kull von Niederlenz, Hans. *Dvořák's Kammermusik,* in
     Berner Veröffentlichungen zur Musikforschung, Heft
     15. Bern: Paul Haupt, 1948. MT 145.D8K8.1948a. x +
     203 pages, 327 examples.
     A basic, thorough, technical study concerned with the
     melody and rhythm in Slavic folk music and in Dvořák's
     music; the 4-voice movement, including non-thematic
     melody, inner voices, and various styles and textures;
     and the forms. Finds that Dvořák rarely uses a melody
     in violin 1 with the rest of the instruments repeating
     chord tones in simple accompaniment as in Haydn, Mozart
     and Beethoven; rather, if his inner voices accompany,
     the parts are wildly moving arpeggios which are mainly
     distinguished from the solo theme in the first violin
     by rhythmic activity. Dvořák's use of pentatonic is
     derived from Slavic folk music originally and is too
     developed in his music to be a casual influence of his
     American years.

*For a non-technical introduction to Dvořák's chamber music,
see John Clapham's essay in Alec Robertson, ed., Chamber
Music {160}.*

854. Beveridge, David. "Sophisticated Primitivism: the
     Significance of Pentatonicism in Dvořák's American

Quartet," in *Current Musicology*, no. 24 (1977), 25-36.
A thorough analysis of the final movement of the quartet and of the underlying pentatonicism of the whole piece. Pentatonicism is more than quotation of the scale, and Dvořák uses it in many works of non-American province in his quest for "important new creative possibilities." It is not an attempt to be American.

855. Krehbiel, Henry Edward. *Antonin Dvořák's Quartet in F Major, Op. 96.* New York: H.A. Rost, 1894. MT 145. D8K7. 7 pages.
An interesting document in the controversy as to what is American in this so-called "American" quartet. Written just after the work's premier in 1893, the author tries to prove the American inspiration for the melodies (from Southern Blacks and American Indians). He emphasizes the beauty of Black songs, genuine American folksongs; because of industrialization, "it is inconceivable that America shall add to her store of folk songs" and therefore they must be preserved and then utilized, as Dvořák has done, in creating American art music.

See also Clapham's analysis of the kind of Indian music Dvořák would have heard {457}.

856. Case, Barbara Betty Bacik. "The Relation between Structure and the Treatment of Instruments in the First Movements of Dvořák's Piano Trios Opus 21, 26, and 65." DMA dissertation. University of Texas, 1977. DAI xxxviii.12A, p. 7011. 64 pages.
Shows how 18th-century concerto features such as tutti, concertino, and solo highlight structural aspects in Dvořák's trios and help clarify the sonata form. Also shows how Dvořák's early instrumentation later becomes more symphonic and coloristic.

857. Stahmer, Klaus Hinrich. "Drei Klavierquartette aus den Jahren 1875/76: Brahms, Mahler und Dvořák im Vergleich," in *Hamburger Jahrbuch für Musikwissenschaft*, vii, *Brahms und seine Zeit* (Hamburg: Laaber, 1984), 113-123.
Compares 2 youthful works by Mahler and Dvořák modeled on a mature work of Brahms. Brahms is the most radical with an original solution to the conflict between classical conception and romantic realization, whereas Dvořák avoids the issue and Mahler is too young to realize the problem.

858. Hadow, Henry. "Dvořák's Quintet for Pianoforte and Strings," in *The Musical Times*, lxxiii (1932), 401-404.

A thematic analysis. Notes that Dvořák thinks harmoni-
cally, not contrapuntally. Discusses the origins of
the term "Dumka" (= elegy) for the slow second
movement.

859. Beveridge, David. "Dvořák's Piano Quintet, Op.81: the
     Schumann Connection," in *Chamber Music Quarterly*
     (Spring, 1984), pages 2-10.
     Hans Hollander ("Schubertsche bei Dvořák -- dargestellt
     am Klavierquintett, op. 81," in *Musica*, xxviii [1974],
     40-43) emphasizes Dvořák's debt to Schubert, especially
     in the second movement, but ignores his debt to Schu-
     mann. This quintet is clearly based on the harmony,
     structure and themes in Schumann's *Piano Quintet*, Op.
     44. Cites Dvořák's own praises of Schumann's chamber
     music, though he never acknowledged the debt of Op. 81
     to Schumann. Shows in detail the parallels between the
     second movements and the differences as well.

Jean-Frédéric Edelmann
1749-1794

860. Saint-Foix, Georges Poullain, Comte de. "Les Premiers
     Pianistes Parisiens [Johann Schobert, Nicolas-Joseph
     Hüllmandel, Jean-Frédéric Edelmann, Henri-Joseph
     Rigel]," in *La Revue Musicale*, III, no. 10 (1922),
     121-136, IV, no. 6 (1923), 193-205, V, no. 8 (1924),
     187-191 and 192-198.
     Gives biographies, evaluates the works, and points out
     the contributions of these 4 composers not only to key-
     board music but to keyboard music accompanied by violin
     or 2 violins. Points the way for later research.

Gottfried von Einem
b.1918

861. Saathen, Friedrich. *Einem Chronik: Dokumentation und
     Deutung*. Vienna/Köln/Graz: Hermann Böhlaus Nachf.,
     1982. HML 2427.15.79. ISBN 3-205-07179-4. 388
     pages.
     Chronological list of Einem's works, including several
     chamber pieces. In his late chamber music Einem re-
     calls the spirit of Schubert. The rest of the book is
     about Einem's reactions to events of his time and the
     reception of his music.

Hans Eisler
1898-1962

862. Grabs, Manfred. *Hans Eisler: Kompositionen-Schriften-
     Literature: ein Handbuch*, in *Veröffentlichung der*

Akademie der Künste der Deutschen Demokratische Republik. Leipzig: VEB Deutscher Verlag für Musik, 1984. HML 2428.15.35.5. 415 pages.
A large, very useful bibliography of Eisler's compositions, of his writings, and of studies on him and his music. Includes at the end a chronological listing of his music, at the beginning a chronology of his life. His chamber works include a Sonata for Flute + Oboe + Harp, a Sonata for Violin + Piano, a String Quartet, and others.

Edward Elgar
1857-1934

863. Maine, Basil. "Chamber Music," in *Elgar: his Life and Works: the Works.* (London: G. Bell & Sons, 1933), pages 259-275. HML 2430.15.53(2).
Notes that Elgar was preoccupied with the key of E Minor when he wrote not only the Cello Concerto but also the sonata for violin + piano and the string quartet. The *Piano Quintet* is in A Minor. Analyzes these 3 chamber pieces separately, paying attention to Elgar's characteristic melody types, forms, and rhythms, with references to other works by him. Also, for historical information, references to the companion volume (*The Life*).

864. [Colles, H.C.] "Elgar's String Quartet," in *The Musical Times*, lx (1919), 336-338.
A thematic analysis of the Op. 83 (1918) string quartet. For reviews of the premiers of the quartet and quintet, see *The Musical Times*, lx (1919), 282.

865. Colles, H.C. "Elgar's Quintet for Pianoforte and Strings, Op. 84," in *The Musical Times*, lx (1919), 596-600.
A thematic analysis of a work which is more impressive in the listening than in the analysis. There is nothing novel or striking to the analyst, but it is a beautiful and cohesive work. See note in {864}.

866. Anonymous, in *The Musical Times,* lx (1919), 162-163.
A review and analysis of Elgar's sonata Op. 82 for violin + piano.

Józef Elsner
1769-1854

867. Nowak-Romanowicz, Alina. *Józef Elsner,* in *Studia i Materialy do Dziejów Muzyki Polskiej*, Vol. 4. Cracow: Polskie Wydawniciwo Muzyczne, 1957. HML 2438.

15.61. 2 vols. I: 352 pages; II: 189 pages of
music. In Polish.
The major study of the Polish composer who besides much
else also wrote a lot of chamber music (listed on pages
314-317) including sonatas for violin + piano, string
and piano trios, quartets, quintets, a septet (for
flute + clarinet + violin + viola + cello + bass +
piano), and others. In the course of the biography the
chamber pieces are discussed and analyzed.

Arnold Elston
1907-1971

868. Lewin, David. "Berkeley: Arnold Elston: Quartet; Seymour Shifrin: Quartet No. 2," in *Perspectives of New
Music*, ii, no. 2 (1964), 169-175.
Reviews premier performances by the Lenox Quartet of
the 2 pieces. Elston's quartet is "saturated with motivic cells which function crucially as carriers of
both line and harmonic progression"; concentrates on
just the third movement. Shifrin's quartet is a "contrasting play of two basic textures": lyricism and
terse fragmentation. The first 2 movements are successful, the third is uncertain. Notes the excitement
in Shifrin's music, which comes from his perception
that a listener must continually test and revise
fundamental assumptions about a piece with repeated
hearings and not accept it as a finished business.

Georges Enesco
1881-1955

869. Voicana, Mircea. *George Enescu: Monografie*. Bucharest: Academiei Republicii Socialiste România, 1971.
HML 2444.15.33. 2 vols. I: xxxvi + 588 pages; II +
696 + i. In Romanian, with a French summary.
List of works includes 3 string quartets, 2 piano quartets, 2 piano quintets, sonatas for violin + piano, a
string trio, a piano trio, and a few others. Historic-
cal background to the pieces and brief analysis in the
course of the biography.

870. Moisescu, Titus. "Cvartetul de Coarde in Creatia liú
George Enescu," in *Muzica*, xxv (June, 1975), 5-11,
(Sept. 1975), 7-14, and (Dec. 1975), 9-14.
Discusses 11 newly discovered string quartets by Enesco
in the Muzeo George Enesco, and the 2 published Op. 22,
nos.1 and 2 quartets.

Alvin Gerald Etler
1913-1973

871. Nichols, William Roy. "The Wind Music of Alvin Etler
     (1913-1973)." DMA dissertation. University of Iowa,
     1976. UMI 77-13154. DAI xxxvii.12A, p. 7396. 255
     pages.
     A biography and chronological list of Etler's wind
     music. Analyzes 5 works, 2 of which are chamber
     pieces: Sonata for Oboe + Clarinet + Viola (1945) and
     Woodwind Quintet No. 1 (1955).

872. Sheldon, Paul Melvin. "Alvin Etler (1913-1973): his
     Career and the Two Sonatas for Clarinet." DMA dis-
     sertation. University of Maryland, 1978. UMI 70-
     20730. DAI: xl.3A, pp. 1146-7. 230 pages.
     A biography and analysis of Etler's compositional style
     and the 2 clarinet pieces. Considers clarinet tech-
     nique and makes performance suggestions.

Victor Ewald
1860-1935

873. Reed, David F. "Victor Ewald and the Russian Chamber
     Brass School." DMA dissertation. University of
     Rochester, 1979. UMI 80-05141. DAI xl.11A, p. 5644.
     322 pages.
     Ewald's 3 brass quintets are the culmination of almost
     a century of brass music composed in St. Petersburg at
     the end of the 19th and beginning of the 20th centuries
     by such people as Alexander Aliabev, Ludwig Maurer,
     Anton Simon, Glazunov, Wilhelm Ramsöe, and Oskar Böhme:
     the Russian Chamber Brass School. Discusses Ewald's
     part in Belaiev's home chamber music sessions -- he was
     a cellist. The 3 quintets are analyzed; they are im-
     portant Romantic works in a repertory not particularly
     noted for Romantic works.

Manuel de Falla
1876-1946

874. Chase, Gilbert, and Andrew Budwig. *Manuel de Falla: a
     Bibliography and Research Guide*, in *Garland Composer
     Resource Manuals*, Vol. 4. New York/London: Garland,
     1986. ML 134.F18C5. ISBN 0-8240-8587-2. xiii + 145
     pages + 14 photographs + 2 letter facsimiles.
     The only chamber works that fit into our definition are
     the early 2-movement *Cuarteto* (piano quartet), *Melodia*
     (cello + piano), *Romanza* (cello + piano), *Serenata
     Andaluza* (violin + piano), and *Mireya* (flute + violin +
     viola + cello + piano). Lists studies on these works.

Giuseppe Maria Fanfani
fl.1723-1757

875. Cole, Malcolm S.   "A Sonata Offering for the Prince of
     Tuscany," in *Current Musicology*, no. 16 (1973), 71-
     78.
     A detailed historical and analytical account of 12
     sonatas (6 da chiesa and 6 da camera) for violin +
     cello by Fanfani, dedicated to Giovanni Gastone de
     Medici between 1723 and 1737.

Arthur Farwell
1872-1951

*For a catalogue of Farwell's chamber music, see Brice Far-
well, A Guide to the Music of Arthur Farwell and to the
Microfilm Collection of his Work (Briarcliff Manor [New
York]: Brice Farwell, 1972), page 60. ML 134.F25G8. ISBN
0-9600484-0-5.*

Johann Friedrich Fasch
1688-1758

876. Sheldon, David Alden.   "The Chamber Music of Johann
     Friedrich Fasch."   PhD dissertation.   Indiana Univer-
     sity, 1968.   UM 68-13704.   DA xxix.4A, p. 1246.   x +
     243 pages.
     A history of 28 sonatas (16 a3, 12 a4) previously
     evaluated by Hugo Riemann and others.   Primarily an
     analysis of style, themes, forms with motivic repeti-
     tion, texture, and harmony.   While Fasch is no more
     advanced in many respects than his contemporaries, he
     stands out for a "firm adherence to a mid-eighteenth-
     century sonata-allegro principle of form and thematic
     development."

Gabriel-Urbain Fauré
1845-1924

877. Barshell, Margaret Louise.   "Gabriel Fauré: a Biograph-
     ical Study and a Historical Style Analysis of his
     Nine Major Chamber Works for Piano and Strings."   DA
     dissertation.   Ball State University, 1982.   DAI
     xliii.7A, p. 2148.   211 pages.
     A historical and cultural background to Fauré's cham-
     ber music and an explanation of his choice of sonata
     form, some rhythmic peculiarities, certain church modal
     progressions, and certain harmonies and melodic turns.

878. Favre, Max. *Gabriel Fauré's Kammermusik.* Zurich: Kom-
     missionsverlag von Max Niehans, 1949. MT 145.F4F4.
     272 pages, 93 examples (on poor quality paper).
     An important, basic study of French chamber music for
     scholars, performers and laypersons. Although techni-
     cal in its discussion of melody, harmony and form, the
     level of analysis -- objective and not poetic -- is
     clear, unencumbered by jargon, formulas and *a priori*
     theories. An erudite book based exclusively on readily
     available documents (printed scores only) and on
     studies of the music (no secondary sources cited). Be-
     gins with a study of early 19th-century French Romanti-
     cism and the romance, a musical genre which paved the
     way for a renewed interest in chamber music later in
     the century. The first half of the 19th century was
     dominated by opera and by German instrumental music.
     Berlioz, who wrote no chamber music, paved the way for
     it in France by placing instrumental (orchestral) music
     on a plane with opera. Chopin contributed an interest
     in color (harmonic, tonal, formal, melodic)-- a French
     preoccupation and important for Fauré -- and almost
     totally avoided larger instrumental works as in Ber-
     lioz. In the second half of the century César Franck
     wrote religious music and counterpoint, contrary to
     prevailing trends and essential to Fauré's chamber
     music style. Saint-Saëns's music influenced Fauré, his
     close friend, in formal problems and by opening up
     chamber music to a new French style. Chief mark of
     Fauré's chamber music: assumes the new technical
     achievement of the Romantic but not in the Romantic
     spirit. Contains a biography that stresses the
     importance of chamber music in Fauré's life. The bulk
     of the book is thematic, tonal and formal analysis of
     the music.

879. Tubergen, David Gene. "A Stylistic Analysis of Select-
     ed Violin and Piano Sonatas of Fauré, Saint-Saëns,
     and Franck." PhD dissertation. New York University,
     1985. UMI 85-21996. DAI xlvi.10A, pp. 2852-3. 274
     pages.
     A comparison of 3 famous French sonatas for violin +
     piano written 1876-1886 under the aegis of the Société
     Nationale de Musique. Analysis based on LaRue's termi-
     nology (sound, harmony, melody, rhythm, and growth),
     with additional comments on performance. Notes that
     Franck writes regular melodic phrases, the other 2 ir-
     regular ones; Franck is the most daring harmonically
     and Saint-Saëns the least so; all 3 are masters of
     polyphony.

880. Halbreich, Harry. "La Musique de Chambre de Fauré,"
     in *Harmonie*, no. 151 (Oct. 1979), 42-51.
     A popular article on the greatness of Fauré despite de-
     bunkers of the past and some neglect today. His cham-
     ber music is his best writing. He was responsible for

a renewed interest in French chamber music in 1876,
continuing the 18th-century tradition. Lists his 10
chamber pieces and discusses their style in metaphoric,
not theoretic, terms. Compares him to Bach and Bruckner; contrasts him with Schumann, Brahms and Beethoven.

881. Jones, Jonathan Barrie. "The Piano and Chamber Works
      of Gabriel Fauré." PhD dissertation. Cambridge
      University, 1974.
     Not seen.

882. Boneau, Denise. "Genesis of a Trio: the Chicago Manu-
      script of Fauré's Opus 120," in *Current Musicology*,
      no. 35 (1983), 19-33.
     Discusses the autograph manuscript of the third move-
     ment of the trio. Apparently Fauré conceived the trio
     for clarinet + cello + piano, but changed it to violin
     + cello + piano. The published version differs from
     this manuscript in meter and tempo as well as in other
     details. Often states that something is significant
     without explaining why. Compares James McKay, "Le Trio
     Op. 120 de Fauré: une Esquisse Inconnue du troisième
     Mouvement," in *Études Fauréennes, Bulletin de l'Asso-
     ciation des Amis de Gabriel Fauré*, no. 19 (1982), 8-17.

883. Ferguson, David Milton. "A Study, Analysis and Recital
      of the Piano Quartets of Gabriel Fauré." EdD disser-
      tation. Columbia University, 1969. UMI 70-4569.
     DAI xxx.9A, pp. 3970-1. 213 pages.
     Studies the influences on Fauré of Schumann, Schubert
     and Chopin, the modality of the quartets, their contra-
     puntal style, their forms, and the continual develop-
     ment found in them. Emphasizes the implications of
     these matters for performance.

                       Joseph Fennimore
                          b. 1940

884. Hoyle, Wilson Theodore. "Joseph Fennimore: his Biogra-
      phy and Works together with an Analysis of his *Quar-
      tet (After Vinteuil)*." DMA dissertation. Manhattan
      School of Music, 1981. DAI xlii.4A, p. 1365. 168
      pages.
     A study of the Quartet for clarinet + viola + cello +
     piano. Considers structure and the program based on
     the fictional composer Vinteuil (from Marcel Proust's
     Remembrance of Things Past). Includes comments by the
     composer.

Michael Christian Festing
c.1680-1752

885. Krantz, Eldon LaVar. "Practical Edition of Six Sonatas for Violin and Piano by Michael Christian Festing." DMA dissertation. Eastman School of Music, 1973. UMI 73-31572. DAI xxxiv.8A, p. 5231. 178 pages.
The introductory commentary has a biography, a discussion of the form and style of the 6 sonatas, the rationale for the continuo realization, and performance suggestions. Festing, who died in London, was a pupil of Geminani and demonstrates considerable technical feats as well as expressive melodies.

Zdenko Fibich
1850-1900

See Vladimir Hudec {457}.

John Field
1782-1837

886. Piggott, Patrick. *The Life and Music of John Field 1782-1837: Creator of the Nocturne.* Berkeley/Los Angeles: University of California Press, 1973. ISBN 0-520-02412-5. xvi + 287 pages.
Chapter 15 discusses Field's works for piano with string quartet, which were written for performance in the salons of Russia where an accompanying orchestra would have been impossible. Usually the piano dominates, but occasionally the quartet is of equal importance. This type of chamber music has precedents in Haydn and Beethoven and continues with Clara Schumann and Mendelssohn. Gives historical background and some basic thematic analysis.

Johann Anton Fils
1733-1760

887. Holzbauer, Hermann. *Johann Anton Fils (1733-1760): ein Eichstätter Komponist der Mannheimer Klassik: Ausstellung zum 250. Geburtstag*, in *Schriften der Universitätsbibliothek Eichstätt*, No. 2. Tutzing: Hans Schneider, 1983. ISBN 3-7952-0406-2. 99 pages + viii pages of facsimiles.
Fils wrote many trio sonatas and other chamber works. Not a complete catalogue of his works but a catalogue of the exhibition, which includes numerous facsimiles (in addition to the ones at the end) showing chamber music title pages, letters, documents, portraits, and

(no. 48) a string quartet performing c.1790 where all
but the cellist are standing. No analysis or history.

Ross Lee Finney
b.1906

888. Haines, Don Robert. "The Eight String Quartets of Ross
Lee Finney." DMA dissertation. University of
Rochester, 1973.
Divides the 8 quartets (1935-1960) into 3 groups according to different phases in the composer's quartet
style. After a biography, a discussion of each quartet
in turn with reference to traditional compositional
techniques. Form, harmony, and tonality change over
the 8 quartets, but the other elements remain consistent. The later quartets are more polyphonic, the
earlier ones more chordal; the later ones are also more
chromatic, eventually serial. The first 6 are cyclic,
the last two circular.

Richard Flury
1896-1967

889. Flury, Richard. *Lebens-Erinnerungen.* Derendingen
(Switzerland): Habegger, 1950. HML 2543.14.   260
pages.
Memoirs of a Swiss composer whose chamber music consists of 4 string quartets, a piano quintet, string
trio, piano trio, 7 sonatas for violin + piano, 2
sonatas for cello + piano, suite for oboe + piano, and
other pieces. No musical analyses but recounts many
personal events surrounding the composition and performance of his own chamber music.

Emanuel Aloys Förster
1748-1823

See *{625}* and Rey M. Longyear, *"Förster,"* in The New Grove
{1}, vi, 717-718.

Josef Bohuslav Foerster
1859-1951

890. Bachtík, Josef. "Komorní Skladby," in Josef Bartos,
ed., *J.B. Foerster: Jeho Zivotní Pout a Tvorba 1859-
1949* (Prague: Národní Hudební Vydavatelství Orbis,
n.d.), pages 95-148.   HML 2547.15.30.
Analysis of Foerster's chamber music. On pages 377-378
of the same volume, a list of the chamber music which
includes a nonet (woodwind quintet + violin + viola +

cello + bass), a woodwind quintet, a piano quintet, 4
string quartets, trios, and sonatas.

Giovanni Battista Fontana
d. 1631

891. Bartleman, Donald L. "Violin Technic in the Early
     Seventeenth Century as Exhibited in the Violin Sona-
     tas of Giovanni Battista Fontana." PhD dissertation.
     Chicago Musical College-Roosevelt University, 1954.
     DD xxi (1954), p. 254. 185 pages.
     Not seen.

Arthur Foote
1853-1937

*For a catalogue of Foote's chamber music, see Wilma Reid
Cipolla, A Catalogue of the Works of Arthur Foote 1853-1937,
in Bibliographies in American Music, No. 6 (Detroit: College
Music Society, 1980), pages 71-78 and 92-98. ML 134.F6C5.
ISBN 0-89990-000-3.*

John Herbert Foulds
1880-1939

892. MacDonald, Calum. "John Foulds and the String Quar-
     tet," in *Tempo*, no. 132 (March, 1980), 16-25.
     A brief biography and discussion of Fould's 11 string
     quartets. Four of the first 5 are lost; describes the
     the remainder. Regards *Quartetto Intimo*, which
     contains some bizarre moments, as his masterpiece.

César Franck
1822-1890

893. Jardillier, Robert. *La Musique de Chambre de César
     Franck: Étude et Analyse.* Paris: Mellottée, [1929].
     MT 145.F7J2. 228 pages, 159 examples.
     Considers the 4 early trios, the organ works, and the
     mature chamber music (quintet, 2 solo piano pieces, the
     violin + piano sonata, and the string quartet). The
     late works had precursors in the early ones which were
     influenced in turn by Schubert and Weber. Gives a
     brief history of each genre leading to Franck. Shows
     how cyclic unity is achieved in different ways in each
     piece. Franck's main contribution is the regeneration
     of French chamber music and French music in general.
     Saint-Saëns, Fauré and Lalo all wrote chamber music be-
     fore Franck, but only Franck showed that simple chamber

music could express as much as an orchestral piece --
the first to do so since Beethoven and Schumann.

894. DeMuth, Norman. "The Chamber Music," in *César Franck*
     (London: D. Dobson/New York: Philosophical Library,
     1949), pp. 123-142. ML 410.F82D35.
     An analysis in essay form, in chronological order, of
     each of Franck's chamber pieces. Subjective remarks
     interspersed with specific aspects of form, harmony,
     texture, variation, cyclic unity, and historical
     influences and events. A good introduction to the
     chamber music for the student.

See {881} for a discussion of the violin + piano sonata.

895. D'Indy, Vincent. "Le Quatuor en Ré Majeur," in *César
     Franck*, in *Les Maîtres de la Musique* (Paris: Librai-
     rie Félix Alcan, 1919), pp. 163-179. ML 410.F82I6.
     Original 1906. Trl. Rosa Newmarch, "The Quartet in D
     Major," in *César Franck* (London/New York: John Lane,
     1910), pp. 182-197. ML 410.F82I63.
     Analyzes the form, especially of the first and fourth
     movements, of his teacher's quartet. Notes the over-
     lapping of song and sonata forms in the first movement
     and the recurrence of various motives in the third and
     fourth movements. With just a few brief comments cap-
     tures the formal essence of the quartet: a model of re-
     levancy for modern-day theorists. Also provides some
     personal recollections of Franck and his methods of
     composition; gives preliminary sketches of the opening
     of the first movement without detailed commentary. In
     addition emphasizes the need for maturity in writing a
     string quartet, and points to Beethoven's late quartets
     as his really great quartets.

Benjamin Franklin
1706-1790

See Hubert Unverricht in {932}.

Girolamo Frescobaldi
1583-1643

896. Harper, John M. "The Instrumental Canzonas of Girola-
     mo Frescobaldi: a Comparative Edition and Introduc-
     tory Study." PhD dissertation. University of Bir-
     mingham, 1975. 4 vols. I: vi + 333 pages; II-IV:
     645 pages of music.
     Not seen.

897. Mead, Ernest Campbell, Jr. "The Instrumental Ensemble
     Canzonas of Girolamo Frescobaldi." PhD dissertation.

Harvard University, 1983. UMI DA 83-11899. DAI
xliv.3A, pp. 607-8. 2 vols. 709 pages.
Discusses the canzonas in relation to Frescobaldi's
biography and overall oeuvre. Establishes the chronology of the canzonas in 1628 and analyzes their style,
form, rhythm, notation and harmony. Vol. II: transcription of the 1634 edition of the canzonas.

Johann Joseph Fux
1660-1741

898. Rutherford, Charles Leonard. "The Instrumental Music
of Johann Joseph Fux (1660-1741)." EdD dissertation.
Colorado State College, 1967. RILM 68-1891. UMI
68-454. DAI xxviii.10A, pp. 4202-3. 450 pages.
Discusses Fux's *Concentus Musico-Instrumentalis*, which
contains ensemble music for dinner or entertainment at
court or for amateurs gathered for an evening's chamber
music. Transcribes a few movements for woodwind and
brass ensembles.

Florian Leopold Gassmann
1729-1774

*For a catalogue of Gassmann's chamber music, see George R.
Hill, A Thematic Catalog of the Instrumental Music of Florian Leopold Gassmann, in Music Indexes and Bibliographies,
No. 12 (Hackensack [New Jersey]: Joseph Boonin, 1976), pages
46ff. ML 134.G37A2. ISBN 0-913574-12-0.*

899. Leuchter, Erwin. "Die Kammermusikwerke Fl. L. Gass-
manns." PhD dissertation. University of Vienna,
1926. ii + 207 pages.
An important scholarly survey of the 74 chamber pieces
and analysis of their form, melody, rhythm, obligato
accompaniment, orchestration and counterpoint. Considers Gassmann's position in the Viennese School and
in the development of 18th-century chamber music.
Finds his music conservative for the period 1760-1774,
though there are many interesting and beautiful moments; and sees no common thought between Gassmann and
Haydn and no influence of Gassmann on Mozart. A thematic catalogue (duets, trios and quartets of strings
and trios and quartets for other settings).

*See Eve Meyer's "Florian Gassmann and the Viennese Diverti-
mento" {342}.*

900. Meyer, Eve R. "The Oboe Quartets of Florian Leopold
Gassmann," in *The Music Review*, xxxiv (1973), 179-
188.

A brief biography, followed by descriptions of the 9 oboe quartets, each in 3 movements (slow-fast-slow). Considers Gassmann's influence on Salieri and Haydn. A history of the quartets, not an analysis. They do not compare with the masterpieces of the time.

901. Craig, Steven Douglas. "Florian Leopold Gassmann and his Quartets for Oboe and Strings." DMA dissertation. University of Cincinnati, 1984. UMI 85-09466. DAI xlvi.3A, p. 548. vi + 228 pages.
Considers the life and oeuvre of Gassmann, the oboe in the 18th century, the oboe quartet, and Gassmann's specific contributions. Includes illustrations of the 18th-century oboe and its manufacturers. His music "stands midway between the polyphonic style of the late Baroque and the rising prominence of homophony in the early Classical period." Good bibliography.

Pierre Gaviniès
1728-1800

902. Ginter, Robert Leon. "The Sonatas of Pierre Gaviniès." PhD dissertation. Ohio State University, 1976. UMI 76-24600. DAI xxxvii.5A, pp. 2479-80. xi + 374 pages.
A stylistic study of 15 sonatas for violin + continuo and 6 sonatas for 2 violins by "the leading French violinist-composer of the second half of the eighteenth century." The sonatas show no technical advance over Leclair, but they are important historically in the transition from the Baroque to the Classical French sonata. The duets, included in score in an appendix, are typical of popular late-18th-century French music.

Francesco Geminiani
1687-1762

903. McArtor, Marion. "Francesco Geminiani, Composer and Theorist." PhD dissertation. University of Michigan, 1951. UMI 51-107. DA xi.2, pp. 374-5. 387 pages.
A discussion of Op. 1 sonatas and Op. 3 concertos and a comparison of them to Handel's similar works.

Roberto Gerhard
1896-1970

904. Nash, Peter Paul. "The Wind Quintet," in *Tempo*, no. 139 (Dec., 1981), 5-11.
Discusses and analyzes the Wind Quintet (1928) for flute-piccolo + oboe + clarinet + bassoon + horn. Con-

siders its serialism and thematic development, and compares it to Schoenberg's *Wind Quintet* of 1924.

Friedrich Gernsheim
1839-1916

905. Meier, Adolf. "Die Kammermusik Friedrich Gernsheims," in Friedrich Wilhelm Riedel and Hubert Unverricht, eds., *Symbolae Historiae Musicae: Helmut Federhofer zum 60. Geburtstag* (Mainz: B. Schott's Söhne, 1971), pp. 263-271. ML 55.F32.1972.
A cursory analysis of the basic forms of the movements of Gernsheim's 17 chamber pieces (sonatas for violin + piano or cello + piano, piano trios, piano quartets, piano quintets, string quartets and quintets, and a sextet-divertimento for flute + 2 violins + viola + cello + bass). A distinguished German pianist, conductor, teacher (of Humperdinck), and composer, Gernsheim was most influenced by Mendelssohn, Schumann, Brahms, and Bruch.

Orlando Gibbons
1583-1625

906. Dart, Thurston. "The Printed Fantasies of Orlando Gibbons," in *Music and Letters*, xxxvii (1956), 342-349.
A history of Gibbons's 9 published 3-part fantasias (1620-1622). Analyzes scoring: 4 for violin + lyra viol + bass viol + continuo, and the other 5 for 2 violins + bass viol + chamber organ. All were written for the private use of King James I.

Alberto Ginastera
1916-1983

For a catalogue of Ginastera's chamber music, see Anon., Alberto Ginastera: a Catalogue of his Published Works ([London]: Boosey & Hawkes, 1976), pages 18-19. ML 134.G54B6.

Alexander Konstantinovitch Glazunov
1865-1936

907. Raaben, Lev Nikolaevich. "Kamerno-Instrumentalnie Sochinenira," in I.V. Golubovskii, ed., *Glazunov: Issledobanuia, Mameruale, Piablukachii, Pusma, i* (Leningrad: Muziuz, 1959), 245-290. HML 2785.15.49. In Russian
A detailed analysis of Glazunov's chamber music.

908. Cherbuliez, Antoine-Elisée. "Alexander Glasunows Kammermusik," in *Musik des Ostens*, iv (1967), 45-64.

A scholarly essay for the layperson on Glazunov and the history and meaning of his chamber music. Before 1860, Russians were Romantics who found the rigid forms of chamber music too Classical. Glazunov wrote between 1882 and 1930 7 string quartets, 2 suites for string quartet, 1 string quintet, an isolated quartet movement for trumpet + horn + tenor trombone + bass trombone, a saxophone quartet (4 saxophones), and a few other movements. Under the influence of Brahms, Glazunov combines an European style with Russian motivic and rhythmic elements. His chamber music evinces a reserved personality that is appropriate for this kind of music.

909. Abraham, Gerald. "Glazunov and the String Quartet," in *Tempo*, no. 73 (Summer, 1965), 16-21.
On the origins of Glazunov's 7 string quartets and numerous other pieces for string quartet. Also mentions some other composers of Russian string quartets not generally known, such as Aliabev (see {524}).

Christoph Willibald Gluck
1714-1787

For a catalogue of Gluck's sonatas, see Cecil Hopkinson, A Bibliography of the Works of C.W. von Gluck 1714-1787 *(London: the author, 1959), pages 60-61.* ML 134.G56H6.

910. Bergmann, Walter. "Gluck's Trio Sonatas," in *The Musical Times*, ciii (1962), 161.
Reviews an edition of the 8 sonatas, analyzes them, gives historical commentary, and makes valid criticisms of details.

Richard Franko Goldman
1910-1980

911. Lester, Noel K. "Richard Franko Goldman: his Life and Works." DMA dissertation. Peabody Institute of the Johns Hopkins University, 1984. UMI 84-17660. DAI xlv.5A, p. 1236. 360 pages.
Biographical and bibliographical information on Goldman and, in chapter VII, a list of chamber music with dates, publishers, style, and reviews.

Karl Goldmark
1830-1915

912. Altmann, Wilhelm. "Karl Goldmarks Kammermusik," in *Die Musik*, xiv.2 (1914-1915), 209-221, 255-256.

Finds Goldmark an individualist always true to his own
style, and especially strong in his rhythms and harmonies. Non-technical analysis of the 8 chamber pieces
(1865-1893), beginning with a piano trio Op. 4 and end-
ing with a piano quintet.

Berthold Goldschmidt
b.1903

913. Matthews, David. "Berthold Goldschmidt: the Chamber
     and Instrumental Music," in *Tempo*, no. 145 (June,
     1983), 20-25.
     Assesses Goldschmidt's career and analyzes his first
     and second string quartet (1926 and 1936). The second
     is a masterpiece.

François Joseph Gossec
1734-1829

914. Clauser, Charles Theodore. "François Gossec: an Edi-
     tion and Stylistic Study of Three Orchestral Works
     and Three Quartets." PhD dissertation. University
     of Iowa, 1966. UM 66-11649. DA xxvii.5A, pp. 1392-
     3. 2 vols. I: xiv + 235 pages; II: 199 pages of
     music.
     Brief biography of Gossec and analysis and comparison
     of the 6 works. The quartets are nos. 1, 2, and 4 from
     Opus 14 (1769). Bibliography and critical notes.

Percy Aldridge Grainger
1882-1961

915. Slattery, Thomas Carl. "The Wind Music of Percy Al-
     dridge Grainger." PhD dissertation. University of
     Iowa, 1967. UM 67-9104. DAI xxviii.2A, p. 713. 265
     pages.
     List and discussion of Grainger's wind chamber music
     contained in his biography and the bibliography.

Johann Gottlieb Graun
c.1702-1771
and
Karl Heinrich Graun
1704-1759

*For discussion of the role of the Graun brothers in the
transition from trio sonata to cembalo-obligato sonata, see
David Sheldon's article {231}. See also {220}.*

916. Wendt, Matthias. "Die Trios der Brüder Johan Gottlieb
     und Carl Heinrich Graun." Inaugural dissertation.
     University of Bonn, 1983. 340 pages.
     An extensive review of the bibliography on the Grauns,
     an attempt to define the trio as explained by 18th-cen-
     tury theorists (Mattheson, Majer, Walther, Quantz,
     Scheibe, Joh. Adam Hiller, Joseph Martin Kraus, Johann
     Samuel Petri, and Heinrich Christoph Koch), a survey of
     the sources of the Grauns's trios, and a description of
     their form, dates, instrumentation, ornamentation, the
     tonal relationships among movements, and the inner
     structure of the movements. Gives special attention to
     thematic structure and thematic development. Also con-
     siders duets by the Grauns.

                    Edvard Hagerup Grieg
                         1843-1907

*For a catalogue of Grieg's music including chamber pieces,
see Dan Fog, Grieg-Katalog (Copenhagen: Dan Fog Musikforlag,
1980), 143 pages. In Danish and German. ML 134.G84F6.
ISBN 87-87099-21-7.*

917. Frank, Alan. "The Chamber Music," in Gerald Abraham,
     Grieg: a Symposium (London: Lindsay Drummond, 1948;
     Norman: University of Oklahoma Press, 1950), pp. 32-
     44. ML 410.G9A47.
     Discusses Grieg's 5 complete chamber works (3 sonatas
     for violin + piano and 1 for cello + piano, and 1
     string quartet) and his incomplete string quartet.
     Surveys Grieg's strengths and weaknesses as a composer
     of chamber music and analyzes keys, form, melodies and
     general style, with special emphasis on the third
     violin + piano sonata and the quartet. Notes the cy-
     clic nature of the quartet, Grieg's greater success in
     non-sonata-form slow movements, and the importance of
     the descending melodic pattern tonic - leading tone -
     dominant (for example, B-flat - A - F). Speculates on
     the potential masterpiece -- a piano quintet in B-flat
     -- which survives only in a fragment. Compares the
     strengths and weaknesses of the chamber music with
     those of the concerto and shows how some of the unfor-
     tunately heavy, continuous triple stops of the quartet
     are avoided in the incomplete string quartet. Intelli-
     gently written for the informed layperson and student.

918. Kortsen, Bjarne. *Zur Genesis von Edvard Griegs G-moll
     Streichquartett Op. 27.* Haugesund: typewriter repro-
     duction by the author, 1967. ML 410.G9K63. 148
     pages. In German with English and Norwegian summa-
     ries. Kortsen's English essay "Grieg's String Quar-
     tet and Robert Heckmann," in *Music and Letters*, xlix
     (1968), 21-28, covers much of the same material.

A source book of information on the quartet. Studies a collection of 17 letters from Robert Heckmann (1848-1891), famous German violinist and quartet leader, to Grieg and 1 from Grieg to Heckmann, in which Heckmann makes many suggestions for bowings, double stops, and other practical matters, some of which Grieg accepted (the relevant musical passages are given and the exact nature of the suggestions demonstrated). Points out large number of errors in the standard published editions as revealed by a study of the original manuscript. Grieg allowed Heckmann to work out the details, since his quartet was to premier it and it is dedicated to Heckmann. Part of the correspondence touches on Peter's rejection of the score and its first publication by Fritzsch in Leipzig. Notes that Debussy based his quartet on this one by Grieg.

919. Yarrow, Anne. "An Analysis and Comparison of the Three Sonatas for Violin and Piano by Edvard Grieg (1843-1907)." PhD dissertation. New York University, 1985. UMI 85-10783. DAI xlvi.7A, pp. 1777-8. 404 pages.
Uses Jan LaRue's *Guidelines for Style Analysis* (New York: W.W. Norton, 1970) as basis for stylistic analysis of the sound, harmony, melody, rhythm and growth of the 3 works. A theoretic study that aims at helping the performer; includes interpretive suggestions.

Charles T. Griffes
1884-1920

For a catalogue of Griffes's chamber music, see Donna K. Anderson, The Works of Charles T. Griffes: a Descriptive Catalogue, in Studies in Musicology, No. 68 (Ann Arbor: UMI Research Press, 1983), pages 379-410. ML 134.G85A73.1983. ISBN 0-8357-1419-5.

Marie-Alexandre Guénin
1744-1835

920. Robert, Frédéric. "Une Découverte Musicologique: Trois Quatuors Opus VII de Marie-Alexandre Guénin (1744-1835)," in *"Recherches" sur la Musique Française Classique*, I (Paris: A. & J. Picard, 1960), 145-152. ML 270.R43.
Rediscovery of 3 quartets mentioned by Fétis, *Biographie Universelle*, ed. Didot (1861), IV, 132, but lost when La Laurencie discusses Guénin (*L'École Française de Violon de Lully à Viotti* {236}). An analysis with musical illustrations of the second one, in G Minor and in 4 movements. Mozart-like in some passages, Mendelssohn-like in others.

Louis-Gabriel Guillemain
1705-1770

921. La Laurencie, Lionel de. "Un Virtuose Oublié: Louis-
    Gabriel Guillemain (1705-1770)," in *Le Courrier
    Musical*, ix (1906), 489-500.
    A scholarly biography of this French violinist, point-
    ing out his duties at the French court from 1738 on and
    his continual financial woes. Gives a temporary list
    of 16 oeuvres containing among other types many sonatas
    a1, a2, and a4 with bass, as well as duets without
    bass. Analyzes the music and demonstrates Guillemain's
    considerable violinistic technique.

922. Snyder, Robert Charles. "The Twelve Quartets of Opus
    XII and XVII by Louis-Gabriel Guillemain in Histori-
    cal and Stylistic Analysis." DMA dissertation. Uni-
    versity of Missouri at Kansas City, 1973. RILM 68-
    3680. UM 73-25947. DA xxxiv.5A, p. 2688. 2 vols.
    519 pages.
    A biography followed by analyses of texture, keys,
    form, melodic contour, and harmony in the 12 quartets.
    Homophonic style and rapid interchange of leading parts
    and accompaniment characterize these Rococo products of
    Louis XV's court, where they served as light background
    music.

Iain Hamilton
b.1922

923. Thompson, Randall Scott. "The Solo Clarinet Works of
    Iain Hamilton." DMA dissertation. University of
    Maryland, 1976. UMI 76-29017. DAI xxxvii.6A, p.
    3262. 141 pages.
    An analysis, assessment of the treatment of the clari-
    net, and historical discussion of 4 early works: Quin-
    tetto, Three Nocturnes, Concerto, and Sonata.

George Fredrich Handel (= Georg Friedrich Händel)
1685-1759

*For a catalogue of Handel's chamber music, see Bernd Baselt,
Thematisch-systematisches Verzeichnis: Instrumentalmusik,
Pasticci und Fragmente, in Händel-Handbuch, Band 3, supplement to Hallische Händel-Ausgabe (Kassel: Bärenreiter,
1986), pages 130-209. ML 134.H16A19.Bd.3. ISBN 3-7618-
0716-3. For a bibliography of studies of Handel's sonatas,
see Konrad Sasse, Händel Bibliographie (Leipzig: VEB Deutscher Verlag für Musik, 1961), pages 212-214, and discography pages 252-253. ML 134.H16S27.*

924. Best, Terence. "Handel's Solo Sonatas," in *Music and Letters*, lviii (1977), 430-438.
Authenticates the solo sonatas of Handel and their scoring. Handel's autographs are precise in their scoring indications even if the prints are ambiguous: 15 sonatas are authentic, 14 survive in autograph; of these 5 are for violin + continuo, 6 are for recorder + continuo, 2 for flute + continuo, and 2 for oboe + continuo. Best is the editor of volume 3 of solo sonatas in *Hallische-Händel-Ausgabe* (Series iv, vol. 18).

See also Bern Baselt, "Zu einigen Fragen der Authentizität in G.F. Händels Kammermusik für ein Soloinstrument und Basso Continuo," in {161}, pages 47-49.

925. _____. "Further Studies on Handel's Solo Sonatas," in *Händel-Jahrbuch*, xxx (1984), 75-79.
A highly technical study of the watermarks on the manuscript copies of the 12 English solo + continuo sonatas in order to date the sonatas more accurately (*Händel Werkverzeichnis* [HWV] 378: c.1707; 363a-b: 1712-1716; 366: 1712; 364: 1724; 359a: 1724; 377: 1724-5; 367a: 1724-6; additions to 367a: 1725-6; 360, 362, 365, 369: 1725-6; 361:1725-6; 379:1727-8; 371: c.1750).

926. Horton, John. "The Chamber Music," in Gerald Abraham, ed., *Handel: a Symposium* (London: Oxford University Press, 1954), pp. 248-261. ML 410.H13A66.
Useful information on the music for the informed layperson despite errors in dates and authentication (corrected in {924} and {925}). Analyzes specific collections, Handel's debt to Corelli in sonate da chiesa and da camera, and technical achievements in the composition of specific movements. The principal value in this chapter is in pointing to Handel's reuse of previous motives, melodies and whole movements.

927. Pook, Wilford. "Notes on the Violin Sonatas of G.F. Handel," in *The Strad*, lxv (1954), 186, 188, 190, 192, 194, 196.
A bibliographic discussion of early and recent editions of these sonatas. Describes bowing, dynamics, trills, cadences, improvisation, and realization of the figured bass -- from the publisher's standpoint but obviously of concern to the performer, too.

928. Gould, Albert Oren. "The Flute Sonatas of Georg Friedrich Handel: a Stylistic Analysis and Historical Survey." EdD dissertation. University of Illinois, 1961. UM 62-607. DA xxii.12, p. 3690. 206 pages.
Attempts to recreate the image of the sonatas in their 18th-century setting, and compares Handel's flute and violin sonatas and other flute sonatas of the time. Traces the evolution of the transverse flute.

929. Meyer, Eve R. "Has Handel Written Works for Two Flutes
     without a Bass?" in *Music and Letters*, xvi (1935),
     293-295.
     A collection of 6 duos for 2 flutes attributed to Han-
     del is by G.Ch. Schultze (1729), and other duos for 2
     flutes are arrangements (by others?) of opera and ora-
     torio excerpts. Handel never wrote for 2 flutes alone.

Roy Harris
1898-1979

930. Mendel, Arthur. "The Quintet of Roy Harris," in *Modern
     Music*, xvii (1939), 25-28.
     A favorable critique and brief analysis of the quintet
     for piano and strings. All themes are typically Har-
     ris, yet each is 12-tone. Harris also achieves more
     variety of texture and color than in earlier chamber
     music pieces. The quintet makes a good initial impres-
     sion on the general chamber music audience, which can
     love it before it understands it.

Joseph Haydn
1732-1809

*For a catalogue of Haydn's chamber music, see Anthony van
Hoboken, Joseph Haydn: thematisch-bibliographisches Werkverzeichnis, I: instrumental works (Mainz: B. Schott's Söhne,
1957), xxi + 848 pages, and III: register, addenda and corrections (1978), 424 pages. ML 134.H272H6 (vol. 3: ISBN 3-
7957-0003-5). For Haydn's own catalogues of his chamber
music, see Jens Peter Larsen, Three Haydn Catalogues: Drei
Haydn Kataloge: Second Facsimile Edition with a Survey of
Haydn's Oeuvre (New York: Pendragon Press, 1979), xlvi + 119
pages. ML 134.H272A1.1979. ISBN 0-918728-10-X. For a non-
technical introduction to Haydn's chamber music, see Rosemary Hughes's essay in Alec Robertson, ed., Chamber Music
{160}.*

931. Landon, H.C. Robbins. *Haydn: Chronicle and Works.*
     Bloomington/London: Indiana University Press, 1976-
     1980. ML 410.H4L26. ISBN: 0-253-37001-9/37002-
     7/37003-5/37004-3/37005-1. 5 vols. I: 655 pages;
     II: 799 pages; III: 639 pages; IV: 656 pages; V: 495
     pages.
     A basic reference for historical information on all
     Haydn music. Part I of each volume is a year-by-year,
     month-by-month, even day-by-day chronicle of Haydn's
     life, with references to chamber music in the index of
     cited works at the end of each volume. Part II of each
     volume considers specific genres of works, with exten-
     sive descriptions of sources and historical background
     and some analysis. Chamber music has at least one

large chapter in each volume (vol. I, 1732-1765, is subdivided differently and has at least 3 large sections on chamber music within 3 different chapters).

932. Larsen, Jens Peter, Howard Serwer and James Webster, ed. *Haydn Studies: Proceedings of the International Haydn Conference Washington, D.C., 1975.* New York/ London: W.W. Norton, 1981. ML 36.I59593.1975. ISBN 0-393-01454-1. xvii + 590 pages.
A collection of papers and discussions on various aspects of Haydn research, among which are the following on chamber music: "Round Table: Problems of Authenticity -- 'Opus 3'" (pages 95-106) [an agreement that Op. 3 is not by Haydn and is probably by Hoffstetter]; Hubert Unverricht, "Haydn and Franklin: the Quartet with Open Strings and Scordatura" (pages 147-154) [shows that these 2 works are neither by Haydn nor Franklin but by some unknown, possibly South German composer c.1790]; "Workshop 3: String Quartets (pages 227-233) [no. 2 on problems in the sources that affect performance]; Unverricht, "The Instrumentation of the Lowest Part in the *Divertimento à Quattro* (pages 233-235) [considers the second inversion chord that results from only a cello scoring and finds it acceptable]; Webster, "The Scoring of Haydn's Early String Quartets" (pages 235-238) [reviews his other essays: a bass is unlikely through Op. 1 and Op. 2 because of range problems for the instrument, although it could double the cello; a cello is probable for Op. 9 and 17; a cello alone most likely from Op. 20 on]; "Workshop 6: Piano Trios" (pages 267-274) [on the instruments used, the musical expression or rhetoric, performance markings in the autographs, and articulation]; Isidor Saslav, "The *alla breve* 'March': its Evolution and Meaning in Haydn's String Quartets" (pages 308-314) [considers how certain rhythmic patterns from Op. 50 on were notated differently prior to then-- Mozart's influence -- and how this is affected by tempo]; Webster, "Did Haydn 'Synthesize' the Classical String Quartet?" (pages 336-339) [warns against an evolutionary approach to "Classical" -- a stylistic consideration -- as proposed by Sandberger when he refers to a late synthesis of earlier styles]; "Round Table: Webster, 'Remarks on Early Chamber Music'" (pages 365-367) [shows how similar Haydn's melodies are to his contemporary Austrian and Bohemian colleagues]; Somfai, "Haydn's London String Quartets" (pages 389-392) [the London quartets Op. 71 - Op. 74 were not in his old *chamber* style but meant for public audience in concert halls]; various articles on Mozart and Haydn influencing each other in their chamber works (pages 405-414); Orin Moe,Jr., "The Significance of Haydn's Op. 33" (pages 445-450) [finds Op. 50 is the first to present all classical style elements, not Op. 33, but while not denying the importance of Op.

33, notes the important return in Op. 50 of equal voice treatment experimented with in Op. 20]; Lester S. Steinberg, "A Numerical Approach to Activity and Movement in the Sonata-Form Movements of Haydn's Piano Trios" (pages 515-522); and Webster, "Freedom of Form in Haydn's Early String Quartets."

933. Fruehwald, Scott. "Authenticity Problems in Franz Joseph Haydn's Early Instrumental Works: a Stylistic Investigation." PhD dissertation. City University of New York, 1984. UMI 84-23057. DAI xlv.7A, p. 1908. 297 pages.
Uses 2 tests to determine authenticity of a Haydn work: quantitative (harmonic and textural rhythm, and the number of impacts per beat) and checklists (traits that usually or rarely appear in Haydn's authentic works). The criteria were conditioned by analyzing known Haydn works and those definitely not by Haydn. Works included 1) accompanied keyboard divertimenti (authentic: *Haydn-Gesamtausgabe* XIV.12, 13, C1, C2, XVIII.F2; spurious: Concertino in D); 2) keyboard trios (authentic: XV.1, 34-38, 40, 41, C1, F1); 3) string trios (authentic: V.C1, C4, D1, D3, F1, G1, G3, G4, A2, A3, B1; spurious: V.C2, C3, C5, C6, C7, C8, D4, D, Eb2-5, Eb11, E2, F7, F9, G5, A8, B4, B7), Op. 3 string quartets (spurious); divertimentos, and other categories.

934. Landon, H.C. Robbins. "Doubtful and Spurious Quartets and Quintets Attributed to Haydn," in *The Music Review*, xviii (1957), 213-221.
An exhaustive listing and discussion of sources of "Haydn's" string quartets Opera XI, XVIII, XXI, and XXVIII, string quintets Opus XXII, and flute quartets Opus XXV, all of which are by other composers. In addition, 32 single string quartets and 10 single string quintets are listed and discussed and attributed to other authors -- many of these omitted from Larsen's catalogue (sections ix and iii).

935. Rosen, Charles. *The Classical Style: Haydn, Mozart, Beethoven.* New York: The Viking Press, 1971. 2nd, rev. ed. New York: W.W. Norton/Toronto: George J. McLeod, 1972. ML 195.R68.1972. ISBN 0-393-00653-0. 467 pages.
Although the entire book is important, 3 chapters are especially relevant: on Haydn's string quartets (pp. 111-142), Mozart's string quintets (pp. 264-287), and Haydn's piano trios (pp. 351-365). On the quartets, points out the different approaches to "wrong keys" and "false" tonal openings in C.P.E. Bach's and Haydn's sonatas, and then extends this to the Op. 33 quartets where the logic is more rigorous and the dramatic force far more compelling. The voices are not equal and independent (a Baroque characteristic) but melody and

accompaniment with one transforming into the other.
Haydn's climaxes are just after the start of the recapitulation, not before. The small detail systematically functions in the whole, whereas in earlier works
(before Op. 33) some details never recur or have no
bearing on the movement as a whole. Draws parallel
between the scherzi designation for the minuet movements and the comic operas that preoccupied Haydn
especially from 1776 on, and traces the new rapid pace
of the quartets to the rapid pace of comic opera. The
"sense that the movement, the development, and the
dramatic course of a work all can be found latent in
the material...[and that the music] is literally im-
pelled from within -- this sense was Haydn's greatest
contribution to the history of music." Analyzes later
Haydn quartets, especially Op. 50, nos. 1 and 6, and
Op. 55, no. 3, with special emphasis on the new Haydn
energy. The ideal string quartet lasts only from Haydn
to Schubert, yet most people equate chamber music with
string quartet. This is because the classical string
quartet "is the natural consequence of a musical language in which expression is entirely based on dissonance to a triad." On the trios it notes the feeling
of improvisation in the solo keyboard and the need for
recognition by modern performers of the proper balance
of the 3 instruments in 18th-century terms. Contains a
good overview of the piano trios. The Mozart quintets
are treated chronologically, emphasizing Mozart's debt
to Haydn (for example in K.174 to Haydn's Op. 20).
Notes that the first movement of K.515 is the largest
sonata-form movement before Beethoven and is revolutionary also for its expansion, its pacing, and its
phrasing. Such expansion was needed to give more room
to the greater density of 5 rather than 4 instruments.
"The essence of Mozart's 'classicism' is the equilibri-
um between the intensity of the expression and the tonal stability which fixes the dimensions of each work."

General Studies of the String Quartets:

*For lessons to be learned from a study of the autographs of
Haydn string quartets, see the essays by László Somfai,
James Webster, and Georg Feder in Christoph Wolff, ed., The
String Quartets of Haydn, Mozart, and Beethoven {617}.*

*Since the origins and early development of the Haydn
quartets are synonymous with the origins and early history
of the genre itself, many studies of the early string
quartet (in Chapter 2) could just as suitably be included
here. The most important such study is Ludwig Finscher's
Studien zur Geschichte des Streichquartetts {173}, which
exhaustively documents Haydn's quartets and their style and
structure up through Op. 33 (1781). See also Adolf Sandberger, "Zur Geschichte des Haydnschen Streichquartetts" {176}.*

936. Webster, James. "The Chronology of Haydn's String
     Quartets," in *The Musical Quarterly*, lxi (1975), 17-
     46.
     A definitive study, based on 50 years of research by
     leading Haydn scholars, on the authenticity and chrono-
     logy of Haydn's 68 string quartets. The first 10 quar-
     tets pose the greatest problems but probably date from
     the late 1750's; all others are precisely dated or
     nearly so. Based on the chronology, the quartets fall
     into 2 groups: those through Op. 33 (1781), composed
     sporadically, and those from Op. 42 to Op. 103 (1785-
     1803), composed on a regular basis.

937. _____. "Haydn's String Quartets," in *Haydn-
     fest: Music Festival: September 22-October 11, 1975:
     International Musicological Concerence: October 4-11,
     1975* (Washington, D.C.: Kennedy Center Program,
     1975), pp. 12-17. ML 410.H4H4.1975.
     A brief, accurate description of the Haydn quartets,
     their style, historical development, and significance.

938. Barrett-Ayres, Reginald. *Joseph Haydn and the String
     Quartet*. New York: Schirmer Books, 1974. ML 410.
     H4B2445.1974. 417 pages, 208 musical examples.
     Chronological, historical discussion of the quartets
     with chapter-length diversions comparing them with
     those by Mozart and Beethoven. Technical discussion of
     style but attempts to explain technical terms for the
     layperson. Valuable as a basic reference to the quar-
     tets, with useful indices.

939. Somfai, László. "Die Entstehung des klassischen Quar-
     tettklanges in den Streichquartetten von Haydn" ("A
     Klasszikus Kvartetthangzas Megszületése Haydn Vonós-
     négyeseiben"), in Bence Szabolcsi and Dénes Bartha,
     eds., *Haydn Emlékére Zenetudományi Tanulmányok VIII*
     (Budapest: Akadémai Kiadó, 1960), pages 295-420. ML
     410-H4S98. In Hungarian, with a German summary pages
     417-420.
     Characterizes the string quartet genre and all chamber
     music in Classical Vienna through an analysis of the
     Haydn quartets. Notes the steady development of idio-
     matic string quartet writing distinct from orchestral
     and divertimento types and the growth of Haydn's own
     idioms. A very scholarly, extremely important study
     which is available unfortunately only to those who read
     Hungarian. An early attempt to disprove Haydn's au-
     thorship of Op. 3; see {956}.

940. Hughes, Rosemary. *Haydn String Quartets*, in *BBC Music
     Guides*, no. 6. Seattle: University of Washington
     Press, 1969. MT 145.H2H8.1969. Originally London:
     BBC, 1966. 56 pages, 17 musical examples.

A non-technical, very elementary introduction to the quartets.

941. Svensson, Sven Erik Emanuel. *Joseph Haydns Strakkvartetter*. Stockholm: H. Geber, 1948. MT 145.H2S8. 250 pages. In Swedish.
Discusses each of Haydn's authentic quartets from Op. 20 on and summarizes the early quartets including Op. 3 and others no longer attributed to Haydn. Simple programs for the layperson.

942. Keller, Hans. *The Great Haydn Quartets: their Interpretation*. London: J.M. Dent/New York: George Braziller, 1986. ML 410.H4K29.1986. ISBN 0-8076-1167-0. vii + 253 pages.
Highly personal yet fascinating discussion of nearly all the quartets from Op. 20 on (and Op. 9 No. 4). Considers whatever is deemed important for performers and others in each case: rhythm, form, tonality, range, texture, technique, and so on.

943. Demaree, Robert W., Jr. *Involvement with Music: Introduction to the Haydn Quartets*. New York: Harper's College Press, 1976. MT 145.H2D4. ISBN 0-06-161010-1. 42 pages.
A text for students who read music. A history and analysis of the structure and style of the quartets in general, and explanations of basic forms and other concepts. Then concentrates on Op.33 No. 2, Op. 64 No. 5, and Op. 76 No. 5: analyzes primarily form in each movement but also melody, rhythm and tonality. Appendix A lists Haydn's quartets (erroneously includes all of Op. 2) with dates; appendix B gives modern printed editions and discography.

944. Blume, Friedrich. "Joseph Haydns künstlerische Persönlichkeit in seinen Streichquartetten," in *Jahrbuch der Musikbibliothek Peters für 1931*, xxxvii (1932), 24-48. Reprint in Blume, *Syntagma Musicologium*, i (Kassel: Bärenreiter, 1963), 526-551 and 899-900. Reprint of the *Jahrbuch* Vaduz: Kraus Reprint Ltd., 1965.
The artist's personality is revealed in his reworking of a single genre of music without destroying the central idea of that genre. String quartets are a single genre, and although he continually reshapes the details, Haydn does not alter his basic idea of the quartet. This idea is not irrational but something that can be defined and understood. Not concerned with the origins of the Haydn quartet but, rather, concentrates first on the dating, ordering, form, and style of the early quartets (here encompassing all of Op. 1 and 2). Op. 3 is called experimental since it has nothing to do with Op. 1 and 2. With Op. 9 Haydn

begins to aim toward the central idea with technical
achievements (4 movements, sonata form, deepening the
thoughts through repetition, variation and modulation
of themes as part of sonata form development, and defining the purposes of the non-sonata-form movements).
Op. 17 bear the first real evidence of Haydn's personality through the first real achievement of the *idea*; 3
changes over Op. 9: deeper inner relationship among
movements, closer integration of the 4 instruments --
except in slow movements -- and more organized thematic
work within movements. Op. 20 was too radical and led
nowhere (picked up possibly by late Beethoven).
Rather, Haydn needed 10 years to redirect his means to
the *idea*. He achieved unity in Op. 20 but lost the expressive polarity of contrast. In Op. 33 there is thematic relationship, but this is set against greater
contrasts; this is classical maturity. Op. 17 = Die
Räuber; Op. 20 = Don Carlos; Op. 33 = Wallenstein.
Blume has much less to say about the later quartets.
Now the personality of Haydn that emerges is not the
"Papa" image as presented to children; rather, Haydn
was a strong-willed, dramatic man with a hot heart and
a cool head. The evolution of the quartet idea shows
these characteristics.

945. Silbert, Doris. "Ambiguity in the String Quartets of
     Joseph Haydn," in *The Musical Quarterly*, xxxvi
     (1950), 562-573.
     Draws attention to William Empson's *Seven Types of Am-
     biguity*, 2nd ed. (New York: 1947), and thereupon care-
     fully defines "ambiguity" in musical terms (harmonic,
     rhythmic and melodic) and then applies it to various
     Haydn quartets. Ambiguity "results from the impact of
     some kind of counter movement upon the cumulative
     movement."

946. Kroher, Ekkehart. "Die Polyphonie in den Streichquar-
     tetten Wolfgang Amadeus Mozarts und Joseph Haydns,"
     in *Wissenschaftliche Zeitschrift der Karl-Marx-
     Universität Leipzig*, v (1955-1956), 369-402.
     Assesses the polyphonic training of Haydn and Mozart
     and the influence of polyphonists on them. Studies the
     fugue finales of their quartets (specifically Haydn's
     Op. 20 no. 2 and Op. 50 no. 4 and Mozart's K.173 and
     K.387) and their use in the string quartets of canon;
     fugato; simple, double, and related counterpoint; con-
     trary motion; inversion; pedal point; and strict and
     free imitation. Haydn's Op. 20 influenced Mozart's K.
     168 and K.173 quartets in their use of fugues for fi-
     nales, but there is no such connection between Op. 54
     no. 4 and K. 387. Considers the use of fugues by other
     contemporaries even if it was regarded as outmoded.

947. Wiesel, Siegfried. "Klangfarbendramaturgie in den
Streichquartetten von Joseph Haydn," in *Haydn-Studien*, v (1982), 16-22.
Finds symmetric patterns for Haydn's choice of melodic
instrument among the 4 of the string quartet.

See also Saslav's and Webster's contributions in {932}.

948. Demaree, Robert William, Jr. "The Structural Proportions of the Haydn Quartets." PhD dissertation.
Indiana University, 1973. UM 74-9419. DA xxxiv.10A,
pp. 6682-3. 264 pages.
Finds 22 basic compositional procedures in the quartets, "six structural effects of these operations and
several types of apparent meaning believed to be communicated to the listener as the results of architectural
modifications." Then compares the movements based on
this system and also on tonal and rhythmic organization. Identifies "certain proportional patterns ...
common in the Haydn quartets" and re-evaluates the
terms "symmetry" and "regularity" in light of this research. A thought-provoking, systematic analysis of
the quartets from an unusual angle.

949. Reed, Carl Hadley. "Motivic Unity in Selected Keyboard
Sonatas and String Quartets of Joseph Haydn." PhD
dissertation. University of Washington, 1966. UM
66-7893. DA xxvii.2A, p. 501. 178 pages, 56
examples.
Diagrams and studies motivic unity in 17 movements from
the keyboard sonatas and 28 movements from the string
quartets. Reviews secondary discussion of the subject
from 1813 to 1965. Proposes the term "unimotivic" to
replace the term "monothematic."

950. Hinderberger, Adolf. *Die Motivik in Haydns Streichquartetten*. Turbenthal: Robert Furrers Erben, 1935.
ML 410.H4H5. vii + 88 pages, 169 musical examples.
Inaugural dissertation. University of Bern, 1933.
A study of the construction of the principle themes in
Haydn's string quartets. Scholarly but mostly analytical. Analyzes the themes by themselves; divides them
into those composed of the repetition of the same motive (exactly or altered), those composed of 2 different motives, and those composed of 3 motives. The argument is not weakened by inclusion of Op. 3 and other
quartets no longer recognized as Haydn's. Realizes
that despite the dissection, the themes are unities
that cannot always be cleanly divided. Although Haydn
gives the appearance of folk-like simplicity, in many
cases the structure is complicated.

951. Germann, Jörg. *Die Entwicklung der Exposition in
     Joseph Haydn's Streichquartetten.* Bern: Kunz-Druck,
     1964. MT 145.H2G5. viii + 207 pages, 91 examples.
     Inaugural Dissertation. University of Bern, 1962.
     Technical, scholarly study of the expositions, with
     whole chapters on each part of the exposition (princi-
     pal theme, bridge, contrasting theme, and closing
     theme).

952. Pankaskie, Lewis V. "Tonal Organization in the Sonata
     Movements of Haydn's String Quartets." PhD disserta-
     tion. University of Michigan, 1956. UM 21344. DA
     xvii.6, p. 1352. 338 pages (DA = 341 pages).
     Analyzes the sonata-form movements of the string quar-
     tets without considering Haydn's antecedents.

953. Cuyler, Louise E. "Tonal Exploitation in the Later
     Quartets of Haydn," in H.C. Robbins Landon, ed.,
     *Studies in Eighteenth-Century Music: a Tribute to
     Karl Geiringer on his Seventieth Birthday* (London:
     Georg Allen and Unwin, 1970), pp. 136-150. ML
     55.G24S8. ISBN 0-04-780016x.
     Explains the keys of the movements of a quartet; most
     have 1 movement in the dominant, subdominant, or
     relative major, but 9 of Haydn's do not. These 9 can
     be explained by Haydn's advanced conceptions of modal-
     ity. Haydn "explored ... [tonal] resources that were
     not fully realized until a century after his death."

954. Sondheimer, Robert. *Haydn: a Historical and Psycholo-
     gical Study Based on his Quartets.* London: Edition
     Bernoulli, 1951. ML 410.H4S7. viii + 196 pages, 118
     examples.
     A nasty, emotional study basically disregarded by to-
     day's Haydn experts but the center of much Haydn dis-
     cussion at the time it appeared. Picks out Franz Beck
     who, it is proposed, reached the developmental level of
     Beethoven c.1760, far in advance of Haydn (a contention
     that cannot be verified). Refers to "musical dialec-
     tic," an ability to produce well-written material with-
     out originality of thought, a characteristic of Haydn
     before Op. 20. Sondheimer comes up with specific
     theories about Haydn's quartets which he then imposes
     on a study of them, and he has some rather unsubstan-
     tiated theories on the importance of Franz Beck to
     music in general and Haydn in particular. Since the
     book is dated and highly personal, it is to be avoided
     by laypersons and students until they have a good un-
     derstanding of the history and significance of Haydn's
     quartets from more reliable sources, including the
     scores themselves and especially the Haydn-Gesamtaus-
     gabe. At an advanced level Sondheimer does challenge
     some accepted theories and suggests areas of comparison

(Haydn with Boccherini, with Mannheimers, with Mozart) that need further elucidation.

For a discussion of whether the cello or string bass is to be used for the "basso" line in Haydn's string quartets and other chamber music, see James Webster, "Violoncello and Double Bass in the Chamber Music of Haydn and his Viennese Contemporaries, 1750-1780" {178} and "The Bass Part in Haydn's Early String Quartets" {179}.

Specific Quartets in Chronological Order:

The most important development in Haydn string quartet studies in the mid-1960's was the elimination of unauthentic quartets from what until then was known as the authentic "83".

955. Landon, H.C. Robbins. "On Haydn's Quartets of Opera 1 and 2: Notes and Comments on Sondheimer's *Historical and Psychological Study*," in *The Music Review*, xiii (1952), 181-186.
   An important scholarly study authenticating the 10 early quartets and eliminating Op. 1 No. 5; Op. 2 Nos. 3 and 5; and all of Op. 3. *See also {184, 932, 954, 956-958, and 1010}.*

956. Somfai, László. "Zur Echtheitsfrage des Haydn'schen 'Opus 3,'" in *The Haydn Yearbook: das Haydn Jahrbuch*, iii (1965), 153-165.
   One of several convincing essays disproving Haydn's authorship of the 6 string quartets Op. 3, and also the 3 spurious quartets of Op. 1 in B-flat and Op. 2 in E-flat and D. Points out the shallow grounds on which the earliest sources of Op. 3 stand vis-a-vis Haydn and then points to stylistic features of Op. 3 that are inconsistent with the other, authentic Haydn quartets.

957. Feder, Georg. "Apokryphe 'Haydn' - Streichquartette," in *Haydn-Studien*, iii (1974), 125-150.
   Originally intended for inclusion in the critical notes to *Haydn-Gesamtausgabe*, xii.1, this study first examines all the sources for Op. 3 and explains why Pleyel included them and others not by Haydn in his edition of Haydn: he relied on previous publications and not on direct contact with Haydn. Then lists with many incipits and discusses almost 100 other spurious Haydn quartets.

958. Brantley, Daniel Lawrence. "Disputed Authorship of Musical Works: a Quantitative Approach to the Attribution of the Quartets Published as Haydn's Opus 3." PhD dissertation. University of Iowa, 1977. UMI 77-21118. DAI xxxviii.4A, p. 1723. v + 92 pages.

"A report on the techniques of the author's research in authorship discrimination, using the [Haydn] Op. 3 question as a point of departure." Studies the basic works on the subject (Tyson, Landon, Somfai, Unverricht, Finscher, Barrett-Ayres, and others), compares similar problems in literature, brings in computer programs, and ends up with statistics that prove Opus 3 is by Hoffstetter. *See {1010}*.

959. Moe, Orin, Jr. "Texture in Haydn's Early Quartets," in *The Music Review*, xxxv (1974), 4-22. An excerpt from "Texture in the String Quartets of Haydn to 1787," PhD dissertation, University of California at Santa Barbara, 1970, RILM 70-507, UM 71-11482, DA xxxi.11A, p. 6100. 385 pages.
Notes 3 basic tendencies in the apparent simplicity of the first 10 quartets which will lead to important stylistic traits of the later quartets: rapid alternation of different textures in the fast movements, interruption of regular motion (mostly "changes between upbeat and downbeat rhythmic grouping"), and the gradual equalization of the 4 instruments.

960. Fry, J. "Haydn's String Quartets, Op. 20," in *The Musical Times*, lxxxv (1944), 140-142.
Designed as an introduction to these quartets for the amateur performer. Brief descriptions and comparisons with some of his other quartets.

961. Tepping, Susan. "Form in the Finale of Haydn's String Quartet, Op. 64, No. 5," in *Indiana Theory Review*, iv, no. 2 (1981), 51-68.
A Schenkerian analysis of the last movement of the "Lark" Quartet, which is a ternary ABA movement at the surface level but binary at the background level. Justified since the surface level is the time form and the background level the harmonic or tonal form.

962. Somfai, László. "A Bold Enharmonic Modulatory Model in Joseph Haydn's String Quartets," in H.C. Robbins Landon, ed. *Studies in Eighteenth-Century Music: a Tribute to Karl Geiringer on his Seventieth Birthday* (London: George Allen and Unwin, 1970), pp. 370-381. ML 55.G24S8. ISBN 0-04-780016x.
Haydn uses enharmonic spellings to make music easier to play but it makes analysis less clear. Shows in a few movements of late quartets (Op. 71 - Op. 103) that Haydn anticipates Romanticism in his modulations. "Haydn's innovation" is the stepwise transition to the enharmonic spelling, for example G-flat Major to F Major but not G-flat Major to F# Major.

963. Trimmer, Maud Alice. "Texture and Sonata Form in the Late String Chamber Music of Haydn and Mozart." PhD

dissertation. City University of New York, 1981.
UMI 82-03335. DAI xlii.9A, p. 3805. 594 pages.
A technical analysis of textural activity in the first
movements (primarily expositions) of 27 string quartets
and quintets by Haydn and Mozart. Notes the homogenei-
ty of themes in the expositions and the contrast of 2
keys. Uses a system of score annotation which involves
graphs and explains how the system evolved.

964. Randall, J.K. "Haydn: String Quartet in D Major, Op.
76, No. 5," in *The Music Review*, xxi (1960), 94-105.
A Schenkerian analysis of the quartet.

965. Löher, Burckhard. *Strukturwissenschaftliche Darstellung der ersten und letzten Sätze der sechs Streichquartette Op. 76 von Joseph Haydn*, in *Veröffentlichungen zur theoretischen Musikwissenschaft*, Bd. 5.
Münster: reproduced typescript by University of
Münster, distributed by Bärenreiter-Antiquariat,
1983. MT 145.H2L63.1983. 177 pages.
Following structural methods of Werner Korte and Ursula
Götze, analysis of the 12 individual opening and clos-
ing movements of these 6 quartets. A highly theoretical interpretation which strives for a *workmodel* for
Op. 76. Each movement is diagrammed according to the
function of the morphemes (smallest substantial relationship factors or constructive elements). The dependence on statistics and mathematically produced generalities becomes the basic weakness of the system: the
generalities are actually found in none or few movements, so that they tell us little or nothing about the
individual quartet movement of Op. 76.

966. Drury, Jonathan Daniel. "Haydn's *Seven Last Words*: an
Historical and Critical Study." PhD dissertation.
University of Illinois, 1976. UM 76-16125. DAI
xxxvii.1A, p. 23. 376 pages.
In the course of discussing the various versions of
this work, considers the string quartet version and
compares it to the orchestral and vocal (?) versions.

Haydn's Other Chamber Music:

967. Brown, Alfred Peter. "The Solo and Ensemble Keyboard
Sonatas of Joseph Haydn: a Study of Structure and
Style." PhD dissertation. Northwestern University,
1970. UMI 71-1805. DAI xxxi.8A, p. 4195. 3 vols.
442 pages.
Considers the sonatas first historically and biblio-
graphically, then as a series of movements with specific forms (3-part sonata form, binary, theme and variations, "additive part" [rondo, ternary and freer], and

minuet-trio). Also discusses the choice of a particular instrument for a given work.

968. Bell, A. Craig. "An Introduction to Haydn's Piano
    Trios," in *The Music Review*, xvi (1955), 191-197.
    Traces the neglect of Haydn's trios during the 19th and
    first half of the 20th centuries and explains the ori-
    gins of the trios, which are basically obligato piano
    sonatas with cello and violin accompaniment. While
    many of the questions raised are correct, not all the
    answers are so. Lists 31 trios in Larsen's chrono-
    logical order and with both Larsen's and Peter's
    numbers. *See also {970} and Steinberg in {932}.*

969. Feder, Georg. "Haydn's Piano Trios and Piano Sonatas,"
    trl. by Howard Serwer, in *Haydnfest: Music Festival:
    September 22-October 11, 1975: International Musico-
    logical Conference: October 4-11, 1975* (Washington,
    D.C.: Kennedy Center Program, 1975), pp. 18-23. ML
    410.H4H4.1975.
    A brief, accurate description of the piano trios (early
    ones with harpsichord) -- some for flute or optional
    flute. Describes sources briefly, dedicatees, scoring,
    and forms. A general introduction for the layperson.

970. _____. "Haydns frühe Klaviertrios: eine Unter-
    suchung zur Echtheit und Chronologie," in *Haydn-
    Studien*, ii (1970), 289-316.
    Reviews Haydn's early piano trios as published for the
    first time in 200 years in the *Haydn-Gesamtausgabe*.
    Previously little was known or authenticated -- only
    the 29 piano trios from 1784 on and 2 early ones.
    Simultaneously to the new edition Landon published
    45 piano trios {971}; considers here the 15 which date
    before 1784 (Hob. xv.1-2, 33-41 + 3 others). Checks
    authenticity, then chronology. With great care, docu-
    mentation and stylistic analyses, proves most authen-
    tic, but questions especially the 3 proposed by Landon.
    With the establishment of a specific Haydn contribution
    to the early piano trio c.1760, Haydn must now be
    brought into the history of the early piano trio along
    with Schobert, Anton Filtz, F.X. Richter and others.

971. Landon, H.C. Robbins. *Die Klaviertrios von Joseph
    Haydn: Vorwort zur ersten kritischen Gesamtausgabe*.
    Munich/Vienna: Doblinger, 1970. HML 3091.68.7. 28
    pages. Forward in German and English. Includes a
    chronological, thematic list of 45 Haydn piano trios.
    The trios fall into 3 groups: the early ones c.1755-
    c.1760, the middle ones 1780's-1790's, and the late
    ones probably written in England. Discusses
    sources, instrumentation, titles, arpeggios, and so on.

972. Steinberg, Lester. "Sonata Form in the Keyboard Trios
     of Joseph Haydn." PhD dissertation. New York Uni-
     versity, 1976. UM 77-16528. DA xxxviii.2A, pp. 541-
     2. 377 pages.
     Builds on Landon's chronology of the keyboard trios
     {971}. Analyzes the basic elements of each and re-
     duces them to arithmetic terms. The early trios still
     have Baroque rhythms. The middle trios have a much
     more developed sonata form, more expansive melodies and
     a larger harmonic vocabulary, which results in less
     activity than in the early trios. The late trios are
     more dynamic and orchestral, with virtuosic piano
     parts, more activity, and expanded harmony.

     See also {932}.

973. Tyson, Alan. "Haydn and Two Stolen Trios," in *The
     Music Review*, xxii (1961), 21-27.
     A thorough, scholarly study of the 2 piano trios Op.
     40 Nos. 1 and 2 (Hoboken xv.3-4), which have been
     ascribed to either Joseph or Michael Haydn. Shows
     conclusively that they are by Ignaz Pleyel, Joseph
     Haydn's pupil. See {974}.

974. Schwarting, Heino. "Über die Echtheit dreier Haydn-
     Trios," in *Archiv für Musikwissenschaft*, xxii (1965),
     169-182.
     Considers the trios in C, F, and G (Hob.xv.3-5) and
     "proves" on stylistic grounds alone that the first 2
     are not by Haydn. See {973}.

975. Benton, Rita. "Resumé of the Haydn - Pleyel 'Trio
     Controversy' with some Added Contributions," in
     Haydn-Studien, iv (1978), 114-117.
     Supplies further evidence that Pleyel, not Haydn, com-
     posed the first 2 trios (or sonatas) Hob.xv. 3-4.
     Among other things, shows the striking relationship of
     the second trio to a symphony by Pleyel (Ben. 136),
     also surviving under a Haydn attribution (Hob.i. F14).

976. Fillion, Michelle. "Eine bisher unbekannte Quelle für
     Haydns frühes Klaviertrio Hob.xv.C1," in *Haydn-
     Studien*, v (1982), 59-63.
     A discussion of a manuscript copy of the Haydn trio at-
     tributed to Wagenseil. On stylistic grounds primarily
     shows that Haydn still is the probable composer.

977. Landon, H.C. Robbins. "Joseph Haydn: a Sketch to Piano
     Trio No. 30 (Hob.xv:17)," in *The Haydn Yearbook*, xiii
     (1982), 220-227.
     A brief but important scholarly discussion of the only
     extant sketch of a Haydn trio between 1786 and 1794, "a
     period particularly rich in this form." Compares the
     sketch to the equivalent measures of the modern edi-

tion. Discusses the data known about the composition of the trio (1790) and its early publication.

978. Brook, Barry S. "Haydn's String Trios: a Misunderstood Genre," in *Current Musicology*, no. 36 (1983), 61-77. The string trio refers to works usually for 2 violins + cello, occasionally violin + viola + cello or rarely 2 violins + viola. Originally it was called divertimento a tre, sonate a tre, or terzetto. Very popular in the second half of the 18th century -- even more so than the string quartet -- over 2000 were written by over 200 composers. Presents some of the problems in distinguishing authentic from unauthentic Haydn trios. Believes Haydn's trios are early works (1755-1765) -- the earliest string quartets seem to predate them, based on harmonic and stylistic achievements of the trios.

979. Strunk, W. Oliver. "Haydn's Divertimenti for Baryton, Viola, and Bass (after Manuscripts in the Library of Congress)," in *The Musical Quarterly*, xviii (1932), 216-251. An important pioneering study, including a history of the baryton and an analysis of baryton technique, the term "divertimento," the forms and styles of the trios, and the historical development of Haydn's style. Includes 2 detailed photos of a baryton built in 1779, a list of the 125 trios, and extensive sources in manuscripts, old editions, and modern prints.

980. Csuka, Béla. "Haydn és a Baryton," in Bence Szabolcsi and Dénes Bartha, eds., *Kodály Zoltán 75. Születésnapjára*, in *Zenetudományi Tanulmányok*, VI (Budapest: Akadémiai Kiado, 1957), pp. 669-728. ML 55.S995. German summary "Haydn und das Baryton," pp. 761-762. A study of the baryton instrument and the chief performers on it (Karl Franz, Anton Kraft, Josef Weigl and Prince Nicolas Esterházy) in the second half of the 18th century. It was an Austro-Hungarian phenomenon, unknown in Italy. Includes a thematic catalogue of Haydn's baryton pieces with incipits, list of movements, meters, manuscript location, and publication information. Replaced by A. von Hoboken in his *Verzeichnis* (Mainz: 1957). Includes photos of surviving barytons and facsimiles of 2 complete baryton pieces.

981. Unverricht, Hubert. "Zur Chronologie der Barytontrios von Joseph Haydn," in Friedrich Wilhelm Riedel and Hubert Unverricht, eds., *Symbolae Historiae Musicae: Hellmut Federhofer zum 60. Geburtstag* (Mainz: B. Schott's Söhne, 1971), pp. 180-189. ML 55.F32.1972. Scholarly study of receipts and other documents leading to the conclusion that Haydn's 126 or 127 baryton trios were composed 1765-1774, the first 100 in 1765-1771.

982. Wollenberg, Susan. "Haydn's Baryton Trios and the
    'Gradus,'" in *Music and Letters*, liv (1973), 170-178.
    A study of the fugue finales of some of Haydn's baryton
    trios and their relation to Fux's *Gradus ad Parnassum*.
    Finds that Haydn drew heavily from Fux.

983. Gerlach, Sonja. "Neues zu Haydns Baryton-Oktett Nr. 5
    (Hob.x:1)," in *Haydn-Studien*, v (1983), 125-134.
    The manuscript of the octet was recently rediscovered
    in the manuscript collection formerly in Berlin, now in
    Cracow; it is the complete piece, as opposed to a re-
    construction which appears in the *Haydn-Gesamtausgabe*.
    A detailed description and comparison with the pub-
    lished version.

984. Smith, Carleton Sprague. "Haydn's Chamber Music and
    the Flute," in *The Musical Quarterly*, xix (1933),
    341-350 and 434-455.
    Asks the question "Why did Haydn write for the flute?"
    and considers the chamber music only: the English
    solicited flute works from him.

[Johann] Michael Haydn
1736-1806

985. Zehetmair, Helmut. "Johann Michael Haydns Kammermu-
    sikwerke a Quattro und a Cinque." PhD dissertation.
    University of Innsbruck, 1964.
    Not seen.

986. Hess, Reimund. "Serenade, Cassation, Notturno und Di-
    vertimento bei Michael Haydn." PhD dissertation.
    Johannes Gutenberg University of Mainz, 1963. ML
    410.H44H4. 2 vols. I: 215 pages; II: 99 pages of
    206 examples.
    Studies an important genre of instrumental music by M.
    Haydn, compares it to similar works of Mozart and other
    contemporaries, and traces its evolution. Among the 33
    works, mostly divertimenti, for various combinations of
    strings, winds, timpani, and bass, are some quartets
    and quintets. Lists the works and their movements, but
    finds no really valid generalizations about them. The
    serenades are orchestral, the divertimenti, chamber,
    the others either orchestral or chamber; this is a
    Salzburg phenomenon applicable to both Mozarts as well.
    M. Haydn is a Rococo composer who never moved on to the
    mature classicism of his brother; Joseph separated his
    art music (Classical) from his social music (Rococo).

Bernhard Heiden
b.1910

987. Langosch, Marlene Joan. "The Instrumental Chamber
     Music of Bernhard Heiden." PhD dissertation.
     Indiana University, 1974. UM 74-9431. DA xxxiv.10A,
     p. 6688. 303 pages.
     Examines structures, procedures and the various other
     parameters in the 45 pieces of chamber music by Heiden,
     an American of German birth and pupil of Hindemith. He
     is a conservative composer.

*For an analysis of his sonata for saxophone + piano see
Robert Sibbing's dissertation {826}.*

Hans Werner Henze
b. 1926

988. Nestler, Gerhard. "Das Bläserquintett von Hans Werner
     Henze," in *Melos*, xxvii (1960), 141-142.
     A brief but careful analysis of Henze's woodwind quin-
     tet (1952), a 12-tone dance. The row is presented
     first in the clarinet in the first 4 measures, and then
     it is basically ignored in this analysis.

Paul Hindemith
1895-1963

989. Wolff, Helmuth Christian. "Die Kammermusik Paul Hin-
     demiths," in *Hindemith Jahrbuch*, iii (1974), 80-92.
     Same article in {457}.
     Considers "varying estimations" of Hindemith's chamber
     music 1921-1963, his resurrection of strict polyphony,
     his novel rhythm and melody, his vocal style, his idio-
     matic instrumental writing, and the special demonstra-
     tion in the *Octet* of 1957 of many 20th-century devices.

990. Mason, Colin. "Some Aspects of Hindemith's Chamber
     Music," in *Music and Letters*, xli (1960), 150-155.
     Praises Hindemith as one of a few modern composers who
     writes true chamber music, that is, music for the ama-
     teur or professional to be played at home. Yet criti-
     cizes him for using traditional string sounds too rou-
     tinely. He has not exploited the color characteristics
     of all instruments in his chamber music. On the other
     hand, he exploits formal potentialities.

*See Landau's "The Harmonic Theories of Paul Hindemith in Re-
lation to his Practice as a Composer of Chamber Music"
{511}.*

991. Strobel, Heinrich. "Neue Kammermusik von Paul Hinde-
     mith," in *Melos*, iv (1925), 541-548.
     An important early review of Hindemith's linear poly-
     phonic writing in the third and fourth string quartets
     and Op. 34 string trio. Compares the fugues in Op. 34
     and the fourth string quartet.

992. Adorno, Theodor [Wiesengrund]. "Kammermusik von Paul
     Hindemith," in *Die Musik*, xix.1 (1926), 24-28.
     Notes the dialectic between Hindemith's choice of tra-
     ditional, objective, *a priori* forms and his vital, sub-
     jective, artistic self. Traces this dialectic in quar-
     tets Op. 22 to Op. 32 to the Op. 34 string trio to non-
     chamber pieces Op. 35 and Op. 36. Hindemith's use of
     Classical form does not make these pieces Classical.
     He needs forms and these are good ones, but his vitali-
     ty extends beyond the limits of these particular forms.

993. Hymanson, William. "Hindemith's Variations: a Compari-
     son of Early and Recent Works," in *The Music Review*,
     xiii (1952), 20-33.
     A study of Hindemith's concept of theme and variation.
     The early works include string quartet Opus 10, move-
     ment 2 (1919), sonata for viola + piano, op. 11 No. 4
     (1922), and String Quartet No. 4, op. 32, last movement
     (1924). The late works include String Quartet in E-
     flat, movement 3 (1944), *Symphonic Metamorphoses*, move-
     ment 2 (1945), and *The Four Temperaments*, for piano +
     strings (1946). In the early works Hindemith uses
     the theme as "a springboard for fanciful transforma-
     tions often related to the original only through remote
     similarities." The late works operate on the old
     cantus firmus and ostinato ideas.

*On Hindemith's ambiguous understanding of the term "chamber
music," see Helmut Haack in {457}.*

994. Espey, Sister Jule Adele. "Formal, Tonal, and Thematic
     Structure of the Hindemith String Quartets." PhD
     dissertation. Indiana University, 1973. RILM 73 -
     43. UM 74-9422. DA xxxiv.10A, pp. 6683-4. 193
     pages.
     Analyzes form, tonality, and thematic structure in the
     6 quartets without reference to Hindemith's theories.
     Reviews other writings on the quartets.

995. Pütz, Werner. *Studien zum Streichquartettschaffen bei
     Hindemith, Bartók, Schönberg und Webern*, in *Kölner
     Beiträge zur Musikforschung*, Band 36. Regensburg:
     Gustave Bosse, 1968. MT 140.P84. iv + 217 pages.
     Despite some dated information, a thorough and careful-
     ly worked out scholarly and theoretic discussion of the
     formal unity and color of these quartets and their out-
     growth from earlier quartets. The rejuvenation of

string quartet writing in the first half of the 20th
century results in the most quartets since the 18th
century. Discusses the development of motivic unity in
the quartet from Haydn's immediate predecessors to
Reger. Leans on Sandberger. Also stresses the divi-
sion of parts of a theme among the different instruments. After Beethoven nothing new is added to these
basic concepts of organic unity, but Schubert added
refined chromaticism and technical devices like tremolos, Brahms added orchestral elements, Reger added
intensive, chromatic polyphony, and Debussy emphasized
color as a main element.

996. Doflein, Erich. "Die sechs Streichquartette von Paul
     Hindemith," in *Schweizerische Musikzeitung*, xcv
     (1955), 413-421.
     A good, non-technical analysis of all 6 quartets with
     more attention to nos. 5 and 6. Brief mention of
     style, forms, and themes. Much greater concern for
     Hindemith's relationship to other composers and to
     tradition.

997. Kostka, Stefan Matthew. "The Hindemith String Quar-
     tets: a Computer-Assisted Study of Selected Aspects
     of Style. PhD dissertation. University of Wiscon-
     sin, 1969. UMI 70-3590. DAI xxxi.2A, p. 786. 349
     pages.
     After a review of earlier computer projects in music, a
     coding of the string quartets nos. 2, 3, 5, and 6 with
     keypunching according to a specific, defined system and
     7 primary FORTRAN programs for analysis. Studies
     chords and root movements.

998. Dorfman, Joseph. "Hindemith's Fourth Quartet," in
     Hindemith-Jahrbuch, vii (1978), 54-71.
     A detailed analysis of each of the movements. The
     first, a triple fugue, is full of stretti, episodes,
     and other typical devices but is also a duality of 2
     opposing musical images. The greatest attention is
     given to the structure of the fourth movement -- a
     passacaglia. Emphasis on the contrapuntal and cyclic
     nature not only of this quartet but of other Hindemith
     chamber music as well.

999. Kolneder, Walter. "Hindemiths Streichquartett V. in
     Es," in *Schweizerische Musikzeitung*, xl (1950), 92-
     96.
     A detailed analysis of the sixth quartet (1943), writ-
     ten 19 years after the fifth and thus reflecting a
     later development in Hindemith's style. It has 7
     themes, which finally come together, often in counter-
     point, in the fourth (last) movement. Shows how
     Hindemith altered his themes -- metamorphosed them
     (at the same time as the writing of his *Symphonic
     Metamorphoses*).

1000. Hambourg, Klement. "Three Sonatas for Violin and Piano by Paul Hindemith: a Stylistic and Interpretive Study." DMA dissertation. University of Oregon, 1977. DAI xxxviii.10A, pp. 5786-7. 270 pages.
The 3 works (E-flat, 1918; E, 1935; and C, 1939) share certain features, such as Gebrauchsmusik, neo-classicism, expanded tonality, melody, rhythm and texture. The 1918 sonata is stylistically ambivalent: various influences of Brahms, Strauss, Reger and Debussy. The other 2, however, are clearly tonal and have a semitonal connection between movements and sections; they are rhythmically fluent and free.

1001. Payne, Dorothy Katherine. "The Accompanied Wind Sonatas of Hindemith: Studies in Tonal Counterpoint." PhD dissertation. University of Rochester, Eastman School of Music, 1974. UM 74-21530. DA xxxv.4A, p. 2325. 227 pages.
A non-technical analysis of form, counterpoint and tonality in each of the 10 sonatas Hindemith wrote 1936-1955 for solo wind instruments + piano.

1002. Kidd, James C. "Aspects of Mensuration in Hindemith's Clarinet Sonata," in *The Music Review*, xxxviii (1977), 211-222.
Investigates the rhythm of mm.12-25 of the second movement of this sonata and its similarity to late-14th century mensuration whereby 6/8 and 3/4 often occur simultaneously. This similarity must be understood by performers so that bar-lines are ignored in favor of the overall rhythmic-melodic patterns.

For an analysis of the sonata for saxophone + piano see Robert Sibbing's dissertation {826}.

1003. Ohlsson, Jean Mary. "Paul Hindemith's Music for Flute: Analyses of Solo Works and Stylistic and Formal Considerations of Chamber Works." DMA dissertation. Ohio State University, 1975. UMI 76-3361. DAI xxxvii.1A, pp. 27-8. 98 pages.
Analyzes the role of the flute *per se* and in ensemble in 4 works: *Acht Stücke für Flöte allein*, Sonata for Flute + Piano, Echo for Flute + Piano, and *Kanonische Sonatine für zwei Flöte*. Considers the nature of stylistic and formal problems and solutions and ponders their relationship to Hindemith's expressed ideas on them in *The Craft of Musical Composition*.

1004. Townsend, George David. "Stylistic and Performance Analysis of the Clarinet Music of Paul Hindemith." EdD dissertation. University of Illinois, 1967. UMI 68-1873. 250 pages.

Analyzes 5 works (4 are chamber pieces) involving the
clarinet: Quintet (1923), Quartet (1938), Sonata
(1939), Concerto (1947), and Octet (1957-1958). Includes historical data on the pieces and analyzes form,
melody, rhythm, texture, harmony and performance problems of range, registration, articulation, dynamics,
fingerings, and ensemble.

1005. Koper, Robert Peter. "A Stylistic and Performance
Analysis of the Bassoon Music of Paul Hindemith."
EdD dissertation. University of Illinois, 1972. UM
72-19863. DA xxxiii.1A, p. 349. 364 pages.
Of 4 compositions analyzed, 1 is the Sonata for bassoon
+ piano (1938) and 1 is the woodwind quintet from
Kleine Kammermusik (1922). Elaborates 3 points: Hindemith's scoring for the bassoon (he was against coloristic effects *per se*), technical problems (he writes
simply), and implications for teaching (excellent for
teaching at the college level).

1006. Willis, James D. "A Study of Paul Hindemith's Use of
the Trombone as Seen in Selected Chamber Compositions." DMA dissertation. University of Missouri at
Kansas City, 1973. UM 73-25951. DA xxxiv.5A, p.
2689. 139 pages.
Analyzes tessitura, dynamics, and melodic patterns in
10 chamber works by Hindemith calling for trombone.
Considers articulation, the trombone as solo or as bass
line, special techniques, and scoring.

1007. Wörner, Karl H. "Hindemiths neueste Oktett," in
Melos, xxv (1958), 356-359.
Briefly places the piece in historical context, and
analyzes in detail the 5 movements: themes, techniques,
and style. It is scored for violin + 2 violas + cello
+ bass + clarinet + bassoon + horn.

John Hingeston
c.1610-1683

1008. Bock, Emil William. "The String Fantasies of John
Hingeston (*ca.*1610-1683)." PhD dissertation.
University of Iowa, 1956. UM 56-1528. DA xiv.5, p.
969. 2 vols. I: xi + 251 pages; II: ii + 287 pages.
Shows the importance of Hingeston's 77 string fantasies
to both Commonwealth and Restoration England. His
later fantasias use violins rather than viols, and a
continuo rather than written-out organ that doubled the
strings. Includes biography and bibliography and a
stylistic analysis of the music. Vol II: 24 fantasias
in transcription.

Ernst Theodor Amadeus Hoffmann
1776-1822

For a catalogue of Hoffmann's chamber music, see Gerhard Allroggen, E.T.A. Hoffmanns Kompositionen: ein chronologisch-thematisches Verzeichnis seiner musikalischen Werke mit einer Einführung, *in Studien zur Musikgeschichte des 19. Jahrhunderts, Band 16 (Regensburg: Gustav Bosse, 1970), pages 37-38 and 77-78. ML 134.H575A4.*

1009. Georgieff, Katherine Pejkarjanz. "The Instrumental and Vocal Works of Ernst Theodor Amadeus Hoffmann." PhD dissertation. Washington University, 1973. UMI 73-24882. DAI xxxiv.5A, p. 2679. 260 pages. Discusses songs and instrumental works. Points out that Hoffmann was more a Classical than Romantic composer and that none of his musical works can measure up to the greatness of his literature. A list of all extant and lost instrumental works.

Roman Hoffstetter
1742-1815

1010. Unverricht, Hubert, with assistance of Adam Gottron and Alan Tyson. *Die beiden Hoffstetter: Zwei Komponisten - Porträts mit Werkverzeichnissen, in Beiträge zur mittelrheinischen Musikgeschichte,* Band 10. Mainz: B. Schott's Söhne, 1968. ML 390.U65. 80 pages.
A brief but intense study of the lives of Roman Hoffstetter and his twin brother Johann Urban Alois Hoffstetter (1742-after 1808), both composers. Of special importance are Roman's 6 string quartets, op. 26, published by Bailleux in Paris in 1777, which Ignaz Pleyel republished in 1800-1802 as Haydn's Op. 3. Gives authentic documents for the biographies of the brothers and lists in detail (with themes) all their known works. Roman wrote in all 20 quartets composed between c.1765 and c.1780; also viola concertos and vocal works. His brother wrote symphonies and songs.

See Philip Olleson's The Rise of the String Quartet {184} for a facsimile of the title of the "Opus 3" quartets showing Hoffstetter's name. See also {932}.

Leontzi Honauer
1737-c.1790

1011. Keillor, Frances Elaine. "Leontzi Honauer (1737-ca. 1790) and the Development of Solo and Ensemble Keyboard Music." PhD dissertation. University of Toronto, 1976. DAI xxxix.3A, p. 1181.

Biographical and analytical study of the Frenchman and
his compositions, including accompanied sonatas, suites
for keyboard and winds, and keyboard quartets, which
were known to Mozart.

Arthur Honegger
1892-1955

*For a catalogue of Honegger's chamber music, see [Walter
Labhart], Arthur Honegger: Liste des Oeuvres: Werkverzeich-
nis (Zurich: Archives Musicales Suisses, 1975), pages 11-12.
ML 134.H77S4.*

Nicolas Joseph Hüllmandel
1756-1823

1012. Benton, Rita. "Nicolas Joseph Hüllmandel and French
      Instrumental Music in the Second Half of the 18th
      Century." PhD dissertation. University of Iowa,
      1961. UM 61-4019. 384 pages.
      Biography and social milieux of Hüllmandel, and discus-
      sion of his compositions, most of which are sonatas for
      keyboard with violin. Considers the problem of the
      harpsichord - continuo replaced by the piano. Excerpts
      appeared in "Nicolas-Joseph Hüllmandel (1756-1823):
      Quelques Aspects de sa Vie et de son Oeuvre," in *Revue
      de Musicologie*, xlvii (Dec. 1961), 177-194.

See also the article by Saint-Foix {860}.

Johann Nepomuk Hummel
1778-1837

1013. Zimmerschied, Dieter. *Die Kammermusik Johann Nepomuk
      Hummels*. Mainz: typescript reproduction with errors
      and corrections, 1966. MT 145.H84Z5. 554 pages.
      Inaugural dissertation. University of Mainz, 1967.
      A scholarly study of Hummel's 2 string trios, 3 string
      quartets, clarinet quintet, 7 violin + piano sonatas (3
      = also flute + piano sonatas, 1 = also mandoline +
      piano sonata), cello + piano sonata, viola + piano
      sonata, 8 piano trios, piano quartet, piano quintet,
      and 2 septets. A movement-by-movement description and
      analysis with somewhat subjective characterizations of
      principal themes and forms. Historical background and
      comparisons are the more important parts of the study.

J.S. (= ?John) Humphries
c.1707-before c.1740

1014. Thomas, Alan Rowland. "The Trio Sonatas of J.S. Humphries." DMA dissertation. University of Illinois,
1966. UMI 66-7819. DAI xxvii.3A, p. 793. 270
pages.
A biography and background material for an edition
of the sonata.

Jacques Ibert
1890-1962

1015. Timlin, Francis Eugene. "An Analytic Study of the
Flute Works of Jacques Ibert." DMA dissertation.
University of Washington, 1980. DAI xl.5A, p. 1832.
141 pages. Sound tape.
An analysis of 11 works with flute, most of which are
chamber pieces.

Andrew Imbrie
b.1921

1016. Boykan, Martin. "Andrew Imbrie: Third Quartet," in
Perspectives of New Music, iii, no. 1 (1964), 139-
146.
Analyzes the quartet, which is in fairly traditional
forms: movement 1 paraphrases sonata form, movement 2
is a scherzo and trio, and movement 3 is a Lied. Only
the first movement is serial, though it "continues to
exert an influence" in the second movement. The overall melodic sounds are wholetone. Finds "an Italian
elegance which is unusual in American music," and contrasts Imbrie's simpler and clearer music -- his personal tone -- with Sessions's more complicated music.

Charles Edward Ives
1874-1954

*For a catalogue of Ives's chamber music, see Dominique-René
De Lerma,* Charles Edward Ives, 1874-1954: a Bibliography of
his Music *(Kent [Ohio]: Kent State University Press, 1970),
pages 166-169 for systematic index. ML 134.I9D4. ISBN 0-
87338-057-6.*

1017. Bader, Yvette. "The Chamber Music of Charles Edward
Ives," in *The Music Review*, xxxiii (1972), 292-299.
Surveys the problems of identifying what is truly chamber music in Ives's output and considers briefly the
rubrics and "folk" tunes that Ives puts into some of
his chamber pieces. Also points out the unique contributions of Ives.

1018. Hitchcock, H. Wiley. "The Chamber Music," in *Ives: a Survey of the Music*, in *I.S.A.M. Monographs*, no. 19 (New York: Institute for Studies in American Music, at Brooklyn College of the City University of New York, [1983]). Reprint with corrections in *Oxford Studies of Composers*, no. 14 (London: Oxford University Press, 1977), pp. 57-72.
An excellent introduction to Ives's chamber music for the student and professional, with emphasis on the 4 violin + piano sonatas and 2 string quartets. Concerned with style, Ives's manifold characteristics, the borrowed American tunes, and the effect and purpose of the pieces. Points out the unity of the 4 sonatas and the personal argumentation of the second string quartet (an expansion of the conversation idea). Not technical but requires musical sophistication.

1019. Quackenbush, Margaret Diane. "Form and Texture in the Works for Mixed Chamber Ensemble by Charles Ives." MA thesis. University of Oregon, 1976. RILM 76-3179. 125 pages.
Analyzes 19 pieces of Ives that are programatic.

1020. Maske, Ulrich. *Charles Ives in seiner Kammermusik für drei bis sechs Instrumente*, in *Kölner Beiträge zur Musikforschung*, Band 64. Regensburg: Gustav Bosse, 1971. ML 410.I94M4. ISBN 3-7649-2068-8. xi + 164 pages, 71 examples. PhD dissertation. University of Köln, 1971. RILM 73-3829.
An exhaustive, scholarly study of melody, harmony, meter, beat, rhythm, dynamics, form and programs in some of Ives's chamber music. Gives the basic problems in dealing with Ives's chaotic manuscripts and accepts John Kirkpatrick's *The Music Manuscripts of Charles Edward Ives* (New Haven: Yale, reproduced typescript, 1960). Since the aim of the book is to characterize Ives's style and not to understand his concepts of chamber music, this book has relatively little relevance to a study of chamber music *per se*. However, in so far as Ives's stylistic characteristics are demonstrated in specific chamber works, these can be useful in attempting elsewhere a study of the chamber music. No one piece is analyzed as a piece, only for a specific aspect.

1021. Walker, Gwyneth. "Tradition and the Breaking of Tradition in the String Quartets of Ives and Schoenberg." DMA dissertation. University of Hartford, 1976. RILM 76-15604. 109 pages.
Analyzes and compares form, harmony, rhythm, meter, texture, and themes in Ives's and Schoenberg's first 2 string quartets.

1022. Schermer, Richard. "The Aesthetics of Charles Ives in Relation to his 'String Quartet No. 2.'" MA thesis. California State University in Fullerton, 1980. UMI PSE 13-14856. Masters Abstracts xviii.4, p. 304. 184 pages.
Ives's concern for New England Transcendentalism, humor, and politics is expressed in this quartet by quotations of American hymn-tunes, patriotic songs, and "incongruous combinations of melodies, rhythms, harmonies, and other musical matters." Analyzes these elements much further in order to understand "the correlation between the composer's aesthetic principles and his art."

1023. Cantrick, Susan Birdsall. "Charles Ives's *String Quartet No. 2*: an Analysis and Evaluation." MM thesis. Peabody Conservatory of Music, 1983. MAI 322234. MAI xx (1984), p. 280. 153 pages.
Comparison of the holograph and a recent miniature score. "Analysis of compositional language and procedure [and] an examination of stylistic heterogeneity as the definitive characteristic of this and Ives's music in general."

1024. Gratovich, Eugene. "The Sonatas for Violin and Piano by Charles E. Ives: a Critical Commentary and Concordance of the Printed Editions and the Autographs and Manuscripts of the Yale Ives Collection." MAD dissertation. Boston University, 1968. UMI 71-14561. DAI xxxi.12A, pp. 6646-7. 242 pages.
A scholarly study of the 4 pieces written 1903-1915 (3 not published until the 1950's). Discusses sources and editions, one chapter for each sonata. A fifth chapter deals with unpublished music for violin + piano, including sketches for a fifth sonata. No analyses.

For a discussion of Ives's Sonata No. 2, see Paul Carlson's "An Historical Background and Stylistic Analysis of Three Twentieth Century Compositions for Violin and Piano" {250}.

1025. Gingerich, Lora Louise. "Processes of Motivic Transformation in the Keyboard and Chamber Music of Charles E. Ives." PhD dissertation. Yale University, 1983. UMI 83-29230. DAI xliv.9A, p. 2617. 288 pages.
Discovers ways in which Ives modifies, varies, and develops motives in his pieces. Analyzes 2 piano works and the Sonata No. 4 for violin and piano.

1026. Milligan, Terry Gilbert. "Charles Ives: a Study of the Works for Chamber Ensemble Written between 1898 and 1908 which Utilize Wind Instruments." DMA dissertation. University of Texas, 1978. UMI 78-17608. DAI xxxix.4A, p. 1919. 178 pages.

In his early years Ives wrote at least 25 pieces using
wind instruments prominently. Concentrates on "From
the Steeples and the Mountains," "Scherzo: Over the
Pavements," and "Central Park in the Dark."

Giuseppe Maria Jacchini
c.1663-1727

1027. Pickard, Alexander L., Jr. "A Practical Edition of
the Trumpet Sonatas of Giuseppe Jacchini." DMA
dissertation. Eastman School of Music, 1974. UMI
74-21522. DAI xxxv.4A, pp. 2325-6. 310 pages.
Preceding this edition of 7 sonatas for trumpet + continuo composed between 1690 and 1703, a historical
introduction and practical suggestions for performance.

Gordon Jacob
1895-1984

1028. Lee, Walter Fulford. "Analysis of Selected Compositions by Gordon Jacob for Solo Oboe: Sonata for Oboe
and Piano, Sonatina for Oboe and Harpsichord, Two
Pieces for Two Oboes and Cor anglais, and Concerto
No. 2 for Oboe." DMA dissertation. Peabody Conservatory, 1978. UMI 78-23478. DAI xxxix.6A, p. 3213.
121 pages, 53 musical examples.
Analyzes form, melody, pulse, articulation, textures,
tonality, and historically stylized techniques in 4 of
the 23 pieces Jacob has written for solo oboe and English horn. A complete works list, list of oboe works,
discography, and correspondence.

1029. Pusey, Robert Samuel. "Gordon Jacob: a Study of the
Solo Works for Oboe and English Horn and their Ensemble Literature." DMA dissertation. Peabody Conservatory of Music, 1980. DAI xli.4A, p. 1275. 411
pages.
A biography of Jacob, a discussion of stylistic influences on his music, and an analysis of 7 works, 5 of
which are chamber pieces: Sonatina for oboe + harpsichord, Sonata for oboe + piano, Trio for flute + oboe +
harpsichord, Sextet for piano + winds, and 3 Inventions
for flute + oboe. Bibliography of newspaper reviews
and discussions.

Leos Janáček
1854-1928

1030. Vogel, Jaroslav. *Leos Janáček: a Biography*, trl. from
Czech by Geraldine Thomsen-Muchová, rev. by Karel
Janovicky. London: Orbis Publishing, 1981. ML

410.J18V712.1981. ISBN 0-85613-045-1. 439 pages.
1st ed. Prague: Artia, 1962. 1st English trl.
London: Paul Hamlyn, 1962.
Within the biography, the historical position of each
chamber work, including lost and fragmentary pieces.
Analysis of the more important works (2 string quartets, Youth Wind Sextet, violin + piano sonata, and
Sonata "Fairy Tale" for cello + piano) and some extra-
musical description. Points out ethnic scales and
tunes.

1031. Pestalozza, Luigi. "Leos Janáček," in *L'Approdo Musicale*, iii (April-June, 1960), 3-74, section 17,
"Musica da camera," pp. 59-62. In Italian.
A brief but intelligent discussion of Janáček's principal chamber music, commencing with the violin + piano
sonata. Points to popular Moravian influences in
timbres and dance rhythms.

1032. Horsbrugh, Ian. *Leos Janáček: the Field that Pros-
pered*. London: David & Charles/New York: Charles
Scribner's Sons, 1981. ML 410.J18. ISBN 0-7153-
8060-5. 327 pages.
Discusses the chamber music in the course of the biography, especially the 2 string quartets and the third
Violin + Piano Sonata. Considers programs and analyzes
the music largely subjectively.

1033. Kaderavek, Milan R. "Stylistic Aspects of the Late
Chamber Music of Leos Janáček: an Analytic Study."
DMA dissertation. University of Illinois, 1970.
RILM 72-1976. DAI xxxi.12A, p. 6649. 2 vols.
Characterizes the chamber music as naive, with an intensely personal idiom and dramatic realism. Analyzes
the peculiar disjointed aspects of the music and its
ties to folk music in 2 string quartets, *Mládí* (Youth)
for wind sextet, and larger works. Considers Janáček's
speech melody, as well as other basic elements.

*See Martin Wehnert's discussion of semantics in Janáček's
string quartets {457}.*

1034. Gerlach, Reinhard. "Leos Janáček und die Erste und
Zweite Wiener Schule: ein Beitrag zur Stilkritik
seines instrumentalen Spätwerks," in *Die Musikforschung*, xxiv (1971), 19-34.
Studies 2 string quartets (1923 and 1928) and their
relationship to the 18th- and 20th-century Viennese
schools. Briefly characterizes the quartets of Haydn,
Mozart and Beethoven, considers the 19th century Romantic quartets as attempts to carry on from Beethoven,
then treats the nationalistic quartets of Smetana, and
finally Smetana's influence on Janáček. After lengthy
analyses of the Janáček quartets, turns to Schoenberg's

5 quartets and considers the fact that there is no connection between the quartets of the 2 composers. Janáček, despite his quartal harmony, is not concerned with
the same problems as Schoenberg.

1035. Bek, Josef. "Neznámy Fragment Janáčkova Kvarteta," in
      Slezsky Sbornik, lviii (1960), 374-378. NYPL *QUA.
      In Czech.
      A detailed description of a 14-folio manuscript of a
      fragment of a Janáček string quartet.

Émile Jaques-Dalcroze
1865-1950

1036. Martin, Frank, and others. *Émile Jaques-Dalcroze:*
      l'Homme, le Compositeur, le Créateur de la Rythmique.
      Neuchâtel: Éditions de la Baconnière, 1965. HML
      3431.15.23. 595 pages.
      A list of the chamber music (pages 472-476) shows a
      string quartet, string quartet movements, various works
      for violin, flute and other instruments + piano, and so
      on. Discusses rhythmic peculiarities (such as mixed
      meters) in the pieces (pages 257-268).

John Jenkins
1592-1678

1037. Warner, Robert Austin. "The Fantasia in the Works of
      John Jenkins." PhD dissertation. University of
      Michigan, 1951. UM 2365. DA xi.2, pp. 378-9. 2
      vols. 331 pages.
      Describes the cultural climate, musical background,
      and biography of Jenkins. Then analyzes and discusses
      transcription problems of 105 of his 114 fantasias for
      instrumental ensemble. The earlier fantasias (c.1625-
      1640) are a4-6 viols, conservative, 16th-century motet
      style with elaborations; the later fantasias (1654 and
      especially 1661-1674) are progressive and scored for a2
      trebles + bass. The level of chamber music is extreme-
      ly high here and fills a gap between the madrigalists
      and Purcell in English music history.

1038. Ashbee, Andrew. "The Four-Part Instrumental Composi-
      tions of John Jenkins." PhD dissertation. Universi-
      ty of London, 1966. RILM 70-1650. 3 vols. I: 256
      pages; II: 238 pages; III: 76 pages.
      Not seen.

1039. Warner, Robert Austin. "John Jenkins' Four-Part Fancy
      (Meyer, No. 14) in C Minor: an Enharmonic Modulation
      around the Key Circle," in *The Music Review*, xxviii
      (1967), 1-20.

Discusses this unusual fancy that goes through the circle of fifths. An edition of the music, critical notes, and 4 facsimiles of 8 pages of the manuscript.

1040. Ashbee, Andrew. "Music for Treble, Bass and Organ by John Jenkins," in *Chelys*, vi (1975-1976), 25-42. Discusses 19 manuscript pieces by Jenkins for this consort and considers concordances. Includes sonata, aria, fantasia, dances and other types.

Karel Boleslav Jirák
1891-1972

1041. Tischler, Alice. *Karel Boleslav Jirák: a Catalog of his Works*, in *Detroit Studies in Music Bibliography*, No. 32. Detroit: Information Coordinators, 1975. ISBN 9-11772-74-X. 85 pages.
Czech composer who lived in Chicago 1947-1972. Annotated list of works including 2 string trios, a woodwind trio, 7 string quartets, a piano quintet, a wind quintet, a sextet and a nonet.

Joseph Joachim
1831-1907

1042. Maas, Gary L. "The Instrumental Music of Joseph Joachim." PhD dissertation. University of North Carolina, 1973. UMI 74-15364. DAI xxxv.1A, pp. 500-501. xi + 316 pages.
Discusses the design, melody, tonality and harmony, rhythm and texture of Joachim's compositions, concenrating on 40 movements but making reference to all his music. Conservative in nature, Joachim's music varies in quality and, even when technically well written, lacks "genius and inspiration." Includes biography and appended lists of all known works with dates, dedications, publishing data, location of manuscripts, and discography. This would seem to replace the old standard Joachim work by Moser {1043}.

1043. Moser, Andreas. *Joseph Joachim: ein Lebensbild*. 1st ed. 1898. 2nd ed. 2 vols. Berlin: Deutsche Brahms-Gesellschaft, 1908-1910. HML 3440.16.57. I: xii + 225 pages; II: 401 pages.
The standard biography, though not by any means the last word (for example, Moser cannot bring himself to mention Joachim's Jewishness). Lists Joachim's works and discusses them historically as part of the biography.

Benjamin Johnston
b.1926

1044. Shinn, Randall. "Ben Johnston's Fourth String Quartet," in *Perspectives of New Music*, xv, no. 2 (1977), 145-173. The entire 1-movement quartet is given on pp. 161-173 (a theme and 9 variations).
A detailed, highly technical analysis of the quartet (1973) and its basic structural aspect: proportionality ("the relationship between the elements of a system are determined by comparing the values [frequency, duration, etc.] of the elements themselves to each other as ratios, and not by reference to any equally segmented linear scale or measurement"). "The Fourth Quartet explores the potential of fluctuating proportional complexity; it uses as few as five proportional divisions of the octave and as many as twenty-two." Johnston's use of the hymn "Amazing Grace" brings in inevitable comparison with Ives. But most of the discussion is of mathematical proportions.

André Jolivet
b. 1905

1045. Jolivet, Hilda. *Avec...André Jolivet*. Paris: Flammarion, 1978. HML 3453.15.42. ISBN 2-08-064061-5. 305 pages.
After a biography, a discussion of Jolivet's string quartet, suite for string trio, flute + piano sonata, flute + clarinet sonatina, and oboe + bassoon sonatina. A brief description of the piece and a brief account of how it came to be.

Friedrich Kalkbrenner
1785-1848

1046. Nautsch, Hans. *Friedrich Kalkbrenner: Wirkung und Werk*, in *Hamburger Beiträge zur Musikwissenschaft*, Band 25. Hamburg: Karl Dieter Wagner, 1983. HML 3490.50.58. ISBN 3-921-029-96-1. xii + 255 pages.
A biography and study of the works of this famous German pianist, including a chapter on the chamber music: over 30 works from duets to septets. Gives history of each and a few cogent points about the music.

Ernst (= Ernest) Kanitz
1894-1978

For an analysis of his sonata for saxophone + piano see Robert Sibbing's dissertation {826}.

Hugo Kaun
1863-1932

1047. Schaal, Richard. *Hugo Kaun: Leben und Werk (1863-1932): eine Beitrag zur Musik der Jahrhundertwende.* Regensburg: Josef Habbel, [?1946]. HML 3500.15. 185 pages.
A biography of this German composer who lived in Milwaukee 1887-1902, where he led choirs. A chapter on chamber music, including pieces for violin or cello + piano, a string quintet (= piano quintet), octet (string quartet + clarinet + bassoon + horn + bass), a piano trio, and 4 string quartets.

Ivan Khandoshkin
1747-1804

1048. Mischakoff, Anne. *Khandoshkin and the Beginning of Russian String Music.* Ann Arbor: UMI Research Press, 1983. ML 410.K3935M6. ISBN 0-8357-1428-4. xx + 197 pages, 136 examples. Originally "Ivan Evstaf'evich Khandoshkin and the Beginnings of Russian String Music." DMA dissertation. University of Illinois, 1978. DAI xxxix.12A, p. 7048. 268 pages.
An extensive study of the life and works of Khandoshkin, whose variations and sonatas for violin alone or with another violin or with bass constitute some of the first publications by a Russian in St. Petersburg. He wrote many variations of Russian songs and arias to please Catherine the Great. Studies the violinist's technique and compares it to that of his great French and Italian predecessors and contemporaries. Uncovers misprints in some of his works. Good description of musical life in Russia 1760's-1804, especially chamber music clubs and concerts, with the importance of foreign artists.

Leon Kirchner
b.1919

1049. Anthony, Carl Rheinhardt. "Formal Determinants in Four Selected Compositions of Leon Kirchner." PhD dissertation. University of Arizona, 1984. UMI 84-21962. DAI xlv.10A, p. 3022. 202 pages.
One of the 4 works is the string quartet no. 2. Contains a biography, discusses his style and the influences of Schoenberg, Berg, Bartók and Stravinsky on Kirchner. "Durational elements are the most useful in formal delineation at all structural levels."

Jakob Friedrich Kleinknecht
1722-1794

1050. Schmidt, Günther. "Die Musik am Hofe der Markgrafen
      von Brandenburg-Ansbach." Inaugural dissertation.
      Ludwig-Maximilians-Universität (Munich), 1953. ML
      275.S29. v + 183 pages.
      Brief history of the musical life in Ansbach before
      1565, and very detailed history from that year with the
      establishment of the Court Kantorei. The focus is on
      church music and opera but chamber music is found
      occasionally. A separate chapter on Kleinknecht's
      chamber music goes into great detail on the meaning of
      chamber music in the 18th century and the solo and trio
      sonatas of Kleinknecht.

Zoltán Kodály
1882-1967

1051. Mason, Colin. "Kodály and Chamber Music," in *Studia
      Musicologica*, iii (1962), 251-254. This volume is
      also entitled *Zoltano Kodály Octogenario Sacrum*
      (Budapest: Akademiai Kiadó, 1962).
      Kodály wrote mostly chamber music until 1921, then
      never wrote any more. The early works synthesize
      Debussy's harmony with Hungarian folk music. Formally
      he prefers slow rhapsodic movements and fast rondos of
      a folk-like character -- rarely sonata form. Kodály
      abandoned chamber music when he realized that his
      desire to create a national music could not reach the
      masses in chamber music but only in symphonic music. A
      concise, easy to read article and a good introduction
      to the chamber music for the layperson.

1052. Brewer, Linda Rae Judd. "Progressions among Non-
      Twelve-Tone Sets in Kodály's 'Sonata for Violoncello
      and Piano, Op. 4': an Analysis for Performance Inter-
      pretation." DMA dissertation. University of Texas,
      1978. UMI 78-17606. DAI xxxix.4A, p. 1913. 77
      pages.
      Shows how Kodály has integrated Eastern European folk
      elements into a post-tonal style of music and "how
      pitch collections (cells) build on tritone combinations
      [to] permit progression between larger diatonic and
      octatonic sets." Contends this theoretical interpreta-
      tion will lead to a more insightful performance.

Charles Koechlin
1867-1950

*For a catalogue of Koechlin's compositions including chamber
music see L'Oeuvre de Charles Koechlin: Catalogue (Paris:
Max Eschig, 1975), ii + 109 pages. ML 134.K6504.*

1053. Kirk, Elise K.   "The Chamber Music of Charles Koechlin
      (1867-1950)."   PhD dissertation.   Catholic Universi-
      ty, 1977.   DAI xxxviii.4A, pp. 1728-9.   xii + 390
      pages.
      A pupil of Fauré and teacher of Poulenc, Koechlin wrote
      over 40 pieces of chamber music that spring from an im-
      pressionist's color and light yet mix in a wide variety
      and disparity of compositional aspects (tonality and
      atonality, diatonicism, chromaticism, and so on).   His
      use of dynamic with static elements influenced Milhaud.
      Considers his critical writings, his views of America
      as the result of 4 visits, diaries, autobiographies,
      commentaries, and other materials.

1054. Calvocoressi, M.D.   "Charles Koechlin's Instrumental
      Works," in *Music and Letters*, v (1924), 357-364.
      Despite the title, this is a study of primarily the
      violin + piano sonata, through which Koechlin's style
      in general is characterized.   The viola sonata also
      gets some attention in this poetic analysis.

Marck Kopelent
b. 1932

1055. Pukl, Oldrich.   "Marek Kopelent," in *Hudebni Rozhledy*,
      xxiii (1970), 423-428.   In Czech.
      "A discussion of Marck Kopelent (b. 1932), a Czech com-
      poser who writes mainly chamber music."

Leopold Koželuch
1747-1818

*See Christa Flamm's "Leopold Koželuch: Biographie und stil-
kritische Untersuchung der Sonaten für Klavier, Violine und
Violoncello nebst einem Beitrag zur Entwicklungsgeschichte
des Klaviertrios" {295}.   Roger Hickman's "Leopold Koželuch
and the Viennese Quatuor Concertant," in College Music
Symposium, xxvi (1986), 42-52, arrived too late to be annotated here.*

Joseph Martin Kraus
1756-1792

1056. Pfannkuch, Wilhelm. "Sonatenform und Sonatenzyklus in
      den Streichquartetten von Joseph Martin Kraus," in
      Georg Reichert and Martin Just, eds., Gesellschaft
      für Musikforschung, *Bericht über den internationalen
      musikwissenschaftlichen Kongress Kassel 1962* (Kassel:
      Bärenreiter, 1963), pp. 190-192. ML 36.I5K3.1962.
      Reviews the 9 string quartets by Kraus, written 1770's
      - 1780's. Considers number of movements, nature and
      form of the movements, and whatever elements (seemingly
      little concrete) that makes each one cyclic.

Johann Ludwig Krebs
1713-1780

1057. Horstman, Jean. "The Instrumental Music of Johann
      Ludwig Krebs." PhD dissertation. Boston University,
      1959. LC Mic 59-3465. DA xx.4, p. 1387. 314 pages.
      Discusses some chamber works: 4 sonatas for violin +
      continuo, 6 trios for 2 flutes + continuo, and 8
      sonatas for flute + harpsichord. A pupil of J.S. Bach,
      Krebs mixes Baroque and Galant styles overall, but the
      chamber music is principally Galant.

Ernst Krenek
b.1900

1058. Erickson, Robert. "Krenek's Later Music (1930-1947),"
      in *The Music Review*, ix (1948), 29-44.
      Analyzes the row and its functions in String Quartet
      No. 6 (1936). The first 3 movements each exploit only
      1 passive function of the row; the last movement com-
      bines all these functions and fully develops the themes
      that emerge from them.

1059. Krenek, Ernst. "Zu meinen Kammermusikwerken 1936-
      1950," in *Schweizerische Musikzeitung*, xciii (1953),
      102-104.
      Reviews his own chamber music mostly written in exile
      in America: *String Quartet No. 6* (discusses his use of
      a row, sonata form, and a fugue), *Suite for cello solo*,
      Sonatine für Flöte + Klarinette, *Sonata for Viola Solo*
      (the only one to use 2 different rows), *Sonata for
      Violin and Piano* (1944 -- his new idea of rotation,
      taking groups of 3 notes from a row and seeking a
      variety of harmony from them), *String Quartet No. 7*
      (the same idea), and some other works. Krenek has
      evolved his style of writing from strict 12-tone to a
      flexible one which depends more on the variety of sound
      than on obedience to rules.

Fritz (= Franz) Krommer
1759-1831

1060. Walter, Hans. "Franz Krommer: sein Leben und Werk, mit besonderer Berücksichtigung der Streichquartet-te." PhD dissertation. University of Vienna, 1932. Not seen.

1061. Riehl, Wilhelm Heinrich von. "Franz Krommer: ein Bei-trag zur Geschichte der Quartettmusik," in *Musikali-sche Charakterköpfe: ein Kunstgeschichtliches Skiz-zenbuch*, II, 7th ed. (Stuttgart: J.G. Cotta, 1899), 213-254. ML 60.R551.
A biography and historical analysis of the 65 quartets (a few with flute) and 22 quintets (which are his best works). Also considers the wind chamber music a3 to a9. Though the book is old, it still contains many good ideas. Seeks to learn why Krommer, whose quartets were popular during his lifetime and demonstrate a steady evolution from Haydn-like to Beethoven, Rossini, Spohr and Weber-like, was so quickly forgotten by per-formers and historians. The string works passed out of favor because they are second-rate; Krommer did not have Beethoven's genius to keep a long movement going. The wind works passed out of favor, in addition, because by the late 19th century wind chamber music was no longer fashionable.

1062. Wessely, Othmar. "Zur Neuausgabe eines Bläsersextetts von Franz Krommer," in *Die Musikforschung*, xiii (1960), 194-195.
Krommer was one of the most successful Czech musicians in Vienna in the late 18th century, and in the 61 years since Riehl's study much of his music has been repub-lished. Yet points out that a wind sextet (Partita in E-flat), originally published by Peters in Leipzig in 1817 under Krommer's name and republished in Leipzig (Hofmeister, 1955), is definitely not by Krommer (cites Krommer's own statement to that effect).

See Hoff's dissertation {829}.

Joseph Küffner
1777-1856

For information on a clarinet quintet see Ulrich Rau's "Von Wagner, von Weber?" {554}.

Friedrich Kuhlau
1786-1832

*For a catalogue of Kuhlau's chamber music see Dan Fog,
Kompositionen von Fridr. Kuhlau: thematisch-bibliographi-
scher Katalog (Copenhagen: Dan Fog, 1977), page 14 for systematic listing. ML 134.K97A16.1977. ISBN 87-87099-09-8.*

1063. Fairbanks, Ann Kozuch. "Music for Two, Three, and
      Four Flutes by Friedrich Kuhlau." DMA dissertation.
      Ohio State University, 1975. UMI 76-3360. DAI
      xxxvi.8A, p. 4837. 85 pages.
      A biography of Kuhlau, a history of the pre-Boehm
      flute, and analyses of the duets Op. 10a, 39, 80, 81,
      87, 102, and 119 (the last with piano), the trios Op.
      13, 86, and 90, and the flute quartet Op. 103. Lists
      Kuhlau's music categorically, provides publication
      information on it, and translates reviews on Op. 10a
      and 87 from *Allgemeine musikalische Zeitung.*

Elisabeth Jacquet de La Guerre
1659-1729

1064. Bates, Carol Henry. "The Instrumental Music of Eliza-
      beth-Claude Jacquet de la Guerre." PhD dissertation.
      Indiana University, 1978. DAI xxxix.5A, pp. 2605-6.
      3 vols. 899 pages.
      Biography and history of La Guerre's works. Vols. II
      and III are modern editions of 6 unpublished trio sona-
      tas (c.1695), the 14 pieces in *Pieces de Clavecin qui
      peuvent se Joüer sur le Viollon* (1707), and the 6 *Sona-
      tas pour le Viollon et pour le Clavecin* (1707).

Heinrich Eduard Josef von Lannoy
1787-1853

1065. Suppan, Wolfgang. *Heinrich Eduard Josef von Lannoy
      (1787-1853): Leben und Werke,* in *Steirischer Ton-
      künstlerbund, Musik der Steiermark,* Reihe 4: *Beiträge
      zur steirischen Musikforschung,* Band 2. Graz: Akade-
      mische Druck, 1960. HML 3691.60.83. 100 pages.
      A biography and brief discussion of a string quintet, a
      quintet for piano + oboe + clarinet + bassoon + horn, a
      piano trio, a clarinet trio, and others. No analysis
      and not much history.

William Lawes
1602-1645

1066. Lefkowitz, Murray. *William Lawes.* London: Routledge
      and Kegan Paul, 1960. ML 410.L334L4. x + 350 pages,

41 examples, 5 complete movements for consort.
The definitive biography and study of the consort music
of this important English composer.

Jean Marie Leclair
1697-1764

1067. Zaslaw, Neal Alexander. "Materials for the Life and
Works of Jean-Marie Leclair l'Aîné." PhD dissertation. Columbia University, 1970. UMI 73-8995. DAI
xxxiii.10A, p. 5771. 529 pages.
New data on Leclair's biography documented by about 200
items. Leclair was a violinist trained in Italy but
active in France. Discusses the styles of each movement of the 89 works of Leclair's 15 opera (many sonatas) and gives an exhaustive catalogue with incipits
and complete bibliographic information. The major
scholarly work on Leclair.

1068. Preston, Robert Elwyn. "The Forty-eight Sonatas for
Violin and Figured Bass of Jean-Marie Leclair,
l'Aîné." PhD dissertation. University of Michigan,
1959. LC Mic 59-4972. DA xx.5, p. 1821. 656 pages.
A historical and stylistic study of the 4 books of 12
sonatas each (1723, 1728, 1734, and 1738). Discusses
such performance questions as figured bass realization
and ornamentation, and analyzes each of the sonatas.
Notes specifically Leclair's expansion of violin technique (double stops) and unusual harmonic progressions,
his diverse treatment of the standard slow - fast -
slow - fast pattern of movements, and his stylistic
flexibility between Baroque and Rococo.

1069. Appia, Edmond. "The Violin Sonatas of LeClair," in
The Score, no. 3 (1950), 3-19 (a complete sonata on
pages 11-19).
A brief biography and overall stylistic analysis of the
sonatas, primarily for performers. Points to frequent
monothematicism and the cyclic use of a single motive
throughout all 4 movements (43 out of 48 sonatas); ex-
cessive double, triple and even quadruple stopping,
which revolutionized both left and right hand techniques; and duo concertante between bass and violin.
Gives performance suggestions for the reproduced sonata. Emphasizes Leclair's role in founding a truly
French style.

1070. La Laurencie, Lionel de. "Le Rôle de Leclair dans la
Musique Instrumentale," in *La Revue Musicale*, iv, no.
3 (1923), 12-20.
Evaluates Leclair's influence on French violin music
(sonatas in particular) and on other types of music as

well. For example, he eliminates dance movements from
sonatas, and others basically follow him in this.

1071. Zaslaw, Neal. "Handel and Leclair," in *Current Musi-
      cology*, no. 9 (1969), 183-189.
      Demonstrates convincingly Leclair's knowledge of and
      debt to Handel's sonatas and other chamber works.

Jean-Xavier Lefèvre
1763-1829

1072. Harman, Dave Rex. "Six Quartets for Clarinet, Violin,
      Viola, and Cello by Jean-Xavier Lefèvre (1763-1829):
      a Critical Score with Analysis and Historical Per-
      spective." DMA dissertation. University of Roches-
      ter, 1974. UM 75-581. DA xxxv.7A, p. 4586. 2 vols.
      I: vi + 108 pages; II: ii + 151 pages of music.
      Discusses the development of the clarinet in Lefèvre's
      time (he was the first professor of clarinet at the
      Paris Conservatory and had other important performing
      positions) and his role in that development. Uses
      Lefèvre's own *Méthode* (1830) by which to judge him.
      Analyzes the forms and harmonies of the quartets.

René Leibowitz
1913-1972

*For a catalogue of Leibowitz's 9 string quartets and other
chamber pieces see Jacques-Louis Monod, Rene Leibowitz,
1913-1972: a Register of his Music and Writings (Hillsdale
[New York]: Mobart Music Publications, 1983), 32 pages. ML
134.L45M66.1983. Forward in German and English by Rudolf
Kolisch.*

1073. Ogdon, Wilbur Lee. "Series and Structure: an Investi-
      gation into the Purpose of the Twelve-note Row in Se-
      lected Works of Schoenberg, Webern, Krenek and Leibo-
      witz." PhD dissertation. Indiana University, 1955.
      UMI 56-551. DA xvi.2, p. 351. 341 pages.
      Analysis of the 12-tone technique and its influence on
      other factors of composition of the Third String Quar-
      tet and 3 other non-chamber-music works.

György Ligeti
b.1923

*For a brief catalogue of Ligeti's chamber music see Anon.,
György Ligeti: Werkverzeichnis (Mainz: B. Schott's Söhne,
1977), p. 14. ML 134.L5A1.*

1074. Kaufmann, Harald. "Ligetis zweites Streichquartett,"
in *Melos*, xxxvii (1970), 181-186.
A lengthy review of the quartet (1968). Recognizes new
criteria with which to judge the piece -- the old criteria do not apply, even though Ligeti is developing
from his historical antecedents. Seeks in Beethoven's
late quartets answers for the aesthetic questions posed
by Ligeti's music.

1075. Häusler, Josef. "Wenn man heute ein Streichquartett
schreibt," in *Neue Zeitschrift für Musik*, cxxxi
(July-August, 1970), 378-381.
An interview in 1968 with Ligeti, who is about to write
his second string quartet. Mindful of the tradition of
string quartets, Ligeti makes no effort to write Hausmusik. It is difficult to follow Bartók, Schoenberg,
and Berg. Ligeti hopes to create something new, yet to
hark back to tradition (he uses concrete quotations
sometimes -- as in the first string quartet, movement
5, from Bartók -- just as Berg quotes from Wagner's
Tristan in the *Lyric Suite*). Discusses 1-movement or
more than 1-movement string quartets, and static form
and broken-up form. Ligeti characterizes the motion in
each of the 5 movements of his quartet.

1076. Ligeti, György. *In Conversation with Péter Várnai,
Josef Häusler, Claude Samuel and Himself*, trl. Geoffrey Skelton. London: Eulenburg Books, 1983. HML
3788.15.50. ISBN 0-903873-68-0. 140 pages.
A brief biography and list of compositions to 1983
includes a Trio for horn + violin + piano (1982).
Várnai's interview has Ligeti state that his most important work is his second string quartet, and the
interview begins with Ligeti explaining it. The second
interview with Häusler has little to do with chamber
music until near the end where again the second string
quartet is discussed. No more chamber music in the
book. Supplements Kaufmann's and Häusler's works,
above.

1077. Morrison, Charles D. "Stepwise Continuity as a Structural Determinant in György Ligeti's *Ten Pieces for
Wind Quintet*," in *Perspectives of New Music*, xxiv
(Fall-Winter, 1985-1986), 158-182.
How Ligeti creates the structural means for centricity
-- the function of junctures in the music as relating
to a central organization of a piece. In traditional
music these junctures are cadences that relate to the
tonal center. In this work "stepwise connections in
bilinear instrumental parts ... and twelve-note patterns of pitch-class unfolding ... [effect] disected
linear continuities toward established structural
goals."

Pietro Locatelli
1695-1764

1078. Dunning, Albert. *Pietro Antonio Locatelli: der Virtuose und seine Welt.* 2 vols. Buren (The Netherlands): Frits Knuf, 1981. ISBN 90-6027-380-x (paper: 90-6027-411-5). I: xv + 346 pages; II: v + 260 pages (thematic catalogue, iconography, and documents). An in-depth study of Locatelli's sonatas Op. 2, 5, 6 and 8, with a thorough catalogue including bibliography, editions, and much other data. Many musical examples illustrating instrumental technique, harmony, and style. Shows thematic resemblances from one sonata to another. Supplants to some extent Arend Koole, *Pietro Antonio Locatelli da Bergamo 1695-1764: Italiaans Musycqmeester tot Amsterdam* (Amsterdam: Jasonpers Universiteitspers, n.d.).

1079. Calmeyer, John Hendrik. "The Life, Time and Works of Pietro Antonio Locatelli." PhD dissertation. University of North Carolina, 1969. UMI 70-3210. DAI xxx.9A, pp. 3967-68. 481 pages. A detailed account of Locatelli, the late Baroque violinist, and his concerto-caprices. Of particular importance are his trio sonatas for violin + cello + keyboard.

Mathew Locke
c.1630-1677

For a catalogue of Locke's chamber music, see Rosamond E.M. Harding, A Thematic Catalogue of the Works of Mathew Locke with a Calendar of the Main Events of his Life (Oxford: Alden Press, 1971), pages 90-128. ML 134.L79H4.

Loeillet family
18th century

1080. Skempton, Alec. "The Instrumental Sonatas of the Loeillets," in *Music and Letters*, xliii (1962), 206-217.
Establishes the existence of 3 rather than 2 members of the Loeillet family and gives specific bibliographic information on their various sonata publications (including contents): 5 sets of sonatas for solo and continuo (54 works) by Jean Baptiste L'Oeillet de Gant (Amsterdam: Roger, c.1710-1717), 3 sets of trio sonatas (18 works) by John Loeillet (London: Walsh, 1722-1729), and 2 sets of sonatas (6 solo and 6 trio) by Jacques Loeillet (Paris: Boivin, 1728).

Louis Ferdinand, Prince of Prussia
1772-1806

1081. McMurtry, Barbara Hughes. "The Music of Prince Louis Ferdinand." PhD dissertation. University of Illinois, 1972. UMI 72-19880. DAI xxxiii.1A, pp. 351-2. 365 pages, 154 examples.
Eleven of the 13 published works of Louis Ferdinand are chamber music with piano: 3 piano trios, 2 piano quartets, 1 piano quintet, Andante with Variations for piano quintet, Larghetto with variations for piano quintet, a nocturne, an octet, and a rondo. The other 2 pieces are for solo piano. Devotes an entire chapter to the relationship between the music of the Prince and that of Beethoven, Field, Weber, Chopin, and especially Dussek, who was a close friend and edited his posthumous works. Considerable biographical information on this statesman, warrior, and scholar, and descriptions of German Romanticism and Berlin c.1800.

Jean-Baptiste Lully
1632-1687

For a list of his Trios de la Chambre du Roi *(1667ff.)*, see *Herbert Schneider,* Chronologisch-thematisches Verzeichnis sämtlicher Werke von Jean-Baptiste Lully (LWV), *in* Mainzer Studien zur Musikwissenschaft, *Bd. 14 (Tutzing: Hans Schneider, 1981), pages 139-146. ML 134.L956S358. ISBN 3-7952-0323-6.*

Witold Lutoslawski
b.1913

1082. Stucky, Steven. *Lutoslawski and his Music.* Cambridge: Cambridge University Press, 1981. ML 410. L965. ISBN 0-521-22799-2. ix + 252 pages.
An extensive bibliography of works about the music. The only piece of chamber music since 1961 is the string quartet. Detailed analysis for the scholar of motives, quarter tones, microrhythmic gestures, and much more. Finds limited aleatorism, traditional sounds (no attempt to go further than Bartók), and "powerful formal structure."

1083. Selleck, John. "Pitch and Duration as Textural Elements in Lutoslawski's String Quartet," in *Perspectives of New Music*, xiii (1975), no. 2, pp. 150-161.
Finds that Lutoslawski subordinates pitch, rhythm and interval to textural considerations (color) in his string quartet (1964). Analyzes pitch and interval. Pitch is of 4 types: interval classes 1 and 6, all in-

terval classes, octaves, and quarter tones. All elements in conjunction produce a succession of dramati-
cally contrasting sections. There is a logical relationship from one section to the next as individual
elements reappear, but the texture is what is heard as
the main surface element and it contrasts from section
to section.

For other discussions of the String Quartet (1964), see
Michael Coonrod {504}, and Peter Gülke {457}.

Gustav Mahler
1860-1911

For a comparison of Mahler's early piano quartet with those
by Brahms and Dvořák, see Klaus Stahmer's article {857}.

Artur Malawski
1904-1957

1084. Schäffera, Boguslawa, ed. Artur Malawski: Zycie i
      Twórczosc. Cracos: Polskie Wydawnictwo Muzyczne,
      1969. HML 3937.45.80. 419 pages. In Polish.
      A study of the life and works of the Polish violinist
      Malawski, with a special synthesis of his style and do-
      cuments. Includes analyses of specific works by other
      writers, especially Zygmunt Wachowicz, "Il Kwartet
      Smyczkowy" (pages 112-118) and Zbigniew Ciechen, "Trio
      Fortepianowe" (pages 118-126).

Biagio Marini
c.1587-1665

1085. Dunn, Thomas Dickerman. "The Instrumental Music of
      Biagio Marini." PhD dissertation. Yale University,
      1969. RILM 69-3620. UM 70-16260. DA xxxi.3A, p.
      1307. 2 vols. 502 pages.
      Analyzes all Marini's instrumental works with equal em-
      phasis on his more successful solo + continuo and trio
      sonatas (2 trebles + continuo), and his less successful
      canzonas, dances, and variations. Marini uses techni-
      cally difficult violinistic passages sparingly and only
      when they contribute to the music.

1086. _____. "The Sonatas of Biagio
      Marini: Structure and Style," in The Music Review,
      xxxvi (1975), 161-179.
      Reviews the sonata before Marini (especially by Giovan-
      ni Paolo Cima and Salomone Rossi), and describes the
      contents of Marini's Affetti Musicale, op. 1 (1617),
      Sonate, op. 8 (1629), and Sonate, op. 22 (1655). Ana-

lyzes basic forms, textures and styles. An important
introduction to the early history of sonatas.

1087. Stuart, David Henry. "A Comprehensive Performance
Project in Trombone Literature with an Essay Consisting of the Use of the Trombone in Selected Chamber
Compositions of Biagio Marini." DAM dissertation.
University of Iowa, 1981. DAI xlii.5A, pp. 1847-8.
239 pages.
A study of Marini's use of the trombone as a continuo
instrument as well as a concertante instrument -- in
the latter case sometimes for 2 or more trombones with
or without violins.

Frank Martin
1890-1974

*For a systematic list of Martin's works, see Werner Misteli,
ed., Frank Martin: Liste des Oeuvres (Zurich: Archives
Musicales Suisses, 1981), chamber music on pages 35-36.*

1088. Martin, Bernard. *Frank Martin ou la Réalité du Rêve.*
Neuchâtel (Switzerland): Éditions de la Baconnière,
1973. HML 3991.15.52. 230 pages.
A study of Martin's aesthetics, including topics such
as "Responsibility of the Composer," musical language,
lyricism, and so on. A small chapter on chamber music
(pages 174-183) fits the music into Martin's aesthetics. Not a history or musical analysis.

Donald Martino
b.1931

1089. Weinberg, Henry. "Donald Martino: Trio (1959)," in
Perspectives of New Music, ii, no. 1 (1963), 82-90.
Analysis of the trio (violin + clarinet + piano), a 12-
tone work based on hexachords. The analysis is entirely concerned with serialism in the piece.

Bohuslav Martinů
1890-1959

1090. Perry, Richard Kent. "The Violin and Piano Sonatas of
Bohuslav Martinů." DMA dissertation. University of
Illinois, 1973. UM 73-17621. DA xxxiv.2A, pp. 812-
3. 126 pages.
Analyzes in detail the form in 4 of the 5 sonatas (the
first sonata existed only in manuscript in Czechoslovakia in 1972 and Perry had no access to it then).
Characterizes them as neo-classical (sonata in D Minor,
1926), jazz influenced (No. 1, 1929), French influenced

(No. 2, 1931), and American (No. 3, 1944). Includes
correspondence with Angel Reyes who premiered No. 3 (=
5) in New York in 1945.

1091. Pettway, B. Keith. "The Solo and Chamber Compositions
for Flute by Bohuslav Martinů." DMA dissertation.
University of Southern Mississippi, 1980. UMI 81-
09889. DAI xli.11A, p. 4537. 154 pages.
Biography, bibliography, and description of the Scherzo
(1929) and Sonata No. 1 (1945), both for flute + piano.

For a discussion of Martinů's Sonatina for clarinet + piano
see Jennings's dissertation {1207}.

1092. Cable, Susan Lee. "The Piano Trios of Bohuslav Martinů." DA dissertation. University of Northern
Colorado, 1984. UMI 84-29822. DAI xlv.10A, p. 3022.
203 pages.
Analyzes the 4 piano trios in context with his other
works and with other piano trios of the 20th century.
Discusses his use of motivic cells, neo-classicism,
folk music, and rhythmic drive.

1093. Kerman, Joseph. ["The Chamber Music of Bohuslav
Martinů,"] in The Musical Quarterly, xxxv (1949),
301-305.
An informed, intelligent review of chamber works by
Martinů performed while the composer was in residence
at Princeton. Notes Martinů's "real sensitivity to
harmonic effect" and his "nice sense of musical color."
Finds the second cello sonata (1945) weak and the 3
madrigals (violin + viola, 1947) "sparkling, delight-
ful" if unpretentious; concentrates on the Piano
Quintet (1944) as more serious and distant.

Michele Mascitti
c.1664-1760

1094. Dean, Robert Henry. "The Music of Michele Mascitti
(ca.1664-1760): a Neapolitan Violinist in Paris."
PhD dissertation. University of Iowa, 1970. UMI 71-
5733. DAI xxxi.9A, p. 4815. 2 vols. 662 pages.
Discusses the life and works of Mascitti, which include
99 sonatas for violin + continuo, 1 divertissement for
violin + continuo, 12 trio sonatas, and 4 concerti a
sei (all published 1704-1738). Among the earliest sonatas published in France, they are conservative in
technique and style and show Corelli's influence. Vol.
II reproduces 7 solo, 3 trio sonatas and 4 concertos.

1095. Ullom, Jack Ralph. "Michele Mascitti: an Analysis and
Performing Edition of Three Sonatas for Violin and
Cembalo, Opus 1, Nos. 1 and 3, and Opus 4, No. 8."

DMA dissertation. University of Oregon, 1978. DAI
xxxix.10A, p. 5796. 216 pages.
A study of the life and sonatas of Mascitti, who was a
pupil of Corelli. Considers the sonatas in context of
the Baroque solo violin sonata and the violin and bow
of the time. (Mascitti's Op. 7, 1727, are the first
concerti grossi composed and published in France.)

Daniel Gregory Mason
1873-1953

1096. Mason, Daniel Gregory. "Adventures in Chamber Music,"
in *Music in My Time and Other Reminiscences* (Freeport
[New York]: Books for Libraries Press, 1938; reprint
1970), pages 163-178. ML 410.M397A2.
Recounts his trials in writing a violin + piano sonata
and piano quartet. **Personal reminiscences of daily**
events, Philip Hale's attack on his quartet, a lengthy
interview with Paderewski, and others's opinions,
covering the years 1907-1911.

Nicholas Maw
b.1935

1097. Payne, Anthony. "Nicholas Maw's String Quartet," in
Tempo, no. 74 (Fall, 1985), 5-11.
A detailed, technical analysis of themes and form.

Ascanio Mayone
c.1570-1627

1098. Kelton, Raymond Harrison. "The Instrumental Music of
Ascanio Mayone." PhD dissertation. North Texas
State University, 1961. LC Mic 61-1297. DA xxi.11,
pp. 3480-1. 381 pages (DA = 389 pages).
The biography of this Neapolitan composer. Transcribes
all his known instrumental works, which are 18 ensemble
ricercare (a3; 1606) -- important early 17th-century
representatives of chamber music.

Johann Georg Anton Mederitsch (= Gallus)
1752-1835

1099. Aigner, Theodor. "Johann G.A. Mederitsch: sein Leben
und sein kammermusikalisches Schaffen mit thematischen Verzeichnis." PhD dissertation. University of
Salzburg, 1973. The catalogue published as *Thematisches Verzeichnis der Werke von Johann Mederitsch
detto Gallus*, in *Publikationen des Instituts für
Musikwissenschaft der Universität Salzburg*, Band 8.

Munich: Musikverlag Emil Katzbichler, 1974.   ML 134.
M49A5. ISBN 3-87397-102-X. xxviii + 285 pages.
Dissertation not seen. A private music teacher in
Vienna and Lemberg, Mederitsch was a writer of some
Singspiels and operas, Catholic liturgical music, and a
large number of instrumental pieces including typical
chamber music of the time. He was known to Mozart,
collaborated with Schikaneder, and taught Franz
Grillparzer and Mozart's son. Includes Grillparzer's
description of W.A. Mozart and a letter from Mozart's
son to Moscheles discussing his father, W.A. Mozart.

Felix Mendelssohn
1809-1847

1100. Horton, John. *The Chamber Music of Mendelssohn*, in
      The Musical Pilgrim. London: Geoffrey Cumberlege of
      Oxford University Press, 1946. MT 145.M5H6. Reprint
      Mendelssohn Chamber Music. London: BBC/ Seattle:
      University of Washington Press, 1972. MT 145.M5H6.
      1972. 65 pages, 40 examples.
      An amazingly thorough treatment of Mendelssohn's cham-
      ber music for such short space. The genesis and first
      performances of the music and sympathetic criticism of
      the individual pieces (sonatas, trios, quartets,
      quintets, sextet and octet).

*For a non-technical introduction to Mendelssohn's chamber
music see Andrew Porter's essay in Alec Robertson, ed.,
Chamber Music {160}.*

1101. McDonald, John Allen. "The Chamber Music of Felix
      Mendelssohn-Bartholdy." PhD dissertation. North-
      western University, 1970. UM 71-1916. DA xxxi.8A,
      p. 4205. I: vii + 333 pages; II: 159 pages of music.
      An analysis of 57 chamber works, many of which survive
      only in manuscript, and a thematic catalogue. Divides
      the chamber music into 4 groups: ensemble works with
      piano, string quartets, solo instrument + piano, and
      works for larger string ensemble. Describes each
      piece. Also includes 140 reviews of Mendelssohn's
      chamber music taken from periodicals 1824-1849 arranged
      by year, a survey of fugues for string quartet, and
      transcriptions and facsimiles.

1102. Krummacher, Friedhelm. *Mendelssohn - der Komponist:
      Studien zur Kammermusik für Streicher*. Munich: Wil-
      helm Fink, 1978. ML 410.M5K8. ISBN 3-7705-1431-09.
      612 pages, 160 examples, facsimiles of Mendelssohn's
      manuscripts and transcriptions. Habilitation disser-
      tation. Erlangen-Nürnberg University, 1972.
      Huge, scholarly study of the chamber music; verbose,
      but lots of information and detailed treatment of

specific problems. In 3 parts: I: chamber music in
Mendelssohn's total work, origins of the chamber music,
autograph sketches and the compositional process; II:
themes and how he conceives them and develops them in
the different movements; III: the form of the movements. At the end assesses Mendelssohn historically
and aesthetically, especially in Germany, where anti-
semitism clouded the German mind. Challenges Eric
Werner's hypothesis that a reevaluation of Mendelssohn
will come from new and more careful biographical information and new assessments of his early works; rather,
that reevaluation must come from a better understanding
of the mature masterworks. The chamber music belongs
to the mature masterworks. It must be evaluated not
only in terms of historical aesthetics but also in
terms of present-day aesthetics. Notes the peculiari-
ties of Mendelssohn, which, in so far as he is consistent with them, form the basis of his own style; there
are no absolutes in aesthetics or in criticism of his
music.

1103. Todd, Ralph Larry. "The Instrumental Music of Felix
Mendelssohn-Bartholdy: Selected Studies Based on
Primary Sources." PhD dissertation. Yale University, 1979. DAI xl.6A, p. 2978. 558 pages.
Analyzes in detail Mendelssohn's workbook 1819-1821
with composition exercises written for C.F. Zelter, and
studies among other genres the string octet and string
quintet. Much previously unpublished documentation.
The chamber music is more traditional than other
genres.

1104. Filosa, Albert James, Jr. "The Early Symphonies and
Chamber Music of Felix Mendelssohn Bartholdy." PhD
dissertation. Yale University, 1970. RILM 70-1944.
UM 71-16236. DA xxxi.12A, p. 6646. i + 195 pages
Analyzes works written by Mendelssohn between the ages
of 11 and 16, considers them as music and as products
of a prodigy, and discusses Mendelssohn's family background and musical training. Looks for early signs of
characteristics of the composer's later musical works.

1105. Kohlhase, Hans. "Studien zur Form in den Streichquartetten von Felix Mendelssohn Bartholdy," in *Hamburger
Jahrbuch für Musikwissenschaft*, ii (1977), 75-104.
Dismisses Wilcke's dissertation {1106} as incomplete
and McDonald's dissertation {1101} as superficial.
Considers cyclic and sonata forms in the movements of
the string quartets (21 of 32 are in sonata form). An
exhaustive, detailed, technical analysis of form for
the scholar. Notes that cyclic form -- use of the same
motives in more than one movement -- is found in Mendelssohn's earliest quartets, then abandoned.

1106. Wilcke, Gerhard. *Tonalität und Modulation im Streich-
      quartett Mendelssohns und Schumanns.* Leipzig: Carl
      Merseburger, 1933. ML 1160.W66.T7.1933. 87 pages.
      Highly technical, theoretical treatise on various as-
      pects of tonality and modulation as evinced in the 31
      movements of Schumann's and Mendelssohn's quartets.
      A methodical presentation, with graphs and statistics,
      of the problems of tonal organization in specific works
      and of chromaticism and chromatic modulation in an em-
      phatically tonal style. Studies modulation in the
      music itself and then in the light of theories by Dehn,
      Tiersch, Wienand, Richter, Sering, Schmitz, Ernst
      Kurth, Hauptmann, Jadassohn, Helm, Louis and Thuille,
      Weigl, and Tenschert. Shows how in most cases the
      rules of these theorists do not apply to Mendelssohn
      and Schumann. Agrees with Schenker that chromaticism
      strengthens tonality and is not a non-tonal intrusion
      into tonal music. Assumes the reader knows the quar-
      tets; prime interest is in the theory, not the music.

1107. Molnár, Antal. "Die beiden Klaviertrios in d-Moll von
      Schumann (op. 63) und Mendelssohn (op. 49): eine
      Stiluntersuchung," in *Sammelbände der Robert-
      Schumann-Gesellschaft,* i (Leipzig: 1961), 79-85.
      Compares the 2 trios in tonal ethos, melody, harmony,
      treatment of theme, and form. Mendelssohn's (1838)
      came first and borrows from Mozart; Schumann's (1847)
      borrows from Mendelssohn. Mendelssohn's is found to be
      superficial melancholy, while Schumann's is deep and
      dark. Designed for the educated layperson.

1108. Whittaker, W. Gillies. "Mendelssohn's Octet," in *The
      Musical Times,* lxxiv (1933), 322-325, 427-429.
      Regards chamber music as in general too intimate, too
      introspective for Mendelssohn. A detailed analysis of
      the octet, though presented mostly measure by measure.

1109. Pound, Gomer. "Mendelssohn and the Baermanns," in
      Woodwind World, ii (May, 1958), 4.
      A brief comment on the dedication of *Concertpiece No.
      1,* Op. 113, in F Minor by Mendelssohn to Baermann,
      which shows close ties between the composer and the
      father-and-son clarinet virtuosos.

Martin-Joseph Mengal
1784-1851

1110. Andrews, Ralph Edwin, Jr. "The Woodwind Quintets of
      Martin-Joseph Mengal." PhD dissertation. Florida
      State University, 1970. ADD, 1971-1972, p. 267. v +
      305 pages.
      Not seen.

Olivier Messiaen
b.1908

1111. Bernstein, David Stephen. "Messiaen's *Quatuor pour le Fin du Temps*: an Analysis based upon Messiaen's Theory of Rhythm and his Use of Modes of Limited Transposition." DMA dissertation. Indiana University, 1974. RILM 74-633. 133 pages.
Uses this famous piece for violin + clarinet + cello + piano to test Messiaen's theories of rhythm and modes as stated in his *La Technique de mon Langue Musical* (Paris: Alphonse Leduc, 1944), trl. by J. Satterfield, *The Technique of My Musical Language* (Paris: Leduc, 1956), MT 6.M4482. Analyzes each of the 8 movements of the quartet with regard to pitch and rhythm and assesses the piece's contribution to contemporary music.

1112. Ross, Mark Alan. "The Perception of Multitonal Levels in Olivier Messiaen's *Quatuor pour la Fin du Temps* and Selected Vocal Compositions." PhD dissertation. University of Cincinnati, 1977. DAI xxxviii.9A, p. 5117. 253 pages.
An analysis of the quartet in light of Messiaen's own theoretical principles as stated in his *La Technique de mon Langue Musical*. Considers the psychological relationship of colors and sounds especially in movement 2 of the quartet. A detailed, technical analysis of a much talked-about work.

Nikolai Yakovlevitch Miaskovsky
1881-1950

1113. Nikolaeva, N. *Trinadtsatyi Kvartet*, in *V Pomosh Slushteliu Muzyki N. IA. Miaskovskogo*. Moscow: Muzyka, 1953. MT 145.M6N5. 43 pages. In Russian.
Biography and overall works, then a general description of the thirteenth string quartet. It discusses more about moods than technical features.

Darius Milhaud
1892-1974

For a catalogue of Milhaud's works including chamber pieces, see Madeleine Milhaud, Catalogue des Oeuvres de Darius Milhaud (Geneva/Paris: Slatkine, 1982), 251 pages. ML 134.M55M5.1982.

1114. Mason, Colin. "The Chamber Music of Milhaud," in *The Musical Quarterly*, xliii (1957), 326-341.
Historical data and a few comments on the styles of Milhaud's 18 string quartets: an enormous output, often dull to listen to but always well-written and interest-

ing to play. Comparison with Hindemith. Also touches
on string quintets and trios and sonatas for piano and
1 soloist (violin, clarinet, oboe).

1115. Cherry, Paul Wyman. "The String Quartets of Darius
        Milhaud." PhD dissertation. University of Colorado,
        1980. UMI 81-03081. DAI xli.8A, p. 3312. 536
        pages.
      After completing his eighteenth string quartet in 1951,
      Milhaud claimed that he had no system of composition
      and his works demonstrate no progression or growth.
      Shows that Milhaud did indeed have systems, which he
      used regularly in his quartets, and though the progres-
      sion is not a straight line, there is growth. Includes
      background on musical aesthetics in France, analyses of
      the 18 quartets, and an extensive bibliography.

1116. McCarthy, Peter Joseph. "The Sonatas of Darius Mil-
        haud." PhD dissertation. Catholic University, 1972.
        UM 73-4353. DA xxxiii.8A, pp. 4458-9. 147 pages.
      Abstract unclear if solo keyboard only or ensemble
      sonatas are being discussed. Divides the sonatas into
      3 chronological groups: 1911-1927, 1931-1945, and after
      1949, and finds specific stylistic differences among
      the groups. The early ones are dramatic and tonal, the
      middle ones neo-Baroque and polytonal, and the late
      ones lighter, shorter, less traditional, and frequently
      modal.

1117. Laughton, John Charles. "The Woodwind Music of Darius
        Milhaud." DMA dissertation. University of Iowa,
        1980. UMI 81-14323. DAI xlii.1A, p. 14. 86 pages.
      Complete list of the woodwind music with scoring, date
      and place of composition, publisher, duration, movement
      titles, discography, and historical information. Ana-
      lyzes Sonata Op. 47 for flute + oboe + clarinet + piano
      (1918), Sonatina Op.100 for clarinet + piano (1927),
      Suite Op. 157b for violin + clarinet + piano (1936),
      and 2 non-chamber pieces.

*See Nancy Mackenzie's "Selected Clarinet Solo and Chamber
Music of Darius Milhaud" {1497}.*

1118. Petrella, Robert Louis. "The Solo and Chamber Music
        for Clarinet by Darius Milhaud." DMA dissertation.
        University of Maryland, 1979. UMI 80-16728. DAI
        xli.2A, p. 455. 105 pages.
      Contrasts the Sonatine Op. 100 for clarinet + piano
      with the clarinet concerto Op. 230, and discusses the
      clarinet as part of the woodwind ensembles of the 1918
      sonata for flute + oboe + clarinet + piano and the 1958
      Divertissement for woodwind quintet. Other pieces for
      clarinet also considered. Historical background for

each work and analysis of tonality, form, thematic treatment, rhythm, and clarinet technique.

For a discussion of Milhaud's Duo Concertante *for clarinet + piano see Jennings's dissertation {1207}.*

1119. Helm, Everett. "Milhaud: xiv + xv = Octet," in *Melos*, xxii (1955), 71-75.
Points out the pros and cons of Milhaud's spontaneous outpouring of easy-flowing music, which is fresh but sometimes also superficial. Describes motives, form, and counterpoint of these 2 quartets, which can also be performed as an octet (1949). Finds quartet no. 14 successful, no. 15 less so, and the octet as sounding like 2 quartets played simultaneously.

Bernhard Molique
1802-1869

1120. Schröter, Fritz. *Bernhard Molique und seine Instrumentalkompositionen: seine künstlerische und historische Persönlichkeit: ein Beitrag zur Geschichte der Instrumentalmusik des 19. Jahrhunderts, mit einem Verzeichnis aller nachweisbaren Werke Molique's.* Stuttgart: Berthold und Schwerdtner, 1923. ML 410. M687S3. ix + 125 pages.
A biography and analysis of the music of Molique, an important German violinist and composer, pupil of Spohr, who was also active in London. Among his compositions are string quartets, violin duets, a flute quintet, a piano quartet, piano trios, violin + piano sonatas, and fugues (1 a4 and 6 a3). Includes some photos, musical examples, a catalogue of his works, bibliography of newspaper criticism of Molique, list of his students, letters to and from Molique by important musicians, and a concert calendar.

Jean-Joseph Cassanéa de Mondonville
1711-1772

1121. Borroff, Edith. "The Instrumental Works of Jean-Joseph Cassanéa de Mondonville." PhD dissertation. University of Michigan, 1959. LC mic 59-2099. DA xix.12, pp. 3319-20. 2 vols. I: 351 pages; II: 55 pages of music.
Studies in detail Mondonville's trio sonatas Opus 2 (1734), sonatas for violin with continuo, Op. 1 and 4 (1733 and 1738), and his sonatas for harpsichord with accompaniment of violin Op. 3 and 5 (1734 and 1748). The last is among the first sonatas for violin and obligato keyboard (completely written-out keyboard).

Bassols Xavier Montsalvatge
b.1911

1122. Klugherz, Laura Jean. "A Performer's Analysis of
      Three Works for Violin and Piano by Contemporary
      Spanish Composers." DMA dissertation. University of
      Texas, 1981. UMI 81-19244. DAI xlii.3A, p. 909.
      Analyzes the style, compositional procedures, and
      violin technique of Rodrigo's Sonata Pimpante (1966),
      Turina's Movimiento (1978), and Montsalvatge's Para-
      frasis Concertante (1972). Includes biography.

Wolfgang Amadeus Mozart
1756-1791

For a catalogue of Mozart's compositions with chamber music
included, see Ludwig Ritter von Köchel, Chronologisch-thematisches Verzeichnis sämtlicher Tonwerke Wolfgang Amadé Mozarts (6th ed. Wiesbaden: Breitkopf & Härtel, 1964), cxliii
+ 1024 pages. ML 134.M9K55.1964. Also useful for identifying themes from Mozart's chamber music is George R. Hill
and Murray Gould, A Thematic Locator for Mozart's Works, as
Listed in Koechel's Chronologisch-thematisches Verzeichnis-
Sixth Edition, in Music Indexes and Bibliographies, no. 1
(Hackensack [New Jersey]: Joseph Boonin, Inc., 1970), vii +
76 pages. ML 134.M9H54.1970. For a bibliography of writings about Mozart's chamber music see Rudolph Angermüller
and Otto Schneider, eds., Mozart-Bibliographie (bis 1970),
in Mozart-Jahrbuch 1975, vii + 363 pages, ISBN 3-7618-0516-
0. For a non-technical introduction to Mozart's chamber
music see Eric Blom's essay in Alec Robertson, ed., Chamber
Music {160}.

1123. King, A. Hyatt. Mozart's Chamber Music, in BBC Music
      Guides, no. 4. London: BBC, 1968/Seattle: University
      of Washington Press, 1969. MT 145.M7K55.1969. 68
      pages, 18 examples.
      A non-technical overview of the sonatas for 2 instru-
      ments, string quartets, piano + string combinations,
      and some other genres of Mozart's chamber music.

1124. Keller, Hans. "The Chamber Music," in H.C. Robbins
      Landon and Donald Mitchell, The Mozart Companion (New
      York: Oxford University Press, 1956; reprint New
      York: W.W. Norton, 1969), pp. 90-137. ML 410.
      M9L24.1956.
      Mostly an analysis of the string quartets, especially
      K.387, based on theories of Reti, Schenker and Schoen-
      berg as synthesized by Keller and directed toward the
      chamber music performer. Also discusses briefly the
      string quintets, string trio and duos, and works invol-
      ving flute, oboe and clarinet with strings. Believes
      the purpose of analysis is to find the unity of a work
      in its diversity; following Freud (Interpretation of
      Dreams) seeks the latent unity behind the manifest di-

versity of the chamber piece as it unfolds. Highly
subjective (for example, dismisses the early Mozart
string quartets as "quite abominable" and accepted by
"our age's unmusical musicological snobbery"). Gives
performance suggestions based on the nature of motives
that are only fully explained in other contexts; "all
great music is latently monothematic and, if in more
than one movement, cyclic." An interesting, penetrating analysis that is thought-provoking even if contro-
versial; a little forbidding at first sight, it is not
beyond the comprehension of serious students and more
advanced performers.

1125. _____. "Mozart -- the Revolutionary Chamber
Musician," in *The Musical Times*, cxxii (1981), 465-
468.
Because Mozart has been unequalled in the sureness of
his ear, some of his innovations came out so perfect
that he left no room for real followers. For example,
the piano quartet K.478 and the viola quintets, though
the latter had Mendelssohn for a successor. Points to
the [almost] unique use of mutes in K.516. A revolutionary musician, however, must have followers, so
points out structural innovations of Mozart's that led
to later things; for example, the key and themes interacting in inverse order for the second "theme" of the
first movement of K.516.

*See Siegmund-Schultze's study {457} on how Mozart conceived
of the term chamber music.*

String Quartets:

1126. Dunhill, Thomas F. *Mozart's String Quartets*, in *The
Musical Pilgrim*. London: Geoffrey Cumberlege for
Oxford University Press, 1927. 49 pages. Reprint
Westport (Connecticut): Greenwood Press, 1970. MT
145.M7D9. 44 pages, 137 examples.
Brief musical descriptions of what the author believes
to be the salient moments in each of the string quar-
tets. Meagre historical information.

1127. King, Alexander Hyatt. "Mozart's String Quartets," in
The Listener, xxxiv (1945), 633.
Traces briefly but cogently the development of Mozart's
quartet writing from his first one in 1770 K. 80 under
Italian influence, and shows the gradual influence of
Haydn with, among other things, the actual copying of
Haydn's Op. 20 No. 4 Finale for the slow movement of K.
168, the addition of minuets to his second set of quar-
tets K.168-173, and the use of a final fugue in K.173.
But the influence of Op. 33 on Mozart took longer to
digest: 1782-1785 -- the reconciliation of Mozart's

Italian training and vocal instincts with Haydn's instrumental techniques and "Germanic tone." The last 3
quartets seem to be a reversion to the earlier quartets, but there are great movements here, too. A
well-written, sensible, brief introduction to the
Mozart quartets for anyone.

1128. Abert, Hermann. "Sechs unter Mozarts Namen neu aufge-
      fundene Streichquartette," in *Mozart-Jahrbuch*, iii
      (1929), 9-58.
      An attempt to verify these 6 quartets that once be-
      longed to Johann Anton André, who published Mozart's
      "Nachlass." The 6 are Italian quartets in 2 or 3 move-
      ments, which would make them similar to Mozart's earli-
      est quartets, but after comparing these 6 to the au-
      thentic ones, it seems clear they are not Mozart's.

1129. Finscher, Ludwig. "Mozarts 'Mailänder' Streichquar-
      tette," in *Die Musikforschung*, xix (1966), 270-283.
      Proves that the 3 quartets K.Anhang 20.01, 20.02, and
      20.04 are, like 20.03, not by Mozart but by Joseph
      Schuster. Discusses these and other quartets of
      Schuster.

1130. Emerson, Isabell Putnam. "The Role of Counterpoint in
      the Formation of Mozart's Late Style." PhD disserta-
      tion. Columbia University, 1977. DAI xxxviii.2A,
      pp. 536-7. 330 pages.
      Studies the development of Mozart's contrapuntal
      writing in his Vienna years 1781-1791, the result of
      Mozart's contact with the music of J.S. Bach and his
      contrapuntal studies 1781-1783. Looks closely at
      string quartet K.387, string quintets K.593 and 614,
      concerto K.459 and symphony K.551. Mozart's new con-
      ceptions based on unification of a small amount of ma-
      terial are best exemplified in his string quartets
      first and then later in other types of music. See
      {496} and {495} for other discussions of Mozart's use
      of fugue and counterpoint in his string quartets.

*For important lessons to be learned from the autographs of
Mozart's string quartets, see the studies by Ludwig Finscher, Marius Flothuis, Alan Tyson, and Christoph Wolff in
Christoph Wolff, ed. The String Quartets of Haydn, Mozart,
and Beethoven {617}.*

1131. Gerstenberg, Walter. "Über den langsamen Einleitungs-
      satz in Mozarts Instrumentalmusik," in Hans Zingerle,
      ed., *Festschrift Wilhelm Fischer zum 70. Geburtstag
      überreicht im Mozartjahr 1956*, in *Innsbrucker Bei-
      träge zur Kulturwissenschaft*, Sonderheft 3 (Inns-

bruck: Sprachwissenschaftliche Seminar der Universität Innsbruck, 1956), pp. 25-32. ML 55.F5Z5.
Discusses the special nature of slow introductions to Allegro movements by late 18th- and 19th-century composers, and lists those symphonic and chamber works by Mozart which use it -- mostly in works written after Mozart moved to Vienna (chamber works K.171, 424, 452, 454, 465, 593, serenades, and divertimenti).

1132. Salvetti, Guido. "Mozart e il Quartetto Italiano," in Friedrich Lippmann, ed., *Colloquium "Mozart und Italien" (Rom 1974)*, in *Analecta Musicologica*, xviii (Köln: Arno Volk, 1978), pages 271-289.
Points to the large number of Italian composers of chamber music and other instrumental music which Mozart certainly knew on his early trips to Paris and London before his trip to Italy in 1770 (see {1133} for a better discussion of the first quartet). The first 13 quartets show the influence of Boccherini, but afterwards Mozart regards both Italian and French string quartets as too much concertant and so turned increasingly to Haydn. When Mozart writes flute quartets and even the oboe quartet, however, he turns to Italian cantilena melodies, and while the later Mozart quartets are far removed from Italian styles, nevertheless the cantabile element (from Italy) often occurs.

1133. Finscher, Ludwig. "Mozarts erstes Streichquartett: Lodi, 15 März 1770," in Friedrich Lippmann, ed., *Colloquium "Mozart und Italien" (Rom 1974)*, in *Analecta Musicologica*, xviii (Köln: Arno Volk, 1978), pages 246-270.
Traditionally (Saint-Foix and others) this first Mozart quartet is regarded as simply an imitation of Sammartini and in no way interesting. Reviews the history of the quartet and, while not claiming it to be a great work, finds some interest in its story. Written originally in 3 movements at 7 p.m. on March 15, 1770, it had a fourth movement added between 1772 and 1774, and Mozart kept the piece with him even in 1778 after he had already written 12 more mature quartets and other chamber music under the influence of Haydn. Shows no Sammartini influence; much more like a Boccherini trio (not quartet) where the order of movements remains slow - fast - minuet and all are in the same key. Analyzes the historical position of each movement: 2 Italian, 1 Austrian, and 1 later French movement. Therefore a conscious attempt by Mozart to mix styles, not according to precepts of Quantz so as to create a German style, but to show his abilities in different national styles and so that the French would accept him with his use of a French movement.

1134. Einstein, Alfred. "Mozart's Ten Celebrated String
      Quartets: First Authentic Edition, Based on Auto-
      graphs in the British Museum and on Early Prints," in
      The Music Review, iii (1942), 159-169.
      A preface to Einstein's edition which was delayed be-
      cause of the War. A history of the autographs of the
      quartets (in the Paul Hirsch Library, now in the Bri-
      tish Library), which show that the printed editions of
      the 19th and much of the early 20th century are inaccu-
      rate. A comparison of the earliest 3 prints (under
      Mozart's supervision) and the autographs; prefers the
      autographs.

1135. Gerber, Rudolf. "Harmonische Probleme in Mozarts
      Streichquartetten," in *Mozart-Jahrbuch*, ii (1924),
      55-77.
      A look at the harmony of Mozart's string quartets in
      isolation from meter and form, in order to see if there
      is an independent harmonic system. Does not mean to
      imply that harmony is not interrelated with meter and
      form. Concerned only with the 10 mature quartets K.
      387, 421, 428, 458, 464, 465, 499, 575, 589, and 590.
      While Haydn achieved thematic development in Op. 33
      (1782), Mozart achieved harmonic changes or modula-
      tions. While Haydn and Beethoven found in metric
      structure the logic for their formal drive, Mozart
      found this in the harmonic and melodic succession. The
      choice of unexpected modulations to unexpected tonali-
      ties gives the piece its inner motion. This play is
      the most outstanding side of Mozart's artistic
      personality.

The Debt to Haydn:

1136. Cherbuliez, Antoine-Elisée. "Bemerkungen zu den
      'Haydn'-Streichquartetten Mozarts und Haydns 'Russi-
      schen' Streichquartetten," in *Mozart-Jahrbuch* (1959),
      pages 28-45.
      Reviews the literature on Mozart's debt to Haydn's Op.
      33, finds it wanting, and thus presents a study as to
      what degree the debt is true based on Mozart's own
      statements as well as the works themselves. Points out
      the personal relationship between the 2 and their simi-
      lar reactions to their times. Generalizes about basic
      structural aspects -- tonality and form -- and finds
      the similarities between the 2 composers, which are
      then compared in a table. Extensive bibliography.

1137. Cuyler, Louise E. "Mozart's Six Quartets Dedicated to
      Haydn," in Gustave Reese and Rose Brandel, eds., *The
      Commonwealth of Music in Honor of Curt Sachs* (New
      York: The Free Press/London: Collier-Macmillan,
      1965), pp. 293-299. ML 55.S13R4.

Mozart's 6 quartets are often unjustly ranked as imita-
tions of Haydn's Op. 33 rather than as pioneer works in
their own right. Mozart preferred concertos and operas
-- contrasting bodies of sound, so the homogeneous
quartet presented a problem. Thus Mozart's juxtaposi-
tions relied on musical elements: chromatic vs. diatonic, abrupt rhythmic transformations, unusual tonal
levels. Also, besides Haydn, Mozart was influenced by
J.S. Bach. Each of the 6 quartets is considered in
turn, with the opening of K.465 as the culmination.
Technical but very readable.

1138. Siegmund-Schultze, Walther. "Mozarts 'Haydn-Quartet-
te,'" in Bence Szabolcsi and Dénes Bartha, eds., *Bericht über die internationale Konferenz zum Andenken
Joseph Haydns (Budapest 1957)* (Budapest: Verlag der
Ungarischen Akademie der Wissenschaften, 1961), pp.
137-146. ML 410.H4M15.
Not an attempt to identify Mozart's models nor to compare Mozart and Haydn quartets nor to analyze the form
and motivic structure, but an attempt to describe what
Mozart was trying to express in the music, especially
as a dramatist in music. A dramatic intensity pervades
all movements, in contrast to other moods in Haydn.
The uniqueness of each work is perceptible in the re-
shaping of traditional forms, in the careful choice and
contrast of themes, and in the demonic *Sturm und Drang*
tones of pure humanity (chromaticism, minor keys). A
characterization of each of the quartets and of Mozart
himself: the great dramatic realist.

1139. Bruce, I.M. "Notes from an Analysis of Mozart's *Quartet in G Major, K.387*," in *The Music Review*, x
(1949), 97-110.
A fairly rigorous analysis of the forms of the movements based on harmony and melody.

1140. Grebe, Karl. "Das 'Urmotiv' bei Mozart: Strukturprin-
zipien im G-Dur-Quartett KV 387," in *Acta Mozartiana*,
vi (1959), 9-14.
The use of a single germ motive to generate a whole
movement is rare in Mozart's music; its use in the
"Jupiter" Symphony is extraordinary and not found in
any other of his symphonies. In the G-major String
Quartet, however, Mozart uses not a germ motive for all
4 movements but rather a single germ idea, the antithesis between a standard diatonic interval of a third,
fourth, fifth, sixth or octave and a chromatic line.
This is a dialectic antithesis.

1141. Mitchell, William J. "Giuseppe Sarti and Mozart's
Quartet, K.421," in *Current Musicology*, no. 9 (1969),
147-153.

Reviews a critical account of Mozart's 2 quartets K.421
and 465 by Sarti and shows that minute quibbling over
details often obscures the logic of the details in a
much broader context. A good lesson for the theorist
or historian who loses touch with the larger issues.

1142. Elvers, Rudolf. "Ein unbekannter Entwurf zum Menuett
      des Jagd-Quartetts," in *Mitteilungen der Internatio-
      nalen Stiftung Mozarteum* no. 18, (Dec. 1956), 2-5.
      About the discovery of a manuscript page from the
      Minuet of Mozart's String Quartet K.458 in an autograph
      book, which is also bound with a manuscript of a Haydn
      Scottish song. The start of a movement which was then
      discarded. Briefly compares the finished version with
      this scrap.

1143. Klockow, Erich. "Mozarts Streichquartett in C-Dur,"
      in *Deutsche Musikkultur*, vi (1941-1942), 67-75.
      Finds Mozart moving from a sonata form with loosely
      connected elements (1782-1783) to a tightly-knit sonata
      form (Jan. 1785) where the first theme leads to the
      rest of the movement and where the whole is more than
      the sum of its individual parts. While this is evident
      in the A-major quartet, Mozart handles it more natural-
      ly in the C-major. A scholarly analysis, not without
      some subjective reactions.

1144. _____. "Mozarts Streichquartett in A-Dur,"
      in *Mozart-Jahrbuch*, iii (1929), 209-241.
      Reviews Mozart's struggle with sonata form from 1781 to
      1784 wherein he recognizes the need for motivic deve-
      lopment, not just big beautiful themes. Then analyzes
      the A-major Quartet K.464 to see how the motives are
      handled. An intensive study of the style and form of
      the piece as affected by the motivic treatment. The
      individual motives serve not only as passing moments of
      interest but are subsumed into a whole, an uninter-
      rupted functional unity.

1145. Vertrees, Julie Anne. "Mozart's String Quartet K.465:
      the History of a Controversy," in *Current Musicology*,
      no. 17 (1974), 96-114.
      Opposed to Mitchell's largely theoretical put-down of
      Sarti's criticism of K.421 (see {1141}). Gives a most-
      ly historical account of the criticism of the opening
      of K.465 ("The Dissonance"), which extends from a 1787
      criticism to a 1925 attack by Ernest Newman (who consi-
      dered Sarti correct and Mozart wrong).

1146. Chailley, Jacques. "Sur la Signification du Quatuor
      de Mozart K.465, dit 'Les Dissonances,' et du 7ème
      Quatuor de Beethoven," in Bjorn Hjelmborg and Soren-
      sen, eds., *Natalicia Musicologica Knud Jeppesen*

Septuagenario (Copenhagen: Wilhelm Hansen, 1962), pp. 283-292. ML 160.N3J3. Since both quartets shocked their audiences initially and are not shocking today, perhaps only because of the fame of their authors, a comparison of the 2 works to see if the cause of the initial shock lies in the similarity of their initial conception. While the 18th and 19th centuries deplored the "mistakes" of Mozart's opening, the 20th century regrets that Mozart did not continue the dissonances beyond the introduction. Why did Mozart do it? Believes it represents the Masonic initiation (= introduction) where Mozart was blindfolded and made to endure the trials by land, water, air and fire, after which (= rest of quartet) he removed the blindfold and suddenly confronted the light of revelation. Mozart was initiated on December 14, 1784; the quartet is dated January 14, 1785. The preceding quartet in A, finished January 10, 1785, is also Masonic-inspired: 3 sharps, and question-and-answer between violin 1 and the other instruments. There is precedence for such chromaticism, and Haydn, to whom the quartet is dedicated and who was himself a Mason, did the same sort of thing later in his "Creation." The Beethoven parallel is at the beginning of the Scherzo to Op. 59 No. 1, perplexing to performers and audiences of the time (1806) for its 3-time presentation of repeated notes. Convincingly shows Beethoven's Masonic connections and both the second and third movements of Op. 59 No. 1 reveal this. No absolute proof, but suggests a strong possibility. Also Andrei Razumovsky probably had such connections. Shows musical elements in the quartet that relate to Masonic ideas, just as in Mozart's quartet.

1147. Cherbuliez, Antoine-Elisée. "Zur harmonischen Analyse der Einleitung von Mozarts C-Dur Streichquartett (K. V.465)," in Erich Schenk, ed., *Bericht über die musikwissenschaftliche Tagung der Internationalen Stiftung Mozarteum in Salzburg von 2. bis 5. August 1931* (Leipzig: Breitkopf & Härtel, 1932), pages 103-111. Recognizes Mozart's contrapuntal thinking in this famous introduction, which allows him to reach some unusual harmonic situations. Nonetheless, attempts an harmonic analysis.

1148. Krummacher, Friedhelm. "Kantabilität als Konstruktion: zum langsamen Satz aus Mozarts Streichquartett KV465," in Werner Breig, Reinhold Brinkmann and Elmar Budde, eds., *Analysen: Beiträge zu einer Problemgeschichte des Komponierens: Festschrift für Hans Heinrich Eggebrecht zum 65. Geburtstag*, in *Beihefte zum Archiv für Musikwissenschaft*, xxiii (Stuttgart: Franz Steiner Verlag Wiesbaden, 1984), pp. 217-233. ML 5.A63 Suppl. Bd.23. ISBN 3-515-03662-8.

Notes that analytical studies of Mozart's quartets are
rare and seldom adequate, and that such studies concentrate on the first and last movements and ignore the
slow movements because of their irregularity. Therefore concentrates here on one such internal movement,
with reference to the slow movement of K.387 in G Major
as well. Dismisses the 19th-century practice of Koch
and Marx in relating everything to sonata form. In
K.465 the slow movement structure evolves out of the
cantabile of the opening theme and continues to evolve
until the end of the movement. This is quite different
from form based on contrast. The form is not transferable; it depends on the particular cantabile melody.
Such structure is hard to analyze with words.

1149. Hümmeke, Werner. *Versuch einer strukturwissenschaft-*
      lichen Darstellung der ersten und vierten Sätze der
      zehn letzten Streichquartette von W.A. Mozart, in
      Veröffentlichungen zur theoretischen Musikwissen-
      schaft, Band 2. Munster: photocopy of typescript,
      1970. ML 410.M9H88. 273 pages.
      Proposes to present the scientific structure of the
      first and fourth movements so that Mozart's quartets
      can be properly compared to Haydn's and the extent of
      borrowing and originality in them properly assessed.
      Criticizes older methods of analysis whereby an indi-
      vidual work is to be understood in terms of *a priori*
      forms and concepts; a scientific analysis deals first
      with the individual work and the interactions of its
      constituent parts into an order planned by the compo-
      ser. Taking only what exists in a work and nothing
      else to determine the piece's work-model, the personal
      style and spirit of the piece can be scientifically
      fixed. Based on Ursula Götze, "Darstellung der Werk-
      struktur," in Johann Friedrich Klöffler, University of
      Munster dissertation, 1965, pages 203ff. The scienti-
      fic elements of a piece are determined through compari-
      son, and their interaction is first described by recur-
      rence or non-recurrence (recurrence subdivided into
      identical, like, similar, associated, equivalence).
      The elements of a movement are built out of morphen and
      larger parts, and integration exists between smaller
      elements and of the whole. The methodology is ex-
      plained at length and signs for these given. Using
      these concepts, the 20 movements of the Mozart quartets
      are then analyzed with the help of 42 oversized, pull-
      out graphs, 3 pull-out charts, and numerous other
      tables. In conclusion gives percentages when certain
      types of recurrences occur or when they do not. In
      first movements, the openings are less important than
      the endings; in last movements openings are more
      important and then usually recur at the ends. *See also*
      {965}.

1150. King, Alexander Hyatt. "Mozart's 'Prussian' Quartets in Relation to his Late Style," in *Music and Letters*, xxi (1940), 328-346.
Tries to explain how these 3 quartets (and *Così fan Tutte*) were products of a new period of creativity of Mozart's, after a lull during which he renewed himself. Finds new, adventuresome elements of form, counterpoint and melody and such new stylistic traits as the prominence of the cello in these quartets. Opposes those who would denegrate these pieces (especially Dunhill) and in this seemingly long article emphasizes the transparent lightness of texture and vitality of craftsmanship.

1151. Benestad, Finn. "Mozarts Strykekvartett in D-Dur (KV575)," in O.M. Sandvik, ed., *Norsk Musikkgranskning: Arbok 1959-61* (Oslo: Johann Grundt Tanum, 1961), pages 74-89. In Norwegian.
Reviews Mozart's quartets up to 1789 and K.575, and analyzes for the historian this quartet to show Mozart's "deepfelt simplicity and artistic satisfaction." A history of Mozart's writing the quartet. Scholarly, thoughtful, not too technical.

1152. St. Foix, Georges de. "Le Dernier Quatuor de Mozart," in *Studien zur Musikgeschichte: Festschrift für Guido Adler zum 75. Geburtstag* (Vienna/Leipzig: Universal-Edition, 1930), pp. 168-173. ML 55.A2S8.
Mozart wrote his last 3 quartets for Frederick Wilhelm II of Prussia, Boccherini's great patron and himself a cellist. Having just finished reorchestrating 2 Handel works, Mozart was under the influence of Bach and Handel in 1790 when he wrote the last 2 quartets: thematic unity and, especially in the finale of the last quartet in F, exceptional counterpoint that makes the movement the high point of the whole quartet. While the 6 "Haydn" quartets were written to please Haydn and show the ultimate in taste and science, the last 3 quartets were written to show the fullness of his powers and genius. Reacts against the prevailing opinion in 1930 (by H. Abert and others) that these 3 quartets are inferior to the 6 "Haydn" quartets. Believes the finale of the last quartet -- like the finale of the Jupiter Symphony -- is the beginning of a new Mozart in depth of expression and the 2 traits of thematic unity and contrapuntal expertise.

Mozart's Other Chamber Music:

1153. Forsberg, Carl Earl. "The Clavier-Violin Sonatas of Wolfgang Amadeus Mozart." PhD dissertation. Indiana University, 1964. UMI 65-3477. DA xxvi.2. 312 pages.

Analyzes each of Mozart's 44 sonatas and traces the influences of Leopold Mozart, Schobert, Johann Gottfried
Eckard, J.C. Bach, Hermann Friedrich Raupach, Sammartini, Veracini, Honauer, and others. Finds the sonatas
fit into chronological groups: the earliest are composed for keyboard with accompanying violin; the next,
few in number, show Boccherini's influence (K.46d, 46e,
55-60); then come K.301-6, under the influence of
Schuster's divertimenti; these are followed by K.376-
80, and 296, all in 3 movements; K.402-4 and 372 show a
growing interest in Baroque counterpoint; finally
K.454, 488, and 526 -- the concert years -- the most
perfect violin + keyboard sonatas before Beethoven.
K.547 seems out of place.

1154. Cherubini, Ralph. "Leopold Mozart's *Violinschule* as a
      Guide to the Performance of W.A. Mozart's Sonatas for
      Violin and Keyboard." PhD dissertation. Case Wes-
      tern Reserve University, 1976. UM 77-11997. DA
      xxxviii.1A, p. 15. 327 pages.
Assumes that Wolfgang, as a pupil of his father, was
influenced by his father in writing and performing his
violin + piano sonatas. Discusses Leopold's treatise:
violin technique, ornamentation, and musical style;
interprets Wolfgang's sonata K.296 accordingly.

1155. Hunkemöller, Jürgen. "W.A. Mozarts frühe Sonaten für
      Violine und Klavier: Untersuchungen zur Gattungsge-
      schichte im 18. Jahrhundert." PhD dissertation.
      Heidelberg University, 1968. RILM 70-3263. 144
      pages. Published in *Neue Heidelberger Studien zur
      Musikwissenschaft*, Band 3. Bern/Munich: Francke,
      1970. ML 410.M9H89. 144 pages.
Mozart wrote 32 violin + piano sonatas from 1762 to
1788, which have been discussed in important studies
elsewhere (see Forsberg {1153}) and which cover all his
compositional metamorphoses. Discusses them here as
part of the history of the genre. The earlier sonatas
are accompanied keyboard sonatas, the later ones dialogue violin + piano sonatas. Concentrates on the
earlier ones since they are generally neglected, they
are the source for the later ones, and they reveal the
growth of the child Mozart. Compares the earliest ones
to their original version for Klavier alone; few real
changes, the violin being added as improvised variation
and simply doubling the right hand melody in unison,
parallel thirds, or sixths, or joining the accompaniment figures of the left hand or inner voices. Discusses the technical difficulty of the violin part
(compares to L. Mozart's book), goes into tonal and
formal structure, considers Mozart's models especially
in London and Paris, and investigates the extent to
which Leopold wrote parts of the early sonatas. Analyzes and compares the early and later sonatas by

Mozart and Mozart's contemporaries Giardini (1716-1796), Pellegrini (1715-1767), Boccherini, J.C.F. Bach, and Schuster (1748-1812). Concludes with an analysis of the genre "violinsonata" as reflected in the works of Mozart, with special consideration of the role of the piano and with the sociological role of the sonatas, including whether they were published in series or not.

1156. Eppstein, Hans. "Warum wurde Mozarts KV 570 zur Violinsonate?" in *Die Musikforschung*, xvi (1963), 379-381.
This piano sonata was published by Artaria in 1796 with a violin part and until recently it was considered as a violin + piano sonata. Now that it has returned to its rightful position as a piano sonata, an investigation into how it became a violin sonata. Mozart himself could not have done this since this keyboard + violin accompaniment type of sonata was well behind him at this point of his career and stylistically is not typical of Mozart. Speculates that the composer of the violin part wanted to improve the sound (not the melody or form). Concentrates on the second movement, where he finds fault with Mozart's piano alone and sees a concerto origin. Speculates further that perhaps the composer knew Mozart and saw these problems and offered a solution.

1157. Marguerre, Karl. "Mozarts Klaviertrios," in *Mozart-Jahrbuch* (1960-1961), 182-194.
Considers the 6 late piano trios that Mozart wrote 1786-1788 as neglected masterpieces, yet they are not good for the players -- especially the cellist -- and are less weighty than the late quartets and quintets. Looks upon these trios as continuation of the evolution out of the accompanied piano sonata and along a further path past the violin + piano sonatas. Thus there is a lot of experimentation in the relationships among the 3 instruments (the scoring changes in the 1788 collection to clarinet or violin + cello + piano).

1158. Newman, William S. "The Duo Texture of Mozart's K. 526: an Essay in Classic Instrumental Style," in Gustave Reese and Robert J. Snow, eds., *Essays in Musicology in Honor of Dragan Plamenac on his 70th Birthday* (Pittsburgh: University of Pittsburgh Press, 1969), pages 191-206. German trl. "Die Duo-Struktur in Mozarts Violinsonate KV 526: ein Versuch über den klassischen Instrumentalstil," in Gerhard Schuhmacher, *Zur musikalischen Analyse* (Darmstadt: Wissenschaftliche Buchgesellschaft, 1974), pages 96-114.
A study of texture in this violin + piano sonata. Considers texture as "the balance between two instruments; the fullness of the part-writing; the euphony of the

scoring; the contrapuntal activity and other busyness within the texture; the technique of voice-leading; and the idiomatic treatment of the individual instruments." Puts this analysis in historical perspective by comparing the chosen sonata to the accompanied violin sonata of the Baroque and the accompanied keyboard sonata with obligato violin of the mid-18th century.

1159. Einstein, Alfred. "Mozart's Four String Trio Preludes to Fugues of Bach," trl. by Marianne Brooke, in *The Musical Times*, lxxvii (1936), 209-216.
Considers Mozart's preludes a3 and his arrangements of part of the exposition of the fugue of Bach's *Well-Tempered Klavier*, II.13. Reviews the relationship of Baron von Swieten to the Bachs -- he learned of J.S. from Frederick the Great and received copies of the *Well-Tempered Klavier* from C.P.E. -- and the influences of the Bachs on Mozart via von Swieten. For Von Swieten Mozart arranged 4-part fugues (WTK II.2, 5, 7, 8 and 9) for string quartet and 3-part fugues (WTK I.8, II.13 and 14, plus other J.S. and W.F. fugues) for violin + viola + cello. For the 3 trio fugues and W.F. Bach's fugue, Mozart composed his own slow preludes -- only 1 other piece by Mozart for string trio. Points to Florian Gassmann's quartets wherein the first movement Adagio or Andante is followed by a fugue, and Albrechtsberger's quartet in 6 movements (3 pairs of slow prelude + fugue) as possible evidence that they could have written the Mozart trios, but dismisses them on stylistic grounds and concludes that these are authentic Mozart

For an analysis of Mozart's late string chamber music, including the quintets, see Maud Trimmer's dissertation {963}. For a penetrating analysis and critique of the quintets, see Charles Rosen's The Classical Style {935}.

1160. Cleary, Nelson Theodore. "The D-Major String Quintet (K.593) of Wolfgang Amadeus Mozart: a Critical Study of Sources and Editions." PhD dissertation. Michigan State University, 1973. UM 74-6022. DA xxxiv. 9A, pp. 6020-1. vi + 227 pages.
A study of the various early editions and autograph score of this piece, with attention to discrepancies here and in later editions to the present. The most significant finding is that Mozart probably did not revise the chromatic theme in the finale. Cleary's findings were anticipated in {1161}.

1161. Hess, Ernst. "Die 'Varianten' in Finale des Streichquintettes KV 593," in *Mozart-Jahrbuch* (1960-1961), 68-77.
Considers in detail the differences between the autograph manuscript of the quintet and its earliest published versions. Points out Einstein's mistakes as

well, based on not recognizing changes in the manuscript score not made by Mozart but by someone else.
Includes 2 facsimiles of the autograph.

1162. Dubiel, Joseph Peter. "The First Movement of Mozart's
C-Major Quintet." PhD dissertation. Princeton University, 1980. UMI 80-18655. DAI xli.3A, p. 843.
139 pages. Vol. I only.
Compares the opening material of the movement to its
exact repetition in the repeat of the exposition, to
its development, and to its return in the recap in
order to see how the material functions differently.

1163. Montgomery, Michael Francis. "A Critical Analysis of
the Modulations of W.A. Mozart in Selected Late Instrumental Works." PhD dissertation. New York University, 1976. UMI 76-19036. DAI xxxvii.2A, p. 682.
Considers the string quartets and quintets K.590, 593,
and 612, as well as piano sonatas, symphonies, and concertos.

1164. Keller, Hans. "Functional Analysis of Mozart's G
Minor Quintet," in *Music Analysis*, iv (March-July,
1985), 73-94.
An analysis without words, using musical adaptations of
Mozart's score to demonstrate stylistic and functional
happenings through special emphasis, thinning out,
rests, expansion, reordering, juxtaposition, and omis-
sion. Believes that a musical conception often cannot
be expressed in words, but still leaves the reader
guessing on a lot of points.

1165. Newman, Sidney. "Mozart's G Minor Quintet (K.516) and
its Relationship to the G Minor Symphony (K.550)," in
The Music Review, xvii (1956), 287-303.
Reviews the obvious though precarious thematic relationships between the 2 pieces and proposes that the
symphony develops out of discarded material for the
conclusion of the quintet. The discussion is based
upon comparison of a Mozart autograph of the quintet,
formerly in the Berlin Staatsbibliothek and viewed
there in 1937 by the author, to an autograph "Erinner-
ungsblatt" auctioned in 1929 (and, as revealed in *The
Music Review*, xviii (1957), 4-7, now in Japan), apparently of the same time as the other manuscript.
Interesting essay on the origins of the quintet.

1166. Riemann, Hugo. "Das Adagio und Menuett von Mozarts G-
moll-Streichquintett: Analytische Studie," in *Prälu-
dien und Studien: gesammelte Aufsätze zur Ästhetik,
Theorie und Geschichte der Musik*, III (Leipzig: 1901;
reprint Hildesheim: Georg Olms, 1967), pp. 69-82. ML
60.R56.1967. Originally in *Musikalisches Wochenblatt*
(1889), no. 7-10.

A fairly technical analysis of several themes from these 2 movements. Points out the changing metrical and motivic structure and their part in periodization. Seeks the location of stressed notes in the musical phrase. For the more advanced performer.

For Mozart's treatment of the viola in his chamber music see J. Arthur Watson's "Mozart and the Viola" {1491}.

1167. Ward, Martha Kingdon. "Mozart and the Flute," in *Music and Letters*, xxxv (1954), 294-308.
     Mozart rarely used the flute in chamber music. Gives 1 paragraph to the flute quartets K.285a, 298, and App.171, which the author believes to be inferior.

1168. Leavis, Ralph. "Mozart's Flute Quartet in C, K.App. 171," in *Music and Letters*, xliii (1962), 48-52.
     Briefly authenticates the works Mozart wrote for the flutist De Jean and concentrates on the 1 work not previously authenticated, K.App.171. Points to a fragment of it definitely by Mozart in an autograph manuscript given in facsimile in the *Neue-Mozart-Ausgabe* by L. Finscher (Ser. viii/20, Abb.1, Bd. 3, p. 150). Considers the possibility of an arrangement by someone else, but has no conclusive evidence that K.App. 171 as it stands is entirely authentic.

1169. Maxwell, John. "The Finale of Mozart's Oboe Quartet, K.370: a Reductive Analysis," in *Indiana Theory Review*, iv, no. 2 (1981), 33-50.
     A Schenkerian analysis of a movement that appears to be an incomplete rondo but, through this analysis, is shown to be a sonata-rondo movement.

1170. Ward, Martha Kingdon. "Mozart and the Clarinet," in *Music and Letters*, xxviii (1947), 126-153.
     Briefly points out Mozart's contacts with the clarinet and clarinetists and something about the late-18th-century instrument. Then discusses all the works by Mozart which include it. After accounting for his infrequent uses of the clarinet before he moved to Vienna, divides the works in the Vienna period by genre, among which is chamber music (pp. 145-148). Gives a concise list of works containing the clarinet.

1171. Kratochvìl, Jiìì. "Betrachtungen über die Urfassung des Konzerts für Klarinette und des Quintetts für Klarinette und Streicher von W.A. Mozart," in Pavel Eckstein, German editor, *Internationale Konferenz über das Leben und Werk W.A. Mozarts: Praha 27.-31. Mai 1956: Bericht* (Prague: Mìr, novin. závody, [1956]), pp. 262-271. ML 410.M9M474.
     Mozart wrote these 2 works for a newly invented bassett-klarinette by Anton and Johann Stadler. Since the

original manuscripts are lost, bases the argument on the ranges of the instruments and stylistic factors in the music compared to a known use of the bassett-klarinette in *La Clemenza di Tito* (Aria 9).

1172. Ward, Martha Kingdon. "Mozart and the Bassoon," in *Music and Letters*, xxx (1949), 8-25.
Except for brief mention of serenades and divertimenti, discusses the bassoon in every context other than chamber music. Considers the question of sonority in combination with other winds or strings.

See also Eric Ohlsson, "The Quintets for Piano, Oboe, Clarinet, Horn and Bassoon by Wolfgang Amadeus Mozart and Ludwig van Beethoven" {685}.

1173. Leeson, Daniel N., and David Whitwell. "Mozart's 'Spurious' Wind Octets," in *Music and Letters*, liii (1972), 377-399.
A scholarly study of the authenticity of K.Anh.C.17.01-5 and 17.07 wind octets and 10 movements in a Prague manuscript. Extensive evidence for Mozart's having written many octets from 1781 to 1787; importance of term *Harmonie* in Vienna c.1782-1825 for wind octet of 2 oboes + 2 clarinets + 2 horns + 2 bassoons; Constanze's letters and dealings with Johann Traeg, who sold a lot of Mozart's music for Constanze including 4 Partitas for Harmonie which are now in the Prague University Library. All of this supports the authenticity of these octets.

Georg Muffat
1653-1704

1174. Gore, Richard Taylor. "The Instrumental Works of Georg Muffat." PhD dissertation. University of Rochester, 1955. v + 260 pages.
Concentrates on the organ music but also considers sonatas and string suites.

For Muffat's influence on Corelli's Sonate da Camera, see John Daverio's article {209}.

Thea Musgrave
b.1928

For a catalogue and discography of Musgrave's chamber music and studies about it, see Donald L. Hixon, Thea Musgrave: a Bio-Bibliography, in Bio-Bibliographies in Music, No. 1 (Westport [Connecticut]: Greenwood Press, 1984), pages 27-36. ML 134.M967H6.1984. ISBN 0-313-23708-5.

Jacques-Christophe Naudot
c.1690-1762

1175. Underwood, Troy Jervis. "The Life and Music of Jac-
      ques-Christophe Naudot." PhD dissertation. North
      Texas State University, 1970. UMI 71-573. DAI
      xxxi.7A, p. 3588. 373 pages.
      Biography and analysis of Naudot's 24 published flute
      works (1726-1752), among which are some sonatas.

Franz Christoph Neubauer
1760-1795

1176. Sjoerdsma, Richard Dale. "The Instrumental Works of
      Franz Christoph Neubauer (1760-1795)." PhD disserta-
      tion. Ohio State University, 1970. RILM 70-1898.
      UM 71-7568. DA xxxi.9A, p. 4825. 2 vols. I: xv +
      398 pages; II: ii + 63 pages.
      A biography and discussion of the works, which besides
      11 symphonies and 3 concertos is mostly chamber music:
      22 quartets (6 are flute quartets), 16 trios, 43 duos,
      and miscellaneous pieces for piano with others. Basic-
      ally a conservative, yet Neubauer employs far-ranging
      modulations in his development sections. In some quar-
      tets the 4 instruments are equal; in others the first
      violin dominates.

Christoph Nichelmann
1717-c.1761

*For a catalogue of his music, see Douglas A. Lee, The Works
of Christoph Nichelmann: a Thematic Index, in Detroit Studies in Music Bibliography, No. 19 (Detroit: Information
Coordinators, 1971), 100 pages. ML 134.N4L4.*

1177. Lee, Douglas Allen. "The Instrumental Works of Chris-
      toph Nichelmann." PhD dissertation. University of
      Michigan, 1968. RILM 68-3373. UM 68-13348. DA
      xxix.4A, pp. 1242-3. 2 vols. I: 307 pages; II: 130
      pages.
      Biography and a chapter devoted to the chamber music by
      Nichelmann, primarily known as a keyboard player. The
      chamber music is apparently his least important music.

Carl Nielsen
1865-1931

1178. Simpson, Robert, "The Chamber Music," in *Carl Nielsen: Symphonist* (New York: Taplinger, 1979), pp. 153-161. ML 410.N625S48. ISBN 0-8008-1260-3.
Simplistic analyses of the major chamber pieces: 4 string quartets, 2 sonatas for violin + piano, and a wind quintet (other works are mentioned). Highly subjective comments, with vague references to the works of other composers.

1179. Hamburger, Povl. "Orchestral Works and Chamber Music," in Jürgen Balzer, ed., *Carl Nielsen: Centenary Essays* (Copenhagen: NYT Nordisk Forlag - Arnold Busk, 1965), pages 19-46. HML 4281.15.6.
Accounts for the early chamber music (string quartet [1888, rev. 1900 as Op. 13], and string quintet [1888]). Analyzes briefly the Quartet in F Minor Op. 5 (1890), Sonata in A for violin + piano (1895), String Quartet in E-flat Op. 14 (1898), String Quartet in F Op. 44 (1906, rev. 1923), and Violin + Piano Sonata No. 2 (1912). Also mentions the Woodwind Quintet Op. 43.

Luigi Nono
b. 1924

1180. Metzger, Heinz-Klaus. "Wendepunkt Quartett?" in *Musik-Konzepte*, xx *Luigi Nono* (July, 1981), 93-112.
Concern that Nono, the Italian Communist leader and publicist, has turned to a 19th-century middle-class art medium: the private, non-political string quartet. But shows that Nono considers this quartet a political message with the smallest means of expression -- there are messages for the players to feel and think even if not expressed aloud.

Pauline Oliveros
b.1932

1181. Subotnick, Morton. "Pauline Oliveros: Trio," in *Perspectives of New Music*, ii, no. 1 (1963), 77-82.
The trio is for flute + piano + page turner, whose role is to properly prepare the piano. Concerned with the lack of growth as the piece progresses -- the opening development is not later expanded except in time. The work contrasts 2 basic motivic units.

Georges Louis Onslow
1784-1853

1182. Franks, Richard Nelson. "George Onslow (1784-1853): a
      Study of his Life, Family, and Works." PhD disserta-
      tion. University of Texas, 1981. UMI 81-19290. DAI
      xlii.11A, p. 4639. 1044 pages.
      An extensive biography with a complete list of his
      works and discussion of all his compositions in order
      of their composition.

1183. Nobach, Christiana. *Untersuchungen zu George Onslows
      Kammermusik.* Kassel: Bärenreiter, 1985. x + 393
      pages.
      Scholarly study and thematic-chronological catalogue.
      Establishes sources and dates and analyzes the chamber
      music in 4 stylistic periods. Attention to the nature
      of particular movements, thematic development, and
      form. Large number of string quartets and quintets,
      piano trios, a piano quintet, a piano sextet, a wood-
      wind quintet, and a nonet and septet for mixed instru-
      ments.

1184. Hayes, Robert. "Onslow and Beethoven's Late Quar-
      tets," in *The Journal of Musicological Research*, v
      (1985), 273-296.
      A fascinating, well-documented study of the reaction of
      the French public of c.1830-1860 and in particular of
      Onslow to the late Beethoven quartets. Onslow wrote 70
      string quartets, mostly after 1830. Although since the
      second half of the 19th century it has been assumed
      that Onslow was primarily influenced by Mozart, Onslow
      was thoroughly acquainted with every note in Beetho-
      ven's quartets. The influences of Beethoven's Op. 18
      and 59 are obvious, but Op. 132 and the other late
      quartets also affected Onslow. Before 1850 the Beetho-
      ven influence on Onslow was recognized by the French
      public, but afterward it was not. The change in atti-
      tude toward the Beethoven influence on Onslow was the
      result of the growth of the Beethoven cult by the
      1850's; it was inconceivable after 1850 that Onslow
      would be so presumptuous as to risk comparison with
      Beethoven and that he could add to Beethoven, so
      Mozart, who was held in less esteem, was substituted.

Carlos d'Ordoñez
1734-1786

For a catalogue of his music, see A. Peter Brown, Carlo
D'Ordonez 1734-1786: a Thematic Catalogue, *in Detroit
Studies in Music Bibliography, No. 39 (Detroit: Information
Coordinators, 1978), 234 pages. ML 134.072A15. ISBN-
911772-89-8.*

1185. Brown, A. Peter. "The Chamber Music with Strings of Carlos d'Ordoñez: a Bibliographic and Stylistic Study," in *Acta Musicologica*, xlvi (1974), 222-272.
An exhaustive, scholarly attempt to authenticate the chamber music (including 27 string quartets, 21 trios for 2 violins + bass, and other combinations) and date it approximately. Stylistic and formal analyses.

Johann Pachelbel
1653-1706

1186. Nolte, Ewald Valentin. "The Instrumental Works of _ Johann Pachelbel (1653-1706): an Essay to Establish his Stylistic Position in the Development of the Baroque Musical Art." PhD dissertation. Northwestern University, 1954. UMI 54-2584. DA xiv.10, p. 1758.
Concentrates on the keyboard works but makes passing reference to chamber music. Seems superficial.

1187. Beckmann, Gustav. "Johann Pachelbel als Kammerkomponist," in *Archiv für Musikwissenschaft*, i (1918-1919), 267-274.
Brief discussion of the chamber music and reproduction of a sarabande for 2 violins + 2 violas + cembalo and a canon for 3 violins + cembalo.

Niccoló Paganini
1782-1840

For a catalogue of his works, including chamber music, see Maria Rosa Moretti and Anna Sorrento, Catalogo Tematico delle Musiche di Niccoló Paganini *(Genoa: Comune di Genova, 1982), xxvi + 422 pages. ML 134.P145A2.1982.*

John Knowles Paine
1839-1906

1188. Schmidt, John C. "Chamber Music," in *The Life and Works of John Knowles Paine*, in *Studies in Musicology*, no. 34 (Ann Arbor: UMI Research Press, 1980), pp. 311-338. 32 examples. ML 410.P138S3. ISBN 0-8357-1126-9.
Discusses each chamber piece -- an early quartet, piano trio, violin + piano sonata and other works for violin + piano. Gives sources, history, and describes each movement's themes and keys. No real analyses. The first half of this large book is a biography; the second half deals with Paine's compositions.

Johann Christoph (= John Christopher) Pepusch
1667-1752

1189. Fred, Herbert William. "The Instrumental Music of Jo-
      hann Christoph Pepusch." PhD dissertation. Univer-
      sity of North Carolina, 1961. UM 62-3121. DA xxiii:
      2, pp. 648-9. 2 vols. I: iv + 101 pages; II: 150
      pages of music.
      Biography, bibliography, and analyses of 127 violin
      sonatas, 14 flute sonatas, and other chamber works.
      They merge da chiesa and da camera characteristics and
      retain the Baroque slow-fast-slow-fast order of move-
      ments, mostly in binary form with continuous expansion.

Giovanni Battista Pergolesi
1710-1736

For a catalogue of his chamber music, see Marvin E. Paymer,
Giovanni Battista Pergolesi 1710-1736: a Thematic Catalogue
of the Opera Omnia with an Appendix Listing Omitted Compositions, in Thematic Catalogues in Music, No. 1 (New York:
Pendragon, 1977), pages 3-12. ML 134.P613A35. ISBN 0-
918728-01-0.

1190. Claydon, Humphrey. "Three String Quartets Attributed
      to Pergolesi," in *Music and Letters*, xix (1938), 453-
      459.
      Documentation and stylistic analysis of 3 quartets
      copied in England in the late 18th century attributed
      to Pergolesi. No final statement on the authenticity
      of Pergolesi's name, but enthusiastic regard for the
      works.

1191. Stover, Edwin L. "The Instrumental Chamber Music of
      Giovanni Battista Pergolesi." PhD dissertation.
      Florida State University, 1964. UM 65-306. DA
      xxvi.3, p. 1690. 160 pages.
      Pergolesi's miscellaneous orchestral sonatas are more
      Baroque than Classical (for example, the movements are
      slow-fast-slow-fast), but the chamber trio sonatas are
      more progressive and point to Classical concepts (the
      movements are fast-slow-fast, with many first movements
      and some others as well showing sonata form). Assumes
      these works are actually by Pergolesi, but see {1192}.

1192. Cudworth, C.L. "Notes on the Instrumental Works
      Attributed to Pergolesi," in *Music and Letters*, xxx
      (1949), 321-328.
      Among these works are several miscellaneous sonatas
      which may or may not be genuine, but the 14 trio
      sonatas certainly are not by Pergolesi but by a
      slightly later composer.

Carlo Perinello
1877-1942

1193. Cantarini, Aldo. "Nuovi Compositori Italiani di Musica da Camera: Carlo Perinello," in *Rivista Musicale Italiana*, xxii (1915), 690-715.
Analyzes a quartet and quintet (1905) by Carlo Perinello. In the quintet the melodic and harmonic climaxes are influenced by Brahms and Schumann. The quartet (1908-1909) borders on a masterpiece and is performed often in Germany; it has a more plastic form, is more impressionistic, and resembles Beethoven's late quartets.

John M. Perkins
b.1935

1194. Spies, Claudio. "John M. Perkins: *Quintet Variations*," in *Perspectives of New Music*, ii, no. 1 (1963), 67-76.
An analysis of the quintet (flute + clarinet + trumpet + piano + percussion). It is in 31 sections, which enables Perkins to use all possible combinations of instruments and solos.

George Perle
b.1915

1195. Moss, Lawrence. "George Perle: String Quintet," in *Perspectives of New Music*, iii, no. 1 (1964), 136-139.
A brief review of the quintet (1958; 2 violins + 2 violas + cello), which is amazingly catholic considering the highly advanced theoretical works of Perle. Symmetrical vertical and horizontal construction.

Goffredo Petrassi
b.1904

For a catalogue of his chamber music, see Claudio Annibaldi, Goffredo Petrassi: Catalogo delle Opere e Bibliografia (Milan: Suvini Zerboni, 1971), systematic index p. 110. ML 134.P615A6.

1196. Stone, Olga. "Petrassi's *Sonata da Camera* for Harpsichord and Ten Instruments: a Study of Twentieth-Century Linear Style," in *The Music Review*, xxxvii (1976), 283-294.
A simple, not too technical analysis of the motives of this piece for harpsichord + flute + oboe + clarinet + bassoon + 2 violins + 2 violas + cello + bass. Regards

this piece as transitional in Petrassi's career from neo-classic to serial.

Johann Pezel
1639-1694

Although Pezel's Turmmusik was never considered chamber music in the 17th century (it was outdoor music), it has been considered chamber music by 20th-century wind players since it fits the modern definition of chamber music as solo ensemble music. For a catalogue of his music, see Elwyn A. Wienandt, Johann Pezel (1639-1694): a Thematic Catalogue of his Instrumental Works, in Thematic Catalogues in Music, No. 9 (New York: Pendragon, 1983), xxxiii + 102 pages. ML 134.P618A35.1983. ISBN 0-918728-23-1.

1197. Wattenbarger, James Albert. "The Turmmusik of Johann Pezel." PhD dissertation. Northwestern University, 1957. UMI 58-4372. DA xviii.2, p. 609. 298 pages.
    History and analysis of Pezel's *Hora Decima* (40 sonatas) and *Fünffstimmigte blasende Musik* (76 pieces), based on incomplete evidence and the writings of Arnold Schering. Post-World War II political conditions inhibited this study. Twenty-nine pieces reproduced in score in an appendix.

Hans Pfitzner
1869-1949

1198. Henderson, Donald Gene. "Hans Pfitzner: the Composer and his Instrumental Works." PhD dissertation. University of Michigan, 1963. UM 63-4965. DA xxiv.2, p. 766. 437 pages.
    Analyzes 13 specific works, most of which are chamber music, and surveys all the instrumental works categorically by form, harmony, melody, orchestration, meter and rhythm, and expression. Considers the social conditions in which Pfitzner worked and all of his writings on music. Pfitzner's creativity stretched from the period of Brahms through Schoenberg and exhibits changing characteristics of the times.

1199. Rectanus, Hans. "Ein wiederaufgefundenes Streichquartett Hans Pfitzners," in *Die Musikforschung*, xxii (1969), 489-495.
    Rediscovers a string quartet in D Minor which Pfitzner wrote in 1886 when he was 17 and which he had entered into a contest in Frankfurt am Main. A brief description, with excerpts of all 4 movements.

1200. Truscott, Harold. "The Importance of Hans Pfitzner: II: The Chamber Music," in *Music Survey*, i (1948), 37-42.

Dwells at length on Pfitzner's use of non-dominant
preparation of returns to the tonic -- a device he
learned from Schubert (the most important model for
Pfitzner). Concentrates on the Piano Quintet Op. 23.

1201. Rectanus, Hans. "Pfitzners Jugend-Trio B Dur (1886),"
in *Mitteilungen der Hans Pfitzner-Gesellschaft*, no.
43 (Sept. 1981), 105-109.
Pfitzner wrote 3 early trios in B-flat, E-flat and E,
which were presumed lost, but now the B-flat one is
found: movement 1 in Vienna and movements 2 and 3 in
Strassburg. The work was performed in 1980 and several
review are printed.

Wenzel (= Václav) Pichl
1741-1805

1202. Postolka, Milan. "Pichl, Václav," in *The New Grove*
{1}, xiv, 731-732.
A brief biography and outlined bibliography of works by
and about Pichl, a Czech violinist well known to Haydn
and Mozart. See also R. Kolisko, "Wenzel Pichls Kammermusik" (PhD dissertation, University of Vienna,
1918, not seen). According to Slonimsky {4}, p. 1772,
Pichl wrote 172 string quartets and much other chamber
music for strings, but Postolka mentions only 18 string
quartets, 45 string or flute trios, and duets.

Willem Pÿper
1894-1947

1203. Hoogerwerf, Frank William. "The Chamber Music of
Willem Pÿper (1894-1947)." PhD dissertation.
University of Michigan, 1974. UM 75-718. DA
xxxv.8A, pp. 5445-6. xiv + 469 pages.
A historical, biographical, and analytical study of
the most important Dutch composer since Sweelinck. The
pieces include 5 string quartets, 4 wind ensembles, 2
piano trios, various sonatas for violin, cello and
flute, and a few other pieces, all composed 1913-1946
but most of them during the 1920's. Pÿper achieved
unity through the use of germ cells which grow during a
piece. Melody dominates, and the resulting harmony and
counterpoint become polytonal. Analyzes in detail
String Quartets Nos. 1, 3-5, Cello Sonata No. 1, Violin
Sonata No. 2, Flute Sonata, and the Septet.

1204. Dickinson, Peter. "The Instrumental Music of Willem
      Pÿper (1897 [*sic*]-1947)," in *The Music Review*, xxiv
      (1963), 327-332.
      Brief overview of Pÿper's works, which include many
      chamber pieces. Points out his use of "germ cells"
      after 1919 as the basis of construction, as in the
      Septet (1920), String Quartets No. 2 (1920), No. 3
      (1923), and No. 4 (1928), and Sonata No. 1 for violin +
      piano (1919). Includes short bibliography.

1205. Ritsema, Herbert. "The Germ Cell Principle in the
      Works of Willem Pÿper (1894-1947)." PhD disserta-
      tion. University of Iowa, 1974. UMI 75-1247. DAI
      xxxv.7A, p. 4601. 134 pages, 106 examples.
      History of Dutch music c.1900, Pÿper's biography, and
      a definition of "germ cell" as derived from César
      Franck and Vincent D'Indy and used in Pÿper's works.
      Among the works analyzed are the septet, sextet, and
      sonata for flute + piano.

1206. Hoogerwerf, Frank W. "The String Quartets of Willem
      Pÿper," in *The Music Review*, xxxviii (1977), 44-68.
      An informative analysis of form, melodic and scalar
      organization, timbre, cyclic elements, and tonality in
      each of the 5 quartets. Since the quartets span
      Pÿper's lifetime, they demonstrate considerable changes
      in attitude and structure. Compares them to Bartók's
      and Ravel's quartets.

Boris Pillin
b.1940

1207. Jennings, Vance Shelby. "Selected Twentieth Century
      Clarinet Solo Literature: a Study in Interpretation
      and Performance." DME dissertation. University of
      Oklahoma, 1972. UMI 73-9159. DAI xxxiii.10A, p.
      5765. 331 pages.
      Concerned with interpreting for performance and teach-
      ing chamber pieces by Pillin, Milhaud, Martinú, Ward-
      Steinman, and Rochberg. Includes annotated list of
      solo clarinet literature of the 20th century.

Paul Pisk
b.1893

1208. Collins, Thomas William. "The Instrumental Music of
      Paul A. Pisk." DMA dissertation. University of
      Missouri at Kansas City, 1972. UM 72-29457. DA
      xxxiii.5A, p. 2408. 207 pages.
      A survey of Pisk's instrumental works, almost half of
      which is chamber music. Basic sound is atonal with
      motivic unity, as befits a pupil of Schoenberg.

Walter Piston
1894-1976

1209. Pollack, Howard. *Walter Piston*. Ann Arbor: UMI Research Press, 1982. ML 410.P593P6.1982. ISBN 0-8357-1280-X. PhD dissertation. Cornell University, 1981.
A biography and stylistic analysis of Piston's composi-tions, including numerous chamber works. The analyses often quote others's opinions. Particularly valuable for its extensive bibliographies, including a separate bibliography for each major Piston composition.

1210. Donahue, Robert. "A Comparative Analysis of Phrase Structure in Selected Movements of the String Quar-tets of Béla Bartók and Walter Piston." DMA disser-tation. Cornell University, 1964. UMI 64-8732. DA xxviii.8A, pp. 3207-8. 161 pages.
Compares Piston's Quartet No. 4, movement 2 to Bartók's Quartet No. 2, movement 1, and Piston's Quartet No. 2, movement 4, to Bartók's Quartet No. 5, movement 1. Considers form and phrase structure in a historical framework from the Classical era to the 20th century and in the 4 movements. Contrasts the Romantic freedom more evident in Bartók with the Classic order and sym-metry more apparent in Piston. In other regards the 2 composers are very much alike.

Ignaz (= Ignace) Joseph Pleyel
1757-1831

The basic catalogue of Pleyel's music is *Rita Benton, Ignace Pleyel: a Thematic Catalogue of his Compositions, in Thema-tic Catalogues in Music, No. 2 (New York: Pendragon, 1977), xxx + 482 pages. ML 134.P74A13. ISBN 0-918728-04-5.*

1211. Zsako, Julius. "The String Quartets of Ignace J. Pleyel." PhD dissertation. Columbia University, 1975. UM 75-27478. DAI xxxvi.6A, pp. 3207-8. 2 vols. I: 414 pages; II: 353 pages.
Although capable of writing movements as good as Mozart's or Haydn's, Pleyel could not sustain such standards throughout a work. He "was often unable to prolong intensity in thematic growth." Biography and discussion of the authentic 57 string quartets, with bibliography, in vol. I. Two thematic catalogues with 370 incipits, bibliographical information, and tran-scription of 3 selected quartets in vol. II. Analyzes styles and forms of the quartets and places them in their sociological milieu.

1212. Klingenbeck, Josef. "Ignaz Pleyel: sein Streichquar-tett im Rahmen der Wiener Klassik," in *Studien zur Musikwissenschaft: Beihefte der Denkmäler der Ton-*

kunst in Österreich, Band 25, also entitled *Fest-schrift für Erich Schenk* (Graz/Vienna/Köln: Hermann Böhlaus Nachf., 1962), pp. 276-297. ML 55.S324 (= ML 113.S44). "Pleyel: sein Leben und seine Komposition für Streichquartett." PhD dissertation. University of Munich, 1928.
Points out Pleyel's debt to Haydn, his teacher. A well-documented, in-depth look at this relationship from a biographical and stylistic standpoint. Unfortunately the author relies on mostly outdated material in discussing Haydn. Considers also the Italian influence on Haydn and on Pleyel. Concludes that Pleyel cannot be measured against Haydn, Mozart and Boccherini, but on a lower plain he has much to offer. Those 3 were pioneers, while Pleyel was dependent on traditional Classical form and expression; they wrote for connoisseurs, while Pleyel wrote for the public.

1213. Wright, Ben Ernest. "The Three Quintets for Flute, Oboe, Violin, Viola and Violoncello by Ignaz J. Pleyel: Edition and Commentary." EdD dissertation. University of Northern Colorado, 1971. UMI 72-3322. DAI xxxii.8A, p. 4056. 299 pages.
A non-scholarly edition designed to teach young performers an 18th-century style of performance. Discusses ornaments and editing of phrasing, articulation, and bowing.

Quincy Porter
1897-1966

1214. Frank, Robert Eugene. "Quincy Porter: a Survey of the Mature Style and a Study of the *Second Sonata for Violin and Piano*." DMA dissertation. Cornell University, 1973. UMI 73-16070. DAI xxxiv.1A, pp. 352-3. 303 pages.
Biography and stylistic survey of the mature works. Linear analysis, harmonic reduction, and rhythmic, motivic and scalar analysis of the sonata. Porter achieved tonal stability and a scalar organization -- termed "scalar modulation" -- which may be Porter's most original contribution to 20th-century American music.

Francis Poulenc
1899-1963

1215. Daniel, Keith W. "Chamber Music," in *Francis Poulenc: his Artistic Development and Musical Style* (Ann Arbor: UMI Research Press, 1982), pp. 101-133. ML 410.P787D3. ISBN 0-8357-1284-2. Revision of PhD dissertation. State University of New York, Buffalo, 1980.

General comments about the chamber music and non-technical analyses of styles and forms in 13 pieces. For
students and laypersons. The chamber music is mostly
for woodwinds, rarely for strings or brass, with the
piano often assuming a leading role. They fall into 3
periods: 1917-1939, 1940-1950, and 1957-1963.

1216. Poulin, Pamela. "Three Stylistic Traits in Poulenc's
Chamber Works for Winds." PhD dissertation. University of Rochester, 1983. UMI 83-15558. DAI xliv.5A,
p. 1238. 281 pages.
Notes 3 principle styles in Poulenc's chamber music:
experimental, neo-classic, and popular, and finds all 3
throughout his career, even sometimes in the same
piece. Divides the works chronologically (early
1920's, late 1920's - 1944, and 1957-1962).

Ferdinand Praeger
1815-1891

1217. Ryberg, James Stanley. "Four String Quartets by Ferdinand Praeger: an Analytical Study." PhD dissertation. Northwestern University, 1978. UMI 79-03355.
DAI xxxix.8A, p. 4587. 284 pages.
A Schenkerian analysis of quartets nos. 11, 16, 21, and
22, found in a late 19th-century manuscript in the
Moldenhauer Archive at Northwestern University. Claims
that this analysis will assist performers.

Sergey Sergeyevitch Prokofiev
1891-1953

1218. Soroker, IAkov L'vovich. *Kamerno-Instrumental'nye
Ansambli S. Prokof'eva*. Moscow: Sovetskii Compositor, 1973. MT 145.P8S7. 104 pages. In Russian.
A scholarly study of Prokofiev's chief chamber music
piece by piece. A moderately technical analysis of
harmony, rhythm, bowing styles (for example, why staccato is used), and so on. For performers and students.
International discography.

1219. Blok, V. *Violenchel'noe Tvorchestro Prokof'eva*.
Moscow: Muzyka, 1973. 184 pages. In Russian.
Extensive musical analysis of Prokofiev's works for
cello without orchestra: Ballade Op. 15, Adagio Op. 97
bis, and 2 sonatas Op. 119 and 133.

Gaetano Pugnani
1731-1798

1220. Müry, Albert. *Die Instrumentalwerke Gaetano Pugnanis:
ein Beitrag zur Erforschung der frühklassischen In-*

strumentalmusik in Italien. Basel: G. Krebs, 1941.
ML 410.P9M8. vii + 109 pages. PhD dissertation.
1940.
A substantial biography of Pugnani, pupil of Somis and
teacher of Viotti, and a history of the violin sonata
from Corelli to Pugnani. Considers his violin sonatas,
violin duets, trio sonatas, harpsichord + flute +
violin + viola + cello quintet, string quartets and
quintets, and also his orchestral music. Dwells
laboriously on tempos, meters, forms, and keys and
makes shallow generalizations. Within a scholarly
framework the analyses are simplistic.

Henry Purcell
c.1659-1695

*For a catalogue of Purcell's chamber music, see Franklin B.
Zimmerman, Henry Purcell 1659-1695: an Analytical Catalogue
of his Music (London: Macmillan/New York: St. Martin's,
1963), pages 372-399. ML 134.P95Z5. To identify a given
melody by Purcell, see Zimmerman, Henry Purcell 1659-1695:
Melodic and Intervallic Indexes to his Complete Works
(Philadelphia: Smith-Edwards-Dunlap, 1975), xi + 133 pages.
ML 134.P95A42. SBN 8443-0068-3.*

1221. Tilmouth, Michael. "The Technique and Forms of
        Purcell's Sonatas," in *Music and Letters*, xl (1959),
        109-121.
        Places the sonatas in historical perspective and
        considers the sources of the 1683 and 1697 sonatas,
        their compositional techniques, and the influences of
        especially Cazzati, Colista, and G.B. Vitali upon him.

1222. Dart, Thurston. "Purcell's Chamber Music," in *Pro-
        ceedings of the Royal Musical Association*, lxxxv
        (1958-1959), 81-93.
        A review of the sources, in 4 categories: 12 trio
        sonatas (1683), 10 trio sonatas (1697), 15 fantasias
        and *In Nomines*, and miscellaneous dances, grounds, and
        other works. Adds a few "footnotes" to Tilmouth's
        article. The chamber organ was Purcell's preferred
        continuo instrument. The simplified continuo part for
        organ allows the bass viol to go off freely (not needed
        for sustaining). Thus criticizes the wrong treatment
        of the continuo and bass viol in modern editions of the
        1697 collection and similarly in the isolated sonata in
        G Minor for violin + continuo (which must originally
        have been for violin + bass viol + organ). Considers
        the introduction of ornaments, the dating of the
        fantasias and *In Nomines*, and the use of continuo.

1223. Parsons, Pleasants Arrand. "Dissonance in the Fanta-
       sias and Sonatas of Henry Purcell." PhD disserta-
       tion. Northwestern University, 1953. UMI 53-2079.
       DA xiii.6, pp. 1218-9. 208 pages.
       Analyzes the concept "dissonance" as described in 17th-
       century treatises and as found in Purcell's works.

Sergi Vasil'evich Rachmaninoff
1873-1943

*For a systematic catalogue with bibliography and disco-
graphy, see Robert Palmieri,* Sergei Vasil'evich Rachmaninoff: a Guide to Research, *in Garland Composer Resource Manuals, Vol. 3 (New York/London: Garland, 1985), pages 28-31.
ML 134.R12P3.1985. ISBN 0-8240-8996-0. A chronological catalogue and listing by opus number is found in Robert Threlfall and Geoffrey Norris,* A Catalogue of the Compositions of
S. Rachmaninoff *(London: Scolar Press, 1982), 218 pages. ML
134.R12T5.1982. ISBN 0-85967-617X.*

Jean-Philippe Rameau
1683-1764

*See Franciszek Wesolowski, "Pièces de Clavecin en Concerts
von J. Ph. Rameau als Beispiel der französischen Kammermusik
für Klavier mit Begleitung anderer Instrumente," in {161},
pages 50-52.*

Maurice Ravel
1875-1937

*For a catalogue of Ravel's chamber music see Fondation
Maurice Ravel,* Catalogue de l'Oeuvre de Maurice Ravel
(Paris: Durand et Cie., 1954), pages 42-45. ML 134.R23F6.

1224. Orenstein, Arbie. *Ravel: Man and Musician.* New York/
       London: Columbia University Press, 1975. ML 410.R23
       073. ISBN 0-231-03902-6. xviii + 291 pages.
       The definitive biography based on considerable documen-
       tation not previously available, and important discus-
       sion of Ravel's aesthetics, musical language, and crea-
       tive process. Gives historical background and analyzes
       the important chamber music. Assesses the violin +
       piano sonata, for example, as Ravel's building on the
       incompatibility of the violin and piano, and in a move-
       ment-by-movement analysis discusses harmony, influences
       (the Blues in movement 2), style, and so on. Discogra-
       phy of major works 1912-1939, catalogue of works with
       important bibliography, and general bibliography.

1225. Braun, Jürgen. *Die Thematik in den Kammermusikwerken von Maurice Ravel*, in *Kölner Beiträge zur Musikforschung*, Band 33. Regensburg: Gustave Bosse (reproduced typescript with typeovers), 1966. MT 145. R19B7. 174 pages.
    Assesses Ravel's position as a "loner" among French composers of his time and the history and style of his 5 main chamber pieces. Analyzes themes (tonality, rhythm, motive, motivic development and melody building) and thematic relationships of String Quartet, Introduction and Allegro (harp + flute + clarinet + string quartet), Piano Trio, Duo (= Sonata) for Violin + Cello, and Sonata for Violin + Piano. The special problem of impressionistic music is that the impressionist ideal -- to capture the character of conditions, the atmosphere of a movement -- is impossible in music where the sound disappears immediately; to overcome this Ravel (following Debussy) does not use harmonic motion and thematic development but dwells on the isolated sound -- as close as music can come to the impressionism in visual arts. Also, Ravel uses masks to diguise deeper feelings, and belongs to the movement of French dandyism -- opposition to the vulgarization of art -- and looks to the past with aristocratic reserve (a type of neo-classicism). Shows traditional elements in Ravel's forms (such as sonata form in the first movement of the Sonata for violin + piano) as well as his use of modern sounds (such as the Blues in the second movement of the same piece). Following H. Mersmann (*Musikhören*, Frankfurt, 1952, p. 160), sees Ravel's chamber music progressing from an impressionistic style to a much more polyphonic style.

    For a comparison of Ravel and Debussy as miniaturists who think homophonically, see Shera's Debussy and Ravel *{834}. See also {831} and {833}.*

    See Stephen Hartke {835} and Eugene Wilson {831} for discussions of the Ravel String Quartet.

1226. Sannemüller, Gerd. "Die Sonate für Violine und Violoncello von Maurice Ravel," in *Die Musikforschung*, xxviii (1975), 408-419.
    Analyzes motives, rhythms, and intervals in this duet (1920-1922). Thorough and well documented.

Alan Rawsthorne
1905-1971

1227. Cooper, Martin. "Current Chronicle: England: Three New Works by Alan Rawsthorne," in *The Musical Quarterly*, xxxv (1949), 305-311.

Describes the Violin Concerto, the Cello + Piano Sonata, and the Quartet for clarinet + violin + viola + cello. The sonata is rhapsodic, based on a germ motive, but the quartet is more traditional and contrapuntal without any pregnant motive.

1228. Howells, Herbert. "A Note on Alan Rawsthorne," in
Music and Letters, xxxii (1951), 19-28.
A shallow, verbose analysis of the quartet for clarinet
+ violin + viola + cello (1948) as a means for understanding Rawsthorne's music as a whole. The composer
uses minor seconds and ninths a great deal.

Max Reger
1873-1916

For a catalogue of Reger's chamber music, see Fritz Stein,
Thematisches Verzeichnis der im Druck erschienenen Werke von
Max Reger einschliesslich seiner Bearbeitungen und Ausgaben
mit systematischem Verzeichnis und Registern *(Leipzig:*
Breitkopf & Härtel, 1953), pages 500-501, 502-503. ML
134.R33S82. A brief general introduction to Reger's chamber
music is:

1229. Trutzschler, Heinz. "Max Reger's Chamber Music," in
Music Journal, xxiii (May, 1965), 32, 69, 71.
A short biography and general description of Reger's
style of composition and output. Brief characterizations of much of the chamber music.

1230. Leichtentritt, Hugo. "Max Reger als Kammermusikkomponist," in *Neue Zeitschrift für Musik*, 72. Jahrgang,
Band 101 (1905), 866-868.
An important study by a contemporary writing during the
composer's lifetime. Omits the earlier works and begins with the 2 clarinet sonatas Op. 49 and concludes
with the Op. 84 violin sonatas. Points out Brahms's
influence in form and structure, especially the violin
sonatas of Brahms on the Op. 49 sonatas of Reger; yet
Reger was his own man -- his humor (fantastic, grotesque, bizarre) is found in all his chamber music.
Defends Reger's melody, his recitative line as rich,
yet something very new. This he gets from Bach.
Another characteristic of Reger's is his use of
variation form in slow movements. This article appears
in an issue of the *Neue Zeitschrift für Musik* devoted
to the music of Reger.

1231. Desderi, Ettore. "Max Reger e la sua Musica Strumentale da Camera," in *Rivista Musicale Italiana*, xxxiii
(1926), 590-603.
Many misconceptions of Reger's music exist because most
people are ignorant of it. Begins with a defense of

Reger in general, then turns to the chamber music.
Discusses sonata form and sonata and concludes with a
discussion of "fugues" in Reger's chamber music. An
analysis for students, laypersons and anyone who wants
an introduction to the chamber music, but not comprehensive and not in great theoretical depth.

1232. Bücken, Ernst. "Die Grundlagen der Kunst Max Regers,"
in *Führer und Probleme der neuen Musik* (Köln: P.J.
Tonger, 1924), pages 108-125. ML 60.B913.
Reger was the first one to return respectability to
pure music among the middle classes; his predecessors
and contemporaries followed Wagner. He did this
through his substantial chamber music, which dominates
his first 89 opus numbers. At first under the spell of
Brahms, Reger turned to Bach and created neo-classicism. He always remained tonal -- true to his teacher
Hugo Riemann (even after they were no longer friends).
He is not impressionistic. An excellent, thought-
provoking commentary on Reger in general with chamber
music as a central part of the discussion.

1233. Möller, Martin. *Untersuchungen zur Satztechnik Max
Regers: Studien an den Kopfsätzen der Kammermusik-
werke*, in *Schriftenreihe des Max-Regers-Instituts
Bonn-Bad Godesberg*, Vol. 3. Wiesbaden: Breitkopf &
Härtel, 1984. ISBN 3-7651-0190-7. 232 pages.
A highly technical, scholarly treatise on Reger's
style in the first movements of his chamber music.
Establishes polyphony as basic and studies the rela-
tionship of this polyphony to his homophonic style.
Analyzes 38 pieces, 31 of which we define as chamber
music. Shows Reger's theoretical relationship to his
teacher Riemann.

For a discussion of the string quartets, see Wilke {197}.

1234. Taylor, Paul Garvin, Jr. "Thematic Process and Tonal
Organization in the First Movement Sonata Forms of
Max Reger's Nine Sonatas for Violin and Piano." PhD
dissertation. Catholic University, 1982. UMI 82-
21465. DAI xliii.4A, p. 970. 417 pages.
Analysis of the thematic process and tonal organization
of these 9 movements based on Schenker and Salzer.
Reger used traditional outer forms and tonal structures, but his inner forms and "the prolongation of the
tonal structure" are his own.

1235. Simon, Eric. "The Clarinet Works of Max Reger," in
Clarinet, no. 20 (Fall, 1955), 12-14.
Rates Reger's clarinet works as satisfying "musical
requirements and [proving] technically interesting and
rewarding" but not aspiring to greatness. Discusses 3
sonatas, the clarinet quintet, and 2 little pieces.

1236. Wilson, Keith. "An Analysis of the First Movements of
      the Sonatas for Clarinet and Piano, Opus 49, by Max
      Reger." MA thesis. University of Illinois, 1942.
      Not seen.

1237. Häfner, Roland. *Max Reger: Klarinettenquintett op.*
      146, in *Meisterwerke der Musik*, Heft 30. Munich:
      Wilhelm Fink, 1982. MT 145.R4H3.1982. ISBN 3-7705-
      1973-6. 64 pages, 21 musical illustrations + 7 pages
      of examples.
      A carefully written introduction to Reger's quintet,
      including the history of the piece and reviews. The
      bulk of the book deals with an analysis designed for
      music students, which is summarized in outline at the
      end.

Anton Reicha
1770-1836

1238. Laing, Millard Myron. "Anton Reicha's Quintets for
      Flute, Oboe, Clarinet, Horn, and Bassoon." EdD
      dissertation. University of Michigan, 1952. UM
      3697. DA xii.4, pp. 432-3. 622 pages.
      An analysis of the 24 quintets (4 in detail) with his-
      torical data such as the performers for whom they were
      written. Vol. I also gives the biography of Reicha,
      based largely on his autobiography (included here in
      both French and English), and Vol. II includes the com-
      plete scores for the 4 works analyzed in detail.

1239. Reicha, Anton. "The Woodwind Quintet: a Symposium:
      Reicha, Herald of the Quintet," in *Woodwind Magazine*,
      vii (Nov. 1954), 5.
      An excerpt from Reicha's autobiography in which he
      takes up the challenge that woodwinds are considered
      inferior to strings in chamber music.

See also Alena Krutová, "Les Quintettes pour Instruments à
Vent d'Antoine Reicha," in {457}, pages 127-130.

Wallingford Riegger
1885-1961

1240. Freeman, Paul Douglas. "The Compositional Technique
      of Wallingford Riegger as Seen in Seven Major Twelve-
      Tone Works." PhD dissertation. University of Ro-
      chester, Eastman School of Music, 1963. UMI 69-4146.
      DAI xxxi.6A, p. 2955. 344 pages.
      Among the works chosen are String Quartet No. 1, Op.
      30; Duos for Three Woodwinds, Op. 35; Nonet for Brass,

Op. 49; and Variations for Violin and Viola, Op. 57. A
detailed analysis of the rows and their interaction
with harmony, rhythm, form and style.

1241. Buccheri, Elizabeth Bankhead. "The Piano Chamber
Music of Wallingford Riegger." DMA dissertation.
University of Rochester, 1978. DAI xl.2A, p. 524.
173 pages.
A brief biographical sketch of Riegger, followed by a
chapter-length analysis of the form, style and other
relationships of each of 6 works: Piano Trio (Op.1),
Whimsey (Op.2), Sonatina (Op. 39), Piano Quintet (Op.
47), Concerto (Op. 53), and *Movement* (Op.66). A final
chapter tackles performance problems: rhythm, balance,
technique, and pianistic techniques.

1242. Schmoll, Joseph Benjamin. "An Analytical Study of the
Principal Instrumental Compositions of Wallingford
Riegger." PhD dissertation. Northwestern Universi-
ty, 1954. UM 55-6. DA xv.1, pp. 130-1. 348 pages.
An analysis of the Trio for violin + cello + piano
(1919-1920) and other works.

Henri-Joseph Rigel
1741-1799

*For a discussion of Rigel's role in French sonata music see
Saint-Foix's article {860}.*

Peter Ritter
1763-1846

1243. Elsen, Josephine Caryce. "The Instrumental Works of
Peter Ritter (1763-1846)." PhD dissertation.
Northwestern University, 1967. RILM 67-1655. UMI
67-15226. DAI xxviii.7A, pp. 1710-11. 2 vols. viii
+ 490 pages.
Gives a descriptive catalogue and general analysis of
the instrumental works of Ritter, a Mannheim composer
who stayed there after the court moved back to Munich
in 1778. Ritter's chamber music includes 23 quartets,
as well as quintets, trios and duos. Appendix II
gives the scores of 3 complete works: a duo for 2
cellos, a string quartet, and a cello concerto.

George Rochberg
b.1918

1244. Smith, Joan Templar. "The String Quartets of George
Rochberg." PhD dissertation. University of Roches-

ter, 1976. UMI 76-21657. DAI xxxvii.5A, p. 2488.
vi + 331 pages.
Discusses influences, basic compositional techniques,
forms, vertical sonorities, sets, texture, dynamics and
rhythm in each of the 3 quartets (1952, 1959-61, 1972).
Notes Rochberg's aesthetics at the time of composition.

1245. Wood, Hugh. "Thoughts on a Modern Quartet," in *Tempo*,
no. 111 (December, 1974), 23-26.
Concern with Rochberg's conscious imitation of different past styles. No analysis or historical commentary.

*For a discussion of Rochberg's Dialogues for clarinet +
piano see Jennings's dissertation {1207}.*

Joaquin Rodrigo
b.1902

*For a discussion of Sonata Pimpante (1966) for violin +
piano see Klugherz's dissertation {1122}.*

Hilding Rosenberg
1892-1985

1246. Wallner, Bo. "Kammermusikalks Sammanfattning: om
Hilding Rosenbergs Strakkvartetter nr 7-12," in *Dansk
Musiktidsskrift*, xxxv (1960), 82-87. In Danish.
Lengthy review of the Swedish composer's string quar-
tets nos. 7-12.

Albert Roussel
1869-1937

*For a catalogue of Roussel's chamber music, see Catalogue de
l'Oeuvre d'Albert Roussel (Paris/Brussels: Editor, 1947),
pages 79-90. ML 134.R88C3.*

1247. Ferroud, P.-O. "La Musique de Chambre d'Albert
Roussel," in *Revue Musicale*, special issue (April,
1929), 52-64.
General statements about Roussel's character, life, and
chamber music, which falls into an early period (Op. 2,
6 and 11) and a late one (Op. 27, 28 and 30). Gives a
brief history of each and brief descriptions of the
forms and themes.

Edmund Rubbra
b.1901

1248. Rubbra, Edmund. "String Quartet No. 2 in E flat, Op.
      73: an Analytical Note by the Composer," in *The Music
      Review*, xiv (1953), 36-44.
      An analysis of tonality and motives.

Archduke Rudolph
1788-1831

1249. Kagan, Susan. "The Music of Archduke Rudolph, Beetho-
      ven's Patron, Pupil and Friend." PhD dissertation.
      City University of New York, 1983. UMI 83-19773. DA
      xliv.5A, p. 1236. 411 pages.
      A scholarly biography and bibliography, followed by an
      analytical discussion of the music, some of which is
      chamber.

Charles-Camille Saint-Saëns
1835-1921

1250. Harkins, Elizabeth Remsberg. "The Chamber Music of
      Camille Saint-Saëns." PhD dissertation. New York
      University, 1976. UMI 77-5409. DAI xxxvii.9A, p.
      5430. 216 pages.
      A history of the 52 chamber pieces Saint-Saëns wrote
      from age 5 to 86.

See {879} for a discussion of his violin + piano sonata.

Giovanni Battista Sammartini
1701-1775

1251. Mishkin, Henry G. "Five Autograph String Quartets by
      Giovanni Battista Sammartini," in *Journal of the
      American Musicological Society*, vi (1953), 136-147.
      Examines the 5 late string quartets by Sammartini pre-
      served in an autograph manuscript in the Paris Conser-
      vatory (now in the Bibliothèque Nationale). A brief
      account of the other printed and manuscript collections
      of Sammartini's chamber music. He combines homophonic
      and melodic elements to form a new kind of counter-
      point, a dialogue with a new-found equality of parts.
      Tonal structure is important.

1252. Cesari, Gaetano. "Sei Sonate Notturne di G.B. Sammar-
      tini," in *Rivista Musicale Italiana*, xxiv (1917),
      479-482.
      Briefly describes these 6 sonatas, which in 1917 were
      in the possession of Count Giorgio Casati, and compares

them with an entirely different collection of *Sei Sonate Notturne, Op. VII*, in Paris.

1253. Churgin, Bathia. "New Facts in Sammartini Biography: the Authentic Print of the String Trios, Op. 7," in *Journal of the American Musicological Society*, xx (1967), 107-112.
Discovery of an authentic edition of the trios reveals connections between Sammartini and the Duke of Parma, Don Fillipo, and establishes a firm date of 1760 for the start of the composer's most mature period (beginning with the trios). Also important for the clear absence of a continuo part. Detailed, scholarly essay.

Johann Christian Schickhardt
c.1682-1762

1254. Moore, J. Robert. "*Six Sonatas for Transverse Flute, Oboe or Violin and Basso Continuo*, Op. 20, Volume II, by Johann Christian Schickhardt (ca.1682-1762): a Performance Edition with Historical Commentary, including an Ornamented Solo Part, Figured Bass Realization and a Comparison with Other Contemporary *Sonate da Camera*." DMA dissertation. University of Rochester, Eastman School of Music, 1981. DAI xlii.8A, pp. 3342-3. 273 pages.
Not seen.

Johann Heinrich Schmelzer
c.1623-1680

1255. Aschböck, E. "Die Sonaten des Johann Heinrich Schmelzer." PhD dissertation. University of Vienna, 1979. DAI (Europe), xliv.2, p. 254.
A history and simple analysis of the sonatas (most are for 2 or more instruments), with a thematic catalogue.

Johann Schobert
c.1740-1767

1256. Riemann, Hugo. "Johann Schobert," in *Ausgewählte Werke von Johann Schobert*, in *Denkmäler deutscher Tonkunst*, 1. Folge, xxxix (Leipzig: Breitkopf & Härtel, 1909), pages v-xxii. M 2.D39.Bd.39.
A thematic catalogue of Schobert's works and an essay on Schobert's life and position within the older generation of Mannheimers. Schobert's fame and importance lie with his chamber music for obligato keyboard with strings, which demonstrates the new aesthetics of mid-18th-century Europe, when the keyboard (= piano) no longer accompanies but is accompanied. Relates Scho-

bert's chamber music to earlier, contemporary, and
later composers. Assembles a lot of information on
Schobert -- a pioneering study that remains the
basis for all future studies.

1257. David, Hans Theodore. *Johann Schobert als Sonatenkom-
ponist*. Kassel: Bärenreiter/Borna-Leipzig: Universi-
tätsverlag von Robert Noske, 1928. ML 410.S282D2.
1928. vii + 76 pages + pullout (unnumbered, with
list of Schobert's works Op. 1-20 and 5 additional
pieces).

A thorough and comprehensive scholarly discussion of
Schobert's sonatas: historical and bibliographic back-
ground, Schobert's style, analysis of the sonatas, analysis of form in general and in specific movements,
Schobert's development techniques, and Schobert's significance aesthetically and historically. Compares
Schobert to his contemporary harpsichordists in Paris:
Leontzi Honauer and Johann Gottfried Eckard. Notes
that the keyboard has become the main instrument, and
Schobert contrasts his stark, simple, compact accompaniment with sudden bursts of heightened emotions (a
Mannheim symphony on the keyboard). His straight-
forward harmony is interrupted by an isolated, novel
modulatory chord or passage that is striking for its
rarity. Schobert was affected by *Sturm und Drang*, yet
this was within a framework of classicism: the emotional modulations occur only at the beginning of the development sections. Despite assertions to the contrary
by Riemann, Schobert was closer to Vienna than to Mannheim. The sonatas are considered *per se* and not merely
as precursors of the violin + piano sonata or any other
later genre. Although David is primarily concerned
with the keyboard aspects, his penetrating analyses and
bibliographic contributions on Schobert make this work
important for all chamber music historians, students
and scholars.

*For an early study of Schobert's importance for the French
sonata see Saint-Foix's article {860}.*

Arnold Schoenberg
1874-1951

*For a catalogue of Schoenberg's music including the chamber
pieces, see Josef Rufer, Das Werk Arnold Schönbergs (Kassel:
Bärenreiter, 1959), trl. by Dika Newlin The Works of Arnold
Schoenberg: a Catalogue of his Compositions, Writings and
Paintings (London: Faber & Faber, 1962), 124 pages + 37
illustrations. ML 134.S33R83.1962.*

1258. Wellesz, Egon. "Arnold Schoenberg," in *Zeitschrift der internationalen Musikgesellschaft*, xii (1911), 342-348.

Discusses Schoenberg's music from Op. 1 to Op. 10 and dwells on Op. 4 ("Verklärte Nacht," string sextet) and especially on Op. 10 (String Quartet No. 1). Schoenberg is first concerned with melodic expansion so he writes songs. Then he is concerned with the highest perfection of the Classical form, so he writes instrumental music (Op. 4). In the third stage -- Op. 10 -- he tackles both problems together: he writes melodic fragments that make sense as an organism only in terms of the whole piece, and the interaction of these fragments combines both melodic unity and the form of the piece. Op. 10 is at the threshhold of this new style, while Op. 11 piano pieces are completely in it.

1259. Whittall, Arnold. *Schoenberg Chamber Music*, in BBC *Music Guides*, no. 21. Seattle: University of Washington, 1972. MT 145.S26W5.1972b. 64 pages, 17 examples.

A non-technical discussion of the string quartets, string trio and wind quintet, designed for the erudite layperson.

For a documentary study of Schoenberg's string quartets, see Ursula von Rauchhaupt's Schoenberg, Berg, Webern: The String Quartets, {201}. For their historical position in the first part of the 20th century, see Werner Pütz's Studien zum Streichquartettschaffen {995}.

1260. Steiner, Fred. "A History of the First Complete Recording of the Schoenberg String Quartets," in *Journal of the Arnold Schoenberg Institute*, ii (1978), 122-137.

A chronicle of the events and personalities in the private recording of the 4 quartets by the Kolisch Quartet in Hollywood in May, 1936. The arrangement of the recording by Schoenberg's pupil Alfred Newman at United Artists Stage 7, and the subsequent pressing of probably 25 copies by RCA Victor for private distribution with liner notes by Schoenberg. Newman's copy is now at the University of Southern California Library; Harvard, Bennington College, and Smith College have copies. Important for a reprint of Schoenberg's notes and a transcript of his and Newman's and the Kolisch Quartets's conversations from the original discs. LP copies made in 1949-1950.

1261. Gradenwitz, Peter. "The Idiom and Development in Schoenberg's Quartets," in *Music and Letters*, xxvi (1945), 123-142.

The composer's 4 stylistic periods reflected in each of his string quartets. Detailed analysis of form, mo-

tive, tonality or atonality, and style. Important analysis and background for understanding the quartets.
Concludes with a chronology of Schoenberg's total
output, which is divided into the 4 periods.

1262. Musgrave, Michael Graham. "Schoenberg and Brahms: a
Study of Schoenberg's Response to Brahms's Music as
Revealed in his Didactic Writings and Selected Early
Writings." PhD dissertation. University of London,
1980. DAI (Europe) xliv.1, p. 5. 522 pages.
An attempt to show Brahms's influence on Schoenberg's
harmonic and tonal relationships, thematic processes
and phrase structure, contrapuntal relationships, and
formal relationships. Chooses 3 early chamber pieces
of Schoenberg in which to demonstrate these: String
Quartet in D Major (1897), *Verklärte Nacht* (1899), and
String Quartet in D Minor (1905).

1263. Thieme, Ulrich. *Studien zum Jugenwerk Arnold Schönbergs: Einflüsse und Wandlungen*, in *Kölner Beiträge
zur Musikforschung*, Bd. 107. Regensburg: Gustav
Bosse, 1979. HML 5040.15.86. ISBN 3-7649-2205-2.
vi + 234 pages. "Schönbergs frühe Kammermusik." PhD
dissertation. University of Köln.
An attempt to understand the developing ideas in
Schoenberg's mind as he wrote his earliest pieces.
While not limited in the book to chamber music, chamber
music does figure prominently (complete and fragmentary
string quartets, string sextet). Considers the influence of Brahms, Dvořák, and Zemlinsky and analyzes
rhythm, counterpoint and development.

See also Wilke {197}.

1264. Gerlach, Reinhard. "War Schönberg von Dvořák beein-
flusst?: zu Arnold Schönbergs Streichquartett D-Dur,"
in *Neue Zeitschrift für Musik*, cxxxiii (1972), 122-
127.
From childhood on Schoenberg knew intimately Dvořák's
chamber music, and this influenced his early string
quartet (1897). Zemlinsky worked with Schoenberg on
the piece and probably had Schoenberg eliminate a lot
of the Dvořák influences since he (Zemlinsky) was completely dominated by Brahms at this time. Uses primarily Dvořák's *Bagatelles* Op. 47 (2 violins + cello +
harmonium) and the 3 string quartets Op. 61, 80 and 96.
A scholarly analysis. Same thesis proposed in {457}.

*For a parallel between Schoenberg's and Ives's first 2
string quartets, see Gwyneth Walker's dissertation {1021}.*

1265. Schîndler, Kurt. *Arnold Schönberg's Quartet in D
Minor Op. 7: an Introductory Note by Kurt Schindler
as Delivered by Him at the Private Performance by the*

Flonzaley Quartet, at the Cort Theatre, New York, December 28th, 1913: followed by an Index of Musical Themes. New York: G. Schirmer, 1914. 787 Sch63S. iii + 10 pages + 5 pages of music.
Most of the essay is an attempt to characterize Schoenberg the composer (and painter!) who has attracted great attention abroad but is little known in America. Finds that Schoenberg's compositions fit into 3 periods: the early one is romantic, the second is contrapuntal, the third is mad. The quartet fits into the second period. Divides this 52 minute, 1 movement quartet into 3 parts: I = sonata (with fugato between first and second themes + scherzo with trio; II = Durchführung (development), and III = recapitulation + Rondo finale. Notes the logic of its construction based on thematic development: Schoenberg always thinks contrapuntally. Paraphrases Betti who finds Schoenberg closer to Beethoven's quartets than late Beethoven was to Haydn's early quartets.

1266. Neff, Severine. "Ways to Imagine Two Successive Pieces of Schoenberg: the Second String Quartet, Opus 10, Movement One; the Song, 'Ich darf nicht dankend,' Opus 14, No. 1." PhD dissertation. Princeton University, 1979. DAI xxxix.12A, p. 7048. 121 pages.
A detailed, technical analysis of the structure of the quartet movement that shows basic major and minor third symmetries which link into minor second symmetries at cadences.

1267. Glasow, Glenn Loren. "Variation as Formal Design and Twelve-tone Procedure in the *Third String Quartet* by Arnold Schoenberg." DMA dissertation. University of Illinois, 1967. UMI 68-8088. DAI xxviii.12A, pp. 5089-90. 243 pages.
Seeks the relationship between variation as form and variation as a 12-tone procedure. The particular movement was chosen because it has both types in it. A detailed theoretic discussion. Concludes that the relationship is inconsistent and unpredictable.

1268. Dietrich, Norbert. *Arnold Schönbergs Drittes Streichquartett op.30: seine Form und sein Verhältnis zur Geschichte der Gattung*, in *Beiträge zur Musikforschung*, Band 12. Munich/Salzburg: Emil Katzbichler, 1983. MT 145.S26D54.1983. ISBN 3-87397-261-1. 195 pages. PhD dissertation. University of Heidelberg, 1981.
A technical but readable analysis for advanced students and scholars on a crucial aspect of 12-tone composition. After a brief but important introduction, a lengthy discussion of each of the 4 movements of this first atonal quartet in history. With the absence of tonality Schoenberg had to discover a means to sustain

longer forms (longer forms in tonal systems depend on
tonality). In this quartet he sticks strictly to the
clear forms of a classical string quartet: 4 movements,
the first most important and in sonata form, the fourth
next in importance but lighter, the inner movements
even less weighty but contrasting. The analysis starts
from the premise that there is a connection between
pure 12-tone structure and the musical content; opposes
Ch. Möllers, *Reihentechnik und musikalische Gestalt*
(1977), who finds no point in using 12-tone technique
since it is meaningless for form. Since tonality is
out, Schoenberg accepts traditional form *per se* and
criteria other than tonality. Puts this problem in
context of historical quartets (Beethoven, Mozart,
Haydn) and Schoenberg's first 2 quartets. Considers
the smallest elements of formal sections in relation to
the 12-tone row, then those sections within the larger
formal scheme, and at times the historical precedence
in any genre of composition for what Schoenberg is
doing.

1269. Peles, Stephen V. "Interpretations of Sets in
        Multiple Dimensions: Notes on the Second Movement of
        Arnold Schoenberg's *String Quartet #3*," in *Perspec-
        tives of New Music*, xii (1983-1984), 303-352.
     Highly technical discussion of the movement based on
     Schoenberg's own belief that the row (set) is a "super
     motive" that acts as organizing factor in the thematic
     world of the piece and not only as "uninterpreted
     pitch-class succession." Thus considers the movement
     from the standpoint of the interaction of the set on
     the piece, the nature of the compositional decisions
     which relate to the set and piece, and "that interpre-
     tational universe wherein chosen compositional repre-
     sentations may impose crucial adjacency relations upon
     set elements which are otherwise distinctly non-
     adjacent when regarded in their precompositional, unin-
     terpreted state." Studies the implications of the set
     for this movement as an abstract set, and then focuses
     on the interpolations into those implications in the
     movement as Schoenberg wrote it.

1270. Stein, Erwin. "Schoenberg's New Structural Form," in
        Modern Music, vii (June-July, 1930), 3-10.
     Demonstrates Schoenberg's new 12-tone system in the
     third string quartet. Emphasizes the idea of "series"
     as "the tonal material of a composition ... borrowed
     from the chromatic scale and grouped in a special
     arrangement." The manipulations of the series leaves
     Schoenberg with much room to express his musical ideas
     and in no way restricts the profile of a melody. Does
     not present a numerical accounting of the use of the
     row in the quartet but rather selects specific uses of
     the row to demonstrate some of the things Schoenberg

does. Designed as an introduction to Schoenberg's method for the layperson; still useful today.

1271. Mangeot, André. "Schönberg's Fourth String Quartet," in *The Music Review*, iii (1942), 33-37.
A thematic and harmonic analysis that does not even mention "row." Stresses Schoenberg's morbid "humor" which results from the frequent diminished ninths and major sevenths.

1272. Neighbour, Oliver W. "A Talk on Schoenberg for Composers' Concourse," in *The Score*, no. 16 (June 1956), 19-28.
Analyzes the first movement of the Fourth String Quartet, which is in sonata form. The row and rhythmic idea merge at the opening and recur together; different forms of the row require different rhythms. Justifies a tonal-based reaction to hearing the opening.

1273. Cubbage, John Rex. "Directed Pitch Motion and Coherence in the First Movement of Arnold Schoenberg's Fourth String Quartet." PhD dissertation. Washington University, 1979. UMI 80-02443. DAI xl.7A, p. 3613. 303 pages.
Defines "directed pitch motion" as pitch patterning, and demonstrates it in an atonal work. Contains graphs. Highly technical, theoretical work.

For discussion of the woodwind quintet, see Erwin Stein's article {506}; Langdon Corson's Arnold Schoenberg's Woodwind Quintet, Op. 26: Background and Analysis, ed. by Roy Christensen {507}; and:

1274. Greissle, Felix. "Die formalen Grundlagen des Bläserquintetts von Arnold Schönberg," in *Musikblätter des Anbruch*, vii (1925), 63-68.
Written by the conductor of the premier (also Schoenberg's son-in-law). Analyzes Schoenberg's use of the row in the Wind Quintet.

1275. Jordan, Roland Carroll, Jr. "Schoenberg's *String Trio, Op. 45*: an Analytic Study." PhD dissertation. Washington University, 1973. UM 74-7046. DA xxxiv. 12A, p. 7808. 279 pages.
History and bibliography of the trio, including a review of previous studies of the piece and an investigation into "Schoenberg's use of hexachords with invariant content." Proposes a general system of related transposition that defines a comprehensible shape for the work. Studies the rows and other serial elements as well, and concludes with "an experiment in the establishment of relationships between the description of the trio and its technical organization." Appen-

dices include rows, analysis, and a list of errors in the published score.

1276. Peel, John M. "On Some Celebrated Measures of the Schoenberg String Trio," in *Perspectives of New Music*, xiv, no. 2 and xv, no. 1 (1976), 260-279.
A detailed, mathematical analysis of measures 12 to 17.5 of the Trio, which form a completed phrase and synthesize previous elements which will be exploited later. Corrects the score, and then goes into the complex details of intervals and pitches and their set implications. For professional theorists only.

1277. Hymanson, William. "Schönberg's String Trio (1946)," in *The Music Review*, xi (1950), 184-194.
A detailed analysis of the use of the row in the trio. Schoenberg has a plan within a plan, that is, a larger plan based on a 12-tone row or some motivic development, and a smaller plan or unit sometimes using only a half-row and not dependent on the order. For additions to and a few corrections of Hymanson, see O.W. Neighbour, "Dodecaphony in Schoenberg's String Trio," in *Music Survey*, iv (1952), 489-490.

1278. Hill, Richard S. "Arnold Schoenberg: String Trio," in *Notes*, viii (1950), 127-129.
An analysis of the trio solely from the standpoint of Schoenberg's use of 4 rows subdivided into hexachords.

1279. Staempfli, Edward. "Das Streichtrio opus 45 von Arnold Schönberg," in *Melos*, xxxvii (1970), 35-39.
On the origins of this trio written just after Schoenberg's near-fatal illness of 1946. It is revolutionary and conservative at the same time. A detailed analysis coupled with reflexion on Schoenberg's total output and on Webern's String Trio op. 20.

1280. Pfannkuch, Wilhelm. "Zu Thematik und Form in Schönbergs Streichsextett," in Anna Amalie Abert and Wilhelm Pfannkuch, eds., *Festschrift Friedrich Blume zum 70. Geburtstag* (Kassel: Bärenreiter, 1963), pp. 258-271. ML 55.B58A2.
Scholarly, highly technical analysis of "Verklärte Nacht," Op. 4, as a chamber piece. The 1-movement piece is a contraction of numerous movements into a single, tightly organized, non-sonata-form movement.

1281. Stein, Erwin. "Zu Schoenbergs neuer Suite Op. 29," in *Musikblätter des Anbruch*, ix (1927), 280-281.
A brief description of the structure of the 4-movement Suite for 3 clarinets (or other optional woodwinds) + violin + viola + cello + piano. Constant play between the 3 bodies of sound: woodwinds, strings and piano.

The movements are formally based on typical Baroque suite movements. Stands out for its rhythm.

Johann Schop
c.1590-1667

1282. Moser, Andreas. "Johann Schop als Violinkomponist," in Max Friedlaender, Henri Hinrichsen, Max Seiffert and Johannes Wolf, eds., *Festschrift Hermann Kretzschmar zum siebzigsten Geburtstage überreicht von Kollegen Schülern und Freunden* (Leipzig: C.F. Peters, 1918), reprint *Festschrift Hermann Kretzschmar zum 70. Geburtstage überreicht von Kollegen, Schülern und Freunden* (Hildesheim/New York: Georg Olm, 1973), pp. 92-95. ML 55.K845.1973.
An assessment of the virtuoso technique of the German violinist Schop as demonstrated in works which survive in *T'Uitnement Kabinet* (Amsterdam: Paulus Matthyss, 1646). The pieces by Schop include a Praeludium for solo violin, dances for violin + bass, 6 allemands a3, and 2 pieces for 2 violins or 2 viole da gamba + another instrument.

Franz Peter Schubert
1797-1828

The standard catalogue of Schubert's music including chamber works is Otto Erich Deutsch, Schubert: Thematic Catalogue of All his Works in Chronological Order *(New York: W.W. Norton, [1951]), xxiv + 566 pages. ML 134.S38D44.1951a. German trl. and ed. by Werner Aderhold,* Franz Schubert: Thematisches Verzeichnis seiner Werke in chronologischer Folge, supplement to Neue Ausgabe sämtlicher Werke, Series viii, Bd. 4 *(Kassel: Bärenreiter, 1978), xxiii + 712 pages. ML 134.S38D445.1978. ISBN 3-7618-0571-3. A paperback edition (Kleiner Ausgabe), ed. by Werner Aderhold, Walther Dürr, and Arnold Feil (Munich: Deutscher Taschenbuch/Kassel: Bärenreiter, 1983), 303 pages. ML 134.S38D45.1983. ISBN 3-423-03261-8; 3-7618-3261-3.*

For a non-technical introduction to Schubert's chamber music see the essay by William Mann in Alec Robertson, ed., Chamber Music *{160}.*

1283. Westrup, Jack A. *Schubert Chamber Music*, in BBC Music *Guides*, no. 5. Seattle: University of Washington Press, 1969. MT 145.S28W48.1969. 63 pages, 40 examples.
A non-technical discussion, for the layperson, of each of Schubert's principal chamber works. An index of works by genre with Deutsch number and bibliography.

1284. Laciar, Samuel L. "The Chamber-Music of Franz Schubert," in *The Musical Quarterly*, xiv (1928), 515-538.
A general, brief analysis of the form and style of the chamber music, with special emphasis on the quartets and piano trios.

1285. Schauffler, Robert Haven. *Franz Schubert: the Ariel of Music*. New York: G.P. Putnam's Sons, 1949. ML 410.S3S25. Chapters 32-37, pp. 203-262 of Part II, are devoted to chamber music.
A popular biography and discussion of the more important works. Each movement is described briefly with the principle melodies quoted and delicious metaphors. Brings in personal anecdotes from the author's perspective as professional cellist.

1286. Huschke, Konrad. *Das Siebengestirn der grossen Schubertschen Kammermusikwerke*. Pritzwalk: Adolf Tienken, 1928. ML 410.S3H8. 64 pages.
A non-scholarly survey of Schubert's chamber music with special emphasis on the masterpieces of 1824-1828: Octet Op. 166, String Quartets in A Minor, D Minor and G Major, the 2 piano trios, and Quintet Op. 163. The analyses are designed for laypersons, with emotive metaphors fairly accurately drawn and comparisons to Beethoven's works.

1287. Chusid, Martin. "The Chamber Music of Franz Schubert." PhD dissertation. University of California, 1961.
Shows how Schubert in his chamber music resolved the contrast between Classical clarity of harmony, tonality and forms based on tonal direction and Romantic ambiguity of harmony, tonality and forms based on thematic organization. Considers different stages in Schubert's output and analyzes specific movements with regard to harmony, texture, melody and form.

1288. Straeten, Edmund van der. "Schuberts Behandlung der Streichinstrumente mit besonderer Berücksichtigung der Kammermusik," in *Bericht über den internationalen Kongress für Schubertforschung Wien 25. bis 29. November 1928* (Augsburg: Dr. Benno Filser, 1929), pp. 131-140.
Schubert inherited a high level of violin technique from Viotti and Rode and as demanded by Beethoven and developed it further in his own way. His melodies may come from heaven, but his violin technique he understood from the violinists whom he knew -- Böhm, Mayseder, and Hellmesberger -- as well as the cellist Linke. From them he learned bowed staccato for longer passages. Schubert tended to orchestral string writing in his quartets. Considers trills and the higher

ranges of the instrument. The later works add little
to the technical demands of the earlier pieces.

1289. Denny, Thomas Arthur. "The Finale in the Instrumental
Works of Schubert." PhD dissertation. University of
Rochester, Eastman School of Music, 1982. DAI xlii.
9A, p. 3801. 284 pages.
Refutes the accusation that Schubert's instrumental
finales are flawed. Goes into considerable depth in
showing that Schubert had other ideas of the recapitulation than standard theorists and uses the B-flat
trio, E-major symphony, and Quartettsatz to prove the
point. Schubert was not interested in "heavy" finales,
and when he attempts heavy finales, he is far less successful than when he uses lighter ones.

1290. Sachse, Hans-Martin. *Franz Schuberts Streichquartette*. Münster in Westfalen: Max Kramer, reproduced
typescript, 1958. MT 145.S23S3. iii + 333 pages.
PhD dissertation. University of Münster, 1958.
A scholarly study which dates and locates source material for the string quartets, including fragments and
lost quartets. Analyzes all the first movements, then
all the second movements, and so on. Divides the
quartets into early, middle and late; the first two
groups are important only in so far as they pave the
way for the late quartets. Lengthy analyses of the
early and middle quartets are tiresome. Value of the
book is largely in the opening and in a final chapter
that assesses the obviously strong influences of Haydn,
Mozart and Beethoven on Schubert (primarily in the
middle, not the outer movements).

1291. Deutsch, Otto Erich. "The Chronology of Schubert's
String Quartets," in *Music and Letters*, xxiv (1943),
25-30.
An important, brief discussion of Schubert's 19 or so
string quartets that dates the manuscripts and the
early publications. Lists the 19 known quartets (4 of
which are completely or partially lost), cites dates of
publication, key, opus number, complete edition locations, dedications, first performances, first publication, and some additional information, and gives excellent but dated bibliography on the subject.

1292. Ruff, Philipp. "Die Streichquartette Franz Schuberts." PhD dissertation. University of Vienna,
1929.
Not seen.

1293. Coolidge, Richard A. "Form in the String Quartets of
Franz Schubert," in *The Music Review*, xxxii (1971),
309-325.

Challenges the common opinion that Schubert was incompetent or dull in musical form. Briefly analyses the forms of the movements of each of the 15 fully surviving quartets and concludes that Schubert is not weak but different in his handling of large forms.

1294. Wolff, Christoph. "Schubert's 'Der Tod und das Mädchen': Analytical and Explanatory Notes on the Song D531 and the Quartets D810," in Eva Badura-Skoda and Peter Branscombe, eds., *Schubert Studies: Problems of Style and Chronology* (Cambridge: Cambridge University Press, 1982), pages 143-171. ML 410.S3S996.1982. ISBN 0-521-22606-6.
The most important essay on the D-Minor Quartet. A detailed, analytical study of Schubert's setting of the song, noting its dramatic and operatic characteristics. A brief analysis of the quartet and the song's penetration of it. Rejects a "cyclic" subject of death throughout the piece but finds that purely structural elements recur and that the spirit of the song affects all movements.

1295. Truscott, Harold. "Schubert's D Minor String Quartet," in *The Music Review*, xix (1958), 27-36.
Yet another attempt to prove that Schubert was, contrary to popular belief, a master of structure, based on arches of tonality. The author fails to convince that the tonal structure is of greater importance than Schubert's lyricism and that the literal repetition of whole sections or melodies is a structural strength.

1296. Siegfried, E. "Das 'Andante con moto' aus dem Quartett D Moll von Franz Schubert," in *Neue Zeitschrift für Musik*, xcviii (1902), 265-266.
Views this movement as the battle between life and death. A detailed description of the "Death and the Maiden" theme and its variation in this quartet movement.

1297. Brent-Smith, Alexander. *Schubert: Quartet in D Minor and Octet*, in *The Musical Pilgrim*. London: Oxford University Press, 1927. MT 145.S28.B7. 55 pages, 82 examples.
Analyzes thematic motives, rhythms, and tonalities in these 2 pieces, punctuated with occasional extramusical rhapsodizing. Gives brief historical comments, and concludes that "Death and the Maiden" shines in its spontaneous color, harmony and energy despite some faulty architecture, unbalanced rhythms, and obscure harmonies. Compares the Schubert Octet with Beethoven's Septet Op. 20.

1298. Truscott, Harold. "Schubert's String Quartet in G Major," in *The Music Review*, xx (1959), 119-145.

A sequel to the same author's analysis of the D Minor
Quartet. *See Gillet's commentary {1299}.*

1299. Gillet, Judy. "The Problem of Schubert's G Major
String Quartet (D.887)," in *The Music Review*, xxxv
(1974), 281-292.
Previous critics of this quartet have discredited part
or all of it, and even Truscott {1298}, in trying to
prove the worth of the last movement, fails to recognize the unity of the whole work. Truscott proposes
that since the first 3 movements reach the "sublime,"
the fourth movement, in its "grotesqueness," must serve
to bring the listener back to earth. Believes Truscott
is on the right track here, even if he does not follow
it up, and pursues more fully the concepts of "sublime"
and "grotesque" as unifying as well as contrasting
principles throughout the quartet. An important,
thought-provoking analysis.

1300. Dahlhaus, Carl. "Über Schuberts Sonatenform: der
erste Satz des G-Dur Quartetts D.887," in *Musica*,
xxxii (1978), 125-130.
Warns against judging Schubert by using form and theory
as practiced by Beethoven, since Schubert may not have
been aware of Beethoven's theory and in any case had
his own things to say. Schubert works in a kind of
timelessness, especially in the second theme of this
movement -- as opposed to Beethoven's dramatic drive.
He works so that the later ideas grow out of earlier
ones, yet this does not obscure the basic contrast of
themes of the exposition (in other words, the merger of
sonata and variation form). Analyzes the movement to
prove this.

1301. Wells-Harrison, W. *Schubert's Compositions for Piano
and Strings: a Critical Study*, in *"The Strad" Hand-
books*, no. 2. London: John Leng/New York: Charles
Scribner's Sons, 1915. 787 Sch7115. iv + 94 pages.
Describes for the layperson the chronological events of
each of the compositions discussed. Despite some gross
inaccuracies (Schubert died at 39, and "his technique
was on a slightly lower plane to his inspiration") this
is the only book devoted to this repertory.

1302. Orel, Alfred. "Franz Schuberts 'Sonate' für Klavier,
Violine und Violoncell aus dem Jahre 1812," in *Zeitschrift für Musikwissenschaft*, v (1922-1923), 209-
218.
Discovers this lost early chamber work in the Vienna
Stadtbibliothek (MH 126) and discusses the manuscript,
handwriting, and errors. Considers why this piece was
omitted from the complete works, along with other early
pieces. Briefly considers the style of the sonata
(trio), its chronological significance in Schubert's

development of sonata form, and its position vis-a-vis
his other chamber music (string quartets in particular)
in rating early Schubert music.

1303. Badura-Skoda, Eva. "The Chronology of Schubert's
    Piano Trios," in Eva Badura-Skoda and Peter Brans-
    combe, eds., *Schubert Studies: Problems of Style and
    Chronology* (Cambridge: Cambridge University Press,
    1982), pages 277-295.
    Briefly mentions an early trio fragment D28, but con-
    centrates on the 2 famous trios Op. 99 and 100 and a
    late fragment D897 (a rejected earlier version of the
    slow movement of Op. 99). Since the autograph for Op.
    99 is lost, it cannot be dated precisely, but based on
    new water-mark evidence as well as a lot of other evi-
    dence, October-November, 1827 seems likely. Op. 100
    can be dated in November, 1827 because it so states in
    Schubert's handwriting on the 2 surviving autographs (1
    a draft).

1304. Geiringer, Karl. "Schubert's Arpeggione Sonata and
    the 'Super Arpeggio,'" in *The Musical Quarterly*, lxv
    (1979), 513-523.
    A brief history of this sonata and the peculiar "bowed
    guitar" for which it was written. The 5-note arpeggios
    Schubert wrote are idiomatic for the arpeggione instru-
    ment but not for the cello. Since this is one of Schu-
    bert's masterpieces, we must expect cellists to perform
    it, but with special care to recreate the arpeggione's
    arpeggios.

1305. Weiss, Piero. "Dating the 'Trout' Quintet," in
    Journal of the American Musicological Society, xxxii
    (1979), 539-548.
    Schubert based his unusual scoring of the Quintet
    (1819) on a quintet arrangement by Hummel of Hummel's
    own Septet Op. 74. Schubert also borrowed melodies
    from the Hummel piece.

1306. Abert, Anna Amalie. "Rhythmus und Klang in Schuberts
    Streichquintett," in Heinrich Hüschen, ed., *Fest-
    schrift Karl Gustav Fellerer zum sechzigsten Geburts-
    tag am 7. Juli 1962* (Regensburg: Gustav Bosse, 1962),
    pp. 1-11. ML 55.F35H8.
    The addition of a fifth instrument to the C-major Quin-
    tet Op. 163 allowed Schubert a synthesis between cham-
    ber and symphonic music which he apparently unwillingly
    had suppressed in his quartets. In the quartets, espe-
    cially the late ones of the 1820's, there is already a
    dichotomy or rhythmic counterpoint between melody-group
    and rhythmic-group (often ostinato) instruments. In
    the quintet this dichotomy now becomes a basic princi-
    ple in all but the scherzo. Brahms does this as well.

A scholarly, erudite yet always readable essay that helps anyone to understand Schubert's chamber music.

1307. Gülke, Peter. "In What Respect a Quintet? On the Disposition of Instruments in the String Quintet D956," in Eva Badura-Skoda and Peter Branscombe, eds., *Schubert Studies: Problems of Style and Chronology* (Cambridge: Cambridge University Press, 1982), pages 173-185. ML 410.S3S2996.1982. ISBN 0-521-22606-6.

In this quintet Schubert started a new structural and psychological exploration: "the contrast between concord and conflict in the relationship of structure and scoring as an important element of the composition." An analysis of the piece from this standpoint, and an effort to disprove Brown's statement (M.J.E. Brown, *Schubert: a Critical Biography* [London: 1958], p. 292) that Schubert could have picked a more reasonable ensemble for his ideas.

G. Ch. Schultze

For a discussion of his collection of 6 duos for 2 flutes (1729) attributed to Handel, see Eve R. Meyer's "Has Handel Written Works for Two Flutes without a Bass?" {929}.

Robert Schumann
1810-1856

For a catalogue of Schumann's chamber music, see Kurt Hofmann and Siegmar Keil, Robert Schumann: thematisches Verzeichnis sämtlicher im Druck erschienenen musikalischen Werke mit Angabe des Jahres ihres Entstehens und Erscheinens, 5th enl. and rev. ed. (Hamburg: J. Schuberth, 1982), systematic list p. 147. ML 134.S4A2.1982. ISBN 3-922074-02-2. 4th ed. 1868. An alphabetical list is Michael Ochs, Schumann Index PT.1: an Alphabetical Index to Robert Schumann Werke, in MLA Index Series, No. 6 (Ann Arbor: Music Library Association, 1967), pages 9-14. ML 134.S4S4.v.1.

For a non-technical introduction to Schumann's chamber music see Joan Chissell's essay in Alec Robertson, ed., Chamber Music {160}. And by the same author:

1308. Chissell, Joan. "Chamber Music," in *Schumann*, in *The Master Musicians Series* (London: J.M. Dent & Sons, 1948; 2nd ed. 1956; 3rd ed. 1967, reprinted 1971; 4th ed. 1977), pp. 155-168. ML 410.S4C4.1977. ISBN 0-460-03170-8.

A survey of Schumann's most important chamber music, with brief historical data and brief but cogent analysis of his unity of motive and form. Except for the 3 string quartets, all the chamber music includes piano,

though not always as successfully as in the piano quintet. Points to specific weaknesses in form, rhythm and
style (Schumann was not a contrapuntalist).

1309. Dickinson, A.E.F. "The Chamber Music," in Gerald
      Abraham, ed., *Schumann: a Symposium* (London: Oxford
      University Press, 1952), pp. 138-175. ML 410.S4
      A6317.
      A few general remarks for the layperson, followed by an
      analysis of form, tonality and motives of each of the
      movements of the major chamber pieces. Seeks Schu-
      mann's models. A lot of cogent if opinionated observa-
      tions without any details.

1310. Gardner, John. "The Chamber Music," in Alan Walker,
      ed., *Robert Schumann: the Man and his Music* (London:
      Barrie & Jenkins, 1972; reprint 1976), pp. 200-240.
      ML 410.S4W26.1976. ISBN 0-214-66805-3.
      An analysis for the educated layperson of interesting
      form, thematic treatment, rhythm and other technical
      items in each of Schumann's chamber pieces. Character-
      izes Schumann's overall chamber style and notes the
      powerful influence he had on the chamber music of his
      19th-century contemporaries and successors (even more
      than Beethoven!).

1311. Kohlhase, Hans. *Die Kammermusik Robert Schumanns:*
      stilistische Untersuchungen, in *Hamburger Beiträge*
      zur Musikwissenschaft, Band 19. Hamburg: Karl Dieter
      Wagner, 1979. TF 2.S392K0. ISBN 3-921-02962-7. 3
      vols. I: xi + 249 pages; II: iv + 224 pages; III:
      121 pages + 9 facsimiles of autograph sketches. PhD
      dissertation. University of Hamburg, 1978.
      An attempt to understand the chamber style, to see if
      there is a consistent growth, and to determine if there
      is any interruption of this style or its growth once
      Schumann became mentally ill. Precise analysis con-
      fronts some concepts that are imprecise, especially
      what is "poetic" (= associative motivic citation and
      reminiscence), but Schumann himself placed a great deal
      more emphasis on the technique of composition than has
      hitherto been assumed. Emphasizes analysis of form,
      especially cyclic forms, and the manuscripts (sketches,
      complete drafts, fragments, autographs, proofs) to show
      compositional processes. Considers historical docu-
      ments (for example written views and reminiscences of
      Clara Schumann, Brahms and Joachim) as well as musical
      evidence (besides the manuscripts, the printed versions
      and borrowings as arrangements or reminiscences of
      earlier material by himself or others such as Bach,
      Beethoven, and Mendelssohn).

1312. Fuller-Maitland, John Alexander. *Schumann's Concerted*
      Chamber Music, in *The Musical Pilgrim*. London:

Humphrey Milford for Oxford University Press, 1929.
MT 145.S29F8. 47 pages, 34 examples.
A brief but comprehensive discussion of Schumann's
duets, trios, quartets, and quintet. Historical data
and non-technical analyses, arranged by genres.

1313. Helms, Siegmund. "Der Melodiebau in der Kammermusik
Robert Schumanns," in *Neue Zeitschrift für Musik*,
cxxxi (1970), 194-196.
An interesting study of Schumann's concept of melody,
especially in his chamber music. Schumann sought a melody quite different from Italian ones, which are like
bird calls. Melody must have feeling much more than
understanding. Schumann used melodies with Romantic
feeling even in the larger works. It was important
that listeners feel, not understand, the melodies. His
melodies are restricted (syncopated) much more than
driving; they are practically devoid of ornamentation.
In chamber music he is much more chromatic than in the
Lied. Compares his earlier to later melodies and to
Brahms's.

1314. Roesner, Linda Correll. "Studies in Schumann Manuscripts: with Particular Reference to Sources Trans-
mitting Instrumental Works in the Larger Forms." PhD
dissertation. New York University, 1973. UMI 74-
13369. DAI xxxiv.12A, p. 7811. 2 vols. 604 pages.
Discusses among other pieces the string quartets Op. 41
in Chapter V. A scholarly study of the manuscripts,
their shape, size, format, foliation, pagination, type
of paper, bindings, layout, and writing media and im-
plements. The sketches for Op. 41 are presented in
vol. II "in complete diplomatic transcription, and
accompanied by a critical apparatus." This is apparently an expansion of her earlier article {1315}.

1315. Correll [Roesner], Linda E. "Structural Revisions in
the String Quartets Opus 41 of Robert Schumann," in
Current Musicology, no. 7 (1968), 87-95.
Studies the sketches and fair copy of the 3 quartets
op. 41 (1842) as well as other supporting documents,
and compares them to the printed edition. Thereby
demonstrates Schumann's preoccupation with large
structural problems. Refutes to some degree the popular notion that Schumann was a spontaneous, improvisa-
tory composer and not capable of extended works that
required a lot of working out.

*For a study of Schumann's use of chromaticism and modulation
in his string quartets, see Gerhard Wilcke's Tonalität und
Modulation im Streichquartett Mendelssohns und Schumanns
{1106}.*

1316. Melkus, Eduard. "Eine vollständige 3. Violinsonate
    Schumanns," in *Neue Zeitschrift für Musik*, cxxi
    (1960), 190-195.
    A major study of this sonata and its curious history.
    The slow and last movements were written in 1853 as
    part of a 4-movement work for Joachim by Schumann,
    Brahms and Albert Dietrich. Later Schumann added his
    own first and third movements. After Schumann's death
    Clara Schumann, Brahms and Joachim felt it would bring
    disgrace to Schumann's good name so they suppressed it.
    A formal and thematic analysis. See also articles by
    Oliver Neighbour, "Schumanns dritte Violinsonate," in
    Neue Zeitschrift für Musik, cxvii (1956), 423-425;
    Heinrich Düsterbehn, "Ein Beitrag zur Entstehung der
    FAE-Freundschafts-Sonate," in *(Neue) Zeitschrift für
    Musik*, ciii (1936), 284-286; Erich Valentin, "Die FAE-
    Sonate: das Dokument einer Freundschaft," in *(Neue)
    Zeitschrift für Musik*, cii (1935), 1337-1340; and
    Joachim Herrmann, "Schumanns dritte Violinsonate," in
    Musica, xii (1958), 226-227.

*See {1107} for a comparison of Schumann's and Mendelssohn's
piano trios.*

1317. Boetticher, Wolfgang. "Das frühe Klavierquartett c-
    moll von Robert Schumann," in *Die Musikforschung*,
    xxxi (1978), 465-467.
    Explains the origins of this early piano quartet and
    its conceptual transformation into a symphony as docu-
    mented in Schumann's diaries. This is a companion to
    an edition of the quartet which Boetticher published
    (Wilhelmshaven: 1978).

1318. Krummacher, Friedhelm. "Schwierigkeiten des ästheti-
    schen Urteils über historische Musik: Anmerkungen zu
    Schumanns Klavierquartett op. 47," in Heinrich Poss,
    ed., *Festschrift Ernst Pepping zu seinem 70. Geburts-
    tag am 12. September 1971* (Berlin: Merseburger,
    1971), pp. 247-268. ML 55.P47F5. ISBN 3-87537-003-
    1.
    Comparison between negative 20th-century judgements of
    the piece and negative mid-19th-century judgements: the
    20th-century ones are based on the emotional qualities
    of the piece and not on its structure or its historical
    position, while the mid-19th-century ones are based on
    form, content, and theme in context of "modern" music
    of the time (part of a historical development). An
    analysis of the music in order to understand the 19th-
    century positions, with consideration of the limited
    success of anyone's piano quartets in the first half of
    the 19th century and the differences in approach to
    structure by Schumann and Mendelssohn. For example,
    the 19th-century critic is judging themes on their
    ability to be developed, not their sweetness or senti-

mentality, with monotony through repetition to be avoided. Should Schumann's own statements on his aesthetics be the criteria on which to judge him? Clearly he was as much concerned with structure as with the poetic character of his pieces, and his comments are not a system of aesthetics. The basis of music aesthetics is determined less from laws of nature than through historical development. There cannot be any absolute modes or dogmas by which to judge a given piece at all times, but each period has its own different criteria which we must understand. As we move further from the 19th century, the temptation to consider the works of the 19th century as having been written with the same aesthetics as our own is less valid and full of difficulties, just as the belief that the greater distance in time gives us objectivity is false.

1319. Hollander, Hans. "Das Variationsprinzip in Schumanns Klavierquintett," in *Neue Zeitschrift für Musik*, cxxiv (1963), 223-225.
The continual variation principle so popular later on is already used by Schumann in some of his works. In variation movements he is less interested in harmonic-melodic variation than in a thematic and structural metamorphosis. Such happens in the Piano Quartet with the first 4 notes (which reflect the happy stage after his marriage with Clara) which recur -- metamorphosed -- in all 4 movements. A convincing analysis.

1320. Westrup, Jack. "The Sketch for Schumann's Piano Quintet Op. 44," in Heinrich Hüschen and Dietz-Rüdiger Moser, eds., *Convivium Musicorum: Festschrift Wolfgang Boetticher zum sechzigsten Geburtstag am 19. August, 1974* (Berlin: Merseburger, 1974), pp. 367-371. ML 55.B6.1974. ISBN 3-87537-085-6.
A discussion of the sketch which was given to Jean-Joseph-Bonaventure Laurens (1801-1891) in 1853 by Schumann and which is in the Bibliothèque d'Inguimbert in Carpentras, France. The sketch throws light on Schumann's working methods and "includes the draft of a movement ... not ... in the finished work." Points out the most significant differences between the sketches and the final quintet version and disproves a Niecks contention that Schumann completely rewrote trio 2 of the Scherzo after Mendelssohn disapproved.

1321. Simon, Eric. "Schumann's Fantasy Pieces," in *Clarinet*, no. 13 (Winter, 1953-1954), 4-7.
A brief discussion of the discrepancies between the published version (Breitkopf & Härtel, ed. by Clara Schumann) of Op. 73 *Fantasy Pieces* and Schumann's manuscript.

Ruth Crawford Seeger
1901-1953

1322. Gaume, Mary Matilda. "Ruth Crawford Seeger: her Life
      and Works." PhD dissertation. Indiana University,
      1973. UMI 74-04672. DA xxxiv.9A, pp. 6021-2. xvii
      + 312 pages.
      A biography and thematic catalogue. Includes a separ-
      ate chapter on the String Quartet (1931), as well as
      discussions of the Wind Quintet (1952), the 4 Diaphonic
      Suites (1930) for various small combinations of instru-
      ments, and several early chamber suites. Analyzes
      rhythm, harmony and motives.

1323. Perle, George. "Atonality and the Twelve-Note System
      in the United States," in *The Score*, no. 27 (July,
      1960), 51-66.
      Analyzes Crawford-Seeger's String Quartet (1931) on
      pages 58-60. Concentrates on the final movement that
      has suggestions of "a preconceived numerical plan."

For another discussion of her String Quartet see Michael
Coonrod's dissertation {504}.

Mátyás Seiber
1905-1960

1324. Weissmann, John S. "Die Streichquartette von Mátyás
      Seiber," trl. by Willi Reich, in *Melos*, xxii (1955),
      344-347 and xxiii (1956), 38-41.
      Assesses and analyzes Seiber's 3 string quartets. The
      3-movement first (1924) is under the influence of Kodá-
      ly, but with some Bartókian dissonances. The second
      (1934-1935) is a 12-tone piece that is at the end of
      his period of searching for his own style and at the
      beginning of that new style. The third (1951) is a
      complicated serial piece that is more contrapuntal than
      the second.

Roger Sessions
1896-1985

1325. Olmstead, Andrea. *Roger Sessions and his Music*. Ann
      Arbor: UMI Research Press, c.1985. ML 410.S47304.
      1985. ISBN 0-8357-1633-3. xvii + 218 pages.
      A study of Sessions's life and works based on 6 years
      of weekly, taped interviews of the composer and on
      criticisms of students, colleagues, and performers.
      Simple thematic, contrapuntal and formal analyses of
      significant pieces, including the Duo for violin +
      piano, 2 string quartets, and the String Quintet. Also

includes the composer's own statements on composition and publication of the music.

1326. Henderson, Ronald Duane. "Tonality in the Pre-Serial Instrumental Music of Roger Sessions." PhD dissertation. Eastman School of Music, 1974. UMI 74-21528. DAI xxxv.4A, pp. 2319-20. 474 pages.
A detailed tonal analysis of 7 instrumental works divided into 3 periods: 1923-1930 (no chamber music), 1935-1940 (string quartet in E Minor), and 1942-1950 (no chamber music). Less detailed discussions of a few other pieces of chamber music: Duo for Violin + Piano and String Quartet No. 2. Incorporates Sessions's own comments and Hindemith's theories of harmonic and melodic progression.

1327. Cone, Edward T. "Roger Sessions String Quartet," in *Modern Music*, xviii (1941), 159-163.
Analyzes tonality in Sessions's quartet (1936) and demonstrates in the opening of the first movement the centrality of E minor with modulation to E-flat minor. Briefly points out a few other factors in the piece.

James Sherard
1666-1738

1328. Tilmouth, Michael. "James Sherard: an English Amateur Composer," in *Music and Letters*, xlvii (1966), 313-322.
Biography of the amateur violinist who published 2 works: 12 trio sonatas Op. 1 (no date) and 12 trio sonatas Op. 2 (between 1706 and 1716). Briefly characterizes the sonatas, which are based on Corelli's.

Seymour Shifrin
1926-1979

For a review of his String Quartet No. 2, see David Lewin's review of Arnold Elston's quartet {868}.

Dmitri Dmitrievitch Shostakovich
1906-1975

For a catalogue of his chamber music, see Derek C. Hulme, Dmitri Shostakovich: Catalogue, Bibliography & Discography (Muir of Ord [Ross-shire]: Kyle & Glen Music, 1982), pages 37-40. ML 134.S48H8.1982. An introduction to Shostakovich's chamber music is:

1329. Bobrovskii, Viktor Petrovich. *Kamernye Instrumental' nye Ansambli D. Shostakovicha.* Moscow: Sovetskia

Compositor, 1961. MT 145.S45B6. 257 pages. In
Russian
A study of all the chamber music then written. Numerous musical examples, facsimile of music manuscripts,
and photos of performers of the chamber music with the
composer. Includes the violin + piano Sonata, string
quartets nos. 1-8, Quintet, and Trio. A technical
analysis of Shostakovich's harmonic and melodic
language and his sequencing scales. Finds a strong
classical influence in the chamber music.

*An excellent introduction to Shostakovich's string quartets
is the following:*

1330. Barry, Malcolm. "Shostakovich's Quartets," in *Music
        and Musicians*, xxvii (February 1979), 28-30, 32, 34.
     In advance of a series of performances in London by the
     Fitzwilliam String Quartet of all 15 Shostakovich quar-
     tets, an essay on their history and on the relationship
     of this particular performing group to Shostakovich
     (they worked together during the last 3 years of the
     composer's life). Considers the quartets as they fit
     into the composer's total oeuvre (and the Soviet sys-
     tem) and as they fit into the history of 20th-century
     quartets from around the world. Each quartet is dis-
     cussed from these 2 standpoints. Written for the
     student and informed layperson.

1331. Roseberry, Eric. "Ideology, Style, Content and Thema-
        tic Process in the Symphonies, Cello Concertos, and
        String Quartets of Shostakovich." PhD dissertation.
        University of Bristol, 1982. DDM, p. 26.
     Not seen.

1332. O'Loughlin, Niall. "Shostakovich's String Quartets,"
        in *Tempo*, no. 87 (Winter, 1968-1969), 9-16.
     An analysis of the first 11 string quartets from the
     standpoint of unity of form.

See also Ekkehard Ochs's remarks on the quartets {457}.

1333. Munneke, Russell Edward. "A Comprehensive Performance
        Project in Viola Literature and a Stylistic Study of
        String Quartets 1-13 of Dmitri Shostakovich." DMA
        dissertation. University of Iowa, 1977. UMI 77-
        21185. DAI xxxviii.4A, p. 1731. 276 pages.
     A description of each of the first 13 quartets, a
     stylistic comparison of the quartets with themselves
     and with other important works by Shostakovich, and
     some historical and biographical background.

1334. Dyer, Paul Eugene. "Cyclic Techniques in the String
        Quartets of Dmitri Shostakovich." PhD dissertation.

Florida State University, 1977. DAI xxxviii.9A, p. 5113. 328 pages.

A study of string quartets nos. 2-13 and the cyclic procedures in them that lead from multi-movement works to a single, unified movement (no. 13). The analysis of the cyclic elements includes cyclic themes and motives and, in a few cases, harmonies.

1335. Smith, Arthur Duane. "Recurring Motives and Themes as a Means to Unity in Selected String Quartets of Dmitri Shostakovich." DMA dissertation. University of Oklahoma, 1976. UMI 76-24392. DAI xxxvii.5A, pp. 2487-8. 480 pages.
Discusses quartets nos. 7 to 10. Notes the D-S-C-H motive of no. 8.

1336. Keldysh, Yury. "An Autobiographical Quartet," in *Sovyetskaya Muzyka* (1961), trl. by Alan Lumsden, in *The Musical Times*, cii (1961), 226-228.
Sees in Shostakovich's music both an attempt to glorify the Russian people and an introverted lyricism. The latter is Shostakovich's way of meditating on the fate of humanity in the modern world. The Eighth String Quartet is based on both these views. The Eighth has strong links to earlier compositions (First and Tenth Symphonies, Piano Trio, and others). It is monothematic, built on his own name D-S-C-H. Reads into it a program of the suffering of World War II. Criticizes Shostakovich's rather mechanical repetitions of melodic fragments.

1337. Keller, Hans. "Shostakovich's Twelfth Quartet," in *Tempo*, no. 94 (Fall, 1970), 6-15.
Attempts to understand Shostakovich's seemingly banal, repetitive music by recognizing its debt to Schoenberg's First Chamber Symphony. Keller loves and respects Shostakovich, and assails those whose hate shuts their ears to understanding.

1338. Fay, Laurel Elizabeth. "The Last Quartets of Dmitri Shostakovich: a Stylistic Investigation." PhD dissertation. Cornell University, 1978. UMI 79-02266. DAI xxxix.7A, p. 3905. 158 pages.
Analyzes quartets 12 to 15, which reveal Shostakovich's sudden interest (1968-1975) in atonality, 12-tone rows, pointillism, melodic and spatial effects, and intervallic manipulation, all within a simple style. Deals with harmony, melody, rhythm, and so on in each quartet. The 4 last quartets are related to Shostakovich's other compositions.

1339. Maróthy, János. "Harmonic Disharmony: Shostakovich's Quintet," in *Studia Musicologica*, xix (1977), 325-348.

A lengthy discussion of Shostakovich's quintet, his
first significant chamber work (1940); only the sonata
for violin + piano (1934) and the first string quartet
(1938) predate it. The duality in his music ("super-
Romantic subjectivity" versus "trivial objectivity") is
interpreted in socialist realist terms; these 2 poles
are synthesized into a "new harmony of a world which
has been surveyed and taken possession of, and through
the bridge of which the particularity of the trivial
'masslike' can also rise into human height in a fuller
sense of the term." The piano quintet is "an island of
harmony in the sea of disharmony"; the disharmony of
duality resolves into harmony.

1340. Shochman, G. "Piatdesiat Let i Sem Vetserov: Festival
      Muzyka D.D. Shostakovicha," in *Sovetskaia Muzyka*
      (1982), no. 5, pages 79-86. In Russian.
      Description and review of a chamber music festival in
      honor of Shostakovich's 75th birthday, with 7 concerts
      in all, performed by leading artists and groups.

Jean Sibelius
1865-1957

1341. Layton, Robert. "Chamber and Instrumental Music," in
      Sibelius, in *The Master Musicians Series* (London:
      J.M. Dent & Sons, 1965; 2nd ed. 1978), pp. 135-142.
      ML 410.S54L35.1978. ISBN 0460-03169-4 (hard cover);
      0460-02193-1 (paperback).
      A brief survey of Sibelius's chamber music, most of
      which falls into his very early years when, as a stu-
      dent, he wrote for home consumption. His only sub-
      stantial chamber music afterwards is his string quartet
      entitled "Voces Intimae" (1909) and the "Sonatina" for
      violin + piano, op. 80 (1915). Subjective descriptions
      with only passing reference to thematic recurrences.

Christopher Simpson
c.1605-1669

See Margaret Meredith's dissertation "Christopher Simpson
and the Consort of Viols" {365}.

Bedřich Smetana
1824-1884

For a non-technical introduction to Smetana's chamber music
see John Clapham's essay in Alec Robertson, ed., Chamber
Music {160}.

1342. Janeček, Karel. *Smetanova Komorní hudba: Kompoziční výklad.* Prague: Editio Supraphon, 1978. ML 410.S63 J28. 466 pages. In Czech. "Smetana's Chamber Music: Compositional Interpretation." Reviewed in *Notes,* xli, no. 2 (Dec.1984), 270-2.

See also Janaček's study of the final movement of Smetana's Second String Quartet in {457}, pages 143-145.

1343. Ginzburg, Lev. "On Performing the E-minor Quartet ("From My Life") by Bedřich Smetana: an Experiment in Comparative Analysis," in Vladimir Grigor'ev and Vladimir Natanson, eds., *Muzykal'noe Ispolnitel'stvo, X* (Moscow: Muzyka, 1979). RILM 79-1608. Not seen.

Daniel Speer
1636-1707

1344. Sirman, Mitchel Neil. "The Wind Sonatas in Daniel Speer's Musicalisch-Türckischer Eulen-Spiegel." PhD dissertation. University of Wisconsin, 1972. UM 72-29512. DA xxxiii.8A, p. 4462. 183 pages.
A lengthy and definitive biography, a survey of his writings and music, and an analysis of 6 wind sonatas for cornets, trumpets, and trombones. Discusses the original scoring and suggests their performance on modern instruments.

Ludwig (= Louis) Spohr
1784-1859

For a systematic list and detailed catalogue of the chamber music of Spohr, see Folker Göthel, Thematisch-bibliographisches Verzeichnis der Werke von Louis Spohr (Tutzing: Hans Schneider, 1981), pages 512-516. ML 134.S68G7.1981. ISBN 3-7952-0175-6.

1345. Brown, Clive. *Louis Spohr: a Critical Biography.* Cambridge/New York/London: Cambridge University Press, 1984. ML 410.S7B8.1984. ISBN 0-521-23990-7. viii + 364 pages.
An important account of the life, works and chamber music activities of one of the most important chamber music personalities in history. Spohr performed chamber music publicly and privately nearly his entire life and composed an immense amount of chamber music of all kinds. The book discusses *ad passim* his chamber music activities and analyzes informally some of the music. Points out the use of a string trio to accompany his virtuosic playing, rather than a piano (c.1800);

his writing of duets for his pupils; his championship
of Beethoven's quartets despite his unhappiness with
the later ones; his writing of chamber music including
harp for himself and his harpist wife; analysis and
history of all his 36 quartets; and Spohr's violin
technique: portamento and legato separate bows on
rapid passage work.

1346. Glenewinkel, Hans. *Spohrs Kammermusik für Streichin-
      strumente: ein Beitrag zur Geschichte des Streich-
      quartetts im xix. Jahrhundert.* Nienburg (Weser):
      C.J. Georg Glenewinkel, [1912]. NL fV415.34. 144
      pages. Inaugural dissertation. Ludwigs-Maximilians-
      University in Munich, 1912.
      For the time an excellent history of the string quartet
      written by a pupil of Sandberger. Includes a brief
      biography of Spohr and characterizes the chamber works
      of Spohr's contemporaries who are of the second rank
      but who nonetheless were important in their time:
      Krommer, Danzi, Andreas Romberg, Reicha, Pierre Rode
      (1774-1830), Hummel, Ries, Onslow, Johann Peter Pixis
      (1788-1874), Friedric Wilhelm Pixis (1786-1842), and
      Fesca (1789-1826). Objective analysis of each of
      Spohr's 36 string quartets and other chamber works (4
      double quartets, 7 quintets, 1 sextet). Spohr's melody
      is a fine line delineated by an extraordinary sense of
      beauty, where chromaticism has a signficiant Romantic
      role. Speculates that the decline in popularity of
      Spohr's chamber music is because the "quatuor
      brillante" passed out of fashion.

1347. Berrett, Joshua. "Characteristic Conventions of Style
      in Selected Instrumental Works of Louis Spohr." PhD
      dissertation. University of Michigan, 1974. UMI 75-
      633. DAI xxxv.7A, p. 4582. 252 pages.
      A lengthy biography and analysis of selected chamber
      music and violin concertos. Spohr's style is charac-
      terized by "seamless legato and the prolongation of
      linear strands of string sound... chromatic appoggia-
      turas..." Spohr looks both forward and backward in
      his compositions.

1348. Kahl, Willi. "Louis Spohr: Quintett für Klavier und
      Bläser, op. 52, Hrsg. v. Eugen Schmitz. Bärenreiter
      ... (1950)...," in *Die Musikforschung*, v (1952), 283-
      285.
      A brief historical description of the writing of the
      piece and a review of the present edition.

*See also Hartmut Becker and Rainer Krempien, eds., Louis
Spohr: Festschrift und Ausstellungskatalog zum 200. Geburtstag im Auftrage der Internationalen Louis Spohr Gesellschaft
und der Staatsbibliothek Preussischer Kulturbesitz. Kassel:
Georg Wenderoth, 1984. 288 pages. ML 55.S696L8.1984. ISBN*

3-87013-019-9. Includes 11 scholarly articles in German on various aspects of Spohr's life and works. Discusses Spohr's discography (chamber music on pages 140-144), the 17 Spohr works (some chamber pieces) for harp with or without others instruments (written for his first wife), and so on.

Carl Stamitz
1745-1801

For a discussion of his Quartets for Bassoon + Violin + Viola + Cello see Helen Hoff's dissertation {829}.

Wilhelm Stenhammar
1871-1927

1349. Wallner, Bo. "Wilhelm Stenhammar och Kammarmusiken," in *Svensk Tidskrift för Musikforskning*, xxxv (1953), 5-73. In Swedish with brief English summary. Stenhammar is a rare figure in Swedish music c.1900 since in addition other types of music he composed chamber music and especially 7 string quartets. Analysis of these quartets and his Sonata for violin + piano from 3 standpoints: thematic development, dependence on precursors (notably Beethoven and Brahms), and creation of a national Swedish style. An introspective musician, Stenhammar used the intimacy of chamber music to develop his thoughts about form. Written from 1894 to 1916, they show his growth from an "improvising Sturm-und-Drang style to a more pregnant, concentrated form." Includes an annotated list of all his chamber music (which also includes a piano trio).

1350. _____. "Wilhelm Stenhammars Straakkvartetts-kisser," in *Svensk Tidskrift för Musikforskning*, xliii (1961), 355-373. This volume also entitled *Studier Tillägnade Carl-Allan Moberg 5 Juni 1961*. In Swedish with a German summary. A study of the relatively large number of sketches for Stenhammar's 7 string quartets which show even more how central these pieces were to his musical thought.

Alessandro Stradella
1642-1682

1351. McCrickard, Eleanor Fowler. "Alessandro Stradella's Instrumental Music: a Critical Edition with Historical and Analytical Commentary." PhD dissertation. University of North Carolina at Chapel Hill, 1971. UMI 72-10749. DAI xxxii.9A, p. 5272. 528 pages. A biography and description of Stradella's milieu. Analyzes the form, rhythm, tonality, harmony and coun-

terpoint in 12 pieces for violin + continuo, 9 pieces
for 2 violins + continuo, 2 pieces for violin + cello +
continuo, and 3 concerti grossi by Stradella. Considers the performance problems caused by ambiguous
language and symbols.

Michele Stratico
c.1721-1782

1352. Roeder, Michael T. "Sonatas, Concertos, and Symphonies of Michele Stratico." PhD dissertation. University of California at Santa Barbara, 1971. UM 72-
7466. DA xxxii.8A, pp. 4651-2. 2 vols. I: xiii +
188 pages; II: ii + 247 pages of music.
Discusses, *inter alia*, the 156 sonatas (written 1740's
- 1750's) for violin + basso in a manuscript at the
University of California at Berkeley. They are slow-
fast-fast with the slower movements more unified mo-
tivicly than the faster ones. The middle movements are
often the longest and are virtuosic. The last movements are lighter. Of historic, not intrinsic, worth.

Richard Strauss
1864-1949

For a catalogue of Strauss's chamber music and in many cases
where further information can be found, see Erich H. Mueller
von Asow, Richard Strauss: thematisches Verzeichnis, 3 vols
containing 29 installments in 17 bands (Vienna/Wiesbaden to
1959, then Munich: L. Doblinger, 1959-1974), 1688 pages.
Systematic list of chamber music p. 1537. ML 134. S94M8. A
condensed works list with additions and corrections in Franz
Trenner, Richard Struass: Werkverzeichnis (Vienna:
Doblinger, c.1985). ML 134.S94T7.

1353. Dubitzky, Franz. "Richard Strauss' Kammermusik," in
Die Musik, xiii.3 (1914), 283-296.
A list of Strauss's chamber music, which occupied his
attention almost exclusively during his youth (Op. 2-9,
11, 13, 18 and some without opus number; includes works
not regarded as chamber music in our definition). His
string quartet was primarily under the influence of
Beethoven, but also of others including Meyerbeer.
Shows already an original sense of tonal relationships.
Strauss develops his own style gradually. He was
following the advice of many -- and later his own in-
clination -- to study the classics before grappling
with the present.

Igor Feodorovitch Stravinsky
1882-1971

*For a chronological and alphabetical catalogue of his works,
see Clifford Caesar,* Igor Stravinsky: a Complete Catalogue
(San Francisco: San Francisco Press, 1982), 66 pages. ML
*134.S96C3.1982. ISBN 0-911302-41-7. For a systematic index
of chamber music, see Dominique-René de Lerma,* Igor Fedoro-
vitch Stravinsky, 1882-1971: a Practical Guide to Publications of his Music *(Kent [Ohio]: Kent State University
Press, 1974), pages 119-131.* ML 134.S96D44. ISBN 0-87338-
158-0.

1354. Mason, Colin. "Stravinsky's Contribution to Chamber
       Music," in *Tempo*, no. 43 (Spring, 1957), 6-16.
       The chamber music comes mostly just after *The Rite of
       Spring* and in his late years. He rarely conforms to
       traditional forms and media: even his "string quartets"
       are not so titled and the *Concertino* is simply 1 long
       movement. Considers serialism and tonality versus
       atonality in the late works and Stravinsky's acknow-
       ledgement of Webern, Schoenberg and Bartók.

1355. Kielian-Gilbert, Marianne. "Relationships of Symme-
       trical Pitch-Class Sets and Stravinsky's Metaphor of
       Polarity," in *Perspectives of New Music*, xxi (1982-
       1983), 209-240.
       Takes Stravinsky's comment in *Poetics of Music* that
       "All music being nothing but a succession of impulses
       and repose, it is easy to see that the drawing together
       and separation of poles of attraction in a way deter-
       mine the respiration of music," and follows Arthur
       Berger's analysis of the meaning of polarity to trace
       "polarity" in *Three Pieces for String Quartet*, the
       Octet, and 2 non-chamber works (*Symphony of Psalms*,
       second movement, and the introduction to *The Rite of
       Spring*). By polarity Berger means "the denial of
       priority to a single pitch-class precisely for the
       purpose of note deflecting from the priority of a whole
       complexe sonore." In other words, the "opposite ends"
       of a pole are closely related to each other, and these
       paired poles in music imply an equivalent interval
       structure of each end of the pole. Analyzes the pitch-
       class sets of a polarity.

1356. Stahmer, Klaus Hinrich. "Der Klassik näher als dem
       Klassizismus: die Streichquartettkompositionen von
       Stravinsky," in *Hindemith-Jahrbuch*, xii (1983), 104-
       115.
       Describes the *Three Pieces for String Quartet*, dedi-
       cated to Ansermet, premiered by the Flonzaley Quartet
       in Chicago in 1915; the *Concertino* written for the
       Flonzaley Quartet in 1920; and the *Double Canon for
       String Quartet* of 1959. Both earlier works he later

orchestrated -- he was not thinking like other 20th-
century string quartet composers who emphasized the
intimacy and special color of the quartet. Stravinsky
treats these works as trifles. He gives names to the 3
pieces when orchestrated: Dance, Eccentric, and
Canticle. The quartets are truely classic, rather than
neo-classic.

See also Paul Carlson's discussion of the Duo Concertante
{250}.

1357. Stein, Erwin. "Stravinsky's Septet (1953), for Clari-
      net, Horn, Bassoon, Piano, Violin, Viola, & Violon-
      cello: an Analysis," in *Tempo*, no. 31 (Spring, 1954),
      including a facsimile of a page of the manuscript.
      A technical, detailed analysis, with rows and emphasis
      on the counterpoint, which is found to be much further
      developed than in earlier Stravinsky pieces.

1358. Schilling, Hans Ludwig. "Zur Instrumentation in Igor
      Stravinskys Spätwerk aufgezeigt an seinem 'Septett
      1953,'" in *Archiv für Musikwissenschaft*, xiii (1956),
      181-196.
      Sees 3 special techniques used by Stravinsky: unison or
      octaves between instruments proceeding in different
      rhythms, breaking up of melodies among instruments of
      different families, and dynamics glossed over so all
      the instruments sound on the same dynamic level. Notes
      the special care Stravinsky takes with tone color.

1359. Schatz, Hilmar. "Igor Stravinsky: Septett," in *Melos*,
      xxv (1958), 60-63.
      An important, somewhat technical analysis of this tran-
      sitional work for listeners who, though enjoying the
      sound, might otherwise miss Stravinsky's technical a-
      chievement. With movements 2 and 3 based on 8, not 12,
      tones, it is the bridge between his neo-classic and
      serial periods. Gives evidence of the row, also in the
      first movement where 5 notes are used. A cyclic unity
      achieved by the row.

1360. Craft, Robert. "The Chronology of the *Octet*," in *Per-
      spectives of New Music*, xxii (1983-1984), 451-463.
      Traces the evolution of this Octet in the sketch books
      starting in 1919 and finishing in 1922. Follows with
      comments from 1923, including a note from Koussevit-
      zky's secretary to Stravinsky concerning the importance
      of the piece.

Giuseppe Tartini
1692-1770

1361. Brainard, Paul. "Die Violinsonaten Giuseppe Tarti-
      nis." PhD dissertation. University of Göttingen,

1959. Published with some additions and corrections: *Le Sonate per Violino di Giuseppe Tartini: Catalogo Tematico*, in *Le Opere di Giuseppe Tartini, Seziona Terza: Studi e Ricerche di Studiosi Moderni*, vol. 2. Milan: Studi e Ricerche dell' Accademia Tartiniana di Padova, 1975. ML 134.T2B7. xl + 145 pages.
A careful, scholarly catalogue of most of Tartini's sonatas for violin and continuo, drawn from manuscript collections, individual manuscripts and printed sources. The sonatas are listed according to tonality, with thematic incipits of each of the movements and tempo designations. Lists the sources for each work, including concordances, the number of measures in each section of each movement (usually but not always binary), and significant variances among the concordances. Also recognizes the sources for borrowed material: opera arias, concertos, and so on. Gives dates, in most cases somewhat tentatively (as discussed in the introduction). Also lists isolated movements for violin + bass or violin alone. The sources are carefully studied in the introduction. A basic tool for any scholar, layperson or performer who wants to study the repertory of Tartini's violin sonatas.

Peter Ilyitch Tchaikovsky
1840-1893

For a catalogue of Tchaikovsky's chamber music, see B. Jurgenson, Catalogue Thématique des Oeuvres de P. Tschaikowsky *(Moscow: P. Jurgenson, 1897; reprint London: H. Baron, 1965), p. 156. ML 134.C4I8.1965. In Russian and French.*

1362. Findeisen, Nikolai Fedorovich. *Kamarnaia Musyka Chaikovskoge*. Moscow: Gosudarsive'oe Isdate'stve, 1930. MT 140.C5F5. 38 pages. In Russian.
A moderately technical introduction to the chamber music of Tchaikovsky presented in chronological order. Concerned with form.

1363. Brown, David. *Tchaikovsky: the Early Years 1840-1874*. New York: W.W. Norton, 1978. ISBN 0-393-07535-2. 348 pages. *Tchaikovsky: the Crisis Years 1874-1878*. London/New York: W.W. Norton, 1982/1983. ISBN 0-393-01707-9. 312 pages. ML 410.C4B74.
The most recent major study of the life and works. Includes historical data on the chamber music and much less technical than cultural analyses of the most important works. Compares the quartets to other works by Tchaikovsky and especially those by Mozart and Schubert. Each volume has its own index of names and cited chamber works.

1364. Auerbakh, Lev Davydovich. *Trio Chaikovskogo Pamiati*
      Velikogo Khudozhnika. Moscow: Muzyka, 1977. MT
      145.C43A9. In Russian.
      A serious analysis of the Piano Trio, with historical
      background. Believes that this piece ends the N. Ru-
      binstein phase of Tchaikovsky's life (it is dedicated
      to Rubinstein in 1881, the year of the latter's death).
      The composer basically hated the combination of piano
      and 1 or 2 strings (stated in a letter of 1880 to
      Madame Von Meck), but to honor Rubinstein he had to
      write a non-orchestral piece with a virtuoso piano part
      that was more than just a solo one. He ultimately was
      satisfied with the piece, though he worried it might be
      too orchestral. The analysis describes all the themes
      and formal aspects, including thematic developments and
      derivatives. Although there are only 2 ostensible
      movements, the variations at the end of movement 2 are
      so long as to constitute a third one. Continual
      references to other works of Tchaikovsky.

Georg Philipp Telemann
1681-1767

For a catalogue of Telemann's chamber music, see Martin
Ruhnke, Georg Philipp Telemann: thematisch-systematisches
Verzeichnis seiner Werke, Band 1, instrumental music, sup-
plement to Georg Philipp Telemann: musikalische Werke (Kas-
sel/Basel/London: Bärenreiter, 1984), pages 107-228. ML
134.T3R8.1984.Bd.1. ISBN 3-7618-0655-8. For a bibliography
of studies of his chamber music, see Hermann Wettstein,
Georg Philipp Telemann: bibliographischer Versuch zu seiner
Leben und Werk 1681-1767, *in* Veröffentlichungen der Hamburger Telemann-Gesellschaft, *Bd. 3 (Hamburg: Karl Dieter Wag-*
ner, 1981), pages 35-37. ML 134.T3W5. ISBN 3-921-029-79-1.

For an overall study of Telemann's chamber music see Günter
Fleischhauer, "Zur instrumentalen Kammermusik Georg Philipp
Telemanns," in {457}, pages 345-360.

1365. Dadelsen, Georg von. "Telemann und die sogenannte Ba-
      rockmusik," in Richard Baum and Wolfgang Rehm, eds.,
      Musik und Verlag: Karl Vötterle zum 65. Geburtstag am
      12. April 1968 (Kassel: Bärenreiter, 1968), pp. 197-
      205. ML 55.V537M9.
      Concerned primarily with rehabilitating Baroque music
      other than Bach's, and with correcting the outdated as-
      sumption that Telemann's music is synonymous with the
      pejorative qualities of Baroque music and especially
      with the amateur performance of it. A probing and pro-
      voking essay (originally a lecture) that aims to upset
      prejudiced misconceptions among educated laypersons but
      not among scholars. Considers, for example, the mean-
      ing of "originality." Monteverdi is orginal not for

inventing new devices; originality is simply the manner of absorbing new and old devices into a personal style expressing human affections. We tend to regard all Baroque music the same, but Telemann (among others) has his own originality in effects in his concertos and chamber music. His music is more immediately appealing to performers. Questions the attacks on Uraufführungs-praxis, which has its merits even for those who do not practice it. This is especially important for Tele-mann, who wrote so idiomatically for different instru-ments -- much more so than for Bach.

See DuBois's dissertation on Telemann's recorder music {242}, and Günter Fleischhauer's "Bemerkungen zum 'Tele-mannischen Geschmack' in der Sonata a Cinque e-Moll," in {161}, pages 77-90.

1366. Funk, Floyd R. "The Trio Sonatas of Georg Philipp Telemann (1681-1767)." PhD dissertation. George Peabody College, 1954. DD, xii (1955), p. 245. 320 pages.
 Not seen.

Giuseppe Torelli
1658-1709

1367. Norton, Richard Edward. "The Chamber Music of Giuseppe Torelli." PhD dissertation. Northwestern University, 1967. UM 68-3207. DA xxviii.10A, p. 4202. xii + 171 pages + 55 pages of music.
 A study of his sonatas da chiesa and da camera written 1686-1698 under the influence of Giacomo Antonio Perti. Opus 2 is unique in Bologna for violin + cello without continuo. The other sonatas range from violin + con-tinuo to 2 violins + cello + continuo. Also considers the concertos in Op. 5 and 6.

Joaquin Turina
1882-1949

1368. Sher, Daniel Paul. "A Structural and Stylistic Analy-sis and Performance of the Piano Trios of Joaquin Tu-rina." EdD dissertation. Columbia University Tea-chers College, 1980. DAI xli.4A, pp. 1276-7. 258 pages.
 A stylistic analysis of the 3 trios Op. 35 (1926), Op. 76 (1933), and Op. 91 (1936). The first is a blend of neo-classic elements and Spanish folk music and is influenced by Albéniz. The second is a more subtle blend of these 2 elements. Trio no. 3 continues the Spanish folk influence but avoids the neo-classicism of the first 2 trios.

Ferdinando Gasparo Turrini (detto Bertoni)
1745-1829

1369. Conter, Fulvia. *La Musica da Camera di Ferdinando
      Gasparo Turrini detto Bertoni.* Brescia: Ateneo,
      1974. ML 410.T96C7. 144 pages.
      The life, works and significance of Turrini, a minor
      but interesting Italian pianist and composer. Because
      he went blind in 1773, he was incapable of studying new
      scores and therefore developed in his own expressive
      way. Lists his works, which are almost entirely key-
      board music, but there is one collection of 6 sonatas
      for harpsichord or piano with violin accompaniment.
      The violin could be omitted and it would work as a solo
      keyboard sonata.

Burnet Corwin Tuthill
1888-1982

*For an analysis of his sonata for saxophone + piano, see
Robert Sibbing's dissertation {826}.*

Marco Uccellini
1610-1680

1370. Pajerski, Fred Mitchell. "Marco Uccellini (1610-1680)
      and his Music." PhD dissertation. New York Univer-
      sity, 1979. DAI xl.11A, pp. 5643-4. 758 pages.
      A documented, scholarly biography of Uccellini, whose
      principal surviving works are violin sonatas. Compares
      them to contemporaneous works and conveys a portrait of
      a violinist's life at the time. Includes musical exam-
      ples representing different facets of Uccellini's
      style, with some contemporary works for comparison.

Bernard Van Dieren
1884-1936

1371. Riley, Patrick Robert. "The String Quartets of
      Bernard van Dieren." PhD dissertation. University
      of Iowa, 1985. UMI 85-18869. 636 pages.
      Not seen.

1372. Williams, L. Henderson. "'Philandering Round' Mr. Van
      Dieren's Quartets," in *The Sackbut*, xi (1931), 325-
      329.
      A highly subjective survey of van Dieren's 6 string
      quartets (premier dates: 1912, 1917, 1919, 1923, 1931,
      and 1928, respectively). The first is dedicated to
      Paganini ("its aspect is that of a quadruple cadenza"
      based on some of Paganini's caprices). Rates nos. 3,

4, and 5 as better than any by Hindemith or Honegger. No. 4 is for 2 violins + viola + string bass; no. 5 was originally for violin + viola + cello + string bass but then arranged for normal string quartet. The earlier quartets are very difficult and experimental.

Johann Baptist Vanhal (= Wanhal)
1739-1813

1373. Jones, David Wyn. "The String Quartets of Vanhal." PhD dissertation. University of Wales, 1978. UMI 81-70007. DAI (Europe) xlii.2C, p. 217. 671 pages. A biographical and bibliographical account of the possibly 74 (54 proven) string quartets. The authentic quartets are dated 1768-1787 and then analyzed formally and stylistically. More superficial than Haydn's quartets, they are in 3 to 4 movements, the outer ones fast; they show harmonic and tonal coloring; and the influence of the concerto is obvious in the slow movements.

Edgard (= Edgar) Varèse
1883-1965

1374. Ramsier, Paul. "An Analysis and Comparison of the Motivic Structure of *Octandre* and *Intégrales*, Two Instrumental Works by Edgard Varèse." PhD dissertation. New York University, 1972. UMI 72-26609. DAI xxxiii.4A, p. 1772. 206 pages. Varèse uses either germ motives or development of motives throughout these 2 works. He develops by rhythmic variation and fragmentation and rarely uses exact repetition. Detailed analysis of the motives and how they are used.

1375. Tyra, Thomas Norman. "The Analysis of Three Twentieth-Century Compositions for Wind Ensemble." PhD dissertation. University of Michigan, 1971. UM 71-23895. DA xxxii.3A, p. 1558. 223 pages. Stylistic analyses, formal analyses and performance problems in Stravinsky's *Symphonies of Wind Instruments*, Varèse's *Octandre*, and Penderecki's *Pittsburgh Ouverture*. Some biographical information. Highly technical analyses for advanced students and professional theorists.

Ralph Vaughan Williams
1872-1958

*For a list of Vaughan Williams's chamber music, see Michael
Kennedy,* A Catalogue of the Works of Ralph Vaughan Williams,
*rev. ed. (London: Oxford, 1982), page 311. ML 134.V3K39.
ISBN 0-19-315452-8. Original edition London: Oxford, 1964.*

1376. Howes, Frank Stewart. "Chamber Music," in *The Music
of Ralph Vaughan Williams* (London/New York/Toronto:
Oxford University Press, 1954), pp. 211-226. ML 410
V3H6.

Brief descriptions of the forms, melodies, and peculi-
arities of Vaughan Williams's 2 string quartets, 1
string quintet (2 violas), "Household Music" and "Suite
for Pipes" (a string quartet with optional horn and
optional substitutions for the other parts, too). The
quintet, dedicated to W.W. Cobbett, is in 4 movements
without break and cyclic. Gives details on its creation and first performance. Less attention to the
other works: the "Household Music" is in 3 movements,
each based on Welsh hymns, and the "Suite for Pipes"
(for home-made bamboo pipes similar to recorders) is in
4 movements. The viola is favored in all his chamber
music.

Francesco Maria Veracini
1690-1768

1377. Hill, John Walter. *The Life and Works of Francesco
Maria Veracini*, in *Studies in Musicology*, No. 3. Ann
Arbor: UMI Research Press, 1979. ML 410.V39H5. ISBN
0-8357-1000-9. xii + 540 pages. PhD dissertation.
Harvard University, 1974. UM 74-16720.
A detailed, thoroughly documented biography of this important Italian violinist based not only on printed
sources but on manuscript ones as well (unlike previous
biographies). Also detailed bibliographic and stylistic analyses of the sonatas. A very good study of violin sonata practice in the generation after Corelli.

1378. Clarke, Mary Gray. "The Violin Sonatas of F.M. Veracini: Some Aspects of Italian Late Baroque Instrumental Style Exemplified." PhD dissertation. University of North Carolina, 1967. UMI 68-6728. DAI
xxviii.11A, p. 4657. 601 pages.
Veracini is a transitional figure from Baroque to
Classical with both old-fashioned and progressive elements. Old-fashioned are passé time signatures, hemio-
la, minor modes, single-affect part forms, counterpoint, and continuous expansion of melodies. Progressive ones are the primacy of first beats, slower harmonic rhythm, and lighter texture. Discussion based on
3 sonata collections with both da chiesa and da camera
elements.

Giuseppe Verdi
1813-1901

*For a list of editions of Verdi's string quartet from 1876
to 1958 see Cecil Hopkinson,* A Bibliography of the Works of
Giuseppe Verdi 1813-1901, *vol. I: Vocal and Instrumental
Works (New York: Broude Brothers, 1973), pages 77-79; see
also p. 84. ML 134.V47H6.vol.1. For a discussion and
analysis of the quartet, see Bruun,* Kammermusik *{146}, iii,
179-182.*

1379. Budden, Julian. "Chamber Music," in *Verdi,* in *The
     Master Musicians* (London/Melbourne: J.M. Dent & Sons,
     1985), pages 310-313. ML 410.V4B9.1985. ISBN 0-460-
     03165-1.
       Brief analysis of the string quartet.

Heitor Villa-Lobos
1887-1959

For a catalogue of Villa-Lobos's chamber music, see Villa-
Lobos: sua Obra *([Brasil]: Museu Villa-Lobos, 1965 [1967]),
pages 59-67 and 131-135. ML 134.V65V5.*

1380. Farmer, Virginia. "An Analytical Study of the Seven-
     teen String Quartets of Heitor Villa-Lobos." DMA
     dissertation. University of Illinois, 1973. UMI 73-
     17533. DAI xxxiv.1A, p. 352. 135 pages, 76
     examples.
       History and analysis of Villa-Lobos's quartets. There
     was no viable tradition of string quartet writing in
     Brazil before him, so he created one. He avoids tra-
     ditional forms and structures and utilizes many folk
     rhythms especially in his middle quartets; he achieves
     coloristic effects through polychords as well as in-
     strumental timbres; he writes either cantabile or
     driving melodies; and his quartets have a personal,
     distinct sound.

1381. Estrella, Arnaldo. *Os Quartetos de Cordas de Villa-
     Lobos.* Rio de Janeiro: MEC, Museu Villa-Lobos, 1970.
     MT 145.V54E8. 141 pages.
       An introduction and guide for the student to the 17
     quartets, which fall into 4 groups: nos. 1-4 (1915-
     1917), 5 (1931), 6 (1938), and 7-17 (1942-1957).
     Discusses essential features of each quartet movement.
     Chamber music is a third of the composer's total out-
     put, and he was capable of working within the limited
     colors of the quartet (the orchestral works are much
     better known). He avoids sonata form and fugues but
     writes continual variations (the Quartet No. 1 is an
     exception), often atonal. Considers the folk music
     influence, especially from the fifth quartet on.

Villa-Lobos's own ability at playing the cello manifests itself especially in nos. 1 and 5.

1382. França, Eurico Nogueira. *A Evoluçâo de Villa-Lobos na
      Música de Câmera.* Rio de Janeiro: MEC/DAC-Museu
      Villa-Lobos, 1976. ML 410.V76F68. 97 pages.
      A historical and stylistic analysis of Villa-Lobos's
      chamber music other than string quartets, which in-
      cludes duos and trios up to a nonet, for various combi-
      nations of bowed strings, piano, guitar, harp, celesta,
      and winds (including saxophone).

Giovanni Battista Viotti
1755-1824

*For a catalogue of Viotti's chamber music (string and flute
quartets, trios for 2 violins + cello, string duets with
some arrangements for winds, and solos with bass or piano
accompaniment), see Chappel White,* Giovanni Battista Viotti
(1755-1824): a Thematic Catalogue of his Works, *in* Thematic
Catalogues, *No. 12.* New York: Pendragon, 1985. *ML 134.V67
A35.1985. ISBN 0-918728-43-6. xx + 175 pages. For a study
of Viotti's violin duets, see Riehl's article {312}.*

1383. Fleischmann, Hugo Robert. "Giovanni Battista Viotti."
      PhD dissertation. University of Vienna, 1911.
      Not seen.

Gasparo Visconti
1683-17??

1384. Monterosso, Raffaello. "Gasparo Visconti, Violinista
      Cremonese del Secolo xviii," in *Studien zur Musikwis-
      senschaft: Beihefte der Denkmäler der Tonkunst in
      Österreich,* Band 25, also entitled *Festschrift für
      Erich Schenk* (Graz/Vienna/Köln: Hermann Böhlaus
      Nachf., 1962), pp. 378-388. ML 55.S324.
      A scholarly study of the life and works of Visconti, an
      aristocratic, amateur violinist, whose 2 surviving col-
      lections are 6 sonatas for violin + basso (Amsterdam:
      Roger/London: Walsh & Hare, 1703; 4 da camera and 2 da
      chiesa) and 6 concertos (Amsterdam: Le Cène, c.1728).
      Concentrates on the sonatas, with the inevitable com-
      parison to Corelli's Op. 5; also notes the friendship
      between Visconti and Tartini.

Giovanni Battista Vitali
1632-1692

1385. Suess, John Gunther.   "Giovanni Battista Vitali and
      the Sonata da chiesa."   PhD dissertation.   Yale Uni-
      versity, 1963.   UM 69-20385.   DA xxx.6, p. 2564.   267
      pages + musical supplement.
      After historical and biographical background, an ana-
      lysis and historical discussion of Vitali's 3 sonata da
      chiesa collections.   Shows their debt to Mauritio Caz-
      zati, his teacher, who codified "the character of the
      three basic types of movements" and reduced the large
      number of sections of the canzona to the 4 or 5 move-
      ments of the sonata.   Vitali's own contributions, espe-
      cially in Op. 9, are his variation techniques and a
      more unified style for all movements "through a common
      contrapuntal foundation without losing the individual
      character of each type of movement."

Tomaso Antonio Vitali
c.1663-after 1719

1386. Reich, Wolfgang.   "Sein oder nicht sein?   Nochmals zur
      'Chaconne von Vitali,'" in *Die Musikforschung*, xxiii
      (1970), 38-41.
      Questions the designation of Tomaso Vitali as author
      of the famous G-minor Chaconne and gives rather the
      title "Dresden Chaconne" after the location of the only
      manuscript copy.

Antonio Vivaldi
1678-1741

For a catalogue of Vivaldi's chamber music, see Peter Ryom,
Verzeichnis der Werke Antonio Vivaldis (RV): kleine Ausgabe
(Leipzig: Deutscher Verlag für Musik, 1974), pages 21-33.
ML 134.V7R98.1974b.   And its supplement by Ryom, Ergänzungen
und Berichtigungen zu dem Verzeichnis der Werke Antonio
Vivaldis: kleine Ausgabe (1974) *(Poitiers: Association*
Vivaldi de Poitiers, 1979), 36 pages.   ML 134.V7R98.1974b
supplement.

1387. Rarig, Howard Raymond, Jr.   "The Instrumental Sonatas
      of Antonio Vivaldi."   PhD dissertation.   University
      of Michigan, 1958.   LC Mic 58-7779.   DA xix.6, p.
      1406.   455 pages.
      Brief biography and bibliography, followed by detailed
      analyses of many solo, trio and other sonatas by Vival-
      di which show a minimal debt to Corelli and much more
      Vivaldi's own originality.   Points the way to classical
      form, tonality, and motivic treatment.

For an attempt to characterize the "76" known sonatas by
Vivaldi, see William S. Newman's "The Sonatas of Albinoni
and Vivaldi" {521}.

1388. Talbot, Michael. "The Instrumental Music: Sonatas,"
in Vivaldi, in The Master Musicians Series (London/
Toronto/Melbourne: J.M. Dent & Sons, 1978), pp. 124-
137. ML 410.V82T34. ISBN 0-460-03164-3.
A survey discussion of the "90" sonatas by Vivaldi "authenticated" in Ryom's Verzeichnis and Antonio Vivaldi:
Table de Concordances des Oeuvres (Copenhagen: 1973),
together with the Dresden quartet sonata. Total: 61
solo sonatas (with bass), 27 trio sonatas, 3 quartet
sonatas. Starts with the 12 Op. 1 trio sonatas (1705)
which show a debt to Corelli, and continues with the
rest of the trio sonatas, which show Vivaldi's more
mature style, often similar to the concertos with 3
movements, ritornello form, and variety of instruments.
The solo sonatas start with Op. 2 (1709): 12 sonatas
for violin + continuo under Corelli's influence. The
Op. 5 solo sonatas show a less contrapuntal bass; the
next set is more lyrical; eventually, by the 1740 collection, they are in 4 movements. Rates the solo sonatas as Vivaldi's best chamber works. Op. 13 "Il Pastor
Fido" sonatas are not authentic Vivaldi; they are arrangements by Parisian publishers of Vivaldi's and
others's works. The quartets, in 2 movements (slow -
fugue), are religious works.

Johann Christoph Vogel
1756-1788

See Helen Hoff's dissertation {829}.

Robert Volkmann
1815-1883

1389. Brawley, Thomas Michael. "The Instrumental Works of
Robert Volkmann (1815-1883)." PhD dissertation.
Northwestern University, 1975. UM 75-29584. DAI
xxxvi.7A, p. 4093. v + 297 pages.
A comprehensive life and works of this German-born com-
poser-teacher who spent most of his adult life in Budapest. Chapter 3 is devoted to an analysis of his
chamber music (piano trios, string quartets, violin-
piano pieces). Shows the influence of Hungarian music
as well as that of Beethoven, Mendelssohn, and
Schumann. Important bibliography.

Georg Christoph Wagenseil
1715-1777

For a catalogue of Wagenseil's chamber music, see Helga
Scholz-Michelitsch, *Das Orchester- und Kammermusikwerk von
Georg Christoph Wagenseil: thematischer Katalog, in
Österreichische Akademie der Wissenschaft, Tabulae Musicae
Austriacae, Bd. 6 (Vienna: Hermann Böhlaus Nachf., 1972),*
pages 161-221. ML 134.WO8S43. ISBN 3-205-03175-X.

Richard Wagner
1813-1883

For a discussion of the Adagio for clarinet + string quintet
formerly assumed to be by Wagner but in fact by Heinrich
Joseph Baermann see Ulrich Rau's article {554}.

Johann Jakob Walther
1650-1717

1390. Krout, Karen June. "Performance Editions of Selected
Works from Johann Jakob Walther's *Hortulus Chelicus*
with Historical and Editorial Notes." PhD dissertation. Texas Tech University, 1982. DAI xliii.8A,
pp. 2488-9.
An edition of 4 works from the collection: 2 absolute
music, 2 program music; 1 easy and 1 difficult; a
suite, a capriccio (= passacaglia with 50 variations)
and 2 sonatas. Gives biography of Walther, a general
discussion of the entire collection, and detailed
analyses of the 4 works with performance suggestions.

William Walton
1902-1983

1391. Tierney, Neil. "Chamber Music," in *William Walton:
his Life and Music* (London: Robert Hale, 1984), pp.
242-246. ML 410.W292T5. ISBN 0-7090-1784-7.
A readable, subjective description of Walton's 2 string
quartets, piano quartet, violin-piano sonata, 2 other
works for violin + piano, and solo cello pieces. Some
historical data on each.

1392. Murrill, Herbert. "Walton's Violin Sonata," in *Music
and Letters*, xxxi (1950), 208-215.
Approaches analysis from the standpoint of how Walton
deals with "high tension."

1393. Howes, Frank. "Pianoforte Quartet," in *The Music of
William Walton*, in *The Musical Pilgrim*, i (London:

Oxford University Press, 1942, reprint 1965), pp. 10-
21. MT 92.W16H6.1965.
A brief history and detailed analysis of Walton's only
chamber piece (by 1942), written when he was 16: a
youthful, romantic piano quartet. Analysis of themes
and tonalities; discussion of its traditional forms
(sonata, sonata-rondo, song and scherzo). Points out
an "authorized" change by Walton not in the original
score of the third movement.

David Ward-Steinman
1922-1983

For a discussion of his Three Songs *for clarinet + piano see*
Jennings's dissertation {1207}.

Carl Maria von Weber
1786-1826

1394. Sandner, Wolfgang. *Die Klarinette bei Carl Maria von*
      Weber, in *Neue musikgeschichtliche Forschung,* Bd. 7.
      Wiesbaden: Breitkopf & Härtel, 1971. HML 5725.15.81.
      ISBN 3-7651-0058-7. 257 pages. "Die Behandlung der
      Klarinette bei C.M. von Weber." PhD dissertation.
      University of Frankfurt.
      Considers the use of the clarinet in all of Weber's
      works, including operas, concertos and chamber music.
      Gives historical events leading to the composition, and
      analyzes motives and tonality, clarinet technique and
      expression in each piece.

For discussion of a Theme and Variations *for clarinet +*
string quartet assumed to be by Weber, but in fact by Joseph
Küffner, see Ulrich Rau's article {554}.

1395. Simon, Eric. "Weber's Clarinet Compositions," in
      Clarinet, i (Fall, 1950), 7-10.
      Comments on the efforts to determine Weber's authentic
      or original version of his clarinet pieces by looking
      at the original autograph scores. Concentrates on the
      Concertino, but the basic question pertains to the
      chamber music as well.

1396. Bellison, Simeon. "Weber's Variations," in *Clarinet,*
      i (Spring, 1952), 5-11.
      A description of each variation of Weber's work for
      clarinet + piano, Op. 33, and an account of Weber's
      other clarient pieces and his relationship with Carl
      and Heinrich Baermann.

Anton von Webern
1883-1945

For a catalogue of the works of Webern including chamber music, see Zoltan Roman, Anton von Webern: an Annotated Bibliography, *in Detroit Studies in Music Bibliography, No. 48 (Detroit: Information Coordinators, 1983), 219 pages. ML 134.W39A6.1983. ISBN 0-89990-015-1.*

1397. Mason, Colin. "Webern's Later Chamber Music," in *Music and Letters*, xxxviii (1957), 232-237.
Postulates that Webern's serialism is an outgrowth of canonic writing and analyzes briefly his works from Op. 15 on with emphasis on the String Trio Op. 20, Quartet Op. 22, Concerto Op. 24, and String Quartet Op. 28.

For a documentary study of Webern's string quartets see Ursula von Rauchhaupt's Schoenberg, Berg, Webern: the String Quartets *{201}. For an analysis of Webern's string quartets within their historical setting of the early 20th century, see Werner Pütz's* Studien zum Streichquartettschaffen *{995}.*

1398. Vander Weg, John Dean. "Symmetrical Pitch- and Equivalence-Class Set Structure in Anton Webern's Opus 5." PhD dissertation. University of Michigan, 1983. UMI 83-24302. DAI xliv.7A, p. 1969. 161 pages.
A criticism and emendation of Allen Forte's theory of sets in atonal music, with Webern's piece serving as an example in which to apply them. Shows "that the five pieces are an interrelated 'set of pieces' based on five symmetrical tetrachords, their subsets, and related embedding supersets."

1399. Persky, Stanley. "A Discussion of Compositional Choices in Webern's *Fünf Sätze für Streichquartett*, Op. 5, First Movement," in *Current Musicology*, no. 13 (1972), 68-74.
A highly technical, theoretical analysis of the pitches in this pre-12-tone movement. Webern chose pitches largely from the opening few notes.

1400. Archibald, Bruce. "Some Thoughts on Symmetry in Early Webern: Op. 5, No. 2," in *Perspectives of New Music*, x, no. 2, (1972), 159-163.
Finds 4 symmetrical chords in this movement (for example, a minor sixth on either side of the tritone E-flat - A), and seeks to determine if the listener can recognize symmetrical chords as destinations or origins of nearby near-symmetrical chords (parallel to the expectation and fulfillment of dissonance-to-consonance in tonal harmony). This is not an analysis of the movement but a theoretical point using some aspects of Webern's movement to demonstrate it.

1401. Pousseur, Henri. "Webern's Organic Chromaticism," in
      Anton Webern, in Die Reihe, ii (Vienna: Universal
      Edition, 1955), English trl. by Leo Black (Bryn Mawr:
      Theodore Presser, 1958), pp. 51-60. ML 410.W33 A77.
      A highly technical discussion of Webern's treatment of
      chromaticism as exemplified in several passages from 3
      movements of his Bagatelles Op. 9 for string quartet.

1402. Stein, Erwin. "Webern's New Quartet," in Tempo, no.
      4 (July, 1939), 6-7. Reprint Millwood (New York):
      Kraus Reprint Co., 1974, pages 52-53.
      An analysis for the music student of Webern's String
      Quartet Op. 28 (1938), in which several different forms
      overlap. Discusses for the layperson in very simple,
      non-technical language Webern's use of a row.

1403. Eimert, Herbert. "Interval Proportions: String Quar-
      tet, 1st Movement," in Anton Webern, in Die Reihe, ii
      (Vienna: Universal Edition, 1955), English trl. by
      Leo Black (Bryn Mawr: Theodore Presser, 1958),
      pp. 93-99. ML 410.W33A77.
      A highly technical analysis of the row of the first
      movement of String Quartet Op. 28.

1404. Stockhausen, Karlheinz. "Structure and Experimental
      Time," in Anton Webern, in Die Reihe, ii (Vienna:
      Universal Edition, 1955), English trl. by Leo Black
      (Bryn Mawr: Theodore Presser, 1958), pp. 64-74.
      ML 410.W33A77.
      A highly technical analysis of a part of the second
      movement of Op. 28. Interested in "what organic con-
      nection [there is] between structure and experiential
      time" (the actual different lengths of time for the
      processes of alteration in the music and also our per-
      ception of the different lengths of time). In this
      example even the actual appearance of equal note values
      is perceived with altered time. There is a structural
      division of the passage which follows from this.

For a discussion of Webern's Four Pieces Op. 7 see Paul
Carlson's "An Historical Background and Stylistic Analysis
of Three Twentieth Century Compositions for Violin and
Piano" {250}.

1405. O'Leary, Jane Strong. "Aspects of Structure in We-
      bern's Quartet, Op. 22." PhD dissertation. Prince-
      ton University, 1978. UMI 78-23512. DAI xxxix.6A,
      pp. 3214-5. 98 pages.
      A study of Webern's Quartet for violin + clarinet +
      saxophone + piano and its relationship to the scherzo
      from Beethoven's piano sonata Op. 14 No. 2. Finds lots
      of similarities in harmony and technique.

1406. Stein, Erwin. "Anton Webern," in *Neue Musikzeitung*,
xlix (1928), 517-519.
An analysis of Webern's *Trio for Violin + Viola +
Cello*, Op. 20, in which the row is shown as the source
for variations built from the usual transformation of
the row; yet the piece uses traditional classical rondo
and sonata forms.

1407. Newlin, Dika. "Anton von Webern: Quintet for String
Quartet and Piano," in *Notes*, x (1953), 674-675.
An analysis of this youthful, tonal, 1-movement sonata-
form chamber work. Points to parallels with early
music of Berg and Schoenberg and to the influence of
the latter and Brahms, and shows where certain elements
of this piece presage later works of Webern.

1408. Spinner, Leopold. "Analysis of a Period: Concerto for
9 Instruments, Op. 24, 2nd Movement," in *Anton Webern*, in *Die Reihe*, ii (Vienna: Universal Edition,
1955), English trl. by Leo Black (Bryn Mawr: Theodore
Presser, 1958), pp. 46-50. ML 410.W33A77.
A highly technical discussion of Webern's treatment of
motives and rows in the opening section of this "concerto" movement.

Egon Wellesz
1885-1974

1409. Benser, Caroline Coker Cepin. "Egon Wellesz (1885-
1974): Chronicle of a Twentieth-Century Musician."
PhD dissertation. University of Iowa, 1981. UMI 82-
9964. DAI xlii.11A, p. 4637. 610 pages.
Includes a chapter on Wellesz's chamber music.

Alec Wilder
1907-1980

1410. Bowen, Glenn Hamel. "The Clarinet in the Chamber
Music of Alec Wilder." DMA dissertation. University
of Rochester, 1968. iv + 218 pages.
Analyzes the form, harmony, melody and rhythm of 6
chamber pieces by Wilder, including 3 woodwind quintets, a trio for clarinet + horn + piano, a clarinet
sonata, and a solo clarinet suite. Notes Wilder's bre-
vity, contrapuntal skill, cyclic forms, tertial harmony, remote tonal centers, and jazz style for the clarinetist. Also considers some performance problems.

Peter Winter
1754-1825

1411. Zeller, Gary Lee. "The Instrumental Chamber Music of
      Peter Winter (1754-1825)." PhD dissertation. Catho-
      lic University, 1977. UM 77-15063. DA xxxviii.1A,
      p. 22. 361 pages.
      Describes all the chamber music by Winter, who worked
      in Mannheim and Munich. Analyzes in depth the 6 string
      quartets (1798-1810), which are influenced by Haydn's
      Op. 20 yet avoid imitation and use few motives for
      development. Harmony is more naive than other ele-
      ments. Three are in 3 movements, one quartet is in 2;
      sonata form movements usually are monothematic. Well-
      written music, better than most minor masters.

Joseph Wölfl
1773-1812

1412. Baum, Richard. *Joseph Wölfl (1773-1812): Leben, Kla-
      vierwerke, Klavierkammermusik und Klavierkonzerte.*
      Kassel: Bärenreiter, 1928. ML 410.W785B3. 90 pages.
      Inaugural dissertation. Ludig-Maximilian University
      in Munich, 1926.
      A definitive account of this relatively minor bravura
      pianist-composer who was born in Michael Haydn's house
      in Salzburg and who was a friend and pupil of Leopold
      Mozart. W.A. Mozart helped him obtain his first posi-
      tion in Warsaw, and later in Vienna he was highly re-
      garded by Beethoven, to whom Wölfl dedicated his 3 Op.
      6 piano sonatas. Only 5 pages deal with the chamber
      music: violin, cello or flute sonatas with a predomi-
      nant piano part (Op. 14 is a potpourri of tunes from
      Haydn's *Creation*). After 1800 the chamber music is
      Hausmusik. Historical, not analytical; easily read by
      the layperson.

Hugo Wolf
1860-1903

1413. Aber, A. "Hugo Wolf's 'Italian Serenade,'" in *The
      Musical Times*, lxxxii (1941), 56-58 and 138-139.
      The quartet was written over a period of time: started
      as a quartet in 1887, arranged for orchestra (not fin-
      ished?) in 1893-1894, continued as quartet to his
      death; the finished orchestral version is by Max Reger
      (discusses this at length). Compares the orchestral
      and quartet versions.

Ermanno Wolf-Ferrari
1876-1948

1414. Hamann, Peter. "Die frühe Kammermusik Ermanno Wolf-
Ferraris." Inaugural dissertation. University of
Erlangen, 1975. DAI (Europe) xxxvii.1, p. 4. ML
410.W82H3. iii + 363 pages.
After introductory chapters on musical history at the
end of the 19th century and on the works of Reger,
Pfitzner, Schoenberg and Rheinberger, a description of
5 of Wolf-Ferrari's chamber pieces. He is always ex-
perimenting, but though aware of his contemporaries, he
remains tonal. Gives a complete list of works that
shows he wrote a number of chamber pieces later in his
career, too.

Charles Wuorinen
b.1938

1415. Kuchera-Morin, JoAnn. "Structure in Charles Wuorinen's String Trio." PhD dissertation. University of
Rochester, Eastman School of Music, 1984. UMI 84-
20072. DAI xlv.6A, p. 1568. 111 pages.
Analysis of the Trio (1967-8) "based on a set-theoretic
approach, incorporating pitch-class structure with
rhythm and texture in a three-dimensional overview.
The use of different pitch, rhythmic and textural con-
tours makes it possible to divide the work into twelve
sections." Finds an abundance of interrelationships in
this highly unified piece.

Yannis Xenakis
b.1922

For discussions of his String Quartet St/4-1,080262 *(1962)*
see Michael Coonrod's dissertation {504} and another by
Rosalie Sward {529}.

Francesco Zannetti
1737-1788

1416. Unverricht, Hubert. "Francesco Zannettis Streichtrios," in Siegfried Kross and Hans Schmidt, eds.,
Colloquium Amicorum: Joseph Schmidt-Görg zum 70.
Geburtstag (Bonn: Beethoven-Haus, 1967), pp. 410-427.
ML 55.S35C6.
Undertakes here the first definitive, scholarly study
of the string trios of Zannetti, an Italian who never
left Italy and who therefore represents the Italian
evolution of the string trio from the trio sonata.
Lists in detail each of Zannetti's 7 collections of 6
trios each and lost trios as well. Attempts to date

both published and manuscript trios, from c.1760 to
1782. Most are fast-slow-fast, only a few with minuets
for the third movement (which contradicts Sandberger).
Most are for 2 violins or 2 flutes + bass (= cello),
but Op. 2 is for violin + viola + cello. The first
violin is more difficult to play in the earlier trios,
and uses fugue-like technique in the fast movements,
but Zannetti is not as prone to the concerto trios as
are composers outside Italy.

Jan (Johann) Dismas Zelenká
1679-1745

1417. Sadie, Stanley. "18th-century Chamber," in *The Musi-*
cal Times, civ (1963), 49.
Brief reviews of editions of sonatas by Corelli (Op.
5), Zelenká (Trio Sonata No. 3 in B-flat) and a number
of others. Places Zelenká in perspective as an awk-
ward, uninspired technician -- despite what the editor
says.

1418. Unverricht, Hubert. "Zu Schönbaums Ausgaben von Ze-
lenkas Bläsersonaten," in *Die Musikforschung*, xxii
(1969), 340-343.
Corrects Camillo Schönbaum (*Hortus Musicus*, no. 147);
the autograph of Zelenká's wind sonatas survives in
Dresden, where he worked, and should have been
consulted.

Alexander von Zemlinsky
1872-1942

1419. Weber, Horst. *Alexander Zemlinsky*, in *Österreichi-*
sche Komponisten des xx. Jahrhunderts, Band 23.
Vienna: Verlag Elisabeth Lafite, 1977. ISBN 3-215-
02085-8. 141 pages.
A biography and discussion of the principal chamber
works, including the 4 string quartets and the clarinet
trio. Analyzes form, thematic content, and relationships to Brahms and Schoenberg. Includes a list of
Zemlinsky's chamber music.

1420. Oncley, Lawrence Alan. "The Published Works of Alexander Zemlinsky." PhD dissertation. Indiana University, 1975. UMI 75-17061. DAI xxxvi.2A, p. 591.
499 pages.
In the course of discussing biography and works, gives
considerable attention to the 3 string quartets and
1 piano trio. The early works show a strong Brahms
influence, while the later ones show parallels with the
music of Schoenberg and Bartók.

CHAPTER IV. PERFORMANCE PRACTICE OF CHAMBER MUSIC

GENERAL ADVICE ON PERFORMING CHAMBER MUSIC

1421. Fuller-Maitland, John Alexander. "Concerted Chamber
Music," in *The Consort of Music: a Study of Interpretation and Ensemble* (Oxford: Clarendon Press, 1915),
pp. 32-106. Reprint Freeport (New Jersey): Books for
Libraries Press, [1973]. MT 75.F89.1973.
Ensemble (= consort) is "that kind of cooperation in
music in which each performer bears some share of responsibility for the general effect, as well as for the
correct execution of the notes set before him." While
good ensemble must come from experience in playing together, this book hopes to speed the process by remind-
ing the reader of the basics. Begins with a remarkably
archean discussion of the absence of need for ensemble
in pre-Haydn and post-Brahms chamber music. Briefly
(incorrectly) tries to interpret appoggiaturas of the
18th century and makes a few general remarks on good
ensemble. Mixed ensembles are easier than homogeneous
ensembles because the important melodies automatically
stand out, and in any case important melodies should
always be made to stand out and the other parts recede
to accompaniment. Pays tribute to Joachim and cites
the violinist's flexibility in interpretation in a performance of a Brahms *Hungarian Dance* in D when the author performed it with Joachim. Concentrates on how to
perform Beethoven's Op. 47 violin + piano Sonata,
Brahms's Op. 76 violin + piano Sonata, Franck's violin
+ piano Sonata, Schubert's B-flat Trio, Mozart's G
Minor Piano Quartet, Beethoven's Op. 74 String Quartet,
Schumann's Piano Quintet, and Brahms's Clarinet Quintet. Discusses articulation, balance, rhythmic distortions, piano pedaling, dynamics, ornaments (even when
written out), tempo, character, fingering, portamento,
intonation, and so on. The slight emphasis on chamber
music with piano and on the piano part itself is no
doubt owing to the author being a pianist. The interpretations are dated but nonetheless valid and worthy
of imitation and study by modern ensembles -- if for no
other reason than to understand how chamber music was
interpreted by competent performers c.1900. Especially
valid for Brahms and Franck. Most remarks are very
specific about a specific group of notes.

1422. _____. "Ensemble," in *The
Musical Quarterly*, i (1915), 83-92.
An intelligent discussion of the concept "ensemble,"
primarily in chamber music. Good ensemble requires of

its participants technical accomplishment, stylistic
insight, and rapport with the other players.

1423. Celentano, John P. "Chamber Music: Challenge and
      Opportunity," in *Music Educators Journal*, lxxx
      (1966), no. 2, 103-107.
      A positive assessment, by an important performer of
      chamber music, of the burgeoning of amateur chamber
      musicians and ensembles in America and the need for
      teachers and performing musicians to influence and
      direct them. Many useful suggestions for teachers to
      prepare chamber music including 1) teaching the mastery
      of essentials in mechanics, 2) coaching to coordinate
      correct mechanical means with musical ends, 3) inspir-
      ing by playing examples, and 4) criticizing musical
      intentions and realizations and limiting amateurs to
      the possible.

1424. Busch, Adolph. "The Art of Ensemble Playing," in
      Etude, lvi (1938), 499-500.
      A call for all string players to play chamber music,
      first of all for the fun of it, but also because it is
      excellent drill. An ensemble requires congenial people
      who can work together. Ensemble playing teaches
      musicianship -- "to strive to perfect a musical concep-
      tion of the work as a whole, and then to translate
      those inner thought values into tonal expression." Two
      or more players discussing and sharing such thought
      values help clarify the thoughts. Also stresses the
      need to understand the notation and expression marks as
      the composer meant them -- *piano* meant something
      different for Beethoven, for example, from what it
      means for us. The music must be studied away from the
      instrument first. String quartets are the best type of
      ensemble for players new to ensemble music. The 2
      violinists "must be of absolute equality" technically
      and musically.

1425. Wyatt, Theo. "The Technique of Consort Playing," in
      Recorder and Music vi (1980), 288-292.
      Designed for teachers and amateur players. Suggests
      how to read music while playing so as not to forget the
      other players but also not to lose place. Provides ex-
      ercises. Considers the difficulties of rests, the im-
      portance of bar lines, and the recognition of cadences.
      Defines a good ensemble and pleads for good intonation.

1426. Ball, Arthur L. "Ensemble Playing," in *The Strad*,
      xli (1930), 233-234.
      Advice to good but inexperienced chamber ensemble
      players: don't speed or drag, keep the tempo when
      changing rhythmic figures, observe rests carefully as
      if they are notes, do not change tempos during crescen-
      do or decrescendo, give short notes their full value in
      slow tempos, keep the rhythm even in each part when

there is 2 against 3 or any other polyrhythm, balance
the tone of the ensemble to the ensemble and allow
other members to come forth when they are more important, know the other players's parts, and sense the
feeling of the work.

1427. Hauser, Emil. *Interpretation of Music for Ensemble.*
New York: author, 1952. MT 728.H28. 31 pages + 2
pages of music.
"A working draft of a complete manual" (still in preparation?) for string players. It is presented in outline and, although it covers material any good string
chamber player knows, it is not presented in a way that
anyone but a good string player would understand. Most
of the book is devoted to phrasing and dynamics and to
signs to indicate all the subtleties of phrasing and
dynamics. Phrasing is related to language in a superficial way. Much appears to be in the form of preliminary notes that should not have been published.

See also Campanha {8}.

1428. Ledbetter, Lynn Frances. "A Compendium of Chamber
Music Excerpts (1750-1890) Selected and Organized
Pedagogically for the Violin According to Technical
Requirements." DMA dissertation. University of
Texas at Austin, 1984. UMI 85-13176. DAI xlv.4A,
p.833.
Presents more material than other pedagogical studies
of chamber music, although the bibliography clearly
shows the author's ignorance of other such studies (for
example {1441-1447}, {672}, and so on). A unique
tract for student violinists who need to develop violinistic techniques for playing chamber music. Systematically presents bowing, left hand, and "special"
techniques, in every case giving examples from the
chamber music repertory (usually by famous composers).
Unfortunately, the musical examples are printed so
small that they are nearly useless.

1429. Stratton, George, and Alan Frank. *The Playing of
Chamber Music,* in *The Student's Music Library.* London: Oxford University Press, 1935. 2nd ed. London:
Dennis Dobson, 1951. MT 728.S91P4.1951. x + 80
pages. Reprinted in *The Strad,* 1 (1939), 66-67, 114-
116, 162, 164, 213-216, 247-249, 279-281, 311-313,
354-360, 375-377, and 407-409.
A practical guide by an ensemble coach for performers
who want to play chamber music: how to rehearse and
technical suggestions. Three string quartets (Mozart
K.465, Beethoven Op. 59 no. 3, and Debussy) are interpreted from the standpoint of how the 4 players are to
blend together: dynamics, bowings, fingerings, vibra-

tos, and so on. A brief chapter on other types of
chamber music.

*A historically interesting discussion of the difference
between practice and rehearsal is in John Hullah's Music in
the House {168}.*

1430. Aulich, Bruno. *Alte Musik, recht verstanden --*
      richtig gespielt. Mit einem Verzeichnis sämtlicher
      Neudrucke. Munich: Ernst Heimeran, 1957. 226 pages.
      2nd rev. ed. *Alte Musik für Hausmusikanten.* Munich:
      Heimeran, 1968. ML 195.A84.1968. 288 pages.
      A book on Baroque (1650-1750) chamber music designed to
      aid the amateur performer at home. Specifically not
      for the professional musician or musicologist. General
      history of Baroque chamber music, general hints on per-
      formance of ornaments, form and stylistic traits of
      such music. Concludes with lists of repertory.

1431. Sutter, Milton. "Francesco Galeazzi on the Duties of
      the Leader or Concertmaster," in *Consort*, xxxii
      (1976), 185-192.
      The first Italian discussion of seating plans and make-
      up of ensembles both orchestral and chamber (in and out
      of church) is in Galeazzi's "Del Regolare, o sia de
      Doveri di un Primo Violino," in *Elementi Teorico-*
      Pratici di Musica, Chapter I, (1791). Also information
      on tempos, ensemble, and tuning.

*On the business aspects of organizing professional chamber
music:*

1432. Helmen, Lillian Campbell. *Organizational Manual for*
      Chamber Music Ensembles. [New York]: Chamber Music
      America, 1981. ML 3795.H445. ISBN 0-941398-00-5.
      vi + 139 pages. "Organizational Alternatives: a
      Study of the Organizational Formats of Chamber Music
      Ensembles." MA thesis. American University, 1983.
      UMI PSE 13-20607. Masters Abstracts xxi.4 (1983), p.
      360. 119 pages.
      The difference between the thesis and the book is that
      the former is aimed at a scholarly readership and the
      latter at the performing public and those who want to
      promote chamber music. Discusses the legal types of
      chamber music organization; federal and other taxes;
      income, funding, and support; organizational structure;
      administration; and 3 case studies. Surveyed 143 Amer-
      ican chamber ensembles of different types: sole pro-
      prietorships, partnerships, corporations, unincorpor-
      ated associations, and ensembles under the aegis of a
      larger organization. Gives alternative solutions.

On the organization of amateur chamber music:

See Oskar Vetter's "Warum und wie spielen wir Kammermusik?" {483} with a defense of amateur chamber music and how it is played, and Adorno's chapter on chamber music {486} which describes the role of amateur Hausmusik.

1433. Piastro, Mishel. "On the Fingerboard," in *Symphony*, iv (June, 1950), 11.
Does not believe a string quartet player can play in an orchestra or an orchestral player in a string quartet. The orchestral player wants to be led by the conductor, and his value as a player in the orchestra is his response to the conductor. The chamber player seeks equality and is part of the decision-making process.

BIBLIOGRAPHIES OF PERFORMANCE PRACTICE FOR CHAMBER MUSIC

1434. Newman, William S., coordinator. "Bibliography of Performance Practices," in *Current Musicology*, no. 8 (1969), 5-96.
List of studies directly bearing on the performance of music from c.1100 to c.1900. Although most articles on instruments pertain to the execution of fingering, bowing, embouchure, and ornamentation of individual instruments, some of the items also are relevant to performance of chamber music, especially before 1780.

1435. Garretson, Homer Eugene. "An Annotated Bibliography of Written Material Pertinent to the Performance of Chamber Music for Stringed Instruments." EdD dissertation. University of Illinois, 1961. UMI 61-4295. DA xxii.5A, p. 1654. 96 pages.
Provides "a ready means of access to all books and periodical literature written since 1900 pertaining to the performance of chamber music for stringed instruments," designed for teacher or scholar. Also includes a selective list of Baroque and early Classical chamber music suitable for public school use. All issues of 37 European and American periodicals were covered for relevant materials, and 3 major libraries were searched for all relevant holdings.

1436. Squire, Alan Paul. "An Annotated Bibliography of Written Material Pertinent to the Performance of Woodwind Chamber Music." EdD dissertation. University of Illinois, 1960. UMI 60-3999. DA xxi.6, pp. 1587-1588. 135 pages.
Comparable to Garretson and Rutan, a bibliography commissioned by the Music Educators National Conference, designed for woodwind students who need to

learn ensemble and specific music by means of harmonic
and structural analysis, historical importance, and
aesthetic value, all of which affect balance, intonation, articulation, phrasing, and so on. Concentrates
on articles, books and critical editions in English,
though some French and German are included separately.
Also gives a graded list suitable for performance by
high school groups. Includes chamber music for a
majority of woodwind instruments as well as 1 woodwind
with piano. Bibliography includes 1) history and
development of woodwind instruments; 2) acoustical and
playing characteristics of woodwind instruments;
3) history and development of woodwind chamber music;
4) musical interpretation of woodwind chamber music;
5) harmonic and structural analyses of woodwind chamber
music; 6) ensemble rehearsal and performance practices;
7) specific playing techniques of woodwind instruments;
and 8) related German and French books and articles.

1437. Rutan, Harold Duane. "An Annotated Bibliography of
      Written Material Pertinent to the Performance of
      Brass and Percussion Chamber Music." EdD disser-
      tation. University of Illinois, 1960. LC 61-196.
      DA xxi.11, pp. 3481-3482. iv + 369 pages.
      A list of books and articles pertaining to performance
      of brass chamber music and a graded list of such music
      for schools. Organizes the bibliographical material
      first by articles in foreign language journals, then
      articles in English language journals, then selected
      books, dissertations, essays, catalogues and pamphlets.
      Many of the citations are on structural and technical
      features of the instruments that are only incidentally
      related to chamber music, on orchestral uses, on vocal
      works with brass, on pre-17th-century works, and only a
      few on actual chamber music.

PERFORMANCE ADVICE FOR THE OVERALL CHAMBER MUSIC OF SPECIFIC PERIODS AND COMPOSERS

1438. Schmitz, Hans-Peter. "Les Possibilités d'Instru-
      mentation ad Libitum dans la Musique de Chambre
      Française pendant la Première Moité du 18ème Siècle
      (en Tenant Particulièrement Compte de la Flûte et de
      sa Littérature)," in Édith Weber, ed. *Couperin
      Colloque: l'Interprétation de la Musique Française
      aux xviie et xviiie Siècles: Colloques Internationaux
      du CNRS, 537: Paris, 20-26 Oct 1969.* Paris: CNRS,
      1974. RILM 74-3824.
      Stresses the liberty taken at the time in instrumenta-
      tion, tessitura, tonality, tempo, rhythm, nuance,

phrasing, and ornamentation, "as long as the meaning or spirit of the work was not modified."

1439. Fry, J. "Brahms' Conception of the Scherzo in Chamber Music," in *The Musical Times*, lxxxiv (1943), 105-107.
Notes 2 types of scherzos: in the lighter-scored (some sonatas, quartets, quintets) and in the heavier-scored (2 sextets and piano chamber music). In the former, Brahms cautions against too scherzando an effect -- he uses words with "scherzo" (such as "un poco Allegretto") or avoids the word altogether. The other type is noisy, vigorous, and without the lightness in the first type. This distinction also applies to the trios following the scherzos.

1440. Barnes, James. "Mozart's Chamber Music," in *Music Journal*, xiv (March, 1956), 24, 41-42.
Recognizes the problems as well as the truths in the extremes of literal interpretaion or a performer's instinctive interpretaion of Mozart. Tempo is relative and personal within limits. Dynamics are less extreme than in Mannheimers or Beethoven but mature Mozart requires strength. Phrasing must not be mechanical but also must not be too full of rubatos.

ADVICE ON PERFORMING STRING QUARTETS

1441. Norton, Mary Dows Herter. *String Quartet Playing: a New Treatise on Chamber Music, its Technic and Interpretation.* New York: Carl Fischer, 1925. MT 728. H37.1925. 144 pages, 132 examples. New ed. 1952. Rev. ed. *The Art of String Quartet Playing: Practice, Technique and Interpretation, with a Preface by Isaac Stern.* London: V. Gollancz, 1962. MT 728.H37.1962. Paperback edition New York: W.W. Norton, 1966. 785.7 N82S. 190 pages, 132 examples.
Sound advice to performers by an experienced player on how best to play string quartets: how to rehearse, matters of phrasing, style, rhythm, and so on. Technical discussion of bowing, fingering, and ensemble. Valuable for all ensembles, not just string quartets. The 1966 edition excludes the old first chapter and adds a chapter on rehearsal; it also expands some of the other material.

1442. Page, Athol. *Playing String Quartets.* Boston: Humphries/London: Longmans, 1964. MT 728.P32. vii + 131 pages.
An experienced quartet player (member of the Manchester String Quartet) presents a practical guide to persons

wanting to play string quartets. Discusses such details as the types of mutes, methods of tuning, intonation, vibrato, bowing, pizzicato, ensemble, rehearsal,
performance, and interpretation. All these comments
are intelligent and any quartet musician will follow
them. However, the comments on specific compositions
are subjective and superficial, and an introduction on
the precursors of the quartet is best ignored.

1443. Borciani, Paolo. *Il Quartetto*. Milan: Ricordi,
      1973. MT 728.B67. 164 pages, 324 examples.
      A detailed, thorough, practical guide for string quar-
      tet players, amateurs, and mostly young professionals,
      by the original first violinist of the Quartetto Ita-
      liano. Part I deals with organizational factors, con-
      cert requirements (for example, the program, the
      seating arrangement), the life of a quartet (study
      habits, tours, and so on). Part II deals with the
      actual playing: intonation, the sound (intensity,
      dynamics, balance, pizzicato), types of bowing, vi-
      brato, portamento and changing strings, rhythm, and so
      forth. There are ample illustrations of each point,
      and additional examples in the appendix, from Haydn to
      Webern but mostly Beethoven. A special chapter is de-
      voted to some technical and interpretive problems in
      Schubert's D Minor Quartet D.810, first movement.

1444. Raaben, Lev Nikolaevich. *Voprosy Kvartetnogo
      Ispolnitel'stva*. 2nd ed. Moscow: Musyka, 1960. MT
      728.R22.1960. 108 pages.
      A book on performance of chamber music for performers,
      including problems of melody, polyphony, harmony, rhy-
      thm, intonation, tone, dynamics, and vibrato. Gives
      examples of specific standard works in regard to these
      questions (Schumann, Beethoven, Borodin, Tchaikovsky,
      Glazunov, Ravel and others).

1445. Fink, I., and C. Merriell, eds. *String Quartet
      Playing: with the Guarneri String Quartet*. Neptune
      City (New Jersey): Paganiniana Publications, 1985.
      ISBN 0-86622-007-0. 191 pages.
      Interviews with the players of the Guarneri String
      Quartet on how to play quartets, with lots of advice on
      how to "achieve top performance in string quartets."
      Considers tone production, ensemble, and much more.
      Analyzes for performance 5 movements: Mozart's "Disso-
      nance," movement 1; Beethoven's Op. 59 No. 2, movement
      1; and Ravel, movements 1-3.

1446. Pochon, Alfred. *A Progressive Method of String-
      Quartet Playing*. New York: G. Schirmer, 1928. MT
      728.P6. 2 parts. I: xi + 66 pages (elementary; in
      English [original], French, and Spanish); II: 86
      pages, 53 examples (advanced; in French [original]

and English, trl. by Theodore Baker). Each part has
commentary followed by examples; the examples include
score (for which the above page references pertain)
and a set of parts.
Part II is the best practical instruction book for more
advanced student quartet players. It covers a wide
range of performance questions, such as interpretation,
tone-vibrato, bowings; special technique questions like
scales, saltati, rhythms, pizzicato, chromatic
fingerings; and some special topics, for example,
"things to be avoided," harmonics, how to practice.
The instructions are clear, precise, and effective.
Examples in Part II range from Beethoven to Webern.
Does not touch upon organizational matters, concert
behavior, and the like.

1447. Léner, Jenó. *The Technique of String Quartet
Playing.* London: J. & W. Chester, 1935. ML 810.
L57T4. Score (iv + 42 pages) and parts (25 or 26
pages each). In English, French, and German.
An equivalent to the Pochon {1446}, it consists of
exercises for string quartet ensembles in scales,
dynamics, tone color and bowing with examples drawn
from Kreutzer, Haydn, Beethoven, J. Jongen and
Malipiero. Not as large as Pochon, and it does not get
as difficult. Verbal instructions are given.

1448. Spohr, Louis. "On the Delivery or Style of Performing Quartetts," in *Celebrated Violin School*, trl.
by John Bishop (London: R. Cocks & Co., [1843]), pp.
232-233. MT 262.S82.1843. Originally published
Violinschule (Kassel:, 1831; Vienna: T. Haslinger,
1832). MT 262.S8.
Refers the violinist to a section on concertos for performance of solo quartets (= *quatuors brillans* = *quatuors concertants*), while here is emphasized the
"genuine quartet" where the soloist must step aside and
which requires "a higher degree of sensibility, a more
refined taste, and a knowledge of composition." The
violinist should first play second violin in order to
learn to accompany and accommodate himself to the first
violinist. The first violinist must study and mark his
part and must know the entire score before he plays it.
The violinist has to make his part violinistic -- add
bowings, fingerings, and so on -- but with great care
to achieve the ideas of the composer and to balance the
instruments properly.

1449. Sharp, J. Wharton. "Quartet Playing," in *The Strad*,
xviii (1908), 412-413; xix (1909), 29-30, 49-50, 90-
92, and 121-124.
Since so many "quartet parties" have been formed (one
of the most perfect was Joachim's), some advice for
them when they start out. "Intuitive playing together"

(ensemble playing) is most important. All 4 players
are equal, though the first violinist has a responsibility to see that everyone works together. All should
coordinate dynamics, and concentrate especially on very
soft passages. Learn to accompany without losing interest. Stresses the ability to read well. Then goes
into specific repertory for the new ensemble, starting
with Mozart's 6 "Haydn" quartets, then Haydn, with
details on performance on some points. Also talks
about how to perform a Beethoven string trio (*The
Strad,* xix 158-162).

1450. Aulich, Bruno, and Ernst Heimeran. *Das stillvergnüg-
te Streichquartett.* Munich: Ernst Heimeran, 1936.
English trl. by D. Millar Craig, *The Well-Tempered
String Quartet: a Book of Counsel and Entertainment
for All Lovers of Music in the Home.* London: Novel-
lo/New York: H.W. Gray, 1938. Revised edition 1949.
ML 67.A843.1949. iv + 147 pages.
A handbook for amateur string quartet players with suggestions for rehearsing, making up programs, and (the
bulk of the book) an alphabetical list of composers of
chamber music with a brief discussion of their principal chamber pieces. At the end a discussion of trios,
quintets and other larger types of chamber music, and a
discussion of chamber music to play when a member of
the quartet does not show up or extra players do.

1451. Kehr, Günter. "Kammermusikalische Selbstverständ-
lichkeiten," in *Musikleben,* iii (1950), 279-282.
Discusses the basic elements of playing chamber music:
rhythm, intonation, dynamics, phrasing and expression.
Sound advice for students or teachers involved in chamber music. The ethics of chamber music requires cooperation and the importance of the music over the
individuality of each player.

1452. Kornstein, Egon F. "How to Practise a String-Quar-
tet," trl. by Dorothy Holland, in *Music and Letters,*
iii (1923), 329-334.
A chatty discussion of how the Hungarian Quartet, of
which Kornstein was a member, rehearses a new work (it
premiered Bartók's First Quartet). Four stages: deciding who has the relatively important material at a
given time, deciding on the right quality of sound,
reassembling the quartet with the right tempos (at this
point the composer can be invited in), and re-study to
obtain the final conception.

1453. Brown, James. "The Amateur String Quartet," in *The
Musical Times,* lxviii (1927), 508-9, 600-602, 714-
716, 798-800, 907-909, and 1078-1081.
Advice to teachers on how to recruit and train young
performers in playing string quartets. They must not

be too young. They should listen to each other. Indicates what the teacher should listen for in a violinist, violist, and cellist. Tells not only how to train their ears and hands but also how to give them discipline in rhythm, tone, phrasing, style, and quality. Although written in an archaic manner, it is an interesting manual.

1454. Tertis, Lionel. "The String Quartet," in *Music and Letters*, xxxi (April, 1950), 148-150.
A famous violist in numerous quartets and coach of still others gives a few suggestions for quartet playing: great executive powers, a close relation in tone-quality among the 4 players, and agreement in style and outlook. Also a strong leader and team spirit. Suggestions on bowing and pizzicatos, and some remarks for the pianist who joins in.

1455. Betti, Adolfo. "Quartet Playing," in *Music and Letters*, iv (1923), 1-5.
This important violinist (member of the Flonzaley Quartet) discusses the role of the first violinist in a quartet: he is a part of a whole, not a dictator like an orchestral conductor. "The quartet is a conversation between four friends, not a lecture by one of them with the others just nodding agreement." The first violinist must be a psychologist in order to work so closely with 3 other players. The quartet is more delicate than a symphony and needs many more rehearsals -- 30 to 35 for an important new work ("the Flonzaley Quartet needed fifty-five to produce Schönberg's Op. 7"). While the first violinist should know the whole score, no work is really known until it is performed *very accurately*. Tempi are extremely important but also extremely elusive. Interpreters must recreate the inspiration in the music from inadequate and ambiguous expression signs on the score. Finds that Mozart and Haydn quartets carry better in big halls (3000 to 4000 people) than Tchaikovsky or Smetana. *See also {472}*.

1456. Gertler, André. "Advice to Young Quartet-Players," in *The Score*, no. 5 (Aug., 1951), 19-32.
Instead of a list of do's and don't's, ambles along with anecdotes commenting on the depth of Beethoven as opposed to the shallowness of Wieniawski, the need for ensembles to practice, the need for a quartet player to subordinate him/herself to the composer yet be capable of great technique and wide variety of tone color, and so on. Gives personal recollections of Bartók and the composer's alterations of his own printed tempos. Calls for a metronome -- good discipline. A useful article, especially for the student chamber ensemble, even if presented in a rambling fashion.

1457. Murnighan, J. Keith. "Many Hands across the Sea: a
      Social Scientist Looks at the British String Quar-
      tet," in *American Ensemble,* vi, no. 3 (1983), 10-11.
      A sociological study of 20 British string quartet en-
      sembles who were interviewed at length (82 actual
      interviews). Analyzed both the individual player's
      issues and those pertaining to the group as a whole.
      Some generalities: most started studying their instru-
      ment at age 7, most came from musical families, most
      married musical persons, almost unanimous reverence for
      the quartet literature, and a continuous search for the
      ideal sound. Also considers rehearsal questions,
      particular instrument's peculiarities, and who leads
      the quartet.

*Advice on performing the string quartets of specific compo-
sers:*

*For performance practice in Bartók's quartets, see Myron
Kartman's "Analysis and Performance Problems in the Second,
Fourth and Sixth String Quartets by Béla Bartók" {577}.*

*For some performance suggestions of the Beethoven string
quartets, see Hugo Riemann's Beethoven's Streichquartette
erläutert {611}.*

1458. Schmid, Willi. "Zur Interpretation von Beethovens
      Streichquartetten," in *Melos,* vii (1928), 396-404.
      Notes that the best musicians have interpreted these
      quartets, each according to personal, natural and his-
      toric criteria of expression. The Czech quartets are
      freer, the Viennese stricter, in interpretation. Also,
      the different styles of violin playing influence inter-
      pretation. General remarks on style rather than de-
      tailed ways to play particular phrases or notes. The 3
      kinds of expression -- lyric, dramatic, and oratoric --
      are difficult to separate in the late quartets. Con-
      cerned with line, with dynamics, and with tempo.
      Criticizes Riemann for being too theoretical and not
      practical.

1459. Todd, Donald Clarke. "The Problem of Bowing in the
      Joachim-Moser Edition of Beethoven's String Quar-
      tets." DMA dissertation. University of Illinois,
      1967. UMI 68-1869. DAI xxviii.8A, p. 3214. 248
      pages.
      Concentrates on the alterations in bowing and articula-
      tion which Joachim made to Beethoven's Op. 59 No. 3
      quartet and then to the previous 8 quartets. Compares
      Joachim's version to the Urtext edition and the surviv-
      ing quartet manuscripts. Identifies changes made for
      expediency -- easier bowings -- and then shows how some
      are actually inferior to Beethoven's suggestions. Joa-

chim did not have the manuscripts of Op. 18 at his dis-
posal.

1460. Keller, Hans. "The Interpretation of the Haydn
Quartets," in *The Score*, xxiv (Nov. 1958), 14-35.
An introduction commiserates with students on the sad
state of modern chamber music: fewer and fewer people
know how to play a genuine string quartet. To play any
string quartet or to understand it, one must start with
Haydn. The literature on the Haydn string quartets is
faulty because the writers are not performers of those
pieces. Urges violinists and violists to exchange
parts to learn the whole quartet. The rest of the
essay is on performance suggestions of specific Haydn
quartets, presented "chronologically" by opus number.
Includes Op. 3. Discusses pizzicatos, phrasing,
rhythm, and other topics. A must for anyone who plays
the Haydn quartets, even if some of Keller's suggestions are obvious or arguable. See also {941} and
{1304}.

1461. Robinson, Edith. "Some Reflections on the Interpretation of Haydn's Quartets," in *The Strad*, xliii
(1932), 530-532.
A plea from a violinist whose training was in Leipzig
1884-1894 to return to a pure style of playing Haydn,
without exaggerated tempi and dynamics, with less of a
vibrato, and with bow strokes known to Haydn. Haydn is
not dainty or graceful; he is witty. Gives specific
advice on tempos, ornaments, and so on, which help
characterize a style of quartet playing of the late
19th century in Germany and England.

1462. Somfai, László. "Zur Aufführungspraxis der frühen
Streichquartett-Divertimenti Haydns," in Vera
Schwarz, ed., *Der junge Haydn: Kongressbericht Graz
1970: Beiträge für Aufführungspraxis*, i (Graz: Aka-
demische Druck- und Verlagsanstalt, 1972), pages 86-
97.
Haydn's real quartets begin with Op. 9. The 10 or 12
earlier ones are divertimenti. Does not attempt to
give the absolute way they should be performed but to
outline the difficulties in trying to perform them
accurately: 1) soloistic or orchestral, 2) with or
without continuo, 3) who plays the bass, and 4) what is
the solution to the viola part which often causes
voice-leading problems. After that come questions of
ornamentation, phrasing and dynamics. Each of the 4
first questions discussed with examples.

*For insight into performing Mozart's string quartet K.387,
see Hans Keller's "The Chamber Music" {1124}.*

1463. Berkley, Harold. "Grace Notes in a Mozart Quartet,"
      in *Etude*, lxx (Dec. 1952), 25.
      In 3 very brief paragraphs (only the first part of the
      article), tells a questioner how to perform the "grace"
      notes in mm. 3-4 of Mozart's K.575, movement 1: they
      take the value they indicate, always on the beat.

1464. Steuermann, Clara. "In Memory of Rudolf Kolisch
      (1896-1978)," in *Perspectives of New Music*, xvi, no.
      2 (1978), 247-250.
      A brief tribute to Kolisch and some personal recollec-
      tions on the life and work of this famous string quar-
      tet violinist and brother-in-law of Schoenberg. Des-
      cribes the main events of his career, preparation for a
      performance of a Schoenberg quartet in 1944, and his
      personality. Useful for anyone planning to play a
      Schoenberg quartet.

*For advice in performing Smetana's E-minor Quartet see
{1343}.*

ADVICE ON PERFORMING SONATAS

1465. Seagrave, Barbara Ann Garvey. "The French Style of
      Violin Bowing and Phrasing from Lully to Jacques
      Aubert (1650-1730): as Illustrated in Dances from
      Ballets and Dance Movements from Violin Sonatas of
      Representative Composers." PhD dissertation.
      Stanford University, 1959. UMI 59-1452. DA xix.12,
      pp. 3322-3323. 309 pages.
      Tries to explain terms and markings in 17th-century
      French violin music, rules for bowing not in the music,
      effects of the nature of the instrument of the time on
      bowings, rhythmic conventions of the time not notated,
      and the relationship between dance and music. Relies
      heavily on French and foreign treatises of the time and
      on dance music and sonatas. Concludes that bowing pat-
      terns correspond in length to dance patterns in France
      but were much more freely interpreted in Italy.

1466. Rubinstein, Seymour Z. "A Technical Investigation
      and Performance of Three French Violin Sonatas of the
      Early Twentieth Century (1915-1927), Debussy, Ravel
      and Fauré." EdD dissertation. Columbia University
      Teachers College, 1976. UMI 76-17292. DAI xxxvii.
      2A, p. 684.
      An investigation into "the problems of violin technique
      inherent in the interpretation of these works. These
      problems include bow control and angles of application,
      glissando, spiccato, pizzicato, variety in vibrato
      effect, and special fingerings." The 3 sonatas are
      compared to Debussy's string quartet, Ravel's string

quartet and sonata for violin + cello, and Fauré's
piano quartet Op. 45.

1467. Robison, John O. "The Messa di Voce as an Instrumental Ornament in the Seventeenth and Eighteenth
Centuries," in *The Music Review*, xliii (1982), 1-14.
The term "messa di voce" is discussed in the leading
treatises of the 18th century (L. Mozart, Quantz,
Corrette, C.P.E. Bach, and others) and is a specific
ornament in slow movements of violin sonatas: a swell
and taper. Relevant to the music from Corelli to
Geminani and Tartini.

*For performance questions in 19th-century American violin
works see James Starr's dissertation {247}. For "possible
solutions to violinistic problems" in 20th-century Spanish
works for violin and piano, see Laura Klugherz's dissertation {1122}. For technical problems in 20th-century
American violin sonatas, see Tyska's thesis {251}.*

Advice on performing sonatas by specific composers:

1468. Fenley, John Franklin. "The Ornamentation in Seven
Flute Sonatas Composed by, or Attributed to, J.S.
Bach." EdD dissertation. University of Illinois,
1976. UMI 77-8987. DAI xxxvii.10. 477 pages.
Using Putnam Aldrich's "The Principal Agréments of the
Seventeenth and Eighteenth Centuries: a Study in Musical Ornamentation" (PhD dissertation, Harvard University, 1942) as a basis, interprets the ornamentation in
Bach's 7 flute sonatas. Amasses much material (editions, treatises, theses, recordings, and articles) to
interpret the 195 ornaments found in the 7 pieces in
addition to those probably improvised.

1469. Baron, Samuel. "The Flute Music of J.S. Bach," in
Symphony, iv (Nov. 1950), 9-10, and (Dec. 1950 - Jan.
1951), 9-10.
After a distinction between flute and recorder sound
and a review of Bach's flute writing in cantatas and
other types of music, concentrates on the 3 sonatas for
obligato clavier + flute and the 3 sonatas for flute +
continuo. After description of all 6, suggests how to
perform the staccatos and how to pace the breaths in
all the flute works. Answers 2 questions: where to
take a breath, and what kind of breath to take.

1470. Scott, Marion Margaret. "The Violin Music of Handel
and Bach," in *Music and Letters*, xvi (1935), 188-199.
Historical and critical essay, without footnotes,
bibliography or other full documentation, on the violin
in the lives and solo works of these 2 composers.
Much information is given, some of it apparently

hearsay, but most probably factual. A performer's analysis of the music, rather than a theoretician's.

For a valuable study of the performance of Beethoven's violin + piano sonatas, see Gail Johansen's dissertation {672}.

1471. Rostal, Max. *Beethoven: the Sonatas for Piano and Violin: Thoughts on their Interpretation.* Trl. by Horace and Anna Rosenberg. New York/London: Toccata, 1985. MT 145.B422R713.1985. ISBN 0-907689-05-1. 219 pages, 207 examples. Original *Die Sonaten für Klavier und Violine.* Munich: R. Piper, 1981. A detailed, intense presentation of performance suggestions for the 10 sonatas, including bowing, phrasing, tempo, dynamics, and style. Far more involved than {1472}.

1472. Szigeti, Joseph. *The Ten Beethoven Sonatas for Piano and Violin*, ed. Paul Rolland. Urbana: American String Teachers Association, 1965. MT 145.B42S9. 55 pages. Defends these 10 sonatas as masterpieces, often quoting famous musicians over 150 years and dropping in suggestions for performance. Does not analyze but romanticizes over keys and fine points. Quotes Bartók in writing his sonata for violin + piano No. 2 as finding it impossible to write the same material for both instruments and therefore, after 1923, never writing another violin + piano sonata. Szigeti differs and shows how the 2 can complement each other in the same material. Many technical problems with his own (sometimes other's) solutions -- fingering, bowing, phrasing, dynamics, tempo, choice of string, and so on. An appendix capsulizes Szigeti's basic performance suggestions for each sonata. (While Szigeti was a seasoned, intelligent musician, he had a terrible bow technique, and his large fingers made his fingerings useless for most violinists with much smaller fingers.)

1473. Herwegh, Marcel. *Technique d'Interprétation sous Forme d'Essai d'Analyse Psychologique Expérimentale Appliqué aux Sonates pour Piano et Violon de Beethoven.* [Paris: Victor Allinger, n.d.] Paris: Pierre Schneider, 1926. MT 145.B5H58. 254 pages. A serious, detailed study of interpretation of music for performers. It requires considerable knowledge of the sonatas in advance and the use of the score while studying. Each sonata is treated in 2 ways: an analysis of the phrases, forms, rhythms and designs of each sonata, and a discourse on the violinist's interpretation of his/her part (the main interest for our discussion). To interpret is to make known to the listener unambiguously the rhythmic, harmonic, and melodic role of each note of a phrase, of a polyphony, and to keep

in mind the continuous expressive flow of the whole
piece. Does not propose to dictate interpretation of
the Beethoven sonatas but to control the details and
free the performer from a servile and sterile obei-
sance to the printed page. Objects to trying to repro-
duce Beethoven on Beethoven's instruments; "time
marches on" and these works sound better with modern
instruments. Be aware of historical facts, but interpret within one's own time frame. Understand the psy-
chology of music for a more profound interpretation.
Music is nuances and nuances of nuances. The phrase is
divided into initial, intermediate, and cadential
group; no matter how long or short, how homogeneous or
heterogeneous, the phrase must be considered in terms
of rhythm, harmony, tonality, and melodic design. This
is then applied to the Beethoven sonatas, gradually to
other Beethoven compositions, and then to various works
by others. Rhythmic interpretation is the main focus.
Basically flexible enough to recognize contingencies
based on acoustics or other physical problems of a
hall.

1474. Altmann, Gustav. "Ein Fehler in Beethovens erster
Violin-Sonate," in *Die Musik*, xi.3 (1912), 28-29.
Questions the phrasing and resultant rhythm of the
upbeat to measure 17 in the slow movement of Op. 12 No.
1. The upbeat should be an eighth, not a sixteenth.
Makes sense.

1475. Pečman, Rudolf. "Zur Frage der Interpretation der
Violinsonaten Frantisek Bendas," trl. by Jan Gruna,
in Eitelfriedrich Thom, ed., *Zu Fragen des Instrumen-
tariums, der Besetzung und der Improvisation in der
ersten Hälfte des 18. Jahrhunderts: Konferenzbericht
der 3. wissenschaftlichen Arbeitstagung Blankenburg/
Harz 28./29. Juni 1975*, in *Studien zur Aufführungspraxis und Interpretation von Instrumentalmusik des
18. Jahrhunderts*, Heft 2 (Blankenburg/Harz: Rat des
Bezirkes Magdeburg, c.1975), pages 38-48. HML 175.
898.
Refers to the 157 violin + continuo sonatas by Benda,
which in general are different from North German examples and Baroque ones. They usually are in the major
mode, 3 movements fast-slow-fast, not yet sonata form
but binary. Then analyzes the ornamentation which survives for many of them, comparing them to those by Tartini and L. Mozart. Since different ornaments exist
for the same music, it is evident that the surviving
ornaments are to be taken as typical but not definitive. The ornamentation never distracts or exists for
its own sake; it and all expression serve the music.
Clearly used dynamic shading -- crescendo and decre-
scendo -- and echo effects. Unlike C.P.E. Bach and L.
Mozart, Benda began all trills on the written note and
then went up.

For another discussion of the embellishments of sonatas for violin + bass by Franz Benda, see Douglas Lee's article {690}. For discussion of embellishments of Corelli's sonatas, see articles by Hans Joachim Marx {818} and David Boyden {819}.

1476. Babitz, Sol. "Corelli in the 20th Century," in *International Musician*, lii (July, 1953), 28-29.
On Corelli's 300th birthday, a call to perform his music in an authentic style. The focus is on ornamentation, with short examples written out (including simplification of a J.S. Bach unaccompanied sonata movement to look like Corelli's printed edition).

1477. Pook, Wilfred. "Thoughts on Corelli," in *The Strad*, lxix (1958), 152, 154, 156, 204, 206, 208, 210, 278, 280, 282, and 284.
A very personal account of one man's becoming interested in pre-Mozart violin music. A brief account of Corelli's total oeuvre and the gradual return of interest in Correli's music. A description of new editions and detailed discussion of the ornamentation.

For performance suggestions for sonatas for violin + piano by the 18th-century Michael Festing, see Eldon Krantz's dissertation {885}. For discussion of the bowing, dynamics, trills, cadences and improvisation of the violin part, and realization of the figured bass in Handel's violin + keyboard sonatas, see the article by Pook {927}.

1478. Berkley, Harold. "Handel Sonata in D Major," in *Etude*, lxix (Jan., 1951), 25 and 53, (March, 1951), 25 and 52.
Primarily for the violinist, a technical interpretation of the sonata, with bowings, vibratos, dynamics. Berkley was a pupil of Franz Kneisel.

1479. Kehr, Günter. "Wir studieren eine Hindemith-Violinsonate," in *Melos*, xiv (1947), 109-111.
An attempt to explain to the performer wary of performing contemporary music how to go about learning a new piece. The Hindemith sonata is used as an example.

For an analysis of the violin + piano sonatas by Hindemith and its effect on performance, see Klement Hambourg's dissertation {1000}. For a discussion on how knowledge of the interval structure in a Kodály sonata affects performance, see Linda Brewer's "Progressions among Non-Twelve-Tone Sets in Kodaly's 'Sonata for Violoncello and Piano, Op. 4': an Analysis for Performance Interpretation" {1052}. For a discussion of such performance questions as figured bass realization and ornamentation in the sonatas of Leclair, see Robert Preston's dissertation {1068}, and for another essay on performing Leclair see Appia's article {1069}. Jack

*Ullom {1095} discusses performance problems (including the
nature of the bow and instrument) in the sonatas of
Mascitti.*

1480. Norden, James Clarence.   "Franz Schubert's Sonata in
      D Major for Piano and Violin, D.384: a Text-Critical
      Study." DMA dissertation. University of Iowa, 1976.
      UMI 77-3788. DAI xxxvii.8A, p. 4687. 141 pages, 22
      examples, facsimile of first edition.
      After historical and bibliographical data, including
      errors and variances in manuscripts and editions, gives
      critical commentary on pitch and time, articulation,
      and dynamics to assist performers and teachers in
      interpreting the sonata.

1481. Fleischhauer, Günter. "Zu einigen Besetzungsfragen
      im Instrumentalmusikschaffen Georg Philipp Tele-
      manns," in Eitelfriedrich Thom, ed., *Zu Fragen des
      Instrumentariums, der Besetzung und der Improvisation
      in der ersten Hälfte des 18. Jahrhunderts*, in *Studien
      zur Aufführungspraxis und Interpretation von Instru-
      mentalmusik des 18. Jahrhunderts*, Heft 2: *Konferenz-
      bericht der 3. wissenschaftlichen Arbeitstagung Blan-
      kenburg/Harz 28./29.Juni 1975* (Blankenburg/Harz: Rat
      des Bezirkes Magdeburg, c.1975), pages 33-37.
      Briefly discusses the instruments which Telemann de-
      signates for his concertos, orchestral suites, and
      chamber music, and on the basis of Telemann's own
      comments and contemporary reports makes 3 suggestions:
      1) use only the instruments which he designates since
      he writes idiomatically for them, 2) in the published
      chamber music it is perfectly acceptable to substitute
      instruments when Telemann allows that -- like harpsi-
      chord with or without cello or cello without harpsi-
      chord if the title so says, and 3) flute, violin and
      oboe are interchangeable in orchestral works when they
      are not soli.

1482. Pepper, William Bloomfield, II. "The Alternate
      Embellishments in the Slow Movements of Telemann's
      Methodical Sonatas." PhD dissertation. University
      of Iowa, 1973. UMI 74-7418. DAI xxxiv.9A, p. 6027.
      365 pages.
      Telemann published 6 sonatas each in 1728 and 1732 for
      violin or flute + continuo. Each sonata has a slow
      movement for which Telemann has provided alternate
      embellishments. Compares the embellishments to the
      originals in order to devise rules, which take into
      account repeated phrases, polyphony, harmonic syntax,
      and rhythm.

ADVICE ON PERFORMING WIND ENSEMBLES

1483. Baron, Samuel. "The Woodwind Quintet: a Symposium,"
      in *Woodwind Magazine*, vi (March-April, 1954), 4, 6,
      (September) 6-7, 14.
      A contribution to a symposium on woodwind quintets (see
      also Barrows {1484} and Schuller {1485}). Points out
      the different tone qualities necessary for a chamber
      music player as opposed to the single, penetrating,
      brilliant sound of the orchestral woodwind player.
      Also discusses rhythmic ensemble.

1484. Barrows, John. "The Woodwind Quintet: a Symposium:
      the Technique of Rehearsal," in *Woodwind Magazine*, vi
      (May-June, 1954), 4-5, 10-11.
      Runs through typical rehearsal situations experienced
      while the author was part of the New York Woodwind
      Quintet, beginning with arrival at the rehearsal,
      tuning, repertory from simple to a new, complex work,
      resolving differences, balance and blend, and so on.

1485. Schuller, Gunther. "The Woodwind Quintet: a
      Symposium: Specific Charges," in *Woodwind Magazine*,
      vi (March-April, 1954), 5-6 and 10-11.
      After listening to bad performances of woodwind quin-
      tets by excellent performers, the author initiated this
      symposium (see also Baron {1483} and Barrows {1484}).
      The performance was bad because the players did not
      blend, their sounds were mediocre, and their intonation
      was poor.

*Advice on performing wind ensemble music of specific compo-
sers:*

1486. Craft, Robert. "Performance Notes for Schoenberg's
      Quintet," in *Woodwind Magazine*, iv (June, 1952), 6-7
      and 15.
      A discussion of the Wind Quintet Op. 26 (1924) by
      Schoenberg. Considers the value of a conductor for
      tempo, balance and dynamics; the form and style; and
      the suitability for winds. Advises that groups inten-
      ding to play it practise as individuals first. It is
      unnecessary to understand its 12-tone structure, but
      that does account for its severity.

*For performance suggestions on modern instruments of the
wind sonatas by Daniel Speer, see Mitchel Sirman's dissertation {1344}.*

ADVICE ON PERFORMANCE OF OTHER TYPES OF CHAMBER MUSIC

*For a performer's discussion of Beethoven's Piano Trio Op.
70 No. 1, see Delbanco, The Beaux Arts Trio {1553}.*

1487. Sprissler, Alfred. "Piano Trios and the Student," in
     Etude, xliii (1925), 747.
     Contrary to Adolf Busch {1424}, thinks piano trios are
     best for the student who wishes to start ensemble play-
     ing. Recommends starting with Mozart K.502, 542, 548,
     564, and 254, beginning with 548. Warns several times
     to maintain the chosen tempo. Then Reissiger's Op. 25
     and 77, Mendelssohn's Op. 49, and Beethoven's trios.
     Always play the whole trio, not just one movement.

1488. Packard, Dorothy R. "Leonard Pennario Talks of the
     Joys of Chamber Music," in *Clavier*, iii (Nov.-Dec.,
     1964), no. 6, 14-17.
     Starts with Pennario's statement that he learned more
     from playing chamber music with Heifetz and Gregor
     Piatigorsky than from any piano teacher. Reviews his
     career as a chamber pianist from c.1950 at Tanglewood,
     and concentrates primarily on his preparations -- with
     Heifetz and Piatigorsky -- for concerts and recordings.
     For example, how they tried out in private many forgot-
     ten or new trios which were really bad. And stresses
     the broadening aspects of any pianist in playing cham-
     ber music.

1489. Bayes, Jack Russell. "The Proposed Use of Improvised
     Embellishment in the Instrumental Ensemble Music of
     Giovanni Gabrieli: the Canzone and Sonate from the
     Sacrae Symphoniae of 1597." DMA dissertation.
     University of Washington, 1977. DAI xxxix.2A, p.
     531. 119 pages.
     Suggested embellishments of Gabrieli's works based on
     descriptions of improvised embellishments in Girolamo
     Dalla Casa's *Il Vero Modo di Diminuir* (1584) and Gio-
     vanni Bassano's *Ricercate Passaggi et Cadentie* (1585).

*For performance suggestions for Purcell's chamber music, see
Thurston Dart's "Purcell's Chamber Music" {1222}. For performance suggestions for Johann Jakob Walther's suites and
sonatas, see Karen Krout's dissertation {1390}.*

ADVICE ON PERFORMANCE OF INDIVIDUAL INSTRUMENTS IN CHAMBER
                              MUSIC

See Francisco di Caffarelli's Gli Instrumenti ad Arco e la
Musica da Camera *{319} in which he discusses the natural and
learned ways of playing.*

1490. Clarke, Rebecca. "The History of the Viola in Quar-
      tet Writing," in *Music and Letters*, iv (1923), 6-17.
      A chronological account of the viola from Haydn and
      Mozart to 1923, based solely on the use of the viola in
      a limited number of quartet masterpieces. No documen-
      tation, no historical discipline, but a useful intro-
      duction to the problem of the viola in chamber music by
      a respected performer.

1491. Watson, J. Arthur. "Mozart and the Viola," in *Music
      and Letters*, xxii (1941), 41-53.
      A non-technical discussion of the use of the viola in
      Mozart's String Quintet K.174, Duos for Violin and
      Viola, K.423-424, Clarinet Trio K.498, the Quintets
      K.515, 516, 593, and 614, and Divertimento in E-flat,
      K.563 (also the Sinfonia Concertante K.364).

1492. Uscher, Nancy Joyce. "Performance Problems in
      Selected Twentieth Century Music for Viola." PhD
      dissertation. New York University, 1980. DMA
      xli.6A, p. 2350. 586 pages.
      Analysis of 8 20th-century compositions with prominent
      viola parts; chamber music includes Debussy's Sonata
      for flute + viola + harp, Schoenberg's String Trio Op.
      45, Bartók's String Quartet No. 6, Berg's *Lyric Suite*,
      Hindemith's String Quartet No. 3, Op. 22, and Boulez's
      Le Marteau sans Maître. A group of viola performers
      was quizzed as to performance problems and possible
      solutions. The various solutions are compared. Con-
      clusions show that much must be done to improve per-
      formance practices of contemporary music so as to prove
      that viola literature is important in the 20th century.
      Direct links between historical background and inter-
      pretive problems.

1493. Stanfield, M.B. "The Cellist in Chamber Music," in
      The Strad, lxiii (1952), 46, 48, 90, 92.
      Advice for cellists in chamber music: recognize the
      violinist as leader and be ready to adapt -- a diffi-
      cult role if any individuality is desired. For the
      amateur who is not experienced, remember to count and
      mark the first beat of each measure slightly in the
      cello, play other than forte or mezzoforte at least
      some of the time, play lightly to hear the others,
      exaggerate crescendo and decrescendo. A-string tenor-
      clef melodies are probably important and should be
      brought out. Think the main tunes through before

playing to have some idea how they should go. If
practising beforehand is possible, do so with a metronome since the cello gives the rhythm. Also, study the
score in advance. Do not lose tone in piano passages
-- the cello rhythm must always be heard; use more
vibrato and bow nearer the bridge.

1494. Teplow, Deborah A. *Performance Practice and Technique in Marin Marais'* Pièces de Viole, in *Studies in
Musicology*, No. 93. Ann Arbor: UMI Research Press,
1986. MT 145.M37T4.1986. ISBN 8357-1714-3. xi +
156 pages.
Aimed at the viol player and student. Based on 17th-
and 18th-century sources, a treatise on how to play the
viol in the late 17th century and how to interpret
specific works by Marais in his *Pièces de Viole* (Paris:
1686, 1689, 1701, 1711, 1717, and 1725). Useful glos-
sary explains French terms for ornaments and style.
Useful for all chamber music in which a viol was the
original instrument (solo or as part of the continuo).

1495. Vertress, Julie Anne. "The Bass Viol in French
Baroque Chamber Music." PhD dissertation. Cornell
University, 1978. UMI 78-17846. DAI xxxix.4A, pp.
1922-1923. 352 pages.
Discusses French secular chamber music with *basse de
viole* obligato, 1695-1740. Considers performance practice, textural functions of the viol, and the solo viol
idiom. Traces the rise and fall of the instrument in
French chamber music of the time and shows Italian influences on it. Also shows how it later was transform-
ed into the violin sonata.

1496. Wölki, Konrad. "Zupfinstrumentenspieler als Haus-
musikpartner," in *Hausmusik*, xxi (1957), 80-82.
Points to the possibilities of plucked string instruments in home chamber music. Notes the advantages, not
disadvantages of its unsustaining tones, and its use in
18th-century and again in recent chamber music. Considers its range and its technique within ensembles.
Aimed at composers and arrangers of chamber music: how
to make the guitar, lute and mandolin work.

*For a discussion of ornaments and rhythmic alteration in
18th-century French flute duets, see Walter Jones's dissertation {266}. For a discussion of late-18th-century performance practice in clarinet works, see Dale Kennedy's dissertation {846}. For a measure-by-measure master-class discussion of Debussy's* Première Rhapsodie *for accompanied clarinet, see Dennis Nygren's dissertation {841}.*

*See Jennings's "Selected Twentieth Century Clarinet Solo
Literature: a Study in Interpretation and Performance"
{1207}.*

1497. MacKenzie, Nancy Mayland. "Selected Clarinet Solo
and Chamber Music of Darius Milhaud." DMA dissertation. University of Wisconsin, 1984. UMI 84-13263.
DAI xlv.7A, p. 1911. 363 pages.
Discusses performance of pieces for 5 or fewer performers that are not transcriptions. Includes history of
each piece and analyses relevant to performance.

*For performance suggestions of Alvin Etler's 2 sonatas for
clarinet, see Paul Sheldon's dissertation {872}. For a
discussion of the performance problems (range, registration,
articulation, dynamics, fingerings and ensemble) in the
clarinet music of Hindemith, see George Townsend's dissertation {1004}. For a study of the performance problems (technique, balance, intonation, tonal matching, projection,
articulation, fingers, range) in the clarinet chamber works
of the 20th-century Danish composer Bentzon, see Ronald
Monsen's dissertation {692}.*

1498. McAninch, Daniel Arthur. "Technical Problems of the
Oboe in the Woodwind Quintet." PhD dissertation.
Eastman School of Music, 1956. v + 172 pages.
Reviewed in *Council for Research in Music Education
Bulletin*, no. 4 (Winter, 1965), pp. 64-65.
A highly specialized discussion for the advanced oboist
on special technical problems and their solutions in
order to perform woodwind quintets. After a lengthy
discussion of the oboe's idiomatic problems *per se*
(range, tonguing, intervals, trills, tremolos and difficult fingerings, passage work, and physical endur-
ance), considers the oboe in ensembles (balance and
blend, intonation, ensemble, and unison-octave
doublings with the other 4 instruments). While all
these problems are important, "of utmost importance ...
is the development of proper concepts of timbre, dynamic levels, and intonation suitable for quintet performance." The oboist needs "a highly sensitive feeling
for tempo and rhythm."

*For practical performance suggestions for the trumpet sona-
tas of Giuseppe Jacchini, see Alexander Pickard's dissertation {1027}. For discussion of various new techniques required to play contemporary American trumpet chamber music,
see the dissertations by James Tuozzolo {286} and Dalvin
Boone {283}. For some comments on performance of specific
trumpet parts from brass quintets, see Michael Tunnell's
dissertation {285}. For performance suggestions for tuba
ensembles, see Gregory Lonnman's dissertation {282}.*

1499. Holetschek, Franz. "Das Klavier in der klassischen
Kammermusik," in *Österreichische Musikzeitschrift*,
xiii (1958), 178.

Holetschek, who as pianist has performed with leading
European chamber groups, makes a few points briefly:
the piano is as important as the strings and should not
be treated as second rate, as it often is; the pianist
should practice separately with some of the strings,
not all of them, and work on coordinating phrasing and
color with each of the different string instruments.
Students of today (1958) are aware of style in chamber
music even as far away from Vienna as, for example,
Japan.

1500. Stern, Milton.   "The Pianist in Chamber Music."   PhD
      dissertation.   Columbia University Teachers College,
      1955.   DD xxii (1955), p. 245.   930 pages.
      Not seen.

See *Lionel Tertis's article above {1454}.*

1501. Lewis, Enid.   "The Piano in Chamber Music," in *Making
      Music*, no. 32 (Autumn, 1956), 7-8.
      Advice to pianists on how to play chamber music.   The
      pianist must develop all the expressive qualities of
      the piano and then use them in partnership with the
      other musician(s).   Tone color is especially important;
      the piano in ensemble with clarinet + cello must play
      with different color from an ensemble with horn +
      violin.   Considers different combinations and how this
      affects the piano.

1502. Sauzay, Eugène.   *L'École de l'Accompagnement.*   Paris:
      Firmin Didot Frères, fils et cie, 1869.   Reprint
      Bologna: Forni Editore, 1972.   ML 1100.S29.1972.   ix
      + 269 pages.
      A mid-19th-century witness to taste and conceptions of
      chamber music by an important pedagogue, professor at
      the Paris Conservatory.   The second half of the book --
      "Principles de l'Accompagnement" -- is advice, from a
      teacher of much experience, to piano students for play-
      ing ensemble music.   Nothing has changed in most of
      this.   The teacher ought to explain to the student what
      the work is about based on the teacher's experience,
      and to direct the student in his/her execution so as to
      realize the composer's ideas.   The pianist must listen
      to, hear, and understand what the other player(s)
      has (have) to do.   Advice on playing sonatas, on
      reading music, on how to work on various moods of
      sonatas, on making good programs, on the minute details
      of a concert, on nuances and accents, on expression, on
      performance of older music, on scales, on consonances
      and dissonances, on modulations, and on dealing with
      mistakes, on fugues, on silences, on ornaments, and so
      forth.
      For *performance problems in the piano chamber music of
      Wallingford Riegger, see Elizabeth Buccheri's "The Piano
      Chamber Music of Wallingford Riegger" {1241}.*

SUGGESTIONS ON THE USE OF CONDUCTORS FOR CONTEMPORARY
CHAMBER MUSIC

See Robert Craft's article on Schoenberg's quintet {1486}.

1503. Bradshaw, Susan. "Whatever Happened to Chamber
      Music?" in *Tempo*, no. 123 (Dec. 1977), 7-9.
      A complaint on the lack of distinction in present-day
      concert life between chamber and orchestral music.
      Symptomatic is the use of conductors for much new cham-
      ber music, especially when the performers are hetero-
      genious. Traces the phenomenon back to *Pierrot Lu-*
      naire. Such heterogenious performers do not perform
      together regularly, so ensemble is lost.

ADVICE ON ORNAMENTATION

1504. Mersmann, Hans. "Beiträge zur Aufführungspraxis der
      vorklassischen Kammermusik in Deutschland," in *Archiv*
      für Musikwissenschaft, ii (1920), 99-143.
      Questions the scoring of particular chamber works
      c.1750 and their performance. Scoring concerns not
      only which instrument but also orchestral vs. soloistic
      scoring. Performance involves ornamentation, which is
      the bulk of the article, with numerous musical illus-
      trations. While dated, still very useful and a
      historically noteworthy article.

1505. Conrad, Ferdinand. "Verzierung langsamer Sätze in
      der Barockmusik," in *Zeitschrift für Hausmusik*, xv
      (1951), 38-44.
      A careful analysis of the problem of ornamentation in
      connection with an edition of methodic sonatas by Tele-
      mann which give the ornamentation by the composer him-
      self. Ornamentation must take into account the music
      and its symbols on the page of music, and also it must
      follow basic rules from the witnesses of the time.
      Basically there are 3 issues: the reduction of longer
      notes into shorter ones by means of expressive orna-
      ments (which are either essential or arbitrary); the
      distinction between essential and arbitrary ornaments;
      and the distinction between ornaments clearly called
      for by signs (French Baroque style) and those which the
      performer can freely choose where and when he/she wants
      (Italian style). Telemann's sonatas do not always make
      clear the distinction between French and Italian
      styles. Details Telemann's choice of ornaments.

For another study of embellishments in Telemann, see William
Peppers's dissertation {1482}. For embellishments in Gio-
vanni Gabrieli's canzone and sonate, see Jack Bayes's dis-
sertation {1489}. For ornamentation in flute sonatas by J.
S. Bach, see John Fenley's dissertation {1468}.

1506. Valasek, Marion Louise. "Flute Quartets from the
Second Half of the Eighteenth Century." MusAD dissertation. Boston University, 1977. UMI 77-21694.
DAI xxxviii.4A, pp. 1733-1734. 171 pages.
Preparation of performance editions of flute quartets
by Adam Kroll, Franz Anton Schubert (1768-1827),
Viotti, Haydn, and Charles Henri Kunze. History of
these quartets within the Viennese classical style,
harmonic and formal analyses, performance practice, and
ornamentation.

For treatment of grace notes in Mozart's quartet K.575, see
Harold Berkley's article {1463}. For embellishments of
sonatas by Franz Benda, see Douglas Lee's article {690} and
Rudolf Zelenka's article in {161}, pages 62-66. For embel-
lishments of Corelli's sonatas, see articles by Babitz
{1476}, Pook {1477}, Marx {818}, and Boyden {819}.

DISCUSSION OF TEMPO

1507. Saslav, Isidor. "Tempos in the String Quartets of
Joseph Haydn." DMA dissertation. Indiana University, 1969. RILM 69-1160. 185 pages.
"Attempts to establish authentic historical guidelines
in one area of 18th-century performance practice, tempo...Correlates in detail the various movements of the
quartets with 18th-century tempo theory so as to provide the performers of these works, whether professional or amateur, with historically authentic, detailed, and specific information" on their tempos.
Uses Landon's *The Symphonies of Joseph Haydn* (1955) as
a model, though it recognizes conflicting evidence and
seeks not absolute tempos but tempo areas for types of
movements following the lead of Erwin Bodky, *The Inter-*
pretation of Bach's Keyboard Works (1960). Accepts and
rejects large portions of Fritz Rothschild, *The Lost*
Tradition in Music: Rhythm and Tempo in J.S. Bach's
Time (1953) and *Musical Performance in the Times of*
Mozart and Beethoven: the Lost Tradition in Music, Part
2 (1961). A thoughtful and well-researched paper.

1508. Gertler, André. "Souvenirs sur Béla Bartók," in
Revue Musicale, no. 224 (1955), 99-110.
Famous Hungarian violinist, friend of Bartók's, who
spent much time in Belgium, recalls chamber music

performances with Bartók and Bartók's agonizing over details of his chamber music. Presents a detailed chart of the Fifth String Quartet with precise metronome indications of how Bartók wanted the tempos to be and other indications. Extremely important document for all string quartet ensembles who play this piece.

1509. Kolisch, Rudolf. "Tempo and Character in Beethoven's Music," in *The Musical Quarterly*, xxix (1943), 169-187 and 291-312.
Tries to prove the importance of metronome markings for the interpretation of tempo and character in Beethoven's music in general. Gives a biography of Mälzel and Beethoven's relationship to him. Then deals with the relationships between meter and tempo, Italian-designated tempos and metronome tempos, movement location and form in relationship to tempos. Many chamber works are covered and all are tabulated so that the interpreter can find the appropriate metronome number for any movement of any Beethoven piece.

1510. Mueller, Hannelore. "Möglichkeiten der Besetzung des Basso Continuo in der Kammermusik des Barock: Probleme der Kombination von Harmonie- und Melodieinstrumenten," in Peter Reidemeister and Veronika Gutmann, eds., *Alte Musik: Praxis und Reflexion: Sonderband der Reihe "Basler Jahrbuch für historische Musikpraxis" zum 50. Jubiläum der Schola Cantorum Basiliensis* (Winterthur: Amadeus, 1983), pages 272-287.
The automatic use of a sustaining instrument to support a keyboard or plucked-string instrument in the 17th- and 18th-century continuo is incorrect from the standpoint of particular countries or epochs or the wishes of particular composers, let alone from the color of Baroque music. The instrumentation of the continuo is varied and this variation of timbres is an important part of Baroque music. Systematically studies 17th- and 18th-century Italian, English, German and French title pages, continuo treatises, instrument manuals and contemporary reports to determine the varieties of realization possible within those national and chronological frames. Many ambiguities remain, but that is the nature of the realization.

In late 18th-century music, there is the question of what instrument or instruments plays the bass line. For Haydn quartets, see {177}, {178}, and {179}; see also {180}.

1511. Bär, Carl. "Zum Begriff des 'Basso' in Mozarts Serenaden," in *Mozart-Jahrbuch* (1960-1961), 133-155.
Does the cello or the string bass or both play the bass line in Mozart's works when in all cases only "basso" is given? Studies this ambiguity in the serenades since all 3 possibilities exist there. In K.239 a

string bass is designated by "violone" and in K.525 both cello and string bass are designated. Concludes that in most serenades Mozart meant only the string bass, not the other 2 possibilities. Includes various means of proof, including contemporary descriptions and the functions for which such music was written, the tone quality of the string bass, and comparisons with the known examples K.239 and 525. Considers the orchestral as well as chamber serenades, and the greater number of bassists than cellists in Mozart's Salzburg.

DISCUSSION OF ACOUSTICS

1512. George, William H. "The Acoustics of the Chamber Music Room," in *The Musical Times*, lxxii (1931), 123-125.
Advice to chamber musicians on how to control the acoustics of a small room so as to achieve maximum satisfaction. In a small room echo does not occur, but a sound may not die as soon as the player stops (reverberation). To deaden or enliven the sound, absorbant material should be put on or removed from the floors or ceilings or walls. What is satisfactory to one ensemble may not be so to another, so each musician should know what to do. Less absorbant materials are best near the players, more absorbant materials at the opposite end.

1513. Shackford, Charles Reeve. "Intonation in Ensemble String Performance: an Objective Study." PhD dissertation. Harvard University, 1954. DD, xxi (1954), p. 254. ix + 269 pages.
A scientific approach to determine how instrumentalists in an ensemble with variable intonation on their instruments play "in tune." Starts from the elementary over-tone series to demonstrate the problem of intonation, and uses tape recorders, filters, amplifiers and oscilloscopes to measure the sound. Reviews ancient and Renaissance discussions of the problem and continues up to modern discussions. Considers especially vibrato. Contains charts, mathematical proportions, and graphs.

CHAPTER V. PERFORMERS OF CHAMBER MUSIC

In this chapter we consider the history and criticism of the performers of chamber music: the groups as groups and the individual artists who form the groups.

GENERAL LISTS AND DISCUSSIONS OF PERFORMANCE GROUPS

The New Grove {1} has entries (often very short) on the following groups:

String Quartets
Aeolin, Allegri, Amadeus, Australian, Avramov, Bartók, Beethoven, Budapest, Busch, Cleveland, Composers, Curtis, Czech, Dartington, Dimov, Dvořák, Fine Arts, Flonzaley, Gabrieli, Gaudeamus, Griller, Guarneri, Hart House, Heutling, Hungarian, Italian, Janáček, Joachim, Juilliard, LaSalle, Léner, London (2 such groups), Melbourne, Melos, Moravian (2 such groups), Ondricek, Orford, Paganini, Parrenin, Prague, Pro Arte, Rome, Rosé, Smetana, Tatrai, Tel-Aviv, Tokyo, Végh, Vlach, and Waldbauer-Kerpely.

Other Groups
Adelaide Wind Quintet, Beaux Arts Trio, Boccherini Quintet, Busch Chamber Players, Chigi Quintet, Classical Concert Society, Contemporary Chamber Ensemble of New York, Czech Nonet, Danzi Wind Quintet, Gabrieli Ensemble, Hungarian Wind Quintet, Israel Woodwind Quintet, Bach-Abel Concerts, Melos Ensemble, Music Group of London, Trio di Bolzano, and Trio di Trieste.

Important Chamber Musicians
Adolf Busch, Josef Joachim, Rudolf Kolisch, William Kroll, Arnold (Josef) Rosé, Josef Suk (i), Walter Trampler, and Sándor Végh.

For other general lists of performing groups see {148}, {151}, and:

1514. *Chamber Music America: Membership Directory 1985.* New York: Chamber Music America, 1985. ML 19.C5.1985. iv + 41 pages.
    Separate lists of ensembles, promoters, festivals, training programs, chamber orchestras, schools and programs, service organizations, managers, businesses and individuals who are members or associate members of CMA, each listed alphabetically by state and within state. Includes title, address and telephone number, and description. General index and index by type of ensemble. An annual list.

1515. American Chamber Music Players, Inc. *1986-1987 North and Central American Directory*. New York: ACMP, 1986. 111 pages.
Lists amateur chamber players alphabetically by state, province and country, with addresses, telephone numbers, instrument, and ability. American directory issued every other year. Alternate years an overseas directory is issued. Address: 215 Park Avenue South, New York, New York 10003.

For descriptions of French chamber groups 1828-1871, see Jeffrey Cooper's dissertation and book The Rise of Instrumental Music and Concert Series in Paris 1828-1871 *{374}. For citations of specific performing groups in Hamburg in the 19th century see Emil Krause's* Die Entwicklung der Kammermusik *{387}. For information on Canadian performers of chamber music of the 19th and early 20th centuries see Marcus Adeney's "Chamber Music" {350}. For a history of Soviet chamber ensembles, see Raaben {434}.*

DISCUSSIONS OF STRING CHAMBER GROUPS, ESPECIALLY STRING QUARTETS

For extensive information on the French chamber violinists from Lully to Viotti, see La Laurencie's L'École Française de Violon de Lully à Viotti *{236}.*

1516. Payne, Albert (pseud. W. Ehrlich). *Das Streich-Quartett in Wort und Bild*. Leipzig: A.H. Payne, [1898]. ML 398.P196S8. vii + 83 pages.
A major source of information on and portraits of 19th-century string quartets. Forty quartets featured (treats Joachim's London and Berlin quartets as 2) and a Leipzig sextet. A page of biographical and historical information, followed usually by a full-page photo. Includes the Soldat-Roeger female quartet.

1517. _____. *Berühmte Geiger der Vergangenheit und Gegenwart: eine Sammlung von 88 Biographien und Portraits*. Leipzig: A.H. Payne, 1893. ML 398.P19. xi + 316 pages. 2nd ed. 1902. ML 398.P192. xiv + 350 pages (104 biographies and portraits). 3rd ed. trl. into English by Robin H. Legge. London: The Strad/Boston: O. Ditson, 1913. 287 pages. The London edition is in *The Strad Library*, No. 4. ML 398.P195.1913.
A major source for information on mostly 19th-century violinists, many of whom played in quartets (such as Heinrich Karl Hermann de Ahna [1771-1842, second violinist of the Joachim Quartet], Pierre Marie François Baillot de Sales, Karl Louis Bargheer, and so on).

1518. Bachmann, Alberto. *Les Grands Violinistes du Passé.*
      Paris: Librairie Fischbacher, 1913. ML 398.B2. vi +
      469 pages.
      Contains 40 chapters each devoted to a violinist or a
      family of violinists. The chapters are arranged alpha-
      betically from Delphin Alard to Wilhelmj, each with
      portraits, biography, bibliography, and in some cases
      thematic indices. Nearly all the violinists composed
      and/or performed chamber music.

See Antoine Vidal's Les Instruments à Archet {56}.

For an enormously valuable source book for information on
string quartet performers from the 1820's to the 1920's, see
Ivan Mahaim's Beethoven {650}. For a glimpse of the activi-
ties of the quartets in Vienna 1824-1825, see {652}.

1519. _____. *An Encyclopedia of the Violin.*
      Ed. by Albert E. Wier, trl. by Frederick H. Martens,
      Introduction by Eugène Ysaÿe. New York/London: D.
      Appleton, 1925. Repr. New York: Da Capo, 1966, with
      new introduction by Stuart Canin. ML 800.B13. ISBN
      0-306-70912-0. xiv + 470 pages, 78 illustrations
      (mostly portraits and violins).
      Twenty-five chapters each devoted to a different aspect
      of the violin (The Origin of the Violin, Violin Makers
      in Europe, Violin Teaching and Study, How to Practice,
      Analyses of Master Violin Works, Biographical Diction-
      ary of Violinists, and so on). Of particular concern
      for chamber music are chapters 19 (Chamber Music) and
      25 (A List of Music for the Violin). Chapter 19 is
      useless for its history of chamber music but valuable
      for its list of 51 international string quartets and 2
      quintets, with portraits of some and a brief descrip-
      tion of each. Chapter 25 lists music generically,
      starting with etudes and eventually including a huge
      amount of chamber music from duets for violin + cello
      to octets. Not scholarly and not completely trustwor-
      thy, but useful and important for student violinists.

1520. Pincherle, Marc. *Les Instruments du Quatuor.* Paris:
      Presses Universitaires de France, 1948. 3rd ed.
      1970. ML 750.P5.1970. 128 pages.
      Much of the discussion is treated better elsewhere,
      such as descriptions and histories of the violin,
      viola, cello and string bass as instruments, and the
      history of string quartet music. Most valuable for
      discussion of quartet ensembles, from the Schuppanzigh
      Quartet to the Capet, mentioning such others as the
      Jansa, Hellmesberger, Rosé, Baillot, Tilmant, Chevil-
      lard-Alard, Arvinrent (Eduard Lalo as violist), Koella,
      Müller Brothers, Joachim, Italian, and Hungarian
      quartets.

1521. Mlejnek, Karel. *Smetanovci, Janáčkovci a Vlachovei.*
      Prague: Státní Hudební Vydavatelství, 1962. ML
      1122.M6. 154 pages.
      A history of the Smetana, Janáček, and Vlach Quartets.
      Includes photos, concert. schedules, foreign tours,
      repertory, and discography.

1522. Gennadiev, B. "Sorevnuyutsia Kvartete," in *Sovets-
      kaia Musyka* (1984), no. 4, pages 136-137. In
      Russian.
      About a competition of Soviet quartets entitled Borodin
      Competition in Tallinin (Estonia) in October, 1983.
      Describes the winners and interpretation problems.

      *See Jan Boublìk's "Czech Chamber Ensembles" {356} for string
      chamber groups in Czechoslovakia since World War II.*

1523. Tsibiu, G. "Forum Kamirnoi Musyki v Plovdive," in
      Sovetskaia Musyka (1980), no. 3, pages 125-128. In
      Russian.
      About a Bulgarian chamber music festival with partici-
      pation of Czech, German, Italian, Soviet and other
      ensembles (some chamber, others chamber orchestra).
      Gives highlights and some criticism of the groups.

Wind Ensembles:

1524. Semple, Arthur E. "The Making of the Flute Litera-
      ture: Some Composers and their Flutist Friends," in
      Woodwind Magazine, ii (Sept., 1949), 4, (Oct., 1949),
      4, 11, (Nov., 1949), 6.
      Emphasizes the influence of great flute players on
      great composers who write for the flute. Includes the
      influence of Karl Weidemann and Quantz on Handel and
      C.P.E. Bach, of J.P. Wendling on Mozart, of Doppler on
      Schubert, of A.B. Fürstenau on Weber, of Boehm on
      Molique and Rossini, of Degenart on Beethoven, and
      others. Many resulting compositions are chamber music
      with flute.

1525. Baron, Samuel. "The Rebirth of the Woodwind Quintet
      in America: Looking Back from the Forties to Today,"
      in *American Ensemble*, vi, no. 3 (1983), 15-17.
      An important article by a leader in the growth of wood-
      wind quintets in America since the late 1940's, ex-
      plaining the problems he encountered and goals he set
      forth. Notes the new groups that have been organized
      and the new compositions they have stimulated.

1526. Pilka, Jiri. "Czech Creativity for Brass Ensembles," in *Music News from Prague*, no. 3-4 (1983), p. 3. A brief discussion of current Bohemian ensembles of brass players (horn quartets, brass quintets, trombone ensembles, and so on) and compositions written for them, organized from duets to quintets, in the 1950's to the 1970's.

STUDIES OF INDIVIDUAL PERFORMING GROUPS

String Quartets:

1527. Snowman, Daniel. *The Amadeus Quartet: the Men and the Music*. London: Robson Books, 1981. ML 421.A44S6. 160 pages, 45 photos, 16 document facsimiles, discography, and 13 examples. Biographies of the 4 members and discussion of the musical climate of London from 1940 to 1980 from the perspective of chamber music. A diary of the activities of the quartet from September to December 1979, and a general evaluation of its work. Especially important is the quartet's association with Benjamin Britten.

For the Amar String Quartet see {576}.

1528. "Betchoventzam-60!" in *Sovetskaia Muzyka* (1983), no. 12, pages 62-63. In Russian. A short description and history of the Beethoven Quartet; started in 1923 and since 1943 has remained unchanged in membership.

1529. Shochman, G. "Radost Vzaimobonimania," in *Sovetskaia Muzyka* (1984), no. 2, pages 52-60. In Russian. An interview with the Borodin Quartet, which covers history, conception of quartet playing, repertory, and style. This is the Borodin Quartet founded after the defection of the original members in the 1970's.

1530. Wechsberg, Joseph. "The Budapest," in *The New Yorker*, xxxv (Nov.14, 1959), 59-60, 62, 64, 67, 69-70, 72, 74, 76, 78-80, 82, 87-89, 91-92, 94, 97-98, 100-102, 104, 106, 108-112. A lengthy biographical account of the Budapest Quartet and its 4 principal members: Boris Kroyt, Alexander and Mischa Schneider, and Joseph Roisman. After a brief attempt at defining chamber music and giving a history of the string quartet, concentrates on the Budapest. Interviews each member and his wife (if married), and produces a wealth of data on this famous ensemble.

Should be a starting point for any critical evaluation
or history of the group.

1531. Kvet, J.M. *Zpameti Ceského Kvarteta.* Prague: Edice
      Corona, 1936. HML 196.45.103. 136 pages. In Czech.
      Various anecdotes concerning the Czech Quartet; its
      members; its interactions with such persons as Brahms,
      Dvořák, Tolstoy, and Cosima Wagner; and Josef Suk's
      comments on Beethoven. Photos.

1532. Ginzburg, Lev. "The 'Czech Quartet' in Russia," in
      Malcolm Hamrick Brown, *Russian and Soviet Music:
      Essays for Boris Schwarz* (Ann Arbor: UMI Research
      Press, 1984), pp. 201-209. ML 55.S398.1984. Origin-
      ally published in Czech in *Ceská Hudba Svétu, Svét
      Ceské Hudbé* (Prague: 1974). See Ginzburg's book on
      the same topic, *Ganush Vigan i Cheshskii Kvartet
      [Hanus Wihan and the Czech Quartet]* (Moscow: 1955).
      A history of the early years of the Czech (= Bohemian)
      Quartet, organized c.1891 at the Prague Conservatory
      under cellist Hanus Wihan: Karel Hoffmann (1872-1936),
      Josef Suk (1874-1935), Oscar Nedbal (1874-1920), and
      Otakar Berger (1873-1897). Wihan succeeded Berger for
      most of the remaining time-span included in this essay.
      Stresses the quartet's appearances in Russia (12 times
      from 1895 to 1912) with descriptions of the concerts
      and the quartet's reception from letters and reviews.
      Discusses repertory (it regularly performed Borodin,
      Tchaikovsky, Glazunov and Taneev, as well as Dvorák,
      Smetana, Beethoven and Schubert). Mentions the rela-
      tionship of the quartet to Leo Tolstoy, at whose home
      the ensemble performed, and to the Belaiev circle.

1533. Herbort, Heinz Josef. "Wir müssen Idealisten sein:
      das Star-Ensemble der Zukunft: das Emerson String
      Quartet aus New York," in *Die Zeit*, xl (Sept. 28,
      1984), p. 49.
      A description of a performance of the quartet and a
      history of the quartet, including the family back-
      grounds and the members's instruments. The name
      Emerson was picked in 1976 from Ralph Waldo Emerson.
      Points out a peculiarity of this group: the 2
      violinists alternate on first and second parts.

1534. Mason, Daniel Gregory. "The Flonzaley Quartet," in
      Music in My Time and Other Reminiscences (Freeport
      [New York]: Books for Libraries Press, 1938, reprint-
      ed 1970), pp. 148-162. ML 410.M397A2.
      Anecdotes from and on the Kneisel Quartet, a discus-
      sion of the lack of taste of American audiences, and
      an essay on the Flonzaley, its members, their person-
      alities, their championship of new music, and their
      correspondence to Mason. Also about the de Coppet
      musicales from October 1886, describing the amateurs

who participated and the social events. Mason dispar-
ages Stravinsky and Schoenberg and claims that the
Flonzaley Quartet succeeded with much more difficult
music by Mozart. Highly personal and opinionated
account by an important American witness.

1535. Parker, Henry Taylor. "The Righteous 'Flonzaleys,'"
in *Eighth Notes: Voices and Figures of Music and the
Dance* (1922; reprint Freeport [New York]: Books for
Libraries, 1968), pages 175-183. ML 60.P175.1968.
A tribute to the greatness of the Flonzaley Quartet and
what it has accomplished in ensemble and repertoire.
Mentions the patrons of the time and the members of the
quartet.

1536. Ruttencutter, Helen Drees. *Quartet: a Profile of the
Guarneri Quartet.* New York: Lippincott and Crowell,
1980. ML 398.G83. ISBN 0-690-01944-0. ii + 153
pages. Originally "Profiles: String Quartet," in *The
New Yorker*, liv (October 23, 1978), 45-131 (some
interruptions for advertisements).
A lengthy, in depth interview with the Guarneri Quartet
and description of its personnel, a recording session,
and a rehearsal. Also briefly outlines the history of
string quartets in America and their situation in 1978.
Popular writing, not scholarly or particularly well-in-
formed on general matters, but does give excellent
coverage of the Guarneri. The book is an updated and
expanded version of *The New Yorker* article, with discography. *See also {1445}.*

1537. "The Havlák Quartet," in *Music News from Prague*
(1983), no. 2, p. 8.
A brief account of this young Czech string quartet,
formed in 1976.

*See {1452} for an inside view of how the Hungarian Quartet
rehearsed in 1923.*

1538. Gay, Harriet. *The Juilliard String Quartet.* New York/
Washington/Hollywood: Vantage Press, 1974. ML 398.
J84. SBN 533-01322-4. vi + 89 pages, 38 photos.
A subjective, adulatory, non-scholarly history of the
quartet organized at William Schuman's instigation at
the Juilliard School in 1945. Basically consists of
long interviews with Schuman and the members of the
quartet. Some factual errors and inconsistencies.
Biographies of 4 members as of 1972: Robert Mann, Claus
Adam, Samuel Rhodes, and Earl Carlyss. Description of
the personal side of tours and Library of Congress
concerts.

1539. Hoffman, Eva. "Juilliard: a Renewed Quartet," in *The
New York Times Magazine* (Oct. 5, 1986), pages 28-29,
32, 34, 36, 38.

An interview with and observation of the quartet simi-
lar to {1538}, but now with Joel Smirnoff and Joel
Krosnick replacing Adam and Carlyss. Recounts how
Smirnoff was selected.

1540. Davidian, R. *Kvartet imeni Komitasa.* Erevan: Izda-
telstvo Aëastan, 1974. HML 279.91. 96 pages.
A history of the Komitas Quartet founded in 1924 by
A.K. Gabrialian (b.1899), who was still with it in
1974. Biographies and photos of all the members of the
quartet during its 50-year history.

1541. Berko, Mikhail. "Vtoraya Molodost 'Kometagovtsev,'"
in *Sovetskaia Muzyka,* (1985), no. 11, pages 51-53.
A description and history of the Komitas String Quartet
from Armenia. Photo.

1542. Molnár, Antal. *A Léner-Vonósnégyes,* in *Nagy Magyar
Elöadómüvészek,* no. 6. Budapest: Zenemökiadó, 1968.
HML 279.75. 36 pages.
A history of the Léner Quartet (flourished 1919-1939).
Opens with an essay on chamber music history and on
chamber music in the concert hall, on new chamber music
developments, on financial questions, then on Jenó
Léner and the Léner Quartet

1543. Borovik, M. *Kvartet imeni Lesenka (do 25-Richya Ve-
konavs'koe Diial'nosti).* Kiev: Musika Ukraina, 1976.
HML 279.97.3. 79 pages. Enl. ed. N.[sic] Borovik.
Kvartet imeni Lesenko. Kiev: Musika Ukraina, 1980.
HML 279.97. 96 pages. In Russian.
A study of the Lesenka String Quartet from the Ukraine,
founded in 1951 by members of the Ukrainian State Phil-
harmonic. Gives repertory (extensive, including many
Soviet composers unknown in America). Also gives
cities in which it has played, and biographies of the
musicians. Named after Mykola Lyšenko, Ukrainian composer of string quartets.

1544. Bagdanskis, Jonas. *The Lithuanian Musical Scene,*
trl. by Olimpija Armalyté. Vilna: Mintis Publishers,
1974. HML 198.48.14.
Brief accounts of the Lithuanian String Quartet (founded 1945; see {1545} for another date) and the Vilnius
String Quartet (founded 1968) with membership, accom-
plishments, repertory, tours, and photos.

1545. Katkus, Donatus. *Lietuvos Kvartetas.* Vilna: no.
publ., 1971. HML 196.48.9. 128 pages. In Lithuanian with brief Russian and English summaries.
A history and documentation of the Lithuanian String
Quartet with many photos. Information on all members,
past and present. Founded in 1946 (see {1544}), the
book commemorates the group's 25th anniversary.

1546. Parker, Henry Taylor. "The Zestful Londoners," in
      Eighth Notes: Voices and Figures of Music and the
      Dance (1922; reprint Freeport [New York]: Books for
      Libraries Press, 1968), pages 184-186.
      About a New York visit of this London-based quartet,
      which has more emotional fire than the Flonzaley and
      recalls the Kneisel Quartet in its earliest years.

1547. Vratislavsky, Jan. Moravské Kvarteto, 1923-1955.
      Prague: Kniznice Hudebních Rozhledni, 1961. ML
      1151.C95M7. 130 pages. In Czech.
      A history of the Moravian Quartet from 1923 to 1955,
      including lists of works performed, premiers given,
      tours, and biographies.

1548. Köhler, Louis. Die Gebrüder Müller und das Streich-
      Quartett. Leipzig: Heinrich Matthes, 1858. ML 398.
      K72. 50 pages.
      A long essay paying homage to the Müller family quar-
      tets. Concentrates on the tastes of recently past and
      present audiences and quartet performers and on the
      Müller brothers's performances. Gives some biograph-
      ical information on both the older and younger Müller
      Quartets.

1549. Ris, A. "Imeni Prokoféva," in Muzikalnaia Zhiz'n
      (1986), no. 5, page 7.
      Discussion of the Prokofiev Quartet in Moscow, an all
      female quartet formed about 30 years ago. A review of
      a concert and discussion of their style of playing.

1550. "New Friends of Music," in Musical America, lxxi (Dec.
      1, 1951), 12 and 16.
      Short review of the debut in Town Hall of the Quartetto
      Italiano (Nov. 4, 1951) in a program dedicated to the
      memory of Artur Schnabel. See also Douglas Watt, "No-
      thing Like It," in The New Yorker, xxvii (Dec. 22,
      1951), 66-67 for a review of the same concert.

1551. Dalinkiavichus, G. "Imeni Tchurlionisa," in Sovets-
      kaia Muzyka, (1982), no. 8, pages 65-66.
      Description of the Tchurlionis String Quartet of Lithu-
      ania, founded in 1968.

1552. Dvarionas, Yu. "Tchetrero iz Vilniusa," in Sovets-
      kaia Muzyka, (1982), no. 8, pages 67-68.
      Description of the Vilna String Quartet, founded in
      1965 and winner of an international competition in
      Liège. Played all "83" Haydn quartets. See also
      {1544}.

See also {651}, {1516}, {1519}, {1520}, and {1521}.

Other individual performing groups:

1553. Delbanco, Nicholas. *The Beaux Arts Trio.* New York:
      William Morrow, 1985. ML 421.B42D4.1985. ISBN 0-
      688-04001-2. 254 pages.
      Extensive interviews with the performers of this Trio
      by the author, a relative of the cellist, covering
      about 10 years. A history, a detailed description of a
      single concert, a behind-the-scenes description of a
      recording session, and a discussion of performance
      problems: a round table discussion among David Blum and
      the Trio, and detailed performers's analyses of Beet-
      hoven's Op. 70 No. 1 by each of the Trio members. In-
      cludes discography and a list of concerts for the 1983-
      1984 season. See also Heidi Waleson, "Beaux Arts Trio,
      an Enduring Sound," in *The New York Times Magazine*
      (Nov. 18, 1984), 76-86.

For a description of an amateur chamber music society in
France 1860-1910 (to which Saint-Saëns belonged), see Lucien
Augé de Lassur's La Trompette {376}.

1554. Schonberg, Harold C. "Musicians Need for Chamber
      Music," in *The New York Times*, xcix (June 4, 1950),
      section 2, p. 7.
      A very brief interview with William Kroll and Joseph
      Fuchs about their founding the Musicians Guild in 1947,
      whose function is to perform chamber music. A tribute
      to their teacher Kneisel. Explains how the Guild
      works, its finances and its programming.

1555. McKay, James R. "Report from Chicago: the Contempor-
      ary Chamber Players," in *Current Musicology*, No. 15
      (1973), 15-17.
      A brief account of the founding of this important per-
      forming ensemble and what it has accomplished.

1556. Block, Steven D. "The Making of a New Music Ensem-
      ble," in *Perspectives of New Music*, xx (1981-1982),
      592-599.
      Presents the history of the Pittsburgh New Music Ensem-
      ble conducted by David Stock. Considers how they have
      attracted audiences (for example, by the use of cele-
      brities), nature of their repertory (90% American and
      not limited to New England composers), funding, radio
      broadcasts with Martin Bookspan, its relationship to
      the Pittsburgh Symphony, and its taking over of the
      Harvey Gaul contest. No specific mention of chamber
      music, but included here since most of its repertory
      would inevitably be chamber music.

1557. "Wind Instrument Chamber Musical Society," in *Musical
      Opinion*, xvi (Jan. 1, 1893), 230.

A brief account of this woodwind society organized in London in 1889, about the music it has engendered, and about a concert given in the 1892-1893 season. Repertory included, besides new works, such works as Mozart's C Minor Serenade. Names performers.

1558. "The Distin Sax-Horn Quintet," in *American Art Journal*, xl (Dec. 22, 1883), 145-146.
About an English saxophone quintet organized by Henry Distin, that introduced the instrument to America in 1849. Describes the group's American tour.

1559. "The Raschèr Saxophone Quartet," in *Music News from Prague* (1984), no. 4, p. 2.
A brief account of this ensemble's career. Founded in 1969, it has had numerous works written for it.

1560. "Leblanc Fine Arts Saxophone Quartet," in *Woodwind World*, x (Sept. 1971), 7.
About a Milwaukee-based sax quartet formed in 1967, its membership, and a discography. Photo.

1561. "Diller's Classical Cornet Quartet," in *American Art Journal*, xxxv (Sept. 3, 1881), 361-362.
About an ensemble organized in New York in 1857 by Francis X. Diller and consisting of 2 cornets, an E-flat tenor and a baritone or basso. They played original works composed for them as well as many arrangements of string chamber music. The performances are private, in small halls, and only occasionally with invited quests.

1562. Woltzenlogel, Celso. "Villa-Lobos Wind Quintet of Rio, Brazil and the Children," in *Woodwind World*, v (June 1, 1964), 6.
A brief account of this Brazilian quintet's activities in front of children. Photos, repertory, and membership. The quintet was part of a "Caravan of Culture" which played for children (and adults) throughout the country.

1563. "The University of Arizona Woodwind Quintet," in *Woodwind World*, v (June 1, 1964), 6.
A brief account of the formation of the group in 1959, its membership, repertory, and activities. Photo.

1564. Snavely, Jack. "University of Wisconsin-Milwaukee Woodwind Art Quintet," in *Woodwind World*, xi (April, 1972), 22, 26.
About the formation of the quintet in 1966 and details on its members.

1565. Astel, A. "Brass-Quintet Bolshogo Teatra," in *Muzikalnaia Zhizn* (1985), no. 16, p. 6. In Russian.

The Bolshoi Theatre Orchestra brass quintet, founded in
1982. The membership and repertory (primarily of the
16th to 18th centuries and some modern works).

STUDIES OF INDIVIDUAL PERFORMERS OF CHAMBER MUSIC

1566. Tenney, Wallace R. "Baermann and Von Weber," in *Wood-
      wind Magazine*, i (Feb., 1949), 3, 6.
      Biography of Heinrich Baermann (1784-1847), great
      German clarinetist for whom Mendelssohn wrote 2 trios
      (clarinet + basset horn + piano) and who had a special
      relationship to Carl Maria von Weber. Describes their
      concert tours and their performances with Spohr. Baer-
      mann inspired Weber to write the Concertino, 2 concer-
      tos, a Grand Duo for clarinet + piano, a quintet for
      clarinet + string quartet, and a set of variations.

1567. Toenes, George. "Baermann - Father and Son," in
      Clarinet, no. 22 (Spring, 1956), 19-20.
      A brief biography of the 2 Baermanns (H.J., father, and
      Carl, son), the former who inspired Weber to write much
      clarinet music (some chamber) and the latter (1811-
      1885) who developed the Baermann method or system.

1568. Guynemer, C. *Essay on Chamber Classical Music.* Lon-
      don: author, 1846. NL V2.6098(2). 24 pages.
      A lengthy biography of Pierre Baillot (1771-1843), the
      author's violin teacher. Defines chamber music, which
      includes piano solo and excludes "those compositions
      which are the ephemeral effusions of fashion, or are
      intended for the display of any *peculiarity of execu-
      tion....*" Stresses the need for ensemble playing and
      quotes Baillot's interpretation of chamber music. If
      the listener is intent on following the details of a
      chamber score with his nose on the notes, he will miss
      many of the nuances that the performers give to the
      notes during performance -- the mind can concentrate on
      only so much (Baillot was particularly annoyed at
      Meyerbeer for following scores rather than listening).
      Appendix gives some of Baillot's programs 1814-1840, as
      well as programs and program notes for concerts of the
      Beethoven Quartet Society and the Musical Union in
      1845. Spends some time on the Beethoven Quartet
      Society (founded 1845), its concerts and its manage-
      ment, as well as other London chamber societies and
      patrons from 1822 to 1846.

1569. Berezowsky, Alice. *Duet with Nicky.* Philadelphia/
      New York: J.B. Lippincott, 1943. HML 1553.15. 239
      pages.

A highly romanticized personal biography of Nicolas Berezowsky (1900-1953) by his wife. He was a violinist and composer, who for 5 years was a member of the Coolidge String Quartet of the Library of Congress. He also played in other quartets and gave many sonata recitals. In addition, he wrote some chamber music, including a string quartet which the Flonzaley performed.

See Clara Steuermann's "In Memory of Rudolf Kolisch" {1464}; for Kolisch's own writing see {1509}.

1570. Richard, Albert, ed. *Alfred Loewenguth: 70 Ans - 50 Ans d'Activité,* in *La Revue Musicale,* no. 347 (1981). 48 pages.
    A tribute to the distinguished French violinist and leader of the Loewenguth String Quartet. Includes biography (b. 1911), photos, accomplishments. Loewenguth has been very active in French chamber music as performer and teacher.

1571. Toenes, George. "Richard Muehlfeld," in *Clarinet,* no. 23 (Summer, 1956), 22-23.
    A brief biography of Mühlfeld and his influence on Brahms's Trio Op. 114, Quintet Op. 115, and 2 Sonatas Op. 120. Quotes an "eyewitness" who describes Mühlfeld's playing as musical but not up to modern technical standards. He established the clarinet as a true solo (and chamber) instrument.

For a brief autobiographical account of his involvement in playing chamber music (specifically piano trios), see Dorothy Packard's interview of Leonard Pennario {1488}. For a discussion of the career of the virtuoso violinist and chamber musician Gaetano Pugnani, see Daniel Heartz's article {1596}. For information on the 17th-century German chamber violinist Johann Schop, see Andreas Moser's "Johann Schop als Violinkomponist" {1282}.

1572. MacArdle, Donald W. "Beethoven and Schuppanzigh," in *The Music Review,* xxvi (1965), 3-14.
    Detailed, scholarly, well-documented study of the relationship between Beethoven and the violinist Ignaz Schuppanzigh (1776-1830), who premiered many of Beethoven's chamber pieces including the late quartets.

For a biography of Spohr as a chamber artist as well as soloist, see Clive Brown's Louis Spohr: a Critical Biography {1345}.

1573. Toenes, George. "Clarinetists who Influenced Mozart," in *Clarinet,* no. 17 (Winter, 1954-1955), 13-14.

Very brief mention of the clarinetists Mozart knew and
the works they caused him to write. Special attention
to Anton and Johann Stadler.

For information on the life of the early 18th-century Ital-
ian chamber violinist Francesco Maria Veracini see John
Hill's dissertation {1377}. For information on Viotti as
violinist in duets, see W.H. von Riehl's article {312}. The
violist Lionel Tertis is discussed by Thomas Tatton {320}.

CHAPTER VI. MISCELLANEOUS TOPICS

PATRONAGE AND CONCERT SERIES

1574. "Chamber Music: its Sponsors and Backers," in *International Musician*, lxi (Feb. 1963), 30-31, 35.
      A sizeable list of resident professional university chamber music groups, university chamber music concert series, museum and library concert series, foundations (Clarion, Gertrude Clarke Whittal, Elizabeth Sprague Coolidge), governments (Canadian), trust funds, ticket sales, and sponsors.

For information on the patronage of the Prussian Queen Sophie Charlotte and Frederick the Great, see Karla Höcker's Hauskonzerte in Berlin *{167}. See Walter Pass's study of Gottfried van Swieten's importance for chamber music, especially that by Haydn and Mozart (457).*

1575. Subirá, José. *La Música en la Casa de Alba: Estudios Historicos y Biograficos.* Madrid: Sucesores de Rivadeneyra, 1927. xxii + 374 pages.
      A study of the musical life surrounding the House of the Dukes of Alba from the 15th to the 19th centuries, based on many types of documents, some of which are quoted here. Evidence for chamber music is scattered throughout, including many foreign publications of sonatas and trios and by natives (especially Francesco Montali) of the 18th century in the library and 6 quartets by Manuel Canales (1747-1786) in the Madrid Biblioteca Nacional dedicated to the Twelfth Duke of Alba.

1576. Sunderman, F. William. *Musical Notes of a Physician: 1980-1982.* Philadelphia: Institute for Clinical Science, 1982. ML 60.S888.1982. v + 255 pages.
      Speeches and program notes by a physician almost entirely on string quartets. A fanciful, undocumented, out-of-date, incorrect volume that is enjoyable reading and which presents the perspective of the amateur enthusiast. Especially interesting are the accounts of 3 19th-century physicians -- Helmholtz, Borodin, and especially Billroth, who were involved with chamber music. Discovered a lost Borodin Sextet while in Moscow, but no further details (the first 2 movements have been known, the last 2 unknown). Billroth was particularly important for his support of Brahms.

1577. Bedford, William Charles. "Elizabeth Sprague Coolidge: the Education of a Patron of Chamber Music: the Early Years." PhD dissertation. University of

Missouri, 1964. UMI 64-13280. DAI xxv.7, pp. 4073-
4. 350 pages.
A biography and history of Mrs. Coolidge's patronage of
chamber music, beginning with her inheritance in Chicago in 1915, her first quartet (the Berkshire) in 1916,
the Berkshire Festival (1918f.) in Pittsfield, Massa-
chusetts, the Library of Congress Auditorium in 1925,
and the Coolidge Foundation to support chamber music.
Concerned with how Mrs. Coolidge's fortune and career
came to be and how she interacted with American institutions of the time.

1578. Batchelder, Alice Coleman. *Coleman Chamber Concerts*
      1904-1944. Pasadena, CA: The Coleman Chamber Music
      Association, 1945. ML 1111.8 P3C6. 73 pages.
History of this Pasadena-based chamber concert series
with charts listing all compositions played, all performers, and all patrons. Gives a good representation
of what chamber music was heard in California during
its period of growth from frontier state to principal
home of major chamber music composers and performers.

1579. Slosberg, Helen S. *An Air of Distinction: a Chronicle*
      of the Brookline Chamber Music Society, Inc., Brook-
      line, Massachusetts. Boston: Thomas Todd, 1976. ML
      1111.8 B72B77. v + 161 pages, 40 photographs.
An informal, homey description of chamber music in the
Boston area by a devotee (Slosberg), with special emphasis on her creation in 1945 of the BCMS, a chamber
music society designed primarily to bring chamber music
to students in Brookline. Many well-known Boston Symphony Orchestra performers and other musicians featured
in its programs. Programs are free to students during
regular school hours.

1580. Hammer, Mari Sweeney. "History of Louisville's Cham-
      ber Music Society." MA thesis. University of Louis-
      ville, 1981. UMI PSE13-17032. 209 pages.
Presents and systematizes all programs, repertory, and
performing groups of the Louisville Chamber Music Society since its founding in January, 1938. Special emphasis on new music and on ensembles of significance to
the Society and Louisville.

1581. Walls, Brian Scott. "Chamber Music in Los Angeles,
      1922-1954: a History of Concert Series, Ensembles and
      Repertoire." MA thesis. California State University
      at Long Beach, 1980. UMI PSE13-15169. 234 pages.
Uncovers materials relating to chamber music in Los
Angeles 1922-1954 and then organizes this material and
evaluates it.

1582. Schmidt, Ferdinand August. "Die Kammermusikfeste des
      Beethoven-Hauses in Bonn vom Jahre 1890 ab," in *Deut-*

sches Beethoven-Fest Bonn vom 21. bis 31. Mai 1927
(Bonn: Carthaus, [1927]), pages 9-102.
A brief history of the founding and development of a
Beethoven chamber music festival in Bonn at Beethoven's
birthplace. Such outstanding groups as the Joachim and
Petri Quartets participated at the first festival in
1890, the Rosé Quartet at the second festival in 1893;
later festivals in 1897, 1899, c.1901, and every 2
years to 1913 and from 1918 to 1926 (when this article
was written). Gives performers and some of the works
performed.

1583. Freed, Isadore. "American Chamber Music," in *Music
  Clubs Magazine*, xxxi (May 1952), 23-24.
  A tribute to the Society for the Publication of American Music, founded in 1919, which has published about
  70 complete chamber works by American composers (23
  string quartets, 13 trios, quartets and quintets with
  piano, 17 solo sonatas, and other kinds of chamber
  music) and thereby encourages chamber music in America.
  Also has annual competitions. Gives a list of the 15
  most highly regarded string quartets by Americans (Copland, Moore, Piston, V. Thomson, Barber, Porter, Norman
  Lockwood, Finney, Bernard Wagenaar, and D.G. Mason).

*For a few chamber concert series and patrons in other coun-
tries, see the studies by Hanslick {343}, Heller {346}, Augé
de Lassur {376}, Gottron {383}, Cooper {374}, Fabricus
{359}, Guynemer {1568}, Seaman {413} and {414}, Prochazka
{355}, Gut {377}, Broman {426}, Engländer {386}, Hedin
{424}, Kammermusikforeningen {358} and Ping-Robbins {87}.*

*For suggestions on improving the patronage of chamber music
see:*

1584. Benedict, Stephen. *Opportunities in Chamber Music:
  Report on a Meeting*. Washington, D.C.: Cultural Resources, Inc., 1979. ML 1111.B46. iii + 20 pages.
  Report of a meeting in Washington of artists, arts
  managers, and philanthropic officers, to explore ways
  of strengthening American chamber music institutions.
  Under the aegis of the National Endowment for the Arts.
  Deals with professional chamber music only; includes
  vocal chamber music. Many practical topics affecting
  the careers and livelihood of chamber musicians.

EDUCATION

*Many collections of chamber music are for beginners, such as
Wesley Sonntag, ed., An Introduction to String Quartet Playing: a Collection of Movements from the Early Quartets of*

Haydn and Mozart *(New York: S. Fox, [1963]), MT 728. S6616,
and only a few have more advanced written instructions.*

1585. Booth, Roscoe Martin. "Baroque String Chamber Works
      Incorporating Techniques Essential to the Development
      of Performing Ability of Violinists." EdD disserta-
      tion. Colorado State College, 1964. UMI 64-10601.
      DA xxv.5, p. 3015. 202 pages.
      Chooses 12 works by known composers written 1685-1756
      which can be used by high school violin students to en-
      hance right arm and left hand techniques. Findings
      sound naive to anyone with more than a modicum of
      violin playing or listening experience. Uncertain
      whether the ensembles are chamber or orchestral.

*For assistance in listening to selected 20th-century string
quartets, see Mary Beth Walker's dissertation {199}.*

1586. Zorn, Jay Daniel. "The Effectiveness of Chamber Music
      Ensemble Experience for Members of a Ninth Grade Band
      in Learning Certain Aspects of Music and Musical Per-
      formance." MED dissertation. Indiana University,
      1969. UMI 70-11945. DAI xxxi.1A, p. 420. 151
      pages.
      Compares the results of groups of students rehearsing
      in chamber ensembles with the results of students per-
      forming in band sectionals and finds no musical differ-
      ences other than attitude: the attitude of those in
      chamber ensembles improved significantly.

1587. Sagul, Edith. "Development of Chamber Music Perfor-
      mance in the United States." EdD dissertation. Co-
      lumbia University, 1952. Summarized in 3 articles:
      "Audience Education for Chamber Music," in *Etude,*
      lxxi (March, 1953), 18, 58, 64.
      After analyzing the status of chamber music activities
      in 30 of the largest United States cities and 168 in-
      stitutions of higher education with music departments,
      found very litle being done to educate audiences in
      chamber music other than concert attendance. This con-
      trasts sharply with orchestra and opera programs. How-
      ever, things are seen to be improving. The National
      Association of Amateur Chamber Music Players, founded
      by Mr. L.A. Strauss of Indianapolis, encourages more
      amateurs to play chamber music, and Young Audiences,
      founded by Mrs. Nina Perrera Collier of Darlington,
      Maryland, brings performers to schools. Describes how
      the New Music Quartet functions with children in such a
      situation.

      "The Developing Interest in Chamber Music," in *Educa-
      tional Music Magazine,* xxxii (March-April, 1953), 26,
      34-40.

Finds healthy the college's role in preparing and edu-
cating students and the community in chamber music by
participation, professional ensembles-in-residence,
variety of scoring, concerts, expanding repertoire,
study of chamber music in general and specific courses,
encouraging professionals, and creating an audience.
Surveys what specific colleges are doing in order to
make all colleges aware of what the others are doing.

"Problems and Possibilities of Chamber Music," in
Music Journal, xiv (Oct., 1956), 28-29.
Sees 2 areas of concern for expanding chamber music in
America: 1) to expand the concept of chamber music from
merely string quartets to all kinds of chamber music,
with increased repertory; 2) to educate the public to
chamber music.

For instruction on chamber music listening for lay audiences
there are many articles and books. See, for example, Alfred
Heuss's Kammermusikabende *{491}.*

1588. Hughes, Charles William. *Chamber Music in American*
Schools. New York: Freybourg Printing Co., 1933. MT
728.H87. iii + 205 pages. Publication of PhD dissertation. Columbia University, 1933.
Concerned primarily with the educational values in
teaching chamber music in schools: it teaches initia-
tive and individual learning, as opposed to group cooperation in orchestras and large choruses, and it
teaches the child to play in ensemble and go beyond
being a passive listener. Describes the social background for "chamber music" in various societies, then
the training of the professional or amateur to fulfill
these roles; includes folk music, organ music, pre-
17th-century music, concerto grosso, symphonies and
orchestral works. Although the history is often simplistic, the treatment of ethnic music naive, and the
bibliographies and discography out-dated, the basic
thesis on the value of chamber music in education is
valid.

1589. National Association of Schools of Music. *Chamber*
Music: Performance and Study at Music Training Insti-
tutions. Reston (Virginia): N.A.S.M., 1982. MT 728.
N25.1982. iii + 49 pages.
A statistical survey of the teaching of chamber music
at 413 American schools of higher education belonging
to N.A.S.M. Collectively, for example, over 6000 student chamber concerts were given in 1 year to approximately 450,000 audience members, and approximately 1800
ad hoc faculty chamber ensemble concerts for over
210,000 people. Questions were asked pertaining to
facts and to attitudes; distinctions were made as to
resident faculty ensembles, *ad hoc* faculty ensembles,

guest faculty ensembles, undergraduate and graduate
ensembles. The academic requirements were also analyzed. Includes a bibliography of chamber music
bibliographies.

For an important account of the 19th-century German music
pedagogue Carl Reinecke, see Karl Fellerer's study {492}.
See also August Reissmann's Die Hausmusik {479}.

1590. Crone, Tan. "Kamermuziek voor Kinderen in Amerika,"
      in *Mens en Melodie*, xxi (1966), 108-110.
      Reports on Young Audiences and its impact on American
      children ages 10 to 12, who hear concerts of 45 to 50
      minutes, with discussion and questions about the music,
      the musicians, and the instruments. It has 640 young
      musicians who form all sorts of chamber groups which
      then play 5300 concerts a year in 26 states.

1591. Watson, J. Arthur. "String Chamber Music: the Lesser
      Combinations," in *Music and Letters*, x (1929), 292-
      298.
      Comments on the large numbers of competent amateur
      players of strings in England, and tries to guide
      these amateurs to literature other than string quartet
      and piano trio. Begins with works for 2 strings (2
      violins, violin + viola, violin + cello), 3, and 1 or 2
      strings with piano. Not a list but a few representa-
      tive examples given and including a few arrangements.

1592. Standen, B.P. "Children and Chamber Music," in *Music*
      and Letters, xiv (1933), 51-54.
      Recognizes the value to character-building that cham-
      ber-playing gives to youngsters, and makes suggestions
      on how average children can participate. Cautions the
      piano accompanist to learn to subdue his or her eager-
      ness for the sake of the ensemble. Mentions arrange-
      ments suitable for the child. Orchestral playing can
      be a disaster for the child.

1593. Pancernova, T. "The Path to Chamber Music," in Ljud-
      mila Miheeva, ed., *Muzyka-detjam: Voprosy Muzykal'no-*
      Esteticeskogo Vospitanija, Vol. 3. Leningrad: Muzy-
      ka, 1976. RILM 76-4206. In Russian.
      A contribution to the aesthetics of music education.

                              ICONOGRAPHY

Many studies include pictures which aid in an understanding
of chamber music. Sometimes they indicate how or where
chamber ensembles assembled, the instruments used, perfor-
mance practices, and types of audiences. In a few icono-
graphic studies the illustration is the focus of the study.

1594. Schwab, Heinrich W. *Konzert: öffentliche Musikdarbie-*
      tung von 17. bis 19. Jahrhundert, in *Musikgeschichte*
      in Bildern, Band 4: *Musik der Neuzeit,* Lieferung 2.
      Leipzig: VEB Deutscher Verlag für Musik, 1971. ML
      89.M9.Bd.4, Lfg. 2. 230 pages.
      Discussion of 165 illustrations of concerts primarily
      in Europe from the 17th through the 19th centuries.

1595. Salmen, Walter. *Haus- und Kammermusik: Privates Musi-*
      zieren im gesellschaftlichen Wandel zwischen 1600 und
      1900, in *Musikgeschichte in Bildern,* Bd. 4, Lfg. 3.
      Leipzig: VEB Deutscher Verlag für Musik, 1969. ML
      89.M9. 203 pages.
      With 1 exception, 117 black-and-white reproductions of
      paintings and drawings, mostly of chamber ensembles
      made up of amateurs in private rooms. Each illustra-
      tion is described, dated, and located, and then briefly
      discussed historically with commentary on the perfor-
      mers, instruments, music performed, social situation,
      and significance. Includes some vocal and solo key-
      board music, too. A lengthy introduction defines Haus-
      musik and then gives a history with reference to some
      of the illustrations. Also defines chamber music and
      salon music and different genres of chamber music, and
      considers the special circumstances, instruments,
      social conditions and so on of different periods.

1596. Heartz, Daniel. "Portrait of a Court Musician: Gaeta-
      no Pugnani of Turin," in Tilman Seebass and Tilden
      Russell, eds., *Imago Musicae I: 1984 (International*
      Yearbook of Musical Iconongraphy) (Basel/Kassel/Lon-
      don: Bärenreiter/Durham [North Carolina]: Duke Uni-
      versity Press, 1984), pp. 103-119. ML 85.I42 vol.I.
      Biography of Pugnani with 4 black-and-white drawings
      and paintings, 1 beautiful full-page color portrait, 1
      title page, and 1 facsimile. Identifies the music in
      the portrait (trio sonata) and gives the movement (3
      musical examples).

1597. Finlay, Ian F. "Musical Instruments in 17th-century
      Dutch Paintings," in *The Galpin Society Journal,* vi
      (1953), 52-69.
      Concerned with 17th-century Dutch representations of
      musical life in the homes of ordinary Dutch citizens.
      The paintings are accurate in details; little is fanci-
      ful. Discusses the instruments shown, proceeding sys-
      tematically instrument-by-instrument from strings to
      winds, keyboard, percussion and miscellaneous. Men-
      tions ensembles that occur commonly: violin + gamba,
      violin + lute + gamba, violin + lute, lute + transverse
      flute, lute + gamba, violin + bagpipes, and violin +
      cittern.

1598. Pilipczuk, A. "Das Musizieren am Tisch: ikonographi-
      sche Bemerkungen zur Spielpraxis vom Spätmittelalter
      bis zur Einführung des Quartett-Tisches im 18. Jahr-
      hundert," in *Die Musikforschung*, xxxii (1979), 404-
      16.
      Discusses the shape and function of musical tables --
      furniture -- about which musicians sat while playing
      ensemble music, especially in the 17th and early 18th
      centuries. These tables and the musicians are often
      represented in paintings on porcelain.

1599. Ulsamer, Josef, and Klaus Stahmer. *Musikalisches Ta-
      felkonfekt*. Würzburg: Stürtz, 1973. ML 1100.U43.
      ISBN 3-8003-0066-4. 95 pages, 76 illustrations, 8
      musical examples, including a 7" LP record.
      A multimedia book (art, music, and German history) that
      traces the use of music at tables primarily in Germany
      and the Low Countries from c.1400 to c.1970 with most
      material c.1600-1790. Designed for the layperson in
      its overall approach and text, but the paintings and
      drawings are valuable for the chamber music scholar as
      well in their depiction of specific instrumental (some-
      times also vocal) ensembles. Ensembles vary from 1
      instrument to 10 or more. Sometimes depictions are of
      chamber music, sometimes Hausmusik, sometimes aristo-
      cratic, and sometimes peasant or bourgeois. Grouped by
      situation.

1600. Leppert, Richard David. "Musical Instruments and Per-
      forming Ensembles in Flemish Paintings of the Seven-
      teenth Century." 3 vols. PhD dissertation. Indiana
      University, 1973. UMI 74-392. DAI xxxiv.8A, p.
      5232. 551 pages.
      Analysis and catalogue of the musical content of 770
      Flemish paintings. It is suggested that this repre-
      sents half the total number of such surviving paint-
      ings; those omitted here include anonymous paintings
      and mythological representations of music. Emphasis on
      the social functions of the instruments.

*See also Holzbauer {887} and Gert Oost, "Die Bedeutung der
niederländischen Hausorgel in der Kammermusik der ersten
Hälfte des 18. Jahrhunderts," in {161}, pages 34-46.*

Inevitably, this index is highly selective. Only those terms which the editor belives to be the ones most likely to be researched are included: the genres of chamber music, the instruments, and basic forms, styles and techniques. Since the terms violin, viola and cello are so ubiquitous in the book, they are omitted here, but see under *sonata*. Italicized numbers refer to pages, the others to entry numbers.

INDEX OF PERSONS

This index is of all persons referred to in the book except
authors and publishers. Italicized numbers refer to pages,
the others to entry numbers.

INDEX OF AUTHORS

The following is an index of authors cited in the book. Authors cited in the course of an entry are indicated by page numbers in italics; the authors of the main entries are indicated by the entry number in regular numerals.

INDEX OF CHAMBER GROUPS

The following is an index of groups of performers of chamber music in which there are at least 3 performers. It also is a list of chamber music societies which sponsor performance, composition, publication or education of chamber music. All performing groups are string unless otherwise stated.